The BiblioPlan Companion, Year Four: A Text for

MODERN HISTORY

U.S. and World History from 1850 – 2000

with Missionary Highlights and U.S. Geography

HARDCOVER EDITION

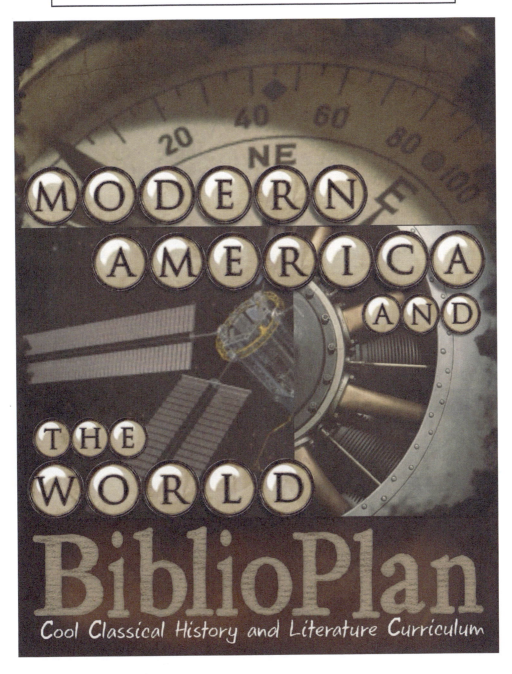

Rob and Julia Nalle

Copyright ©2014, Rob and Julia Nalle. All rights reserved.
Printed in the USA.

Published in Palmyra, Virginia by BiblioPlan for Families.

ISBN 978-1-942405-07-8

BIBLIOPLAN COPYRIGHT POLICY

All of the text, reading lists, explanations, directions, schedules, questions, maps and other content contained in these pages are copyrighted materials owned by BiblioPlan for Families. Please DO NOT reproduce any of these materials on websites or e-mail.

Families who purchase these materials may make as many copies of the Cool History assignments, Maps, Timelines or Coloring Books as they need for use WITHIN THEIR FAMILY ONLY.

Co-ops and schools MAY NOT photocopy, e-mail or reproduce ANY of BiblioPlan's materials.

Co-ops and schools who wish to use BiblioPlan's materials should e-mail us at contactus@biblioplan.net for bulk purchasing options.

Please see BiblioPlan's website at www.biblioplan.net or email contactus@biblioplan.net to let us know how we may best serve your family, co-op or school.

This Book is dedicated to Rob's father, Edward Lester Nalle.

"For the Lord himself will come down from heaven, with a loud command, with the voice of the archangel and with the trumpet call of God, and the dead in Christ will rise first. After that, we who are still alive and are left will be caught up together with them in the clouds to meet the Lord in the air. And so we will be with the Lord forever."

— 1 Thessalonians 4:16-17

Welcome to the BiblioPlan Companion!

The BiblioPlan Companion is a textbook for a four-year, Christian-worldview survey of Biblical History, World History and U.S. History. BiblioPlan offers four Companions, each with 34 chapters for 34 weeks of study:

Year One, Ancients covers Ancient and Biblical History from Creation to the Fall of Rome with World Geography

Year Two, Medieval covers Medieval and Church History from the Fall of Rome to the Renaissance with World Geography

Year Three, Early Modern covers U.S. and World History from 1600 – 1850 with Missionary Highlights and U.S. Geography

Year Four, Modern covers U.S. and World History from 1850 – 2000 with Missionary Highlights and U.S. Geography

Notes on Scope and Sequence

Year One, Ancients
For Year One, BiblioPlan's scope is based mainly on the Bible. Because Biblical History begins with Creation and ends before the Fall of Rome, the Bible makes an excellent framework for a study of ancient history. We study topics from secular history wherever they fit best with Bible history. For example, topics from Egypt are woven into the stories of Biblical figures who lived in Egypt, such as Abraham, Joseph and Moses.

Most chapters include a section on World Geography.

Year Two, Medieval
For Year Two, BiblioPlan's scope is heavy on Western European and Church History. The first 15 weeks focus mainly on Western Europe. The next few weeks move on to Asia. From there, we move to Africa; then to pre-Columbian America; and then to the Age of Discovery. Finally, we return to Europe to cover the Renaissance, the Protestant Reformation and Elizabethan England.

Most chapters include a section on World Geography. Church History topics include the early church, the medieval church, the Great (East-West) Schism, the Avignon Papacy, the Western Schism, the Protestant Reformation, the Counter-reformation and more.

Year Three, Early Modern
Year Four, Modern
Year Three covers U.S. and World History from 1600 – 1850; while Year Four covers U.S. and World History from 1850 – 2000.

Our scope covers U.S. History as chronologically as possible from beginning to end in years Three and Four. Some chapters cover U.S. History exclusively; some are divided between U.S. and World History; and a few cover World History exclusively. We also cover World History as chronologically as possible, but with one proviso: to avoid the confusion that comes with jumping back and forth from region to region too often, we have organized our studies of Asia, Eastern Europe, Western Europe, the Middle East, Australia, Africa and South America into units. Whatever part of the world we study, we always provide the background students need to understand what came before and what comes next.

Most chapters include a section on U.S. Geography. Church History topics in Year Three include the Scottish Reformation, the King James Bible, the Thirty Years' War, the English Civil War, the Great Awakening, the Second Great Awakening and more. The Church History in Year Four covers mainly missionary biographies.

Notes on the Companion

The Companion is both a textbook and an enrichment supplement:

- For older students, the Companion serves as a textbook, providing a running historical narrative from Creation through modern times. Teachers who try to follow a pure Living Books approach sometimes find that their students lack a framework for understanding where those books fit into the overall narrative of history. For example, a student who reads a biography of Oliver Cromwell may learn stories from Cromwell's life without ever understanding the key context of that life, the English Civil War. The Companion provides a framework for understanding the conflicts that led to the English Civil War, how Cromwell fits into that war and what happened after the war.
- For younger students, the Companion serves as an enrichment supplement filled with Fascinating Facts to excite student interest.

Each Companion interweaves God's Word and Church History with the overall narrative of history, helping students understand the Christian themes and connections that reappear throughout humanity's story.

The Companion is designed in a colorful style that grabs students' attention. The narrative of history appears in regular black-on-white text in prose form, timeline form or combined prose/timeline form. Fascinating facts, unique characters, definitions, tables and the like appear on colored backgrounds, making them easier to find and study.

Although the Companion is easy to read, parents must sometimes choose which portions are appropriate for children of different ages. Of necessity, the Companion sometimes describes cruel, violent deeds performed by villains with base, selfish motives. Parents may judge some of this material to be beyond the maturity level of younger readers. We judge the vast majority of this material to be appropriate for independent reading by older middle school and high school students. A few sections have parental warnings attached, and parents should use their discretion with these.

Notes on BiblioPlan

BiblioPlan for Families is a classical Christian History and Literature curriculum for homeschoolers, homeschool cooperatives and Christian schools. BiblioPlan offers simple, family-friendly lessons that enrich your children's studies of all of these subjects:

Ancient History	Medieval History	World History
Bible Studies	Church History	Missionary Studies
Geography	Social Studies	U.S. History
Literature	Art	Creative Writing

BiblioPlan's survey of history is divided into four years:

- **Year One: Ancients** covers Ancient and Biblical History from Creation to the Fall of Rome
- **Year Two: Medieval** covers Medieval and Church History from the Fall of Rome to the Renaissance
- **Year Three: Early Modern** covers U.S. and World History from 1600-1850 with Missionary Highlights
- **Year Four: Modern** covers U.S. and World History from 1850-2000 with Missionary Highlights

For each of these years, BiblioPlan offers eight helpful products:

1. The **Family Guide**, a lesson plan that outlines your course of study while providing versatile reading choices and writing assignments for all ages.
2. The **Companion**, a textbook that pulls together each week's lessons while adding plenty of fun and interesting facts to liven up your class time.
3. The **Discussion Guide**, a lesson recap/discussion starter designed to help families and classes get the most out of the teaching time they spend together.
4. **Cool Histories**, weekly homework assignments based on the lessons in the Family Guide and the Companion.
5. **Hands-On Maps**, weekly map assignments based on the lessons in the Family Guide and the Companion.
6. **Timelines**, flowcharts with cutouts of important historical figures for students to assemble.
7. **Craft Books**, collections of arts, crafts and activities that highlight the lessons in the Family Guide and the Companion.
8. **Coloring Books**, collections of simple sketches from history for the little ones to color.

BiblioPlan's goals are:
- To honor God with every word we write.
- To provide an easy-to-follow curriculum that
    1. allows children of all ages to study the same topics at the same time, making life far easier for parents and teachers; while also
    2. providing history and literature readings that are appropriate for each child's reading level.
- To provide literature, lessons and activities that bring the family together.
- To meet the needs of every family member— big or small, young or old, child or adult.
- To provide supplemental materials such as crafts, activities, hands-on maps, timeline figures and coloring books that are fun for kids, but that also educate by fixing lessons in students' minds.
- To provide an adaptable curriculum with plenty of reading options.
- To provide an affordable curriculum.
- To weave God-honoring Bible lessons into the study of history.

To learn more about BiblioPlan for Families, please visit our website: www.biblioplan.net
Or email: contactus@biblioplan.net

TABLE OF CONTENTS

CHAPTER 1: The British Empire, U.S. Slavery and the Underground Railroad — 11

CHAPTER 2: The Crimean War, the Suez Canal, the Beginnings of the U.S. Civil War — 24

CHAPTER 3: The Great Game in Afghanistan, Dr. Livingstone in Africa — 37

CHAPTER 4: U.S. Civil War, Part I — 50

CHAPTER 5: U.S. Civil War, Part II — 68

CHAPTER 6: Reconstruction in the U.S., War in South America, Canada — 82

CHAPTER 7: France, Germany, Lady Liberty — 97

CHAPTER 8: The Transcontinental Railroad, Moving Out West — 112

CHAPTER 9: The Emergence of Japan, Immigration to the U.S. — 124

CHAPTER 10: Women's Suffrage, Prohibition, Colonizing Indonesia, Reform and Relapse in the Ottoman Empire — 137

CHAPTER 11: Jim Crow Laws, Heroes of Black Rights, Colonizing Australia, the Scramble for Africa — 153

CHAPTER 12: Tsarist Russia, the Spanish American War — 168

CHAPTER 13: China, Japan and Korea — 182

CHAPTER 14: Western Pioneer Trails, Indian Wars in the American West — 197

CHAPTER 15: Big Business, the "Robber Barons" — 212

CHAPTER 16: American Inventions, Persia, the Balkan Wars — 225

CHAPTER 17: Revolution in Mexico, World War I (Part I) — 241

CHAPTER 18: Revolution in Russia, World War I (Part II) — 259

CHAPTER 19: The Roaring Twenties, Independence for Ireland and India — 276

CHAPTER 20: The Treaty of Versailles, The USSR under Stalin — 294

CHAPTER 21: The Roaring Twenties (part II), Italy, Egyptian Independence — 307

CHAPTER 22: Nationalism and Communism in China, Japan in Manchuria — 322

CHAPTER 23: The Great Depression — 336

CHAPTER 24: The Spanish Civil War, Germany's Weimar Republic and Rise of Hitler — 350

CHAPTER 25: World War II (Part I), the Holocaust — 367

CHAPTER 26: World War II (Part II) — 385

CHAPTER 27: Dividing Germany, Dividing India — 409

CHAPTER 28: Israel, Egypt and the Suez Crisis — 425

CHAPTER 29: Communism in China, the Korean War — 441

CHAPTER 30: South America, South Africa — 458

CHAPTER 31: The Cold War, Cuba, the Nuclear Arms Race, the Space Race — 477

CHAPTER 32: Civil Rights Struggles in the United States, the Vietnam War — 497

CHAPTER 33: The USSR — 519

CHAPTER 34: Wars in the Middle East — 540

ADDENDUM: Presidents Supplement — 555

ADDENDUM: Year Four Overview — 557

BIBLIOGRAPHY — 560

PHOTO CREDITS — 564

INDEX — 569

Chapter 1

The British Empire, U.S. Slavery and the Underground Railroad

WORLD HISTORY FOCUS

A Brief Review of World History Through 1800

The earliest recorded human history comes from the Middle East and the area around the Mediterranean Sea. Ancient history covers the emerging empires of Egypt and Persia, followed by Greece, then Rome. When Jesus lived, the Roman Empire dominated most of the known world. After the fall of Rome, Europe entered a period called the Dark Ages or the Middle Ages.

The Middle Ages saw the rise of Islam in the Middle East, Africa and Spain. The Christian church divided itself in the Great Schism of 1054. The Roman Catholic Church was dominant in Europe, and its popes held political as well as religious power. The Eastern Orthodox Church spread into Russia, but struggled to survive against the Muslim onslaught in the Middle East, Asia Minor and the Balkans (Greece and northward). The Fall of Byzantine Constantinople marked the end of the Middle Ages.

During the Renaissance (rebirth) that followed the Middle Ages, learning, literature and the arts received renewed attention as ancient Greek and Roman ideas returned to light. Europeans became more aware of the Far Eastern nations of China and India. After Constantinople fell to the Muslims, Europeans were forced to seek new trade routes to China and India. In the process, they discovered the New World of the Americas. The Roman Catholic Church was further divided when a large number of its people objected to some of its established teachings and formed new churches during the Protestant Reformation.

Spain, Portugal, France, the Netherlands and England all founded colonies in the New World. The English colonists thrived in eastern North America, and eventually formed thirteen colonies there. These colonies rebelled against English rule and founded the United States of America in 1776. Back in Europe, France had its own revolution against oppressive royalty a little later, with a less happy outcome. After the French Revolution, France's Emperor Napoleon launched the Napoleonic Wars in an attempt to conquer all of Europe, while England continued to build its empire overseas. The young United States began to overspread the continent of North America. Slavery, which was banned in England in 1833, became an increasingly controversial subject in the United States. The U.S. government compromised in order to preserve a balance between states that allowed slavery and those that didn't. The conflict between North and South, which was present from the nation's founding, was coming to an ugly head.

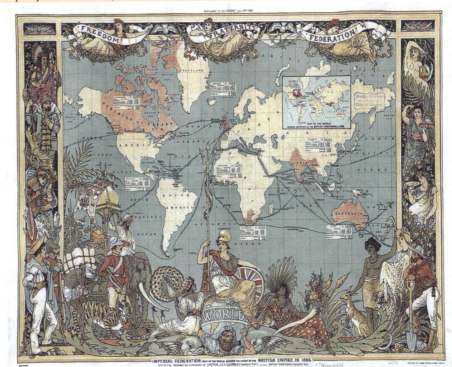

We begin our study of modern history by looking at the British Empire, the superpower whose holdings at its peak are depicted in pink on the map below. These holdings were so vast and widespread that it was said that "the sun never sets upon the British Empire": no matter what time of day it was, it was always daytime somewhere in the British Empire.

THE BRITISH EMPIRE

BRILLIANT BRITONS: Queen Victoria (lived 1819 – 1901, reigned 1837 – 1901)

Queen Victoria was a long-reigning and highly successful Queen of the United Kingdom of Great Britain and Ireland. During the Victorian Age, which lasted from 1837 – 1901, Great Britain grew to be the world's largest empire and greatest superpower.

Victoria was the niece and heir of King William IV, who died in 1837 without a surviving child of his own. Victoria's father, Prince Edward, was the brother of William, and the fourth son of King George III— the same George III whose tyranny drove American colonists to declare independence from Britain in 1776. Having just turned eighteen when King William died, Victoria was just old enough to reign as queen in her own right, without a regent (regents rule in the place of royals who are too young to govern on their own). Through the early years of her reign, Victoria relied on the advice and guidance of her experienced prime minister, Lord Melbourne.

Victoria's first, most important task as Britain's queen was to marry so that she could produce heirs to Britain's throne. Victoria's choice of husbands fell upon her first cousin Albert, heir to Saxe-Coburg and Gotha, a small duchy (dukedom) in Germany. The match between Victoria and Albert was unpopular in Britain at first, for two reasons: because Albert was a German, and because he brought little wealth into the marriage. Albert stood to gain a great deal by marrying the Queen of England. Victoria, too, was unpopular at the time: she wasn't as beautiful and glamorous as the people of Britain expected their queen to be; and she had angered parliament by refusing to allow its new prime minister to appoint new members to her Royal Household. Someone summed up the Victoria/Albert situation with a rather cruel rhyme about the royal couple:

"He comes to take/ for better or worse/ England's fat queen and fatter purse."

After their marriage in 1840, however, their popularity began to improve. Prince Consort Albert became the great love of Victoria's life. During their 21 years of marriage, the royal couple had nine children together. Albert was a great help to Victoria in her duties as Queen, and she relied on him and trusted him completely. Unfortunately, Prince Albert's health began to fail him at an early age. When Prince Albert died in late 1861 at the age of 42, Victoria went into a deep mourning from which she never quite recovered.

Victoria would outlive her husband by 40 years, years in which Britain's empire would spread farther and wider than ever before. In Victoria's time, most of the powers of government belonged to Britain's Parliament, and her responsibilities had more to do with maintaining friendly relationships than with writing and passing laws. Still, she worked closely with each new prime minister, and her opinions on every issue were important because of her influence on the public and on members of Parliament.

Victoria saw herself as the moral leader of a great, enlightened British Christian society. Like many British people of her time, she felt that the less enlightened parts of her empire would benefit enormously from the benevolent influence of that great society. Victorian Britain had little respect for the cultures of its faraway colonies in places like China, India and South Africa. The world would be a better place, Victorians believed, if Britain could replace these colonies' backward cultures with the far more enlightened British culture.

Queen Victoria lived on past the turn of the twentieth century, then died of natural causes in 1901. Her many children and grandchildren married members of royal families all over Europe. Her first grandchild was Kaiser Wilhelm II, the German emperor whose belligerence helped spark the terrible World War I in 1914.

ENORMOUS EVENTS of the Victorian Age:

1837, June 20: Victoria becomes Queen of the United Kingdom of Great Britain and Ireland less than one month after her 18th birthday.	**1857 – 1858:** Indian soldiers rebel against the British East India Company in the Sepoy Rebellion (see below). Most of India becomes British India.
1840, February 10: Victoria marries Albert.	**1861, December 14:** Prince Consort Albert dies.
1840: Britain acquires New Zealand as a colony.	**1867:** Canada becomes a Dominion of the British Empire (see Chapter 6).
1842: Britain acquires its first "treaty ports" in China after defeating China in the First Opium War (see Chapter 13).	**1882:** Egypt becomes a protectorate of Great Britain (see Chapter 21).
1851: Prince Consort Albert organizes and presents the Great Exhibition in London, England (see below).	**1899:** Britain begins the Second Boer War and annexes the independent Boer (Dutch-descended) colonies of South Africa (see Chapter 11).
1854 – 1856: Britain, France and the Ottoman Empire battle Russia in the Crimean War (see Chapter 2).	**1901:** The provinces of Australia unite to form the Commonwealth of Australia, another Dominion of the British Empire.

FASCINATING FACTS: The Kensington System

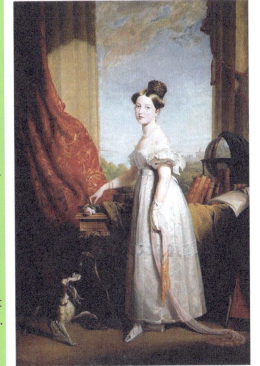

The Kensington System was a set of strict rules for young Victoria's upbringing. Victoria's mother, the Duchess of Kent, devised the Kensington System with the help of her favorite attendant, Sir John Conroy. Under the Kensington System, Victoria was forbidden:

1. To have her own bedroom (she shared her mother's bedroom throughout her childhood);
2. To walk up or down the stairs of her Kensington Palace home without her mother or a trusted member of her staff holding her hand; and
3. To visit with anyone unless her mother or a trusted member of her staff was present in the room with her.

Except for the constant, watchful attendance of her mother the Duchess, Sir Conroy and their staff, Victoria lived out her lonely childhood in melancholy isolation. Even so, she received an excellent education and became an accomplished writer and watercolor artist.

By ruling Victoria, Victoria's mother and Sir Conroy hoped to rule Britain itself. Their fondest wish was that Victoria's uncle, King William IV, would die while Victoria was still a minor so that they could become her regents and rule in her place. For his part, William's fondest wish was to survive past Victoria's 18th birthday so that she, and not her mother, would rule when he was gone. He said so in public at his last birthday celebration in August 1836, and his bitter announcement embarrassed the Duchess terribly. While King William lived, Victoria's mother kept her far away from King William so that he could neither influence her himself nor introduce her to others who might influence her.

In the end, the Kensington System backfired on the Duchess and Conroy. As soon as Victoria became queen upon her uncle's death, she asked for two things: she wanted one hour alone, without her mother or any staff watching her every move; and she wanted her bed moved out of her mother's bedroom. She soon banned Sir Conroy from her presence; she wanted nothing more to do with him. When Victoria married Prince Albert in 1840, she evicted her mother and saw a lot less of her for the rest of her life. Victoria turned out to be as strong-willed as her mother, and the Kensington System failed to change that.

FASCINATING FACTS: The Great Exhibition

By 1850, the Industrial Revolution was well underway, and the British Empire was at the head of that Revolution. Victorian Britain was proud of its vastness, its greatness and its advanced technology. No other nation in the world had ever possessed so many of the world's wonders at one time.

To display all of these wonders, as well as its own superiority, Great Britain invited the world to a spectacular exhibition in London that would become the first World's Fair. From May 1 - October 15, 1851, over six million people visited London's "Great Exhibition of the Works of Industry of all Nations," also known as the "Great Exhibition" or the "Crystal Palace Exhibition."

Perhaps the most stunning sight at the extravagant Great Exhibition was the building that housed it, the Crystal Palace. The Crystal Palace was an enormous structure of glass and iron commissioned by Prince Albert, who promoted the Great Exhibition. The nearly 1 million-square-foot Crystal Palace housed over 13,000

exhibitors from all over the world. Inside were exhibits of every kind imaginable. Daguerreotypes, an early version of photographs, were popular. Factory machines such as industrial looms and cotton mills were on display, as were innovative farm machines. There were also exotic exhibits from around the world. The world's largest known diamond, the 105-carat Koh-I-Noor diamond (now part of the British Crown Jewels) was on display, along with other Indian jewelry.

After the Great Exhibition, the Crystal Palace building was moved to Sydenham Hill in south London, where it became the centerpiece of a 200-acre park. A fire destroyed the building in 1936.

BRITISH INDIA

India spent most of the Middle Ages under the control of Islamic emperors from Muslim dynasties. Most of these emperors tolerated other religions, so India retained its ancient faiths of Hinduism, Buddhism, Sikhism and Jainism. India entered the early modern era under the Moghul Dynasty, which began with Emperor Babur in 1526 and included the well-known Emperors Akbar, Jahangir and Shah Jahan, builder of the Taj Mahal. India's last great Moghul emperor was Aurangzeb, who died in 1707.

Around 1600, the British East India Company began building trading posts and factories in India. One of its largest trading posts was at Calcutta, a city in the East Indian province of Bengal on the northern coast of the Bay of Bengal.

FASCINATING FACTS: The East India Company

A group of English businessmen formed the East India Company (EIC) in late 1600 for the purpose of trading in the Indonesian Islands (the "East Indies"). The East India Company grew wealthy by buying, selling and transporting exotic goods like silk, spices, dyes and even opium-- goods that were valuable because they were unavailable outside the Far East. The company found its greatest fortune in India, where it established several factories and trading posts. During the early 1800s, the company grew so large and important in India that it functioned more like a government than a trade company.

Around 1615, the EIC convinced the British government to negotiate a trade treaty between the Moghul Emperor Jahangir and the British Empire. In order to help the negotiations along, the EIC sent Jahangir valuable gifts. Whatever gifts the EIC sent along must have pleased Jahangir very much, because he excitedly invited Great Britain to send more merchants. Over the next hundred years, the EIC established factories and trading posts at Surat, Madras, Bombay, and Calcutta, among many other places.

Around 1670, King Charles II granted the company new powers so that it could protect these far-flung factories and trading posts. After 1670, the EIC had the power:

- to collect taxes from the people of India;
- to hire police and establish courts of law in the parts of India it controlled;
- to claim territories for itself and maintain law and order inside these territories; and even
- to raise armies of local soldiers to defend its territories.

All of these powers were normally the powers of government, not of a business. The EIC's authority to tax meant that the Indian people were paying their taxes to a business that worked to generate profit for itself, not to a native Indian government created to serve and defend the Indian people.

Whenever the natives of India fought to resist the EIC's expansion, the EIC fought back harder. The EIC took advantage of conflicts between India's different princes: some princes fought on the side of the EIC, while others resisted. By turning India's princes against one another, the EIC eventually defeated nearly all of them. After EIC armies won major victories over Indian princes at the 1757 Battle of Plassey and the 1764 Battle of Buxar, an EIC general named Robert Clive (see picture) became the first British Governor of Bengal, a vast and important region of east India.

By the mid-1700s, the EIC controlled nearly all of India and some large territories farther east, including the future Burma. The line between the EIC and the British government began to blur as the government sent armies to help the EIC conquer more and more Indian Territory. It became difficult to tell the difference between the interests of the EIC and the interests of Great Britain.

During the late 1700s, however, the British government began to realize the dangers of allowing one company to control so much wealth and power. In 1773, the British Parliament passed the first of several laws designed to claim the EIC's territories and its wealth for the British Crown. By 1853, the EIC was hardly a trading company at all anymore: it had lost its exclusive right to trade in the Far East, and existed primarily to maintain control of its vast territories.

The EIC was a harsh government for India. As a proud British company of the Victorian Age, the EIC tended to look down on native Indians and to ignore their religious beliefs. The Indian people suffered under the EIC because they had to obey all of its rules and pay all of its taxes, without gaining in return the protections of a local government that cared about their interests.

The 1857-8 Sepoy Rebellion (see below) meant the end of the East India Company. Most Britons were outraged at native Indians for rebelling against British rule, but Parliament could still see that the EIC's harsh treatment of its subjects had made some sort of rebellion nearly inevitable. <u>In 1858, Parliament dissolved the EIC and established a new government office, the India Office, to govern India directly</u>. Queen Victoria promised that the new British government of India would be both more generous to native Indians and more tolerant of their different religions.

The next period of Indian history, the 89 years from the 1858 dissolution of the East India Company through Indian independence in 1947, became known as the British *Raj*. Victoria would claim the title "Empress of India" in 1876.

The Sepoy Rebellion (1857 – 1858)

The word *sepoy* comes from the Persian word for "soldier." Most the East India Company's foot and cavalry soldiers were native Indians known as sepoys, who served under trained British military officers. The Sepoy Rebellion happened when these sepoys rebelled against their British officers, trying to cast out the British *imperialists* (empire-builders) and restore native Indian rule.

The sepoys accumulated their many reasons for the Sepoy Rebellion over more than 150 years of East India Company domination in India. Among their reasons:

- The East India Company regularly mistreated native Indians. Its officers were racially prejudiced against Indians.
- The EIC ignored Indians' property rights. Under the Doctrine of Lapse, the EIC could take ownership of Indian land if the land's lord died without a male heir of his own.
- The sepoys resented British attempts to Christianize them. Christian missionaries tried to change barbaric Indian practices like *Sati*, the Hindu rite in which widows burned themselves to death on their dead husbands' funeral pyres in order to display their grief. Some British officers required their soldiers to listen to Christian preachers. The sepoys felt that British Christians were trying to stamp out their ancient religious faiths.
- The sepoys resented being forced to serve the East India Company's armies overseas. Hindu sepoys in particular could not remain ritually clean while living on board a ship-- shipboard life interfered with their cleansing rituals.
- The East India Company was ungenerous with native Indians. The sepoys' pay was extremely low, and the company didn't accept Indians into the higher-paid officer corps. Indian taxes went to support wealthy Britons and British interests overseas, while Indians starved at home in India, sometimes in large numbers.

The sepoys' final grievance against the EIC came with the arrival of the new Enfield 1853 Rifle-Musket (see picture). For ammunition, the Enfield used a new, manufactured paper cartridge that was different from the ammunition the sepoys had used in the past. The Enfield cartridges arrived with a coating of some sort of grease to waterproof and lubricate them. In order to load the Enfield, the Sepoys were required to bite off one end of the paper cartridge. Religious sepoys began to fear that the cartridges' grease coating might contain animal fats. If they contained tallow, or beef fat, then they would offend Hindus, to whom cattle were sacred. If they contained lard, or pork fat, then they would offend Muslims, to whom pork was *haraam* (unclean). In either case, the situation proved to many sepoys that the British didn't care about their religions' strict teachings on diet. Some of the sepoys refused to bite the Enfield cartridges, so their British officers imprisoned them for disobeying orders.

The sepoys' first act of open rebellion was to break into the jails and free their comrades who had been imprisoned for refusing to bite the tainted cartridges. Then, the sepoys began their all-out Sepoy Rebellion with the goal of restoring the Moghul Dynasty emperor Bahadur Shah Zafar to power throughout India. The Sepoy Rebellion began to spread over large parts of India, and the British began to lose ground.

The turning point in the Sepoy Rebellion came after a major sepoy victory at Cawnpore, a city in east India. After their victory at Cawnpore, the sepoys made the mistake of slaughtering the British women and children they had captured in the battle. <u>When the British people back home learned of the Cawnpore Massacre, they were outraged.</u> British troops from both the British homeland and the Crimea (a peninsula in the Black Sea) rushed to India to strike back at the rebel sepoys. In many areas, sepoys remained loyal to their British officers and fought against their own rebel countrymen. Before the end of 1857, the rebels began losing ground. The rebel sepoys finally signed a peace treaty with Britain in 1858, after their primary leaders were killed.

Several important things happened in the aftermath of the Sepoy Rebellion:

1. Britain dissolved the East India Company.
2. Britain established a new government office, the India Office, to govern India. It also created a Secretary of State for India in the cabinet of the British Prime Minister, as well as a British Viceroy and Governor-General for India (*viceroy* means "in place of the king.")
3. The British convicted Emperor Bahadur Shah Zafar of treason and exiled him to Burma. He died in exile and never returned to India.
4. The long-standing Moghul Dynasty of India came to an end.
5. Britain would continue to hold British India from 1858 - 1947, a period known in India as the British *Raj*.
6. Queen Victoria proclaimed herself Empress of India in 1876.

FASCINATING FACTS: The Union Flag

The modern flag of the United Kingdom is known as the *Union Flag* or the *Union Jack*. It has appeared in its current form since 1801, when Ireland joined the union of England and Scotland known as Great Britain (England and Scotland formally united in 1707). To symbolize the (often unwilling) union of three independent nations, it combines the crosses of the three patron saints of England, Scotland and Ireland, all over a blue field:

1. The largest cross is the red cross of Saint George, patron saint of England, edged in white.
2. On the diagonal is the white cross of Saint Andrew, patron saint of Scotland.
3. Also on the diagonal is the red cross of Saint Patrick, patron saint of Ireland.

Wales, which was also formerly independent, is not represented on the flag. The kings of England have regarded Wales as part of their territory from the time of King Edward I, and since then, the king's heir has almost always received the title "Prince of Wales."

Southern Ireland became an independent republic in 1922-1937, and has its own flag. However, the United Kingdom retains control of Northern Ireland, so it has retained the cross of St. Patrick on the Union Flag.

MISSIONARY FOCUS

GIANTS OF THE FAITH: George Mueller (1805 – 1898)

George Mueller was a Prussian-born English Christian missionary. Born in 1805, he was by his own admission a selfish child who lied, stole and lived an immoral life. When he was sixteen, he was arrested and jailed. His father left him in jail for three weeks hoping that imprisonment might teach him a lesson, but punishment wasn't the answer. It was only after George heard and believed the Gospel of Jesus Christ at an 1825 prayer meeting that the Lord finally changed his heart.

From that time on, George Mueller dedicated his life to missions. He went to England hoping to train as a foreign missionary to unbelieving Jews, but he changed his mind. Instead, he planted a small church in Bristol, England and expanded it into a thriving ministry. George Mueller believed in the power of personal prayer. At his church and in his private life, he trusted in the Lord for finances. As a pastor he vowed never to take a fixed salary, never to pass an offering plate, and never to go into debt. Instead, he left a donation box at the back of the church, and the Lord met all of his needs. He also helped to establish the Scriptural Knowledge Institution for Home and Abroad, a training seminary for missionaries and pastors which eventually trained 7,000 students.

His greatest work, though, was among orphans. On a day when he had only 50 pence in his pocket, God laid it on George Mueller's heart to build homes for England's many orphans. He did not share his desire with anyone or launch elaborate fund-raising schemes. Instead, he simply prayed that God would provide. People all over the world heard about the orphan ministry through George's autobiography, and sent money without even being asked. In George's lifetime, his ministry received over seven million dollars in donations for building and maintaining its orphanages. When he died in 1898, he had five buildings that housed a total of two thousand orphans (see picture of George's orphanage at Ashley Down, Bristol). In all of the years that his orphanages were open, his orphan children were never without food.

THE FIVE NEW ORPHAN HOUSES, ASHLEY DOWN, BRISTOL.

U.S. HISTORY FOCUS

A Brief Review of the United States in the Years Before the Civil War

The conflicts that divided North and South were evident from the founding of the United States. The "Three Fifths Compromise" in the U.S. Constitution, which allowed the South to count three fifths of its slave population in the census that determined its number of representatives in Congress, was an attempt to find an agreeable balance of power between the slaveholding, farm-loving South and the free, business-minded North. New compromises like the Three Fifths Compromise came every thirty years, beginning in 1790:

- The Compromise of 1790 moved the capital of the U.S. to Washington DC, which lay on land provided by two Southern states, so that power would not reside solely in the already powerful North.
- The 1820 Missouri Compromise declared that no new Louisiana Purchase territory north of the 36° 30' parallel could legally allow slavery, except Missouri.

- The Compromise of 1850 was a complex series of bills which made concessions to both North and South. California was admitted to the Union as a free state, but other states in the South would still have the potential to become slave states. Part of the Compromise of 1850 was the Fugitive Slave Act (see below).

Then came the 1854 Kansas-Nebraska Act, which repealed the Missouri Compromise and set off violent conflicts in Bloody Kansas. Political compromises were losing their ability to hold the Union together. The South was preparing to act on its repeated threats to leave the Union, while the North was considering the use of force to hold the Union together and bend the South to its will.

SLAVERY AND THE UNDERGROUND RAILROAD

The Fugitive Slave Act

The Fugitive Slave Act of 1850 was one of several laws that together made up the Compromise of 1850. Some of the compromise's laws, like the law that admitted California to the Union as a free state, were designed to please Northern abolitionists; but the Fugitive Slave Act was designed to please Southern slaveholders. Under the Fugitive Slave Act, every law enforcement officer, whether from the North or the South, was legally bound to help return escaped slaves to their owners.

Before the Fugitive Slave Act, slaves who managed to escape their owners had only to pass into a free state to win their freedom. Most Northern lawmen considered escaped slaves free, and didn't try to return them to the South. When the Fugitive Slave Act became law, Southern slaveholders were free to pursue their escaped slaves deep into Northern territory, and Northern lawmen were obligated to help them track the slaves down. The act also made it illegal for the people of the North to provide shelter for escaped slaves.

The Underground Railroad

The *Underground Railroad* was not a railroad at all, but rather a secret network of abolitionists that helped slaves escape to freedom. In the decades before the Civil War, the Underground Railroad quietly helped thousands of slaves to escape captivity. Sympathetic homeowners along the slaves' path to freedom silently moved them north, guiding them along secret paths. The runaways usually traveled by night until they crossed the Mason Dixon Line (the line between Maryland and Pennsylvania) into the free states. After the 1850 passage of the Fugitive Slave Act, the Underground Railroad's job was even more complicated, because slave owners or their agents began to pursue escaped slaves far north of the Mason Dixon Line. It became necessary to extend the network all the way to Canada, where the escapees' freedom was assured because Canada had already outlawed slavery.

To confuse its enemies, the Underground Railroad used real railroading terms: the homes along the path were called "stations," the homeowners were called "stationmasters," donors of money and goods were called "stockholders," and guides (like Harriet Tubman) were called "conductors."

AMAZING AMERICANS: Harriet Tubman (1820 – 1913)

Harriet Tubman was a former slave who escaped from slavery in Maryland to freedom in Pennsylvania. Over the course of 10 years, Harriet returned to the South many times and risked her life to lead slaves to freedom along the Underground Railroad. She was also a prominent abolitionist who consulted with Frederick Douglass, William Lloyd Garrison and the radical John Brown. Because she led so many people out of slavery and into the "promised land" of freedom, she earned the nickname "The Moses of Her People."

Harriet decided to escape from the slave state of Maryland to the free state of Pennsylvania in 1849, when she began to fear that her owner was about to sell her to a new owner farther south. When she arrived in Philadelphia, she went to work and began to save money for return trips to Maryland to free her family. In the year after Harriet's escape, 1850, Congress passed the Fugitive Slave Act. After that, escaped slaves had to travel all the way to Canada to win their freedom, not just across the Mason-Dixon Line between Maryland and Pennsylvania. During the 1850s, Harriet became a cunning and experienced "conductor" on the Underground Railroad. She had more than one narrow escape in the South; but despite the rewards Southern slaveholders offered, no one ever captured Harriet or any of the Underground Railroad "passengers" she guided.

Harriet supported the radical abolitionist John Brown in his daring plan to start a slave rebellion at Harper's Ferry, but she may have withdrawn her support before he actually carried out his failed plan (see Chapter 4). When the Civil War began, Harriet served the Union cause by using some of the same skills she learned on the Underground Railroad: she worked as a spy and helped to lead slaves to freedom. She even participated in an armed raid in South Carolina that freed hundreds of slaves. Like Frederick Douglass, she criticized President Abraham Lincoln for waiting so long to officially free the slaves in the 1863 Emancipation Proclamation, but praised him when he finally did so.

Later in life, Harriet worked with Susan B. Anthony to promote voting rights for women. She also donated land for a home for the elderly. She devoted her entire life to helping the slaves, the poor and the underprivileged. Wise, brave Harriet Tubman died of old age and pneumonia in 1913.

FASCINATING FACTS: Uncle Tom's Cabin

Uncle Tom's Cabin is a novel written by Harriet Beecher Stowe, an abolitionist from a New England family of ministers. The novel tells of the ills of slavery from a strongly Christian point of view. When it first appeared in 1852, during a heated national argument over slavery in the United States, it quickly became the most important and widely read abolitionist writing of all time. An instant bestseller, it sold 300,000 copies in its first months and was translated into 13 languages by 1856.

Uncle Tom's Cabin follows the story of Uncle Tom, a Godly and faithful slave, as he is sold to different owners. Tom's story begins in Kentucky, where he holds a dignified and responsible position as his owner's farm manager. Life is good for Tom in Kentucky; but then his master is forced to "sell Tom down the river" in order to repay his debts.

Sold away from his wife and children, Tom begins a journey down the Mississippi River with a slave trader. The farther Tom goes down the river, the worse conditions become for slaves. Arriving in New Orleans, Tom is finally sold to an abusive, villainous farm owner named Simon Legree. Even though Tom serves Legree faithfully, Legree beats him mercilessly. Through all of Legree's abuses, Tom holds fast to his pure Christian faith and prays for his wicked master. Eventually, Simon Legree beats Tom to death (see picture) for refusing to tell him where two runaway slaves have gone.

To the Christian audience of 1800s America, Tom's Christ-like response to his sufferings was inspiring.

Uncle Tom's Cabin argued effectively that it was impossible for a Christian person to support slavery-- Christianity and slaveholding were incompatible. The novel also ridiculed certain Southern ministers, who used passages from the Bible to justify slavery while they turned a blind eye to its obvious evils.

Uncle Tom's Cabin was such an important abolitionist novel that when Abraham Lincoln met Harriet Beecher Stowe during the Civil War, he reportedly said, "So this is the little lady that started this great war."

AMAZING AMERICANS: Frederick Douglass (1818 – 1895)

Frederick Douglass was the most prominent abolitionist leader of the 1800s. Born in Maryland to a slave mother and an unknown white father, Frederick grew up to become a well-known abolitionist speaker and the first black citizen to hold high rank in the U.S. government.

Frederick learned to read at around age 12, even though his master strongly disapproved of his reading because he knew that educated slaves would be more rebellious than uneducated ones. After learning to read himself, Frederick began to teach other slaves to read the New Testament. Frederick's master decided to punish his upstart slave by sending him to a poor farmer who beat his slaves. Frederick rebelled against these beatings and began to fight back. After more than one failed escape attempt, he finally managed to escape to New York by dressing as a sailor and carrying false identification papers.

Frederick began his life of freedom in New England, where he met the famous abolitionist William Lloyd Garrison. He became a regular speaker at Garrison's abolitionist meetings, where listeners were excited to hear him because he had personal experience of slavery and because he was a naturally gifted speaker and writer. He published his first autobiography, *Narrative of the Life of Frederick Douglass, an American Slave,* in 1845, and it became a bestseller.

Frederick's intelligence and education were so obvious in his writings that prejudiced whites refused to believe that he could have produced such eloquent words without help. He was living proof that black slaves possessed the intelligence required to live as free people, no matter what prejudiced whites might believe. He continued to speak, write and work against slavery all of his life.

Douglass was an early advocate (supporter) of integration: instead of keeping the black and white races separate (segregated), he wanted all races to live together in peace and equality. Douglass believed that integrated public schools would provide young blacks with better educations. Based on his own experience, he understood that quality education was the key to freeing the slaves.

Unlike the radical abolitionists William Lloyd Garrison and John Brown, Douglass believed that the U.S. Constitution was an anti-slavery constitution. Later in life, he worked to promote education for southern blacks and to support equal voting rights for both blacks and women.

The Dred Scott Decision

Dred Scott was a slave born in Virginia around 1800. After he was purchased by a U.S. Army Major, he traveled along with his owner to his various military assignments. Two of his owner's assignments were in Illinois and the Wisconsin Territory, both of which were free territories with no slavery allowed. Scott was married in a free territory and had a child in a free territory. Then his owner returned to the slaveholding south. Later, his owner sent for him, so Scott and his family returned to slave territory.

When Dred Scott's owner died, his late owner's wife became his new owner, and she continued to earn money on Scott by hiring him out as a laborer and keeping his wages for herself. Scott tried to purchase freedom for himself and his family; but his new owner needed the money that he earned for her, and refused to sell. So Scott decided to try to win his freedom by suing his owner in a Missouri court. His argument was that he should no longer be a slave: her husband, he said, had technically freed him by taking him to live in the free territories where slavery was illegal.

Aided by abolitionist lawyers, Scott kept up a series of court cases for years in pursuit of his freedom. His suit *Dred Scott v. Sandford* finally appeared before the U.S. Supreme Court in 1857.

The Supreme Court's decision in the Dred Scott case, written by Chief Justice Roger B. Taney, was decidedly pro-slavery. Instead of focusing on Scott's argument-- that his former owner had freed him by taking him to live in free territories-- Taney's decision focused on Scott's right to sue in the first place.

The Supreme Court decided that because he was born a slave, Scott was not a citizen, and therefore had no right to sue anyone at all, for any reason. It also decided that the U.S. Congress had no power to take away a slaveholder's "property" (his slaves) by designating new territories as "free," as it had done in the 1850 Missouri Compromise for every territory north of the 36-30 parallel. To some, this part of the ruling meant that slavery might legally continue to spread throughout all of the United States' unsettled territories.

The Supreme Court's pro-slavery decision in the Dred Scott case was one of many things that upset Abolitionists in the years just before the Civil War. Some abolitionists feared that as more and more slave states were admitted to the United States, Southern representatives would overpower Northern representatives in the federal government. Abolitionists grew increasingly frustrated by the government's many compromises with the supporters of slavery; and certain radical abolitionists, like John Brown, began to resort to violence.

U.S. GEOGRAPHY FOCUS

The Seven Continents

DID YOU KNOW…
- The globe has seven continents: Africa, Antarctica, Asia, Australia, Europe, North America and South America.
- Every continent except Antarctica is inhabited.
- About 70% (seven-tenths) of the globe is covered with water, and about 30% is covered with land.
- The equator is an imaginary line that divides the earth into two sections, the Northern Hemisphere and the Southern Hemisphere. "Hemisphere" means "half-globe."

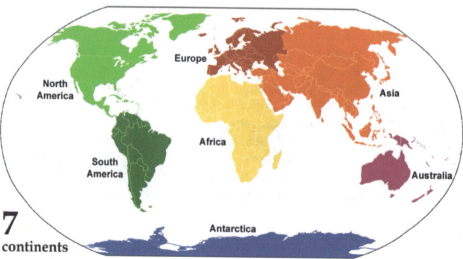

The Five Oceans

DID YOU KNOW...
- The globe has five oceans: the Atlantic Ocean, the Pacific Ocean, the Indian Ocean, the Arctic Ocean and the Southern Ocean.
- The Southern Ocean surrounds Antarctica. It is a fairly recent addition to maps and globes, and may not appear on older ones. Although the definition of "Southern Ocean" is disputed, some geographers define it as the body of ocean water south of the globe's 60th parallel south.
- The oceans have no well-defined boundaries; they are all interconnected. Some geographers refer to all five oceans together as the "World Ocean."

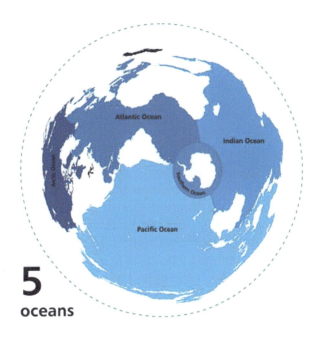

PRESIDENTIAL FOCUS

PRESIDENT #12: Zachary Taylor (1784 – 1850)	
In Office: March 4, 1849 – July 9, 1850	**Political Party:** Whig
Birthplace: Virginia	**Nickname:** "Old Rough and Ready"

Zachary Taylor was an old soldier and a hero of the Mexican-American War who was elected President in 1848. Before he became President, Taylor had never served in political office and had never even voted in an election. Since Taylor refused all postage due letters, he was unaware that he had even been nominated for the Presidency until several days after it happened. Taylor was no cagy politician, but rather a highly practical army general who was well-accustomed to command.

Taylor's Presidency came during the period of conflict before the Civil War. Although he was a Southerner who owned a plantation and slaves in Mississippi, he was loyal to the army and to the Union. At the end of the Mexican-American War, the United States had to decide how to handle the admissions of newly-won California and New Mexico to the Union. When both of these large territories appeared unlikely to allow slavery, some disappointed slave states threatened to secede from the Union. President Taylor responded to their threats with threats of his own: He promised to invade any state that disobeyed its nation's laws by seceding, and to hang any traitors he captured in rebel states.

President Taylor didn't live to fight the Civil War, which started eleven years later. After attending a ceremony at the unfinished Washington Monument on July 4, 1850, he suddenly grew ill. He died five days later, possibly of a heat stroke. His term in office lasted only 16 months.

Other interesting facts about President Zachary Taylor:
- While he lived in the White House, President Taylor kept his warhorse Whitney on the White House lawn. Visitors sometimes plucked Whitney's hairs to keep as souvenirs.
- As a devout Christian, President Taylor refused to take the inaugural oath on a Sunday.
- Although President Taylor indulged in the ungentlemanly habit of chewing tobacco, he also possessed this gentlemanly virtue: when spitting out the juice, he reportedly never missed the spittoon.
- Abraham Lincoln delivered the eulogy at President Taylor's funeral.

Chapter 2

The Crimean War, the Suez Canal, the Beginnings of the U.S. Civil War

WORLD HISTORY FOCUS

RUSSIA

What Has Gone Before

During the early modern era (1600 – 1850), Russian emperors Peter the Great and Catherine the Great worked to elevate their country's backward culture and industry to the advanced level of Western Europe's.

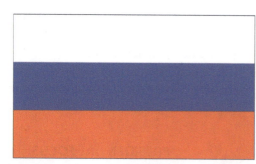

Tsar Nicholas I, who came to power in 1825, followed in Peter and Catherine's footsteps. Like his predecessors, Nicholas sought to elevate Russia to the same level as the greatest powers of his day, Britain and France. Armed with a newly-modernized military, Nicholas hoped to expand his empire south to Constantinople— just as his ancestors, the Kings of Rus, had hoped to conquer Constantinople hundreds of years before (see Year 2). With the all-important port of Constantinople in its grasp, Russia would at last gain free access to the Mediterranean Sea. Russian warships on the Mediterranean would protect Russian trade all over the world, allowing Russia to become as great as Britain and France.

One special circumstance made Tsar Nicholas I's fond hope of conquering Constantinople seem more attainable: the growing weakness of Constantinople's long-time master, the Ottoman Empire.

CRITICAL CONCEPTS: The Eastern Question and the Balance of Power

The Ottoman Empire was an Islamic Empire founded by Sultan Osman I around 1300 AD. After conquering Asia Minor, the Ottoman sultans expanded into the Middle East, North Africa and even southeast Europe (see map). The Ottoman Empire reached its peak in power and size in the 1500s and 1600s, under mighty sultans like Suleiman the Magnificent (reigned 1520 – 1566) and the uncommonly strong Murad IV (reigned 1623 – 1640).

Later, however, the Ottoman Empire grew weak. Its leaders clung to their traditional Islamic way of life, refusing to modernize their backward industry and culture. The empire's once-feared elite army, the Janissary Corps, failed to keep pace with the new weapons and tactics Western armies were using. Far-off territories like Hungary and Egypt began breaking away from Ottoman control. By the mid-1800s, the Ottoman Empire seemed to stand on the verge of collapse.

The decline of the Ottoman Empire gave rise to the **Eastern Question**:

How would the decline of the Ottoman Empire affect the balance of power in Europe? Should the other European powers allow the Ottoman Empire to fall? Or should they prop up the empire to preserve the balance of power? If the Ottoman Empire did fall— as all believed it would— then how should the other European empires divide its territories?

The Congress of Vienna— the body of diplomats that negotiated the end of the awful Napoleonic Wars back in 1815— had sought to avoid future wars by establishing a **balance of power** in Europe. To accomplish this, the Congress had divided Europe's territory and resources as equally as possible between the six major empires of the day: **(1) Britain, (2) France, (3) Austria, (4) Prussia, (5) Russia** and **(6) the Ottoman Empire**. Diplomats hoped that with territory and resources so evenly divided, no empire would bother attacking another, for none would have anything to gain. Thanks to the balance of power established by the Congress of Vienna, 1816 had been the first year of an almost century-long *Pax Britannica*— a "Britannic Peace" during which Europe suffered no continent-wide wars.

Russia's ambitions in Constantinople threatened the Pax Britannica. Britain and France feared that if Russia absorbed too much of the dying Ottoman Empire's territory, then it might upset the balance of power, dragging all of Europe into war. The Crimean War was Britain and France's attempt to accomplish two goals: (1) to preserve the balance of power; and (2) to maintain their navies' great advantages in the Mediterranean Sea.

As of 1853, the Ottoman Empire still held territory all around Constantinople and the Middle East, including the Holy Land of Palestine. However, weakness and internal disagreements threatened the empire's hold on these territories. Like vultures circling over a dying animal, the powers of Western Europe (Britain and France) and Eastern Europe (Russia, Prussia and Austria) argued over how to answer the Eastern Question, a question raised by the Ottomans Empire's coming collapse.

Just before the Crimean War, England and France reconciled their longstanding feud and formed an alliance against Russia. The two former enemies agreed that they must bar Russian warships from the Mediterranean Sea— or else Russia might take over the entire Ottoman Empire, becoming too large to contain.

The Crimean War (1853 – 1856)

Like the Christian-versus-Muslim Crusades of the medieval era, the Crimean War began with an argument over the Holy Land of Palestine. Both Russia and France coveted the Holy Land:

- Russian Orthodox Christians and their emperor, Tsar Nicholas I, had already signed treaties with the Ottoman Empire making Russia the official "protector" of such holy sites as (1) the Church of the Holy Sepulcher in Jerusalem, built on the site of Jesus' burial; and (2) the Church of the Nativity in Bethlehem, built on the site of Jesus' birth. Such treaties, known in the West as the "Ottoman Capitulations," were partly designed to protect Christians who lived under the anti-Christian government of the Ottoman Empire.
- French Catholic Christians and their emperor, Napoleon III, wanted France to take Russia's place as the official protector of the Holy Land.

When Russia and France started arguing over the Holy Land, the Ottomans saw a chance to gain the aid of the mighty French army against their longtime enemies, the Russians. First, the Ottomans signed a new treaty making France, not Russia, the official protector of the Holy Land. In response, Russia advanced troops into two northern provinces of the Ottoman Empire: Moldavia and Wallachia, both of which lay along the Danube River in what is now Romania.

Emboldened by their alliance with France, the Ottomans issued a deadline ultimatum, warning that Russia would face consequences if it failed to remove its troops from Moldavia and Wallachia before the deadline. **When the Russians missed the deadline, the Ottoman Empire launched the first attacks of the Crimean War.**

The Crimean War in 1853

After declaring war on Russia on October 23, 1853, the Ottomans surged across the Danube River, trying to force the Russians out of Moldavia and Wallachia. Predictably, the backward Ottoman army failed to drive out the more modern Russian army. The Ottomans' losses spread to the Black Sea on November 30, when their navy suffered a devastating defeat at the Battle of Sinop.

This Russian victory on the Black Sea gave the French and their new allies, the British, the excuse they needed to join the war. After declaring war on Russia in March 1854, Britain and France repeated the Ottomans' demand that Russia withdraw from Moldavia and Wallachia.

In mid-1854, Russia surprised everyone by agreeing to withdraw. If defending Ottoman territory had been the West's true goal, then the Crimean War could have ended there and then, without any further bloodshed.

Unfortunately, the West's true goal was a more self-interested one: barring Russian warships from the Mediterranean Sea. Therefore instead of accepting the Russian withdrawal, the West piled on more demands; and when Russia failed to meet these new demands, the French and British navies moved into the Black Sea. The Russian fleet waited at its port in Sevastopol, where it remained a constant threat but saw little action.

IMPORTANT PORTS: Sevastopol

Sevastopol is a port city on the southwest coast of the Crimean Peninsula, which lies in the Black Sea. Before the Crimean War, Sevastopol was Russia's chief naval station and most important port. As such, Sevastopol was critically important to Russia's ambitions. With it, the Russian navy could carry Russian troops and supplies all over the Black Sea region. Without it, Russia could not hope to absorb any more of the dissolving Ottoman Empire's territories.

The Siege of Sevastopol

In September 1854, the French, the British and a smaller number of Ottomans landed on the Crimean Peninsula. Their goal was to capture Sevastopol, thus depriving Russia of its best Black Sea naval station.

The Siege of Sevastopol would last almost a year, and would involve disastrous tactical mistakes by both sides. The Battle of Balaclava, which included the ill-fated Charge of the Light Brigade (see below), was only the second of several major battles in the Crimean Peninsula campaign.

One result of these battles was the utter destruction of the Russian navy on the Black Sea. In their desperation to save Sevastopol, the Russians made the best use of their navy they could: they removed their ships' cannon for use in land battles, and then scuttled (deliberately sank) their ships in the entrance to their harbor, barring entry for a time.

Despite these desperate tactics, the Russians finally surrendered Sevastopol in September 1855. With the loss of Sevastopol, Russia no longer held any significant navy or naval station in the Black Sea.

The Treaty of Paris, which ended the Crimean War in 1856, put an end to Russia's hope of capturing Constantinople. The Black Sea was declared neutral territory; both the Russians and the Ottomans agreed not to maintain warships or naval bases on its shores. The blasted ruin of Sevastopol, which had cost the French and the British eleven months and many lives to capture, returned to Russian control— but not as a naval base.

MAJOR RESULTS OF THE CRIMEAN WAR:

Under the terms of the Treaty of Paris, signed on March 30, 1856:

- Russia agreed to withdraw from Moldavia and Wallachia, which remained Ottoman provinces.
- Russia surrendered its right to protect Christians in the Holy Land; France became the Holy Land's protector.
- Both Russia and the Ottoman Empire agreed that the Black Sea was neutral territory. No warships were allowed in the Black Sea, nor could either side maintain naval bases on its shores.

The Treaty of Paris held only until 1871, when Prussia defeated France in the Franco-Prussian War (see Chapter 7). The Franco-Prussian War weakened France tremendously, to the point where it could no longer enforce the Treaty of Paris. Once freed from the threat of French warships, Russia soon re-established its fleet in the Black Sea.

FASCINATING FACTS: The Charge of the Light Brigade and the Thin Red Line

The Charge of the Light Brigade was an ill-fated cavalry charge ordered by British officers at the Battle of Balaclava, a Crimean War battle fought in October 1854. Confusion about the direction of the Light Brigade's charge led to disaster on the battlefield, and a costly defeat for the British.

Balaclava lay near Sevastopol, a critical Russian naval base on the southwest coast of the Crimean Peninsula. British, French and some Turkish (Ottoman Empire) troops were moving toward Sevastopol when the Russians came out to meet them at Balaclava. The Light Brigade and the Heavy Brigade were the two main British cavalry units engaged at the Battle of Balaclava.

The battle began with Russian cannon driving Turkish troops off a ridge called the Causeway Heights (see map next page). The Turks, allies of the British and French, had been trying to build a set of six defensive positions along the Causeway Heights. When the Russians attacked, the Turks fled, leaving behind some very valuable British cannon.

The first time Russian cavalry advanced onto the Causeway Heights, the British managed to drive them back with the successful Charge of the Heavy Brigade. The "Thin Red Line" formed by the Scottish Highland Brigade met and stopped another Russian advance. However, the Russians did manage to capture part of the Causeway Heights, including the British cannon abandoned by the Turks. The British battle commander, Lord Raglan, sent the Light Brigade to recapture those abandoned cannon.

Two circumstances doomed the Charge of the Light Brigade to failure: (1) Raglan's instructions were so vague as to be easily misunderstood; and (2) the aide who carried Raglan's instructions to the Light Brigade, Captain Nolan, was thoroughly overexcited. Raglan intended the Light Brigade to follow the road up the Causeway Heights, near where the Heavy Brigade had fought, and drive the Russians off the heights. Instead, Captain Nolan sent the Light Brigade into the valley below the heights— a valley protected by Russian cannon.

With a reckless boldness inspired by duty and loyalty, the Light Brigade charged directly into the heavily-defended valley. When Captain Nolan saw the brigade going the wrong way, he rode out in front, trying to redirect it; but sadly, enemy artillery cut him down before he could do so. Continuing on its errant course, the Light Brigade charged down the full length of the valley— a distance of about 1-1/2 miles, all under heavy Russian fire. Murderous shot rained down on the Light Brigade, cutting down horse after horse, man after man.

When the Light Brigade reached the far end of the valley, enough cavalrymen survived to launch a successful attack. Despite this temporary victory, though, the Battle of Balaclava ended in a British loss. The Russians managed to retain their positions along the Causeway Heights— positions which the Light Brigade might have captured if it had understood its orders.

The worst disaster was the casualty count. Before its famous charge, the Light Brigade numbered more than six hundred mounted cavalrymen. After the charge, fewer than two hundred remained in fighting condition— a crushing loss of nearly 70 per cent.

The fame of the Light Brigade continues today because of the incredibly brave, dutiful way its soldiers followed orders, even though they must have suspected that their leaders were making a terrible mistake. This bravery is commemorated in the well-known poem by Alfred, Lord Tennyson that includes these famous lines: "Theirs not to make reply / Theirs not to reason why / Theirs but to do and die."

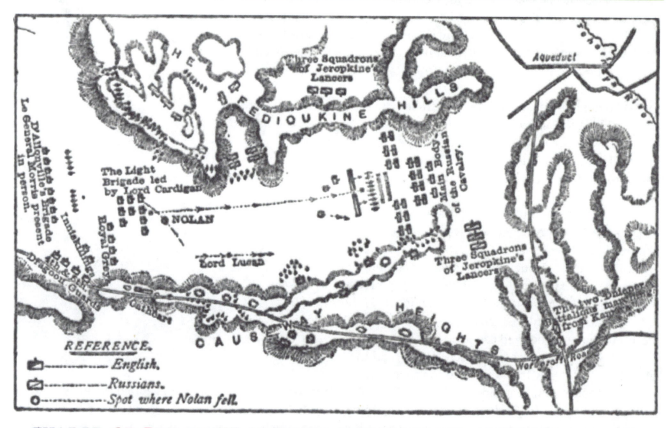

CHARGE OF THE LIGHT BRIGADE AT BALACLAVA, OCTOBER 25th, 1854

The Charge of the Light Brigade
by Alfred, Lord Tennyson

Half a league, half a league, half a league onward,
All in the valley of Death rode the six hundred.
'Forward, the Light Brigade! Charge for the guns!' he said:
Into the valley of Death rode the six hundred.
'Forward, the Light Brigade!' Was there a man dismay'd?
Not tho' the soldier knew someone had blunder'd:
Theirs not to make reply, theirs not to reason why,
Theirs but to do and die:
Into the valley of Death rode the six hundred.

Cannon to right of them, cannon to left of them,
Cannon in front of them volley'd and thunder'd;
Storm'd at with shot and shell, boldly they rode and well,
Into the jaws of Death, into the mouth of Hell
Rode the six hundred.

Flash'd all their sabres bare,
Flash'd as they turn'd in air Sabring the gunners there,
Charging an army, while all the world wonder'd:
Plunged in the battery-smoke right thro' the line they broke;
Cossack and Russian reel'd from the sabre-stroke shatter'd and sunder'd.
Then they rode back,
But not, not the six hundred.

Cannon to right of them, cannon to left of them,
Cannon behind them volley'd and thunder'd;
Storm'd at with shot and shell, while horse and hero fell,
They that had fought so well came thro' the jaws of Death,
Back from the mouth of Hell, all that was left of them,
Left of six hundred.

When can their glory fade?
O the wild charge they made! All the world wonder'd.
Honour the charge they made! Honour the Light Brigade,
Noble six hundred!

FASCINATING FACTS: Firsts in the Crimean War

In several ways, the Crimean War was the first "modern war" – the first major war to make heavy use of modern industrial and communications technology. Here are some "firsts" of the Crimean War:

- Crimean War troops were among the first to use the **Minie ball**, a precisely-manufactured lead bullet with grooves that provided greater accuracy, range and power for riflemen (see picture).
- The Crimean War was the first war to be regularly recorded by a photographer. The photographic technology of the day, called the daguerreotype, required anywhere from several seconds to several minutes of exposure to take a picture.

- The Crimean War was also the first far-off war to be reported back to the British and French homelands by fast-moving telegraph, train and steamship technology. Thus the West heard news of the war soon after it happened, rather than weeks or months later.

BRILLIANT BRITONS: Florence Nightingale (1820 – 1910)

The terrible modern weapons of the Crimean War led to terrible wounds, accompanied by terrible infections. During the war, a British reporter toured the army hospitals in the Crimea and reported that conditions in the British hospitals were far worse than conditions in the French hospitals. The people of Britain were appalled to think that the French treated their wounded better than they themselves did. One Briton who heard these reports was Florence Nightingale.

Florence was born in 1820 to a well-to-do English family living in Florence, Italy. Florence's parents named her for the city of her birth. The usual program for wealthy girls like Florence was formal social gatherings, followed by marriage, followed by children. Florence was different: She shocked her parents when she told them from an early age that she wanted to be a nurse. In her parents' eyes, nurses were little more than servants. Even so, Florence finally convinced her father to allow her to begin her nursing studies in Germany in 1851, when she was thirty-one years old.

In 1854, Florence began to hear news from the Crimean War. Within a few weeks of the first British troops' arrival in the Ottoman Empire, about 8,000 of them died from cholera and malaria. Florence volunteered her services, and received permission to lead a group of thirty-eight nurses to Turkey.

When she arrived in Turkey, Florence found the conditions at the war hospitals there appalling. Many soldiers were dying, not from their war wounds, but from poor care, lack of food, dirty bedding and rampant disease in the hospitals. The wounded were unwashed, lying in filthy and overcrowded tents or rooms. Typhus, cholera and dysentery were spreading.

By working 20 hours per day, Florence and her nurses changed these conditions. They organized a kitchen and laundry, cleaned the hospital and ordered bedding and clothing for their patients. They also worked with a government commission to improve ventilation and sewers. The loving care Florence provided made her a favorite with the wounded soldiers, who called her the "Lady of the Lamp" because she often walked among them during the night, checking their conditions. Some kissed her shadow as it passed over their beds, as if she were an angel. Through the work of Florence Nightingale, thousands of wounded soldiers who might have died were saved.

After the war, Florence founded the Nightingale School and Home for Nurses in London, England. She is honored as the creator of the modern nursing education program.

FASCINATING FACTS: The Sublime Porte

The Sublime Porte was the court in which the Ottoman sultans' highest government official, the grand vizier, received visits from foreign diplomats. The Sublime Porte took its name from the gate of Topkapi Palace, the sublime sultans' official home palace (see picture).

The Divan was a council of the sultans' highest advisers, the viziers.

A bey was a regional governor who ruled a territory of the empire with the sultans' permission.

EGYPT

During the Middle Ages, control of Egypt passed from Saladin's Ayyubid Dynasty to the Mamluk Sultanate. The Mamluks were a class of slaves who were trained from their youth to be warriors, and some of them rose to power in Egypt to form a dynasty of their own. In 1517, the Ottoman Empire conquered the Mamluk Sultanate, just as it had already conquered most of the Muslim world. Even under the Ottomans, however, the Mamluks still held power as the sultans' viceroys in Egypt.

Emperor Napoleon of France briefly conquered Egypt in 1798, but an alliance of Ottoman, Mamluk and British forces expelled him in 1801. In 1805, an Albanian army commander named Muhammad Ali defeated the Mamluks to become the Ottoman sultan's new viceroy in Egypt.

INTERESTING INDIVIDUALS: Muhammad Ali Pasha (1769 – 1848, reigned 1805 – 1848)

Muhammad Ali Pasha was an Ottoman Empire army officer from Albania, a nation in the Balkan region (north of modern-day Greece). He rose to power in Egypt as the Ottoman sultan's viceroy; but because the Ottoman Empire was weakening, Ali ruled Egypt almost independently.

Ali arrived in Egypt in 1801 as part of the Ottoman force that was sent to reclaim Egypt after Napoleon's brief occupation. The still-strong Mamluks also fought for control of Egypt, hoping to cast out the Ottomans. Muhammad Ali was able to calm the chaos that followed France's departure and take the place of the Mamluk former governor. What he needed next was a plan to eliminate future problems with Egypt's powerful Mamluks.

His solution to the Mamluk problem was to invite the Mamluks to a feast, a lavish celebration in honor of his son Tusun Pasha. After the feast, a large Mamluk unit was marching near the end of a military parade inside the Citadel of Cairo. Just as the marching Mamluks were about exit the Citadel, the gates slammed shut. The Mamluks turned to find Ali's Albanian troops behind them, sealing the trap. The many Mamluks were all crowded into the tight space before the gate, defenseless. Ali's men on the high walls of the Citadel rained down fire upon them and destroyed them. In this brutal fashion, Muhammad Ali eliminated his Mamluk rivals and cemented his hold on Egypt.

One of Ali's goals for Egypt was to modernize it. He sent Egyptian students to the West to learn modern military and industrial techniques. He built factories for weapons, ships and uniforms, as well as a military hospital. He also made cotton growing an important national industry. In the process, he "nationalized," or took over, most Egyptian land and industry, until his government essentially owned nearly everything and everyone. He raised taxes to such a high level that farmers were forced to sell their land to the government in order to pay what they owed. He forced cotton growers to sell their cotton to the government so that he could raise the price and resell it later at a profit. He also forced laborers to work at his factories against their will (Forced labor is sometimes known as corvee labor).

As Ali's power grew, he began to claim former Ottoman Empire territories in Sudan (east Africa), Arabia, Syria and Anatolia (Asia Minor, modern-day Turkey). From 1838-1840, Ali even threatened to capture Constantinople (the Ottoman capital) itself and overthrow the Ottoman Empire. Ali's near-capture of Constantinople is known in the West as the Oriental Crisis of 1840.

In fear of Ali, the Ottoman sultan negotiated an alliance with Great Britain and other European nations for protection. In order to preserve the balance of power (see above), Great Britain agreed to support the ailing Ottoman Empire, just as it would later in the Crimean War. In 1840, as in 1854, the British answer to the "Eastern Question" was to prop up the dying Ottoman Empire.

Britain threatened to attack Egypt if Ali attacked Constantinople. Faced with the prospect of hostile British warships bombarding Alexandria, Ali decided to withdraw from Anatolia and leave the Ottoman sultan in power. However, he did receive one major concession in exchange: He became Egypt's hereditary governor, able to pass the governorship down to his heirs. Muhammad Ali Pasha had succeeded in establishing a new dynasty in Egypt and Sudan, and had made Egypt nearly independent of the Ottoman Empire. He died in 1848.

FASCINATING FACTS: The Citadel of Cairo and the Well of Joseph (Saladin's Well)

Cairo is the capital of Egypt, and it sits on the Nile River at the head of the Nile Delta. Its name means "conqueror." The Citadel of Cairo is a medieval castle and fortress on a hill in the center of Cairo, first built by Saladin around 1180 (see picture). The Citadel would remain the seat of Egyptian government until about 1860.

The Citadel of Cairo was surrounded by walls that were about thirty feet high and three feet thick. Round towers projected out from the walls so that defenders could shoot at the flanks of any attackers who tried to scale the walls. Inside the walls' protection were mosques, army headquarters and government buildings.

To provide water for the Citadel in case of a siege, Saladin dug a well called the Well of Joseph. The Well of Joseph is no mere hole in the ground, but rather a large manmade cavern carved through many feet of solid rock. Around its perimeter, circular stairs are carved directly into the rock. The backbreaking labor of digging the Well of Joseph may have been performed by Christian prisoners captured during the Crusades of the Medieval age.

WORLD GEOGRAPHY FOCUS

THE SUEZ CANAL

Muhammad Ali Pasha's son Abbas I succeeded him as governor, reigning from 1848 - 1854. Ali's grandson Said Pasha reigned from 1854 - 1863, and his great-grandson Ismail Pasha reigned from 1863 - 1879. All three of these descendants of Ali were involved with negotiating or building the Suez Canal.

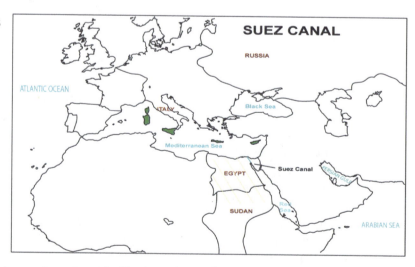

The Suez Canal is a manmade waterway that connects the eastern Mediterranean Sea to the Gulf of Suez, and through the Gulf of Suez to the Red Sea, the Gulf of Aden, the Arabian Sea and finally the Indian Ocean. The canal is about 120 miles long, and its passage by ship requires about half a day. This makes the Suez Canal a vast improvement over the water route it replaced: Before the Suez Canal, a trip from the Mediterranean world to the Far East required a journey of thousands of miles around the southern tip of Africa through perilous seas.

Long ago, the ancient Egyptians built east-west canals to aid transportation from the Nile River to the Red Sea. When Napoleon Bonaparte briefly held Egypt from 1798 - 1801, he found evidence of these canals. Napoleon was interested in the possibility of a north-south canal between the Red Sea and the Mediterranean Sea, because he believed that such a canal in French hands would give him an immeasurable advantage over his enemies the British. Unfortunately, his surveyors told him that there was a 30-foot height difference between the two seas, so that any canal would require an expensive system of locks to raise and lower ships as they traversed it. Napoleon abandoned his canal idea; but even if he had started work on his canal, he would have been forced to abandon it when Britain joined with the Ottoman Empire to drive him out of Egypt in 1801.

The canal idea didn't end with Napoleon. Both French and British engineers studied the problem; and, in 1854 - 1856, a French developer named Ferdinand de Lesseps received permission from Egypt's governor Said Pasha to design and build his canal. De Lesseps formed the Suez Canal Company in 1858 and started work in 1859, using a great deal of forced Egyptian labor (corvee labor). It turned out that the sea levels at the opposite ends of the canal were equal, and that the finished canal was perfectly level, requiring no locks at all. Even so, the canal was a vast excavation and a tremendous engineering challenge.

From the beginning, Britain opposed the Suez Canal project because it threatened their lucrative trade with India and the Far East— such a canal would render the trip to the Far East easy for anyone and everyone. By complaining about the use of corvee labor and encouraging the canal workers to rebel against their French masters, the British managed to halt construction on the canal for a time.

<u>After ten difficult years, however, the Suez Canal finally opened to ships of all nations in November 1869</u>. Its importance was enormous: it enabled the European powers to colonize East Africa, and made travel to the Far East much easier and safer. World travel was a far simpler matter with the Suez Canal in place.

Egypt's governor Ismail Pasha went deep into debt to purchase a large share of the Suez Canal Company, and he soon found himself unable to keep up with the payments on this debt. In 1875, he was forced to sell his share of the company to his lenders: British bankers. Thus Britain, which had opposed the canal's creation, ended up owning over forty percent of the Suez Canal Company; while the Egyptians, on whose territory the canal was built, owned none of it. In 1882, Britain would invade Egypt and assume full control over the all-important Suez Canal (see Chapter 21). When it left Egypt in 1936, Britain would still insist on controlling the canal by maintaining Egypt's Suez Canal Zone.

U.S. HISTORY FOCUS

AMAZING AMERICANS: Clara Barton (1821 – 1912)

Clara Barton was a professional teacher and clerk who worked as a nurse during the Civil War. After the war, she became the first President of the American Red Cross, an agency that still provides medical relief during wars and natural disasters.

Clara was born in Oxford, Massachusetts, the youngest of five children. When she was eleven years old, her older brother David hurt himself badly in a fall from the roof of an unfinished family barn. Clara got her introduction to nursing as she stayed by his side for two years, caring for him.

Later, Clara taught school for several years and even helped to found a school in New Jersey. But when the time came to hire a school administrator, the school board chose a man instead of Clara. Disgusted by the school board's choice, Clara left teaching and moved to Washington DC, where she got a good job as a clerk in the U.S. Patent Office.

When the Civil war broke out, Clara went to work caring for wounded soldiers from her home state of Massachusetts. These wounded were housed in the U.S. Capitol building, for lack of a better place. She discovered that there was a shortage of medical supplies for the wounded, and set out to acquire these supplies. Later, the Union army issued Clara a special pass that allowed her access to supplies from all over the Union. The army also supplied her with wagons so that she could transport medical supplies and wounded soldiers to and from the battlefield. She cared for the wounded day and night, sometimes without sleep, whether they were Confederate or Union. For this she earned the nickname "Angel of the Battlefield."

After the war, Clara made every effort to help war-bereaved families discover what had happened to their lost soldiers. She also became a popular traveling speaker by telling tales of her war experiences. She met Susan B. Anthony and Frederick Douglass, and supported both of their causes (women's voting rights and black civil rights). After learning about the International Red Cross, she founded the American Red Cross in 1881, and served as its President for 23 years.

U.S. GEOGRAPHY FOCUS

The United States

Did you know…
- The United States is a union of 50 individual states. All except one, Hawaii, lie on the continent of North America.
- The capital of the United States is Washington D.C.
- The smallest of the 50 states is Rhode Island, and the largest is Alaska.
- The United States also controls 14 far-flung islands and island chains: American Samoa, Baker Island, Guam, Howland Island, Jarvis Island, Johnston Atoll, Kingman Reef, Midway Islands, Navassa Island, Northern Mariana Islands, Palmyra Atoll, Puerto Rico, U.S. Virgin Islands and Wake Island.
- The lowest elevation in the United States is Badwater Basin in Death Valley, California, which lies 282 feet below sea level.
- The highest elevation in the United States is Mt. McKinley, Alaska, which rises 20,236 feet above seal level.
- The United States shares land borders with only two nations: Canada to the north and Mexico to the south.
- The Rio Grande River forms part of the border between the United States and Mexico.

United States Flag

Did you know…
- The United States flag has thirteen stripes, one for each of the thirteen colonies that rebelled against British rule in the Revolutionary War of 1776 – 1783. Seven of the flag's stripes are red, and six are white.
- The flag also has 50 stars, one for each of the 50 states. There are four rows of five stars each, and five rows of six stars each, all arranged on a blue field.
- The flag's nicknames include "Old Glory" and "the Stars and Stripes."

PRESIDENTIAL FOCUS

PRESIDENT #13: Millard Fillmore (1800 – 1874)	
In Office: July 9, 1850 – March 4, 1853	**Political Party:** Whig
Birthplace: New York	**Nickname:** "Last of the Whigs"

New York-born Millard Fillmore rose through the New York state assembly and the U.S. House of Representatives to win election as President Zachary Taylor's vice president. When President Taylor died of illness after sixteen months in office, Fillmore became president in his place.

Fillmore was one of several pre-Civil War presidents who sought to hold the fast-dividing nation together by compromising with slaveholders. Although he did not believe in slavery himself, he was willing to compromise with those who did. The Compromise of 1850 included concessions to abolitionists, because it admitted California to the Union as a free state and outlawed the slave trade in Washington DC; but it also included a major concession to the supporters of slavery, because it contained the Fugitive Slave Act. President Taylor had opposed the Compromise of 1850; but he was gone, dead of heat stroke. President Fillmore reversed Taylor's position and supported the Compromise of 1850, which passed with great difficulty as a series of five bills. Fillmore's Compromise of 1850 may have kept the states of the Deep South from seceding right away, but it also gave the people of the North more reasons to be angry with the South.

It was President Fillmore who commissioned Commodore Matthew Perry to travel to Japan in pursuit of a trade agreement, an agreement that soon led to the end of Japanese *Sakoku* (isolation) and the opening Japan (see Chapter 9). Fillmore also solidified the United States' tenuous hold on Hawaii by warning off France's Emperor Napoleon III.

Other interesting facts about Millard Fillmore:
- When Millard was young, his family was so poor that his father made his son an indentured servant to a cloth maker (indentured servants worked as slaves until they paid off their debt, or "indenture.") Millard finally escaped this miserable life by borrowing thirty dollars to pay off his indenture.
- Fillmore first entered school in his late teens. He later married his teacher, Abigail Powers.
- The adult Fillmore was a voracious reader who owned a personal library of about 4,000 books.
- Abigail Fillmore installed the White House's first bathtub with running water.

Notable quote from Millard Fillmore:
- "God knows that I detest slavery, but it is an existing evil, for which we are not responsible, and we must endure it, till we can get rid of it without destroying the last hope of free government in the world."

PRESIDENT #14: Franklin Pierce (1804 – 1869)	
In Office: March 4, 1853 – March 4, 1857	**Political Party:** Democrat
Birthplace: New Hampshire	**Nicknames:** "Handsome Frank" and "Fainting Frank"

Franklin Pierce was a New Hampshire politician who unexpectedly won the Presidency in 1852. Pierce was known as a "doughface," a Northern politician who always seemed to side with the South on the issue of slavery. This made him a compromise candidate who was able to combine votes from both North and South in order to win the Presidential election of 1852. President Pierce's willingness to allow slavery in new U.S. territories angered Northern abolitionists and led to conflict in "Bloody Kansas."

After serving in the New Hampshire legislature, Pierce became a U.S. congressman, then a senator. He resigned from the Senate in 1841, possibly because his wife hated Washington DC and refused to live there (Built on a swamp, Washington was not yet the beautiful city that it is today). When the Mexican-American War began, Pierce used his political connections to obtain a commission as a U.S. Army Brigadier General—despite the fact that he had absolutely no military experience. He served under "Old Fuss and Feathers," General Winfield Scott, who would oppose him in the Presidential election of 1852. During the war, Pierce earned the nickname "Fainting Frank" because he lost consciousness after falling off of his horse.

The biggest event of Pierce's Presidency was the passage of the Kansas-Nebraska Act, which repealed the Missouri Compromise of 1820 and allowed the new territories of Kansas and Nebraska to decide for themselves whether or not to allow Slavery. Pierce reluctantly supported the Kansas-Nebraska Act. If Kansas or Nebraska voted to allow slavery, it would mean that slavery would be legal in the North, a possibility that appalled abolitionists. Pro-slavery and anti-slavery settlers alike rushed into the two new territories, both to claim land and to try to influence the slavery vote. In Kansas, the disagreement over slavery became violent. Some of that violence involved the radical abolitionist John Brown (see Chapter 4).

President Pierce also angered the North when he considered annexing Cuba and Nicaragua into the United States, because both would have entered the Union as slaveholding territories or states. Pierce's many compromises on slavery, which had made him electable in 1852, made him untouchable in 1856. The Democratic Party abandoned Pierce and chose James Buchanan to run for President in his place.

Other interesting facts about Franklin Pierce:
- Pierce's secretary of war was Jefferson Davis, who would become the President of the Confederate States of America.
- His son died tragically two months before his inauguration, so he held no inaugural ball.
- He suffered from depression and perhaps alcoholism.
- He was a college friend of the author Nathaniel Hawthorne, who later wrote his biography.

Notable quotes from Franklin Pierce:
- "A Republic without parties is a complete anomaly. The histories of all popular governments show absurd is the idea of their attempting to exist without parties."
- "It must be felt that there is no national security but in the nation's humble, acknowledged dependence upon God and His overruling providence."

Chapter 3

The Great Game in Afghanistan, Dr. Livingstone in Africa

WORLD HISTORY FOCUS

AFGHANISTAN

Independence for Afghanistan

Afghanistan is a mountain-filled nation in south central Asia. Because it has no seacoasts, Afghanistan is said to be **landlocked**. During the 1800s, its neighbors were Persia (Iran) to the west, India to the south and east, and Russia to the north. Its geographical location between three great empires made it a strategic crossroads, a borderland between West and East. For this reason Afghanistan became a war-torn nation, as invaders from both West and East sought to control its mountain passes. These invasions go as far back as Alexander the Great, before 300 BC.

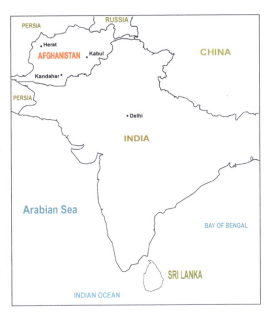

In the Medieval age, Afghanistan was a disunited region peopled by various tribes. Arabs of the Islamic Empire brought Islam to the Afghanistan region during 700-900 AD. Around 1200 AD, Mongols from the Far East led by Genghis Khan's heirs overran the Afghanistan region and forced its people to make tribute payments to the Mongol *khans* (regional governors). The khans retained control of Afghanistan through the 1500s. When the Mongol Empire finally collapsed, the Afghanistan region spent the next 200 years caught between two rival powers: the Moghul Dynasty of India and the Safavid Dynasty of Persia. India claimed southern Afghanistan, and Persia claimed the rest. Both ruled as occupiers and treated the Afghan natives poorly.

In the 1700s, native Afghans began to lead Afghanistan away from Persian control and toward independence. The most successful of these was a former Persian military leader named Ahmad Shah Durrani.

AMAZING AFGHANIS: Ahmad Shah Durrani (1722? – 1773, reigned 1747 – 1773)

Ahmad Shah Durrani was the founder of independent Afghanistan. Upon the death of Nader Shah of Persia, Ahmad liberated his Afghani homeland from Persian rule and established Afghanistan as an independent nation.

Ahmad was a native Afghani who entered the service of Nader Shah of Persia when the Shah was recruiting young Afghanis. He began his military career as Nader Shah's personal attendant, then rose to become the commander of a large unit of 4,000 cavalry. Most of Ahmad's cavalrymen were native Afghanis like himself. Thus, when the time came to break away from Persia, Ahmad already had a small army of loyal Afghanis ready-made.

Ahmad's breakaway opportunity came in 1747, when someone, possibly the Shah's own nephew, assassinated Nader Shah. Upon Nader Shah's death, Ahmad and his cavalry unit decided to abandon the Persian army and head home to Kandahar, Afghanistan.

Along the way, Ahmad was lucky enough to capture an Indian caravan filled with treasure, which made him a wealthy man. Ahmad's combination of wealth, experience and military power made him the logical choice to lead the newly united Afghani people. When an Afghani council at Kandahar elected him as its leader, Ahmad took the name *Durr-i-Durrani,* "Pearl among Pearls," to indicate that his people were all pearls and that he himself was the special pearl at their head. Ahmad's dynasty became known as the Durrani Dynasty.

Ahmad Shah expanded Afghanistan in all directions (picture at right shows soldiers of the Durrani army). He drove the Persians west and the Indians south until his Muslim empire was the second largest in the world, behind only the enormous Ottoman Empire. Ahmad reigned in Afghanistan for 26 years, and died of natural causes in 1773.

Unfortunately, Ahmad Shah Durrani's weaker successors were unable to retain all of the territories he had won for Afghanistan.

Afghanistan struggled and shrank through the remainder of the Durrani Dynasty, which lasted until 1826. Disagreement over who should succeed the great Ahmad Shah Durrani led to civil war between Afghanistan's many clans. The Durrani Dynasty also had great difficulty with the Sikhs from the Punjab region of northern India, who built a Sikh Empire under the leadership of Maharajah Ranjit Singh.

The Great Game in Afghanistan

In the early 1800s, both Britain and Russia became deeply interested in Afghanistan. Britain controlled most of India through the East India Company, and thus bordered Afghanistan on the south. Russia was dominant in the north. Both sides tried to defend their territories by controlling the border region between them– poor, luckless Afghanistan.

> DEFINITION: The political and military duel between Britain and Russia over control of Afghanistan (and Persia) became known as "The Great Game."

> FASCINATING FACTS: Rudyard Kipling's *Kim*
>
> *Kim* is the title of a 1901 novel by the great British author Rudyard Kipling, who often based his writing on India. The novel's title character, Kimball O'Hara, is the orphaned son of an Irish soldier who dies serving the British in India. Without his father, young Kim is forced to survive in India alone, in any way he can. While traveling with a Tibetan Lama, he meets a British officer who is involved in the diplomatic duel between Britain and Russia over control of Afghanistan. Kim secretly delivers messages for the officer, and thus becomes involved in the cagy maneuvering that he begins to call "The Great Game."
>
> This highly appropriate phrase, which Kipling borrowed from a British intelligence officer named Arthur Conolly, soon became well-known. Ever since *Kim* became a popular novel, students of history have known the struggle between Britain and Russia over Afghanistan as "The Great Game."

The maneuvering of the Great Game took place over a period of nearly 100 years, roughly from 1813 - 1907. Early in the Great Game, a new ruler and a new dynasty came to power in Afghanistan: Emir Dost Mohammad Khan replaced the Durrani Dynasty with his new Barakzai Dynasty in 1826. The Barakzai Dynasty would rule Afghanistan until 1973.

A Brief Timeline of the Great Game in Afghanistan

1. In 1837, Russia, which has a great deal of power over Persia, encourages Persia to invade western Afghanistan and capture the city of Herat. If Persia can capture Herat, then Russia can control Herat by controlling Persia, and Russia will be one step closer to its goal: control of Afghanistan. Russia's use of Persia

to fight its battles is an example of a "proxy war," a war in which a powerful nation uses a less powerful nation as a substitute, or "proxy," to capture territory without directly involving its own armies.
2. Britain, which is well aware that Russia is behind Persia's invasion of Afghanistan, threatens Persia with war. Persia backs down and agrees to withdraw from Herat, but continues to occupy Afghani territory.
3. Britain offers Dost Muhammad Khan's Afghanistan large loans to finance its fight against the invaders, Russia and Persia. If Dost Muhammad decides to accept the loans, then he will be firmly on Britain's side of the Great Game because he will owe the British money.
4. The crafty Dost Muhammad refuses Britain's offer of loans, and replies with a counteroffer of his own: If the British truly want to be his allies, he asks, then will they please help him drive his enemies the Sikhs out of southern Afghanistan? That would be a true alliance in Dost Muhammad's eyes. Britain refuses Dost Muhammad's offer of an alliance.
5. Dost Muhammad plays Britain and Russia against one another by asking Russia to join him in an alliance against the Sikhs instead. If Russia accepts Dost Muhammad's offer, it will place Russian troops on the very border of British India, a prospect Britain is absolutely unwilling to accept.
6. Britain attacks Dost Muhammad, launching the First Anglo-Afghan War. In 1839, Britain invades Afghanistan from British India and captures Dost Muhammad's capital city, Kabul. Britain holds Dost Mohammad captive in India. For two years, British forces occupy Kabul while native Afghanis grow ever more angry over the occupation.
7. In 1841, Dost Muhammad's son Akbar Khan leads attacks on the occupying British army. No reinforcements arrive to help the British. The British decide to abandon Kabul and retreat to British India. The results are disastrous: Nearly every man of the British occupying force is killed in the January 1842 Massacre of Elphinstone's Army (see below).
8. In 1843, Dost Muhammad returns to his battle-scarred capital, where he will spend the next twenty years rebuilding Afghanistan.
9. In 1855, Dost Muhammad signs the friendly Treaty of Peshawar with Britain. In the Treaty of Peshawar, both sides agree to respect one another's territory and to defend one another against attack. Dos Muhammad honors this treaty, at least in part, by staying out of the 1857 Sepoy Rebellion against British India (see Chapter 1).
10. In 1863, Dost Muhammad drives the last Persian invaders out of Afghanistan. He dies fourteen days later, leaving Afghanistan independent and free of foreign invaders.

AMAZING AFGHANIS: Dost Muhammad Khan (1793 – 1863, reigned 1826 – 1839, 1843 – 1863)

Dost Muhammad Khan was the Emir of Afghanistan during the early years of the "Great Game" maneuvering between Britain and Russia. Through clever gamesmanship, Dost Muhammad managed to maintain Afghanistan's independence in a time when his small, backward nation could easily have been swallowed by either Britain or Russia.

Dost Muhammad came from the Barakzai clan, one of Afghanistan's leading clans. His father and brother were both leaders (khans) in the Barakzai clan and high officials under the Durrani Dynasty. The last shah of the Durrani Dynasty, Mahmud Shah Durrani, repaid the Barakzai clan's loyalty by assassinating Dost Muhammad's brother. In response, the angry Barakzai clan turned against Mahmud Shah and removed him from power in 1818.

At first, Dost Muhammad ruled only a single Afghani province, the Ghazni Province, and was only one of several Barakzai clan khans. Afghanistan's Barakzai Dynasty began in 1826, when Dost Muhammad added the important Kabul Province to his holdings. By 1835, Dost Muhammad Khan was Afghanistan's undisputed *Emir*, or principal chieftain.

Dost Muhammad spent his reign trying to preserve Afghanistan against grasping invaders like the Russians, the Persians, the British and the Sikhs. Soon after Dost Muhammad came to power, Sikhs led by the Maharajah of Punjab, Ranjit Singh, captured the important fortress of Peshawar near the Khyber Pass. Dost Muhammad fought to regain Peshawar for years, seeking help from both Britain and Russia; but he never succeeded. Peshawar later became part of British India, then part of Pakistan; it never returned to Afghani control.

Dost Muhammad was the key Afghani figure in the Great Game between Britain and Russia. Both Britain and Russia were interested in Afghanistan because it guarded the entrance to India.

"SAVE ME FROM MY FRIENDS!"

The British felt that they could not allow an ambitious Russia to control the valuable passes through Afghanistan's mountains, so they offered Dost Muhammad loans if he would agree to use the money to fight off Russia and Persia. But Dost Muhammad was too wise to spend himself into debt pursuing someone else's goals; and he was far more concerned about regaining Peshawar than he was about defeating the Persians.

When Dost Muhammad refused to play along with the British, they launched the First Anglo-Afghan War against him (see Fascinating Fact below). In 1839, British forces invaded Afghanistan and soon captured Dost Muhammad's capital, Kabul. They removed Dost Muhammad from power and replaced him with Shuja Shah Durrani, a member of the ousted Durrani clan who would serve as a puppet governor and do Britain's bidding.

Dost Muhammad spent the next three years as a captive while the British tried, and failed, to control the rebellious Afghanis. Dost Muhammad's son, Akbar Khan, made life miserable for the occupying British. When the British tried to withdraw from Afghanistan, Akbar Khan hounded their retreat, slaughtered them all and later assassinated Shuja Shah. Britain punished the Afghanis for the Massacre of Elphinstone's Army by sending an Army of Retribution against them in 1842. The Army of Retribution repaid Akbar Khan by slaughtering entire villages of Afghanis, but it did not try to re-occupy Afghanistan.

For after the fiasco of the first Anglo-Afghan War, the British had little interest in possessing rocky, desolate Afghanistan, with its many stubborn warrior tribes. Instead, they sought peace with Afghanistan and tried to prevent Afghanistan from becoming too friendly with Russia. In 1843, one year after the Army of Retribution's murderous visit, Britain made a move toward peace by allowing the captive Dost Muhammad to return to Afghanistan and rebuild his war-torn nation.

Dost Muhammad spent the rest of his life rebuilding Afghanistan. In time, he built a more friendly relationship with Britain. In 1855, Dost Muhammad negotiated the Treaty of Peshawar, a treaty of friendship and alliance, with Britain. And in 1863, he used British help to drive the Persians out of western Afghanistan, leaving his country free, united and independent for the first time in many years.

Only two weeks after this final victory, Dost Muhammad grew ill and died. His dynasty, the Barakzai Dynasty, would remain in power in Afghanistan until 1973.

FASCINATING FACTS: Bribes, Betrayals and the Massacre of Elphinstone's Army

The First Anglo-Afghan War began in March 1839, when a British army of about 20,000 troops (both British and sepoy) crossed into Afghanistan by way of the Bolan Pass. The British captured Kandahar in April and Ghazni, Dost Muhammad's former home fortress, in June. The commander of the fortress at Ghazni had ordered all of the fortress's gates bricked over, but one gate remained unfinished. When the attack began, the British quickly destroyed the unfinished gate and poured into the fortress, capturing it after a short battle.

By the end of 1839, the British had captured Afghanistan's capital city, Kabul, and settled in for a long, comfortable occupation.

Bribe: The first year of British occupation was peaceful because the government paid "subsidies," otherwise known as bribes, to Afghani clans in the area. This bribe money kept the Afghani clans happy and quiet.

However, the British government couldn't afford to keep paying bribes forever; so, around early 1841, they stopped paying the Afghani clans. When the bribe payments stopped, it was far easier for Dost Muhammad's son, Akbar Khan, to convince the Afghanis to rebel against their British occupiers and fight a guerrilla war against them.

The guerrilla war turned into an all-out revolt in late 1841. First, Akbar Khan and his men openly attacked the home of a British officer, murdering him and all of his staff. Next, they launched a surprise attack against the British army camp near Kabul, killing hundreds of troops. After this attack, the British realized that they were in serious trouble, so they made an appointment to negotiate peace with the Afghanis. Their plan was to surrender Kabul and abandon their occupation of Afghanistan in exchange for free passage to their base at Jalalabad, about 90 miles away.

Betrayal: When frightened British officers appeared under a flag of truce to negotiate terms of peace, Akbar and his men treacherously attacked and murdered the entire peace delegation.

Finally, the aged and ill British General Elphinstone reached an agreement with Akbar Khan: the Afghanis promised not to attack the fleeing British occupiers as they traveled to Jalalabad, provided that the British left behind their artillery and most of their gunpowder. On January 1, 1842, about 4,500 British troops and 12,000 camp followers left Kabul for a march through the snowy Khyber Pass to safety. They left their sick and wounded behind, because Akbar Khan had agreed not to harm them.

Betrayal: As soon as the British troops left Kabul, Akbar Khan and his men attacked and killed the sick and wounded they had left behind.

Betrayal: Before the departing British troops had traveled ten miles, Akbar Khan again broke his word and attacked them. Two thirds of them were dead before they had traveled 10 miles.

About forty survivors made their last stand on a lonely hill in the Khyber Pass (see picture) on January 13, 1842. A lone, badly wounded survivor, William Brydon, rode to safety in Jalalabad later that day.

Betrayal: Reportedly, Akbar Khan issued two sets of orders to his troops as they attacked Elphinstone's army: In Persian, which most of the British understood, he shouted "Spare them"; but in Pashtun, which his attacking tribesmen understood, he shouted "Kill them!"

One Final Betrayal: Akbar Khan died in 1847, when his father Dost Muhammad Khan was back in power in Kabul. According to rumor, Dost Muhammad poisoned Akbar because he was afraid that his son might try to kill him and take his place as Emir. To a man who had 66 children and more than 25 wives, perhaps murdering one troublesome son did not seem such a terrible loss.

FASCINATING FACTS: The Brown Bess and the Jezail

The "**Brown Bess**" was a British-made, .75 caliber musket/bayonet. It fired a ¾ inch ball and had a maximum range of about 175 yards. British armies used Brown Bess muskets in one version or another for well over 100 years, from their introduction in 1722 until the introduction of the 1853 Enfield rifle-musket (see Chapter 1). Both sides of the American Revolutionary War used the Brown Bess musket. The Brown Bess's formal name was the "Land Pattern Musket" because it was manufactured in British factories according to a pattern.

The **Jezail** was a longer, heavier musket used by Afghani armies in the Anglo-Afghan wars. Unlike the British, most Afghanis custom-made their own jezails, decorating their curved stocks with elaborate painting and carvings. Some jezails were so long that cavalrymen could rest their jezails' butts on the ground and load them from horseback.

The Afghanis had survived the First Anglo-Afghan War with their freedom intact, but the Great Game wasn't over. In 1878 - 1879, Britain would reinvade Afghanistan in the Second Anglo-Afghan War. This time, Afghanistan would still keep its territory, but would lose its right to manage its own foreign affairs. Britain wanted not to conquer Afghanistan, but to keep it in place as protection against the growing threat from Russia.

FASCINATING FACTS: The Khyber Pass

Geography is important in the history of Afghanistan. Europe and Central Asia are divided from Southern Asia and India by the Hindu Kush mountain range, which is considered a sub-range of the Himalayas farther to the east. The Hindu Kush Mountains are a formidable obstacle for travelers, traders or invaders, and the best route through them is the Khyber Pass.

Rudyard Kipling described the Khyber Pass as "a sword cut through the mountains." In places, it looks like exactly that: it is walled on both sides by steep cliffs that rise almost one thousand feet above the path. It is 33 miles long and only about ten feet wide at its narrowest point. The pass is part of a longer natural route from Afghanistan to Pakistan that begins at Kabul, passes near Jalalabad and ends at Peshawar.

Through the ages, the Khyber Pass was the chosen invasion route for conquerors like Alexander the Great, the Mongol Horde and many others. When Ahmad Shah Durrani first built his nation in Afghanistan, it included Peshawar and the Khyber Pass. Dost Muhammad lost the Pass to the Sikhs, and it later fell under the control of British India. The British controlled the Khyber Pass until they partitioned India and Pakistan in 1947 (see Chapter 27). Today most of the Khyber Pass lies inside Pakistan.

AFRICA

Africa is the world's second largest continent (behind Asia), with an area of about 11.7 million square miles. Nearly all known ancient African history focuses on North Africa, partly because natural barriers like the Sahara Desert made Africa's interior difficult for Europeans to reach. In the mid-1800s, Europeans had seen only Africa's coastal edges. Its center remained a mystery.

Britain gained control of Cape Colony, South Africa in 1806. They captured it from the Dutch, who had founded it in 1652 (later, Cape Colony became the Cape of Good Hope). When Protestant Christian missionaries began active mission work in South Africa in the mid-1800s, they used Cape Colony as a base. It was at this time that Dr. David Livingstone felt called to become a missionary.

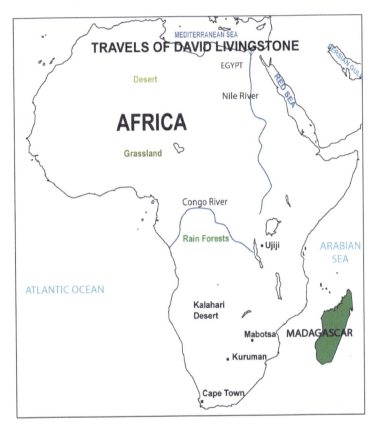

MISSIONARY FOCUS

GIANTS OF THE FAITH: Dr. David Livingstone (1813 – 1873)

Dr. David Livingstone was a Scottish missionary who served in Africa. During the mid-1800s, Livingstone became a legendary explorer who was better known for his well-written and exciting chronicles of perilous trips across untamed Africa than for his mission work.

David came from a strong Christian family of extremely humble means. At age ten David went to work in a cotton mill, where he worked twelve-hour shifts. The mill offered a school, and David studied his lessons from a book propped open on a spinning wheel. Later, he took two years of medical training and attended lectures on theology. He joined the London Missionary Society in the mid-1830s, and expected to be assigned to mission work in China. However, when the First Opium War began in 1839, travel to China became difficult, and David began to consider other possibilities.

In 1840 Livingstone attended a lecture by Robert Moffat, a missionary who was on furlough (leave) from Christian service in Kuruman, a village in South Africa. Moffat described the missionary's challenge in Africa in inspiring language, using lines that might have been poetry:

"I have sometimes seen in the morning sun
The smoke of a thousand villages where no missionary has ever been."

Livingstone caught Moffat's vision for sharing the Gospel of Jesus Christ among an entire continent of people who had never had a chance to hear it. He would remain dedicated to that vision for the rest of his life. He would also marry Robert Moffat's daughter Mary in 1845.

Livingstone arrived in South Africa in 1841. On his first journey to Africa's interior, Livingstone had a famous encounter with an angry lion near a village called Mabotsa. He shot the lion before it could pounce, but it still had enough life left in its powerful body to leave him with eleven tooth scars and a shattered arm. His poorly healed arm gave him trouble for the rest of his life.

Livingstone continued to make long, dangerous trips to the interior of Africa, attended by a small band of native Africans who were fascinated by him and felt honored to help him. At the time, the natives of the interior were likely to assume that any white foreigners they saw were in Africa only to capture slaves. The native Africans who traveled with Livingstone helped him to avoid fights with the natives of the interior. He traveled light, carried few weapons, and kept his band of travelers small-- unlike the slave traders, who traveled in large bands of mercenaries (paid soldiers) bristling with deadly modern weapons.

Along the way, Livingstone saw and recorded things that no other European had ever seen, both natural and cultural. He saw vast deserts and deep rainforests; and he also witnessed the shocking rituals of Africa's native tribes. He discovered Victoria Falls, one of the world's largest and most beautiful waterfalls, and named it for Queen Victoria. He also crossed the Kalahari Desert, a feat that was supposedly impossible for a white man. During a trip back home to Britain, he published a chronicle of his journeys in a book entitled "Missionary Travels." Dr. Livingstone's tales of Africa's mysterious interior and the strange, sometimes savage customs of its natives fascinated the curious and mostly Christian public of mid-1800s Europe and America.

In 1858, the government of Great Britain paid Livingstone to return to Africa on a mission to explore and map trade routes to Africa's interior. This was in tune with Livingstone's motto, which is now engraved on the pedestal of his statue at Victoria Falls: "Christianity, Commerce and Civilization." Like many Britons who lived during the height of the British Empire's power, Livingstone believed that unenlightened, impoverished Africans would benefit greatly if they could learn and adopt Britain's Christian culture. His explorations and maps were the first steps in bringing that culture to Africa's interior.

Livingstone did not, however, approve of the *exploitation* of Africa, the practice of using native Africans and their homeland for financial gain and giving them little or nothing in return. Livingstone was a devoted opponent of black slavery. On his travels, he saw the terrible results of the slave traders' careless attitudes toward native Africans, the people he came to save. He saw their unburied corpses, cast into rivers and lakes after battles with slave catchers. He saw the burned villages that slave traders left behind. He was angry over the mistreatment of Africans, and his letters to abolitionists in Britain and America added fuel to the fire of their anger on behalf of mistreated black slaves.

Livingstone's mission for his last journey to Africa, which began in 1866, was to find the source of the Nile River. On this journey, Livingstone grew ill, and was out of touch with both his friends and the public for six years. When the rumor began to spread that Livingstone had died, the *New York Herald* newspaper paid a journalist named Henry Stanley to travel to Africa and find him.

Henry Stanley began his journey in 1869. He hired a large party of mercenaries and blasted his way into Africa's interior in a brutal manner that was exactly the opposite of Livingstone's. Reportedly, he shot African porters who tried to desert his expedition. Stanley finally found Livingstone in 1871 at Ujiji, a village on the shores of south central Africa's Lake Tanganyika. The *Herald*'s story of Stanley's unlikely meeting with Livingstone reported the following conversation:

Stanley: "Dr. Livingstone, I presume?"
Livingstone: "Yes."
Stanley: "I thank my God I am permitted to see you."
Livingstone: "I feel thankful that I am here to welcome you."

Instead of leaving Africa with Stanley, Livingstone remained behind to continue his mission. When he died a year later, his African friends buried his heart in his beloved Africa. His other remains were returned to Britain, where they were eventually buried in Westminster Abbey.

GIANTS OF THE FAITH: Mary Slessor (1848 – 1915)

Like David Livingstone, Mary Slessor was a Scottish missionary born to a poor family. Also like Livingstone, she worked in a mill from an early age, and attended a school operated by the mill. As a young woman, she became a Sunday School teacher who was willing to take risks for her faith. Reportedly, a group of ruffians once challenged her to stand still while they swung a lead weight on a string in circles closer and closer to her forehead. She continued to stand stock still, even when the weight brushed her forehead. The ruffians admired her courage so much that they joined her Sunday School class.

Mary Slessor would take risks for her faith for the rest of her life. When she was 29, she became a missionary in the Calabar River region of Africa. All too soon she contracted the disease that still plagues missionaries in Africa today, malaria. Her malaria would trouble her for the rest of her life, and would force her to return home several times to recover her health. She returned to Africa each time, and with each return she traveled farther into Africa's interior and ministered among new tribes.

Mary encountered barbaric rituals and practices among some of these tribes, and she took a stand against them. Among them:

- **Twin murder**: Some tribes believed that the birth of twins happened because an evil spirit fathered the second child. These tribes killed both children and shunned the twins' unlucky mother. Mary saved and adopted some of these twins, and she provided care for others. Some of them returned to Scotland with Mary on her furloughs.
- **Resolving disputes with poison**: If two tribesmen argued, some tribes forced both arguers to drink poison. They judged the one who sickened or died first to be the one in the wrong. Over time, the tribes grew to trust Mary so much that they sometimes asked her to judge disputes so that they wouldn't have to judge them with poison.
- **Alcoholism**: Mary took a stand against alcoholism by encouraging idle drunkards to trade their goods with European traders, giving them something to do besides drinking.
- **Warring**: Mary stopped battles between warring tribes simply by standing between the warriors when their battles were about to begin. They didn't want to hurt saintly old Mary, so they postponed or canceled their battles.

Mary Slessor lived a simple life of faith, service and self-denial. For most of her 39 years in Africa, she lived in a tiny mud hut and wore the plainest of clothing. She died in Africa in 1915.

WORLD GEOGRAPHY FOCUS

FASCINATING FACTS: Victoria Falls and the Devil's Pool

Victoria Falls is a huge waterfall that lies on the Zambezi River on the border between modern-day Zambia and Zimbabwe. In 1855, David Livingstone became the first European to see the spectacular falls, and named it for Britain's Queen Victoria. Its African name is *Mosi-oa-Tunya*, "The Smoke that Thunders"; the name refers to the plumes of water vapor that rise high in the sky around the falls and the constant roar of its cascading waters.

One remarkable and unexpected feature of Victoria Falls is a small lagoon at its top called the "Devil's Pool." A shelf of rock just below the water's surface diverts the water and makes the Devil's Pool safe for swimming, as long as the river's water level is not too high. It is possible for a brave swimmer to stretch out over the falls and look straight down into the gorge below. However, it is called "Devil's Pool" for a reason: it has claimed the lives of many reckless or unfortunate swimmers.

FASCINATING FACTS: African Trade Beads

The history of African trade beads began in the 1400s, when Portuguese trading ships first arrived on the west coast of Africa. The Portuguese wanted to buy Africa's many resources, among them gold, ivory and slaves. They needed something to trade to the Africans in exchange for these resources. One item they could trade was, of course, alcohol; but when they discovered that these Africans had no knowledge of glass-making, they began bringing them colorful glass beads from Italy. Such beads were inexpensive in the European world, but the Africans loved them. The Portuguese traders grew wealthy by trading cheap beads for valuable items that brought high prices back in Europe.

The Africans strung their trade beads and wore them as necklaces, bracelets or belts. They used them for protection, to display their status and for simple decoration.

U.S. HISTORY FOCUS

AMAZING AMERICANS: Jefferson Davis (1808 – 1889)

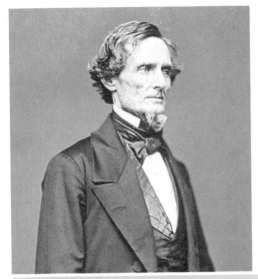

Jefferson Davis was the President of the Confederate States of America, the short-lived nation established by the eleven Southern states that seceded from the U.S. just before the Civil War.

Davis was born in Kentucky, but lived most of his life in Mississippi. He graduated from West Point military academy in New York, then served in the U.S. Army from 1828-1835. He was briefly married to the daughter of the future President Zachary Taylor, until his young wife died of malaria. His second wife would bear him six children, but only one would survive to adulthood.

Davis became a U.S. Congressman from Mississippi in 1845, but then resigned to return to military service in the 1846-48 Mexican War. His unit of Mississippi militia was one of the best in the army, and Davis' bravery earned him high praise from General Taylor, his former father-in-law. After that war he served as a U.S. senator from Mississippi, then as President Franklin Pierce's Secretary of War, then as senator again.

Before the Civil War began, Jefferson Davis had never truly believed that the Southern states should secede from the Union. Before the seven states of the Deep South seceded, Davis argued against secession, both in the U.S. Senate and back home in Mississippi. After the Deep South voted to secede, Davis still hoped to reconcile and rejoin the Union. Nevertheless, like many Southerners, he strongly believed that the Union had no right to use force to prevent the South from seceding. Therefore, when the states of the Deep South seceded and the Union raised troops against them to force them to rejoin the Union, Davis felt that he had no choice but to fight back against what he considered to be an unlawful invasion of the South.

When Davis's home state of Mississippi seceded from the Union on January 9, 1861, he resigned from the U.S. Senate and returned home. A month later, the new Confederate States of America appointed Davis as its first president. He won the Confederacy's first official presidential election in the following November; and, as it turned out, he was the only president the Confederate States of America would ever have.

Having served the United States as Secretary of War, Davis knew very well that the South could never match the North's military resources. The Confederacy's hopes in the Civil War rode on two military objectives: (1) quick, decisive victories that would demoralize the North and make its people reluctant to fight on, and (2) a strong defense. Davis also sought victory through an alliance with the British, who were quite happy to see the young United States tearing itself apart. The alliance with Britain never materialized, partly because the Confederacy believed in slavery, and slavery was already illegal in Britain.

In April 1865, when the South's Civil War effort collapsed and the Confederacy began to unravel, President Davis fled his capital in Richmond and traveled to Danville, Virginia. After General Lee surrendered at Appomattox, Davis became a fugitive on the run from the Union army. Union troops caught up with him in Georgia on May 10, 1865. With his camp surrounded, Davis tried to escape by hiding under his wife's coat. Whether he intended the coat as a disguise or not, his enemies mocked him about trying to escape by dressing as a woman for the rest of his life. The Union indicted him for treason and held him in prison for two years, but the federal government dropped its case against him in 1869.

Jefferson Davis in Prison

U.S. GEOGRAPHY FOCUS

FASCINATING FACTS about ALABAMA:

- <u>Statehood</u>: Alabama became the 22nd US state on December, 14 1819.
- <u>Bordering states/bodies of water</u>: Florida, Georgia, Mississippi, Tennessee and the Gulf of Mexico.
- <u>Area</u>: 52,419 sq. mi (Ranks 30th in size)
- <u>State capital</u>: Montgomery
- <u>Abbreviation</u>: AL
- <u>State nickname</u>: "Yellowhammer State" or "Heart of Dixie"
- <u>State Birds</u>: Yellowhammer (Northern Flicker), Wild Turkey
- <u>State tree</u>: Longleaf Pine
- <u>State flower</u>: Camellia
- <u>State song</u>: *Alabama*
- <u>State Motto</u>: "We Dare Defend Our Rights"
- <u>Meaning of name</u>: "Tribal Town" (translated from Creek language)
- <u>Historic places to visit in Alabama</u>: Desoto Caverns, Alabama Space and Rocket Center, Tuskegee Airmen NHS, Little River Canyon National Preserve, The Alabama Jazz Hall of Fame
- <u>Resources and Industries</u>: coal, limestone, iron, steelmaking, farming (chicken, cotton, corn, peanuts, soybeans)

Alabama State Capital

Flag of Alabama
- Alabama adopted this flag in 1895.
- Its design is known as the "crimson cross of St. Andrew"
- It was modeled on the Confederate Battle flag.
- It can be either square or rectangular, and the bars of its cross must be at least six inches wide.

PRESIDENTIAL FOCUS

PRESIDENT #15: James Buchanan (1791 – 1868)	
In Office: March 4, 1857 – March 4, 1861	**Political Party:** Democratic
Birthplace: Pennsylvania	**Nickname:** "Bachelor President"

James Buchanan was a Pennsylvania attorney who ran for President four times before he finally won in 1856. He could hardly have chosen a worse time to win, because his single term in office coincided with the prelude to the Civil War. Like Franklin Pierce before him, Buchanan was considered a "doughface," a President from the North who often sided with the slaveholding South.

Buchanan became wealthy as a young attorney, and he used his wealth to launch an ambitious political career. He served as a U.S. congressman from Pennsylvania, then as ambassador to Russia, then as a U.S. senator, then as secretary of state under President Polk. President Pierce appointed Buchanan as his Minister to England. Buchanan tried to win his Democratic Party's Presidential nomination in 1844, 1848 and 1852 before he finally won the nomination and the Presidency in 1856.

Although Buchanan was technically from the North, just above the Mason-Dixon Line, he interpreted the Constitution like a Southerner. He was devoted to the law; and, as a lawyer, his opinion was that the Constitution gave Southern states the right to permit slavery if that was their people's choice. Like many in the South, Buchanan believed in sovereign States' Rights. Many in the North agreed with this much, and doubted that the federal government had the power to ban slavery in states that already had slavery.

However, the North did not agree with Buchanan on what to do about slavery in the new territories. Buchanan's inauguration came soon before the Supreme Court's infamous Dred Scott decision, and he may have tried to influence that decision before Chief Justice Taney delivered it. When the Dred Scott decision arrived, Buchanan immediately agreed with the Court's position: that the Constitution did not give Congress the power to prohibit slavery in the new territories, and that those territories must be allowed to decide the issue for themselves. This was not a popular position in the North, where most people wanted to stop the spread of slavery into new territories.

Although the violence in Bloody Kansas had died down by Buchanan's time, the issue of slavery in Kansas was still undecided. When the time came to write a constitution for the new state, Buchanan supported the Lecompton Constitution, a hastily-drawn pro-slavery constitution that had little public support. Later, a new constitutional convention with far more public support drew up an anti-slavery constitution for Kansas. Buchanan's earlier support for the Lecompton Constitution made him look far too eager to promote slavery.

As Buchanan's term wound to a close, the nation spiraled toward civil war, and he was powerless to prevent it. He had promised to serve for only one term. Without a strong candidate, his Democratic Party divided itself between North and South. This allowed the upstart Republican Party candidate, Abraham Lincoln, to win the Presidency in 1860. As Buchanan left office, he warned Lincoln that the government had no right to use force to keep the Southern states in the Union. Judging by Lincoln's actions in the Civil War, he did not agree.

Other interesting facts about James Buchanan:
- He was the first President to send a transatlantic telegram. The telegram went to Britain's Queen Victoria.
- He had an unfortunate incident with his fiancée when he was young. The young lady, Anne Caroline Coleman, broke off their engagement and then suddenly died, possibly of heartbreak or by suicide. Buchanan never got over her death, never revealed any details about the incident and never married. On Buchanan's instructions, his attorneys burned Coleman's letters to him after he died.
- Because Buchanan had no wife to be his first lady, his adopted niece Harriet Lane served as hostess for White House events.
- As a result of an eye problem, Buchanan developed a habit of tilting his head to one side and closing one eye when he spoke.

Chapter 4

U.S. Civil War, Part I

U.S. HISTORY FOCUS

THE WAR BETWEEN THE STATES

The Prelude to the Civil War

Divisions between the Northern states and the Southern states were present from British Colonial days, and are evident in the U.S. Constitution. From the beginning, and for the nation's first 85 years, North and South were held together by political compromises. Among the many contentious issues between North and South:

Economics: The economy of the North was based on industry, mining, trade and transportation, as well as on family farms. In this economy there was little need for slaves, except among traders and businessmen who profited from the slave trade. The North had a large and growing population due to its more numerous cities, high birth rates and immigration from Europe.

The economy of the South was based largely on plantation farming of labor-intensive cash crops like cotton (see picture) and tobacco. This economy made much use of slave labor, especially when the demand for cotton grew high. The South depended on the North for most manufactured goods. Even though only about one third of Southern whites were slave owners, they were the wealthiest and most influential third.

Another economic issue between North and South was taxation. When Southern traders tried to save money by bringing in manufactured goods directly from Europe, bypassing Northern traders and manufacturers, the federal government placed high tariffs (import taxes) on European goods so that the South would be forced to buy from the North. South Carolina, always the boldest Southern state, responded to the federal government's tariffs by issuing the 1832 "Ordinance of Nullification," which declared that the tariffs were illegal and that South Carolina wouldn't pay them.

States' Rights: The United States began in 1776 as a union of 13 independent states. The Continental Congress that produced the Declaration of Independence became the United States' first *federal* government, with limited power over all of the states. Even before the American Revolution, the states argued over how much power to grant to this federal government: men like Alexander Hamilton wanted a strong federal government, while men like Thomas Jefferson wanted

to limit the federal government's power to interfere in the affairs of the states. During the run-up to the Civil

War, people in the South tended to believe in strong state governments, with only limited power for the federal government. People in the North tended to believe the opposite: they wanted a strong federal government, with only limited power for the states.

Slavery: Most Northerners were not active abolitionists. Many in the North were content to allow the Southern states to retain their slaves, and to let the Southern slaveholders retain their slave "property" and their way of life. They resisted, however, when Southerners tried to expand slavery into new territories, or to acquire new slaveholding territories such as Cuba or Nicaragua. For their part, abolitionists were not content with slavery at all, and they stirred Northern feelings against slavery by publishing flyers, newsletters and novels such as *Uncle Tom's Cabin* (see Chapter 1).

The Election of Abraham Lincoln: The last Presidents before the Civil War were "doughfaces," Northern men who sympathized with the South. Presidents Pierce and Buchanan compromised with the South by allowing the possibility of slavery in new territories like Kansas. They also resisted the idea of using force to keep the Union together.

Abraham Lincoln was no doughface. He was decidedly against slavery in the new territories, and he also believed that it was absolutely illegal for any state to secede from the Union. When Lincoln won the Presidential election of 1860, the State of South Carolina was so angry that it issued its "Declaration of the Causes of Secession" almost immediately. Seven states of the Deep South would secede before Lincoln even took office in March 1861. Four more would follow after Lincoln issued a call for army volunteers to reclaim federal property in the Deep South.

FASCINATING FACTS: Naming the Civil War

The people of the South resisted the name "Civil War." That name implied a war between the people of the United States; but after secession, the people of the South no longer considered their land to be part of the United States, so to them the term "civil war" no longer applied. The alternative names people chose gave clues about their political opinions.

Names used among those who sympathized with the South:

The War Against Northern Aggression	The Second American Revolution
The War for States' Rights	The War for Southern Freedom
The War Against the States	The Yankee Invasion
The War Between the States	Mr. Lincoln's War
The Lost Cause	

Names used among those who sympathized with the North:

The War of Attempted Secession	The Confederate War
The War for the Union	The Great Rebellion
The War of the Rebellion	

Other names:

The Late Unpleasantness	The War of North and South
The War of the Sixties	The Brothers' War

A Brief Timeline of the Civil War (through January 1, 1863):

1854: The Kansas-Nebraska Act sparks feuding over the issue of Slavery in Kansas.

FASCINATING FACTS: The Kansas-Nebraska Act

1856 map: slave states (gray), free states (pink), territories (green), and Kansas (white)

    The Kansas-Nebraska Act was the 1854 law that established the new U.S. territories of Kansas and Nebraska. During the run-up to the Civil War, the Kansas-Nebraska Act was controversial because in addition to organizing two new territories, it also allowed the people who settled in those territories to decide for themselves whether or not to allow slavery within their borders. The idea of allowing the people of the new territories to make their own choices about slavery was known as "popular sovereignty."
    Like most acts of Congress, the Kansas-Nebraska Act was a compromise. Congress was eager to see some company build a railroad across North America, and wanted to provide public land for the railroad's route. However, the congressmen could not agree on what route to choose. Northerners wanted the railroad to begin at Chicago and travel west, while Southerners favored a route than began farther south at St. Louis.
    Part of the railroad discussion involved organizing the first territories through which the railroad would run: Kansas and Nebraska. Southern members of Congress brought the issue of slavery into the discussion. They agreed to support the organization of the new Kansas and Nebraska territories-- but only if Northern members of Congress would allow slavery in those new territories. Eventually, North and South agreed to a compromise: the people of the new territories would be allowed to decide the issue of slavery for themselves under the idea of popular sovereignty.
    The Kansas-Nebraska Act included the repeal of an important part of an earlier law, the 1820 Missouri Compromise. The Missouri Compromise had banned slavery in the Louisiana Territory north of 36°30' north latitude. The border between Kansas and Nebraska was the 40th parallel, which of course lay north of 36°30'. All of Nebraska lay north of 36°30', and so did part of Kansas. The repeal of the Missouri Compromise meant that slavery might once again be allowed in the North— a prospect that appalled abolitionists.
    As soon as the new territories of Kansas and Nebraska were opened to settlement, pro-slavery settlers from slaveholding Missouri streamed over the border into Kansas to claim new land for slavery. Northern abolitionist groups provided money for anti-slavery settlers, or "free-staters," to move into Kansas as well. The clash between slave-staters and free-staters led to the violence of "Bloody Kansas," which President Franklin Pierce controlled by sending in federal troops. After several attempts, Kansas finally produced an anti-slavery constitution and entered the Union as a free state in early 1861. Nebraska had to wait for statehood until 1867, after the Civil War.

1859, October 16: Abolitionist John Brown attempts to launch a slave revolt at Harpers Ferry, Virginia.

FASCINATING FACTS: John Brown (1800-1859), Bloody Kansas and the Harpers Ferry Raid

John Brown was a radical abolitionist in the years before the Civil War. Brown had an affinity (liking) for violence. Most abolitionists published newspapers or held meetings to promote their opinions, but John Brown went farther: he joined the free-staters who moved into Bloody Kansas in 1855 and fought battles against slaveholders there. He is best known for his ill-fated 1859 attack on a federal armory at Harpers Ferry, Virginia.

Brown was a New Englander born in Connecticut. His father was vehemently opposed to slavery, and Brown inherited his father's opinions. Brown was active in abolitionist circles, and was well acquainted with prominent abolitionists like Harriet Tubman and Frederick Douglass. Like Tubman, Brown was a conductor on the Underground Railroad. He practiced what he preached by living in a black community: he had a home in a New York state village of "freedmen," former black slaves. Each new outrage committed by the supporters of slavery drove John Brown closer to violence. Brown was particularly enraged by the 1837 murder of Elijah Lovejoy, an abolitionist newspaper publisher.

After the 1854 passage of the Kansas-Nebraska Act, settlers from the neighboring slave state of Missouri poured over the border into Kansas. The Missourians hoped to fill the new territory with slavery supporters so that when the time came to vote for or against slavery in Kansas, slavery would win. In response, Brown and several of his children joined the many free-staters who were moving into Kansas hoping to swing the new territory's votes away from slavery.

John Brown wasn't the only abolitionist involved in Bloody Kansas. Henry Ward Beecher, the minister brother of Harriet Beecher Stowe (author of *Uncle Tom's Cabin*), openly preached against the Missouri-based settlers who were trying to turn Kansas into a slave state like their own. Beecher raised money to buy "Beecher's Bibles," powerful breech-loading rifles that he used to arm the abolitionist free-staters who were moving into Kansas. The slave-staters, Beecher said, wouldn't listen to the Bible, but a Beecher's Bible rifle spoke a language that no one could ignore.

In 1856, a pro-slavery posse attacked Lawrence, Kansas on a mission to destroy free-stater newspapers. This was a common tactic in the war between abolitionists and slavery supporters: for decades, their struggle had been mainly a war of words fought in newspapers and other widely-distributed literature. The posse that attacked Lawrence was so angry over what the abolitionists were printing that it decided to shut them up by destroying their printing presses. John Brown reacted to the Lawrence raid violently: a few days after the raid, Brown formed a posse of his own, including some of his sons, and killed five pro-slavery Kansas settlers near Pottawatomie Creek. Brown was involved in at least two other Bloody Kansas skirmishes before the violence in Bloody Kansas calmed down and he returned to the East.

Brown spent the next two years planning and raising funds for the grandest scheme of his life, an armed raid on Harpers Ferry, Virginia (Harpers Ferry now lies in West Virginia). Harpers Ferry was home to a federal weapons factory; its arsenal was filled to the brim with gunpowder, guns and ammunition. Brown's plan was to build a small army to capture Harpers Ferry, then use its arsenal to provide weapons and ammunition for a larger army of rebel slaves. Brown was convinced that when word reached the ears of Virginia slaves that a slave rebellion was underway, they would all flock to his side and join the rebellion against slavery. With the slaves armed and able to defend themselves, Brown believed, the institution of Slavery would soon collapse all over the United States.

Unfortunately for Brown, support for his raid began to collapse before he even finished planning it. Most abolitionists believed that by planning an attack on a federal armory, Brown was going too far. Abolitionists were prepared to defend themselves, but not to blatantly break the law by joining an armed raid against the U.S. government.

As a result, when Brown began his raid on Harpers Ferry on October 16, 1859, he had just 21 men with him. His small force caught Harpers Ferry by surprise and easily captured the lightly guarded arsenal; however, when the local militia found out what was happening, they soon surrounded the arsenal and pinned Brown's men inside it (see picture). Federal troops arrived at Harpers Ferry within two days. After a brief attempt to negotiate a truce with the stubborn Brown, they attacked the arsenal, routed Brown's small force and captured Brown. The federal government tried John Brown, convicted him of treason, and then hanged him to death on December 2, 1859.

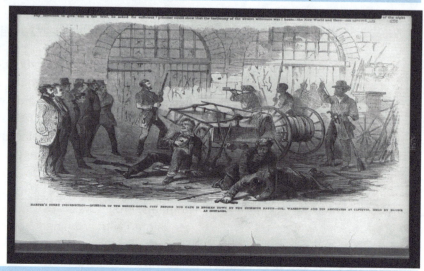

Three important figures, all later Confederate army officers, served the U.S. Army in the Harper's Ferry incident:

1. The commander of the U.S. forces that removed John Brown from the arsenal was Robert E. Lee.
2. The lieutenant who tried to negotiate a truce with John Brown inside the arsenal was J.E.B. Stuart.
3. The leader of the Virginia Military Institute cadets who provided security at Brown's execution was Thomas Jonathan Jackson, later known as Stonewall Jackson.

1860, November 6: Abraham Lincoln is elected President of the United States.

1860, December 20: The South Carolina legislature votes unanimously to secede from the Union. Within weeks, six other Deep South states also secede: Mississippi, Florida, Alabama, Georgia, Louisiana and Texas.

1861, January 9: Cadets of the Citadel, the Military Academy of South Carolina, fire the first shots of the Civil War when they attack the *Star of the West*, a steamer that is trying to deliver troops and supplies to Fort Sumter, South Carolina.

1861, February: The seven seceded states form a new nation, the Confederate States of America. The CSA drafts a constitution based on the U.S. Constitution, except that (1) it protects the institution of Slavery, and (2) it protects States' Rights. Jefferson Davis becomes President of the CSA.

1861, March 4: Abraham Lincoln is sworn in as the 16th President of the United States.

CRITICAL CONCEPTS: President Abraham Lincoln's First Inaugural Address

When Abraham Lincoln took the oath of office and became the 16th President of the United States, seven states of the Deep South had already voted to secede from the Union. The outgoing President Buchanan firmly believed that the U.S. Constitution did not give the federal government the power to force those states to remain in the Union. President Lincoln disagreed just as firmly.

To President Lincoln, seceding from the Union was like committing a crime, then escaping punishment for that crime simply by declaring that one no longer wanted to be a citizen and therefore didn't have to abide by the law. It was the President's job to uphold the law; but to Lincoln, allowing secession was the same thing as allowing anarchy. Here are some excerpts from President Lincoln's First Inaugural Address:

"I hold that, in contemplation of universal law and of the Constitution, the Union of these States is perpetual.

"Perpetuity is implied, if not expressed, in the fundamental law of all national governments. It is safe to assert that no government proper ever had a provision in its organic law for its own termination...

'It follows from these views that no State upon its own mere motion can lawfully get out of the Union; that resolves and ordinances to that effect are legally void; and that acts of violence, within any State or States, against the authority of the United States, are insurrectionary or revolutionary, according to circumstances...

'In your hands, my dissatisfied fellow-countrymen, and not in mine, is the momentous issue of civil war. The government will not assail you. You can have no conflict without being yourselves the aggressors. You have no oath registered in heaven to destroy the government, while I shall have the most solemn one to "preserve, protect, and defend it."

'I am loath to close. We are not enemies, but friends. We must not be enemies. Though passion may have strained, it must not break our bonds of affection. The mystic chords of memory, stretching from every battlefield and patriot grave to every living heart and hearthstone all over this broad land, will yet swell the chorus of the Union when again touched, as surely they will be, by the better angels of our nature."

1861, April 12: Confederate soldiers bombard Fort Sumter, South Carolina.

FASCINATING FACTS: The Battle of Fort Sumter

The secession of the Deep South states posed an immediate problem: what to do about the South's forts? To the North, every Southern military fort, naval station or armory was technically the property of the U.S. government, not of the state in which it lay. The South believed otherwise. After secession, these forts immediately found themselves surrounded by the Confederacy. Most of them surrendered peacefully and were taken over by the Confederacy; but some did not.

One that did not surrender was Fort Sumter, which lay in the harbor of Charleston, South Carolina. Fort Sumter was commanded by Major Robert Anderson, a former slave owner from Kentucky who decided to remain loyal to the Union army. Because Fort Sumter was situated on the South Carolina coast, it was not quite as surrounded as other Southern forts were, and could hope to receive supplies sent by ship from the North. The Confederacy blockaded Fort Sumter and demanded its surrender, but Major Anderson refused to surrender.

No blockaded fort can survive forever without supplies. In January 1861, before President Buchanan left office, he sent a supply ship to Fort Sumter; but cadets from Charleston's Citadel military academy fired on the supply ship and drove it off. In doing so, these eager Citadel cadets fired the first unofficial shots of the looming Civil War. As soon as President Lincoln took office in March, he laid plans to send more supply ships to Fort Sumter.

The Confederacy decided to act before Lincoln's supply ships could arrive. On April 12, 1861, the first battle of the Civil War began when the port of Charleston's other forts began firing their cannon on Fort Sumter. Major Anderson returned fire until he ran out of ammunition, then surrendered. Fort Sumter fell to the

Confederacy on April 13, 1861.

Like most soldiers who chose to remain loyal to the Union instead of joining the Confederacy, Major Anderson and his men were allowed to return safely to the North.

FASCINATING FACTS: Soldiers' Choices after Secession

When the Civil War broke out, U.S. soldiers all over the nation were forced to choose sides between North and South. Southern troops stationed in the North, Northern troops stationed in the South, troops stationed in faraway territories like California-- all had to choose whether to remain loyal to the Union or to resign and join the Confederacy (see picture). Often friends and even brothers made opposite choices, and ended up standing on opposite sides of Civil War battle lines.

When Texas seceded from the Union, Robert E. Lee was serving there under General David E. Twiggs, a Georgian who sided with the South. Twiggs chose to join the Confederate army, while Lee made the opposite choice and remained loyal to the Union. Twiggs' new Confederate troops granted Lee a safe, if uneasy, passage to Washington, where he received a promotion to colonel in the U.S. army.

Weeks later, when Virginia seceded from the Union, Robert E. Lee had another choice to make. As a loyal Virginian, he felt that he could not be part of a Union army that might be sent to invade his homeland; so he decided to resign his new colonel's commission and join the Confederate army.

1861, April 15: President Lincoln calls for 75,000 volunteer troops to help enforce U.S. law and defend U.S. forts in the seven seceded states. The states of the middle South object to being asked to raise troops for what they consider to be an illegal invasion of the deep South.

1861, April 17: Virginia's Secession Convention, which had previously voted twice against secession, suddenly approves secession and submits the question to Virginia voters. Virginia voters overwhelmingly approve the convention's decision, and vote to secede from the Union. Within two months, three other states-- Arkansas, North Carolina and Tennessee-- also vote to secede from the Union.

NEUTRAL: Four states that allowed Slavery before the war-- Delaware, Kentucky, Maryland and Missouri-- never seceded from the Union at all, and remained neutral. West Virginia was also neutral (see West Virginia below).

The divided United States: Blue = Union; Light blue = Neutral; Red = Confederacy; White = Unsettled Territories

AMAZING AMERICANS: Robert E. Lee (1807 – 1870)

Robert E. Lee was the commander of the Confederate Army of Northern Virginia and later the general-in-chief of Confederate forces during the Civil War. Through a number of daring victories against difficult odds early in the war, Lee became the South's most respected and beloved hero.

Lee was born at Stratford Hall Plantation, Virginia, the son of Revolutionary War hero Lighthorse Harry Lee. He married Mary Custis, a great-granddaughter of Martha Washington. Before the Civil War, Lee lived at Arlington when not away in military service. He was a loyal Virginia native, a friend and relative of many whom had known the great George Washington personally.

Lee graduated second in his class at the West Point military academy in New York, where he trained as an army engineer. Like many Civil War officers, Lee served in the 1848 - 1849 Mexican-American War. His exceptional service there as both an engineer and a scout drew high praise from General Winfield Scott, who commanded the inland invasion of Mexico. Lee thus began a friendly relationship with "Old Fuss and Feathers" Scott, the U.S. Army's highest officer. In 1859, General Scott called on Lee to handle the John Brown incident at Harper's Ferry.

On April 12, 1861, Confederate troops from South Carolina fired on Fort Sumter, and war between North and South became inevitable. On April 15, President Lincoln proposed to raise an army of 75,000 troops to reclaim Southern forts and bring the secessionists back into the Union. The aging General Scott recommended promoting Robert E. Lee to the rank of major general and placing him in command of that army.

Before Lee could decide how to answer General Scott, the situation changed. Virginia reacted strongly against the idea of invading the South, and voted to secede from the Union on April 17. Unwilling to lead an invasion force against his home state, Lee made the difficult decision to resign from the U.S. Army, which he had served for over thirty years. He resigned on April 20, then became a Confederate army officer on April 23.

Among other things, Lee's decision to resign cost him his home at Arlington, which lay directly across the Potomac River from Washington DC. Lee's Arlington estate became the property of the U.S. government, and is now the site of Arlington National Cemetery.

Lee became a senior military adviser to Confederate President Jefferson Davis, then Commander of the Army of Northern Virginia. He was a beloved and revered general. The very sight of him inspired his troops to tremendous valor and sacrifice. He was a brilliant and daring commander, and he won notable victories against great odds on his home ground of Virginia. However, his two attempts to invade the North and force an end to the war- at Sharpsburg (Antietam), 1862 and at Gettysburg, 1863- both ended in failure.

Late in the war, Union General Ulysses Grant pushed deep into Virginia, despite terrible Union casualties, and forced Lee to retreat to Petersburg. After a long siege at Petersburg (near the Confederate capital at Richmond, VA), Lee was forced to retreat to the west. He finally surrendered at Appomattox, VA on April 9, 1865. After the war, he became the President of Washington College at Lexington, VA, which later became Washington & Lee University. He died of heart disease in 1870.

1861, April 19: President Lincoln orders a naval blockade of all Confederate ports. After Virginia and North Carolina secede, the blockade is extended to include their ports as well. One particularly important blockade is at Hampton Roads, Virginia. It blocks all shipping from Richmond, the James River and important naval stations like Newport News and Portsmouth.

1861, July 21: The first major battle of the Civil War happens at Bull Run/Manassas.

FASCINATING FACTS: The First Battle of Bull Run/Manassas

In the opening months of the Civil War, the Union sought a quick end to what it considered to be a rebellion, while the South sought to defend itself against what it considered to be an invasion. No one from the North or the South yet had any idea how vast and terrible the Civil War was about to become.

Bull Run is a creek near Manassas Junction, an important railroad junction in Virginia about 30 miles west-southwest of Washington DC. Union General Irvin McDowell proposed to lead 35,000 troops to Manassas Junction and capture it. Possession of the railroad at Manassas, he hoped, would open the way to the Confederate capital at Richmond and a swift victory over the rebels.

Unfortunately, McDowell's plans were not a well-kept secret. Even the public knew about his invasion of

Virginia before it began, and Confederate Generals P.G.T. Beauregard and Joseph E. Johnston learned of the plan in plenty of time to position their troops near Bull Run and defend Manassas Junction.

The Union expected a quick victory over the upstart rebels. As the battle began on July 21, 1861, wealthy civilians and congressmen from Washington looked on from their carriages as though they were watching a military parade. The battle did indeed go well for the Union at first, but then a brigade under Colonel Thomas Jackson reinforced the Confederates, stubbornly holding its ground "like a stone wall."

Jackson's fierce counterattacks turned the tide of the battle. The Confederates routed the Union forces, who fled back to their defensive positions near Washington DC. After the battle, both North and South had a new understanding of the horrors to come in the Civil War.

AMAZING AMERICANS: Thomas Jonathan "Stonewall" Jackson (1824 – 1863)

Thomas Jackson was the commander of the elite "Stonewall Brigade," a military unit he formed early in the Civil War. Promoted through the ranks from colonel to lieutenant general, Jackson became the Confederacy's fiercest fighting commander and a major factor in Confederate victories all over northern Virginia.

A native of what would become West Virginia, Jackson was born in 1824 and orphaned at age 7. Despite little early education, he graduated from New York's West Point military academy in 1846, then served in the Mexican-American War (as did most experienced Civil War officers). He resigned from the army to take a teaching job at the Virginia Military Institute, where his classes were reportedly rather dull. He was a strict Presbyterian Christian, and his faith in God influenced every aspect of his life.

When Virginia seceded from the Union in 1861, Jackson joined the Confederate army and began recruiting troops. He earned his famous nickname "Stonewall" at the July 21, 1861 First Battle of Bull Run, when General Barnard Bee encouraged his troops to take courage from the example of Jackson's brigade "standing firm like a stone wall." Jackson later won a stunning series of victories in Virginia's Shenandoah Valley. His fierce, single-minded aggression in battle and his refusal to retreat made him a legendary figure and an inspiration to every Confederate soldier.

The 1863 Battle of Chancellorsville, Virginia would be Jackson's last. On May 2, 1863, the badly outnumbered Jackson led a daring flanking maneuver against the Union Army of the Potomac in the hours just before dark. His attacking Corps caught the enemy by surprise and raced up the defenseless Union flank, forcing Union soldiers to run for their lives. Jackson's Corps might have trapped the Army of the Potomac against the Rappahannock River and destroyed it entirely if darkness had not stopped him.

Late in the day on May 2, Jackson eagerly pressed forward with his staff officers after dark, seeking to take the best possible advantage of the gains his Corps had made. He soon found himself well beyond his own advancing forward lines. When he tried to return, some of his own troops mistook him for an enemy in the dark and shot him.

Weakened by the wounds he received at Chancellorsville, Stonewall Jackson died of pneumonia on May 10, 1863. General Robert E. Lee wrote of the loss: "I know not how to replace him."

FASCINATING FACTS: The Rebel Yell

At the First Battle of Bull Run, Stonewall Jackson issued an order to troops of the 4th Infantry, part of his Stonewall Brigade:

"Reserve your fire until they come within 50 yards! Then fire and give them the bayonet! And when you charge, yell like furies!"

Yelling "like furies" became a routine for Confederate troops. In battle after battle, charge after charge, entire units of them issued terrible cries that struck fear into the hearts of the often inexperienced Union soldiers. Exactly what sound they made is uncertain; their yells may have resembled Native American war whoops or Scottish battle cries. The "rebel yell" was an especially effective weapon early in the war, when the Union was suffering defeat after defeat under indecisive generals like McClellan, Burnside and Hooker.

1861, July 27: President Lincoln appoints General George B. McClellan to organize and lead the new Army of the Potomac, replacing General Irvin McDowell.

1862, January 31: President Lincoln orders Union naval and land forces to launch aggressive action against the Confederacy by February 22, George Washington's birthday.

1862, February 6-16: Union forces capture Forts Henry and Donelson in Tennessee.

FASCINATING FACTS: Fort Henry and Fort Donelson

The early 1862 Battles of Fort Henry and Fort Donelson were the Union army's first major victories in the "western theater," a series of Civil War battles fought west of the Appalachian Mountains. They were also the first victories for Brigadier General Ulysses S. Grant, who would become the Union's most effective commander.

Fort Henry was a mud walled fort sitting on low ground along the Tennessee River, just south of Tennessee's border with neutral Kentucky. Fort Henry was designed to keep the Union from floating supplies and troops down the Tennessee River, but its low position made it vulnerable. Before the Battle of Fort Henry even began on February 6, 1862, heavy rains flooded much of the fort, and the Confederate ground forces withdrew to nearby Fort Donelson. Ironclad Union navy gunboats pounded Fort Henry into surrender after only about 75 minutes of firing, and General Grant's ground forces never even attacked. Two days later, heavy floods placed the entire fort underwater.

The Battle of Fort Donelson began six days later, on February 12. Fort Donelson lay twelve miles east of Fort Henry on the Cumberland River. Its elevation high above the river made it much more defensible than Fort Henry, and when the Union navy gunboats tried to attack it, they all took heavy damage. Nevertheless, the Confederates feared that they could not continue to hold the fort against the much larger Union forces, which were being reinforced with new troops arriving by boat.

On February 15, the Confederates burst out of Fort Donelson and attacked, hoping to open an escape route and join other Confederate forces. General Grant was away at Fort Henry when the battle began, and the Union forces were disorganized. However, just when their escape route opened up and success was in their grasp, the Confederate commanders lost their nerve and returned to the safety of the fort. On the next day, February 16th, the Confederates surrendered Fort Donelson to the Union.

The fall of the Tennessee and Cumberland "Twin Rivers" helped to open Tennessee for more Union advances. The capital at Nashville would be occupied by the end of the month. Most of Tennessee would spend the rest of the war, from March 1862 on, under the control of a military governor appointed by President Lincoln: the future U.S. President Andrew Johnson.

Other interesting facts about the Battles of Forts Henry and Donelson:

1. Union General U.S. Grant earned his nickname "Unconditional Surrender Grant" at Fort Donelson, when he responded to a Confederate request for terms of surrender with a note that included this sentence: "No terms except immediate and unconditional surrender can be accepted."
2. A Union general named Lew Wallace also participated in the Battle of Fort Donelson. Lew Wallace would later write the well-known Christian novel *Ben Hur: A Tale of the Christ*.

1862, March 8-9: The *Merrimack* and the *Monitor*, two iron-armored gunboats, battle near the Virginia coast.

FASCINATING FACTS: The *Merrimack* and the *Monitor*

The idea of protecting wooden ships by lining their sides with iron armor was less than ten years old when the Civil War began. The Confederates were aware that their navy was far inferior to that of the Union, so they sought to boost their chances by building an iron-armored warship.

In the confusion around the time of Virginia's secession, the Union had abandoned an important naval station at Gosport, Virginia. Gosport lay near Portsmouth and Norfolk, upriver from the Union naval blockade at Hampton Roads. Gosport was simply full of cannon and gunpowder, and it had a dry dock for ship repair. It also had a U.S. steam frigate named the *Merrimack*. The Union had scuttled and burned the *Merrimack* before it left, but Confederate engineers raised its hulk and used Gosport's dry dock to rebuild it into an iron-armored warship. They renamed their odd-looking vessel the *CSS Virginia*, but it was still better known as the *Merrimack*.

On March 8, 1862, the completed *Merrimack* steamed into Hampton Roads on a mission to eliminate the Union blockade there, which had been in place since the war began. The armored warship was an instant success. It rammed and sank the much larger *USS Cumberland*, then helped destroy the *USS Congress*. Cannon shells fired from ship and shore simply bounced off of its heavily armored hull.

On the next day, March 9, the crew of the *Merrimack* got an unwelcome surprise when a second iron-armored ship, the *USS Monitor*, steamed into Hampton Roads. The Union had secretly developed an armored craft of its own. The *Monitor*, too, was an odd-looking vessel. If the *Merrimack* looked like an iron house flooded up to its eaves, the *Monitor* looked like an iron raft with a steam boiler on top. The "boiler" was actually an innovative rotating gun turret that allowed the *Monitor* to fire in any direction except straight ahead, where its guns were blocked by the command bridge.

The *Merrimack* and the *Monitor* battled to a draw that day; neither was able to damage the other significantly. The *Monitor* retreated to shallow water where the heavier *Merrimack* couldn't follow, and the *Merrimack* withdrew upriver. Although both ships remained seaworthy, neither ever fought again. When the Confederates abandoned Norfolk, they burned the *Merrimack* to keep it out of Union hands. Later, when the *Monitor* was ordered to North Carolina, it took on water in heavy seas and sank. Its sunken wreck was rediscovered in 1973, and its recovered turret and other items are on display in Newport News, Virginia.

1862, April 6: North and South fight the Battle of Shiloh on the Tennessee River.

FASCINATING FACTS: The Battle of Shiloh

In the spring of 1862, General Grant stood near Shiloh, Tennessee, waiting for General Don Buell to arrive from Nashville. Grant's Army of West Tennessee had over 48,000 troops; while Buell's Army of the Ohio had over 17,000. When Buell arrived, the two generals planned to head south— hoping to hit the Confederates at Corinth, Mississippi, home to an important railroad junction. Grant camped around Pittsburg Landing, on the west bank of the Tennessee River. He was so confident, or so careless, that he built almost no defenses around his camp.

Confederate General Albert Sydney Johnston wanted to attack Grant before Buell got there; for he knew that once the two linked up, they would be almost unbeatable. With no defenses around the Union camp, Johnston could lead his 44,000 troops almost under Grant's nose before anyone noticed!

The Battle of Shiloh started with a Confederate surprise attack on the morning of April 6, 1862. Johnston gained ground quickly, at first. But then he ran into the "Hornet's Nest"— a heavily wooded position where Union troops fought like heroes. In the hours it took to capture the Hornet's Nest, General Johnston was killed. His second in command, General P.G.T. Beauregard, halted the attack for the evening, just as Buell's army started to arrive.

The next day, Beauregard faced a refreshed and reinforced Union army about twice the size of his own. After more fierce fighting, which he directed from his base at Shiloh Church, Beauregard retreated down the road to Corinth. He left behind the bloodiest battlefield of the war so far. The Union had suffered about 13,000 casualties, and the Confederacy about 10,000. The Confederacy had missed its chance to destroy Grant's army, and the Union would go on to capture Corinth and Memphis.

Other interesting facts about the Battle of Shiloh:
1. After the battle, General Grant was temporarily relieved of command for leaving his army so defenseless at Pittsburg Landing. President Lincoln was asked to fire him, but replied, "I can't spare this man. He fights."
2. Another officer who won fame at Shiloh was William Tecumseh Sherman— the same Sherman who would later fight a horrible "Total War" against the Deep South. This made Sherman a hero to the North, but a villain to the South.

1862, September 17: The Battle of Antietam leads to the deadliest day in US military history.

FASCINATING FACTS: The Battle of Antietam

After an August 30, 1862 victory at the Second Battle of Bull Run, Confederate General Robert E. Lee made plans to invade the North for the first time in the war. President Lincoln had more or less forced the State of Maryland to remain in the Union at the outset of the war (lest Washington DC be surrounded), and Lee hoped to regain at least part of Maryland and bring its people and soldiers into the Confederacy if he could. He also hoped to move the battlefront into the North, and to win a major victory that might encourage Britain to recognize and help the Confederacy. General Lee planned to invade Maryland at the town of Sharpsburg, which lay near Antietam Creek.

Unfortunately, Lee's strategy became well known when the enemy discovered a copy of his battle plan. Union troops found a misplaced copy of Lee's detailed battle plan, "Special Order 191," rolled up around three cigars and tucked inside an envelope on the ground near Frederick, Maryland. With Special Order 191 in hand, Union General George McClellan knew where every unit of Lee's army would be, although he was uncertain of each unit's size.

Thanks to this unexpected gift, McClellan's 90,000-man-strong Army of the Potomac was well positioned to defend against Lee's Army of Northern Virginia invasion force of 55,000. However, despite McClellan's advantages, Lee was able to fight McClellan to a standstill at the Battle of Antietam on September 17, 1862, in what became the bloodiest battle of the war so far.

Some of the Battle of Antietam's worst fighting happened along a sunken road that became known as the "Bloody Lane." Eyewitnesses reported that the very atmosphere along the Bloody Lane turned red with blood. The Union suffered about 12,000 casualties at Antietam, the Confederates about 10,000. These casualties were slightly fewer than the ones at the terrible Battle of Shiloh, but more of Antietam's casualties were dead, not wounded or missing. More soldiers died in that one day at Antietam than in any other day of any battle in any American war.

After the battle, Lee successfully withdrew to Virginia, and his army survived to fight on; but his first attempted invasion of the North was over. Union General McClellan was criticized for failing to pursue Lee with fresh troops, because about one third of his vast army never fired a shot at Sharpsburg. President Lincoln grew impatient with McClellan's caution, and replaced him with a new general before the end of the year.

1863, January 1: President Lincoln issues an executive order called the Emancipation Proclamation.

FASCINATING FACTS: The Emancipation Proclamation

Despite Abraham Lincoln's deserved reputation as "the man who freed the slaves," he was no radical abolitionist. From the beginning of the Civil War, President Lincoln justified his use of force against the South on the basis of upholding the law, preserving the Union and saving the unique American form of government that provided its citizens with so much liberty. Freeing the slaves of the South was not his first goal, nor was it a goal for which many of his volunteer Northern troops wanted to offer their lives.

Nevertheless, freeing the slaves became a more important goal as the Civil War went on. Lincoln came under considerable pressure from both abolitionists and the Congress to address the issue of slavery and make abolition a cause of the war. After the Battle of Antietam, President Lincoln gave in to this pressure and issued an executive order called the Emancipation Proclamation, scheduling it to take effect on January 1, 1863.

The Emancipation Proclamation forever linked the Civil War with the emancipation (freeing) of slaves. Under its terms, all slaves in the seceded states became free. Late in the Civil War, as the Union captured more and more Confederate territory, the proclamation took effect in that captured territory and began to free slaves all over the South. The order also led to the enlistment of 200,000 black soldiers in the Union army.

The Emancipation Proclamation had another important effect: it discouraged Britain from supporting the Confederacy. Slavery was illegal and unpopular in Britain, and the British would not support a Confederate war that was linked to the advancement of slavery. Lincoln's order kept the Confederacy from gaining vital British support that might have turned the tide of the war.

Slave Children

FASCINATING FACTS: The Soldier's "Housewife"

Soldiers in the Civil War often carried a "housewife," a small sewing kit stocked with needle, thread and buttons for repairing their uniforms. Many of them tucked locks of hair from their wives or girlfriends inside their "housewives."

SOBERING STATISTICS: Soldier Deaths in the Civil War

The North and the South fought the United States Civil War from 1861-1865. During those four years about 620,000 soldiers died, along with an unknown number of civilians. It was by far the United States' deadliest war of all time, an unspeakable tragedy. More soldiers died of infected wounds and disease than in actual combat.

U.S. GEOGRAPHY FOCUS

FASCINATING FACTS about WEST VIRGINIA:

- Statehood: West Virginia became the 35th US state on June 20, 1863.
- Bordering states: Kentucky, Maryland, Ohio, Pennsylvania and Virginia
- State capital: Charleston
- Area: 24,230 sq. mi (Ranks 41st in size)
- Abbreviation: WV
- State nickname: "Mountain State" (West Virginia is called the "Mountain State" because its entire territory lies within the Appalachian Mountain Range)
- State Bird: Northern Cardinal
- State tree: Sugar Maple
- State flower: Rhododendron
- State songs: *West Virginia My Home*, *The West Virginia Hills*, *This Is My West Virginia*

- State Motto: "Mountaineers are always free"
- Meaning of name: West Virginia was originally part of Virginia, which was named for Queen Elizabeth I of England (the "virgin queen")
- Historic places to visit in West Virginia: New River Gorge Bridge, Organ Cave, Harpers Ferry National Historic Park, Oil and Gas Museum, Cass Scenic Railroad State Park, Berkeley Springs State Park
- Resources and Industries: mining (coal), tourism, forestry, farming (livestock, dairy), manufacturing (glass, chemicals, steel and iron)

John Brown Fort at Harper's Ferry

Flag of West Virginia

- West Virginia adopted this flag in 1929
- It has a white field bordered in blue, and a coat of arms in the middle.
- The rock on the flag contains the date on which West Virginia became a state.
- The two men on the flag represent farming and mining.
- The flag's lower red banner contains the state motto written in Latin.
- The flowers on the flag are rhododendrons (the state flower).

FASCINATING FACTS: West Virginia Statehood

Early in 1861, Virginia was considered a pro-Union state. Even after President Lincoln's April 15 call for troops, when most Virginians favored secession, the people of western Virginia remained mostly pro-Union. When Virginia's Secession Convention scheduled a statewide vote on secession for May 23, twenty-seven western Virginia counties immediately scheduled a convention of their own in Wheeling, Virginia. At its second meeting, this convention declared that secession was illegal and that all of Virginia's state officers- its governor, its congressmen, and so on- were no longer Virginia's legal representatives. These western counties elected their own governor, senators and congressmen to represent them. This new, alternative government of Virginia was called the "Restored Government of Virginia."

The federal government was eager to retain these counties in the Union, so it proposed to accept them into the Union as a new state. The proposed name for this new state was "Kanawha," but instead it formally entered the Union as West Virginia on June 20, 1863. West Virginia is the only state that entered the Union in this way.

The Flags of the Union and the Confederacy

The Union Flag

There were 34 states in 1861, represented by 34 stars on the Union flag. The Union never acknowledged the secession of the 11 states of the South, and never removed their stars from its flag. West Virginia came into the Union in 1863 as the 35th state, so the flag added its 35th star.

The Confederate Flag

The Confederate States of America used several flags during its four-year existence:

This was the original flag of the Confederacy. Its 7 stars represented the 7 states of the deep South.	
After the 4 additional states of the middle South seceded, the new Confederate flag had 11 stars.	
The similarities between the Union flag and the Confederate flag led to confusion on the battlefield. This flag, known as the "Southern Cross," was used after the First Battle of Bull Run to avoid confusion. It became the Confederacy's most recognized flag, even though the Confederate Congress never officially adopted it. It has thirteen stars, not eleven: The two extra stars represent Kentucky and Missouri, two neutral states that the Confederacy tried to claim.	

PRESIDENTIAL FOCUS

PRESIDENT #16: Abraham Lincoln (1809 – 1865)	
In Office: March 4, 1861 – April 15, 1865	**Political Party:** Republican
Birthplace: Kentucky	**Nickname:** "Honest Abe"

President Abraham Lincoln is best remembered for guiding the United States through the Civil War. Most Americans honor Lincoln as one of the nation's greatest Presidents, although some still criticize him because in their opinion he had no legal right to invade the seceded South. President Lincoln wrote and delivered some of American history's most eloquent speeches.

Lincoln was born in a Kentucky log cabin. He rose from humble circumstances to become an Illinois country lawyer, then a railroad company attorney. Next he served in the Illinois state legislature, followed by the U.S. House of Representatives. When he ran for the U.S. Senate in 1858, he lost to the powerful Illinois Senator Steven Douglas. However, his eloquent performance in the Lincoln-Douglas debates, a series of grueling debates on the issues of slavery and popular sovereignty, made him an admired national figure. Two years later, in 1860, Lincoln won the Presidency.

Like many in the North, Lincoln opposed the expansion of slavery more than he opposed slavery itself. Although he believed that slavery was inconsistent with the human rights outlined in the Declaration of Independence, his primary goal through the first two years of the Civil War was not to free slaves, but to hold the Union together. He took an extraordinary action in pursuit of that goal when he suspended *habeas corpus*, the law that prevented U.S. authorities from holding prisoners without trial. This he did primarily to keep the Upper South border state of Maryland in the Union, because if Maryland had seceded as Virginia did, then Washington DC would have been surrounded by hostile territory.

The character and goals of the Civil War changed when Lincoln's Emancipation Proclamation took effect on January 1, 1863. From that time on, the Civil War began to be identified with liberating the black slaves of the South. Before the war was over, Lincoln's Emancipation Proclamation would free between 3 and 4 million of them. Lincoln also promoted the 13th Amendment to the U.S. Constitution, which finally banned slavery everywhere in the United States when it was ratified. Although he required some coaxing from abolitionists like Frederick Douglass, Lincoln is rightly remembered as a great liberator of slaves.

Five days after General Lee's surrender at Appomattox, actor John Wilkes Booth assassinated President Lincoln at the Ford's Theater in Washington DC. This act of murder enraged the North, and was partly responsible for the North's vengeful attitude toward the South during the period of Reconstruction after the Civil War.

Other interesting facts about Abraham Lincoln:
- At 6' 4" of height, Lincoln was America's tallest President.
- Lincoln was the first president who was photographed at his inauguration (his second inauguration, in March 1865). John Wilkes Booth, who later assassinated Lincoln, is believed to be visible in that picture.
- During the Lincoln-Douglas Debates, Lincoln was beardless. Lincoln grew his beard after an 11 year old girl wrote a letter telling him that he'd look better with whiskers.
- When he worked a lawyer, Lincoln often carried legal papers in his trademark top hat.
- Lincoln and his wife had four children, but only one, Robert Todd Lincoln, survived to adulthood.
- Lincoln had a premonition of death before his assassination.

Notable quotes from Abraham Lincoln:
- "I destroy my enemies when I make them my friends."
- "It is better to remain silent and be thought a fool than to open one's mouth and remove all doubt."
- "America will never be destroyed from the outside. If we falter and lose our freedoms, it will be because we destroyed ourselves."

The Gettysburg Address

(Delivered by President Abraham Lincoln on November 19, 1863 at the dedication ceremony for the new Soldiers' National Cemetery in Gettysburg, Pennsylvania)

Four score and seven years ago our fathers brought forth on this continent, a new nation, conceived in Liberty, and dedicated to the proposition that all men are created equal.

Now we are engaged in a great civil war, testing whether that nation, or any nation so conceived and so dedicated, can long endure. We are met on a great battle-field of that war. We have come to dedicate a portion of that field, as a final resting place for those who here gave their lives that that nation might live. It is altogether fitting and proper that we should do this.

But, in a larger sense, we can not dedicate -- we can not consecrate -- we can not hallow -- this ground. The brave men, living and dead, who struggled here, have consecrated it, far above our poor power to add or detract. The world will little note, nor long remember what we say here, but it can never forget what they did here.

It is for us the living, rather, to be dedicated here to the unfinished work which they who fought here have thus far so nobly advanced. It is rather for us to be here dedicated to the great task remaining before us -- that from these honored dead we take increased devotion to that cause for which they gave the last full measure of devotion -- that we here highly resolve that these dead shall not have died in vain -- that this nation, under God, shall have a new birth of freedom -- and that government of the people, by the people, for the people, shall not perish from the earth.

Chapter 5

U.S. Civil War, Part II

U.S. HISTORY FOCUS

THE WAR BETWEEN THE STATES, PART II

ELITE ENGLISHWOMEN: Elizabeth Blackwell (1821 – 1910)

English-born Elizabeth Blackwell became the first woman in the United States to receive a medical degree and become a doctor. Discrimination against women made it difficult for Elizabeth to practice medicine, but she persisted. She put her education to good use during the American Civil War, when she trained women as nurses. After the war, she joined with Florence Nightingale to help found the Women's Medical College in England.

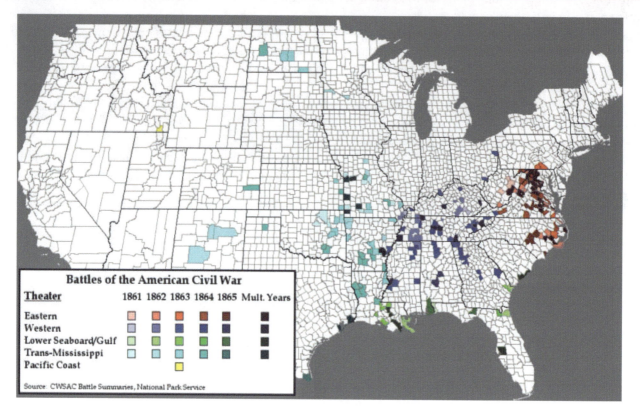

A Brief Timeline of the Civil War (late 1862 - 1865, continued from Chapter 4):

1862, November 7: President Lincoln appoints General Ambrose Burnside as his Commander of the Army of the Potomac, replacing General McClellan.

1862, December 13: General Burnside suffers an embarrassing and costly defeat at the Battle of Fredericksburg, Virginia.

1863, January 25: Lincoln appoints General Joseph Hooker as his Commander of the Army of the Potomac, replacing General Burnside.

1863, January 29: Lincoln appoints General Grant as his Commander of the Army of the West.

see Chapter 7 for more on General Grant

1863, May 4: The Confederate Army of Northern Virginia defeats a much larger Union force at the Battle of Chancellorsville.

> ### FASCINATING FACTS: The Battle of Chancellorsville
>
>
>
> In 1863, the Union's advantages in numbers began to grow overwhelming. Before the Battle of Chancellorsville, Virginia, the Union Army of the Potomac under General Hooker numbered more than 130,000 men. Confederate General Lee's Army of Northern Virginia opposed them with less than half that number, about 60,000. The battle to come would be proof of the Ecclesiastical proverb, "The battle is not always to the strong."
>
> General Hooker's plan was to cross the Rappahannock River near Chancellorsville with a large force, while simultaneously sending a smaller force across the river near Fredericksburg to attack General Lee from the rear. Hooker had so many troops that his "smaller force" contained 40,000 men, two thirds of Lee's entire army, while his "large force" of 70,000 still outnumbered Lee's main force. Hooker assumed that Lee would retreat in the face of such an overwhelming threat and move to defend Richmond.
>
> Instead, General Lee surprised Hooker by dividing his force to meet the two threats. Lee held off Hooker's smaller force of 40,000 at his rear with just 11,000 of his own men. With the rest of his men, he attacked Hooker's 70,000-man attacking force and drove it back inside its defensive lines on May 1, 1863. Hooker retreated because he wanted to fight defensively from the protection of his lines, as the Confederates had done so successfully at the Battle of Fredericksburg during the previous December.
>
> On the next day, May 2, battlefield scouts reported a weakness in the Union lines that Hooker trusted so much: their right flank (the right end of their defensive lines), which should have been well-defended, was almost entirely unprotected. General Lee took advantage of this weakness with a daring maneuver: dividing his army a second time, he sent Stonewall Jackson's 28,000 men around the Union lines to attack that unprotected flank.
>
> General Jackson managed to arrive near the Union flank undetected, or at least unreported. Shortly before dark, he launched a devastating attack that rolled up the defenseless Union flank like lightning, forcing Union troops to retreat in a panic. If darkness had not intervened, Jackson might have destroyed the entire Union force against the south side of the Rappahannock River. That night, Stonewall Jackson was accidentally shot and put out of action by his own troops. About a week later, Jackson died (see Chapter 4).
>
> Despite the success of Jackson's flanking maneuver, a large un-fought Union force remained on the south side of the Rappahannock. Over two more days of fierce fighting, Lee managed to drive Hooker back to the north side of the river. The Battle of Chancellorsville would turn out to be General Lee's greatest victory of the war. However, it was a costly victory: Lee lost 13,000 casualties, nearly a fourth of his fighting force. Hooker lost 17,000: a greater number, but a far smaller fraction of his total force. The South could ill afford such heavy losses, especially when one of those losses was the great Stonewall Jackson.
>
> Author Steven Crane based his well-known short novel *The Red Badge of Courage* on the chaos surrounding the Union side of the Battle of Chancellorsville.

1863, June: Emboldened by his victory at Chancellorsville, General Lee launches his second invasion of the North with almost 75,000 troops. On June 13, he defeats Union forces at Winchester, Virginia, then moves north through Maryland and into Pennsylvania.

1863, June 28: President Lincoln appoints General George Meade as his new Commander of the Army of the Potomac, replacing General Hooker. Meade is the fifth general to take this post since the war began.

1863, July 1-3: In a major turning point of the war, the Union army defeats the Confederates at the Battle of Gettysburg.

FASCINATING FACTS: The Battle of Gettysburg

Emboldened by his victory at Chancellorsville, General Lee sought to press his advantage with a second attempt to invade the North in the summer of 1863. His successes against great odds had given him confidence that his Southern troops were superior fighters, able to defeat far larger numbers of timidly-led Northern troops. Lee hoped to win enough victories to threaten the city of Washington itself and force an end to the war.

Unfortunately for General Lee, the North reached the high ground first in Pennsylvania. Just as Lee's vanguard (leading force) arrived near Gettysburg, Pennsylvania on July 1, 1863, Union cavalry commanded by General John Buford also arrived and occupied high ground north of the town. Because Buford received infantry reinforcements, he was able to hold this high ground long enough for the main force of General Meade's Union army to arrive on the hills south of the town. Before the first day of the battle was over, Meade had established his defenses on a series of high ridges south of Gettysburg, forcing Lee to go on the offense against an entrenched enemy.

On the second day of the battle, Lee concentrated his attacks on the Union's flanks. Lee sent wave after wave of troops against Meade's defenses on now-famous battlegrounds like Culp's Hill, Cemetery Hill, Little Round Top and Devil's Den. The Union only barely managed to survive these flank attacks through the bravery of units like the 20th Maine, commanded by Colonel Joshua Chamberlain (see below).

When his attacks on the Union's flanks failed, Lee spent the third day of the battle attacking the Union's center. The best-known offensive of the Battle of Gettysburg was Pickett's Charge, an assault on entrenched Union forces at another famous battleground, Cemetery Ridge. Pickett led his troops against the very center of the Union lines on Cemetery Ridge, where he hoped that those lines had been weakened by intense Confederate cannon fire. Instead, Union defenses in the center remained as strong as ever, and Pickett lost more than half of his division in the failed assault. Reportedly, when General Lee ordered Pickett to rally his division after the charge, Pickett replied, "I have no division."

The highest point Pickett's Charge reached on Cemetery Ridge has been called "the high water mark of the Confederacy." After the failure of Pickett's Charge and the Confederate army's devastating loss at Gettysburg, the rising tide of Southern rebellion against the North slowly began to recede.

When the Battle of Gettysburg was over, General Lee retreated to Virginia, and General Meade's weary army did not pursue. The loss at Gettysburg was the end of the Confederacy's hopes for victory, and the major turning point of the Civil War. With the draft swelling the Union army's ranks more and more, Union victory became a near certainty after Gettysburg. Even so, the bitter war would drag on for nearly two more years.

AMAZING AMERICANS: Joshua Chamberlain (1828 – 1914)

Joshua Chamberlain was a 34-year-old, well-established college professor with no prior military experience when he volunteered to serve the Union army in August, 1862. Chamberlain's age and position would certainly have exempted him from military service; but he chose to volunteer anyway because he believed in the cause of preserving the Union. As a lieutenant colonel of the 20th Maine Regiment, Chamberlain became part of the Army of the Potomac. He fought in the Union loss at the late 1862 Battle of Fredericksburg, then missed the Union loss at the Battle of Chancellorsville because his unit had been sickened by an overly strong batch of smallpox vaccine.

Chamberlain's finest hour came at the Battle of Gettysburg. On July 2, 1863, the second day of the battle, Chamberlain and the 20th Maine were assigned to defend the Union army's far left flank at Little Round Top. No one on the Union side expected Little Round Top to see much action that day. As it happened, however, that second day was the day when General Lee decided to attack the Union's flanks. When the 15th Alabama Infantry launched its all-out assault on Little Round Top, Chamberlain suddenly found himself responsible for the highly vulnerable left flank of the entire Union army. If the Confederates could bypass that flank, then they might be able to attack the Union army from the rear and destroy it. Chamberlain resolved to hold his position at Little Round Top no matter what the cost.

Chamberlain's 20th Maine determinedly ignored the Confederates' rebel yells as it stood its ground and repulsed wave after wave of attacks. Late in the day, when his unit's ammunition began to run low and the flank was in danger, Chamberlain ordered a desperate, daring bayonet charge. Switching from defense to offense, the troops of the 20th Maine pin-wheeled through the woods of Little Round Top, killing and capturing stunned Confederates as they went. Chamberlain's bayonet charge saved his unit, the Union army's left flank and possibly the Battle of Gettysburg. For his gallant conduct at Little Round Top, Chamberlain won the Medal of Honor, the United States' highest military award.

Chamberlain continued to risk his life in battle throughout the rest of the Civil War. He was shot six times and had six horses shot beneath him. One bullet passed through both of his hips and cost him nearly six months in a hospital. Despite his many wounds, Chamberlain was still fighting when General Lee finally decided to surrender at Appomattox. At the surrender ceremony, the men of the Union army repaid Chamberlain's war-long bravery by granting him the highest honor imaginable: they selected him to lead the troops that stood guard while Confederates laid down their arms and their battle flags.

AMAZING AMERICANS: J.E.B. Stuart (1833 – 1864)

James Ewell Brown "Jeb" Stuart was a Confederate cavalry commander during the Civil War. Stuart cut a dashing figure in his caped uniform and plumed (feathered) hat; and he earned a reputation for horsemanship, battle skills and gallantry that made him a hero of the South.

Jeb Stuart was the sort of hero the South needed early in the Civil War: optimistic, energetic and conscious of the inspiring power of a bold gesture. During the Union's Peninsula Campaign in early 1862, Stuart led 1,200 cavalry troops on a 150-mile reconnaissance mission that rode all the way around the Union army. He returned with good information about the enemy, and he also captured Union troops, horses and supplies. His success embarrassed the North and thrilled the South. He repeated this bold stunt after Lee's failed invasion of the North at Sharpsburg, Maryland (Antietam), again returning with horses and supplies.

Stuart fared less well during Lee's second invasion of the North, in the days just before the Battle of Gettysburg. Operating on unfamiliar ground and faced with more-aggressive Union opposition, Stuart was forced to ride far to the east to avoid fast-moving Union forces. His ride caused minor scares in both Washington DC and Baltimore, and captured some supplies; but in the process, his scouts were cut off from the main body of the Confederate army, and failed to provide General Lee with regular reports about the enemy's location. Stuart finally arrived at Gettysburg on the second day of the battle, far too late for his outdated reports to be of much use to General Lee. Some accused him of betraying the Confederate army by attempting another joy ride around the Union army, with less success this time. Some even blamed the absence of Stuart's cavalry for the Confederate loss at Gettysburg.

Late in the war, the Confederate cavalry began to lose its advantage over the Union cavalry, and the aggressive Union General Phil Sheridan began to take Stuart's place as the Civil War's most celebrated cavalryman. On May 11, 1864, Stuart was involved in a 3-hour cavalry battle near Yellow Tavern, an empty inn a few miles north of Richmond. As Stuart's men drove Union forces off a hilltop, a retreating Union soldier shot Stuart in the midsection. He died in Richmond on the next day, May 12.

1863, July 4: One day after the Union victory at Gettysburg, the Union wins a major western theater victory when the Confederate army defending a Mississippi River stronghold at Vicksburg, Mississippi surrenders.

FASCINATING FACTS: The Siege of Vicksburg

Vicksburg, Mississippi is a small city on a high bluff overlooking a horseshoe bend in the Mississippi River. It lies about 40 miles west of Jackson, Mississippi's capital. Vicksburg's strong natural defenses included the river on its west side, a huge swamp to its north and steep hills all around. During the Civil War, Vicksburg was the key to control of the important Mississippi River. For as long as Vicksburg remained in Southern hands, the Confederacy could control at least part of the Mississippi River and remain united with the Confederate states of Louisiana, Arkansas and Texas on the west side of that river. Both President Lincoln and President Davis considered Vicksburg a key to winning the war.

For the first half of 1863, capturing Vicksburg was General Grant's main focus. Earlier attempts to capture the city by boat had already failed. Positioning his forces in Louisiana on the west side of the Mississippi, Grant made several attempts to bypass Vicksburg's tough natural defenses by digging canals. One of these canals would have diverted the Mississippi River's flow away from Vicksburg if it had succeeded, rendering the city irrelevant. It didn't succeed: the mighty Mississippi River defeated Grant, and his failed efforts to bypass the river became known as "Grant's Bayou Operations."

General Grant finally abandoned the Bayou Operations and instead embarked on a roundabout path toward Vicksburg. He crossed the Mississippi River south of Vicksburg, heading west to east from Louisiana into Mississippi. Then he captured Jackson and approached Vicksburg from the east. When Grant finally arrived at Vicksburg, he launched two all-out assaults on Vicksburg's defenses, one on May 19 and another on May 22. Both failed. Judging that the city's defenses were too strong for a frontal assault, Grant decided to blockade the city and settle in for a siege.

No city can survive under siege forever without supplies, and Vicksburg was no exception. The city's only hope was to await rescue by General Joseph E. Johnston, the Confederacy's western theater commander. But Johnston's army was far too small to attack Grant's, so Johnston never came.

After more than 40 days under siege, Vicksburg's defenders finally surrendered their city to General Grant on July 4, 1863, one day after the Union's big victory back east in the Battle of Gettysburg. With this victory, the Union controlled the upper Mississippi River, and would soon control the entire river. The

Confederacy was divided: Louisiana, Arkansas and Texas were cut off, and supplies could no longer reach the eastern Confederate states by way of Mexico.

For eight decades after the Civil War, the citizens of Vicksburg refused to celebrate American Independence Day on July 4th, because that was also the date of their city's surrender.

1863, September 19-20: The Confederates score a rare western theater victory in the Battle of Chickamauga. Confederate General Braxton Bragg's Army of Tennessee forces the Union Army of the Cumberland to retreat to Chattanooga, Tennessee.

1863, October 16: President Lincoln appoints General Grant to command all Union operations in the western theater of the war.

1863, November 23-25: Grant's Union forces avenge their defeat at Chickamauga with a victory over the Confederates at the Battle of Chattanooga.

1864, March 9: President Lincoln appoints General Grant as his commander of all Union forces. General William Sherman takes Grant's place as commander of western theater operations.

(General William T. Sherman, General Ulysses S. Grant, Lincoln, and Admiral David Dixon Porter discuss military plans for final months of the Civil War)

1864, May: General Grant begins a massive offensive campaign involving all Union armies in all theaters of the war. General Sherman will advance toward Atlanta, Georgia, while Grant advances toward Richmond, Virginia in his "Overland Campaign." On all fronts, Union forces will outnumber Confederate forces by 2 to 1 or more.

1864, May 5-6: The Union suffers terrible casualties at the Battle of the Wilderness near Fredericksburg and Chancellorsville, Virginia. Heedless of the cost, General Grant disengages and begins to maneuver around the Confederates, threatening their capital at Richmond. Lee and the Confederates are forced to retreat to protect their capital. Similar losses and similar retreats happen at Spotsylvania, Virginia on May 8-12 and at Cold Harbor, Virginia on June 1-3.

1864, June 15: The Confederates take up defensive positions around Richmond and the important railroad junction of Petersburg, Virginia. Grant's long Siege of Petersburg begins.

FASCINATING FACTS: The Siege of Petersburg

Petersburg, Virginia was the site of an important railroad junction just south of the Confederate capital of Richmond. The Siege of Petersburg was a nearly 10 month long standoff between Union forces under General Grant and Confederate forces under General Lee.

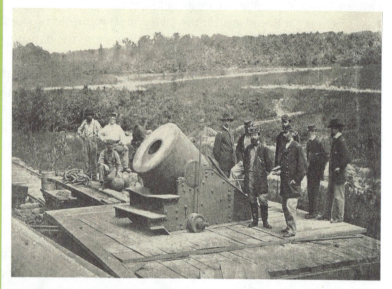

In early 1865, Grant forced his way deep into Virginia in his Overland Campaign to bring an end to the war. He pressed forward in spite of terrible losses at the Battle of the Wilderness and the Battle of Spotsylvania; in both cases, he simply withdrew from the lost battle and maneuvered around Lee's defenses, threatening Richmond. Each time, Lee was forced to retreat and build new defenses. At the next battle, the Battle of Cold Harbor, Grant made the mistake of attacking Lee after he had had plenty of time to engineer his defenses. The result was a one-sided bloodbath that cost Grant thousands of Union casualties. General Grant was quickly earning a reputation with the North as a bungler who recklessly wasted his troops' lives in poorly planned assaults. When Grant withdrew from Cold Harbor and began to threaten Petersburg, he did so with a healthy respect for Lee's defensive capabilities.

For this reason, Grant was slightly more cautious when he began his attack on Petersburg in June, 1864. After one more costly frontal assault, he ordered a series of smaller attacks while he turned his attention to his many other weapons. He ordered an attack in Virginia's Shenandoah Valley, forcing Lee to send some of his troops to reinforce General Jubal Early there. He authorized Sherman's March to the Sea to terrorize the South. And all the while, he maintained constant pressure on Lee, sending out cavalry raids to damage his railroad lines and cut off his supplies. With each assault, Lee had to extend his lines farther and farther until his troops were spread out over defensive lines about 30 miles long.

On March 25, 1865, Lee attacked Union forces at Fort Stedman in a final attempt to break the Siege of Petersburg. When the attack on Fort Stedman failed, Lee's defenses were weaker still, and defeat became inevitable. By now the Union had succeeded in cutting off almost all of the Confederate army's supplies, and Lee's men were starving. When Grant began a series of breakthrough attacks in the Third Battle of Petersburg on April 2nd, Lee was finally forced to abandon Petersburg and Richmond and retreat to the west. (Picture shows Richmond in ruins, April 3rd, 1865).

FASCINATING FACTS: The Battle of the Crater

Near the beginning of the long Siege of Petersburg came a strange battle called the Battle of the Crater. As Union and Confederate forces settled into their defensive lines for the Siege of Petersburg, each probed the other for weakness. One section of the Union lines lay only about 400 feet from Elliot's Salient, a small earth-walled fort along the Confederate lines. This section was manned by the 48th Regiment of Pennsylvania Volunteer Infantry, a unit that happened to include a number of men who worked as Pennsylvania coal miners during peacetime. These miners conceived a plan to dig a mine shaft under Elliot's Salient, fill it with gunpowder, and blow the fort sky-high. Then they planned to use the gap in the lines to break through Confederate lines and capture Petersburg.

The soldiers began work on the tunnel on June 25, 1864, using improvised tools. When they had tunneled about 500 feet, they reached the subsoil directly under the fort. Then they widened the end of the tunnel so that the explosion would make a wider gap in the Confederate lines above. Finally, they filled the tunnel with 8,000 pounds of gunpowder, packed it with sandbags to direct the blast upward, and ran a long fuse back to the tunnel's entrance.

The attack was set for July 30. The miners lit the fuse and waited— and waited some more. Finally, two volunteers had to enter the mineshaft to discover that the fire had fizzled out at a splice in the long fuse. They re-lit the fuse and scurried out. When the charge went off, it did just what the miners had hoped: it destroyed Elliot's Salient, killing almost 300 Confederate troops in the process, and made a wide gap in the Confederate lines.

Unfortunately, the gap in the lines was blocked by the 20-foot deep, steep-sided blast crater (see picture). Instead of attacking around the crater's edges, Union troops gamely charged into the crater, only to find themselves trapped under terrible fire from the fast-recovering Confederate defenders. What had begun as a Union success quickly changed to disaster for the Union. Confederate troops rained down fire on Union troops from the high ground at the crater's edges, while Union troops took cover against the crater's steep sides or struggled to climb out. Union generals finally managed a strong attack around the Crater's edge, but the Confederates soon drove them back to their original lines. The breakthrough opportunity of the crater was wasted, and the Siege of Petersburg went on as before.

1864, September 2: General Sherman captures Atlanta, Georgia.

AMAZING AMERICANS: William Tecumseh Sherman (1820 – 1891)

William Tecumseh Sherman was an Ohio native who graduated from West Point in 1840. As the Union general who destroyed Atlanta, Georgia and led the highly destructive "March to the Sea," Sherman became a war hero to the North and a hated villain to the South.

Early in the war, President Lincoln promoted Sherman for his good performance in the Union loss at the First Battle of Bull Run. From the beginning, Sherman doubted that anyone in the North was taking the war seriously, and the Union's failure at Bull Run proved it to him. The pressures of serving in such an environment led to a nervous breakdown of sorts, and he was temporarily relieved of his duties.

Sherman later returned to service under General Grant in the war's western theater, where he fought at Shiloh, Corinth and Vicksburg. When Grant promoted Sherman as his second in command, some complained that the Union's western armies were being led by a "drunk" (Grant, because of his rumored drinking problem) and a "lunatic" (Sherman, because of his nervous breakdown).

Soon enough, however, military success justified both Sherman and Grant. When Grant returned east, promoted by President Lincoln as commander of all Union forces, Sherman took his place as commander in the west. After the pivotal, back-to-back Union victories at Gettysburg and Vicksburg in July 1863, Grant and

Sherman were ready to begin a two-pronged assault on the Confederacy that would both defeat its armies and demoralize its citizens.

Sherman is best remembered for the two things that came next: his capture of Atlanta, Georgia and the "March to the Sea" that followed. Atlanta was an important Southern capital, a crucial railroad junction and the home of much of the South's limited manufacturing capability. On September 2, 1864, Sherman and his army burned much of Atlanta to the ground, destroying its ability to contribute to the Confederate war effort (picture shows Sherman and his staff outside Atlanta).

The burning of Atlanta was an early example of Sherman's doctrine of "hard war" or "total war": he believed that in order to win decisively, the Union must punish not only the Confederate soldiers who took up arms against the Union, but also the Confederate civilians whose production of food and weapons made their soldiers' rebellion possible.

Sherman followed this "hard war" doctrine on his 285-mile "March to the Sea" from Atlanta to Savannah, Georgia. Leaving behind a large force to deal with the remaining Confederate army in the area, Sherman marched southeast with a smaller army of 60,000 men. Sherman's army confiscated every scrap of food and supplies that it could carry along the way, and it burned everything that it could not. Georgia lay devastated after the March to the Sea, and the South would never forgive Sherman for this devastation.

After he reached the port of Savannah, Sherman planned to load his army aboard steam ships and join General Grant against General Lee in the Siege of Petersburg. Instead, Grant ordered Sherman to attack South Carolina, the bold rebel state that had been the first to secede from the Union back in 1860. Sherman punished South Carolina as he had punished Georgia, burning its capital at Columbia on February 17, 1865 (see picture).

Other interesting facts about William Sherman:

- <u>Sherman's Neckties</u>: One of Sherman's objectives was to destroy the South's railroads. If he had only torn up the iron tracks and left them behind, the South could have easily re-laid them. Instead, he ordered his men to heat sections of the iron tracks around twist them around trees so that they would never lie straight again. These sections of bent, useless tracks became known as "Sherman's neckties."
- <u>40 Acres and a Mule</u>: Under the terms of the Emancipation Proclamation, Sherman liberated Southern slaves with every foot of ground he recaptured from the Confederacy. Early in 1865, Sherman issued special orders that granted freed slaves property of their own, carved from sections of land that he had confiscated from Southern landowners in South Carolina and Georgia. Some freed slaves also received an army mule that they could use to plow their 40 acres. During the Reconstruction that followed the Civil War, President Andrew Johnson revoked the grants of "40 Acres and a Mule" that Sherman had made to 40,000 freed slaves.

1864, October 19: Union General Phil Sheridan defeats Confederate General Jubal Early in Virginia's Shenandoah Valley.

1864, November 8: Thanks in part to Northern good feeling after Sherman's victory in Atlanta, Abraham Lincoln wins reelection as President.

1864, November 15: General Sherman begins his "March to the Sea" (see picture).

1864, December 16: Confederate General John Bell Hood's Army of Tennessee is eliminated at the Battle of Nashville. <u>The western theater of the war will see no more major battles.</u>

1865, March 4: President Lincoln delivers another notable speech at his second inauguration, concluding: "With malice toward none, with charity for all, with firmness in the right as God gives us to see the right, let us strive on to finish the work we are in, to bind up the nation's wounds, to care for him who shall have borne the battle and for his widow and his orphan, to do all which may achieve and cherish a just and lasting peace among ourselves and with all nations."

1865, April 2: Confederate defenses around Petersburg and Richmond collapse in the Third Battle of Petersburg. Confederate President Davis evacuates and moves his capital to Danville, Virginia. With his army starving around him, General Lee begins to retreat westward, hoping to find supplies and then escape by railroad.

1865, April 3: Union troops occupy Richmond and raise the Union flag over the former Confederate capital (picture shows the Confederate capital). President Lincoln briefly sits at President Davis's former desk.

1865, April 7: As the fast-moving Union cavalry commanded by General Sheridan begins to surround General Lee's slower force, General Grant begins negotiating Lee's surrender in the "Surrender Letters."

1865, April 9: General Robert E. Lee surrenders to General Ulysses S. Grant at Appomattox Courthouse, Virginia.

General Lee's Surrender at Appomattox

As the Siege of Petersburg wound to an end, General Lee and his starving Army of Northern Virginia retreated to the west. Lee's hope was to reach a railroad line that the Union Army hadn't cut yet and load his army aboard for a retreat farther south. As Lee's troops moved through the area around Farmville toward Appomattox Courthouse, Virginia, the fast-moving cavalry of Union General Phil Sheridan galloped around them, cutting off their chances to receive supplies by rail. A much larger force under General Grant remained close behind, and units of Lee's army had to fight to keep the main force safe during the retreat.

On April 7, 1865 Grant sent Lee the first of several "Surrender Letters" proposing that Lee surrender his Army of Northern Virginia. Lee's first response denied that he was beaten; but, as his men were forced to march onward mile after long mile with no hope of food, his situation grew desperate, and he asked for a meeting with Grant. With his army finally surrounded on April 9, General Lee met General Grant at Appomattox Courthouse, Virginia.

Lee waited for Grant in the parlor of a private home, tall, stately and dignified in an immaculate general's uniform. When Grant arrived, his poorer uniform bore the marks of a hard night and day's travel. After a long, courteous conversation between the two men, Lee had to remind Grant why they were there.

Getting down to business, Grant proposed that Lee's troops lay down their arms and return to their homes, promising not to fight again. Because he was dealing with "Unconditional Surrender" Grant, Lee had expected far worse terms of surrender, and was relieved to learn that he and his men would not be tried and hanged for treason. He asked that his men be allowed to keep their horses or mules, and Grant agreed. The surrender of artillery and muskets was finished by April 12, with Joshua Chamberlain presiding (see above).

With Lee's surrender at Appomattox, the Civil War was essentially over. The remaining Confederate armies would all surrender before the end of June. In his final address to his army, Lee instructed his surrendered troops to "Go home now, and if you make as good citizens as you have soldiers, you will do well, and I shall always be proud of you."

General Lee Surrenders to General Grant at Appomattox

FUN FACT about the surrender at Appomattox:
- General Lee's surrender at Appomattox Courthouse, Virginia took place in the parlor of a man named Wilmer McLean. McLean's former home in Manassas, Virginia was damaged at the First Battle of Bull Run, so McLean moved to Appomattox to get away from the battleground area around Washington DC. Ironically, the war followed McLean to his new home in Appomattox and ended in his very parlor.

PERFIDIOUS PRISONS: The Confederate Prisoner of War Camp at Andersonville

Andersonville, Georgia was the site of a terrible prison camp that the Confederacy built in 1864 to confine its Union army prisoners of war. Andersonville Prison began as no more than a 16.5-acre, heavy-walled stockade, a walled yard with no buildings inside. If its prisoners desired shelter from the rain, they had to build it themselves (some had tents). A creek that ran through the stockade served as its drinking fountain, washroom and toilet. The Confederates originally designed Andersonville to hold 10,000 prisoners, but the prison's swelling population soon forced them to expand the stockade by another 10 acres. The expanded stockade's population reached about 33,000 at its peak.

33,000 people require a great deal of food every day. Unfortunately for the prisoners at Andersonville, by 1864, the Confederacy was having trouble enough feeding its army, let alone its prisoners. For food, the prisoners at Andersonville always received the least and the worst. Of the roughly 45,000 prisoners that passed through Andersonville in 1864 - 1865, nearly 13,000 died of starvation and disease.

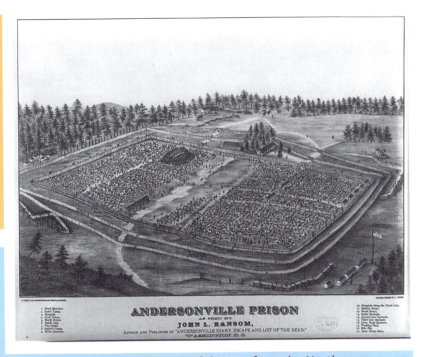

A FINAL NOTE: Sherman's Prediction about the Civil War

Before the Civil War even began, William T. Sherman wrote this prediction to a secessionist friend in the South. We end our study of the U.S. Civil War with this stunningly accurate summary of the war from the Northern perspective, written before either side had fired a single shot:

"You people of the South don't know what you are doing. This country will be drenched in blood, and God only knows how it will end. It is all folly, madness, a crime against civilization! You people speak so lightly of war; you don't know what you're talking about. War is a terrible thing! You mistake, too, the people of the North. They are a peaceable people but an earnest people, and they will fight, too. They are not going to let this country be destroyed without a mighty effort to save it... Besides, where are your men and appliances of war to contend against them? The North can make a steam engine, locomotive, or railway car; hardly a yard of cloth or pair of shoes can you make. You are rushing into war with one of the most powerful, ingeniously mechanical, and determined people on Earth—right at your doors. You are bound to fail. Only in your spirit and determination are you prepared for war. In all else you are totally unprepared, with a bad cause to start with. At first you will make headway, but as your limited resources begin to fail, shut out from the markets of Europe as you will be, your cause will begin to wane. If your people will but stop and think, they must see in the end that you will surely fail."

1865, April 14: John Wilkes Booth assassinates President Lincoln.

INTERESTING INDIVIDUALS: John Wilkes Booth

John Wilkes Booth was a well-known and wealthy actor and Confederate sympathizer before and during the Civil War. Along with several others, Booth plotted to assassinate the top men of the Union government in the days after Lee's surrender at Appomattox.

Booth was born in Maryland, the state that Lincoln essentially forced to remain in the Union at the outset of the Civil War. Booth did not hide the fact that he hated Lincoln as he continued his acting career throughout the Civil War; in fact, he was once arrested for treasonous remarks against the President. He met regularly with Confederate sympathizers in Baltimore, Maryland, and once traveled to Montreal, Canada, where a number of escaped Confederates hid during the war. Through these connections, he made plans during the war to kidnap Lincoln and hold him hostage in exchange for the release of Confederate prisoners; but these plans failed.

Immediately after General Lee's surrender, Booth attended a Lincoln speech in which the President talked about allowing freed slaves to vote. Enraged at this idea, Booth changed his mind about kidnapping Lincoln and decided to assassinate him instead. He also assigned two other men to assassinate Vice President Andrew Johnson and Secretary of State William Seward, hoping to throw the Union into chaos by killing its top three executive officers all at once. Neither of his accomplices succeeded in their attempts; but on April 14, 1865, Booth shot President Lincoln in the back of the head (see picture), then made his broken-legged escape into southern Maryland on horseback.

THE ASSASSINATION OF PRESIDENT LINCOLN.
AT FORD'S THEATRE WASHINGTON D.C. APRIL 14TH 1865.

As a fugitive, Booth read newspaper reports about millions of mourners turning out to see the funeral train that carried the fallen President's remains on a tour of Northern cities. Booth was surprised and disappointed to learn that even in the South, most people did not approve of his act of murder. Feeling sorry for himself, he hid his identity and decided to escape to Mexico, even as the Union announced a large reward for his capture.

U.S. army troops caught up with Booth on April 26, hiding in a barn at the Richard Garrett farm near Bowling Green, Virginia. When he refused to come out, they set fire to the back of the barn; and as Booth waited with a leveled gun for troops to break down the front door, another soldier shot him to death through a gap in the barn's siding. His wound was remarkably similar to the one that had killed President Lincoln.

The Assassination of President Lincoln

As a popular actor of his day, John Wilkes Booth had performed at Ford's Theater in Washington DC many times. President Lincoln himself had seen Booth perform there. Booth's personal friend John Ford owned and operated the theater, and even received mail for him there. When Booth went to Ford's Theater to collect his mail on the Good Friday morning of April 14, 1865, he learned that President Lincoln would be there that evening, and he began to set his assassination plans in motion.

President Lincoln and his wife planned to attend that evening's performance of "Our American Cousin," an 1858 comedy about a coarse American bumpkin who is suddenly introduced to his highly refined British relatives. The Lincolns had invited General Grant and his wife to attend the show as their guests; but the Grants declined, and instead they invited Mrs. Lincoln's younger friend Clara Harris and her fiancé, army Major Henry Rathbone.

Early in the day, Booth had secretly drilled a peephole through the door of the box where he knew the President's party would sit so that he could watch Lincoln during the show. He had also carved a notch in the lockless door so that he could brace it closed from the inside. He planned his attack to take place after a funny line in the play's dialogue, when he hoped that the audience's laughter would conceal the sound of his gunshot. He wanted no one to interfere with his task. Whether by luck or by treachery, Booth gained another advantage: Lincoln's bodyguard was supposed to be watching his box, but instead the bodyguard went to a nearby drinking tavern during the show.

After intermission, as the play progressed and his laugh line approached, Booth waited outside the box with both a pistol and a dagger at the ready. When the laugh line arrived, Booth stepped silently into the box, braced the door closed and shot President Lincoln from behind. Major Rathbone jumped up to grapple with Booth, and Booth slashed Rathbone's arm deeply with the dagger to make him let go. Then he jumped from the box to the stage and shouted "Sic semper tyrannis" ("Thus always to tyrants," Virginia's state motto) in his trademark theatrical style. Many in the audience assumed that this was part of the show, and didn't try to interfere with his escape. He rushed out the backstage door, probably limping on a leg that he broke during his jump, and escaped on his waiting horse.

President Lincoln slumped forward in his seat, unconscious; he never spoke again. An army doctor who rushed to the door of Lincoln's box to help the injured President had to wait for the injured Rathbone to discover Booth's door brace and let him in. Stunned audience members lifted another doctor directly from the stage into the box. The doctors moved Lincoln across the street to a boarding house, where he died the following morning, April 15, 1865.

President Lincoln on His Deathbed

Other interesting facts about Lincoln's assassination:

- Days before the assassination, Lincoln dreamed that he saw his own corpse lying in the White House surrounded by mourners.
- Major Rathbone, the Lincolns' guest at the play, later went insane and murdered his wife Clara.
- After Lincoln died, mourners discovered a $5 Confederate note in his pocket.
- Witnesses disagreed about when Booth broke his leg. Some said that he caught a riding spur on the flag that decorated the railing of the President's box, then landed on the stage badly. He told the doctor who set his leg that his horse had injured it, but he might have lied to the doctor to conceal his identity.

FASCINATING FACTS: The Thirteenth Amendment to the U.S. Constitution

The Union, indignant over Lincoln's murder, acted quickly on one of its dead President's last wishes: the passage of the Thirteenth Amendment to the Constitution, which finally and formally banned slavery everywhere in the United States. Approved by Congress before the President's death, it was quickly ratified by three quarters of the states and adopted in December 1865. The amendment reads:

"Section 1. Neither slavery nor involuntary servitude, except as a punishment for crime whereof the party shall have been duly convicted, shall exist within the United States, or any place subject to their jurisdiction.

Section 2. Congress shall have power to enforce this article by appropriate legislation."

Chapter 6

Reconstruction in the U.S., War in South America

U.S. HISTORY FOCUS

RECONSTRUCTION (1862 – 1877)

Reconstruction under Lincoln

The process of restoring the seceded Southern states to the Union was called "**Reconstruction**." Reconstruction lasted for more than 10 years, beginning during the Civil War and ending with the inauguration of President Rutherford B. Hayes in 1877.

Reconstruction began under President Lincoln, when he established military governments in the territories the Union recaptured from seceded Southern states. Tennessee received its military governor, Andrew Johnson, in March 1862, and other states followed. Early in the war, Lincoln was reluctant to free slaves in these territories for fear of angering neutral border states like Maryland and Kentucky. Lincoln wanted to be as lenient as possible with the seceded states: He planned to allow them to return to the Union as soon as ten percent of their people had sworn loyalty to the Union (the "Ten Percent Plan"). He even planned to allow secessionist leaders to return to government office if they agreed to swear the same oath.

Lincoln also sought a solution for the problem of finding new lives for the United States' 3-4 million freed slaves. For a time, Lincoln proposed to send freed slaves to new colonies of their own in places like Liberia, Africa and Central America; but abolitionists like Frederick Douglass didn't support the idea. The freed slaves wanted to stay in America, the only home most of them had ever known.

The assassination of President Lincoln made the task of reuniting the nation after the war far more difficult. The victorious North was enraged by what it perceived as a cowardly act of vengeance, and was no longer willing to be lenient with the South. President Johnson tried to continue Lincoln's lenient Ten Percent Plan in mid-1865, when Congress was out of session.

Unlike Lincoln, however, President Johnson strongly opposed voting rights for freed slaves. He also revoked the "40 Acres and a Mule" policy, begun under Lincoln and General Sherman, that had granted land confiscated from rebel farmers in South Carolina and Georgia to freed slaves (Picture from the Robert N. Dennis Collection of Stereoscopic Views shows a freed slave with his army mule).

When Congress returned to session in late 1865, it refused to recognize representatives from former slave states. It also wanted to establish voting rights for freed slaves. President Johnson didn't agree with either of these moves; so this was the beginning of a long dispute between Congress and President Johnson that eventually led to his impeachment in early 1868 (see President Andrew Johnson below).

The Radical Republicans

In the election of 1866, a large group of Republicans, members of President Lincoln's former party, won election to Congress. These "**Radical Republicans**" wanted to punish the South-- severely-- for both the Civil War and the assassination of President Lincoln. The Radical Republicans passed a series of laws, including the Fourteenth and Fifteenth Amendments to the U.S. Constitution, that granted voting rights and civil rights to all freed slaves in the South. When President Grant took office in 1869, he supported these laws in order to honor the sacrifices his Union troops had made during the Civil War.

However, the Radical Republicans also had a political reason for passing their voting laws: the Republicans could expect to win very few votes in the South unless the freed slaves had the right to vote for their party, Lincoln's party. Every freed slave in the South would almost certainly vote for the Republicans, and their votes could swing elections. The South was coming back into the Union, and its votes would be extremely important in national elections.

The Ironclad Oath, Scalawags and Carpetbaggers

The Radical Republicans also installed military governments throughout the South. Under these military governments, the forgiveness offered to the South by Presidents Lincoln and Johnson was formally revoked. No Southerner could hold elected office unless he agreed to swear the "**Ironclad Oath**" guaranteeing that he never had and never would take up arms against the U.S. government. Most native Southerners either (1) could not swear the Ironclad Oath with any honesty, or (2) disagreed with the oath and refused to swear it. With so many candidates disqualified from office by the Ironclad Oath, the military governments of the South were usually controlled by two classes of people:

1. **Scalawags**, Southern whites who supported the Radical Republicans, often for selfish reasons; and
2. **Carpetbaggers**, greedy opportunists from the North who moved South to win political office. The carpetbaggers were known by their cheap luggage made from pieces of old rugs. Southerners resented them as enemy occupiers.

The End of Reconstruction

The South continued to struggle under military rule for over ten years, until at last a political opportunity arose. The Presidential election of 1876 was extremely close: Republican Rutherford B. Hayes received a minority of popular (individual) votes, but a tiny majority of electoral (statewide) votes. In order to gain more support and ensure his election, Hayes agreed to remove the last military governors from the South if the South would agree to support him and throw the uncertain election results in his favor. Hayes' angry opponents accused him of fraud for making this shady backroom deal with the South, nicknaming him "Rutherfraud" Hayes. Nevertheless, the arrangement did have the benefit of ending the bitter era of Reconstruction.

After Reconstruction, when the Southern states were finally free to write their own laws as they chose, they established Jim Crow laws that took away the rights of freed slaves. The Jim Crow Laws established "segregation," rules that demanded separation between blacks and whites living in the same community (see Chapter 11). Many Jim Crow laws remained in effect in the South until the passage of the Civil Rights Act of 1964 (see Chapter 32).

FASCINATING FACTS: The Freedmen's Bureau

The Freedmen's Bureau was a government agency created in 1865 to provide for the needs of freed slaves.

After the Civil War, about 4 million former

Southern slaves were suddenly free. Freedom is a wonderful thing, but it is of little use to someone who has no way to feed himself. Most former slaves owned little or nothing, and had no wealthy parents or families to give them anything with which to start a new life. Proposals like Sherman's "40 Acres and a Mule" policy, which would have taken land from rebellious Southerners and given it to freed slaves, were revoked in the name of property rights– the Constitution forbade the government to confiscate citizens' property without legal action. With no other options open to them, most freed slaves were forced to go to work for their former masters for low wages. In this way, Southern slavery would essentially continue under a new name.

The Freedmen's Bureau was the U.S. government's answer to this problem. From 1865-1872, the Freedmen's Bureau helped to provide former slaves with medical care, food, housing, jobs and education. It built more than 1,000 schools, provided teacher training and founded several black colleges.

The Freedmen's Bureau did not, however, provide the former slaves with any land or property of their own. Despite the efforts of the Freedmen's Bureau, it was still very difficult for freed slaves with no property to earn enough money to survive and thrive.

FASCINATING FACTS: The Ku Klux Klan

The original Ku Klux Klan was a secret organization of Southerners who resisted the military governments of the Southern states during Reconstruction. "Ku Klux" is an adaptation of the Greek word for "circle," so the name means "circle of brothers." The words "Ku Klux" also have a sound like that of a sliding rifle bolt.

Ku Klux Klansmen were strong opponents of the Radical Republicans, those members of Lincoln's Republican Party who placed harsh restrictions on former Confederates after the Civil War. Most Klansmen were former Confederate soldiers who, even after they lost the Civil War, still felt strongly that the South should be left to govern itself. They resented the Radical Republicans' restrictions on voting for those who couldn't or wouldn't swear the Ironclad Oath of loyalty to the Union.

Most Klansmen were also racists and white supremacists who felt strongly that former slaves shouldn't have the right to vote, especially if they themselves couldn't vote. Klansmen used terrorism to scare blacks away from voting booths, cloaking themselves in white and pretending to be the ghosts of dead Confederate soldiers come to kill blacks who dared to vote. They also resorted to threats, beatings and murders of blacks and of white Republicans. These tactics were quite effective, and the Radical Republicans lost votes in the South because blacks stayed away from the polls.

By 1870, the Ku Klux Klan was in decline. Some Klansmen grew dismayed by the Klan's reputation for lawlessness, and feared that its tactics would lead to even more harsh laws from the Radical Republicans. By the time Congress authorized military action against the Klan in 1871, the organization was beginning to disappear. Later groups that called themselves "Ku Klux Klan" were only imitators of this original group.

WORLD HISTORY FOCUS

SOUTH AMERICA

PARAGUAY

A Utopia Lost

Paraguay is a landlocked nation in South America bordered by Bolivia (also landlocked), Argentina and Brazil. Its capital, Asuncion, was settled by Spanish explorers around 1537, and Paraguay became a Spanish colony. Jesuit (strict Roman Catholic) priests controlled Paraguay's native *Guarani* tribe through most of its years as a Spanish colony. Paraguay overthrew Spanish rule and gained its independence in May 1811; but the newly independent Paraguay almost immediately fell under a series of dictators.

Paraguay's first dictator was Dr. Jose Gaspar Rodriguez de Francia.

> **INTERESTING INDIVIDUALS: Dr. Jose Gaspar Rodriguez de Francia (1766 – 1840)**
>
> Dr. Jose Gaspar Rodriguez de Francia was the first dictator of independent Paraguay. De Francia was a highly educated philosopher who sought to create a "utopia," or ideal society, in Paraguay. He is remembered in Paraguay as *El Supremo* Francia, the father of his country.
>
> De Francia was born in Paraguay, but educated in nearby Argentina because backward Paraguay had virtually no schools. As a student of philosophy, De Francia grew deeply impressed with French philosophers like Voltaire and Rousseau, whose ideas about the ideal human society also influenced the founding fathers of the United States. However, as dictator of Paraguay, Francia would take those ideas in a very different direction. A bright and highly successful student of

theology and philosophy, Francia became one of Paraguay's only educated citizens. Among the mostly illiterate citizens of Paraguay, he gained a reputation for an almost mystical wisdom.

For this reason, De Francia was the natural choice as Paraguay's leader after it gained its independence from Spain in 1811. Almost no other Paraguayan had any idea how to manage the newly independent nation, which was in real danger of being absorbed by Argentina. De Francia joined the government to aid in negotiations with Argentina because no one else could do it. Over the next three years, he gradually assumed more authority, until he became Paraguay's sole, undisputed *El Supremo Dictador* in 1814. He would retain that role until his death 26 years later in 1840.

De Francia's understanding of philosophy made him a unique sort of dictator. He sought no riches for himself, and usually returned his salary to the public treasury. He cared about the native Paraguayan people and wanted them to thrive. In order to eliminate class differences in Paraguay, he insisted that citizens born in Spain must marry native-born citizens. Under this policy, the elite Spanish-born class of Paraguayans would disappear within a single generation. He sought to elevate the poor and to place every citizen on an equal footing by eliminating private property. De Francia was building an early communist-style utopia in Paraguay.

In order to accomplish all of this, however, De Francia had to insist on absolute power for himself. He involved himself in nearly every decision that was made in Paraguay-- he even approved his citizens' individual marriages. He confiscated private property for the state, whether its owners liked it or not. And he mercilessly imprisoned, tortured or eliminated any citizen who publicly disagreed with him. He closed off Paraguay to outside influences and made it independent and prosperous by the force of his intelligence and will.

Paraguay succeeded under De Francia for two reasons:

1. Because he was a skilled and crafty administrator, capable of single-handedly managing all of his nation's affairs; and
2. Because the surrounding great nations of the day (Argentina and Brazil) were too involved with their own difficulties to interfere in unimportant, backward Paraguay.

After De Francia's death, the situation around Paraguay began to change, and there was no one with Francia's skills to take his place.

De Francia's successor was another well-educated dictator named Carlos Antonia Lopez, who reigned from 1840-1862. Carlos appointed his son, Francisco Solano Lopez, as commander-in-chief of the army; and when Carlos died in 1862, Francisco took his place as dictator.

Neither Carlos nor Francisco had De Francia's talent for administration. It was Francisco who collapsed Paraguay's utopian house of cards by entering the War of the Triple Alliance.

The War of the Triple Alliance (1865 – 1870)

Francisco Solano Lopez grew alarmed for Paraguay's survival when neighboring Brazil, South America's giant, threatened to take over its smaller neighbor Uruguay. Afraid that Paraguay would be next, Francisco sought an alliance with Argentina against Brazil. When Argentina refused, Francisco crossed Argentina on his way to drive Brazil out of Uruguay—drawing Argentina into the war as well. Francisco's opponents thus formed a Triple Alliance against him: Argentina, Brazil and Brazil's puppet Uruguay.

On paper, Paraguay had South America's largest army; but in fact, Paraguay was entirely unprepared for a war against far larger and more modern opponents. The War of the Triple

Brazilian Soldiers in Paraguay

Alliance dragged on from 1865-1870, five of the bloodiest years in South American history.

Late in the war, when Paraguay was overwhelmed and obviously defeated, Francisco refused to surrender and negotiate for peace. With most of his regular army dead or wounded, he forced every Paraguayan male over the age of twelve into military service. Whole divisions of young boys marched into battle and died for Francisco. When Francisco's military leaders and even his own brothers tried to reason with him, begging him to surrender, he order them executed. The War of the Triple Alliance went on until the half-mad Francisco Solano Lopez finally, fortunately died in battle on March 1, 1870.

> The disastrous War of the Triple Alliance tore down everything that *El Supremo* De Francia had built. Paraguay's population went from 525,000 before the war to 221,000 after the war. Astonishingly, only about 28,000 of these-- about 12 percent-- were men. More than 300,000 Paraguayans had died, and only about one Paraguayan man survived for every eight Paraguayan women. After the War of the Triple Alliance, Paraguay surrendered territory to both Argentina and Brazil, and remained occupied by Brazil until 1876.

BRAZIL

From Portuguese Colony to Independent Republic

Brazil was a colony of Portugal, not of Spain. Unlike most other South Americans, modern Brazilians still speak Portuguese instead of Spanish.

Explorers from Portugal began to colonize Brazil around 1500. At first, the only item of value they could discover there was the Brazilwood tree, from which they made a red dye. Later, the Brazilian Gold Rush of the 1690s brought more Portuguese settlers and African slaves to Brazil.

Back in Europe, Portugal suffered a crisis in 1807 when French Emperor Napoleon Bonaparte captured its capital, Lisbon. Prince Regent John VI was forced to flee Portugal and travel to Brazil, where he established the new capital of the Portuguese Empire at Rio de Janiero in 1808. By 1821, with the threat of Napoleon removed, John VI was able to return to Portugal, leaving his son Pedro behind. A year later, with his father's permission, Pedro declared Brazil's independence from Portugal and named himself Emperor Pedro I of Brazil.

Brazil was notoriously difficult to govern. Its citizens were a complex mixture of roughly five different people groups:

1. native Brazilians;
2. African slaves;
3. Portuguese settlers and their descendants;
4. other European immigrants; and
5. Refugees from all over the world.

As a vast and largely unsettled part of the world, Brazil became home to thousands of refugees seeking a new start there. This difficult mixture of people led to frequent political problems and crises.

After one such crisis in 1831, Emperor Pedro I suddenly abdicated his throne in Brazil and returned to Portugal. His five-year-old son, Pedro II, took his place as Emperor of Brazil.

> INTERESTING INDIVIDUALS: Emperor Pedro II of Brazil (1825 – 1891, reigned 1831 – 1889)
>
> Pedro II was the second and last Emperor of Brazil. Pedro helped set Brazil on its feet as a constitutional monarchy and a modern world power during the late 1800s, only to see his government torn down near the end of his life.

Pedro's father, Emperor Pedro I, abdicated his throne and left Brazil in 1831 because of trouble in both Brazil and Portugal. He left his five-year-old son Pedro II behind to serve as Brazil's emperor in his place. A series of regents struggled to manage the chaos in the Brazilian government while Brazil waited for its young emperor to grow up. Pedro II suffered through a lonely childhood spent following the strict education guidelines set by his absent father Pedro I, who died of tuberculosis in 1835.

Because the regency period was so difficult, Brazil decided to place Pedro II in charge of its government early, when he was still only 14. The government hoped that Pedro's royal blood would make him more respected than his ineffectual regents were.

After a rough start, Pedro II proved to be a wise and effective leader for Brazil. When Paraguay threatened Brazil in the War of the Triple Alliance, Pedro demonstrated his bravery by going to the battlefront personally and risking his life. He became Brazil's beloved hero, and his nation prospered through most of his 58-year reign as it filled itself with schools, railroads and growing businesses.

Pedro also took a stand against slavery, which he believed shamed his nation. By law, Pedro could not ban slavery on his own authority, and knew that he would get a violent reaction from slave owners if he tried. Instead, he took a more gradual approach:

- In 1850, Brazil banned the importation of new slaves.
- In 1871, Brazil declared that children born to slave women were free at birth.

By eliminating the sources of new slaves, Pedro managed to reduce the number of slaves in Brazil, so that Brazilians relied on slave labor less and less as time went on.

Pedro II's stand against slavery would contribute to his undoing. Brazil finally banned slavery in 1888, while Pedro was in Europe recovering from an illness. In response, a group of dissatisfied revolutionaries deposed the absent Pedro and installed a new form of government, a republic governed by a strong dictator. Pedro was old, ill and tired of his long life of heavy responsibility; and he had no male heirs to replace him. He gave up his throne willingly, and died two years later in France. Brazil would decline in the years to come under leadership less wise than that of Pedro II.

THE WAR OF THE PACIFIC (1879 – 1884)

The War of the Pacific started over a boundary dispute between Bolivia and Chile, two countries on South America's Pacific coast (see map). Both sought possession of the Atacama Desert, an extremely dry and desolate place which was nevertheless rich in minerals. One of the Atacama Desert's abundant minerals was saltpeter, an important component of both fertilizer and gunpowder.

The border between Bolivia and Chile lay somewhere in the Atacama Desert. Before its minerals were discovered, neither nation knew or cared where this wasteland boundary lay. After its minerals were discovered, however, this boundary became important enough to start a war.

High mountains made access to the Atacama Desert more difficult from Bolivia than from Chile, so Bolivia was always at a disadvantage against Chile. Chile was also wealthier than Bolivia; so most of the mining companies and miners in the Atacama Desert were Chilean, even on the Bolivian side of the border.

A Brief Timeline of the Events Leading to the War of the Pacific

1866: The Boundary Treaty of 1866 establishes the 24th parallel south of the equator as the border between Chile and Bolivia. This line splits the Atacama Desert. The two nations also agree to divide evenly the tax money collected from mining companies operating between the 23rd and 25th parallels. Unfortunately, the treaty doesn't specify exactly what qualifies as "mining," and the two nations continue to bicker over the tax money.

1870s: A major economic depression pushes South American governments to search for extra tax money wherever they can find it. Chile and Bolivia both seek more tax money from the mining of saltpeter.

1873: Peru and Bolivia sign a Treaty of Alliance in which each agrees to defend the other against foreign invasion or aggression. They keep their alliance secret from Chile.

1874: Chile and Bolivia sign a new Boundary Treaty. The 24th parallel remains the legal boundary, but Chile allows Bolivia to receive all tax money from the Atacama Desert region if Bolivia promises to leave taxes on Chilean mining companies unchanged for 25 years.

1878: Bolivia tries to raise taxes on a Chilean mining company operating in the Atacama Desert because it claims that the company's contract was never ratified by the Bolivian congress. When the company refuses to pay, Bolivia confiscates the company's property.

1879, February 14: 500 Chilean troops take control of the Bolivian port city of Antofagasta. There is no fighting because, even though the city lies in Bolivia, most of its inhabitants are Chileans involved in saltpeter mining and mining support (Picture shows Battalion No. 3 of the Chilean Army, formed in columns in the *Plaza Colon*, Antofagasta, Bolivia, 1879).

1879, March 1: Bolivia declares war on Chile and calls on its ally Peru to help.

1879, April 5: Chile declares war on Bolivia and Peru.

FASCINATING FACTS: The War of the Pacific (1879 – 1883)

The War of the Pacific was a struggle between Chile and the Alliance of Bolivia and Peru over control of the Atacama Desert region. Bolivia declared war after Chile occupied Bolivia's primary port city, Antofagasta; and Peru joined the war to help defend its ally, Bolivia.

Early in the war, the primary battlefield was the Pacific Ocean. Since Bolivia had no navy and no seaport after Chile captured Antofagasta, most of the war's sea battles were between Chile and Peru.

Soon after the war began, Chile blockaded the Peruvian port of Iquique with two of its oldest wooden ships, then sent its more modern navy farther north to find and destroy Peru's navy. Unknown to the Chileans, Peru had already sent its two best armored warships south to raise the blockade at Iquique. The two enemy fleets bypassed one another, undetected. When the Peruvians reached Iquique, they were able to pit their two heaviest armored warships against Chile's two aged wooden warships.

However, the battle is not always to the strong: in the Battle of Iquique, Peru's largest and finest warship, the Independencia, ran aground and sank while it was trying to chase down Chile's *Covadonga*. Peru's other warship, the *Huascar*, managed to raise the thin Chilean blockade; but the loss of the powerful *Independencia* rendered the Peruvian navy's defeat inevitable. By the end of 1879, Chile had defeated the Peruvian navy and controlled the sea along the entire Pacific coast of South America.

Chile used its control of the sea to move troops and supplies for its land campaign. In that land campaign, Peru and Bolivia suffered defeat after humiliating defeat. Chile captured and controlled the entire Atacama Desert, then pursued a peace treaty. When Peru and Bolivia would not accept its terms of peace, Chile captured the Peruvian capital of Lima.

With its capture of Lima, Chile won the power to dictate the terms of surrender. Peru lost part of its southern coastline to Chile. Bolivia lost the disputed Atacama Desert, with all of its wealth. More importantly, Bolivia lost its entire Pacific coastline and became a landlocked nation. Bolivia never regained its coastline. Modern Bolivians still bemoan the loss of their only seaports, and still regularly ask Chile to give them back.

FASCINATING FACTS: Rainsticks

A rainstick is a South American noisemaker believed to have the power to call down rainstorms. Rainsticks were invented in either Chile or Peru.

Native South Americans made rainsticks from cactus plants that they hollowed, then dried in the sun. They removed the cactus spines, then drove them through the hollowed-out cactus shells like nails. For noisemakers, they placed small objects like pebbles or dried beans inside their cactus shells and sealed them off. When they turned their finished rainsticks over, the pebbles would fall through them, hitting the spines to mimic the sound of falling rain. The hollow cactus shells amplified the sound. Rainsticks were often decorated with weather symbols.

CANADA

A Brief Timeline of Canadian History

1000 AD: Vikings explore the areas of North America that will become Nova Scotia, Newfoundland and New Brunswick, Canada.

1497: John Cabot, an Italian explorer hired by the English, arrives on Canada's east coast and claims the territory for England.

1534: French explorer Jacques Cartier claims the territory that will become Quebec for France.

1608: Samuel de Champlain founds France's first permanent Canadian colony at Quebec. The French know Canada as "New France." New York's Lake Champlain will be named for Samuel de Champlain.

1763: The Treaty of Paris ends the French and Indian War, seven long years of fighting between France and England in both the New World and Europe. Under terms of the Treaty of Paris, France surrenders its Canadian colonies to Britain. Britain renames New France "The Province of Quebec" in the Royal Proclamation of 1763.

1774: The Quebec Act, an act of the British Parliament, guarantees the Quebec province's Frenchmen the right to retain their French language, culture and laws. The Quebec Act's main purpose is to keep Quebec's people happy so that they won't join the American Revolution. In the Thirteen Colonies, the Quebec Act is viewed as one of the "Intolerable Acts" driving the colonies toward revolution.

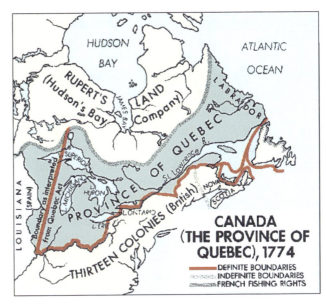

1776: The U.S. invades Canada, trying to drive the British out. With Montreal occupied by U.S. Revolutionary War troops, U.S. ambassadors in Montreal try and fail to convince Canada to join the American Revolution. The arrival of the British navy in the St. Lawrence River forces U.S. troops to withdraw from Montreal. Canada remains under British control and never joins the American Revolution.

1791: England divides the Quebec Province into French-speaking Lower Canada (down the St. Lawrence River, near Quebec) and English-speaking Upper Canada (up the St. Lawrence River, near the Great Lakes and Ontario). Many Upper Canadians are British loyalists ("Tories") who moved to Canada after the American Revolution.

Rebellion against British Rule Begins

Like the Thirteen Colonies before them, both Upper Canada and Lower Canada rebelled against British rule. Upper Canada rebelled in 1837 under the leadership of William Lyon Mackenzie. Lower Canada rebelled in that same year, inspired by Louis Joseph Papineau. The British overcame both rebellions, and both rebel leaders fled to the United States.

Although they both failed, these two rebellions forced the British to consider the possibility of another major North American revolution, this time in Canada. Hoping to avoid this, they dispatched an official named John George Lambton to study the situation in Canada and make recommendations.

FASCINATING FACTS: John George Lambton's *Report on the Affairs of British North America*

John George Lambton, Earl of Durham was a wealthy British official and the son-in-law of a British prime minister. After the 1837 - 1838 rebellions in Upper and Lower Canada, Britain appointed Lambton as the new Governor General of Canada and sent him to Canada with two missions: (1) to investigate the situation in Canada, and (2) to recommend steps Britain might take to prevent any future rebellions.

Lambton summarized his recommendations for Canada in his

1839 *Report on the Affairs of British North America.* In this report, Lambton observed that Canada's problems were largely the result of conflicts between its French Canadian half and its English half. Lambton proposed that the best way to reconcile these conflicts was to gradually replace the French Canadians with good Englishmen. Over time, he wanted to eliminate the laws that allowed French Canada to remain more French than English. Lambton wanted to teach the French Canadians the English language and make them follow English law rather than French law.

As the report went on, Lambton calmly considered different schemes the British might use in order to eliminate French Canadian representatives from the Canadian parliament: holding sham elections to replace French Canadian representatives with English ones, establishing a British dictatorship over French Canada, and so on. He argued against all such schemes, partly because they might anger the freedom-loving people of the nearby United States. The U.S. would never approve if Britain robbed the French Canadians of fair representation in their own government; and if Britain ever lost its grip on Canada, then the U.S. would be in an excellent position to take over Canada and provide Canadians with the freedoms Britain had denied them.

Rejecting these schemes, Lambton proposed instead to unite Upper Canada and Lower Canada and allow them to form a united, representative government. He believed that this government should truly represent the will of its citizens, not that of the British Parliament. Because a majority of the united provinces' population would be English, he said, far more representatives would be English than French Canadian. Lambton firmly believed that the superior English race would eventually replace the less industrious French Canadian race. When that happened, Lambton was sure, a unified Canada would end up with a thoroughly English government and culture. He was also convinced that this unified Canada would remain loyal to Britain, because Britain's gift of self-government would inspire gratitude and loyalty to Britain.

Apparently, Britain's attitude toward its colonies had changed quite a bit. In the 1770s, Britain had refused to grant the Thirteen Colonies representation in the British Parliament. In 1840, however, in order to avoid a second North American revolution, Britain made the surprising decision to adopt Lambton's idea for a nearly independent, representative government in Canada without a fight.

The United Province of Canada

In 1840, the British Parliament adopted Lambton's recommendations and passed the Act of Union, combining Upper Canada and Lower Canada under one government as the United Province of Canada. This government heavily favored Canada's English-speaking half and limited the use of French as an official language. The United Province of Canada was not immediately independent of the British Parliament, but it was headed in that direction.

Responsible Government

In 1848, Britain granted the separate Canadian province of Nova Scotia responsible government status. "Responsible government" meant that Nova Scotia's governor obeyed Nova Scotia's parliament, not Great Britain's. A few months later, Britain also granted the United Province of Canada responsible government status. Although the British crown was still Canada's official head of state, these two provinces of Canada officially became self-governing and independent of the British Empire after 1848. Canada would gradually become more and more independent of Britain in the coming years.

The Dominion of Canada

On July 1, 1867, the provinces of Quebec, Ontario, Nova Scotia and New Brunswick united to form the Dominion of Canada. A "dominion" of the British Empire was a self-governing, independent union of provinces that retained the British crown as its official head of state. Australia, New Zealand South Africa and others would also become dominions of the British Empire. The provinces of Manitoba, British Columbia and Prince Edward Island would soon join the Dominion of Canada.

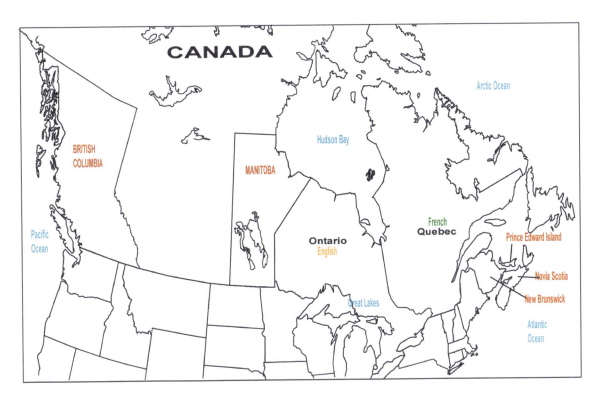

THE TEN PROVINCES OF CANADA

Province	Capital	Joined Canada	Official Languages
Alberta	Edmonton	1905	English
British Columbia	Vancouver	1871	English
Manitoba	Winnipeg	1870	English
New Brunswick	Fredericton	1867	English and French
Newfoundland and Labrador	St. John's	1949	English
Nova Scotia	Halifax	1867	English
Ontario	Toronto	1867	English
Prince Edward Island	Charlottetown	1873	English
Quebec	Quebec City	1867	French
Saskatchewan	Regina	1905	English

FASCINATING FACTS: The Maple Leaf

Maple trees thrive around Quebec, where Canadians have long recognized the maple's strength, beauty and usefulness. The maple leaf and the beaver were both early symbols of Canada. In 1860, the maple leaf became more prominent when Canadian newspapers encouraged the people of Toronto to wear maple leaf emblems for an official visit from Britain's Prince of Wales. The maple leaf appeared on all Canadian coins from 1876-1901. Canada adopted its national flag, with its prominent red maple leaf, in 1965.

MISSIONARY FOCUS

GIANTS OF THE FAITH: Charles Spurgeon (1834 – 1892)

Charles Spurgeon was a British Reformed Baptist preacher during Britain's Victorian era. His God-given talents as a speaker and

writer made him one of the most-published Christian authors of all time.

Through his early teens, Spurgeon went from church to church and listened to sermon after sermon, all without finding the answer to his fundamental question: How could he find forgiveness for his sin? He finally found his answer at a Primitive Methodist church in Essex, England, where the minister exhorted him with the words of Isaiah 45:22: "Turn to me and be saved, all you ends of the earth; for I am God, and there is no other." The answer to his question was to turn himself wholly toward Jesus Christ. When Spurgeon became a preacher himself, he resolved never to preach a message that didn't answer this question for sinners seeking forgiveness.

From his early twenties on, Spurgeon was always in the pulpit. He served as pastor to England's largest Baptist congregation, and was the most popular speaker in England for decades. When his books and printed sermons grew popular as well, Spurgeon hired stenographers to copy down his sermons as he delivered them so that he could edit and publish them almost immediately. He preached more than 3,500 sermons in his lifetime.

Spurgeon was a strong believer in the doctrine of *predestination*, the idea that God chooses the people He will save from damnation without any action whatsoever on their part. To Spurgeon, salvation was all the work of God, and not at all the work of sinful human beings. He loved most of the ideas of Reformed theologian John Calvin, and once traveled to Geneva, Switzerland to preach from the late Calvin's pulpit.

Some interesting quotes from Charles Spurgeon:

- "I believe that nothing happens apart from divine determination and decree. We shall never be able to escape from the doctrine of divine predestination-- the doctrine that God has foreordained certain people unto eternal life.
- "Saving faith is an immediate relation to Christ, accepting, receiving, resting upon Him alone, for justification, sanctification, and eternal life by virtue of God's grace."
- "A Bible that's falling apart usually belongs to someone who isn't."

U.S. GEOGRAPHY FOCUS

FASCINATING FACTS about MAINE:

- Statehood: Maine became the 23rd US state on March 15, 1820
- Bordering states/bodies of water/country: New Hampshire, Canada, the Atlantic Ocean
- State capital: Augusta
- Area: 35,385 sq. mi (Ranks 39th in size)
- Abbreviation: ME
- State nickname: "Pine Tree State"
- State Bird: Chickadee
- State tree: Eastern White Pine
- State flower: Eastern White Pine Cone and Tassel
- State song: *State of Maine Song*
- State Motto: "I Direct"
- Meaning of name: Maine refers to the mainland. It may also refer to the region of Maine, France.

- Historic places to visit in Maine: The White Mountain National Forest, Acadia National Park, The Penobscot Marine Museum, Saint Croix Island, Black Mountain of Maine, Bar Harbor Whale Watch Company
- Resources and Industries: tourism, forestry, shipbuilding, farming (blueberries, potatoes, apples, maple sugar, livestock), fishing (lobster), toothpicks and electronics

Misty Morning, Coast of Maine by Arthur Parton

Flag of Maine

- Maine adopted this flag in 1909.
- The coat of arms lies on a field of blue.
- The North Star at the top of the flag represents Maine's position as the northernmost state (until Alaska joined the union). The motto "I Direct" also refers to the fact that people look to the North Star for direction.
- The two men on the flag represent a farmer and a fisherman.
- The animal in front of the pine tree (the state tree) is a moose (the state animal)

FASCINATING FACTS: Seward's Folly in Alaska

The original check used to pay for Alaska

    In 1867, U.S. Secretary of State William Seward convinced the United States Senate to purchase Alaska's 600,000 square miles of territory from Russia for $7,200,000. This price worked out to about two cents per acre. Many in the U.S. believed that frigid Alaska would offer nothing but fur, and grumbled about "Seward's Folly" in purchasing "Seward's Icebox" of Alaska. Later, when miners discovered gold in Alaska during the 1890s Yukon Gold Rush, Seward's former critics looked back on what they had called Seward's Folly and praised him for his foresight.

    Alaska became a U.S. territory in 1912 and a state in 1959. The many resources discovered there have long since repaid Seward's 7.2 million dollars.

PRESIDENTIAL FOCUS

PRESIDENT #17: Andrew Johnson (1808 – 1875)	
In Office: April 15, 1865 – March 4, 1869	**Political Party:** Democratic
Birthplace: North Carolina	**Nickname:** "Tennessee Tailor"

President Andrew Johnson was a pro-Union man from the Southern state of Tennessee. He served Tennessee as a U.S. representative, as governor, and then as a U.S. senator in the years before the Civil War. Johnson held an unusual mixture of views: He supported slavery, but not the Southern states' right to secede from the Union. Unlike most in the South, he believed in a strong federal government. When Tennessee seceded from the Union against Johnson's will, he became the only U.S. senator from a slave state who didn't choose to resign from the U.S. Senate.

Early in the Civil War, General Grant won several victories in Tennessee and captured its capital at Nashville. From March 1862 on, Union troops occupied much of Tennessee, and President Lincoln appointed Johnson as Tennessee's military governor. Johnson served there through most of the war, until Lincoln needed him for another task.

In early 1864, Lincoln had reason to doubt that he would win re-election in the coming fall. General Grant was racking up terrible casualties in Virginia without achieving any real victories; there was no end to the war in sight, and the North was growing war-weary. Lincoln reasoned that a pro-Union Southerner like Johnson would be the ideal choice as his vice presidential running mate in a nation that he hoped would soon be reunited. After Sherman's victory in Atlanta restored the North's optimism, Lincoln won re-election in a landslide, carrying Johnson along with him as his vice president. Then Lincoln was murdered only about a month after his second inauguration, leaving Johnson to serve most of the second Presidential term that Lincoln had just won.

Most Americans agreed that Lincoln could hardly have made a worse choice than Johnson to replace him. During his first months as President, Johnson cleared the way for the Southern states to return to the Union without allowing freed slaves to vote. This meant a return to power for many of the same people who had supported secession in the first place. After Lincoln's assassination, the Republicans were in no mood to see secessionist Southerners back in their old places in Congress. The Congress objected to Johnson's leniency with the South, and a war began between Congress and President Johnson that would last throughout his Presidency.

Members of Lincoln's party, the Republicans, needed freed slaves to vote if they were to win any elections in the South; so they passed several laws to grant freed slaves voting rights. President Johnson vetoed those laws, but the Republican had enough votes in Congress to override Johnson's vetoes.

Congress added to these insulting veto overrides by passing a law that restricted Johnson's power to fire officials of the federal government without its consent. Johnson resented this, because federal officials worked for the executive branch, and were technically his employees, not Congress's. When Johnson fired Lincoln's Secretary of War Edwin Stanton without Congress's permission, Congress decided to impeach him for violating its new law. In the United States' first-ever Presidential impeachment trial, held in early 1868, Johnson escaped conviction by only one vote. Neither party nominated him for the Presidency in the election of 1868.

Other interesting facts about Andrew Johnson:
- Johnson was apprenticed to a tailor as a boy, and was the only President who made his own clothes.
- Johnson's family was so poor that he received no education as a boy, and only learned to read and figure from his clever wife, Eliza McCardle. His wife also helped him to find money-making investments that enabled him to grow wealthy enough to run for political office in Tennessee.

Chapter 7

France, Germany, Lady Liberty

WORLD HISTORY FOCUS

FRANCE

Chaos in France

Throughout the Medieval era, France was ruled by a hereditary monarchy. Its kings ruled by a Divine Right that the French believed had been granted by God Himself. When French kings died, they passed their thrones on to their heirs according to French Salic Law, which give strong preference to males. This government was known in France as the Ancient Regime.

During the Renaissance and the Enlightenment, French philosophers like Voltaire and Rousseau led the French toward a new understanding of the ideal society and government. Changing religious attitudes made the French doubt their kings' "divine right" to rule, especially when French kings and nobles began to live more and more extravagant lifestyles at the expense of French commoners. The French nobility's disdain for the lives and fortunes of commoners led to the chaotic and highly violent French Revolution of 1789-1799.

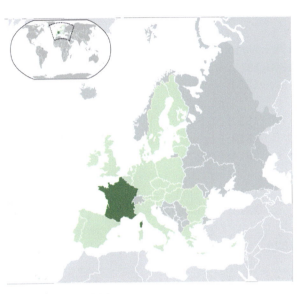

Beginning with the French Revolution, France entered a period of chaos during which governments and constitutions came and went rapidly. The government of France was:

1. A <u>Hereditary Monarchy</u> (king reigns) before the French Revolution (Ancient Regime);
2. A <u>Republic</u> (representative government) during the French Revolution (First French Republic, 1789-1804)
3. An <u>Empire</u> (emperor reigns) under Emperor Napoleon I (First French Empire, 1804-1815)
4. A <u>Hereditary Monarchy</u> again under Louis XVIII and Charles X (restored Ancient Regime, 1815-1830)
5. A <u>Constitutional Monarchy</u> under King Louis-Philippe (July Monarchy, 1830-1848)
6. A <u>Republic</u> again under Louis-Napoleon (Second French Republic, 1848-1852)
7. An <u>Empire</u> again under Emperor Napoleon III (Second French Empire, 1852-1870)
8. A <u>Republic</u> yet again (Third French Republic)

In about 80 years, France underwent seven major changes in government. The Third French Republic would prove to be more stable, and would last until Germany conquered and occupied France near the beginning of World War II in 1940. As of 2010, France is governed by its Fifth French Republic.

A Brief Timeline Review of French History:

1643-1715: Louis XIV, the "Sun King," reigns as King of France.
    1682: The Sun King moves the royal court to his extravagant new Palace of Versailles, 12 miles southwest of Paris.
1715-1774: Louis XV reigns as King of France.

- **1762:** Jean-Jacque Rousseau's *Social Contract* and other works of French philosophy appear, causing the French to question the Ancient Regime and the Divine Right of Kings.
- **1774:** Louis XVI begins his extravagant, decadent reign as King of France.
- **1778-1783:** France supports the cause of liberty in the American Revolution, and French commoners are inspired to desire more liberty for themselves.
- **1789, July 14:** The French Revolution begins with the Storming of the Bastille prison. The Ancient Regime ends, and the First French Republic begins.
- **1793-1794:** Robespierre leads the *Reign of Terror*, in which numerous French nobles and others lose their heads at the guillotine.
  - **1793:** During the Reign of Terror, both King Louis XVI and Queen Marie Antoinette are guillotined for treason. Their young son Louis XVII will die in prison in 1795.
- **1799:** Napoleon Bonaparte becomes First Consul of France, ending the French Revolution.
- **1803-1815:** France fights the *Napoleonic Wars* and expands throughout much of Europe.
  - **1804:** Napoleon I becomes Emperor of France. The First French Republic ends, and the First French Empire begins.
  - **1812:** Napoleon's invasion of Russia fails disastrously, and his empire begins to decline.
  - **1814:** Napoleon is deposed as emperor and goes into exile on the Island of Elba.
  - **1814:** Louis XVIII becomes King of France. The First French Empire ends, and the Ancient Regime is temporarily restored.
  - **1815:** The First French Republic is briefly restored as Napoleon returns for his "Hundred Days" reign.
  - **1815:** Britain's Duke of Wellington defeats Napoleon at the Battle of Waterloo. Napoleon goes into exile on the Island of St. Helena, where he will die in 1821.
- **1824:** King Charles X succeeds King Louis XVIII. Charles X governs as King Louis XVI did, ignoring commoners' rights.
- **1830, July 27-29:** The French revolt against Charles X for "Three Glorious Days." Louis Philippe becomes King of France. The Ancient Regime ends for the last time and a Constitutional Monarchy, also known as the "Orleans Monarchy" or the "July Monarchy," begins.
- **1848:** Louis-Philippe barely escapes another revolution, fleeing to England. The Constitutional Monarchy ends with the creation of a new Republican constitution. Louis-Napoleon, nephew of Napoleon I, wins election as the first president of the Second French Republic.
- **1852:** Louis Napoleon discards the constitution and proclaims himself Emperor Napoleon III of France. The Second French Republic ends, and the Second French Empire begins.

INTERESTING INDIVIDUALS: Louis-Napoleon Bonaparte (1808-1873)

Louis-Napoleon Bonaparte, the nephew and heir of Emperor Napoleon I, won election as the first president of the Second French Republic in 1848. Four years later, Louis-Napoleon discarded the Republic's constitution and proclaimed himself Napoleon III, Emperor of the Second French Empire. He would be France's last monarch.

Louis-Napoleon was born in Switzerland in 1808, when his Uncle Napoleon I was at the height of his power. He spent most of his life in exile outside of France (along with the rest of the Bonapartes), and even spoke French with a slight German accent. Nevertheless, his family name made him popular in France, and he won election as President of France in 1848 with a large majority.

As president, Louis Napoleon grew highly dissatisfied with the section of the Second French Republic's constitution that forbade its presidents from running for re-election. He asked his National Assembly to change the constitution so that he could stay on as president and continue the work he had begun, but the wary Assembly refused. Louis Napoleon proved that the Assembly's fears were justified when he ignored their constitution and proclaimed himself Emperor Napoleon III in 1852.

Napoleon III's ambition to rule the world was nearly as great as his uncle's. He intervened in foreign affairs as far west as Mexico and as far east as Korea. His biggest success was his alliance with France's traditional enemy Britain, which allowed him to succeed (at least partly) where his uncle had failed by defeating Russia in the Crimean War. His biggest failure was also his last: In the Franco-Prussian War, the Prussian army outmaneuvered and defeated Napoleon III at the 1870 Battle of Sedan, France (see below). Napoleon III was forced to surrender himself and his Army of Chalons in a humiliating defeat that cost him his empire. The new Third French Republic deposed him as emperor, and he spent the rest of his life as he had begun it, in exile.

Another interesting fact about Napoleon III:
- Between the reigns of Napoleon I and the decades-later reign of Napoleon III came the very brief reign of Napoleon II. Napoleon II was Napoleon I's son, who was four years old when Napoleon I was forced to abdicate his throne after the Battle of Waterloo in 1815. Napoleon II was technically France's king for two weeks while France awaited the return of King Louis XVIII from exile, but he was never crowned. He died of tuberculosis in 1832, when he was 21 years old. When Louis-Napoleon took over as Emperor in 1852, he remembered his dead cousin's short reign as Napoleon II and took the name "Napoleon III."

1870: Louis-Napoleon is defeated in the Franco-Prussian war, deposed and exiled. The Second French Empire ends, and the Third French Republic begins.

A Brief Summary of France's Foreign Affairs Under Emperor Napoleon III

During the Napoleonic Wars of 1803 - 1815, the mighty French Empire threatened to conquer all of Europe. After Napoleon I's final defeat at Waterloo, however, France's position as a major world power was greatly diminished. The fondest desire of Emperor Napoleon III's heart was to restore the French Empire to the glory it had known under his uncle.

Here are brief summaries of a few of Napoleon III's efforts to restore France's overseas empire to greatness, from west to east:

Extending the French Empire into Mexico (1862 – 1867)

In 1862 - 1863, while the American Civil War diverted the attention of the United States, Napoleon III invaded Mexico and established the Second Mexican Empire there under Emperor Maximilian I. That empire ended in 1867, when Mexican President Benito Juarez overthrew Maximilian and executed him (see Chapter 17).

Aiding Italian Unity, Hindering Italian Unity (1859 – 1871)

Napoleon III helped to restore Italy's long-lost unity by siding with northern Italy's Kingdom of Sardinia-Piedmont in its battle against Austria. In exchange, France received control of the provinces of Nice and Savoy, which lay between Italy and France (see Chapter 21).

On the other hand, Napoleon III worked against Italian unity by helping the popes retain control of Rome and the Papal States. Italy finally recaptured Rome after Prussia defeated France in the 1870 - 1871 Franco-Prussian War (see below).

Battling Russia (1854 – 1856)

Napoleon III joined with Britain and the Ottoman Empire to defeat Russia in the Crimean War. His goal in the Crimean War was to maintain the balance of power in Europe by preventing Russia from conquering the dying Ottoman Empire (see Chapter 2).

Colonizing Vietnam (1861 – 1863)

Napoleon III captured much of the Indochina Peninsula, including the territories that would become

Vietnam and Cambodia, in 1861 - 1863. France would continue to hold Vietnam until the end of the First Indochina War in 1954 (with one interruption during WW II; see Chapter 32).

Battling China (1856 – 1860)

Napoleon III joined Britain against China in the Second Opium War (1856 - 1860). After that war, he established French control over sections of several treaty ports in China (a "treaty port" was a port city in which treaties forced the formerly closed China to allow foreigners to live and trade). France also established a legation (embassy) in China's formerly closed capital city of Peking (Beijing). Every foreign legation in Peking would come under attack during the Boxer Rebellion (1898 - 1901), and would require a dramatic rescue from China's angry Boxers (see Chapter 13).

Battling Korea (1866)

Napoleon attacked Korea to punish the closed, Christian-hating nation for its attacks on French Catholic missionaries who were trying to convert Koreans to Christianity. Korea would remain closed until Japan forced it to open in 1876 (see Chapter 13).

FASCINATING FACTS: The Eiffel Tower

The Eiffel Tower, a.k.a. the "Iron Lady," is an elegant iron tower that stands at one end of a Paris park called the *Champ de Mars*. It was built as a grand entry arch for the 1889 Universal Exposition, a World's Fair timed to celebrate the 100th anniversary of the beginning of the French Revolution. The tower takes its name from its lead engineer, Gustave Eiffel, who also built the frame for the Statue of Liberty (see below).

At first, Eiffel's design was unpopular with Paris's highly refined art community. When Eiffel started building his tower in 1887, three hundred French artists and Parisians signed the following petition:

"We, the writers, painters, sculptors, architects and lovers of the beauty of Paris, do protest with all our vigour and all our indignation, in the name of French taste and endangered French art and history, against the useless and monstrous Eiffel Tower."

Because of such protests, the city granted the tower only a 20-year lease and promised to tear it down when the lease ran out. During those 20 years, however, the Tower became the base for many useful radio antennae, and Parisians began to fall in love with its distinctive beauty. Today it is Paris's best-known symbol and one of the world's most popular tourist attractions.

GERMANY

What Has Gone Before

The history of the part of the world now called Germany is long and complex, filled with migrating tribes and shifting boundaries. Before the Medieval era, a long parade of Germanic Migrations carried Germanic tribes from their homes in central Europe to other parts of Europe: among others, the Allemani and the Franks migrated to France, the Angles and the Saxons migrated to England, the Lombards migrated to northern Italy, and the Visigoths migrated to Spain.

During the Medieval era, much of what is now Germany was part of the Holy Roman Empire. The Holy Roman Empire began when Pope Leo III, the chief bishop of the Roman Catholic Church, crowned the great French King Charlemagne as the first Holy Roman Emperor on Christmas Day, 800 AD.

Charlemagne's dream was to reunite the ancient, vast Roman Empire under a single emperor (himself). Charlemagne achieved part of his dream, and succeeded in building a huge empire that included France and most of central Europe. However, when Charlemagne died, French Salic Laws required his three sons to divide his empire between them. The eastern part of Charlemagne's empire, which included modern-day Germany, would become the Holy Roman Empire under Germanic emperors like Otto the Great (reigned 962-973), Frederick I Barbarossa (reigned 1155-1190) and Charles V (reigned 1516-1556).

Conflicts between Catholics and Protestants tore the Holy Roman Empire apart during the Thirty Years' War of 1618-1648. After the 1648 Peace of Westphalia ended the Thirty Years' War, the Holy Roman Empire was little more than a loose collection of more than 300 Germanic states, each with its own king, duke, prince or bishop. Some of these states were large territories like Bohemia, Saxony, Silesia and Bavaria; and some were no larger than a city or town.

In 1806, France's Emperor Napoleon I issued an ultimatum that forced the Holy Roman Empire to dissolve. Then the large kingdoms of Prussia and Austria began to dominate the former empire, overtaking some of the smaller Germanic states. After Napoleon's final defeat in 1815, about 40 surviving Germanic states united to form the German Confederation.

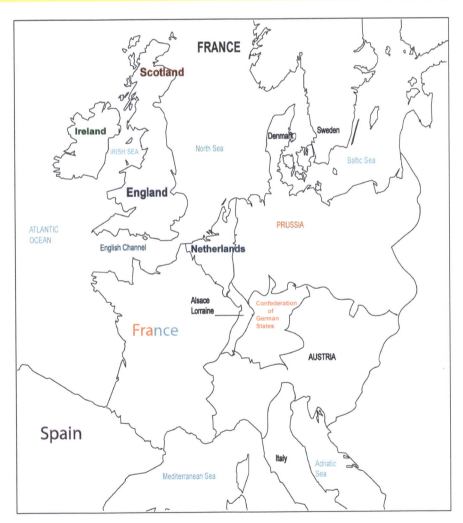

A Brief Timeline of the Progression from Chaos to Unity in Germany:

Before 1806: Central Europe is governed by the Holy Roman Empire, a once-glorious empire that by 1806 is no more than a loose confederation of states.

1806-1815: The Holy Roman Empire dissolves, and larger German-speaking states like Prussia and Austria begin to swallow smaller ones.
1815: About 40 German-speaking states unite to form the German Confederation.
1862: Prussian King Wilhelm I appoints Otto von Bismarck as Prussia's prime minister and foreign minister.
1866: By defeating Austria in the Austro-Prussian War, Prussia takes Austria's place as the most powerful German-speaking nation. The Peace of Prague, the treaty that ends the Austro-Prussian War, dissolves the German Confederation.
1867: The northern German-speaking states, which are dominated by Prussia, unite to form the North German Confederation. Austria is excluded from the North German Confederation, and will later unite with Hungary.
1870: The Franco-Prussian War begins.

CRITICAL CONFLICTS: The Franco-Prussian War (1870 – 1871)

The Balance of Power

From 1815 - 1914, Europe's delicate peace depended upon the balance of power between six major empires:

Britain, France, Russia, Prussia, Austria and Ottoman (see Chapter 2).

When Prussia defeated Austria in the 1866 Austro-Prussian War, it upset that balance of power by demonstrating that Prussia was on the rise, while Austria was on the decline. With the highly ambitious Otto von Bismarck governing Prussia,  and the highly ambitious Napoleon III governing nearby France, war between Prussia and France became nearly inevitable.

The trouble began in 1870, when France's troubled western neighbor Spain considered offering its vacant throne to Prince Leopold of Hohenzollern. Prince Leopold happened to come from the same royal family as King Wilhelm I of Prussia. The French were greatly concerned that if Prince Leopold became the King of Spain, then he might unite Spain with Prussia-- upsetting the balance of power even further, and threatening France from both west and east.

Bad Diplomacy

France decided to take aggressive action. A French ambassador, Count Benedetti, approached Prussia's King Wilhelm I and demanded his guarantee that he would not allow Prince Leopold to become the King of Spain. Benedetti implied that if Wilhelm didn't agree, then France might be forced to go to war with Prussia. Wilhelm disappointed the people of Prussia by agreeing to France's demand. He withdrew Prince Leopold's candidacy for the kingship of Spain, and believed that the matter was closed.

Still unsatisfied, Benedetti approached Wilhelm again and demanded his guarantee that <u>no</u> member of his royal family would <u>ever</u> become the King of Spain. This time, Wilhelm testily replied that he couldn't possibly agree to such vague, hypothetical demand.

The newspaper reports of these encounters between King Wilhelm I and the French ambassador angered both the Prussians and the French. The Prussians felt that Benedetti had behaved disrespectfully toward their royal King Wilhelm I; while the French felt that Wilhelm had been short with Benedetti.

<u>The uproar over these news reports finally led France to declare war on Prussia on July 19, 1870</u>.

The Franco-Prussian War Begins

Although France declared war first, Prussia was far better prepared to fight the war. Under Prime Minister Otto von Bismarck, the "Iron Chancellor," Prussia had thought of little else but war. At the time, Prussia was the only nation in the world with compulsory peacetime military service: Every Prussian male was required to serve in the military, so Prussia was able to send an army of more than one million soldiers against France. Prussia also had superior weaponry: the new Krupp 6-pounder cannon (see below) fired faster, fired farther, and caused far more damage than the older cannon the French were using. In a series of battles from July - September, 1870, Prussian armies defeated French armies time and again.

The Battle of Sedan

Prussia's most decisive victory came at the Battle of Sedan, a town in the Ardennes region near the French-German border. Before the Battle of Sedan, Emperor Napoleon III was personally leading his newly-created Army of Chalons to the rescue of 180,000 French soldiers who had just surrendered to the Prussians at Metz.

Instead of waiting for Napoleon to arrive at Metz, the Prussians counterattacked and drove Napoleon back to Sedan. On September 1, 1870, the Prussians surrounded the Army of Chalons at Sedan and defeated it. On the next day, September 2, Emperor Napoleon III and more than 100,000 of his troops surrendered to Prussia. Prussia had captured not only most of France's armies, but also its haughty and ambitious Emperor Napoleon III (painting shows Napoleon III seated with Otto von Bismarck after the Battle of Sedan).

The Siege of Paris Begins

After the Battle of Sedan, so many French troops had surrendered that the Prussians could find no more French armies to fight. Since most of France's remaining troops had retreated to Paris, Prussia surrounded Paris and began its Siege of Paris on September 19.

Paris was powerless to defend itself from the Prussian onslaught. No French armies remained outside Paris to raise the siege, and no foreign allies sent armies to rescue the city. Inside the city, food and supplies quickly began to run low. Cut off from their regular sources of food during the siege, formerly fine French restaurants were forced to serve dishes made from the meat of horses, dogs, cats and even rats.

The German Empire and the Palace of Versailles

Prussia's great victories in France finished the work of uniting Prussia with its smaller allies. The German allies' common anger with the French had united them, and they were ready to join Prussia in a newly united German Empire.

To honor the foundation of their new empire, the Germans chose a historic and highly symbolic site: the Palace of Versailles, the seat of government for every French king from Louis XIV on. On January 18, 1871, the new German Empire crowned its new emperor, the former King Wilhelm I of Prussia, inside the opulent Hall of Mirrors at the Palace of Versailles. King Wilhelm I of Prussia became Emperor Wilhelm I of Germany. In this way, Germany declared both its unity and its supremacy over the formerly proud, now deeply shamed France.

The Siege of Paris ended when France finally surrendered to Prussia on January 28, 1871.

1870, September 2: Prussia defeats France at the Battle of Sedan, capturing Emperor Napoleon III in the process.
1870, September 4: France establishes a new government, the Third French Republic, and deposes the defeated Emperor Napoleon III. Even though France no longer has any large armies available, the Franco-Prussian War goes on.
1870, September 19: Prussian armies surround France's capital city, Paris, and begin the Siege of Paris.
1871, January 18: The German-speaking states unite to form the German Empire, which will be led by Prussia's "Kaiser" ("Caesar" or Emperor). The German Empire embarrasses its enemy, France, by crowning its first emperor at a highly symbolic site: inside the Hall of Mirrors at the Palace of Versailles, the extravagant palace near Paris built by King Louis XIV.
1871, January 28: Paris falls, and France surrenders to the German Empire.
1871, February: Germany withdraws from Paris, but continues to occupy northeastern France until France pays the war reparations demanded in the treaty that ends the war. Germany also insists on retaining the mineral-rich Alsace-Lorraine, two provinces of France that lie along the French/German border.

INTERESTING INDIVIDUALS: Otto von Bismarck (1815 – 1898)

Otto von Bismarck was the prime minister of the highly militant Kingdom of Prussia from 1862-1890. An extremely capable politician, Bismarck used both warfare and diplomacy to bind together a powerful, unified German Empire dominated by Prussia.

Bismarck began his political career in 1848 as a representative in the Landtag, the Prussian parliament. He was a conservative politician who believed in three things:

1. The Divine Right of Kings to rule,
2. The natural superiority of the German race, and
3. The particular superiority of Prussia.

King Friedrich Wilhelm IV of Prussia chose Bismarck as Prussia's ambassador to the Diet of the German Confederation, an assembly of ambassadors from all German states, in 1851. Bismarck later served as Prussia's ambassador to Russia, then to France. Bismarck's experience as an ambassador made him Prussia's leading expert on foreign affairs.

King Friedrich Wilhelm IV died in 1861. His successor, King Wilhelm I, appointed Bismarck as both prime minister and foreign minister of Prussia in 1862. Wilhelm was content to allow his extremely capable prime minister to manage most of Prussia's affairs, and Bismarck led Prussia to victory after important victory:

1. In the 1864 Second War of Schleswig, Prussia allied with Austria to drive Denmark out of the important German-speaking province of Schleswig.
2. In the 1866 Austro-Prussian War, Prussia defeated Austria to win control of the important German-speaking province of Holstein. After the Peace of Prague ended the Austro-Prussian War, Prussia dominated north central Europe, while Austria's importance in south central Europe faded; Austria would never win another war. The Austrian-led German Confederation dissolved, and was replaced by the Prussian-led North German Confederation in 1867.
3. In the Franco-Prussian War, Prussia defeated Napoleon III and occupied Paris itself. The North German Confederation dissolved, and was replaced with a unified German Empire in early 1871. King Wilhelm I of Prussia became the German Empire's new emperor, receiving his crown in the opulent Hall of Mirrors at the Palace of Versailles in Prussian-occupied Paris. Bismarck became chancellor of the new German Empire, which excluded Austria.

In this way, under Bismarck's care, Germany went from a loose confederation of squabbling states to a unified Empire; and Wilhelm I went from King of Prussia to German Emperor, or Kaiser (Caesar).

Kaiser Wilhelm I was succeeded briefly by his son, Kaiser Friedrich III, in 1888. But Friedrich died of cancer after just 99 days as Kaiser, leaving his crown to his own son, Kaiser Wilhelm II.

Where Friedrich had been moderate and cautious, Wilhelm II was proud and erratic. Wilhelm II refused to be dominated by Bismarck as his grandfather Wilhelm I had been, and he fired Bismarck in 1890. Bismarck died in retirement at age 73.

Other interesting facts about Otto von Bismarck:
- Early in his tenure as Prime Minister, Bismarck famously told the Prussian parliament that Prussia must spend more on its military because "the great questions of the day will not be settled by speeches and majority decisions ... but by iron and blood." Because of this, and because of his willingness to fight wars to achieve his goals, Bismarck was known as the "Iron Chancellor."
- Bismarck's harsh political philosophy earned a name: *realpolitik*. *Realpolitik* may be loosely summarized as "might makes right": In Bismarck's opinion, any nation that had the military power to take what it wanted would always do so eventually, and should simply get on with it without wasting a lot of time wringing its hands over ethics and morals.
- Bismarck was honored with many monuments, both before and after his death. Early in World War II, Germany's largest and proudest battleship was the *Bismarck*, first ship of the Bismarck class. The British Royal Navy sank the *Bismarck* in 1941 (see Chapter 26).
- Kaiser Wilhelm II, who fired Bismarck in 1890, would later be partly responsible for leading most of the world into World War I. Bismarck had predicted that the next great war would begin in the Balkan Peninsula (the European peninsula that includes Greece), and he was right (see Chapter 17).
- Germany's Fuhrer Adolf Hitler described himself as a "second Bismarck" in his autobiographical Nazi propaganda book, *Mein Kampf*.

FASCINATING FACTS: The Krupp 6-Pounder Cannon

The Krupp steel company was Germany's leading weapons manufacturer during the Franco-Prussian War. Krupp's new 6-pounder cannon had several advantages over French cannon:

- The Krupp loaded at a breech in the rear of the barrel, not at the muzzle like the old-style French cannon. Breech loading was faster than muzzle loading, so the Krupp fired faster.
- The Krupp was made of cast steel, not of bronze. Cast steel technology made the Krupp stronger, lighter, more accurate and longer-ranged than the bronze cannon the French were using.
- The Krupp fired a 6-pound hollow shell filled with explosives and smaller shot. These shells exploded on contact, causing far more damage than solid shot.

The Krupp Company continued to build some of the world's most advanced weapons before and during World War I. After World War I, the Treaty of Versailles severely limited German companies' ability to manufacture weapons legally (see Chapter 20); however, with Adolf Hitler's encouragement, Krupp continued to build weapons anyway, illegally. Germany's defeat in World War II finally forced Krupp to stop building weapons.

FASCINATING FACTS: The Grimm Brothers' Fairy Tales

Children's and Household Tales was a collection of children's stories originally published in 1812 by Jacob and Wilhelm Grimm, the "Brothers Grimm." The Grimm brothers published several volumes and editions of their children's collection over the years. They built their collection by gathering German folk tales that had been passed down orally for generations, then editing the tales and publishing them accompanied by plenty of illustrations.

Despite the collection's child-friendly name, parents often considered Grimm Brothers tales too frightening, violent or suggestive for children. Sometimes, the Grimm brothers answered these complaints by making the revised versions of their tales even more violent. For example: in the first edition of *Rumpelstiltskin*, when the queen saves her firstborn child by learning Rumpelstiltskin's name, Rumpelstiltskin simply runs away angry. In the last edition, his angry reaction is far worse: he stomps his right foot so hard that it becomes stuck in the ground, then rips himself in half trying to pull himself out by his left foot.

MISSIONARY FOCUS

GIANTS OF THE FAITH: Abraham Kuyper (1837 – 1920)

Abraham Kuyper was a minister and politician from the Netherlands. Kuyper was important in the Dutch Reformed Church's "Calvinist Renaissance," a time of renewed interest in the Reformed theology of John Calvin.

Kuyper studied theology at Leiden University, a very enlightened and modern school of theology in the Netherlands. His professors were "liberal" theologians who taught him not to take the Bible at face value, but instead to study it in light of modern scientific thought. At Leiden, Kuyper learned to doubt that Jesus' miracles had ever really happened, and even to question whether Jesus was really raised from the dead.

After graduation, Kuyper took a post as a minister among average Dutch men and women who had never heard Leiden University's liberal ideas. Instead of being impressed with Kuyper's learning, they were horrified that a man who was supposedly so educated in Scripture could actually understand so little of it. Through repeated visits to devout believers in his first church, Kuyper came to understand that the liberal ideas his seminary professors had taught him were all wrong.

To replace those ideas, Kuyper turned to the theology of John Calvin for guidance. He soon discarded most of his liberal beliefs in favor of Calvin's Reformed theology. Like Charles Spurgeon (see chapter 6), Kuyper came to believe in predestination and in a God who is Master of all things. He turned a full circle, abandoning liberal theology to become one of its fiercest opponents.

Kuyper was dismayed when, in spite of his best efforts, parts of the Dutch Reformed Church continued to grow ever more liberal. Although Kuyper's Dutch Reformed Church was not strictly a state church, it was close, because members of the Dutch parliament were all expected to be members of the church in good standing. Kuyper helped to found the Antirevolutionary Party, a Christian political party, to spread his reformed thought from the Church into the government. Later, he led a group of churches that left the Dutch Reformed Church. These churches called themselves the *Doleantie* (from the Latin word for sorrow) because it grieved them that the Dutch Reformed Church had wandered so far from God's Word. As the leader of his Antirevolutionary Party, Kuyper was the Netherlands' prime minister for four years, from 1901-1905.

U.S. HISTORY FOCUS

FASCINATING FACTS: The Poll Tax

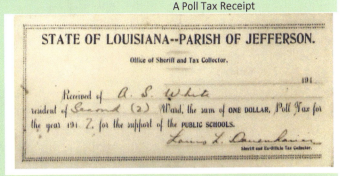

A Poll Tax Receipt

Near the end of Reconstruction, several Southern states established a "poll tax" law that required voters to pay a tax at the polling place in order to exercise their right to vote. Anyone who couldn't afford the tax was turned away from the polls, and lost his chance to vote. Some poll taxes included a "grandfather clause" that allowed anyone who had voted in the past to continue voting, even if he couldn't pay the tax. The "grandfather clause" allowed poor whites who couldn't pay the poll tax to continue voting, while still achieving the poll tax's primary purpose: preventing poor blacks from voting in Southern elections.

Poll tax laws were part of a larger set of "Jim Crow" laws passed to rob Southern blacks of their rights both during and after Reconstruction. Although the "equal protection" clause of the fourteenth amendment (see Chapter 6) seemed to prohibit Jim Crow laws, the South worked around this problem with clever legal arguments. An 1896 Supreme Court decision in the case of *Plessy vs. Ferguson* upheld the idea that government services could be "separate but equal": that is, that laws could maintain the separation between blacks and whites as long as they provided "equal" services to both in order to satisfy the fourteenth amendment.

The United States finally outlawed poll taxes for federal elections in 1964, with the ratification of the 24th Amendment to the Constitution. Later, the courts decided that poll taxes were unconstitutional for all elections anywhere in the United States.

THE 24TH AMENDMENT

Section 1. The right of citizens of the United States to vote in any primary or other election for President or Vice President, for electors for President or Vice President, or for Senator or Representative in Congress, shall not be denied or abridged by the United States or any State by reason of failure to pay any poll tax or other tax.

Section 2. Congress shall have power to enforce this article by appropriate legislation.

FASCINATING FACTS: The Statue of Liberty

The American Revolution might have come to nothing without help from France. The Revolution benefited from French philosophy, French military aid and French money. The French were proud of their role in helping to establish enlightened liberty in the United States, and they wanted to commemorate that role with a monument to celebrate America's 100th birthday in 1876.

The French proposed to build a harbor statue inspired in part by the ancient Colossus that once stood over the harbor of Rhodes, one of the Greek Isles. The new sculpture's title would be "Liberty Enlightening the World," but it would be better known as "The New Colossus." France agreed to build the statue itself, while the U.S. agreed to build its pedestal on Bedloe's Island in New York harbor (Bedloe's Island is now known as "Liberty Island").

The French shipped the finished statue to the U.S. in 350 pieces before the U.S. even completed the pedestal. President Grover Cleveland dedicated the completed monument on October 28, 1886. The torch in the statue's upraised arm was fitted with a light that made it a functioning lighthouse; however, its light never worked very well, and it was extinguished in 1902.

The Statue of Liberty is often seen as a symbol of a free and open immigration policy because, for many years, immigrants passed the statue on their approach to the U.S. immigration center at nearby Ellis Island. This symbolism is reinforced by a poem engraved on a plaque attached to the statue's pedestal:

THE NEW COLOSSUS

Not like the brazen giant of Greek fame,
with conquering limbs astride from land to land;
Here at our sea-washed, sunset gates shall stand
a mighty woman with a torch, whose flame
is the imprisoned lightning, and her name
Mother of Exiles. From her beacon-hand
Glows world-wide welcome; her mild eyes command
The air-bridged harbor that twin cities frame,
"Keep, ancient lands, your storied pomp!" cries she
with silent lips. "Give me your tired, your poor,
Your huddled masses yearning to breathe free,
The wretched refuse of your teeming shore,
Send these, the homeless, tempest-tost to me,
I lift my lamp beside the golden door!"

Poet Emma Lazarus wrote this poem to help with the statue's 1880s pedestal fundraising campaign. Her poem proudly declared America's profound difference from the storied empires of the past: its people were free. After Lazarus died, her friends honored her by creating the plaque and dedicating it at the pedestal.

Other fun facts about the Statue of Liberty:
- The statue's steel frame was designed by French engineer Gustave Eiffel, who also designed Paris's Eiffel Tower.
- A broken chain lies at the statue's feet to represent the broken bonds of oppressive government. The chain is difficult to see from the ground.
- The statue's finished head was displayed at the 1878 World's Fair in Paris.
- A one-fourth scale replica of the statue sits on an island in the Seine River in Paris.

AMAZING AMERICANS: Thomas Nast (1840 – 1902)

Thomas Nast was a talented artist who immigrated to the United States from Germany with his family as a child. At age eighteen, he earned a job as an illustrator at *Harper's Weekly*, which at the time was a new American political magazine based in New York City. Through the Civil War, Reconstruction and beyond, Nast drew political cartoons and caricatures that often attacked corrupt politicians and policies.

It was Thomas Nast's political cartoons that permanently linked the Democratic Party to its Donkey symbol, the Republican Party to its Elephant symbol, and the United States to Uncle Sam. He also created the popular image of Santa Claus as a chubby, smiling, jolly, bearded old gentleman.

U.S. GEOGRAPHY FOCUS

FASCINATING FACTS about IOWA:

- Statehood: Iowa became the 29th US state on December 28, 1846.
- Bordering states: Illinois, Nebraska, Minnesota, Missouri, South Dakota and Wisconsin
- State capital: Des Moines
- Area: 56,272 sq. mi (Ranks 26th in size)
- Abbreviation: IA
- State nickname: "Hawkeye State"
- State bird: Eastern Goldfinch
- State tree: Oak
- State flower: Wild Rose
- State song: *The Song of Iowa*
- State Motto: "Our Liberties We Prize and Our Rights We Will Maintain"
- Meaning of name: Possibly named for the Ioway Indian tribe
- Historic places to visit in Iowa: Rathbun Dam and Reservoir, Spirit Lake, Fenlon Place Elevator, Knoxville's National Sprint Car Hall of Fame and Museum, Boone and Scenic Valley Railroad, Crystal Lake Cave, The Amana Colonies, Fort Atkinson State Preserve
- Iowa's Resources and Industries: farming (hogs, cattle, dairy, corn, soybeans) manufacturing, banking, machinery, chemical products, insurance, food processing

Fenlon Place Elevator

Flag of Iowa

- Iowa adopted this flag in 1921.
- It is patterned after the French flag, because Iowa belonged to the French before the Louisiana Purchase.
- The long ribbon the bald eagle carries contains the state motto.
- A member of the Daughters of the American Revolution name Dixie Gebhardt designed this flag.

PRESIDENTIAL FOCUS

PRESIDENT #18: Ulysses S. Grant (1822 – 1885)	
In Office: March 4, 1869 – March 4, 1877	**Political Party:** Republican
Birthplace: Ohio	**Nickname:** "United States" (during the Civil War, "Unconditional Surrender")

Ulysses S. Grant was born in Ohio and attended the U.S. Military Academy at West Point. After Grant served bravely in the Mexican-American War of 1846-1848, depression and heavy drinking marred his military career. He left the military to do other things; and when the Civil War began, he was a clerk in his father's leather goods shop in Galena, Illinois.

From this lowly status, Grant rose to become General-in-Chief of all Union armies during the Civil War. Late in the war, he became the first American after George Washington to be promoted to the rank of full general (four stars). Grant used superior numbers and resources to grind down the cunning resistance of Confederate General Robert E. Lee. Where earlier Union commanders (McClellan, Pope, Burnside and Hooker) were hesitant, afraid of being routed and embarrassed by Lee, Grant was cool under fire and unmoved by heavy casualties on the battlefield.

Although Grant's reputation suffered ups and downs during the Civil War, he was a Northern hero at its end and a natural candidate for President. Lincoln's Republican Party nominated Grant to replace the highly unpopular democrat Andrew Johnson, and Grant won election easily.

During Reconstruction, Grant was less lenient with the former rebel states of the South than President Johnson had been. Grant's policy as President was to honor the sacrifices of his Union soldiers by defending the things for which they had fought and died: a strong Union and freedom for former slaves. President Grant was not afraid to send U.S. troops against the violent demonstrations of the Ku Klux Klan, nor was he content to allow the same Southern politicians who had voted for secession to return to power after the war.

Unfortunately, more than ten political scandals marred Grant's years as President: the "Salary Grab," the "Whiskey Ring" and several others. Most of these scandals involved officials in Grant's government accepting bribes. Although Grant wasn't directly involved in these scandals, they made him and his Republican Party look bad for hiring and electing so many corrupt politicians.

Other interesting facts about Ulysses S. Grant:

- Grant's parents named him Hiram Ulysses Grant, but he didn't like his initials (HUG). When he got to West Point, he dropped the name "Hiram" and added the middle initial "S," which stood for nothing.
- Grant was an excellent horseman. During Grant's Presidency, a police officer fined him $20 for reckless speeding on his race horse in downtown Washington DC.
- Grant's favorite breakfast dish was cucumbers soaked in vinegar.
- Grant smoked cigars constantly, and his smoking may have contributed to the throat cancer that killed him.
- A memorial statue of Grant stands in front of the U.S. Capitol, at the opposite end of the Mall from the Lincoln Memorial.
- Grant's tomb is in Manhattan, New York City, New York; and yes, Grant is buried in Grant's Tomb.

Notable quotes from Ulysses S. Grant:

- "The art of war is simple enough. Find out where your enemy is. Get at him as soon as you can. Strike him as hard as you can, and keep moving on."
- "There is no great sport in having bullets flying about one in every direction, but I find they have less horror when among them than when in anticipation."

PRESIDENT #19: Rutherford B. Hayes (1822 – 1893)	
In Office: March 4, 1877 – March 4, 1881	**Political Party:** Republican
Birthplace: Ohio	**Nickname:** "Dark Horse President"

President Rutherford B. Hayes' election marked the end of the Reconstruction period after the Civil War. In the extremely close Presidential election of 1876, Hayes became the first Presidential candidate in history to win the electoral (statewide) vote, but lose the popular (individual) vote. In other words, more individual Americans voted for Hayes' opponent, but more states cast the majority of their votes for Hayes.

The outcome of the election was in real doubt, so Congress established an election commission to decide what to do. Hayes needed the South's support to ensure his victory, so he approached Southern members of Congress with a compromise: Hayes would agree to remove the last military governments in the South if Southern congressmen would agree to support his election. Under the terms of this unofficial compromise, known as the "Compromise of 1877," Hayes won the Presidency, and Reconstruction came to an end.

Hayes' critics nicknamed him "Rutherfraud" for his "fraud" in winning the Presidency in such a shady way. However, some of those same critics were almost certainly involved in the terror tactics used to keep blacks, most of them Republicans and Hayes voters, away from the polls in the South. Without their interference, Hayes would have won more Southern votes anyway.

Hayes' Presidency was a transition period during which the U.S. returned to relative peace and calm after the chaos of the Civil War and Reconstruction. He returned U.S. currency to the "gold standard," under which all U.S. money was backed by gold owned by the U.S. Treasury. The gold standard lowered inflation and gave the nation's businesspeople more confidence. By the end of Hayes' single term in office, U.S. businesses were prospering again. Hayes did not seek re-election.

Other interesting facts about Rutherford B. Hayes:
- Hayes served bravely as a colonel in the Civil War, and was the only President who was wounded in that war.
- Hayes' abolitionist wife, Lucy Ware Webb, was nicknamed "Lemonade Lucy" because she refused to serve alcohol in the White House. Lemonade Lucy also banned smoking, dancing and card playing.
- The traditional Easter Egg hunt on the White House lawn began with Hayes' Presidency.
- Hayes was the first President to use a telephone in the White House.

Notable quotes from Rutherford B. Hayes:
- "One of the tests of the civilization of people is the treatment of its criminals."
- "Free government cannot long endure if property is largely in a few hands, and large masses of people are unable to earn homes, education, and a support in old age."
- "Nothing brings out the lower traits of human nature like office-seeking."

Chapter 8

The Transcontinental Railroad, Moving Out West

U.S. HISTORY FOCUS

FASCINATING FACTS: The Pony Express

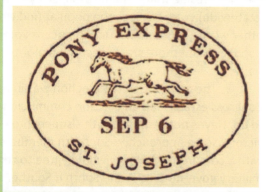

The primary mission of the Pony Express was to deliver news and mail on horseback as quickly as possible between its eastern terminal at St. Joseph, Missouri and its western terminal at Sacramento, California. The distance between these terminals was about 2,000 miles, and the Pony Express usually covered it in about ten days. The Pony Express was in service for just 2 years, 1860 and 1861; but during those two years it became a memorable symbol of the American West.

When the State of California entered the Union in 1850, it was cut off from the eastern half of the nation by a wide, largely unknown expanse of land filled with natural barriers and often hostile Indians. Instead of crossing to California overland, many travelers:

1. Traveled by boat down the east coast of North America and across the Gulf of Mexico to Panama or Nicaragua, where they
2. Crossed Central America at its narrowest point overland (by rail after 1855), and then
3. Caught another boat up the west coast of North America to California.

This journey could take months; but the people of California and the West needed news and letters from back east quickly. To answer this need, three businessmen created the Pony Express, hoping that they would receive a contract from the U.S. Post Office to deliver mail across country to and from California. As it turned out, they never won that contract.

When the Pony Express agency first went into operation, it purchased about six hundred fast, tough horses and hired about seventy-five qualified riders. Each rider could weigh no more than 110 pounds and was required to be:

1. An excellent horseman,
2. Brave,
3. Able to shoot from horseback and
4. Willing to fight Indians when necessary.

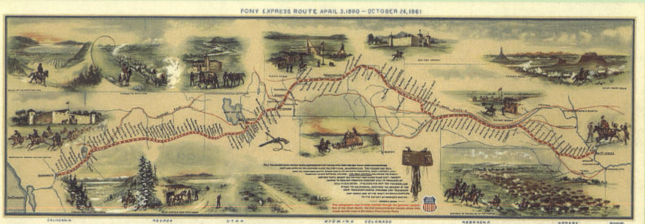

The Pony Express agency established about 190 stations stocked with fresh horses and supplies along the route from St. Joseph to Sacramento, which followed trails blazed by the pioneers. Over good terrain, each rider covered a 60-mile leg of the trip in 6 hours on 6 different horses. Riding at a gallop, a rider would cover about ten miles, change horses, and then cover another ten miles, making an average of 10 miles per hour. Over mountain terrain, of course, each mile took longer.

Other interesting facts about the Pony Express:
- Pony Express mail was expensive. A single half-ounce letter cost $5 to deliver, about $120 in 2010 dollars.
- The best-known Pony Express rider was William Cody, later known as Buffalo Bill.
- The Pony Express closed two days after the completion of the first Transcontinental Telegraph on October 24, 1861.

FASCINATING FACTS: Early Railroads

From as early as 1550, German road builders created "wagon ways" to speed travel for horse-drawn wagons. Wagonways were wooden rails laid down to guide and bear the weight of wagons loaded down with coal or ore. Wagonways allowed horses to do their work far more easily, without the constant danger of becoming stuck on muddy roads. By the late 1700s, as the Industrial Revolution was getting underway, iron rails had begun to replace wooden rails on wagonways.

Other interesting facts about early railroads:
- The first working commercial steam locomotive appeared in Britain in 1804.
- The first American-built steam locomotive was the 1829 *Tom Thumb*, which malfunctioned and lost a race against a horse-drawn rail car on its maiden run. Even though it lost, the *Tom Thumb* was still fast and powerful enough to convince the owners of the Baltimore and Ohio Railroad that steam locomotives would soon replace horses.
- By the 1850s, steam locomotives and railroads had spread all over the eastern United States, and they were critically important during the 1861 - 1865 Civil War.
- The Pullman Company built the first luxury sleeping cars in the late 1850s.
- A Pullman car carried President Lincoln's remains on a tour of Northern states after his assassination in 1865.

The Transcontinental Railroad

The Mexican-American War (1846 - 1848) and the California Gold Rush (1849) combined to make settling and governing California urgent matters for the United States. In an effort to bypass the issue of banning slavery in the proposed California Territory, President Zachary Taylor decided to skip territory status for California and bring it directly into the Union as a State. California became a free State as part of the Compromise of 1850, shortly after President Taylor's death.

But California was divided from the eastern United States by a wide, often treacherous expanse of land filled with natural barriers and hostile Indians. The journey across this "Great American Desert" by wagon train required months, and the water route around South America or across Panama often required just as long. The United States needed a way to unite its two halves. The Transcontinental Railroad, completed in 1869, would bridge the gap between East and West and become the key to the nation's westward expansion.

In 1862, the Pacific Railway Act encouraged private companies to build the Transcontinental Railroad by offering them government bonds (loans) and land grants for each mile of track they completed. Two companies jumped at the opportunity:

1. The **Central Pacific Railroad Company**, which would lay track eastward from Sacramento, California, and
2. The **Union Pacific Railroad Company**, which would lay track westward from Omaha, Nebraska.

At first, the Civil War delayed the Transcontinental Railroad's progress in the East, while difficult terrain and supply problems delayed its progress in the West.

The Transcontinental Railroad was a prodigious feat of engineering. Its 1800-mile length covered two-thirds of the North American continent's width, across every type of terrain imaginable. The only settlement of any size along the entire route was Salt Lake City, founded by the Mormons in 1847 after the Mormon Exodus. The eastern part of the route followed the Platte River valley west from Omaha, just as the Oregon Trail (see Chapter 14) and the Pony Express had done.

The Union Pacific's section of the Transcontinental Railroad was relatively easy. Trains from the east could deliver rails and supplies along the track as the railroad progressed westward. On the High Plains of Nebraska and Wyoming, the ground beneath the track required little preparation at all: the railroad workers could simply lay down the railroad ties, spike the rails to the ties, and move along. As the track approached completion, the Union Pacific had grown so skillful that it needed only twelve hours to lay about ten miles of rails across the easy terrain of the High Plains.

The Central Pacific's section of the railroad was far more difficult. The only supplies the Central Pacific could buy on its end of the line were wooden railroad ties, most of which were cut from California redwood trees. Everything else, from rails and spikes to locomotives, had to be shipped from the east coast by way of Panama or South America. The Central Pacific also faced the extremely difficult terrain of the Sierra Nevada and Rocky mountain ranges, with altitudes up to 8,000 feet, steep grades and mountain snows.

The amount of labor the Central Pacific side of the railroad required was almost beyond imagination. The Central Pacific hired more than ten thousand laborers, many of them from China, to perform the fantastic work of:

1. Carving roads into steep mountainsides and building numerous bridges;
2. Using sledgehammers and dynamite to create 15 tunnels through mountainsides of solid granite, sometimes tunneling from both ends at once; and
3. Building sheds over 37 miles of the route so that they could work through the winter snows.

The Union Pacific and the Central Pacific railroads met and completed their railroad at Promontory Summit, Utah on May 10, 1869. The final spike, made of solid gold, was engraved with these words:

- On top: "The LAST SPIKE"
- On one side: "The Pacific Railroad ground broken Jan. 8th 1863 and completed May 8th 1869"
- On the other side: "May God continue the unity of our Country as this Railroad unites the two great Oceans of the world."

The other two sides were engraved with the names of the railroad companies' heads. Soon after the heads of the Central Pacific and the Union Pacific drove this ceremonial spike, real railroad workers removed it and replaced with an iron one, and the Transcontinental Railroad was finally open for business. <u>The cross country trip that had once required months could now be accomplished in less than five days</u>.

Other interesting facts about the Transcontinental Railroad:
- The president of the Central Pacific Railroad was Leland Stanford, a governor of California and the founder of California's Stanford University.
- The two railroads' joining ceremony had been scheduled for May 8, 1869, the date engraved on the golden spike. After the spike was engraved, however, unforeseen circumstances delayed the ceremony: the unpaid railroad workers of the Union Pacific Company kidnapped their boss, Thomas Durant, and held him for ransom for two days until the company wired him the money he owed them.

FASCINATING FACTS: Buffalo

Before American settlers began to move into the West, uncounted hordes of buffalo, perhaps 50 million or more, roamed the Great Plains in herds. American Indian tribes such as the Arapaho, the Cheyenne, the Kiowa and the Shoshone used buffalo as their primary sustenance. They used buffalo meat, fat, hides, bones, sinews, horns and hooves to make nearly everything they needed to live. Before these tribes gained horses, they sometimes killed buffalo by driving them into a stampede that led the herd over a cliff. After they gained horses, they shot buffalo with bow and arrow from horseback.

This way of life rapidly came to an end after the American settlers began to move west. To the settlers, the buffalo were inconvenient because:

1. Buffalo sustained the American Indian tribes, whom the settlers wanted to remove from the plains and force onto Indian "reservations";
2. Buffalo herds stood on railroad tracks, blocking the trains and refusing to move; and
3. Buffalo herds ate prairie grass that cattlemen wanted for their cattle.

For a short time, American settlers found that the buffalo were valuable and easy to kill. Buffalo presented a money-making opportunity that was hard to ignore: buffalo skins sold for $3 or more apiece, while a laborer putting in a long, hard day's work on the Transcontinental Railroad earned only about $1 (less if he was Chinese).

For some reason, gunfire rarely caused buffalo herds to stampede. Careful hunters could kill one buffalo after another without frightening the herd. Eventually, the herd would catch on to the threat and run off; and then the hunter's skinning crew would move in and pull off the dead buffalos' hides using teams of horses or mules. When the skinners were finished, every part of the buffalo except the hide lay wasted on the plain.

The American settlers' extravagant overuse of the buffalo could not last long. The buffalo herds were large enough to sustain the American Indian population, but nowhere near large enough to sustain the American settler population. During the twenty years from 1869 - 1889, American settlers hunted the buffalo until they were nearly extinct.

Other interesting facts about buffalo:
- Union General Phil Sheridan, who became an Indian fighter after the Civil War, asked Congress to eliminate the buffalo so that it would be easier for the U.S. Army to drive the American Indian tribes onto their reservations.
- Railroad companies sometimes encouraged their bored passengers to shoot buffalo from moving trains, hoping to eliminate the herds in order to keep their tracks clear and their trains on time.
- Two buffalo hunters who went on to later fame were Buffalo Bill Cody and Wyatt Earp.

MOVING OUT WEST

After the U.S. Civil War, the rush to settle the American West began. Both the U.S. government and the settlers were excited about Western settlement:

1. The U.S. government was eager to settle the American West because it knew that the best way to claim and hold Western territory was to fill it with loyal U.S. citizens.
2. The settlers were eager to settle the American West because of the fantastic opportunity it offered poorer Americans. The Homestead Act of 1862 (see below) made the American West just about the only land anywhere in the world that one didn't need to be wealthy to claim.

Newspapermen like Horace Greeley, editor of the New York Tribune, advised the Americans of their day to take advantage of these opportunities: "Go West, young man," Greeley said in 1865, "Go West, and grow up with the country!" An economic depression during Reconstruction (the Depression of 1873) made settlers all the more eager to seek new lands and opportunities out West.

FASCINATING FACTS: The Homestead Act

The Homestead Act of 1862 was designed to encourage settlers to take possession of land in the American West. Under the terms of the Homestead Act, all settlers, including women and freed slaves, were entitled to up to 160 acres

of undeveloped land if they could meet four conditions:

1. They must pay a fee of $10;
2. They must live on their new land for five years;
3. They must "improve" their new land, usually by building a house and/or a barn on it; and
4. They must file their claim with the U.S. Land Office to receive a title of ownership.

160 acres of land was equal to one "quarter section," or one fourth of a square mile. Much of the American Midwest is still visibly divided into the one-square-mile "sections" that surveyors laid out because of the Homestead Act.

Oklahoma Land Runs

From 1889-1895, the U.S. Land Office conducted "Land Runs" to distribute some of the Midwest's last unsettled territories to homesteaders. Most of these unsettled territories were parts of Oklahoma that had been set aside for American Indian tribes during the 1830s, but never occupied.

Before the Land Office began its land runs, two types of people occupied parts of these unsettled Oklahoma lands:

1. Cattlemen who grazed their herds there, renting the land from the American Indian tribes who still technically owned it; and
2. "Squatters" who snuck onto the land, quietly building small homes and raising crops there. The squatters of Oklahoma hoped to take possession of their illegal land claims someday by "squatter's rights," unwritten laws that sometimes allow the person who inhabits and uses a piece of land to become that land's owner.

When the U.S. Land Office planned its land runs, it deliberately ignored "squatter's rights." Instead, it removed all squatters from the unsettled lands so that they became a clean slate, a "no man's land" where no one was allowed to live. Then it announced a fixed date and time when the unsettled lands would be opened to settlement. On the announced date of a land run, hopeful settlers lined up at the unsettled land's border, ready to race each other to stake their claims on the best quarter sections they could find.

The Land Run of 1889 was the Land Office's first official land run. On April 22, 1889, about 50,000 settlers gathered on the borders of the unsettled lands that would soon become six counties in Oklahoma. The U.S. Army was on hand to make sure that no one crossed the borders early. At high noon, a starting gun fired, and those 50,000 settlers rushed to claim the 12,500 quarter sections of land that the Land Office had surveyed for them. Obviously, only one quarter of the settlers were satisfied, and three quarters of them were disappointed. The successful settlers in the Land Run of 1889 established and laid out two towns, Oklahoma City and Guthrie, within a single afternoon on April 22.

The largest land run was the September 16, 1893 Cherokee Strip Land Run, which distributed about 7 million acres of land in Oklahoma's Cherokee Strip. About 100,000 men, women and children, most of them riding horses, wagons or trains, waited for a starter's shot before racing each other to claim about 42,000 quarter sections of available land.

The Land Runs made two types of people famous:

1. The **Boomers**, settlers who drummed up the public's excitement about the unsettled Indian lands and pressured Congress to open the lands for settlement; and
2. The **Sooners**, settlers who cheated on the Land Runs by arriving "sooner" than everyone else. Oklahoma's Sooners (1) secretly crossed the border into the unsettled lands before the land run began, then (2) jumped out of hiding at the right moment and staked their claims before the unlucky settlers who had naively obeyed the rules could arrive. Some Sooners were U.S. Marshals (law officers) who took their jobs as marshals precisely because these jobs allowed them to spy out all of Oklahoma's best land before the land runs began, in territory that was closed to everyone else. The State of Oklahoma honored the opportunism and dubious honesty of the Sooners by adopting "The Sooner State" as its nickname.

Cattle Drives

The treeless plains of Texas and the Midwest were as good for cattle as they were for buffalo; but in the early 1800s, Texas cattlemen had no way to transport large cattle herds to market. Some drove their cattle to California to feed the people of the California Gold Rush, but that was a long and difficult journey.

After the Civil War, when beef prices began climbing steadily, Texas cattlemen began to take advantage of the railroads in Kansas to ship their cattle to the vast markets of the East. To accomplish this, they hired teams of cowboys to drive their herds over the long miles from Texas to Kansas.

Cattle driving teams consisted of about a dozen men, including a trail boss, a cook, several drovers to keep the cattle moving and a couple of wranglers to manage the team's horses. They loaded all of their equipment and supplies aboard a chuck wagon specially designed for cattle drives, then drove their herds from Texas to the railroad at Abilene, Kansas along the Chisholm Trail. At a pace of 10- 15 miles per day, cattle drivers could complete a cattle drive in 1-3 months.

These cattle drivers were the storied cowboys of the American West, men who tasted freedom as few ever have on the boundless, open Midwestern plains of the mid- to late-1800s.

Like the Pony Express and the land runs, these cattle drives lasted for only a short span of years. The arrival of railroads in Texas rendered long cattle drives unnecessary, and they dwindled during the 1880s.

The Fence Cutting War

Texas cattle drivers grew accustomed to the "open range," the nearly limitless free land on which they could graze their cattle wherever they found grass and water. However, as more settlers moved into Texas, more land was claimed by ranchers who wanted to save their land for their own herds and crops. With the arrival of Joseph Glidden's newly-invented barbed wire, patented in 1874, these ranchers found an inexpensive way to build the miles-long fences they needed to protect their Texas-sized ranches. The ranchers' barbed wire fences prevented crop-trampling, grass-stealing cattle herds from crossing their land, and were a major obstacle to open range cattlemen.

The conflict between open range cattlemen and closed ranchers led to the Fence Cutting War of 1883-1884. The ranchers claimed that they built fences only to protect their private property, which was their right. The open range cattlemen claimed that ranchers were fencing in not only their own land, but also public lands that didn't belong to them. Open range cattlemen began to cut fences, and ranchers began to fight back.

But the open range way of life was dying along with the cattle drives, for the same reasons. Declining beef prices, hard winters and the arrival of railroads combined with the ranchers' fences to drive open range cattlemen out of business around the mid-1880s.

FASCINATING FACTS: Time Zones

The invention of telegraphs and the rapid travel made possible by railroads led to some confusion in timekeeping. During the mid-1800s, every town along every railroad line had its own time, measured according to the position of the sun. Each town set its clocks by sextants or sundials that it used to mark high noon. Because of the rotation of the earth, these sundial times were different in every town, east or west, near or far.

As railroads became more common, some railroad stations began to keep one clock for every town along their rail line. Each clock was set to the correct time for its particular town and kept accurate by telegraph. In this way, the railroad could tell its passengers what the local time would be when they arrived at their destinations.

The British were the first to establish "Railway Time," a standard time maintained at rail stations all over Britain. Railway Time was equal to Greenwich Mean Time, the standard time established for oceangoing navigators, and was the same all over Britain. For years, each British town had to keep track of two times: Railway Time and its own local sundial time. During those years, the British fashioned their clocks and watches so that they had two minute hands— one for sundial time, and one for Railway Time.

The United States was far broader than Britain, so a single time for the entire nation wouldn't do. Because of the earth's rotation, high noon in New York equaled only about 9 AM in California. In order to keep clock times reasonably close to sundial times, the United States adopted four time zones— Eastern, Central, Mountain and Pacific— and set all local clocks according to the standard within their time zone. This standard was adopted on November 18, 1883, the "Day of Two Noons," when railroad stations all over the nation adjusted their clocks to the standard time inside their time zone.

AMAZING AMERICANS: Thomas Alva Edison (1847 – 1931)

Ohio-born, Michigan-grown Thomas Edison was the most talented, persistent and successful inventor of his time. From his innovative research laboratory in Menlo Park, New Jersey, Edison patented hundreds of useful inventions that changed lives all over the world. Among them:

1. **The Phonograph**: Before he even built his lab at Menlo Park, Edison invented a device that could record and play back sound. His recording medium was a tinfoil-covered cylinder, and needles attached to diaphragms created and played back the impressions on the tinfoil. His first successful recording was of himself reciting a nursery rhyme.

2. ***The Edison Bulb***: Edison's light bulb was a refinement of an earlier invention, the arc light. The arc light made light with an electric spark that passed between two electrodes. Part of the reason the Statue of Liberty was a failure as a lighthouse was because it used an unreliable arc light. Edison's first refinement to the arc light was to use a glowing filament instead of a spark to carry the electric current. Then he removed the air from the glass bulb that housed the filament, so that the filament couldn't react with the oxygen in the air and burn up.
3. ***The Kinetoscope***: Edison invented equipment to record and play back pictures taken in rapid sequence, giving the appearance of movement. These were the first motion pictures.

Edison also invented other practical things such as the mimeograph machine and waxed paper. He was not always right, though: In the "War of the Currents," Edison stubbornly insisted that his Direct Current system for transmitting electric power was superior to the Alternating Current system championed by Tesla and Westinghouse. Later developments proved that Edison was wrong.

Edison was an eccentric with great powers of concentration and dogged persistence. He never let go of a problem; he even left his bride on her wedding night to attend to some nagging difficulty with one of his ongoing experiments. These Edison quotes highlight his philosophy of persistence:

- "I never did anything by accident, nor did any of my inventions come by accident; they came by work."
- "I have not failed. I've just found 10,000 ways that won't work."
- "Genius is one percent inspiration and ninety-nine percent perspiration."

AMAZING AMERICANS: Cyrus McCormick (1809 – 1884) and Jerome Case (1819 – 1891)

The process of growing and processing wheat changed little from Bible times through the beginning of the Industrial Age. Producing wheat was a labor-intensive process of many steps: plowing, fertilizing, sowing, scything (cutting), binding, drying, flailing (threshing) and milling. In the mid-1800s, two inventors designed machines that could take the place of many men in the work of harvesting and processing wheat: Cyrus McCormick and Jerome Case.

Virginia-born Cyrus McCormick patented his reaper, a machine that took the place of the hand scythe, in 1834. McCormick's horse-drawn reaper could harvest an acre of wheat in an hour, about four to eight times as fast as a man with a scythe. Hand laborers walked behind McCormick's reaper, binding the sheaves of wheat for drying and later threshing. McCormick's company became the International Harvester Company, which later made tractors and other types of farm machinery. Early International Harvester tractors, invented and built decades after McCormick's death in 1884, still bore McCormick's name.

New York-born Jerome Case made several improvements and refinements to the threshing machine, a device for separating kernels of wheat from the straw on which they grow. Case's first commercial thresher appeared in 1844. When they were working well, threshing machines could take the place of many laborers working with flails on a threshing floor.

Case's early wooden-bodied threshing machines were unwieldy contraptions with multi-belted, whirling shafts jutting in every direction. They required almost constant adjustments to account for different grain sizes. For the skilled, patient operator, threshing machines could produce clean wheat and leave almost no grain on the straw. They were powered by windmill shafts, horse-turned shafts or early stationary steam engines. Later, they were powered by steam tractors.

U.S. GEOGRAPHY FOCUS

FASCINATING FACTS about ARKANSAS:

- Statehood: Arkansas became the 25th state on June 15, 1836.
- Bordering states: Louisiana, Mississippi, Missouri, Oklahoma, Tennessee, Texas
- State capital: Little Rock
- Area: 53,179 sq. mi (Ranks 29th in size)
- Abbreviation: AR
- State nickname: "The Natural State"
- State Bird: Mockingbird
- State tree: Short Leaf Pine
- State flower: Apple Blossom
- State songs: *Arkansas* and *Oh Arkansas*
- State Motto: "The People Rule"
- Meaning of name: *Arkansas* is from a Sioux word that means "downstream" or "south wind."
- Historic places to visit in Arkansas: Ozarks, Hot Springs National Park, Blanchard Springs Cavern, Mountain Village 1890, Toltec Mounds Archaeological State Park, Tiny Town, Petit Jean State Park
- Resources and Industries: farming (chickens, eggs, cotton, cattle, dairy, hogs, rice, soybeans, cotton, sorghum) paper and plastics, food processing, diamond mining, oil, steel

Cedar Falls in Petit Jean State Park

Flag of Arkansas

- Arkansas adopted this flag in 1913.
- Its design is by Willie Kavanaugh Hocker, who won a design contest.
- The diamond on the flag represents the fact that Arkansas is the only place in North America where miners have found diamonds.
- The flag's 25 stars represent the fact that Arkansas was the 25th state to join the Union.
- The star above the word *Arkansas* represents the Confederate States of America. The three stars under the word *Arkansas* represent Spain, France and the United States. All four of these nations held Arkansas territory at one time.

PRESIDENTIAL FOCUS

PRESIDENT # 20: James A. Garfield (1831 – 1881)	
In Office: March 4, 1881 – September 19, 1881	**Political Party:** Republican
Birthplace: Ohio	**Nickname:** "Preacher President"

James Garfield was a Civil War officer who was elected to the U.S. House of Representatives in late 1863, while the war was still going on. As a U.S. Representative from Ohio, Garfield became one of the Radical Republicans of the Reconstruction era who sought to punish the South for its rebellion. Garfield and his wife were both abolitionists and strong Christians.

Garfield had served as President for only two months when he was shot in the back by a former campaign supporter, the mentally unstable Charles Guiteau. Guiteau was an attorney who felt that he deserved to be appointed as a well-paid U.S. ambassador because he had helped Garfield win election as President. When President Garfield failed to appoint him ambassador, Guiteau was angry enough and crazy enough to shoot him.

Garfield's doctors tried to pinpoint the location of the bullet, which was lodged in Garfield's spine, using a metal detector provided by inventor Alexander Graham Bell. Unfortunately, the metal springs of Garfield's bed made the metal detector useless. President Garfield died of infection, blood poisoning and other complications about 2 months after the shooting.

Other interesting facts about James Garfield:
- Garfield was the Union's youngest general during the Civil War.
- Garfield was the first left-handed President.
- Although he came from an extremely poor family, Garfield educated himself thoroughly. He could write Latin with one hand and Greek with the other, all at the same time.
- Garfield produced his own original proof of the Pythagorean Theorem, the ancient mathematical theorem which says that the hypotenuse of a right triangle is equal to the square root of the sum of the squares of the remaining two sides.

Notable quotes from James Garfield:
- "Next in importance to freedom and justice is popular education, without which neither freedom nor justice can be permanently maintained.
- "Poverty is uncomfortable; but nine times out of ten the best thing that can happen to a young man is to be tossed overboard and compelled to sink or swim."

PRESIDENT #21: Chester Alan Arthur (1829 – 1886)	
In Office: September 19, 1881 – March 4, 1885	**Political Party:** Republican
Birthplace: Vermont	**Nickname:** "Gentleman Boss"

Chester Arthur was President Garfield's vice president, so he assumed office when Garfield died, becoming the third President within the single year of 1881. Arthur had been a prominent abolitionist lawyer in New York both before and after the Civil War, and he had served the Union army during the war as one of its best quartermasters (supply managers). Arthur had never before served in elected office when he was surprisingly nominated as James Garfield's vice presidential running mate.

As President, Arthur signed the Pendleton Civil Service Reform Act, which was intended to put a stop to the corrupt practice of doling out government jobs to the people who helped government officials win their election campaigns. Before the Pendleton Act, grateful election winners too often handed out valuable government jobs and appointments to those who had helped them win office, without even considering their qualifications for the jobs. The passage of the Pendleton Act was partly a response to President Garfield's assassination: the unstable assassin, Charles Guiteau, had seen so many corrupt political appointments that he assumed that he, too, was owed one. He shot Garfield for refusing him an appointment as a U.S. ambassador.

Other interesting facts about Chester Arthur:
- Arthur spent a good deal of time in Canada. His political enemies once claimed that he was ineligible to be President because, they said, he had been born in Canada.
- Arthur hired a prominent New York designer named Tiffany to spruce up the dreary White House, spending the modern-day equivalent of about 2 million dollars on the project.
- A man of elegant tastes, Arthur owned over 80 pairs of pants and changed his pants several times a day.
- Arthur suffered from a kidney disease that sapped his energy late in his Presidency. He was not nominated for re-election, and died two years after he left office.

Notable quotes from Chester Arthur:
- "Men may die, but the fabrics of free institutions remains unshaken."
- "If it were not for the reporters, I would tell you the truth."

Chapter 9

The Emergence of Japan, Immigration to the U.S.

U.S. HISTORY FOCUS

IMMIGRATING TO AMERICA

An *immigrant* is someone who "migrates in" to a new area or nation. Since the New World was unknown in Europe before 1492, every European settler and colonist who later moved there was technically an immigrant. European immigration to North America began with the Virginia Company's colony in Jamestown, the Mayflower Pilgrims' settlement in Plymouth, the French settlements in Quebec and the Dutch settlements on Manhattan Island. Perhaps half of all pre-Revolutionary War settlers were indentured servants, poor Europeans who paid for their passage over the ocean with years of service to their employers. And of course, many were slaves from Africa.

The Naturalization Act of 1790

After the United States adopted its Constitution in 1787, it needed laws to establish the procedure for becoming a citizen of the new United States. The first such law was the Naturalization Act of 1790, which established these requirements for new citizens:

- **Personal requirements**: New citizens were required to be "free," "white" and "of good moral character." This meant that no indentured servants, no slaves, no blacks, no American Indians, and no criminals could become citizens.
- **Time of residence**: New citizens were required to live in the United States for two years, and in a single state for one year, before they could apply for U.S. citizenship at their local court.

Anyone who met these requirements could become an official citizen of the United States by going to his or her local court and taking an oath to support the U.S. Constitution. Within a few years, the rules changed to increase the required time of residence: in 1795, it went up to 5 years; and in 1798, it went up to 14 years.

The local courts of the individual U.S. states would continue to handle new citizens in this way for 100 years-- until 1890, when the federal government took control of immigration for the first time by establishing the U.S. Citizenship and Immigration Service.

European Immigration from 1820 – 1920

Over the century from 1820 - 1920, millions of Europeans immigrated to the United States. The people of the different European nationalities tended to stick together when they arrived in the United States, so each nationality created its own clusters in cities across the nation: most American cities had an Irish section, an Italian section and so on.

Crisis after crisis in Europe sent wave after wave of European immigrants to the United States:

- *Irish* **immigrants** came to the U.S. seeking better wages and opportunities. About 2 million Irish immigrated to the U.S. during the years from 1820 - 1860. Great numbers of them worked on such massive construction

projects as the Erie Canal and the Transcontinental Railroad. The 1845 Irish Potato Blight caused a major famine in most of Ireland, and gave poor Irish another reason to ship out to the U.S.
- *German* **immigrants** came to the U.S. to escape their dictatorial German governments. The largest waves of German immigrants arrived during the years from 1840 - 1880. The Revolutions of 1848 failed to produce liberty and democracy in Germany, so disappointed German revolutionaries known as the "forty-eighters" left Germany to seek liberty and democracy in the United States.
- *Italian* **immigrants** came to the U.S. to escape the extreme poverty of southern Italy and Sicily. The largest wave of Italian immigrants arrived between 1880 and 1920.
- *Russian* **immigrants** came to the U.S. to escape the atheistic communism that spread throughout Russia after the 1917 Bolshevik Revolution.
- *Jewish* **immigrants** from several nations, especially Russia, came to the U.S. seeking escape from religious persecution and violent pogroms.
- *Chinese* **immigrants** tried to immigrate to the U.S. for better work and wages, and to escape from the disastrous Taiping Rebellion.

FASCINATING FACTS: The Chinese Exclusion Act of 1882

China's Taiping Rebellion of 1850-1864 was one of history's deadliest wars (see Chapter 13), and many Chinese tried to escape it by leaving China behind. The first Chinese immigrants began to appear in California during the 1848-1855 California Gold Rush (see picture).

More Chinese appeared in California during the 1860s, when the Central Pacific Railroad Company was hiring Chinese laborers to build its end of the Transcontinental Railroad. Up to 10,000 Chinese laborers at a time worked for the Central Pacific Railroad, blasting tunnels, building bridges and laying rails through the mountainous American West. Chinese laborers also worked in mining and farming jobs. The Chinese labored hard and well, and they were usually satisfied with lower wages than white laborers demanded.

Americans had always resented poor immigrants who were willing to work for low wages, but they especially resented the Chinese. Racist Americans called poor Chinese laborers "coolies," and criticized them constantly. In 1870s California, a labor group called the Workingman's Party blamed Chinese coolies for low wages in their state, drumming up opposition to Chinese immigration by repeating this slogan over and over: "The Chinese Must Go!"

Plenty of Americans felt the same way. America's racist, anti-Chinese feelings were so strong that in 1882, Congress passed the first highly restrictive immigration law in U.S. history: the 1882 Chinese Exclusion Act. The Chinese Exclusion Act:

1. banned all Chinese from immigrating to the U.S. for ten years, from 1882 - 1892;
2. prevented Chinese who were already living in the U.S. from becoming naturalized U.S. citizens, and
3. made it more difficult for Chinese who left the U.S. to return.

Congress extended the Chinese Exclusion Act for ten more years in 1892, then extended it again in 1902. Thanks to the Chinese Exclusion Act, Chinese immigration to the United States came to a full stop from 1882 on. Then the Immigration Act of 1917 extended the ban on immigration to all Asians. From 1917 on, Japanese, Koreans and other Asians all faced the same immigration restrictions the Chinese faced.

Congress finally repealed the Chinese Exclusion Act in 1943, when the U.S. and China signed a treaty of alliance during World War II. The Chinese Exclusion Repeal Act of 1943 was intended to soothe a sore spot on the irritated skin of Chinese-American relations, but it still placed heavy limits on Chinese immigration and property rights. The Chinese finally received equal treatment under U.S. immigration law in 1965 (see below).

The Contract Labor Law

During the Industrial age of the late 1800s, large American businesses were always looking for ways to reduce their laborers' wages. For businesses that employed thousands of laborers, even a small decrease in each laborers' hourly wages could save a great deal of money.

One of the tactics such businesses used was to recruit poor European laborers, who were often willing to work for lower wages than Americans demanded. These businesses hired recruiters who traveled to Europe and sought out poor Europeans, offering to pay their travel expenses if they would agree to move to the United States and work for their companies. The wages these companies offered were low; but even so, plenty of Europeans were desperate enough to jump at the chance for a one-way, all-expenses-paid trip to America, the land of opportunity. These poor immigrant laborers became known as "contract laborers" because they signed a contract in which they agreed to work for certain (low) wages in exchange for their free passage to America.

The cheap labor that contract laborers offered was good for businesses and their profits, but bad for American laborers and their wages. When poor immigrants arrived in the United States and offered to labor for low wages, American laborers had to accept lower wages as well or risk losing their jobs.

In 1885, the U.S. Congress passed a new immigration law to protect the wages of American workers: the **Contract Labor Law**. The Contract Labor Law kept new contract laborers out of the United States by forbidding American companies to pay immigrants' travel expenses. Under the Contract Labor Law, there were fewer poor immigrants offering to work for low wages, so Americans could demand higher wages from their employers.

More Restrictions on Immigration

In 1890, the federal government took over responsibility for immigration and established the new Bureau of Citizenship and Immigration Services (BCIS). Federal officers of the BCIS inspected and recorded immigrants at all ports where they entered the United States. Their largest immigration station was at Ellis Island in New York Harbor (see below): about 70 percent of all European immigrants entered the U.S. by way of Ellis Island.

During the early 1900s, immigrants continued to arrive in alarming numbers. By then, there were no more large, unclaimed territories available for settlement; but still, the immigrants kept coming. Within the single year of 1907, more than 1,250,000 immigrants arrived in the United States. Americans began to fear that these overwhelming numbers of immigrants would drive prices up and wages down, dragging America down into the very European poverty that the immigrants were coming to America to escape.

In 1917, Congress passed the first in a series of even more restrictive laws designed to clamp down on immigration to the United States. Like the Chinese Exclusion Act, these new immigration laws limited immigration based on the immigrant's race, and were designed to keep certain "undesirable," unwanted types of immigrants out of the United States:

The **Immigration Act of 1917** altogether banned immigration from a newly established "Asian Barred Zone."

The Asian Barred Zone was an area of the globe that stretched from Turkey and the Arabian Peninsula, through India and southeast Europe, all the way to China and Indonesia. The Immigration Act of 1917 extended the Chinese Exclusion Act to all Asians. Japanese, Koreans and many other nationalities were all forbidden to become U.S. citizens. The Act also banned illiterates (those who couldn't read and write) over the age of 16, along with several other types of "undesirables."

The **Emergency Quota Act of 1921** introduced the new idea of "proportional immigration."

Proportional immigration meant that the United States wanted to maintain the mix of races that it already had; it did not want a flood of immigrants from "undesirable" races to upset its racial balance. The U.S. was a mostly white nation, and it wanted to remain a mostly white nation.

The Emergency Quota Act set a quota for yearly immigrants from each foreign nation at three percent of the number from that nation that was already present in the United States. It based its numbers on the most recent finished census, the Census of 1910. For example, if the Census of 1910 showed that the United States contained 1,000,000 Italian-born citizens, then the Emergency Quota Act would allow 30,000 Italians (3% of 1,000,000) to enter the United States each year.

The **Immigration Act of 1924** introduced the "National Origins Formula" that would guide U.S. immigration law for the next forty years.

The National Origins Formula reduced the immigrant quotas laid out in the Emergency Quota Act: It set the new quota for immigrants from each foreign nation at two percent of the number from that nation already present in the U.S. It also introduced a new wrinkle: Instead of basing its quotas on numbers from the Census of 1910, it based them on the earlier Census of 1890, which was taken before too many "undesirable" immigrants had arrived in the United States.

For example, suppose that there were 1,000,000 Italians living in the United States in 1910, but that there had been only 500,000 in 1890. The 30,000 yearly Italian immigrants that would have been allowed under the 1921 Emergency Quota Act would be cut to just 10,000 (2% of 500,000) under the National Origins Formula.

The Immigration Act of 1924 also limited total immigrants from all nations to 150,000 per year. This was far lower than the years before 1920, some of which had seen more than one million immigrants. The total ban on Asian immigrants also continued under the Immigration Act of 1924.

The Immigration and Nationality Act of 1965

The civil rights movement of the 1950s and the 1960s changed Americans' attitudes about racism and discrimination (see Chapter 32). During the early 1960s, Americans began to feel that the National Origins Formula was a racist formula that they could no longer support. Even so, they still wanted to limit the total number of immigrants to the U.S. each year.

The **Immigration and Nationality Act of 1965** finally abolished the National Origins Formula and set a new limit of 300,000 total immigrants per year. This new law allowed 170,000 immigrants from the Eastern Hemisphere, 130,000 from the Western Hemisphere and no more than 20,000 from any one nation. President Lyndon Johnson symbolically signed the Immigration and Nationality Act at Liberty Island, remarking that the National Origins Formula had been "un-American" and that the new law corrected "a cruel and enduring wrong in the conduct of the American nation."

FASCINATING FACTS: Ellis Island

Ellis Island was the United States' largest federal immigration station from 1892-1954. Over the course of those 62 years, about twelve million immigrants entered the U.S. by way of Ellis Island. Crossing the Atlantic Ocean by ship, they entered New York Harbor and passed by the Statue of Liberty on their way to Ellis Island and a new life in the United States.

Not every immigrant who arrived in New York passed through Ellis Island. Those who could afford first or second class tickets were often processed aboard ship and placed ashore in New York or New Jersey, on the theory that the wealthy were unlikely to end up as charity cases. Ellis Island was for the third class ticket holders, the "steerage" passengers who rode in the bowels of the ship— the poor.

Prospective immigrants at Ellis Island had to answer a list of 29 questions so that inspectors could determine their fitness to enter the U.S. They also had to pass a "six-second physical" from a doctor trained to spot major health problems quickly. Not everyone was admitted; applicants for entry could be rejected if they suffered contagious disease or seemed likely to end up as charity cases. Those who failed the admission examinations would suffer the disappointment of starting the long journey back home. For them, Ellis Island would become the "Island of Tears."

The role of Ellis Island changed as immigration laws became more restrictive. After the U.S. began to establish more permanent embassies overseas, those embassies issued visas for prospective immigrants, and Ellis Island processed fewer and fewer immigrants. After the National Origins Act of 1924 became law, the only immigrants processed at Ellis Island were war refugees or other displaced persons.

AMAZING AMERICANS: Jane Addams (1860 – 1935) and Hull House

Jane Addams was a wealthy Illinois woman who founded Hull House, an immigrant aid center in Chicago. Addams was a Universalist Christian who believed in the "social gospel," a gospel that was more concerned with meeting the daily needs of the poor than with converting them to Christianity.

Addams founded Hull House in 1889 as a place where poor immigrants could find a bowl of soup, English lessons and help finding work. Women who went to Hull House could also find rooms to rent, a safe place to hide from abusive husbands and a safe place for their children. Hull House built a playground and offered day care and kindergarten classes. It also offered free medical care for mothers and infants. At

its peak around 1900-1920, Hull House assisted as many as 2,000 immigrants per week.

Hull House was an example of a "settlement house," a model community designed by believers in the social gospel. In the ideal settlement house, the wealthy, educated and privileged people of a community would live alongside the community's poor, illiterate and underprivileged. The educated would share their knowledge, helping the poor and uneducated to elevate themselves. Jane Addams and her helpers at Hull House did just that, living among the immigrants and helping them overcome their problems so that they could prosper in America. Addams was an early example of the modern-day social worker.

Jane Addams won the 1931 Nobel Peace Prize for her work with the poor of Chicago.

WORLD HISTORY FOCUS

JAPAN

What Has Gone Before

For thousands of years, from ancient times through modern times, Japan has always had an emperor, or *Tenno*. Tenno Jimmu founded the Japanese Empire around 660 BC, and every Tenno since has supposedly been descended from Jimmu. Japanese Tennos rule from the Chrysanthemum Throne, which is the symbolic seat of the Tennos' power rather than an actual chair. All Tennos are said to be descended from the Shinto Sun Goddess Amaterasu.

For most of those years, however, the power of the Tennos has been more symbolic than real. The Tennos concerned themselves with lofty matters suited to the descendants of gods, while Buddhist priests, court nobles or mighty warlords conducted the more mundane business of governing Japan.

Japan's Feudal Age

Through the Medieval era and into the early Modern era, powerful lords called *daimyos* governed Japan. Like the feudal lords of Europe, the daimyos owned enormous tracts of land, and reigned over that land and its people like kings. The daimyos' "knights" were the *shoguns*, warlords who governed in the name of their daimyos, and the *samurai*, the shoguns' chief military officers. The age of the daimyos, from 1185-1868, is known as "Japan's feudal age" because it was similar to Europe's feudal age.

The Tokugawa Shogunate (1603 – 1868)

Near the end of Japan's feudal age, the powerful *Tokugawa* shoguns took control of Japan. Because the Tokugawa governed Japan from their capital city at Edo (modern-day Tokyo), their time in power was known as the Edo Period. The Tokugawa government was known as the *bakufu*, or military government.

"TAKAMIKURA," THE SPECIAL SEAT USED BY THE EMPEROR AT THE ENTHRONEMENT.

The Tokugawa Shoguns guarded their power jealously by requiring lower-ranking daimyos to spend part of each year in Edo. In this way, they could keep an eye on the lesser lords and make sure that they weren't trying to lead rebellions (French King Louis XIV used the same strategy to control his nobles, forcing them to spend part of each year at the Palace of Versailles).

The Tokugawa shoguns enforced a strict feudal system that divided the Japanese people into four classes:

1. Shoguns, daimyo and samurai,
2. Farmers,
3. Artisans, and
4. Lowly, greedy merchants.

A Japanese person's class was usually set for life; the Japanese rarely moved between classes.

FASCINATING FACTS: The Four Classes of Japanese Feudalism

The four classes of Japanese feudalism were based on Confucian philosophy, not on wealth as the European classes were. Peasant farmers ranked second, behind the ruling class, because they produced the food and raw materials needed for life. Artisans ranked third, behind farmers, because they only worked with the materials provided by farmers. Merchants ranked at the bottom because they produced nothing, but only benefited from the work of farmers and artisans.

This four-tiered system was more idealistic than practical. In real life, merchants grew wealthy and exercised a great deal of power over farmers and artisans, even though farmers and artisans supposedly outranked them.

Sakoku

For more than 200 years, from 1633-1853, the Tokugawa Shoguns' desire for absolute control was so strong that they decided to isolate Japan from outside influences as strictly as possible. These two centuries of Japanese isolation were known as *Sakoku*.

Sakoku was partly a reaction to the Spanish and Portuguese Catholic missionaries who had begun moving to Japan and trying to convert the Japanese to Christianity. The shoguns were well aware of what had happened when the Spanish and Portuguese explorers conquered the New World, and they did not want Japan to end up as another Spanish or Portuguese colony like Paraguay or Brazil. So the shoguns took several steps against Catholic missionaries in Japan: they

1. Expelled the missionaries;
2. Banned Christianity; and
3. Isolated their island nation as strictly as possible from all foreign influences.

Under Sakoku, Japan was cut off from the outside world: foreigners could not enter Japan, and Japanese could not leave Japan. The shoguns did allow some trade with Dutch, Chinese and Korean merchants; but these merchants were not allowed to come ashore on Japan's main islands. Instead, they traded on certain small islands set aside for them. The Japanese were likely to fire upon foreign ships that came too close to their shores, and they were unlikely to help any foreign sailors who had the misfortune to shipwreck near their shores.

The Tokugawa Shoguns' two-centuries-long *Sakoku* isolation came to an abrupt end with the arrival of four U.S. Navy gunboats under the leadership of American Commodore Matthew Perry.

Commodore Matthew Perry's Japan Expedition (1852 – 1854)

Merchants all over the world wanted to trade in the Far East, and American merchants were no exception. Certain goods were available only in the Far East, and merchants who could not trade freely with the Far East were at the mercy of those who could. American merchants wanted to open Japan to American trade so that they could trade freely there without fear of attacks from angry Japanese.

The desire for Far East trade was one peaceable reason for opening Japan; but there were also military reasons. By the mid-1800s, the young United States was becoming more involved in world affairs. The need to defend U.S. businesses in Central and South America created a cascading series of other needs:

1. The Monroe Doctrine, introduced by President James Monroe in 1823, promised that the U.S. military would defend Central and South America against any European nation that tried to interfere there.
2. In order to enforce the Monroe Doctrine, the U.S. needed a powerful navy with which to defend South and Central America.
3. In order to be truly powerful, the American navy needed the ability to operate all over the Pacific Ocean, so that it could (1) oppose powerful European navies if necessary, (2) defend U.S.-flagged trade ships against piracy and (3) defend America's coast.
4. In order to operate all over the vast reaches of the Pacific Ocean, the American navy's steam ships needed access to coal at convenient ports. By 1848, the U.S. had secured Pacific Ocean coaling ports in California and Hawaii. It needed access to a coaling port in East Asia, and Japan had coal.

The man the U.S. government assigned to negotiate a trade agreement with closed Japan was Commodore Matthew Perry (see picture). Commodore Perry's four U.S. Navy gunboats steamed and sailed into Edo (Tokyo) Bay on July 8, 1853, loaded with gifts for Japanese ambassadors and carrying a letter for the emperor from President Millard Fillmore. They were also loaded with guns and ammunition: Perry's ships carried a total of 52 guns, many of which fired explosive shells.

When the Perry expedition arrived at Edo Harbor, it was instantly surrounded by smaller Japanese ships; however, the expedition had no reason to fear, because Japan's backward junks were no match for America's modern, steam-driven warships. An earlier American expedition captain had ruined his mission by allowing Japanese marine troops to board his ships, but Perry was ready for the Japanese this time: He armed his men and refused to allow any Japanese marines to board.

Perry demanded a meeting with a high Japanese official, either the Emperor himself or his representative, so that he could deliver President Fillmore's letter and discuss a trade agreement. Under the threat of Perry's guns, the shoguns were powerless to refuse him. He went ashore to meet with one of the shoguns, delivered his letter, and then departed to allow the shoguns to consider America's offer. Commodore Perry and his ships spent the winter of 1853 - 1854 near the coast of China.

When Perry returned to Japan during the following spring, he led 8 or 9 ships with a total of about 144 guns. By now, the Japanese had decided to negotiate. At the Convention of Kanagawa on March 31, 1854, Japan and the United States signed a "Treaty of Peace and Amity" that opened Japan to American trade, allowed Americans to purchase Japanese coal and promised fair treatment for American traders and ships. Japan soon signed similar treaties with several European nations. In 1854, Sakoku was over, Japan was open once more, and free trade was the new rule in Japan.

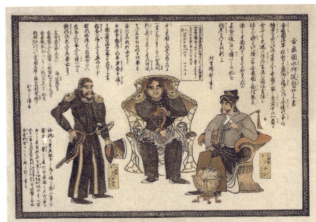

Picture shows a Japanese artist's rendition of Commodore Perry and two other navy officers who negotiated with the Japanese

Other interesting facts about Commodore Perry's Japan Expedition:

- On his first trip to Japan, Perry led three rigged sidewheel steamers and one heavily-armed sail-driven sloop of war. His rigged sidewheel steamers had steam boilers, smokestacks and paddlewheels that jutted from their sides, but they also had three masts that could be filled with sails.
- Most Japanese had never seen steam ships, and some thought that the smoke coming from the ships' stacks meant that Perry's steamers were on fire. They called the steamers the "Black Ships," and some Japanese still hold "Black Ship Festivals" to commemorate Perry's expedition and the opening of Japan.
- Perry's expedition is one of many examples of "gunboat diplomacy," in which powerful nations force weaker ones to negotiate under the threat of cannon.

The Meiji Restoration (1868 – 1912)

Meiji is Japanese for "enlightened rule." After Japan reopened in 1854, some of Japan's daimyos began to understand that Japan was far behind the Western world in technology and learning, and wanted to catch up. The period of years Japan spent catching up with the West, from 1868 - 1912), became known as the Meiji Restoration.

The Boshin War

In 1867, a new, 15-year-old emperor named Mutsuhito ascended the Chrysanthemum Throne and became Japan's Tenno. By the following year, 1868, Tenno Mutsuhito had gained the support of enough powerful daimyos to challenge the Tokugawa shoguns for power. In the 1868 Boshin War, Mutsuhito and his daimyos captured the Tokugawa shoguns' capital at Edo and took control of Japan. Tenno Mutsuhito renamed Edo "Tokyo" and established his Meiji (enlightenment) government there.

Catching Up with the West

The Meiji government's motto was *fukoku kyohei*: "Enrich the country, strengthen the military." Tenno Mutsuhito wanted Japan's technology to catch up with the West's as quickly as possible. He abolished the feudal system of four classes, and instead encouraged all types of Japanese to become involved in the government, the military and industry. He forced the daimyos to surrender their claims to their former lands, and took their place as Japan's highest power.

Under Tenno Mutsuhito, Japan's central government was more powerful than it had ever been under the daimyos. The Meiji government insisted on education for all of its citizens (compulsory education), and Japanese scholars even traveled abroad to study Western science and languages. The Japanese would prove to be fast learners, and Japanese technology and industry would soon achieve Tenno Mutsuhito's dream of catching up with the West. After his death, Mutsuhito would be known in Japan as the Meiji Emperor.

German Influence on Japan

When the Meiji government began work on its first written constitution in 1884, it chose Otto von Bismarck's Prussian constitution as its model. When the Meiji government finally adopted Japan's new constitution in 1889, it created a government much like Prussia's: a constitutional monarchy with a weak elected parliament and a small group of powerful ministers chosen by the emperor.

Bismarck's Prussian influence helped to make the new Japan both (1) *militarist*, devoted to military might, and (2) *nationalist*, patriotically devoted to Japan. Germany's influence on Japan would continue until it led to a national disaster at the end of World War II (see Chapter 26).

FASCINATING FACTS: The Satsuma Rebellion (1877)

The Satsuma *han* (or domain) was home to a large number of samurais who were powerful in the Meiji government. Two Satsuma samurais, Okubo Toshimichi and Saigo Takamori, were among the "three great nobles" who joined Tenno Mutsuhito and helped him lead the Meiji Restoration when it began in 1868. As the Meiji Restoration went on, however, some of the Satsuma samurai began to resist the rapid changes in the Japanese government that were robbing the samurai of their power and wealth.

Japanese samurai obeyed a strict code of honor known as *bushido*, and nothing was more important to the samurai than honor. In 1873, samurai Saigo Takamori wanted to defend Japan's honor by attacking Korea, which he felt had insulted Japan by refusing to recognize Tenno Mutsuhito as emperor. Samurai Okubo Toshimichi opposed Saigo's idea because he felt that Japan was not yet ready to fight a war overseas: Okubo feared that an international war might draw in more advanced nations, giving them an excuse to defeat and capture Japan. Disgusted by Okubo's cowardice, Saigo resigned his office in the government and returned home, taking with him a number of other Satsuma samurai who were feeling as rebellious as he was.

In January 1877, Saigo led his Satsuma samurai in a revolt against the Meiji government. The rebel samurai used modern weapons like the ones the government used, but they were soon overwhelmed by far larger government forces. Like all *bushido*-following samurai, the Satsumas preferred the honor of suicide (by ritual *seppuku* or *hara-kiri*) to the shame of defeat. Soon after the Satsumas' last stand began at the Battle of Shiroyama, Saigo died, either from a bullet wound or by seppuku. With no weapons left to them but their swords, the last forty or so Satsuma samurai bravely charged an imperial government force armed with Gatling guns. The Satsuma Rebellion ended when they all died in a hail of bullets.

FASCINATING FACTS: Noh Masks

Japanese theater actors often use elaborate masks. The most artistic of these are the Noh Masks used in *Noh* plays, slow-paced traditional dramas focused on one main, mask-wearing character. This main character usually does not speak, but instead expresses himself through movement. Some Noh masks are cleverly designed to convey different emotions depending upon the angle from which the viewer sees them (see picture). They represent about five types of characters: gods, demons, men, women and the elderly.

Noh masks cover only the front of the face and have small holes for the eyes, nostrils and mouth. They are lightweight, because actors must wear them throughout a performance that can last for several hours.

MISSIONARY FOCUS

FASCINATING FACTS: *Kirishitans* and *Fumie*

Catholic missionaries from Portugal and Spain moved into Japan during the 1500s. The Japanese called them *Kirishitans*, a Japanese version of the word "Christians." Most of these missionaries were Jesuits, extremely strict Catholics (one famous Jesuit who visited Japan was St. Francis Xavier). The Jesuits were as successful in Japan as they had been in other parts of the world; and by 1600, they had converted as many as 300,000 Japanese to Catholic Christianity.

However, the Jesuits' tactics made the Japanese shoguns wary of them. Jesuit missions were more like fortified towns than churches, and Jesuits sometimes hired troops to advance their gospel. In places like Paraguay, South America, Jesuits acted as if they were Spain's colonial government, controlling the local population and keeping Paraguayan natives in their lowly places. The shoguns had no intention of allowing Japan to become a Portuguese or Spanish colony, so they decided to seal off Japan against these dangerous foreigners. After persecuting Christians for years, the Tokugawa shoguns finally initiated *Sakoku* in the 1630s by closing Japan, banning Christianity and ejecting the Jesuit *Kirishitans*.

Even before *Sakoku* began, the shoguns set about erasing Christian influence from Japan. In order to discover which Japanese were *Kirishitans*, the shoguns subjected suspects to a trial: they showed suspected Christians a carved image of Christ or the Virgin Mary, then asked them to trample it. The carved image was called a *fumie*.

Non-*Kirishitans* would trample the *fumie* willingly, but baptized *Kirishitans* were extremely reluctant to step on the symbols of their faith's most revered figures. Just like the persecuted Roman Christians of the early church, Japanese *Kirishitans* had to decide: should they deny their faith, trample the *fumie* and live on, or should they confess their Christian faith and possibly die for it, becoming martyrs? Among the many who refused to trample the *fumie* were the Twenty-Six Martyrs of Japan, whom the shoguns crucified and speared (like Christ) at Nagasaki in 1597.

After Japan reopened in 1854, Christian missionaries began to return there, even though seeking converts (proselytizing) was still illegal. Returning Catholic priests were stunned to find that there were still secret groups of baptized *Kirishitans* in Japan, even after more than two centuries of Sakoku isolation. These "hidden Christians" were called *Kakure Kirishitans*, and some of them still live in Japan, spiritual descendants of the Jesuits' first Christian converts there. The *Kakure Kirishitans'* largest community is around Nagasaki.

Freedom of religion came to Japan in 1871, during the Meiji Restoration.

U.S. GEOGRAPHY FOCUS

FASCINATING FACTS about MICHIGAN:

- <u>Statehood</u>: Michigan became the 26th US state on January 26, 1837
- <u>Bordering states/bodies of water/country</u>: Wisconsin, Ohio, Indiana, Minnesota (across Lake Superior), Canada and four of the five Great Lakes: Lake Erie, Lake Huron, Lake Michigan and Lake Superior. Michigan is actually made up of two peninsulas.
- <u>State capital</u>: Lansing
- <u>Area</u>: 96,716 sq. mi. (Ranks 11th in size)
- <u>Abbreviation</u>: MI
- <u>State nickname</u>: Wolverine State
- <u>State Bird</u>: Robin
- <u>State tree</u>: Eastern White Pine
- <u>State flower</u>: Apple Blossom
- <u>State song</u>: *Michigan, My Michigan*
- <u>State Motto</u>: "If you are seeking a pleasant peninsula, look around you"
- <u>Meaning of name</u>: *Michigan* is based on a Chippewa Indian word that means "Great Water" or "Large Lake"
- <u>Historic places to visit in Michigan</u>: The Mackinac Bridge, Sleeping Bear Dunes, Seul Choix Point Lighthouse, Iron County Historical Museum, Automotive Hall Of Fame, Alcona Park

The Mackinac Bridge

- <u>Resources and Industries</u>: auto manufacturing, farming (corn, soybeans, vegetables, apples, livestock), tourism, furniture, machinery, food processing, ore transportation and processing

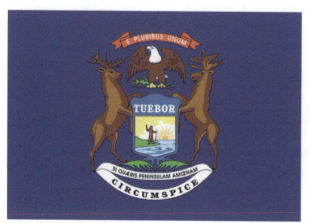

Flag of Michigan
- Michigan adopted this flag in 1911.
- It contains three different mottos, all in Latin: "Out of many, one" (in honor of the USA), "I will Defend" and "If You Seek a Pleasant Peninsula, Look Around" (the state motto).
- The elk and the moose on the flag are symbols of Michigan, and the eagle is the symbol of the USA.

PRESIDENTIAL FOCUS

PRESIDENT #22 and 24: Grover Cleveland (1837 – 1908)	
In Office: March 4, 1885 – March 4, 1889 and March 4, 1893 – March 4, 1897	**Political Party:** Democratic
Birthplace: New Jersey	**Nickname:** "His Obstinacy"

Grover Cleveland was a former Governor of New York who became the only President to serve two non-consecutive terms. President Benjamin Harrison served a single term as President between Cleveland's two terms.

Cleveland believed that a large part of the President's job was to prevent Congress from passing too many laws, especially spending laws intended to dole out federal money to the poor and needy. He believed that private charities, not the government, should help the poor and the needy, so he refused to sign relief bills designed to aid the poor. He rarely proposed legislation of his own, and he vetoed bills passed by Congress 584 times. Cleveland's frequent, ready use of the Presidential veto earned him the nickname "His Obstinacy."

Other interesting facts about Grover Cleveland:
- Cleveland avoided service in the Civil War by paying a Polish immigrant to serve in his place. This practice was legal in the Union and common among the wealthy, even if it was not precisely heroic.
- Cleveland became the only President to be wed in the White House when he married a 21-year-old recent college graduate, the daughter of a former law partner. He himself was 49.
- The Baby Ruth candy bar was named for Cleveland's daughter, Ruth, who was born in 1891.
- Cleveland secretly underwent cancer surgery on his mouth in 1893. The surgery was performed on board a yacht, and was kept so quiet that that it remained a secret until 1917, years after his death.

Notable quotes from Grover Cleveland:
- "I know there is a Supreme Being who rules the affairs of men and whose goodness and mercy have always followed the American people, and I know He will not turn from us now if we humbly and reverently seek His powerful aid."
- "Honor lies in honest toil."
- "Though the people support the government, the government should not support the people."

PRESIDENT #23: Benjamin Harrison (1833 – 1901)	
In Office: March 4, 1889 – March 4, 1893	**Political Party:** Republican
Birthplace: Ohio	**Nickname:** "Kid Gloves Harrison"

Benjamin Harrison was the grandson of the ninth President, William Henry Harrison. He served a single term as a Republican President between the two terms of Democratic President Grover Cleveland.

Harrison was the first of several Presidents who believed that the United States needed more regulations to control big businesses and foreign trade. He supported the high McKinley Tariff of 1890 on foreign imports, and won more authority for himself and future Presidents to negotiate trade agreements with foreign nations. He also supported the Sherman Antitrust Act of 1890, which gave future governments the power to prevent giant businesses from cornering markets and fixing prices to their advantage. President Theodore

Roosevelt would make great use of the Sherman Antitrust Act in the early 1900s.

Harrison ran for re-election in 1892, but he was distracted throughout the election campaign by his wife's illness. His wife died just before the election of 1892, and Harrison lost to Grover Cleveland. A grief-stricken President Harrison told his family that he felt as if his election loss had freed him from imprisonment.

Other interesting facts about Benjamin Harrison:
- Harrison's great-grandfather, Benjamin Harrison V, was one of the signers of the Declaration of Independence.
- When Harrison signed the bills admitting North and South Dakota to the Union as states, he shuffled them so that no one could know which was the 39th state and which was the 40th.
- When electric lights were first installed in the White House, Harrison was afraid to touch the switches, so the lights burned all night.
- Because of a sensitive skin condition, Harrison often wore gloves made of soft kid leather. His kid leather gloves earned him the nickname "Kid Gloves Harrison."

Notable quotes from Benjamin Harrison:
- "The bud of victory is always in the truth."
- "I pity the man who wants a coat so cheap that the man or woman who produces the cloth will starve in the process."
- "No other people have a government more worthy of their respect and love or a land so magnificent in extent, so pleasant to look upon, and so full of generous suggestion to enterprise and labor."

Chapter 10

Women's Suffrage, Prohibition, Colonizing Indonesia, Reform and Relapse in the Ottoman Empire

U.S. HISTORY FOCUS

WOMEN'S SUFFRAGE

The Struggle for Women's Voting Rights in the United States

The Fifteenth Amendment to the U.S. Constitution was one of three "Reconstruction amendments" passed by the Radical Republicans in Congress after the Civil War. Ratified in 1870, the Fifteenth Amendment prohibited anyone from denying a citizen the right to vote because of his "race, color or previous condition of servitude." It was designed to grant freed slaves the right to vote, especially in the South, where Republicans would get few votes if freed slaves were not allowed to vote.

But the Fifteenth Amendment failed to mention another class of people who were also disqualified from voting: women. The amendment was silent on the issue of gender. By tradition, women did not vote in the United States; but long before 1870, some American women were ready to break that tradition.

FASCINATING FACTS: Women's Suffrage and the Nineteenth Amendment

The first women's rights convention in the United States took place in 1848 at Seneca Falls, New York. The 68 women and 32 men of the Seneca Falls convention produced a "Declaration of Sentiments" that was modeled on the Declaration of Independence. Like that Declaration, the Seneca Falls declaration began with "When, in the course of human events..." It went on to list fourteen grievances against the unequal treatment of women under the law, and then presented twelve resolutions that requested equal rights and voting rights for women.

From the beginning, the women's rights movement was friendly with the Abolitionist movement. The same important figures moved in both circles: Abolitionist heroes like Frederick Douglass and Harriet Tubman also supported women's rights; and women's rights heroes like Susan B. Anthony and Elizabeth Cady Stanton also supported Abolition before the Civil War.

However, this friendly association quickly crumbled over the issue of the Fifteenth Amendment. Women's rights supporters like Anthony and Stanton wanted the Fifteenth Amendment to grant voting rights to women as well as to free slaves; but Abolitionists like Douglass supported the amendment as it was proposed, without women's voting rights. To the Abolitionists, the passage of an amendment granting equal voting rights to former slaves was the fulfillment of a dream. They feared that demanding women's voting rights as well might endanger their dream, so they refused to join the women's rights movement in holding out for women's voting rights. The debate over the Fifteenth Amendment drove a wedge between the former allies: after that debate, Anthony and Stanton stopped working for black rights, and started working for women's rights alone.

On Election Day in 1872, Susan B. Anthony

marched into her local polling place and voted for every Republican candidate on the ballot, including President Ulysses S. Grant, who was running for reelection. Two weeks later, she was arrested. At her trial, the court convicted her of violating election law and fined her one hundred dollars. Anthony vowed never to pay her fine, and she never did.

Anthony and Stanton were the founders of the National Woman Suffrage Association, which wrote a women's suffrage amendment to the U.S. Constitution and worked to get it passed in Congress. A parallel organization, the American Woman Suffrage Association, worked to pass women's suffrage amendments in the individual states.

In 1890, the two organizations merged to form the National American Woman Suffrage Association (NAWSA). NAWSA had its first major success in 1893, when Colorado amended its constitution to allow women's voting rights. Several other states, most of them western ones, soon joined Colorado and began allowing women's voting rights as well.

Over the next thirty years, the suffragists of NAWSA staged demonstrations and hunger strikes to make more Americans aware of their grievances and demands. Their ultimate victory came in 1920 with the ratification of the Nineteenth Amendment to the U.S. Constitution:

"The right of citizens of the United States to vote shall not be denied or abridged by the United States or by any State on account of sex. Congress shall have power to enforce this article by appropriate legislation."

Common arguments against women's suffrage, as voiced by anti-Suffragists (not actual quotes):

1. "The woman's place is in the home! Politics is a man's business."
2. "Delicate women should not be exposed to the ugliness of politics."
3. "Women are not sufficiently educated about politics to make an intelligent vote."
4. "Women are too emotional! The stress of voting will upset them and lead them to make irrational decisions."
5. "As the head of the family, the man is responsible to cast the family's vote. A woman will only echo the vote of her husband or father, so women's suffrage won't change the election results."
6. "Allowing women to vote will tear apart the fabric of the family, especially if women decide to vote in opposition to their husbands or fathers."
7. "Women are too compassionate. Their sympathetic hearts will lead them to give away public money or to unfairly regulate behaviors of questionable morality such as drinking and gambling."

The United States granted its female citizens the right to vote in all federal and state elections when it ratified the 19th Amendment to the U.S. Constitution on August 18, 1920.

AMAZING AMERICANS: Helen Keller (1880 – 1968)

Alabama-born Helen Keller was only nineteen months old when an illness, possibly scarlet fever, destroyed both her eyesight and her hearing. At the age of seven Helen was sharp-minded, but unable to learn without eyes or ears to help her. Helen's mother found a teacher for her in the person of Anne Sullivan, a 20-year old former student at Boston's Perkins Institute for the Blind who was herself partially blind. Anne taught Helen her first words by signing into her open palm.

Once Helen figured out what words were, she learned quickly. She attended the Perkins Institute for the Blind herself, followed by two schools for the deaf. At eighteen, she entered the Cambridge School for Young Ladies, a mainstream school not set aside for the deaf or the blind. At twenty, she entered Radcliffe University, the Cambridge, Massachusetts sister school to Harvard University. There, she became the first deaf and blind person to earn a bachelor's degree.

Helen Keller turned out to be a talented writer. Two of her autobiographical works, *The Story of My Life* and *The World I Live In*, told the world about her brave struggles and successes in overcoming her disabilities. Her life story was inspiring to a world that was beginning to understand the evils of prejudice against the weak and disadvantaged.

PROHIBITION

The Temperance Movement in the United States

"Temperance" means "moderation," especially moderation in drinking alcohol. The Temperance Movement in the United States was a well-organized effort to discourage heavy drinking and the many problems that it caused, problems such as alcoholism, poverty, child abuse and wife abuse. The movement reached its peak with the 1919 ratification of the 18th Amendment to the U.S. Constitution, which banned the "manufacture, sale or transportation of intoxicating liquors" throughout the U.S. and its territories. The Prohibition of alcohol in the United States would last from 1920 - 1933.

The Drunkards Progress by Nathaniel Currier

Many of the same people who supported women's rights also supported the Temperance Movement. Some were battered women who suffered abuse from their alcoholic husbands. Others were suffragists like Susan B. Anthony, who saw the ill effects of alcoholism as she labored among poor women during her work for women's rights. Religious figures like Lyman Beecher, the minister father of Harriet Beecher Stowe, spoke out against the dangers of alcohol as early as the 1820s.

Some supporters of temperance followed Transcendentalist writers like Ralph Waldo Emerson and Henry Thoreau, who emphasized self-improvement and high moral standards. Others were believers in the "social gospel" who sought to imitate Christ by helping the poor. Social gospel believers tended to concern themselves more with improving conditions for the poor than with converting the poor to Christianity. Later, most Temperance supporters were also "progressives," people who believed in battling social problems like alcoholism and poverty by banning alcohol and creating government-funded programs to help the poor.

The Anti-Saloon League

As the Temperance Movement began to gain traction among politicians, certain cities, counties and states began passing local laws that banned alcohol. Areas that banned alcohol were known as "dry" areas.

The Anti-Saloon League, formed in 1893, wanted to make the entire nation dry. The Anti-Saloon League published temperance literature and badgered politicians until a majority of congressmen were finally ready to support a temperance amendment to the U.S. Constitution. When the 18th Amendment took effect in 1920, the entire U.S. and all of its territories supposedly became "dry."

The 18th Amendment to the U.S. Constitution banned the "manufacture, sale or transportation of intoxicating liquors" in the United States and its territories. The amendment was ratified on January 16, 1919 and took effect one year later on January 16, 1920.

Determined Drinkers and Gangsters

Unfortunately, staying dry was not as easy as it sounded. As some dry states had already discovered, banning alcohol seemed to make drinkers all the more determined to drink. City drinkers found their alcohol in half-hidden public drinking houses called "speakeasies," named for their secretive nature; tens of thousands of speakeasies sprang up all over the United States. Country drinkers sometimes quietly distilled their own alcohol from corn, sugar or even wood.

Since making and selling alcohol was against the law during Prohibition, only outlaws made and sold alcohol. "Moonshiners" distilled alcohol in hidden stills at night, by the light of the moon (see pictures); and organized crime gangs in Chicago grew wealthy importing alcohol from Canada by way of Lake Michigan. These gangs controlled all alcohol shipments into their territories, and fought over the best territories. Notorious organized crime bosses Al Capone, Lucky Luciano, Bugs Moran and Bugsy Siegel were only a few among dozens of well-known gangsters of the Prohibition Era.

The Bureau of Prohibition

To combat the illegal alcohol business, the federal government established a new law enforcement agency called the Bureau of Prohibition. At first, the Bureau of Prohibition was part of the Bureau of Internal Revenue, the same agency that was responsible for collecting federal taxes. Moonshiners knew Prohibition agents as "Revenuers." A well-known Prohibition Agent named Eliot Ness battled alcohol importers in Chicago and elsewhere. Ness's unit earned the nickname "The Untouchables" because its agents refused to accept the bribes offered to law officers by one of the biggest crime bosses of all, Al Capone (see picture).

Capone was also involved in another well-known incident, one that helped change America's attitude about Prohibition. After one of Capone's competitors, Bugs Moran, stole some of his alcohol shipments, Capone decided to set a trap for Moran. On February 14, Valentine's Day, 1929, Capone's crime gang lured seven men from Moran's gang inside a north side Chicago garage and shot them all to death with Thompson sub-machine guns (tommy guns). This murderous ambush became known as the St. Valentine's Day Massacre, and it demonstrated to Americans just how lawless their nation had become under Prohibition.

The End of Prohibition

Americans also recognized an ironic truth: that crimes bosses like Capone and Moran could never have become so wealthy and powerful if they hadn't had so many willing customers. The problem with Prohibition was that too many Americans still wanted alcohol, whether it was illegal or not. The Anti-Saloon League had convinced Americans' minds that banning alcohol was a good idea, but Americans' hearts remained unconvinced: too many of them still enjoyed the relaxation that alcohol offered. During the late 1920s, public opinion turned against Prohibition, and lawmakers began to consider repealing prohibition laws.

In 1933, the 21st Amendment completely repealed the 18th Amendment, and alcohol was legal in the United States once more (although local laws still banned it in places). When President Franklin Roosevelt signed a new law allowing beer manufacturers to return to work, he famously remarked, "I think this would be a good time for a beer."

> The 21st Amendment to the U.S. Constitution completely repealed the 18th Amendment, which had outlawed "intoxicating liquors." The amendment was ratified on December 5, 1933.

Other interesting facts about Prohibition:

- One Temperance advocate, a woman named Carrie Nation, became well-known for carrying a hatchet into public drinking houses and using it to smash furniture and bottles of alcohol.
- The Prohibition Party, a political party founded in 1869 to promote candidates who supported Prohibition, still backs a Presidential candidate in every major election.
- Because some temperance advocates believed that easy access to cool drinking water would lead to less reliance on alcohol, public drinking fountains known as *temperance fountains* sprang up all over the U.S. Several temperance fountains included a statue of *Hebe*, cup-bearer to the Greek gods.

WORLD HISTORY FOCUS

INDONESIA

FASCINATING FACTS: The Dutch East India Company and the Dutch East Indies

The Netherlands chartered the Dutch East India Company in 1602 to compete with its English counterpart, the British East India Company (see Chapter 1). Known by its Dutch initials, VOC, the Dutch East India Company established successful trading posts all over Indonesia (a large group of islands south of China), as well as in Africa, India, and the Middle East. During Japan's Sakoku (isolation) era, the Netherlands was the only European nation that was allowed to trade with Japan (see Chapter 9).

Like the British EIC, the Dutch VOC controlled territory around its trading posts and factories in order to keep them safe and productive. The Netherlands authorized the VOC to field armies, negotiate treaties and conduct business with surrounding territories just as if it were an independent nation. Through most of the 1600s, the VOC was highly profitable because it was the only company that sold exotic spices like nutmeg and cloves, spices that grew only in Indonesia. The company was less profitable in the 1700s, after competition from other trading companies made its business more difficult.

In 1795, Napoleon of France invaded and occupied the Netherlands, replacing its government with the short-lived Batavian Republic. By then the Dutch East India Company was struggling financially, and therefore didn't hold as much political power as it had before.

In 1796, the Batavian Republic "nationalized" all of the VOC's holdings, taking control of its territories in Indonesia and making them territories of the Dutch Empire.

The VOC dissolved, and the islands of Indonesia became known as the Dutch East Indies.

From 1796-1920, the Netherlands expanded its territories in the Dutch East Indies until they included nearly all of modern-day Indonesia. The Netherlands became independent again in 1815, after Napoleon's final defeat at Waterloo.

The Island of Sumatra and the Aceh War

Sumatra is an Indonesian island just south of south Asia's Malaysian Peninsula. The island is rich in natural resources such as petroleum, coal, gems and gold. After the Netherlands nationalized all of the VOC's holdings, most of Sumatra became part of the Dutch East Indies. However, chaos in the Netherlands during its occupation by Napoleon had made the Netherlands' hold on Sumatra uncertain.

In 1819, Britain established an important trading post at Singapore, which lies on the tip of the Malaysian Peninsula, very close to Sumatra. Both Britain and the Netherlands were interested in Sumatra's resources.

The Anglo-Dutch treaty of 1824 temporarily resolved the Sumatra situation: the British released their claim to Sumatra in exchange for some Dutch holdings in India, where Britain was the dominant power. However, the British required one major concession from the Dutch before they would sign the Anglo-Dutch Treaty: the little Islamic kingdom of Aceh, home to an important trading post on the northern tip of Sumatra, must remain independent. The British did not want to grant the Dutch easy access to a well-established trading post that might overshadow Singapore someday.

Decades later, after Singapore was well established, the British removed the requirement for Aceh's independence in the Sumatra Treaty of 1871. By 1871 other nations, including the United States, were also interested in Aceh; so the Dutch wanted to claim Aceh quickly, before anyone else could. Before they could claim Aceh, however, they first had to deal with Aceh's Islamic sultan and his Muslim subjects.

The Aceh War began in early 1873, when the Dutch tried to blockade Aceh's harbor and capture the sultan's castle. With their fine warships and their modern army, the Dutch expected a quick victory over the backward army of Aceh.

Unknown to the Dutch, however, some European enemy had secretly been helping Aceh modernize its military. The Dutch suspected both Britain and Italy of undercutting them by providing aid to Aceh; but the true source of Aceh's surprising military aid remains a well-kept secret that no one ever told. Instead of winning a quick victory over a backward foe, the Dutch found themselves facing stiff resistance. They were forced to retreat from Aceh with heavy losses.

Later that year, the Dutch returned to Aceh, and this time they managed to capture the city. The Sultan of Aceh escaped into the countryside surrounding the city. From that countryside, the sultan and his people carried on a guerrilla-style war of damaging attacks followed by swift retreats into hiding.

The sultan's guerrilla attacks went on for years. The Dutch continued to hold Aceh, and declared that the Aceh War was over 1880; but in reality, the war went on for about thirty years, from 1873-1904. The high costs of capturing Aceh, both in lives and money, continued to drag the Netherlands down for decades.

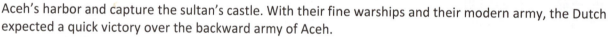

THE OTTOMAN EMPIRE

What Has Gone Before

Sultan Osman I founded the Ottoman Empire around 1300 AD. His Islamic empire grew until it controlled most of the territory that the Byzantine Empire had once held, plus part of Persia to the east. By the time the

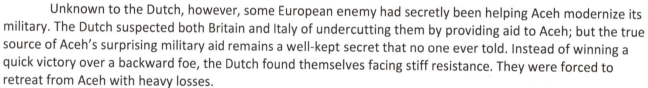

Ottoman Turks captured Constantinople in 1453, they had replaced the Orthodox Christian Byzantine Empire with their own Islamic one.

The Ottoman Empire remained a dominant world power through the rest of the Medieval era and into the early Modern era. The empire's power peaked in the 1600s, then began to subside around 1683 when it failed to capture Vienna, Austria.

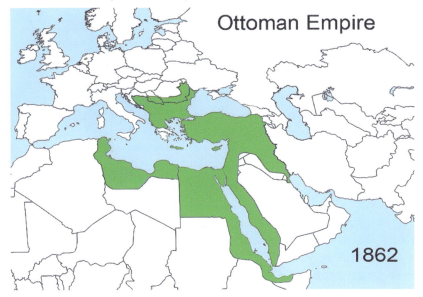

By the 1820s, the Ottoman Empire was in the early stages of collapse. The Ottomans' elite Janissary corps, an army that had once been remarkable for both its skill in battle and its devotion to the sultans, had become obsolete. The corrupt Janissaries of the 1800s resisted change, and attacked every sultan who tried to modernize the Ottoman military. Sultan Mahmud II finally eliminated the Janissary Corps, violently and treacherously, in the Auspicious Incident of 1826.

The ailing empire's worst troubles came from two of its border regions, Egypt and the Balkans. Egypt's Muhammad Ali Pasha nearly captured the empire's capital, Constantinople, in 1839, but was forced to settle for near-independence for Egypt (see Chapter 2). On the Balkan Peninsula, the large European peninsula that lies east of Italy, Orthodox Christian nations began to slip out of the Ottoman Empire's grasp. The Balkan nations of Greece and Serbia both reclaimed their independence around 1830.

As the Ottoman Empire declined, Russia and the other major European empires began to ask the "Eastern Question": What should they do with this ailing empire, this "sick man of Europe"? To the Russians, the answer was clear: they wanted to annex (absorb) neighboring Ottoman territories and use them to achieve their two ancient goals, capturing Constantinople and controlling the Black Sea. Other European powers, especially Britain and France, wanted to prop up the "sick man" to keep Russia from achieving those goals and becoming too powerful in the process. In the 1854-1856 Crimean War (see Chapter 2), Britain and France temporarily succeeded in driving the Russian navy out of the Black Sea– keeping the "sick man" alive, but on life support.

FASCINATING FACTS: The *Tanzimat* and the *Millets*
(The picture in this section is of a Turkish postcard. It includes an angel holding a banner that says "Liberty, Equality, Fraternity"; Abdulhamid II; the Grand Vizier; and the millet governors holding their flags).

In Turkish, *Tanzimat* means "reorganization." In the early 1800s, the sultans of the Ottoman Empire began to realize that their empire had fallen far behind the empires of Western Europe in several areas, including education, technology and military tactics. They also recognized that rebellions from Christian nations within their empire, such as Bulgaria and Armenia, threatened to tear their empire apart. The sultans' Tanzimat reorganization program, which ran from 1839-1876, was a set of reforms designed to hold the Ottoman Empire together and modernize the empire so that it wouldn't be overrun by its more-advanced enemies.

By the 1800s, the Christians of the Balkan Peninsula had been subject to Islamic rule for centuries, some of them since before the capture of Constantinople in 1453. For most of that time, the Ottomans had allowed Christians and Jews to operate separate sub-governments within the imperial government known as *millets* ("sub-nations"). As long as the millets remained loyal to the Ottoman Empire, they were free to do many of the things that governments do: collect taxes, write laws and operate courts.

Even so, the Christians and Jews of the millets remained strongly subordinate to Ottoman Muslims. Christians and Jews could not testify against Muslims in court or serve in the Ottoman military; nor could they ride horses or carry weapons like military men. Sometimes the Ottomans required Christians and Jews to set themselves apart by wearing clothing of a certain color.

When the Ottoman Empire's Tanzimat reorganization began in 1839, the empire's Christians and Jews became slightly less subordinate to Muslims. The sultans lowered or eliminated the special taxes that they had collected only from Christians and Jews; and they also encouraged Christians and Jews to serve in the new, Janissary-free Ottoman military. The sultans were trying to promote "Ottomanism," or loyalty to the Ottoman Empire, instead of loyalty to one's individual millet. They were also trying to smooth over the stark differences between Muslims, Christians and Jews, and make single-minded devotion to Islam less important.

Under Tanzimat, the Ottoman Empire was no longer the world-swallowing Islamic Empire of the 1300s, whose *ghazi* warriors had fought to conquer every nation for Islam. Instead, it became more like a secular empire that was trying to hold itself together by asking its people to become less devoted to Islam.

A Brief Timeline of the Ottoman Empire's Reform, Relapse and Collapse

1804 - 1833: The Balkan nation of Serbia wins its independence from the Ottoman Empire in the Serbian Revolution.

1821 - 1832: The Balkan nation of Greece wins its independence from the Ottoman Empire in the Greek War of Independence.

1839: The Ottoman Empire narrowly escapes being conquered by Egypt's Muhammad Ali Pasha (see Chapter 2).

1839: Ottoman Sultan Abdulmecid I inherits his father's throne and begins the Tanzimat program of reorganization and reform.

1854-1860: Sultan Abdulmecid I borrows a great deal of money from Britain and France in order to finance both the Crimean War and his Tanzimat reforms.

1861: Sultan Abdulmecid dies. His brother Abdul-Aziz takes his place as Sultan and continues the Tanzimat reforms.

1875: The Balkan nations of Bosnia and Herzegovina rebel against two things: (1) the Ottoman Empire's harsh treatment of Christians, and (2) the high taxes the empire demands in order to repay its foreign loans. Their rebellion is known as the Herzegovina Uprising.

1875, October: The Ottoman government declares that it is bankrupt, unable to repay its foreign loans.

1876, April-May: Christians in Bulgaria begin a revolt of their own, known as the April Uprising. The Ottomans respond to the April Uprising with brutal massacres of over fifty Bulgarian villages, some of which were not even involved in the April Uprising. The most notorious massacre is the Batak Massacre, in which Ottoman troops butcher 12,000-15,000 Bulgarian men, women, children and even infants at the village of Batak. When the people of the West learn of the Batak Massacre, they are horrified by the Ottomans' barbaric attacks on Christians.

1876, May 30: The combination of the Christian uprisings in the Balkans, the massacres and the empire's financial meltdown lead the Ottoman government to remove Sultan Abdul-Aziz from office and imprison him. Days later, former Sultan Abdul-Aziz dies under suspicious circumstances.

1876, June 30: Serbia declares war on the Ottoman Empire and invades regions near its borders, trying to recapture territories it held long ago.

1876, May 30-August 31: Abdul-Aziz's nephew Murad V briefly reigns as sultan before the Ottoman government declares him insane and removes him from office.

1876, August 31: Murad V's brother Abdulhamid II takes his place as sultan.

1876, December 11: Russia, the Ottoman Empire and others meet at the Constantinople Conference to discuss the troubled situation in the Balkans. Russia demands independence for Bulgaria, and the Ottomans agree.

1876, December 23: At the end of the Constantinople Conference, Sultan Abdulhamid II announces that he has changed his mind about allowing Bulgaria to become independent, but that it doesn't matter because he is adopting important new Tanzimat reforms: a new, western-style constitution for the Ottoman government and the empire's first elected parliament.

1877: As soon as the Russo-Turkish War begins, Sultan Abdulhamid II suspends the constitution and dissolves the empire's new parliament.

FASCINATING FACTS: The Russo-Turkish War (1877 – 1878)

The Russo-Turkish War was the next major European war after the Crimean War. Its combatants fought for several different goals:

1. **Russia** fought to defend Orthodox Christians in the Balkans, and to reclaim the Balkan Peninsula territories it had lost in the Crimean War.
2. The **Ottoman Empire** fought to hold its territories in the Balkans.
3. The **nations of the Balkan Peninsula** fought for their independence.

The Russo-Turkish War was a struggle between Eastern Orthodox Christians and Muslims; and it was also a struggle for the independence of Balkan nations like Bulgaria and Serbia, nations that had been dominated by foreign empires for centuries.

In 1876, the Balkan nation of Serbia attacked the Ottoman Empire. The Serbians had just won their independence from the Ottomans in 1833, and they were hoping to reclaim neighboring Ottoman territories that they believed rightly belonged to them. The Ottomans blocked the Serbian attack, and then answered it with a strong counterattack that threatened to re-conquer Serbia.

Russia got involved in the conflict because it was the ally and defender of the Orthodox Christians in the Balkans. At the Constantinople Conference of December 1876, Russia insisted on two conditions, among others:

1. That the Ottoman Empire must halt its counter-invasion of Serbia; and
2. That the empire must release its hold on Christian Bulgaria.

At first, Sultan Abdulhamid II agreed to Russia's demands; but as soon as the conference was over, he changed his mind about allowing Bulgaria to become independent. Instead, he asked both Russia and Bulgaria to be satisfied with the western-style freedoms he was offering Balkan Christians under his empire's new constitution. After the peace negotiations at the Constantinople Conference failed, Russia finally declared war on the Ottoman Empire on April 24, 1877.

The Russo-Turkish War began when the Russians crossed the Danube River and attacked the Ottomans in Bulgaria. The Russians were soon joined by native armies from Bulgaria, Romania, Serbia and Montenegro. The Ottomans stayed on the defensive, and were soon overwhelmed. By January, 1878, the Russians and their Balkan allies had conquered the Ottomans' forts in Bulgaria and were marching toward the Ottoman capital at Constantinople.

Russians Crossing the Danube River

The presence of Russian troops in Constantinople was something the mighty British Empire would not allow; so Britain sent a squadron of ships to Constantinople to warn the Russians off. The Russians knew that their real competitors, the major empires of Europe, would never allow them to capture Constantinople; so they decided to heed the British warning. They halted their march at the town of San Stefano, which lay on Constantinople's outskirts.

The Treaty of San Stefano (signed on March 3, 1878)

From this position of strength, Russia brought an end to the Russo-Turkish War by dictating the strong terms of the Treaty of San Stefano. The Treaty of San Stefano required the Ottomans to surrender territories to Russia, Serbia, Montenegro and Romania. Most importantly, it also required the Ottomans to surrender their hold on Bulgaria, allowing the large Orthodox Christian nation of Bulgaria to become independent for the first time in about 500 years.

The Treaty of San Stefano alarmed the other major empires of Europe. These empires were still guarding their delicate balance of power jealously, and they didn't want to see Russia gain such a powerful and grateful ally in Bulgaria. In June, the major empires met at the Congress of Berlin and dictated a new treaty to end the Russo-Turkish War, one that would give far less power to victorious Russia.

The Treaty of Berlin (signed on July 13, 1878)

Under the terms of the Treaty of Berlin, which replaced the earlier Treaty of San Stefano:

1. The large Christian nation of Bulgaria that had been formed by the Treaty of San Stefano was divided into three provinces, in order to keep it from becoming too powerful and too friendly with Russia. One of these provinces, Macedonia and Eastern Thrace, remained under strict Ottoman rule; but the other two, Eastern Rumelia and the Principality of Bulgaria, became semi-independent Ottoman provinces. The Treaty of Berlin was a major setback for Bulgarian independence, but Bulgaria would soon declare its independence again (in 1885, see Chapter 16).
2. Russia, Montenegro, Serbia and Romania all won territories from the Ottoman Empire.
3. The Ottoman Empire promised not to govern rebellious Bosnia and Herzegovina too harshly. Bosnia and Herzegovina remained under Ottoman rule, but would be "supervised" under the watchful eye of Austria-Hungary (which would later claim these territories for itself).

1878: The Treaty of Berlin ends the Russo-Turkish War. The Ottoman Empire loses much of its territory in the Balkans, and will lose more in the coming years.
1885: Eastern Rumelia and the Principality of Bulgaria unite to form a new, independent Bulgaria. The third province of Bulgaria remains in Ottoman hands.
1889: A group of well-educated Ottomans band together to create a reform group known as the *Young Turks*.

1895 – 1897: Abdulhamid II's *Hamidian Massacres* kill as many as 100,000-300,000 Armenian Christians.

DASTARDLY DICTATORS: Abdulhamid II (1842 – 1918, reigned 1876 – 1909)

Sultan Abdulhamid II was the 34th sultan of the Ottoman Empire and the last Ottoman sultan who held absolute power over his empire. Abdulhamid was also among the last of the Ottoman sultans, because the ailing Ottoman Empire, the "sick man of Europe," would finally die shortly after the end of his reign. When World War I arrived in 1914 - 1918, it would bring about the end of the Ottoman Empire.

When Abdulhamid II came to power, the Ottoman Empire's Tanzimat reforms had been going on for decades. These reforms reached their peak near the beginning of Abdulhamid's reign, when he adopted the empire's first Western-style constitution and established its first elected parliament in late 1876. Even though Abdulhamid only offered these reforms under the threat of Russian guns, the Ottoman Empire had never been less like a dictatorship than it was in 1876. Unfortunately, the new constitution didn't last long: When the Russo-Turkish War began in 1877, Abdulhamid II quickly suspended the constitution and dissolved the parliament, returning the empire to his own dictatorial rule.

The Russo-Turkish War was a quick loss for Abdulhamid II. The Ottomans' former allies in the Crimean War, the British and the French, had been horrified by the Ottomans' brutal massacres of Bulgarian Christians in 1876; so, although Britain and France hated to allow a Russian victory, angry public opinion would not allow them to enter the war on the Ottomans' side. As a result, the Russians defeated the Ottomans within less than a year, and the Ottomans were forced to give up Bulgaria and other territories on the Balkan Peninsula.

After the Russo-Turkish War, Abdulhamid II tried to maintain strict control over the territories he had left. Because he feared rebel assassination attempts— he had once survived a would-be assassin's ill-timed bomb— he almost never left his new castle, *Yildiz* ("Star") Castle at Constantinople. From this safe stronghold, he censored (removed from print) any rebellious talk in newspapers or books, and he operated a large network of secret police to spy on potential rebels. Whenever his spies discovered any rebel activity, Abdulhamid was quick to kill or imprison the rebels.

One such rebellion began in Armenia, a small Ottoman-controlled nation that lay between the Black and Caspian Seas, in 1894. Armenia lay on the Ottoman Empire's border with Russia; and, like Russia, Armenia was a Christian nation. The Christians of Armenia rebelled against Sultan Abdulhamid II for several reasons:

1. Because he taxed them heavily;
2. Because he refused to grant them the same rights that Muslims had;
3. Because he failed to protect them from roving bandits; and
4. Because he wouldn't allow them to own their own weapons, which they might have used to defend themselves against the bandits.

Abdulhamid developed a deep hatred for these rebellious Armenian Christians, partly because he knew that they were more loyal to Christian Russia than to the Islamic Ottoman Empire.

In 1895, Abdulhamid began sending armies of "Hamidiye," named for himself, into Armenia to punish the Christian rebels there. When Abdulhamid's Hamidiye attacked the Armenians, they drew no distinctions between peaceful protesters and violent rebels: they simply slaughtered every Armenian they could find. The Hamidiye's brutality was unspeakable: they fired into crowds of Armenian protesters, burned whole buildings full of Armenians, and laid waste of defenseless Armenian villages. These Hamidian Massacres lasted from 1895-1897, and slaughtered uncounted tens of thousands of Armenians. The Hamidian Massacres earned Sultan Abdulhamid II his bloody nicknames: "The Great Assassin," "Abdul the Damned" and "Abdulhamid the Red."

In 1908, the Young Turks launched a successful revolution against Abdulhamid II (see below). When Abdulhamid learned that the Young Turks were marching on Constantinople, he tried to appease their anger by quickly restoring the constitution that he had set aside in 1876. However, his weak attempts to reform his dictatorial government didn't go far enough to satisfy the Young Turks, so they deposed him in 1909. The former sultan died in exile in 1918.

1908: The Young Turks lead the <u>Young Turk Revolution</u> against Sultan Abdulhamid II.
1908, July 24: Abdulhamid II restores the Ottoman constitution that he had suspended back in 1876.
1909, April 27: The Young Turks depose Abdulhamid II.

FASCINATING FACTS: The Young Turks

From 1839-1876, the Ottoman Empire was on a path of modernization and reform under Tanzimat. The government was becoming more like a Western-style constitutional monarchy with an elected parliament; and the millions of Christians and Jews were headed toward more equality with Muslims. Sultan Abdulhamid II himself adopted the Ottoman constitution and convened the parliament in the first months of his reign.

Then, during the 1877-8 Russo-Turkish War, Abdulhamid II abruptly suspended the new constitution and dissolved the parliament. The empire still tried to modernize its technology and education, but its government relapsed to its previous form, an absolute dictatorship under the sultan. Christians and Jews returned to their previous lowly status and paid heavy extra taxes. A network of spies watched the Empire closely for signs of rebellion. Most of the Tanzimat's reforms relapsed, coming to a sudden stop under Sultan Abdulhamid II.

The Young Turks were a revolutionary group that wanted to stop that relapse and put the Ottoman Empire back on its earlier course of reform. The first Young Turks were university students who had been educated in Western schools. They held their first meeting, the Congress of Ottoman Opposition, in Paris in 1902. These students appreciated the representative governments of the West, and wanted the same representation in their own government. The Young Turks wanted an Ottoman equivalent of the U.S. Bill of Rights: freedom of religion, freedom to assemble, voting rights for all citizens and other modern reforms.

In 1906, the Young Turks established a political party known as the Committee of Union and Progress (CUP). Several

Young Turks First Congress

important Ottoman military officers joined the CUP, and soon it had enough high-ranking officers to challenge the sultan for control of the Ottoman military. When the Young Turks began their revolution against Sultan Abdulhamid II in 1908, the sultan suddenly realized that the Ottoman military was no longer under his control.

In desperation, the sultan tried to appease the CUP by restoring the Ottoman constitution that he had briefly adopted in 1876. His weak effort wasn't nearly enough to satisfy the Young Turks, so they deposed him in 1909 and replaced him with a new, far weaker sultan. After 1909, the CUP and the Young Turks controlled the Ottoman government.

Unfortunately, however, the Young Turks never achieved their lofty goals of freedom and equality for all. During World War I, the CUP government grew as suspicious of the Armenian Christians' loyalty to Russia as Abdulhamid II had been. Christian-hating Muslims took over the CUP, and they massacred even more Armenians than Abdulhamid had (see The Armenian Christian Genocide below).

1912-1913: In the Balkan Wars, the Ottoman Empire loses most of its remaining territory on the Balkan Peninsula (see Chapter 16).
1914-1918: The Ottoman Empire sides with the losing Central Powers (Germany, Austria-Hungary, Bulgaria) in World War I (see Chapters 17 - 18).

1915-1917: The Ottomans massacre as many as 500,000-1,500,000 Armenian Christians in the Armenian Genocide (see below).

1922-1923: After losing World War I, the new Republic of Turkey overthrows the last Ottoman sultan and dissolves what remains of the Ottoman Empire.

MISSIONARY FOCUS

The Armenian Christian Genocide

Armenia lies northeast of modern-day Turkey, between the Black and Caspian Seas. Armenia became part of the Ottoman Empire shortly after the Ottomans captured Constantinople in 1453. It had been the first nation in history to embrace Christianity, and most of its people remained loyal Eastern Orthodox Christians long after the Ottomans conquered their nation.

Armenia lay in a troubled border zone between the Ottoman Empire and Russia. As Christians and near neighbors of Christian Russia, Armenians tended to prefer the Russians over the Ottomans; and so the Muslim Ottomans tended to view Armenians as dangerous infidels, traitors, and lovers of their empire's most hated enemy, Russia.

As the power of the Ottoman Empire declined, the Christian nations of the West began to demand protection for Christians who lived under Ottoman rule. The Ottomans agreed to these demands in treaties known as the Ottoman Capitulations. Sultan Abdulhamid II promised to obey these demands more than once; but instead, he allowed a special military force known as the Hamidiye to brutally assault Armenians who demanded equality. As many as 100,000-300,000 Armenian Christians died in the Hamidian Massacres of 1895-1897.

Ottoman persecution of Armenian Christians didn't end with the Hamidian Massacres. During the Young Turk Revolution, Islamic fundamentalists fought back against the Young Turks' program of religious equality. During a failed counter-revolution designed to restore Abdulhamid II to power, Ottoman Muslims murdered as many as 15,000-30,000 Armenian Christians in the 1909 Adana Massacre.

But the worst acts of the Armenian Genocide (race killings) came during World War I. Once again, the Ottomans accused the Armenians of traitorously siding with enemy Russia; and this time, they decided to

Armenians Marched by Turkish Soldiers – 1915

exterminate the Armenians. In a systematic program of racial murder second only to the Nazi Holocaust against the Jews during World War II, the Ottomans subjected Armenians to:

(1) Death camps; (2) Death marches; (3) Mass poisonings;
(4) Mass burnings; (5) Mass drownings; and (6) Forced deportations.

As many as 500,000 to 1,500,000 Armenian Christians died at the hands of Ottoman Muslims during World War I. The Ottomans' attempt to exterminate the Armenians outraged Western Christians, and some of them donated a great deal of money to help the survivors.

A portion of Armenia gained its independence after World War I ended in 1918. Later, Armenia became one of the republics of the USSR.

INTERESTING ITEMS: Armenian Khachkars

Khachkars, or "cross stones," are ornately carved memorial stones made by Armenian Christian

craftsmen to honor people, buildings or events. They first appeared around 800 AD, and their art was at its most refined around 1100-1300. About 40,000 Khachkars still survive in Armenia, and each is unique.

Khachkars are carved from slabs of *basalt* or *tuff*, two types of volcanic rock. The nature of these rocks makes it possible to inject water into them before carving, softening them so that they can be finely crafted. In this way, Armenian craftsman can produce carvings as intricate and delicate as lace.

The symbolism of Khachkars is as intricate as their carving. Among their many ornaments, Khachkars always include a prominent Armenian Cross. Each point of this cross is decorated with three circles to represent the Holy Trinity of Father, Son and Holy Spirit. Some Khachkars include a disc under the cross to represent the sun or the earth. Surrounding the cross are lovely patterns with unending lines to represent God's infinite nature.

WORLD HISTORY FOCUS, continued

FASCINATING FACTS: The Red Cross and the Red Crescent

The International Committee of the Red Cross was founded in Geneva, Switzerland in 1863. The organization was based on ideas from a book by Henry Dunant, a Swiss businessman who was moved by the suffering of wounded soldiers on a battlefield during the Italian Wars for Independence (see Chapter 21). The mission of the International Committee of the Red Cross was to provide medical aid for the victims of terrible modern wars. The Red Cross took no sides: it was designed to be impartial, neutral and independent, and to offer help for anyone who was suffering, regardless of his race or nationality. Its adopted symbol was a red cross on a white field-- the reverse of the Swiss flag, which was a white cross on a red field.

During the 1877-1878 Russo-Turkish War, Ottoman Muslims saw the Red Cross symbol on the battlefield for the first time. Some of the Muslims took offense at the sight of the cross, saying that it reminded them of the crosses that Christians carried during the Crusades of the Medieval era. In order to avoid offending Muslims, aid societies in Muslim nations decided to replace the red cross symbol with a red crescent symbol. Muslim nations now have Red Crescent societies instead of Red Cross societies.

FASCINATING FACTS: The Neutrality of Switzerland

Switzerland is a small, mountainous, landlocked European nation that borders Italy to the south, France to the west, Germany to the north and Austria to the east. The Alpine mountain passes that link Germany, France and Italy lie in Switzerland, and all three of these larger nations have held Swiss territory over the years. Most of the Swiss people speak German (64%), French (20%) or Italian (7%).

For most of its history, Switzerland was a crossroads nation surrounded on all sides by powerful, grasping empires. Its location left it in constant danger of being swept into Europe's frequent, miserable wars. After suffering through these wars for centuries, the Swiss began to look for a way to remain independent and peaceful.

In 1815, the Swiss found their way. The Congress of Vienna, which negotiated the peace at the end of the Napoleonic Wars, declared that Switzerland would be neutral in all future conflicts. Switzerland stayed out of every major war that followed, including World War I and World War II, declaring war on no one and supplying aid to no one. By remaining peaceful and neutral, Switzerland became a popular place for:

1. **Exiles:** Political figures who got into trouble in their home nations could take refuge in Switzerland. Neutral Switzerland did not take sides in other nations' political squabbles; so a man like Vladimir Lenin, the Russian revolutionary who was a criminal to Russia's tsars, could live safely in Switzerland until it was time to launch the Bolshevik Revolution in 1917.
2. **Negotiators:** Neutral Switzerland was an excellent place to negotiate treaties between hostile nations. Because Switzerland never took sides, both sides of any conflict could feel safe there. The treaty that divided North Vietnam from South Vietnam in 1954 was one of the many well-known treaties that were negotiated in Switzerland.
3. **Bankers:** Switzerland's neutrality also made it an excellent place to hide money from greedy or overly curious governments. Swiss banks are well-known for keeping their customers' secrets: unless a foreign government can convince a Swiss judge to intervene, a Swiss bank will reveal nothing about its customers' accounts. During World War II, notorious members of Germany's Nazi Party stored much of their stolen wealth in Swiss banks because they knew that the neutral Swiss would keep their secrets.

U.S. GEOGRAPHY FOCUS

FASCINATING FACTS about WISCONSIN:

- Statehood: Wisconsin became the 30th US state on May 29, 1848.
- Bordering states/bodies of water: Minnesota, Michigan, Iowa, Illinois, Lake Superior and Lake Michigan
- State capital: Madison
- Area: 65,497.82 sq. mi (Ranks 23rd in size)
- Abbreviation: WI
- State nickname: "Badger State"
- State bird: Robin
- State tree: Sugar Maple
- State flower: Violet
- State song: *On, Wisconsin!*
- State Motto: "Forward"
- Meaning of name: Based on an Indian word that might mean "place of beaver" or "grassy place"
- Historic places to visit: Devil's Lake, The House on the Rock, Mount Horeb, Mustard Museum, Noah's Ark, National Fresh Water Fishing Hall of Fame, Hamburger hall of fame, Milwaukee's Summer fest, Eagle River
- Wisconsin's Resources and Industries: farming (milk, butter, cheese, corn, livestock, vegetables, cranberries), paper, electric equipment, fabricated metal products, tourism, beer, shipping

Wisconsin State Capital

Flag of Wisconsin

- Wisconsin adopted this flag in 1913.
- Its blue field has *Wisconsin* and *1848* (the date of its statehood) printed on it in bold white letters.
- One of the men on the flag is a miner, and the other is a sailor.
- The four quadrants of the shield depict 1) an arm and hammer, 2) a plow, 3) a pick and shovel 4) an anchor. These represent Wisconsin's main industries: manufacturing, agriculture, mining and shipping.

Chapter 11

Jim Crow Laws, Heroes of Black Rights, Colonizing Australia, the Scramble for Africa

U.S. HISTORY FOCUS

RACISM AND THE STRUGGLE FOR BLACK RIGHTS IN THE UNITED STATES

Jim Crow Laws

"Jump Jim Crow" was a popular song written by Thomas Dartmouth Rice, a white comedian from New York. Rice's song and dance routine was part of his traveling minstrel show, in which white performers dressed in blackface to portray black slaves as cheerful, funny and musically talented, but not very bright. "Jump Jim Crow" became so well-known that by the 1840s, "Jim Crow" was a common and insulting name for the blacks of the South.

When Reconstruction ended in 1877, the Southern states were once again free to create race laws of their own choosing. Although the Fourteenth Amendment to the Constitution guaranteed Blacks "equal protection of the laws," the Southern states worked around this problem with clever legal arguments. An 1896 Supreme Court decision in the case of Plessy vs. Ferguson upheld the South's idea that government services could be "separate but equal": that is, that laws could maintain a racist separation between blacks and whites as long as they provided "equal" services to both in order to satisfy the fourteenth amendment. In practice, however, the facilities Southern governments provided for Blacks were often somewhat less than equal.

Laws that enforced this separation of whites and blacks became known as "Jim Crow Laws," and they led to separate ("segregated") public facilities of nearly every kind:

- Separate schools, buses, rail cars, restaurants and restrooms;
- Separate hospitals, libraries, prisons, pools and beaches;
- Separate cemeteries; and
- Separate units in the United States Military.

Other Jim Crow Laws were racist customs which, in some places, became law:

- Black men could not offer to shake hands with white men.
- Black men could not offer to light cigarettes for white women.
- White drivers always had the right-of-way over black drivers.

- Black barbers could not cut the hair of white girls or women.
- White nurses could not provide hospital care for black men.
- A black person's testimony in court held less weight than a white person's.

Blacks who resisted the South's Jim Crow laws were risking their homes, jobs and their lives.

FASCINATING FACTS: Lynching in America

A *lynching* is an illegal execution carried out by a mob. The practice of lynching was probably named for Charles Lynch, a Virginia justice of the peace who executed British loyalists (Tories) for treason without trial during the American Revolution.

Lynching was a common punishment for blacks who resisted the Jim Crow Laws. Lynching inspired fear in the black community and maintained "segregation," the separation of the races. The Ku Klux Klan sometimes lynched its victims while it was active during Reconstruction. Later, other racist groups that were inspired by the KKK also lynched their victims. There were almost 3,000 documented lynch mob killings in the United States between 1882 and 1930. This means that on average, racist mobs lynched about one black per week for almost 50 years.

HEROES OF BLACK RIGHTS

Booker T. Washington (1856 – 1915)

Booker T. Washington was born into slavery on a Virginia plantation, the son of a slave mother and a white man from a nearby farm. As a slave boy, one of his jobs was to carry schoolbooks for one of his master's daughters. He longed for the chance to go to school himself, but educating slaves was against the law. In 1865, when the Civil War was over, Booker's master read the Emancipation Proclamation to all of his slaves and released them. Nine-year-old Booker's family moved to West Virginia to find mining work.

In West Virginia, Booker began his long struggle to get a good education. He had to start work at 4 AM each day in order to have enough time to attend school. When he was sixteen, he traveled hundreds of miles on foot for a chance to attend the Hampton Institute, a Hampton, Virginia teacher training school established for freed slaves. At Hampton, Booker became part of a growing group of people who believed that education was key to equality for blacks. Teachers from the Hampton Institute spread out all over the southern U.S. to establish schools and provide freed slaves with a chance to receive a good education. Booker himself was dispatched to establish another teacher training school, Alabama's Tuskegee Institute, in 1881.

Booker's strategy for advancing black equality relied on education and hard work. He believed that blacks could earn the respect of whites by proving their quality through good education, hard work and excellent moral behavior. Booker's 1901 autobiography, *Up From Slavery*, was a bestseller. His positive message earned him the approval of white reformers who wanted to help blacks get on their feet in American society. These reformers helped Booker by donating money for his large and growing education programs. One of them, Julius Rosenwald, donated enough money to help Booker's Tuskegee Institute build nearly 5,000 "Rosenwald Schools" for young black students all over the South. Booker gave speeches all over the United States, and even shared the stage with President Theodore Roosevelt when the President visited Tuskegee Institute.

But Booker's message also brought disapproval from some blacks, who felt that by stressing the need for black self-improvement, Booker was agreeing with white racists and suggesting that blacks weren't as good as whites. Black leaders like W.E.B. Dubois accused Booker of giving in to white racists by accepting too much of their money to fund his schools. Dubois believed that the industrial training blacks received at Booker's schools was not good enough, and that learning to do industrial work would only make blacks permanent slaves to white-owned businesses.

Interesting quotes from Booker T. Washington:
- "Dignify and glorify common labor. It is at the bottom of life that we must begin, not at the top."
- "If you can't read, it's going to be hard to realize dreams."

W. E. B. Du Bois (1868 – 1963)

Massachusetts-born William Edward Burghardt Du Bois was the first black man to earn a Ph.D. from Harvard University. Du Bois became an expert sociologist at Harvard and went on to publish books on the condition of American blacks. Like Booker T. Washington, Du Bois wanted to improve the black condition and work for black equality. But he disagreed with Washington over his methods: Du Bois did not believe that education and hard work alone were enough to achieve that equality. Instead, he believed that blacks would have to stand up for their rights and combat white racism.

In 1909, Du Bois became a co-founder of the National Association for the Advancement of Colored People (NAACP). Through the NAACP, he worked to advance black rights in several ways: by taking a stand for equal voting rights, by resisting Jim Crow Laws, and by highlighting black accomplishments. He served as the NAACP's publishing director, and wrote columns that appeared in newspapers all over the United States. In this way, Du Bois became America's most prominent black rights advocate of the early 1900s.

Over the years, Du Bois became increasingly frustrated with continued racism in America, and he began to seek answers elsewhere. He grew interested in socialism and communism, and became friendly with communist leaders like Joseph Stalin and Mao Tse-tung. Late in his life, both the FBI and the House Un-American Activities Committee investigated him. A defiant Du Bois joined the Communist Party at the age of 93. He died in Ghana, Africa in 1963, on the eve of Martin Luther King's "I Have a Dream" speech in Washington.

Interesting quotes from W.E.B. Du Bois:
- "One ever feels his twoness - an American, a Negro; two souls, two thoughts, two unreconciled strivings; two warring ideals in one dark body, whose dogged strength alone keeps it from being torn asunder."
- "To be a poor man is hard, but to be a poor race in a land of dollars is the very bottom of hardships."

George Washington Carver (1864 – 1943)

George Washington Carver was born into slavery in Missouri around 1864. He struggled throughout his youth to get an education in a system that discriminated mercilessly against black youth. He was twenty-six years old when he was finally accepted at Iowa's Simpson College. At Iowa State Agricultural College, he studied botany and became a skilled plant scientist.

Carver went to work at Booker T. Washington's Tuskegee Institute as head of the agriculture department. In his research there, he found ways to improve Southern soils that had been damaged by continual cotton and tobacco farming. Carver's ideas helped to rebuild Southern agriculture, and gave farmers more and different ways to earn money from their crops. His study of peanuts produced about 300 new uses for peanuts and peanut oil.

In 1921, Carver testified before the U.S. Congress about American peanut farming. Despite racist taunts before the event, his testimony impressed the congressmen so much that they gave him a standing ovation when it was over. At this and other speaking events, Carver's easy manner and obvious intelligence won over his racist audiences. He was living proof that a black man could excel in the scientific studies so long reserved for whites.

> *Interesting quotes from George Washington Carver:*
> - "I wanted to know the name of every stone and flower and insect and bird and beast. I wanted to know where it got its color, where it got its life - but there was no one to tell me."
> - "Learn to do common things uncommonly well; we must always keep in mind that anything that helps fill the dinner pail is valuable."

WORLD HISTORY FOCUS

AUSTRALIA

A Brief Timeline of Australia's History as a British Colony

1606: Dutch explorer Willem Janszoon becomes the first European to discover Australia.
1688: British explorer William Dampier lands on Australia's northwest coast.
1770: British explorer Lieutenant James Cook, sailing on his first "voyage of discovery" aboard HMS Endeavour, lands at Botany Bay (in modern Sydney) and claims eastern Australia for Britain.

1788, January 26: The eleven ships of the First Fleet arrive at Botany Bay to establish Australia's first British penal colony. January 26th will become Australia Day, a national holiday.

1820s: As settlement moves inland, free British immigrants are encouraged to settle in Australia.
1851: The Victorian Gold Rush (named for the Australian province of Victoria) begins, bringing large numbers of settlers to Australia.
1854: In the Eureka Rebellion, British troops attack and kill about 30 miners at the Eureka gold mine. The miners had been protesting high mining license fees and unfair treatment of miners. Public sympathy for the miners leads more Australians to call for freedom and fair government.

A Prison Colony

Explorer James Cook claimed both Australia and New Zealand for Britain on his near-fatal first "voyage of discovery" aboard the HMS Endeavour in 1770.

At around that time, Britain began looking for a solution to the problem of housing its many convicts. British prisons were so full of convicts that jailers were forced to house some of them aboard the "hulks," rotting carcasses of obsolete ships anchored near British shores. Living conditions in both the prisons and the hulks were abominable and shameful to the British. After the Thirteen Colonies won independence in the American Revolution, the British could send no more prisoners to North America; so they hit upon the idea of establishing a penal colony in the unknown land of Australia. The First Fleet of eleven prisoner transport ships arrived at Botany Bay in New South Wales, Australia in 1788.

A series of British governors managed the penal colonies and the settlements that grew up around them. Convicts worked through a probation period until they earned their freedom; the length of their probation depended on their original crime and sentence. Over the years, as the settlements contained more emancipated former prisoners, they began to grow and move inland. Later, more free immigrants began to move into Australia.

The Eureka Rebellion

The Victorian Gold Rush of the 1850s brought a great wave of free immigrants to Australia. The boost in population brought with it railways, telegraphs and other signs of modernization. It also brought conflict with the native population, the Aborigines, some of whom tried to fight back when British settlers claimed their land. A terrible number of Aborigines died from exposure to European diseases for which native Australians had no immunity.

The gold rush also brought a struggle for freedom and a fair, representative government. According to British law, all minerals on British soil belonged to the British crown, and the crown sternly regulated all mining activity. All miners were required to purchase an expensive license in order to claim the mining rights to a small piece of land, whether they found gold there or not. Because only large companies could afford these licenses, only large mining companies could operate mines. The poor were left out.

In the 1854 Eureka Rebellion (see picture), poor miners took a stand in favor of miners' rights and representative government for Australia's poor. The government, of course, favored the wealthy mining companies, and government troops quickly defeated the rebellious miners of the Eureka Rebellion. But the public sympathized with the roughly-treated miners. The public's outrage over the British government's harsh response to the Eureka Rebellion helped put Australia on the road to a more independent self-government.

The government also favored the wealthy in the outback, Australia's vast, wild interior. Wealthy ranchers accumulated vast tracts of good land for their immense sheep herds, while the poor struggled to survive on small, dry patches of barren land. The police did little to protect the rights of the poor, so bandits known as bushrangers gave up on the law and began to steal what they needed to survive. The best-known of these bushrangers was Ned Kelly.

INTERESTING INDIVIDUALS: Ned Kelly (1854 – 1880) and the Bushrangers

The bushrangers were outlaws who used their intricate knowledge of the outback, Australia's "bush" region, to hide from the police. The first bushrangers were convicts who had escaped from Australia's penal colonies. Bushrangers survived by robbing small town banks and inns, holding up travelers at gunpoint or stealing gold shipments.

Bushranger Ned Kelly was the son of Red Kelly, an Irish convict who was sent to an Australian penal colony in 1843. Red Kelly earned his release in 1848, and remained in Australia. When Ned Kelly was young, his father Red was convicted of stealing a cow and sentenced to six months hard labor. The hard labor destroyed Red's health, and he died in 1866, when Ned was only eleven years old. The harsh treatment his father received at the hands of Australia's courts probably contributed to Ned Kelly's rather low opinion of the Australian justice system.

Ned's own outlaw days began shortly after his father's death. After convictions on charges of horse theft, assault and indecent behavior, Kelly served two prison terms. In 1877, faced with more criminal charges and another likely prison term, Ned and his brother decided to go into hiding.

When a band of police came looking for the brothers near Stringybark Creek, Ned Kelly and his gang remained free by shooting and killing three policemen. This was no easy feat: it required excellent marksmanship and a cool head under fire. It also required a certain disregard for the law and for human life. Among those who hated Australia's oppressive police, Ned Kelly was becoming a folk hero; but among the police, he was becoming a notorious and hated outlaw.

After they were joined by fellow outlaws Joe Byrne and Steve Hart, the Kelly brothers committed two major bank robberies at Euroa and Jerilderie. At Jerilderie, the Kelly Gang boldly impersonated police while they

1. Held hostages in the local inn;
2. Cut the telegraph lines so that no one could call for help;
3. Robbed the bank; and finally
4. Made their getaway.

When the police found out about the Jerilderie robbery, they rounded up all of the Kelly Gang's friends and families and jailed them for three months. The police war against the Kelly Gang was escalating.

The defiant Kelly Gang planned to take revenge on the police by counterattacking them at Glenrowan. First, they captured Glenrowan's inn and held hostages inside it. Then they tore up the town's railroad tracks, hoping to derail a police train that was scheduled to come through. But the gang made the mistake of releasing one of their hostages, and this freed hostage ran up the tracks to tip off the police and stop the train before it could derail.

The police stopped their train, raced to Glenrowan and surrounded the Kelly Gang inside the inn. During the siege at Glenrowan Inn, an armored Ned Kelly advanced on the police siege line like an invulnerable action hero until police shot him several times in his unprotected legs (picture shows Ned Kelly's bullet-dented armor). All of the other gang members died in the siege, but Kelly was captured and imprisoned. Months later, he was convicted and hanged at Melbourne.

Other interesting facts about Ned Kelly:
- After the Kelly Gang's bold robbery at Jerilderie, Ned Kelly wrote a long, rambling letter in which he told his side of nearly every incident that had ever got him into trouble with the police. Throughout the letter, and even at his trial, Kelly maintained that he was an innocent victim who was only defending himself from the cruel and aggressive police who had victimized his family.
- All four Kelly Gang members wore heavy iron armor for the siege at Glenrowan. Their armor was probably fashioned from farmers' plowshares.
- As a child, Ned Kelly risked his life to save another boy from drowning, and received a green sash as a reward. He was still wearing that green sash under his armor when he was captured at Glenrowan in 1880.

1855: Australia's New South Wales province becomes the first to achieve "responsible government," which means that its governor must obey the province's elected representatives and not the British parliament. Other provinces follow. Australia remains under the protection of the British crown.
1868: Transportation of British prisoners to Australia ends.
1880: Bushranger Ned Kelly is executed.

1901: The provinces of Australia unite to form the Commonwealth of Australia, a mostly independent constitutional democracy with the British sovereign as its symbolic head of state. Like Canada, the Commonwealth of Australia is considered a Dominion of the British Empire. The new Commonwealth remains strongly bound to Britain: Australia will send troops for British wars, and the British navy will contribute to Australia's defense.

FASCINATING FACTS: Peach Melba and Melba Toast

Peach Melba and Melba Toast were both created by French Chef Auguste Escoffier for his favorite Australian operatic soprano singer, Nellie Melba.

Nellie Melba was born Helen Porter Mitchell in 1861. As a professional singer, she took the stage name "Nellie Melba" in honor of her favorite Australian city, Melbourne. Melba was one of the best-known operatic sopranos of her day, and the first Australian opera star to achieve international fame.

One night in 1892, Nellie Melba performed at the Covent Garden Opera House in London. In honor of her performance, Chef Escoffier created a new dessert made with poached peach halves, vanilla ice cream and raspberry sauce. He displayed his new Peach Melba on a swan-shaped ice sculpture.

On a separate occasion in 1897, an ailing Nellie complained to Chef Escoffier that her bread was too thick. Escoffier coddled his favorite soprano by lightly toasting a fresh piece of bread, dividing it into two thin slices, and re-toasting both. His new creation became known as Melba Toast.

Did you know....
- Australia is the both the world's smallest continent and the world's largest island.
- Australia is the flattest of the 7 continents. Over 90% of Australia is flat and dry.
- Australia's vast, arid and remote plains are known as "the Outback."
- Australia's name comes from the Latin *terra australis incognito*, which means "unknown southern land."
- Australians celebrate "Australia Day" each year on January 26 to commemorate the arrival by ship of its first European colonists.
- The Great Barrier Reef is a huge coral reef off the coast of the northeast Australia province of Queensland.
- Tasmania is a large island about 150 miles south of mainland Australia. It is Australia's southernmost province.

AFRICA

By the late 1800s, Africa's formerly dark interior was coming into the light. David Livingstone and others had mapped Africa's great central lakes, and had located the Nile River's source above Lake Victoria. They had also discovered that Africa was rich with mineral resources like diamonds, gold, copper, tin and oil. Yet in 1880, European nations controlled only about ten percent of the African continent, most of it near the African coast.

All of this would begin to change when King Leopold II of Belgium cast his greedy eye upon the riches of Africa.

TERRIBLE TYRANTS: Leopold II of Belgium (1835 – 1909, reigned 1865 – 1909)

Belgium gained independence from its neighbor, the Netherlands, in the 1830-1831 Belgian Revolution. The newly independent Belgium established a constitutional monarchy with Leopold I as its king. Leopold I's son, Leopold II, was Belgium's second king.

King Leopold II wanted to expand Belgium's power and influence in the same way the other great European powers had: by establishing colonies overseas. The target he chose for Belgium's expansion was central Africa, the last, best "unclaimed" territory in the world. Central Africa was, of course, claimed by its natives; but like most Europeans, Leopold didn't devote much thought to Africa's natives. King Leopold II tried to convince his parliament that Belgium should colonize Africa's interior, but his parliament wasn't interested. The king could have submitted to his parliament's wishes, but that would have thwarted his burning ambition; so instead, he set out to colonize the Congo region on his own.

In 1876, Leopold II established the International African Association, an organization whose stated goals were to explore the Congo region of central Africa and to bring Christian civilization to its natives. Leopold's representatives began negotiating with the tribal chiefs of the Congo, exchanging gifts for land in treaties the natives hardly understood. Through such one-sided treaties, Leopold assumed control over ever-larger portions of the Congo. Finally, in 1885, Leopold organized his colonies as the Congo Free State.

Unfortunately, **"Christian civilization" turned to "exploitation"** when Leopold put the natives of his Congo Free State to work for him. Congolese natives made Leopold wealthy by collecting the sap of rubber plants, which he sold to rubber factories. Leopold's private army in the Congo, the *Force Publique*, established high quotas for rubber collection. Whenever the natives displayed any reluctance to meet those quotas, Leopold's soldiers responded with unthinkable violence. The Force Publique beat, robbed, raped, murdered or cut off the hands of any Congolese natives who failed to meet their rubber quotas. Even though most of the Force Publique's soldiers were Congolese (only their officers were Belgian), they seemed to view the lives of the Congolese natives as worthless. No one knows how many natives of the Congo died during the cruel reign of Leopold's Force Publique, but estimates run from 2 million to 10 million or more.

In the early 1900s, the news of Leopold's brutal, murderous treatment of Congolese natives began to reach the rest of the world. In response to a world outcry, the Belgian parliament insisted on taking control of the Congo out of Leopold's private hands. The Belgian parliament's new colony, established in 1908, became known as the Belgian Congo. The Belgian Congo's area was 75 times that of Belgium itself.

The Democratic Republic of the Congo gained independence from Belgium in 1960 (see Chapter 30).

Other interesting facts about Leopold II:
- The man King Leopold II hired to claim the Congo in his name was Henry Morton Stanley, the reporter and explorer of Africa who found the missing David Livingstone in 1871. It was Stanley who made many of Leopold's treaties with Congolese tribal chiefs in order to acquire the vast Congo Free State.
- *Heart of Darkness*, a well-known short novel by author Joseph Conrad, was inspired by the horrors Conrad witnessed as a steamboat captain on the Congo River during Leopold II's tenure in the Congo Free State.
- American author Mark Twain wrote a mocking satire of Leopold II's "Christianization" of the Congo called *King Leopold's Soliloquy*.

INTERESTING INQUIRY: Why Build an Overseas Empire?

During the Industrial Revolution of the 1800s, European powers like Britain, France, Germany and Belgium built factories that were capable of producing enormous quantities of goods of all kinds. In order to keep their factories operating, those nations needed two things: (1) raw materials for their factories to use (iron, rubber, cotton and so on), and (2) markets in which to sell their goods. Without these two things, these nations' businesses and economies could not grow and prosper as quickly their businessmen and governments wished.

The Scramble for Africa was the European powers' answer to these two problems. Africa was full of untapped raw materials, and its natives had little idea of these materials' value. Africa was also a marketplace for Europe, because Africans were often eager to buy European factory goods like cloth, beads, weapons and whiskey. Africa provided European nations with an opportunity to grow their businesses and economies at the expense of Africa's natives. The truth of this is evident in this quote from Cecil Rhodes, a well-known Briton who grew wealthy in the South African diamond trade:

> "We must find new lands from which we can easily obtain raw materials and at the same time exploit the cheap slave labor that is available from the natives of the colonies. The colonies would also provide a dumping ground for the surplus goods produced in our factories."

The Berlin Conference and the Scramble for Africa

In 1884-1885, thirteen European nations met at a Berlin Conference to discuss how they might fairly divide Africa's spoils among themselves. Germany's Otto von Bismarck called the Berlin Conference in order to avoid unnecessary squabbles between the European nations over African territory. The Berlin Conference was remarkable because it was one of the first times in history when Europeans met for negotiations before, rather than after, they fought a major war.

Under the terms of the 1885 **General Act of the Berlin Conference**, each European nation received the right to acquire territories within its assigned zone, according to the map at right:

Blue = France
Yellow = Belgium
Pale Green = Germany
Deep Purple = Portugal
Pink = Britain
Green = Italy
Purple = Spain
Gray = Unassigned

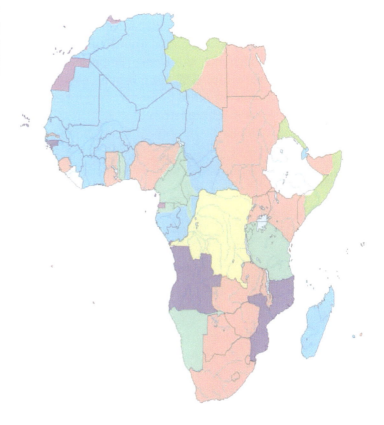

The Berlin Conference did not guarantee possession of these assigned territories; it only guaranteed that the nations of Europe wouldn't have to battle one another for control of the same zone (so long as they obeyed the General Act of the Berlin Conference). Within its assigned zone, each nation would have to acquire territory as Belgium's King Leopold had, by treaty; or, if necessary, it could acquire territory by conquering Africa's natives.

After the Berlin Conference came the **Scramble for Africa**, a race in which the European powers rushed to gain as much African territory for themselves as possible. Because the borders drawn at the Berlin conference paid little attention to the preferences of African natives, native tribes that were enemies often ended up as fellow countrymen under the same foreign government. Most Europeans placed no value on the Africans' often savage culture, and hoped to replace it with an enlightened European Christian civilization.

After the Scramble for Africa, the only two nations in all of Africa that still lived under independent home rule were **Liberia** and **Ethiopia**.

LIBERIA

Liberia is a small coastal nation in West Africa with a unique history.

The American Colonization Society founded Liberia in 1821 as a new home for freed slaves from the United States. Both abolitionists and slaveholders supported "repatriation," or resettling free blacks in Liberia: The abolitionists supported it because they feared that free blacks could never achieve equality in the U.S.; while slaveholders supported it because they feared that free blacks might inspire their own slaves to desire freedom if they stayed too close. Well-known Americans like Senators Henry Clay and Daniel Webster, former Presidents Thomas Jefferson and James Madison, and abolitionist Harriet Beecher Stowe all supported the American Colonization Society.

The new Liberian government was operated by Americo-Liberians, free blacks from the U.S. who were often of mixed race. Because they had been educated in America, Americo-Liberians tended to believe in the superiority of American and European culture. They spoke English, established Christian churches and adopted a constitution similar to that of the United States. Instead of mingling with Liberia's native Africans, they dominated native Liberians and denied them voting rights.

By the early 1840s, the American Colonization Society was bankrupt, unable to sponsor Liberia any longer. Liberia became a free republic in 1847, but it remained under the protection of the United States. Americo-Liberians continued to control the Republic of Liberia until 1980, even though Americo-Liberians never made up more than 5% of Liberia' population.

ETHIOPIA

Ethiopia is Africa's oldest independent nation. Except for a five-year period of Italian occupation from 1936-1941, Ethiopia has always remained independent. Ethiopian Emperor Menelik II (see picture), who reigned from 1889-1913, kept his east African nation ahead of the Scramble for Africa by modernizing it before the empire-hungry Italians could overtake it.

Like all Ethiopian kings, Menelik II claimed to be descended from the ancient Hebrew King Solomon and

his famous visitor the Queen of Sheba (I Kings 10:1-13; ancient Sheba may have been part of the territory that became Ethiopia). He became Ethiopia's emperor in 1889 after his rival, Yohannes IV, died in a war against Sudan. From the moment he took over the emperor's throne, Menelik II had trouble with Italy, because according to the 1885 General Act of the Berlin Conference, Italy alone had the right to colonize Ethiopia.

This trouble arrived in the form of the Treaty of Wuchale, an 1889 treaty between Italy and Ethiopia. In the Treaty of Wuchale, Emperor Menelik II agreed to grant Italy control of several northern provinces of Ethiopia in exchange for Italian money and military aid. However, the emperor soon discovered that the Italian-language version of the Treaty of Wuchale said something very different from the Amharic-language version prepared for the Ethiopians. The Italian version said that all of Ethiopia was a protectorate of Italy, which meant that in the eyes of Italians, Ethiopia had become a colony of Italy. The Ethiopian version said no such thing. An outraged Emperor Menelik demanded that Italy change its version of the treaty, but Italy refused. So Menelik renounced the Treaty of Wuchale; and in response, Italy invaded Ethiopia, setting off the First Italo-Ethiopian War in 1895-1896.

Italy believed that its superior weapons technology would allow it to make light work of the backward Ethiopians. What Italy didn't know was that Menelik had purchased modern weapons of his own from Russia and France. Menelik also had one other major advantage: his loyal Ethiopian troops far outnumbered the Italian invaders.

At the 1896 Battle of Adwa, Emperor Menelik II's Ethiopia dealt Italy the only major military defeat suffered by any European power during the entire Scramble for Africa. The Treaty of Addis Ababa that ended the First Italo-Ethiopian War straightened out the disagreement over the Treaty of Wuchale, making it clear that Ethiopia was independent of Italy. The northern provinces that Ethiopia had ceded to Italy in the Treaty of Wuchale remained part of the Italian Empire, and later became the nation of Eritrea.

SOUTH AFRICA

A Brief Timeline of the South Africa Colonies

1497: Portuguese explorer Vasco da Gama sails around southern Africa near Christmastime, and names its eastern coast Natal in honor of Christ's birth.
1652: The Dutch East India Company founds Cape Town and Cape Colony at South Africa's rocky southern tip, the Cape of Good Hope.
1795: After Napoleon's France gains control of the Netherlands, Britain seizes Cape Colony from the Dutch in order to keep the important seaport out of French hands.
1803: Britain returns Cape Colony to Dutch control.
1806: Britain seizes Cape Colony once again to keep it out of Napoleon's hands.
1820: A group of British settlers known as the 1820 Settlers arrives to settle in the territory that will become South Africa's eastern province of Natal.
1816-1826: The Zulu Empire expands under the leadership of Zulu King Shaka.
1835-1840: In order to escape British domination, the Voortrekkers (Dutch-descended pioneers) leave Cape Colony to establish independent Boer (farmer) colonies in what will become the Natalia Republic, the Orange Free State and the Transvaal Republic.
1843: Britain conquers the closest Boer colony, the Natalia Republic, and makes it a British colony. The remaining Boers move on to Transvaal and the Orange Free State.
1852: In negotiations at the Sand River Convention, the Boers of the Transvaal gain independence from Britain.
1854: In negotiations at the Orange River Convention, the Boers of the Orange Free State gain independence from Britain.
1856: The highly independent Boers of the Transvaal unite to create the Transvaal Republic.
1866: A 15-year-old shepherd boy named Erasmus Jacobs discovers the Eureka Diamond, the first diamond discovered in South Africa, near the Orange River. As a result, the rest of the world suddenly becomes more interested in Africa's interior.
1871: Briton Cecil Rhodes (see below) enters South Africa's diamond mining business.
1877: Britain revokes the Transvaal Republic's independence and annexes (absorbs) the Transvaal.
1879: Britain defeats the Zulus in the Anglo-Zulu War and adds Zululand to its Natal Colony.
1880: Cecil Rhodes helps found the DeBeers diamond mining company, which will become the world's largest and wealthiest diamond company.
1880-1881: In the First Boer War, the Boers of the Transvaal rebel against British control. The Boers defeat the British, and the Transvaal Republic's independence is restored.
1880s: Britain's interest in the Transvaal is renewed when gold is discovered there. Great numbers of British-born "outlanders" begin to move into Boer Transvaal, looking for gold.
1889: Cecil Rhodes founds the British South Africa Company and uses it to establish more British territory north of the Transvaal. The Boer-controlled Transvaal will soon be surrounded by British territory.

1890: Cecil Rhodes becomes Cape Colony's prime minister.

1895: Rhodes and others plan the Jameson Raid, a plot to support an outlander rebellion against the Boers in the hope that the outlanders will overthrow the Transvaal's Boer government. The Jameson Raid fails, and the exposure of Rhodes' plot increases the angry tension between the British and the Boers. Rhodes loses his place as prime minister in early 1896.

The Boers

Boer is the Dutch word for "farmer." The Boers of South Africa were the farmer descendants of Cape Colony's original Dutch settlers. Long after Britain seized Cape Colony from the Dutch, large communities of Boers continued to live there. Most Boers were tough, self-sufficient and highly independent farmers of the African frontier, and many of them owned slaves. They spoke a derivative of the Dutch language known as Afrikaans, and they referred to themselves as Afrikaners. The Boers were not, as a rule, overly fond of Britons.

In the 1830s, the Boers of Cape Colony began a massive northward migration to escape British control. Large groups of Boer *Voortrekkers*, or pioneers, moved across the Vaal and Orange Rivers to areas beyond British control, seeking freedom and independence. Britain allowed the new Boer colonies of the trans-Vaal and the trans-Orange to become independent in the 1850s because, at the time, it had little interest in the territory they claimed.

The First Boer War

All of that changed in 1866, when fifteen-year-old Erasmus Jacobs found a huge diamond on his father's farm in the Transvaal (the 21-carat Eureka Diamond). Geologists soon discovered that South Africa contained far more diamonds than any other place in the world. Britons like Cecil Rhodes began to move into South Africa to take advantage of its diamond wealth, purchasing mining lands in Cape Colony, the Boer territories and beyond.

In 1877, Britain tried to revoke the Transvaal's independence and claim its territory. However, the Boers were tough fighters and accurate marksmen, and their militia soon drove the British out of the Transvaal, winning the short First Boer War in 1880-1881. The Transvaal and the Orange Free State managed to remain free of the powerful British Empire after the First Boer War.

The Jameson Raid

Soon, however, further mineral discoveries made the Boers' land in the Transvaal even more valuable. During the 1880s, miners discovered that South Africa was home to plentiful gold as well as diamonds. The South African Gold Rush of 1886, also known as the Witwatersrand Gold Rush, brought so many British gold-hunting "outlanders" to the Transvaal that the outlanders soon outnumbered the Boers. The Boers knew that if they allowed the British outlanders to vote in their elections, then their nation would soon be overtaken by Britain again.

Cecil Rhodes, who was by now Cape Colony's prime minister, wanted the Transvaal for Britain. His hope was that the many British outlanders in the Transvaal would rebel against the Transvaal's Boer government, conquering it for Britain without the need for a long war. When his outlander rebellion failed to materialize, Rhodes tried to help it along by stationing troops along Cape Colony's border with the Transvaal. The plan for the Jameson Raid, named for its commander, Sir Leander Jameson, was to wait for the expected outlander rebellion to begin, then cross the border to "restore order" and conquer the Transvaal in the process.

Frustratingly, the outlander rebellion in the Transvaal still refused to materialize. Finally, on December 29, 1895, Jameson grew tired of waiting and decided to attack the Transvaal on his own. None of the wishes of Rhodes and Jameson came true: no outlanders joined Jameson's raiders, and the Boers easily defeated his small force soon after his attack began. An embarrassed Cecil Rhodes lost his office as prime minister over the bungled Jameson Raid; and his brother, whom the Boers had captured during the raid, was nearly executed for treason. The Jameson Raid gave the Boers yet another reason to distrust the grasping British.

All of this distrust led to the 1899-1902 Second Boer War, a much longer and nastier affair than the first.

FASCINATING FACTS: The Second Boer War (1899 – 1902)

The Second Boer War was a long, ugly and cruel conflict between the British Empire on one side and the Boers of the Transvaal and the Orange Free State on the other. The Boers had established their two colonies mainly in order to get away from British control, and they were determined to remain independent of Britain. The British wanted the Boers' mineral-rich land, and were determined to have it now that that British-born outlanders outnumbered the Boers in many areas of the Transvaal.

The Second Boer War began as the First Boer War had begun, with a number of Boer victories. Beginning on October 12, 1899, the Boers invaded British-held Cape Colony and Natal Colony, laying siege to ill-prepared British forts at Mafeking, Kimberley and Ladysmith. Unfortunately for the Boers, these sieges lasted too long, leaving the British with plenty of time to call in reinforcements.

In time, an enormous army of British reinforcements arrived and overpowered the Boer militias. Britain captured the Orange Free State's capital, Bloemfontein, in March 1900; and it captured the Transvaal's capital, Pretoria, in June 1900. The hard-fighting Boers lost their independence yet again when Britain annexed (absorbed) both colonies.

Instead of giving up, however, the Boers retreated into the wild and conducted a guerrilla-style war against their British occupiers for two more long, bitter years. The country-wise Boers would emerge from the wild to attack, then disappear again without leaving a trace.

The British responded to the Boers' guerrilla attacks with two dreadful tactics of their own:

1. They launched a "scorched earth" total war on the Boers in which they burned the Boers' farms, poisoned their wells, destroyed their livestock, salted their fields and did everything possible to prevent them from feeding themselves; and
2. They confined captured Boers to concentration camps in which Boer women, children and prisoners of war were locked away and held under miserable conditions. They also held black refugees in camps, under even worse conditions. Lack of food and poor medical care led to as many as 50,000 Boer deaths in Britain's terrible concentration camps.

Left with little way to feed themselves, the last Boer guerrillas finally surrendered in 1902. The Treaty of Vereeniging, which ended the Second Boer War, made British colonies of both the Transvaal and the Orange Free State.

In 1910, all four South African colonies— Cape, Natal, Transvaal and Orange Free State— united to form the Union of South Africa, a dominion of Great Britain. It would remain a dominion until 1961, when it gained full independence from Britain as the Republic of South Africa. But the brutality and misery of the Second Boer War had sown the seeds of a long and fertile hatred between South Africa's three major people groups: the British, the Boer Afrikaners and the native Africans (see Chapter 30 for more on South Africa).

1899: The Second Boer War begins in the Transvaal Republic and the Orange Free State.

1902: Britain defeats the Boers, and the Treaty of Vereeniging ends Second Boer War. The Transvaal Republic and the Orange Free State become British colonies with only limited self-government.
1910: South Africa's British colonies unite to form the Union of South Africa.

INTERESTING INDIVIDUALS: Cecil Rhodes (1853 – 1902)

Cecil Rhodes was a Briton who grew fabulously wealthy mining and selling South African diamonds. He was also a powerful British "imperialist," or empire-builder, who sought to bring as much African territory under British control as possible. Rhodes is perhaps the second most notorious figure of the Scramble for Africa, behind Belgium's King Leopold II.

Rhodes came to South Africa as a teenager in 1871, when diamond mining there was in its infancy. Funded by Rothschild's, a British banking firm, Rhodes bought small mining operations all over the South African colonies. In 1880 he co-founded DeBeers Consolidated Mines, which would become the largest diamond company in the world. Over the next two decades, Rhodes' diamond companies grew until they controlled nearly all of the world's diamond supplies, and Rhodes himself became fabulously wealthy.

Rhodes was a firm believer in the superiority of the British race. As his mine holdings spread north from South Africa, he conceived a vision of a "red line" of British territory all across Africa, from Cape Town, South Africa to Cairo, Egypt. Along this line, he envisioned modern improvements like railroads and telegraph lines that would make it easier for Britain to harvest the fantastic wealth of Africa's interior. A well-known political cartoon depicts a colossal Rhodes standing astride the continent of Africa, with one booted foot in South Africa and the other in Egypt, suspending a telegraph wire in his outstretched arms (the cartoon is a play on the ancient Colossus of Rhodes).

In 1889, Rhodes helped to found the British South Africa Company (BSAC). The BSAC was similar to the British East India Company in both name and purpose: its charter from the British government allowed it to take and hold African territories by purchase, by treaty or even by force if necessary. The BSAC established British colonies for Rhodes in central Africa, north of the Boers' Transvaal; and it protected those colonies with its own private police force. By 1895, two of these colonies were named in Rhodes' honor: Northern Rhodesia and Southern Rhodesia.

When Rhodes became Cape Colony's prime minister in 1890, he used the power of his office to win more British control over Africa and its natives. Because of his faith in British superiority, Prime Minister Rhodes never allowed native Africans to vote. He encouraged any idea that would help drive the natives out of their homelands and make more room for Britons. He also supported the Hut Tax, a tax on every hut (home) in the colony that often forced penniless native Africans to work for Rhodes' mining companies in order to earn money to pay the tax. Rhodes lost his place as Cape Colony's prime minister in 1896 after he supported the Jameson Raid, a failed plot to start a British outlander rebellion against the Boer government in the Transvaal (see above).

Cecil Rhodes died of a heart attack in 1902, at the age of 48. Decades later, when the Scramble for Africa was long past and most African nations had won their independence, native Africans looked back on Rhodes' superior attitude with anger. The African nations that once honored Rhodes by bearing his name do so no longer: his Southern Rhodesia colony now bears the name Zimbabwe, and his Northern Rhodesia colony bears the name Zambia.

Other interesting facts about Cecil Rhodes:
- Between trips to South Africa, young Cecil Rhodes found time to attend Oxford University. When Rothschild's Bank executed Rhodes' will after his death, it established Oxford's well-known Rhodes Scholarships in his name.
- A quote from Rhodes: "Remember that you are an Englishman, and have consequently won first prize in the lottery of life."
- Another quote: "I contend that we are the first race in the world, and that the more of the world we inhabit the better it is for the human race...If there be a God, I think that what he would like me to do is paint as much of the map of Africa British Red as possible..."[1]

FASCINATING FACTS: The Boy Scout Badge

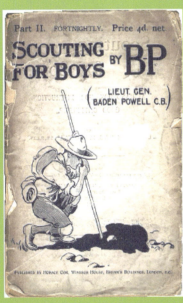

During the Second Boer War, a British military officer named Robert Baden-Powell successfully defended the city of Mafeking, South Africa from the Boers with some help from a cadet corps of boys too young for military service. Baden-Powell also wrote a military manual called Aids to Scouting designed to help the British army train its forward observers. He was surprised to learn that his manual was popular with young boys. The manual's success inspired Baden-Powell and his family to found the Boy Scout movement.

In his manual *Scouting for Boys*, Baden-Powell designed a scout's badge. He chose the *fleur-de-lis* symbol for the badge because it indicated the compass point north on the maps of his day, and because maps were important in scouting. He chose the motto "Be Prepared" for the Boy Scouts because it had the same initials as his name.

Chapter 12

Tsarist Russia, the Spanish American War

WORLD HISTORY FOCUS

RUSSIA

Russia Under the Romanovs

The Russian word *tsar* comes from the Latin word *Caesar*, and means "emperor." The first Russian tsar was Ivan IV the Terrible, who reigned from 1533-1584 and first claimed the title "tsar" for himself in 1547. The tsars ruled in Russia from 1547-1917, with some interruptions during the Time of Troubles from 1598-1613.

From 1613 until the end in 1917, every tsar belonged to the Romanov Dynasty. Michael Romanov, a nephew of Ivan the Terrible's wife Anastasia Romanovna, was the first Romanov Tsar. The best-known Romanov tsars of the early Modern era were Peter I the Great (reigned 1682-1725, see Year 3, Chapter 13) and Catherine the Great (reigned 1762-1796, see Year 3, Chapter 23). Both Peter and Catherine are remembered for modernizing backward Russia, but Catherine is also remembered for her likely involvement in a successful plot to execute her husband, Tsar Peter III.

Under Tsar Alexander I (reigned 1801-1825), Russia survived the threat of France's Napoleon. Alexander I's son and heir was Tsar Alexander II the Liberator.

INTERESTING INDIVIDUALS: Tsar Alexander II the Liberator (1818 – 1881, reigned 1855 – 1881)

Tsar Alexander II came to power in 1855, the first year of the Crimean War. The 1856 Treaty of Paris brought that war to a disappointing end for Russia, which once again lost its chance to capture Constantinople and gain access to the Mediterranean Sea (see Chapter 2).

After the loss of the Crimean War, Alexander began to realize that Russia's economy was far less advanced than the economies of the other European powers. Russia was one of the last places in the world that still retained its version of the feudal system, a system in which peasant serfs owned nearly nothing of their own and depended on Russian nobles for everything. This system had several drawbacks:

1. It kept the serfs so poor that they were often unproductive;
2. It divided farm land inefficiently; and
3. It created an angry underclass of people who were likely to rebel against their lords.

Tsar Alexander II solved these problems with his 1861 Emancipation Manifesto, which freed Russia's serfs. Alexander decided to allow the liberated serfs to purchase land from their lords, and even loaned the former serfs government money with which to do so. In this way, Tsar Alexander liberated over 20 million Russians from serfdom. The money Alexander's government paid the nobles in exchange for their land kept the nobles happy, but it also placed his government deep in debt.

Alexander also gave Russia's people the beginnings of a Western-style representative government. Under Alexander, each town or district elected its own *zemstvo*, or council. He also reformed his nation's corrupt military and its courts. Despite these reforms, however, groups of revolutionaries constantly protested against Alexander, demanding that he give up his absolute rule as tsar and create a constitutional monarchy in Russia like the ones in Western Europe. These revolutionaries accompanied their protests with no fewer than four attempts to assassinate Alexander.

Their fifth assassination attempt succeeded. In 1881, Alexander II was working on a constitution that would have created a new, freer government for Russia, one that would have included a national assembly of elected representatives from each *zemstvo*. While he was still working out the constitution's details, two revolutionaries attacked his traveling carriage with grenades. Their grenades missed their target, and Alexander survived their first attack; but when he got out of his carriage to check on others whom the grenades had injured, a third attacker killed him with another grenade. All hope of a Western-style constitutional monarchy under Russia's tsars died with Tsar Alexander II.

Other interesting facts about Alexander II:
- Alexander II is often compared to U.S. President Abraham Lincoln, for two reasons: (1) because both liberated slaves, and (2) because both were assassinated.

FASCINATING FACTS: Russian Serfs

Like the serfs of Medieval Western Europe, Russian serfs, or *muzhiks,* were peasants who lived to serve their lords. They lived on land and in houses granted to them by their lords, and spent about one third of their time working in their lords' fields. Many Russians became serfs during the 1200s, when the Mongol hordes ravaged much of Eastern Europe and the poor needed protection that only powerful lords could provide. With time, the lords gained more and more power over their serfs. Many of the serfs that Alexander II freed could be bought and sold like slaves, and could neither marry as they chose nor leave their lord's lands without permission.

DASTARDLY DICTATORS: Tsar Alexander III (1845 – 1894, reigned 1881 – 1894)

When Tsar Alexander II's son, Alexander III, was 36 years old, he watched his father's broken body bleed to death from wounds inflicted by revolutionaries' bombs. These revolutionaries had attacked his father despite all of his best efforts to give them what they wanted: a constitutional monarchy that was more like the governments of the West. Alexander III was different from his father: he had grown up believing in the absolute power of Russia's tsars, and he wanted nothing to do with creating a Western-style constitutional monarchy in Russia.

Alexander went in the opposite direction. Instead of granting the Russian people more liberty, he took away what little liberty they had. He controlled Russia's presses and newspapers so that no word of any revolution could spread. His secret police scoured the nation for revolutionaries, gathering information even from the Orthodox Christian priests who heard confessions in church. He sent every revolutionary he found, along with everyone he even suspected of being a revolutionary, to work camps in the far-north, frigid Russian province of Siberia. Alexander III's reign is known in Russia as the Age of Counter Reform.

Tsar Alexander III also hated Jews, and laid much of the blame for his father's assassination at the Jews' feet. To Alexander, Russia's Jews were a convenient target for the bottled-up frustration of the Russian people.

Like other Europeans, Russian Christians were convinced that wealthy Jewish bankers and shopkeepers were the real cause of Russia's poverty problem; so Alexander organized *pogroms*, violent anti-Jewish riots, to make sure that Russia's angry masses blamed their poverty on the Jews and not on his government.

In 1882, Alexander III further restricted the Jews' rights with new anti-Jewish laws known as the **May Laws**. Under the May Laws:
1. Jews were not allowed to settle outside cities and towns;
2. Jews were not allowed to own property or hold mortgages (home loans); and
3. Jews were required to close their businesses on Sundays and during Christian holidays.

The only way the Jews could escape their oppression under Tsar Alexander III was to leave Russia. Alexander III's reign was the beginning of a huge Jewish migration that carried millions of Jews from Russia to America and other havens.

Although Alexander III was a harsh ruler, he was apparently a loving husband and father. He was also a "Russian bear" of a man, uncommonly large and strong. In 1888, Alexander and his family were riding in a railroad dining car when their train suddenly derailed, probably because it was speeding. Reportedly, Alexander III saved his family by holding up the dining car's roof by himself until they could escape. Alexander's train accident became known as the Borki Train Disaster.

Alexander also suffered a kidney bruise in the Borki Train Disaster, a wound that would lead to his early death in 1894. Tsar Alexander III's son, Tsar Nicholas II, would be Russia's last Tsar.

FASCINATING FACTS: Pogroms in Russia

Pogrom is a Russian word for "devastation." During Tsar Alexander III's reign, the word *pogrom* began to refer to the Russian people's devastating attacks on Russia's Jews.

Anti-Semitism, or hatred for the Jews, had a long history in Russia before the time of Tsar Alexander III. In 1791, Empress Catherine the Great established Russia's Pale of Settlement, a bounded area outside of which Jews were not allowed to settle (the word "pale" can mean "fence"). The boundaries of the Pale of Settlement changed over the years, especially after Russia gained territory from Poland in the 1772-1795 Partitions of Poland. Poland had a large Jewish population, and Russian Poland was part of the Pale of Settlement. Most Jews of the Pale of Settlement lived in small Jewish villages called *shtetls*.

Violent pogroms against Russian Jews became far more common after the assassination of Tsar Alexander II in 1881. Alexander III blamed his father's murder on the Jews, so he either encouraged the pogroms himself or at least did nothing to stop them. The first major wave of anti-Jewish pogroms lasted from 1881 - 1884, and another wave lasted from 1903-1906.

Despite Russia's laws against crime, any violent crime against the Jews was legal during a pogrom: the Russian police were willing to tolerate vandalism, theft, rape or even murder, so long as the victim was a Jew. When the Russian authorities refused to protect them, the Jews had nowhere to turn for help. The constant threat of violence forced millions of Jews to leave their homes, sometimes forever.

Russia's violent, anti-Jewish pogroms had two major effects:
- They led millions of Russian Jews to leave Russia and migrate to America and other havens; and
- They led Jews to join the Zionist Organization, a political movement that sought to re-create a Jewish nation

in Palestine. Zionist Jews would finally succeed in recreating their ancient nation of Israel in 1948.

The Broadway musical *Fiddler on the Roof* is set in a Jewish *shtetl* (Anatevka) in the Russian Pale of Settlement, and its plot involves a pogrom that forces all of the *shtetl*'s Jews to leave their homes.

FASCINATING FACTS: The Periodic Table of the Elements
Photo: Sculpture in honor of Mendeleev and the periodic table

Russian scientist Dmitri Mendeleev published his first Periodic Table of the Elements in 1869. Mendeleev's table was a highly useful representation of the repeating properties of the natural elements, and it was a great leap forward in humankind's understanding of the nature of the elements.

U.S. HISTORY FOCUS

THE SPANISH-AMERICAN WAR

Spain's New World Empire

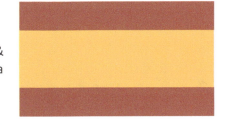

The Spanish Empire in the New World began with Christopher Columbus' 1492 settlement on the island of Hispaniola (modern-day Haiti & Dominican Republic, see picture). From there it spread to Puerto Rico, Cuba and Panama before its *conquistadors* claimed vast holdings for Spain in South, Central and North America. Explorer Ferdinand Magellan carried Spanish influence to the islands of the Philippines and Guam in 1521. At its peak during the late 1500s, Spain controlled more New World territory than any other European power.

The rivers of silver and gold that Spain collected from its New World colonies were both a blessing and a curse. On one hand, they made Spain fabulously wealthy. On the other hand, they led to inflation, raising the

prices of goods so high that they wrecked the Spanish economy. They also led Spanish manufacturers to create fewer goods at home: with so much silver readily available, it was easier to purchase goods from other nations than to create them in Spain. Instead of strengthening the Spanish Empire, all of that easy money weakened it. After the Peace of Westphalia ended Europe's Thirty Years' War in 1648, the Spanish Empire began a long decline.

During the early 1800s, Spain's New World territories began to escape its grasp, largely due to Spain's troubles with Emperor Napoleon of France. In 1800, Napoleon took away most of Spain's North American holdings when he forced Spain to return the Louisiana Territory to France (Napoleon then sold the Louisiana Territory to the U.S. in 1803). And in 1808, Napoleon invaded Spain and deposed King Ferdinand VII, hoping to replace Spain's king with his brother Joseph Bonaparte.

Napoleon's meddling temporarily destroyed Spain's government, leaving Spain's American and island colonies to fend for themselves. The colonies created temporary governments for themselves known as *juntas*. These colonial juntas wanted to remain in power even after the threat from Napoleon was over; and soon all of

Spain's former colonies were becoming independent in the 1808 - 1829 Spanish-American Wars of Independence. By 1830, out of all of its formerly enormous New World holdings, Spain retained only the islands of Cuba and Puerto Rico.

Trouble in Cuba

Although Cuba remained a thriving part of the Spanish Empire, all was not quiet there. Cuban rebels first declared their independence from Spain in 1868, but their Ten Years War against Spanish occupation ended with a loss in 1878. Several American Presidents, including Thomas Jefferson, Franklin Pierce and William McKinley, were interested in annexing (absorbing) Cuba into the United States; but Cuba used slave labor to tend its huge fields of sugar cane, and American abolitionists would not allow Cuba to enter the United States as a slave state.

The Cuban War for Independence

The Cuban War for Independence began in 1895, when exiled Cubans who were living in Florida, Costa Rica and the Dominican Republic invaded Cuba and tried to overthrow the Spanish government there. These poorly-armed, ill-trained rebels were no match for the Spanish army, so the Spaniards quickly defeated them. Instead of surrendering, however, the rebels resorted to a guerrilla-style war-- emerging from hiding to launch swift attacks, then disappearing into hiding again.

In order to crush the guerrillas and cut off their support, the Spanish army began to imprison hundreds of thousands of Cubans in some of the world's first concentration camps (similar to the concentration camps the British would create for South Africa's Boers in 1900). The lack of food and cleanliness inside these Spanish-run concentration camps made living conditions there both miserable and deadly. After about 200,000-400,000 Cubans died in Spanish-run concentration camps, the world began to take notice of Spain's harsh treatment of Cubans.

Enter the United States

Cuba was important to the United States for two reasons: (1) because it was so close to U.S. shores, and (2) because so many U.S. businesses depended on Cuban trade.

Riot and revolution in Cuba were dangerous for Americans who lived in Cuba, as well as for U.S. businesses that operated there. U.S. President William McKinley wanted to protect U.S. businesses in Cuba by ending the Cuban War for Independence peacefully. In 1897, President McKinley offered to purchase Cuba from Spain for 300 million dollars. When Spain rejected that offer, McKinley asked Spain to consider creating a new Cuban government with only limited Spanish control.

In January 1898, as the rioting continued in Cuba, McKinley sent the battleship *USS Maine* into Cuba's Havana Harbor in order to protect about 8,000 Americans who were living there. On February 15, 1898, while the *Maine* was anchored at Havana Harbor, it suddenly exploded and sank.

> FASCINATING FACTS: The Destruction of the USS *Maine*
>
> In early 1898, Cuba stood on the verge of achieving partial independence from Spain, but Cuban revolutionaries were continuing to demand nothing less than full independence. Riots in Havana continued, endangering the roughly 8,000 American citizens who lived there. In order to protect those citizens, diplomats (negotiators) from the United States requested and received Spain's reluctant

permission to send the *USS Maine* into Havana harbor.

The *Maine* was a heavily-armored U.S. battleship that had been launched in 1890 and commissioned for active naval service in 1895. She was a coal-fired steamer with eight boilers, two enormous steam engines and four ten-inch main guns that could each fire a 520-pound shell a distance of 11 miles.

When the *Maine* steamed into Havana Harbor on January 25, 1898, her mission was not to conquer Spanish Cuba, but to preserve its peace. Her captain kept his crew aboard the ship to prevent any unforeseen incidents that might become a cause for war.

Unexpectedly, the *Maine* itself became a cause for war when it suddenly exploded in Havana Harbor on February 15, 1898. 260 American sailors died in the blast, which obliterated the forward third of the ship and quickly sent the rest of it to the bottom of the shallow harbor.

Americans immediately suspected Spain of destroying the *Maine*, because the Spanish resented the United States' intrusion into Spanish-Cuban affairs. Americans who were already angry over Spain's horrible treatment of the Cuban prisoners in their concentration camps now added the destruction of the *Maine* and the murders of her crewmen to their list of grievances against Spain.

The U.S. Navy's investigation into the cause of the *Maine* explosion required four weeks. In the end, the Americans concluded that a submerged mine had struck the *Maine* near her powder magazine, touching off an explosion in the magazine's five tons of highly explosive gunpowder. The Spanish claimed that the navy's investigators were wrong, and that spontaneous combustion-- a fire without a spark, caused by heat buildup in the *Maine*'s coal hold-- had caused the explosion.

Later investigations into the *Maine* explosion have never been able to prove exactly what happened. Another American investigation in 1911 seemed to confirm the Navy's mine theory, but other investigators claimed the opposite. The explosion of the *Maine* remains an unsolved mystery, open to interpretation: Spain's defenders say that imperialist Americans used the *Maine* incident as a convenient cause for a trumped-up war; while America's defenders still believe that someone on the Spanish side mined, torpedoed or otherwise sabotaged the *Maine*.

Other Causes of the Spanish-American War

Spanish atrocities in Cuba and the fate of the *Maine* were not the Spanish-American War's only causes. Long before the war, some Americans sought ways to build up the U.S. Navy and remake the isolated United States as a world power. Among them:

- **U.S. Navy Captain Alfred T. Mahan**, who wrote the influential 1890 book *The Influence of Sea Power upon History, 1660-1783*. Mahan believed that the nation that controlled the seas, controlled the world. He promoted the idea that in order to become a dominant sea power, the U.S. Navy needed control of coal ports all over the Pacific Ocean, ports like Hawaii and the Philippines.

- **U.S. Assistant Secretary of the Navy (and future President) Theodore Roosevelt**. Before the Spanish-American War, Roosevelt ordered U.S. Navy Commodore George Dewey to capture the Philippines immediately if the U.S. went to war with Spain. The Philippines had little to do with liberating Cuba, but much to do with improving U.S. naval power.

The United States had been accused of imperialism (greedy empire-building) in the 1846-1848 Mexican War. The same accusations, and worse, arose over the Spanish-American War.

German chancellor Otto von Bismarck once commented that America had "contrived to be surrounded on two sides by weak neighbors, and on two sides by fish." In the Spanish-American War, the United States ventured outside of those protections to assume a bigger role on the world stage.

A Brief Timeline of the Spanish-American War

1492: Christopher Columbus claims Cuba and Hispaniola for Spain.
1823, 1848 and 1854: U.S. Presidents John Q. Adams, James Polk and Franklin Pierce all offer to purchase Cuba from Spain.
1868-1878: The Ten Years' War, a war for Cuban independence from Spain, ends with Spain still in control of Cuba.
1883: Newspaper publisher Joseph Pulitzer purchases the *New York World.*
1895: The Cuban War of Independence begins.
1895, June: U.S. President Grover Cleveland announces that the U.S. will remain neutral in the Cuban War of Independence.
1895, November: Newspaper publisher William Randolph Hearst purchases the *New York Journal.*
1896, February: Spain places Cuban civilians in concentration camps to prevent them from helping Cuban rebels.
1896, August: The Philippine Revolution begins.
1897, January: *World* publisher William Randolph Hearst sends journalists to Cuba to report on the Cuban War for Independence.
1897, May: American businessmen and bankers appeal to U.S. President McKinley to stop the chaos in Cuba because it is destroying their businesses.
1898, January 25: The *USS Maine* arrives at Cuba's Havana harbor.
1898 February 15: The *Maine* explodes.

FASCINATING FACTS: Yellow Journalism and the Spanish-American War

The term "**yellow journalism**" comes from two New York newspapers, the *New York World* and the *New York Journal*, both of which published versions of a popular color cartoon featuring a character called "The Yellow Kid." The *World* was published by Joseph Pulitzer, and the *Journal* by William Randolph Hearst. Both newspapers competed for the same readers; and in doing so, both sometimes published fantastic pictures and stories that either stretched the truth or jumped to conclusions without examining all of the facts. These newspapers' tactic of appealing to readers' senses, rather than their minds, came to be known as "sensational" or "yellow" journalism.

Both the *World* and the *Journal* were accused of yellow journalism in the days before the Spanish-American War. Both tried to hold their readers' interest by keeping the Cuban War for Independence and Spain's concentration camp abuses on their front pages.

Of the two newspapers, the *Journal* was probably the worse. Before the war, at a time when the Cuban riots had died down, the *Journal*'s Hearst reportedly instructed one of his illustrators to remain in Cuba, telling him "You furnish the pictures and I'll furnish the war." When the *Maine* exploded, Pulitzer's *World* contented itself with a spectacular drawing of the exploding *Maine*; but Hearst's *Journal* treated the *Maine* incident like a crime drama, offering a $50,000 reward for capture of the "perpetrator." After the U.S. finally declared war on Spain, Hearst printed a headline asking "How Do You Like the *Journal*'s War?"

Pulitzer and Hearst's newspaper duel received a great deal of credit for causing the Spanish-American War, but it is difficult to say how much they actually influenced the United States' declaration of war on Spain. Neither newspaper circulated outside New York, but both probably influenced other newspapers that did. The flavor of their reporting influenced the opinion of the American public, and that opinion was one of the main reasons for the American government's decision to go to war. After the destruction of the *Maine*, America's public opinion was strongly against Spain.

AMAZING AMERICANS: Nellie Bly (1864 – 1922)

Female writers of the Victorian Era often used pen names to protect their identity and modesty. *Nellie Bly* was the pen name of Elizabeth Jane Cochran, a journalist for publisher Joseph Pulitzer's *New York World*. Her pen name came from a Steven Foster folk song.

Nellie Bly won fame for two of her assignments at the *World*. The first was an undercover assignment: she pretended to be insane so that she would be committed to an insane asylum, where she could discover first-hand how its patients were treated. After spending ten days in the asylum, she released a scathing report under the headline "Ten Days in a Mad-House" in which she exposed the ill-treatment of New York's mental patients.

The second assignment was a well-publicized journey around the world, taken in honor of Jules Verne's 1873 novel *Around the World in Eighty Days*. Both the novel and Bly's assignment took advantage of excitement about the modern railroads and steamships of the day, which made such rapid and romantic journeys possible. Nellie Bly circumnavigated the globe in the 72 days from November 14, 1889 through January 25, 1890, sending regular progress reports to the *World* by telegraph and by mail. The *World* drummed up excitement about her trip by sponsoring a contest to see which reader could guess the exact moment of her return.

1898, February 17: Before any investigation of the *Maine* explosion can begin, the *New York Journal* accuses Spain of deliberately destroying the *Maine*.
1898, March 21: U.S. Navy investigators conclude that a submerged mine destroyed the *Maine*.
1898, April 21: The United States Navy blockades Cuba.

1898, April 24: Spain declares war on the United States. **The Spanish-American War begins.**

1898, May 1: Commodore George Dewey's naval squadron arrives at the Philippines and defeats the Spanish in the Battle of Manila Bay.

1898, June 10: United States Marines capture Cuba's Guantanamo Bay from Spain (The Marines are in Guantanamo Bay still).
1898, June 12: Filipino rebels declare their independence from Spain. Neither Spain nor the United States recognizes Philippine independence.

The Philippine Revolution

As if the Spanish didn't have enough trouble in Cuba, the people of the Philippines, a group of Spanish-controlled islands in Southeast Asia, supplied them with even more. The Philippine Revolution of 1896-1898 happened at the same time as the Cuban War for Independence. Before the Philippine Revolution was over, it would also lead to a third war: the Philippine-American War of 1899-1902.

The Filipinos' desire for independence had its roots in the work of well-educated reformers known as the *Ilustrados*. One of the *Ilustrados*, Jose Rizal, became a Philippine national hero after the Spanish executed him for exposing Spain's greedy and corrupt treatment of the Philippines. A revolutionary group called the *Katipunan* organized an armed rebellion against Spain that began in 1896. But the *Katipunan*'s rebel troops, armed mainly with spears and bolo knives, continually lost ground against Spanish troops equipped with modern rifles and cannon.

The United States got involved in the Philippine Revolution after it declared war on Spain and blockaded Cuba on April 20, 1898. U.S. Commodore George Dewey's squadron arrived in the Philippines' Manila Bay on May 1 and wiped out the Spanish squadron there within hours, destroying seven Spanish ships and losing none of its own. When the sea battle was over, Filipino troops dug trenches around Manila, the Philippines' capital, and laid siege to the city. Months later, American troops commanded by General Arthur MacArthur (father of the well-known World War II General Douglas MacArthur) broke through the Spaniards' defenses and captured Manila.

After the United States captured Manila, the Filipinos began to wonder whether the Americans had come to liberate them or simply to replace the Spanish as their colonial governors. Nevertheless, after the U.S. defeated Spain, the Philippines declared independence from Spain on June 12, 1898 and established a dictatorship under Emilio Aguinaldo, the leader of the *Katipunan*. American troops held Manila, but Filipino troops still surrounded Manila and held the rest of the islands.

Spanish-American War Timeline, continued:

1898, June 20: Spanish authorities surrender the Island of Guam to the United States (Like the Philippines, Guam was part of the Spanish East Indies in Southeast Asia).
1898, June 22-24: American ground forces land in Cuba near the heavily defended port city of Santiago de Cuba.
1898, July 1: Teddy Roosevelt and the Rough Riders capture Cuba's San Juan Heights, ensuring the capture of Santiago de Cuba.

FASCINATING FACTS: Theodore Roosevelt and the Rough Riders

"The Rough Riders" was a fighting name for the First U.S. Volunteer Cavalry Regiment, a U.S. Army cavalry unit led by Colonel Theodore Roosevelt. The future President Roosevelt was one of the Spanish-American War's biggest supporters; so when the U.S. declared war on Spain, he immediately resigned his position as Assistant Secretary of the Navy and joined the army as a lieutenant colonel. During the Cuban campaign, Roosevelt was promoted to full colonel and placed in command of the Rough Rider regiment.

Unfortunately, a shortage of transport ships meant that most of the Rough Riders' horses had to be left behind in Florida. Although they had been trained to fight from horseback, nearly all of them were forced to fight on foot when they arrived in Cuba. Some of them dubbed themselves the "Weary Walkers" instead of the "Rough Riders."

Roosevelt and his Rough Riders were among the Cuban campaign's most important army units. Roosevelt himself bravely led charges on Cuba's Kettle Hill and San Juan Hill, dodging back and forth on one of his regiment's only horses, "Little Texas." The Rough Riders' capture of the San Juan Heights gave the Americans the high ground around the port city of Santiago de Cuba, and forced a quick end to the war. The fame that Roosevelt won in 1898 at Cuba's San Juan Heights helped him win election as William McKinley's Vice President in 1900.

1898, July 3: After U.S. troops capture the San Juan Heights above Cuba's Santiago de Cuba Harbor, a Spanish navy squadron tries to break out of the harbor. The U.S. Navy destroys the squadron in the Battle of Santiago de Cuba, the largest naval battle of the Spanish-American War.

1898, July 7: The United States annexes independent Hawaii, gaining control of another important coaling port.

1898, July 17: Spain surrenders to the United States at Santiago de Cuba.

1898, August 12: Spain and the United States sign an armistice agreement to end the Spanish-American War.

1898, August 13: Before word of the armistice can reach the Philippines, U.S. General Arthur MacArthur captures the Philippine capital in the Battle of Manila. Filipino troops still surround Manila, and soon MacArthur is holding Manila against the Filipinos.

1898, December 10: The Treaty of Paris ends the Spanish-American War. Under its terms:

- Spain gives up all of its rights to Cuba. Under the *Platt Amendment*, the U.S. leases Guantanamo Bay from Cuba and retains a great deal of control over Cuba.
- Spain surrenders Puerto Rico (West Indies) and Guam (East Indies) to the U.S.
- Spain surrenders the Philippines to the U.S. in exchange for 20 million dollars.

1899, February 2: U.S. and Philippine forces exchange shots near Manila. The Philippine-American War begins.

The Philippine-American War

On February 2, 1899, for reasons that are lost to history, American and Filipino troops exchanged shots across the former siege lines around Manila. These were the opening shots of a new war between two former allies, the U.S. and the Philippines. The Philippine-American War was highly unpopular in the United States, where few Americans could understand why the United States was suddenly fighting the very nation that it had just liberated from Spain.

The American government had several reasons for keeping its troops in the Philippines:

1. The U.S. wanted access to the Philippines' conveniently-placed ports for coaling stations and U.S. trade.
2. The U.S. wanted to protect those ports. The U.S. feared that if it left the Philippines undefended, Spain or some other powerful nation would quickly recapture them.
3. The U.S. distrusted the new Philippine leader, Emilio Aguinaldo. Aguinaldo's first act as the Philippines' leader had been to establish himself as a dictator. The U.S. wanted to help the Philippines establish a free society with a representative government, not leave the newly-liberated nation in the hands of a dictator.

Once the fighting began, neither side was willing to back down. When the Filipinos realized that their battle lines could not hold their ground against the Americans' superior weaponry, they stopped fighting major battles and began a guerrilla-style war like the one the Cubans were fighting against their Spanish occupiers. The Philippines' most-feared guerrilla fighters were the *moros* ("moors" or Muslims).

Both Filipinos and Americans used brutal tactics in the Philippine-American War. The Filipinos were accused of torturing and killing American prisoners in unspeakable ways. The Americans were accused of slaughtering an entire village of Filipinos in response to the killing of one American soldier. Ironically, the Americans found themselves treating the Filipinos as roughly as the Spanish had treated the Cubans during their War for Independence. The Philippine-American War became a source of shame for many Americans, including author Mark Twain, who wondered aloud how it had begun and why it continued.

Philippine dictator Aguinaldo surrendered to the United States in 1901, and the Philippine-American War officially ended in 1902. The United States would not fully recognize Philippine independence until 1946, after the end of World War II.

> *Other interesting facts:*
> - The development of the U.S. Army's well-known, highly powerful Colt .45-caliber automatic handgun began in response to Filipino *moro* guerrillas. Some of the moros were so wildly aggressive that a shot from a lesser weapon than the Colt .45 would not stop them.
>
> - Commodore George Dewey began the Battle of Manila Bay with this memorable command to Captain Gridley, the commander of his flagship *USS Olympia*: "You may fire when you are ready, Gridley."

1902: The Philippine-American War ends with the Philippines under U.S. occupation.

U.S. GEOGRAPHY FOCUS

FASCINATING FACTS: The Panama Canal

Within a matter of months in the year of 1898, the United States suddenly acquired two crucial Pacific island ports in the Philippines and Hawaii. All of a sudden, the U.S. Navy was a dominant power in the Pacific Ocean. But travel between America's east and west coasts (from the Atlantic Ocean to the Pacific Ocean) still involved a trip of thousands of miles around South America's Cape Horn or through the Straits of Magellan. The navy needed a faster way.

The narrowest land route across any of the Americas lay in Central America's Isthmus of Panama, and the French had already tried to build a manmade canal there. Ferdinand de Lesseps, the same French engineer who had completed Egypt's Suez Canal in 1869, tried to recreate that success in Panama beginning in 1880. Unfortunately, the conditions in tropical Panama were far more difficult than the conditions in Egypt. Problems like rampant mosquito-borne malaria and a shortage of machinery forced the French to abandon their canal-building efforts in 1888.

U.S. President Theodore Roosevelt was highly interested in taking up the canal project in Panama, but there was one problem: the Isthmus of Panama was owned by the adjacent South American nation of Colombia, and Colombia wasn't selling. If the U.S. was going to invest a lot of money and effort in the Panama Canal, it needed a treaty guaranteeing U.S. control of a zone around that canal. The U.S. government approached the government of Colombia with just such a treaty, but Colombia refused to ratify it.

Clearly, it was time for a bit of "gunboat diplomacy." When President Roosevelt learned that a group of Panamanian rebels was eager to win Panama's independence from Colombia, he agreed to support their rebellion. On November 2, 1903, when Colombia tried to send troopships to control the rebellion in Panama, they found U.S. Navy ships blocking their sea lanes.

Colombia was forced to admit defeat. Panama declared its independence on November 3, 1903, and signed the Canal Zone Treaty that Colombia had refused to sign on November 6. American engineers began work on the Panama Canal in May, 1904.

The building of the Panama Canal was an immense feat of engineering. Unlike the level, lockless Suez Canal, the Panama Canal required a system of locks and lakes to raise and lower ships up and down Panama's hilly spine. American engineers used steam shovels and rail cars to dig and move earth with stunning efficiency. The Americans succeeded where the French had failed partly because of progress in medical science: by 1904, doctors had discovered that

mosquitoes carried malaria, and the Americans went to great lengths to eradicate mosquitoes in the Canal Zone.

The Panama Canal opened ahead of schedule on August 15, 1914, just as fighting in World War I got underway. Its effect on shipping and travel was almost beyond belief: By spending 10 hours crossing the canal's 50-mile length, a vessel on a journey from New York to San Francisco could save about 8,100 miles of steaming, a distance that required over three weeks of travel time at a steady 15 miles per hour. The U.S. retained control of the Panama Canal Zone until 2000, when Panama took it over.

Some Territories and Possessions of the United States
The map below indicates territories and states that are under U.S. control as of 2010

Territory	Date Acquired	Date of Independence
Midway Islands	1867	
Philippine Islands	1898	1946
Puerto Rico	1898	
Palmyra Atoll	1900 (along with Hawaii)	Divided from Hawaii in 1959, when Hawaii became a state. Remains a territory.
American Samoa	1899	
Guantanamo Bay, Cuba	1903	
U.S. Virgin Islands	1917	
Federated States of Micronesia	1947	Became independent in 1986, but signed a Compact of Free Association with the United States
Northern Mariana Islands	1947	
Republic of Palau	1947	Became independent in 1994, but signed a Compact of Free Association with the United States
Republic of the Marshall Islands	1947	Became independent in 1990, but signed a Compact of Free Association with the United States
Panama Canal Zone	1903	2000
Guam	1898	
Wake Island	1899	

PRESIDENTIAL FOCUS

PRESIDENT #25: William McKinley (1843 – 1901)	
In Office: March 4, 1897 – September 14, 1901	**Political Party:** Republican
Birthplace: Ohio	**Nickname:** "Napoleon of Protection"

Ohio-born William McKinley was a Civil War major who served with Colonel Rutherford Hayes (who was also later a President). McKinley's friendship with President Hayes helped his political fortunes, and he rose to the Presidency through the U.S. House of Representatives and the Ohio governor's office.

McKinley was a friend of American businesses. He earned his nickname, the "Napoleon of Protection," by supporting high tariffs, taxes on goods imported to the United States. McKinley's tariffs raised prices at home, but they also helped U.S. businesses survive competition from foreign manufacturers.

McKinley's friendship with business also helped guide him into the Spanish-American War. The Cuban War for Independence, which had begun before McKinley took office, continued to threaten both American citizens who were living in Cuba and American businesses that were trading in Cuba. McKinley negotiated with Spain, then sent the *USS Maine* to Cuba in order to protect those citizens and those businesses. When the *Maine* exploded and the U.S. Navy blamed Spain, the American public's anger made war with Spain inevitable.

Having committed his nation to expansion in the Pacific, McKinley took bold steps to make that expansion successful. He annexed independent Hawaii to strengthen America's hold there; and he made sure of America's hold on the Philippines, even at the expense of the horrible Philippine-American War. When the Boxer Rebellion threatened to close China, McKinley provided American troops to help keep China open for American trade.

Early in his second term as President, McKinley was greeting the public in Buffalo, New York when a Polish-American anarchist named Leon Cgolcosz suddenly shot him. McKinley died eight days later. Cgolcosz had been influenced by some of the same anarchists who assassinated Russia's Tsar Alexander II in 1881. These anarchist revolutionaries believed that some "great event," such as the assassination of a world leader, would be the single spark that could ignite a world-wide flame of revolution against oppressive governments everywhere. Justice was swift for Cgolcosz: He shot McKinley on September 6, 1901, and was executed in an electric chair on October 29.

Other interesting facts about William McKinley:
- McKinley loved opera, theater and a game of cribbage.
- McKinley's wife, Ida, was an epileptic in delicate health, and McKinley cared for her tenderly. When he was shot, McKinley begged his personal secretary to be careful how he broke the news to Ida.
- McKinley's last words, spoken to his beloved wife Ida, were "It is God's way; His will be done, not ours."

Notable quotes from William McKinley:
- "The free man cannot be long an ignorant man."
- "In the time of darkest defeat, victory may be nearest."

PRESIDENT #26: Theodore Roosevelt (1858 – 1919)	
In Office: September 14, 1901 – March 4, 1909	**Political Party:** Republican
Birthplace: New York	**Nickname:** "Rough Rider"

Theodore Roosevelt was an important national figure before, during and after his Presidency. As Assistant Secretary of the Navy before the Spanish-American War, Roosevelt helped build up the American navy; and he made sure that his navy would capture the Philippines if war with Spain ever came. When the Spanish-American War did come, he immediately resigned his navy job so that he could recruit and train his Rough Rider cavalry regiment, then bravely led the Rough Riders to victory at Cuba's San Juan Heights.

Roosevelt's Spanish-American War fame helped him to win nomination as President McKinley's vice presidential running mate after McKinley's first vice president, Garrett Hobart, died in office. Roosevelt served as vice president through the early months of McKinley's second term, then took office as President after McKinley's assassination.

Having helped push President McKinley toward expansion in the Pacific, Roosevelt supported that expansion with all of his considerable energy. He used "gunboat diplomacy" to capture a U.S.-controlled zone around the proposed Panama Canal, then promoted the canal wholeheartedly. He personally visited the canal while it was under construction; and he minted special keepsake coins for each canal worker, struck from the melted scraps of obsolete steam shovels the French had left behind there.

Although Roosevelt was friendly to business, he also believed in regulating businesses that grew too large. Under former Presidents, wealthy U.S. businesses had grown used to overworking their hordes of immigrant workers and paying them low wages without government interference. The workers fought back by joining labor unions and going out on strike, stopping work so that their money-hungry employers would lose money. Earlier Presidents had helped big business by forcing striking labor unions back to work, but Roosevelt did the opposite: he helped striking workers by threatening to "nationalize" big businesses, taking them over and making them the property of the federal government. He also used the Sherman Antitrust Act of 1890 to break up "monopolies," huge companies that forced their competitors out of business so that they could control prices. Roosevelt liked to call his fair dealings with both business and labor unions "The Square Deal."

Before he left office in 1909, Roosevelt carefully groomed his successor, Republican President William Taft. After Taft took office, though, he failed to continue Roosevelt's reform program to his mentor's satisfaction. Roosevelt grew so angry that he challenged Taft for the Republican Presidential nomination in the election of 1912.

When Taft managed to win the Republican Party's nomination anyway, despite Roosevelt's challenge, Roosevelt decided to establish a new party of his own: the Progressive Party. Like Roosevelt, the Progressive Party believed in using government power to regulate business and solve social problems. In the end, the Progressives and the Republicans divided the voters who usually voted Republican between them, and Democrat Woodrow Wilson defeated them both to win the Presidency.

Other interesting facts about Theodore Roosevelt:
- Roosevelt was a rugged outdoorsman and a big game hunter. Some of the Smithsonian Museum's African big game specimens came from an African safari that Roosevelt took with his son after he left office.
- During one hunting trip, Roosevelt refused a chance to shoot a black bear. The stuffed child's "Teddy Bear" was named in honor of the bear Roosevelt allowed to live.
- His militant motto was "speak softly but carry a big stick." Dozens of Roosevelt supporters gave him large sticks as gifts.
- During Roosevelt's 1912 Progressive Party run for the Presidency, a would-be assassin shot him in the chest. The bullet was slowed by a sheaf of papers in Roosevelt's pocket, but it still wounded him. After examining his wound, Roosevelt remarked that "It takes more than that to kill a Bull Moose," and went on to deliver an hour-long speech before he was rushed to the hospital. For this reason, his Progressive Party became known as the Bull Moose Progressives.

Notable quotes from Theodore Roosevelt:
- "If you could kick the person in the pants responsible for most of your trouble, you wouldn't sit for a month."
- "Nobody cares how much you know, until they know how much you care."

Chapter 13

China, Japan and Korea

WORLD HISTORY FOCUS

CHINA'S COLLISIONS WITH THE WEST

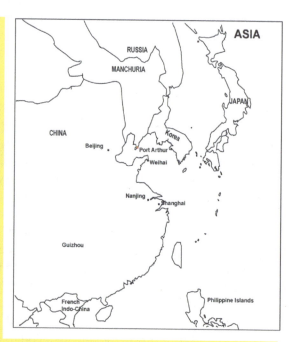

What Has Gone Before

During the Medieval era, China was part of the vast Mongol Empire established by Genghis Khan and his heirs. Genghis Khan's grandson Kublai Khan founded China's Yuan Dynasty in 1279. In 1368, the Mongol Empire dissolved, and China's Yuan Dynasty gave way to the Ming Dynasty. It was under the Ming Dynasty that China completed its Great Wall and created some of its finest art. The rulers of the Ming Dynasty were *Han* Chinese, members of the southern Chinese race that made up most of China's population.

In 1644, a new race took control of China: *Manchu* people from the Manchuria region of northeast China captured the Chinese capital of Beijing and founded a Manchu dynasty known as the Qing Dynasty. The Qing Dynasty insisted on strict separation between Manchu and Han. For many years, Han Chinese could not hold office in the Manchu government, nor could they even enter the Manchu homeland. Manchu and Han did not marry one another; and the Manchu required Han men to wear their hair in a *queue* (a shaved forehead and a long braid in the back) to set themselves apart. The Qing Dynasty would remain in power until 1912, when China became a republic.

The First Opium War (1839 – 1843)

It was during the reign of the Qing Dynasty that China began to have trouble with Western Europeans. The Qing Dynasty distrusted the strange people of the West, so it tried to keep China's contact with the West to a minimum. The Qings allowed Christian missionaries in just two Chinese port cities, Canton and Macau; and they allowed British sea trade only in Canton (Portugal held Macau). These restrictions frustrated Britain's many traders, who wanted the Chinese to open more cities to British trade.

There was also another problem: Chinese merchants at Canton sold plenty of their goods to British merchants, but wanted to buy very few British goods. Instead of trading Western goods for Chinese goods, the British were forced to pay for

Chinese goods with silver. By the 1800s, so much European silver had flowed into China that silver was becoming scarce and expensive in the West. To solve this problem, British merchants hit upon the idea of selling more opium in China so that they wouldn't need so much silver.

This set the stage for the 1839-1843 First Opium War (see Year 3, Chapter 25). The Chinese people loved to smoke opium, but the Qing government had banned opium because it was an addictive drug, harmful to the Chinese people. When a Qing official confiscated and destroyed a great deal of British opium in order to keep it from being sold in China, the British attacked. The backward Chinese navy was completely unprepared for Britain's modern, steam-powered warships, so the First Opium War was a disastrous loss for China. In the **Treaty of Nanking** that ended the First Opium War, Britain won possession of the island of Hong Kong and the opening of five new Chinese port cities to British sea trade. The lopsided loss of the First Opium War badly weakened the Qing Dynasty, making it vulnerable to rebellion.

FASCINATING FACTS: Treaty Ports

Before the First Opium War, China was almost entirely closed to European trade. European traders desperately wanted access to more Chinese ports, but China stubbornly refused to allow it.

The Treaty of Nanking gave British traders what they wanted: free access to five Chinese port cities, or "treaty ports." Within each treaty port, Britain was able to create a British "quarter" or section that was like a little colony of Britain. Under the principle of "extraterritoriality," British citizens living in the British quarter obeyed British law, not Chinese law. The British built exclusive private clubs (no Chinese allowed) and Christian churches within their British quarters, and generally acted as if the treaty ports were British territory. Although China never became a colony of Britain, it often seemed as if it was.

Later, other European nations made similar treaties with China and built their own quarters of certain treaty ports. France, Germany, Austria, Italy, Portugal, Belgium, Russia, Japan and the United States all operated sections of Chinese treaty ports.

Major results of the First Opium War (1839 – 1843) and the Treaty of Nanking:

1. The Island of Hong Kong became a British possession, and Britain gained access to five Chinese "treaty ports": Shanghai, Canton, Ningbo, Amoy and Fuchou.
2. British citizens lived above the local law in the five Chinese treaty ports. Under the principle of "extraterritoriality," they were required to obey only the British ambassador, not Chinese law.
3. China agreed to pay Britain a great deal of money for the destroyed opium and the costs of the war.
4. The beaten and impoverished Qing Dynasty became vulnerable to rebellion from China's majority race, the Han Chinese.

The Taiping Rebellion (1851 – 1864)

Hong Xiuquan

Rebellion against the Qing Dynasty arrived in the person of Hong Xiuquan, a tutor from the area around Canton. Hong was exposed to Christianity as a youth, but never studied the Bible until he suffered some sort of mental breakdown and began having spiritual visions. He interpreted his visions to mean:

1. That the Chinese religions of Confucianism and Buddhism were all wrong;
2. That the Chinese people were really worshipping monsters, demons and idols; and
3. That God had given him a mission to destroy these idols and drive the demons out of China. He began his mission by destroying some of the Canton area's many local idols.

Hong studied the Bible with some Christian missionaries, but he interpreted what these missionaries taught him according to his visions. Hong came to believe that he was a brother of Jesus Christ, sent to establish a heavenly kingdom in China. He wanted that kingdom to be a "utopia," or ideal society, in which every citizen shared everything equally, followed orders and lived a highly moral life.

Hong found followers easily among the Han Chinese. To many of the Han, Hong's race was probably more important than his semi-Christian spiritual teachings; they were eager to follow any Han leader who would oppose the hated Manchu. They also liked Hong's communist idea of sharing everything in common, because it gave the poor a rare opportunity to share in China's wealth. Soon Hong Xiuquan was preaching his unique form of Christian communism to tens of thousands of followers whom he called "God Worshippers." The God Worshippers shared all of their wealth and land in a common treasury, and lived by Hong's rules for good behavior.

The Jintian Uprising

The Taiping Rebellion began in 1851 with the Jintian Uprising, Hong's first armed rebellion against Qing Dynasty soldiers. After defeating the Qings at the Jintian Uprising, Hong and his God Worshippers declared the foundation of the *Taiping Tianguo*, or the "Heavenly Kingdom of Transcendent Peace." Hong himself became the "Heavenly King." The Taiping Rebellion was underway, and Hong's new Heavenly Kingdom spread northward rapidly.

In 1853, Hong's troops were able to defeat Qing Dynasty defenders at the city of Nanking, and Hong established the Heavenly Kingdom's capital there. His troops went on to conquer most of southern China for the Heavenly Kingdom, but only after paying a terrible price: millions of Chinese died in the Taiping Rebellion, both in battle and as a result of starvation and disease.  Meanwhile, wealth and power began to corrupt the supposedly upright morality of Hong's Heavenly Kingdom: Hong began to maintain a harem full of wives as if he were an emperor, and he murdered a man whom he feared might try to take his place as the Heavenly King.

The End of the Taiping Rebellion

The Taiping Rebellion began to wane in 1860, when the God Followers threatened to capture the important seaport of Shanghai. Shanghai was the most important of the treaty ports that had been opened to British trade after the First Opium War; and British troops were stationed in Shanghai to protect Britain's valuable investments in Shanghai's British Quarter. With British help, the Qing Dynasty was able to turn the tide in its war against the Heavenly Kingdom: its soldiers succeeded in defending Shanghai and driving off the Heavenly Kingdom's army.

The Taiping Rebellion officially ended in 1864, when Qing Dynasty troops recaptured Nanking and found Hong Xiuquan dead inside his palace.

> Major results of the Taiping Rebellion (1851 – 1864):
>
> 1. A staggering number of Chinese, perhaps as many as 20-30 million, died, most of them from disease or starvation. The Taiping Rebellion was responsible for immeasurable human suffering and misery.
> 2. Many Chinese fled China to find homes overseas. Refugees from the Taiping Rebellion formed a large part of the Chinese work force that built the western part of America's Transcontinental Railroad.
> 3. Hong's communist ideas planted the seed of communism in China. Decades later, future Communist Party Chairman Mao Tse-tung would use Hong's rebellion as a model for a rebellion of his own.

The Second Opium War (1856 – 1860)

The Arrow Incident

After the First Opium War, China's five "treaty ports" were like occupied cities in some ways. The British did as they pleased in the treaty ports, because under the Treaty of Nanking, they were not subject to Chinese law. The Chinese resented the treaty's harsh terms and did all they could to resist them; while the British watched carefully to be sure the Chinese stuck to the treaty. Each side hated the other. The tense situation needed only a spark to ignite a second war.

The Arrow Incident provided that spark. The *Arrow* was a small Chinese ship that flew a British flag when it worked for British merchants. At the time, pirates sometimes hid behind British flags, because the Treaty of Nanjing prevented Chinese officials from boarding ships that flew British flags. In 1856, Qing Dynasty officials boarded the *Arrow* and arrested twelve Chinese sailors whom they suspected of piracy. The British claimed that the Chinese had no right to board the *Arrow* because it had been flying a British flag. Armed with the thin excuse of an insult to their flag, the British began to bombard forts all along the Canton River.

The war that followed was called the Second Opium War because the British continued to pursue the same goals they had pursued in the First Opium War: they wanted more Chinese cities opened for trade and more freedom for British citizens living in China. Once again, the Chinese were at a disadvantage against the far superior weapons and tactics of the British. They also had a second disadvantage: The Second Opium War ran in the middle of the Taiping Rebellion, so the Qing Dynasty faced trouble on all sides at once.

Poison and Torture

Since they were unable to defend their cities with troops and cannon, the Chinese fought back against the British in other ways. A Chinese baker tried to poison British officials; but he put too much arsenic in their bread, so they vomited up the deadly bread and survived.

Later in the war, the Chinese broke a solemn rule of war when they attacked and captured a group of British military men who were negotiating under a flag of truce. The Chinese tortured and killed their British prisoners using the dreaded "Death by a Thousand Cuts," a horrible form of torture in which the torturers sliced their victims over and over with sharp knives, then used tourniquets to control the bleeding so that their suffering would last longer. Barbaric methods like Death by a Thousand Cuts infuriated the Europeans, and made them hate the Chinese even more.

France, Russia and the United States

The Second Opium War also drew in three other interested nations: France, Russia and the United States. France came into the war after the Chinese murdered a French missionary, Father August Chapdelaine;

and Russia came into the war because it was battling China over their common borders in northeast China (Manchuria).

Officially, the United States was neutral; but an American navy commander named Josiah Tattnall drew the U.S. into the war by going against orders. In 1859, Tattnall's squadron was positioned near Fort Taku, at the mouth of the Baihe River, when the Chinese managed to sink four British gunboats. Despite his orders to remain neutral, Tattnall decided to defend the British by opening fire on Fort Taku. Asked why he intervened on the British side, Tattnall responded that "Blood is thicker than water"– by which he meant that Americans had far more in common with the British than with the strange, often barbaric Chinese.

The Emperor's Summer Palace and the Treaties of Tianjin

By 1860, British and French troops were in position to capture the Chinese capital city, Beijing. The arrival of the European armies forced the emperor and his family to flee their beloved capital, with its Forbidden City and its elaborate Summer Palace. The Europeans wanted to end the war and punish the Chinese for torturing and killing British citizens so brutally; but they did not have enough troops to occupy Beijing, and they did not want to make the Chinese so angry that they would never sign a peace treaty. So instead of destroying the Forbidden City, the Europeans satisfied themselves with destroying the emperor's Summer Palace. With their capital in European hands, the Chinese were forced to negotiate an end to the war.

The **Treaties of Tianjin** ended the Second Opium War on even more humiliating terms than the first war's Treaty of Nanking. Under the Treaties of Tianjin, the Chinese were forced:

1. To open ten more Chinese ports for foreign trade;
2. To allow foreigners the freedom to travel all over China; and
3. To pay the British larger sums of money.

The Second Opium War and the 1860 Treaties of Tianjin opened China to the West as the United States' Matthew Perry expedition had opened Japan in 1854 (see Chapter 9). With more of China open to Europeans, Christian missionaries and others were able to move around China far more freely than before.

Major Results of the Second Opium War (1856-1860) and the Treaties of Tianjin:

1. **Foreigners and missionaries gained the right to travel and live all over China. China was "opened" as Japan had been.**
2. The Chinese opened ten more ports cities to foreign trade.
3. China once again owed Britain a great deal of money.

The Boxer Rebellion (1898 – 1901)

The Boxers

After the Second Opium War opened China to foreigners, more Europeans began to move into China as traders, opium merchants or Christian missionaries. Many Chinese felt that Europeans were ruining their ancient homeland by addicting its people to opium and spreading their strange, foreign religion. China's next generation of warriors, the Boxers, grew out of China's struggle for independence from European influence.

The Boxers were named for their methods. Because the Chinese were unable to match the Europeans' superior weaponry, they sought to defeat the Europeans using spiritual and physical combat, which the English described as "boxing." The Boxers followed strict diet and exercise routines and trained themselves in the *kung fu* martial arts. They believed that with rigorous training and help from their ancestors, they could reach a charged state in which they would be invulnerable to European bullets and able to fly. The "boxer" nickname was reinforced by one of the names the Boxers chose for themselves, the "Society of Righteous and Harmonious Fists." The Boxers had no central organization and no dominant leader. They were simply a collection of Chinese country folk who rallied to the cry, "Support the Qing! Destroy the foreigner!"

When the Boxer Rebellion began in 1898, every foreigner in China was suddenly in danger. The Boxers began with scattered church burnings and attacks against Christian missionaries in southern China. The China Inland Mission, Hudson Taylor's missionary organization, suffered the worst: the Boxers killed 58 of the China Inland Mission's missionaries and 21 of their children. The missionaries who survived raised the alarm about the rebellion, which was rapidly spreading northward.

The Siege of the International Legations

The main military event of the Boxer Rebellion was the 1900 Siege of the International Legations in Beijing (Peking). In the years after the Second Opium War, foreign nations had taken advantage of China's new openness to establish legations (embassies) in Beijing. Eleven foreign legations were clustered in Beijing's Legation Quarter. Alerted to the rebellion, the Legation Quarter called for help; and a mixed force of about 400 soldiers from eight different European nations arrived in the Quarter before the real trouble could begin.

Soon after the legations' 400 defenders arrived, the Boxers surrounded and sealed off the Legation Quarter, beginning a siege that would last for about two months. With their far superior numbers, the Boxers could have overrun the Legation Quarter at any time; only the Boxers' lack of organization saved the Quarter. Even without organization, they came close to routing the Quarter's defenders more than once. Their attacks killed or wounded nearly half of the Quarter's defenders; but the final, concentrated Boxer assault never came.

The Seymour Expedition and the Gasalee Expedition

Caught off guard by the unexpected siege, the foreign governments scrambled to organize a force that could break the siege and rescue their ambassadors and citizens. The first rescue force, the 2,000-man Seymour Expedition, was on its way to Beijing when it was waylaid by the Chinese army. British Vice Admiral Seymour's force had to be rescued itself before it could return to its base at Tianjin.

A second and far larger force, the 55,000-man Gasalee Expedition, finally reached Beijing to break the Boxers' siege. Eight nations (Britain, France, Germany, Austria, Italy, Russia, Japan and the USA) contributed soldiers to the Gasalee Expedition. The American contingent of the Gasalee Expedition actually climbed over

Beijing's city walls to enter the city (see picture), but the British contingent under General Alfred Gasalee entered the Legation Quarter first to receive the welcome of the grateful British ambassador. <u>The Gasalee Expedition captured Beijing, defeated the Boxers and put an end to the Boxer Rebellion.</u>

The arrival of the Gasalee Expedition forced the Qing Dynasty government to flee Beijing again, just as it had done at the end of the Second Opium War. The head of that government was the Empress Dowager Cixi.

INTERESTING INDIVIDUALS: Empress Dowager Cixi (1835 – 1908)

Empress Dowager Cixi was an emperor's concubine who rose to power during the Qing Dynasty as a regent for her young son. Cixi was the true power behind the Chinese throne for 47 years, from her husband's death in 1861 until her own death in 1908.

Cixi joined the Chinese royal family as a concubine in the harem of the Xiangfeng Emperor, the ninth emperor of the Qing Dynasty. Her fortunes improved in 1856, when she bore the emperor his only son. When the emperor died shortly after the Second Opium War, Cixi's five-year-old son became the tenth Qing Dynasty emperor, and Cixi became one of two Empress Dowagers (a "dowager" is a widow who takes charge of her dead husband's wealth).

Cixi's husband the emperor had appointed a group of eight counselors to govern as regents for his son; but Cixi outmaneuvered them to become the real power behind the emperor's throne. Because she was a woman, Cixi ruled China secretly, from "behind the curtain" that formed the backdrop of her son's throne. When her son died at the age of eighteen, Cixi's five-year-old nephew became the eleventh Qing emperor, and she was no longer the emperor's mother. However, Cixi was a more forceful personality than the new emperor's mother, so Cixi continued to rule from behind the curtain in the young emperor's place.

As a young woman, Cixi had witnessed China's disastrous loss in the Second Opium War. At the end of that war, she had been forced to flee Beijing, along with the rest of China's royal family; so she was well aware that her nation's technology was far behind that of the West. However, when she sent young Chinese students to foreign schools to learn the West's secrets, she was horrified with the results: When the students returned, they were full of disrespect and scorn for Chinese traditions. These students' attitudes changed Cixi's mind about Western reforms, and she became a strong defender of Chinese traditions. In 1881, she stopped allowing Chinese students to study overseas; and in 1898, she imprisoned her emperor nephew for attempting a series of Western reforms called the Hundred Days Reform.

During the Boxer Rebellion, Cixi was of two minds: She was pleased that the Boxers hated the West and defended Chinese traditions, but she was also aware that this leaderless mob was beyond her control. So she tried to play both sides: she allowed the Boxers to attack the Legation Quarter, and her troops attacked the Seymour Expedition to keep it out of Beijing; but she also did not help the Boxers overrun the Legation Quarter. In the end, she was powerless against far superior Western forces. When the Gasalee Expedition arrived, Cixi was forced to flee her beloved capital once again, just as she had during the Second Opium War in her youth.

China's collisions with the West were the undoing of the Qing Dynasty. When Cixi returned to her capital after the Boxer Rebellion, her empire was in ruins. The Qing Dynasty would survive for only a few more years after Cixi's death in 1908.

Major Results of the Boxer Rebellion:

1. International armies occupied China for over a year. These armies captured and executed many Boxers.
2. In order to remain in power, Empress Dowager Cixi was forced to agree to several of the Western reforms she hated. Among other things, she once again allowed Chinese students to study in foreign schools, and she banned the Chinese tradition of binding women's feet.
3. China was forced to pay more vast sums of money to the West.
4. The Qing Dynasty was weakened to the point of collapse.
5. Russia occupied northeast China (Manchuria, home of the Manchu Qings) with a large army, so that it could control and protect the area around its vital eastern railroads.

FASCINATING FACTS: Foot Binding

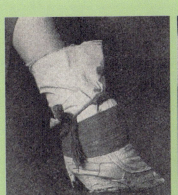
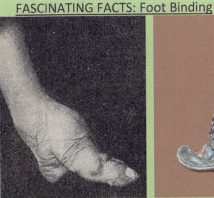

For about one thousand years, from the 900s until the 1900s, Chinese mothers practiced foot binding in order to keep their daughters' feet small. Foot binding was a long and painful process that painfully crippled generation after generation of Chinese women.

No one knows how the practice of foot binding began, but there are a few theories. One is that Chinese women began binding their feet out of sympathy for an empress who was born with clubbed feet. Another is that the women of the Chinese royal court needed small feet in order to mimic the graceful walk of some prince's small-footed concubine.

In the eyes of the Chinese, small feet were a mark of beauty, while large feet were a mark of coarseness and clumsiness. For this reason, not all Chinese women had bound feet. Tiny bound feet were intended to entice men and capture worthy husbands, so no one bothered to bind the feet of slave or servant girls. It was the daughters of the wealthy, and the daughters of the poor who hoped for wealthy marriages, who most often suffered the rigors of foot binding.

To bind a girl's feet, hired professionals or Chinese mothers used cloth bandages ten feet long and two inches wide to wrap each foot tightly, forcing the toes under the sole of the foot. They tightened these bandages a bit more each day, over the course of about two years, until the feet stopped growing. Properly bound feet took on the "lotus shape," named in honor of a Chinese flower prized for its beauty. Women with bound feet learned to keep their balance with a swaying "lotus walk" that Chinese men loved.

Foot binding was excruciating for the young women who endured it. The process often involved breaking several bones in the foot, and these broken bones were left to heal in their broken position. Mothers had to remove the bandages and carefully wash and groom the feet every day, otherwise infection might set in. If the bandages were too tight, poor circulation might cause gangrene (tissue rot). If the toenails were untrimmed, they might cut into the flesh and cause an infection. Bound feet often stank, even after the binding process was finished, because binding created folds in the skin of the foot that were hard to clean. As the Chinese said, "Every small foot costs a bath of tears."

When Christian missionaries began to move into China, the suffering of young Chinese women with bound feet horrified them, and they spoke out against foot binding. After the Boxer Rebellion, China's European occupiers demanded that the Chinese abandon some of their more barbaric traditions. Empress Dowager Cixi banned foot binding in answer to these demands. After the Qing Dynasty's fall, the new Republic of China permanently banned foot binding in 1912.

FASCINATING FACTS: The History of Chopsticks

The Han Chinese developed chopsticks about five thousand years ago when they began using pairs of sticks to retrieve food from hot cooking fires. Confucius, the Chinese philosopher and holy man, taught that the upright man must avoid the slaughterhouse and the kitchen, and he frowned upon knives at the table. This idea made chopsticks more popular. By 500 AD, chopsticks had spread throughout Asia.

Chinese chopsticks tend to be long, square and thick; while Japanese chopsticks tend to be short, round and thin.

Here are a few rules of chopsticks etiquette:
- One must not use chopsticks to make noise or gestures.
- One must not use chopsticks to move bowls or plates around the table.
- One must not use chopsticks to pierce food.
- One must not leave chopsticks standing upright in a bowl, because at Chinese funerals, mourners leave chopsticks standing upright in a bowl of food intended for the deceased.
- It is rude to suck on chopsticks or chew on them.
- It is rude to pass food from one person's chopsticks to another's.
- It is impolite to hold chopsticks with all five fingers.

KOREA AND JAPAN

The First Chinese-Japanese War (1894 – 1895)

What Has Gone Before

Korea lies on an East Asian peninsula between China and Japan. During the 1590s Imjin War, Japan's emperor Hideyoshi invaded Korea; but Korea drove Japan out with help from China's Ming Dynasty (see Year 3, Chapter 8). After the Imjin War, Korea became a closed society like Japan and China. Korea traded with its ally China, but had nothing to do with Japan.

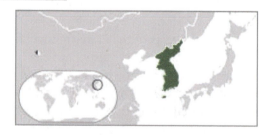

Japan's Meiji Restoration changed all of that. During the late 1800s, China's Qing Dynasty was weakened by its collisions with the West; but Japan's own collisions with the West had opened Japan and set it on the *Meiji* path of "enlightenment" and modernization (see Chapter 9). Japan's Meiji government believed that Korea would be a threat to Japan as long as it remained friendly to China, and Japan now had the modern military might to control that threat.

The Ganghwa Incident

In 1875, Japan forced its way into Korea with an episode of "gunboat diplomacy" known as the Ganghwa Incident. Ganghwa was a Korean island that had already been attacked twice by foreign traders, so its defenses were always on high alert. The Japanese sent one of their modern warships toward Ganghwa on a mission to obtain fresh water, knowing that the Koreans would attack it. When the Koreans predictably fired on the

Japanese warship, they gave the Japanese exactly what they wanted: an excuse to attack Korea.

Against modern Japan, backward Korea was defenseless. The Japanese warship attacked and defeated a Korean port city, then withdrew. Japan's quick victory allowed Japan's diplomats to negotiate a peace treaty, the Treaty of Ganghwa, from a position of strength. Under the terms of the 1876 **Treaty of Ganghwa**:

- Korea opened itself to Japanese trade, just as Japan had opened itself to European trade twenty years before.
- Japan won the right to send a permanent ambassador to Korea and to maintain an embassy there.
- Japanese citizens in Korea lived under the principle of "extraterritoriality," just like Europeans who lived in China's treaty ports. Extraterritoriality meant that Japanese citizens didn't have to obey Korean law-- they only obeyed the laws laid out by the Japanese ambassador to Korea.

The Treaty of Ganghwa made Korea a battleground between China and Japan. The presence of a Japanese embassy and Japanese money in Korea led some Koreans to support Japan, while other Koreans remained faithful to their old ally China. Over the next 18 years, there were several incidents in Korea that nearly led to war between Japan and China. One of the two rivals' efforts to avoid war was the 1885 **Convention of Tientsin**, in which China and Japan agreed:

1. That Korea would remain independent;
2. That both nations would withdraw their armies from Korea and keep them out of Korea; and
3. That each would notify the other if it decided to send troops to Korea for any reason.

The Tonghak Rebellion

This weak arrangement failed in 1894, when Korean peasants set out to destroy their ineffective and oppressive government in the Tonghak Rebellion.

Tonghak was a Korean religion whose followers believed in the equality of all human beings. Tonghak followers naturally resisted Korea's dictatorial ruling class. When the Tonghak Rebellion began, the nearly defenseless Korean king Kojong called upon his friends in China's Qing Dynasty for aid in defeating the rebels.

China responded to King Kojong's call by sending an army into Korea. China obeyed the Convention of Tientsin by notifying Japan of its troop movements; but even so, the Japanese still saw the presence of Chinese troops in Korea as an attempt to capture Korea. In response, Japan decided to send its own, larger army into Korea. The result was the First Chinese-Japanese War, which lasted from 1894 - 1895.

War and Consequences

The First Chinese-Japanese War was a quick loss for China. Japan rapidly overwhelmed China's navy, drove China's troops out of Korea, occupied Korea and even invaded Manchuria (northeastern China). Under the terms of the 1895 **Treaty of Shimonoseki**, which ended the First Chinese-Japanese War:

- China ceded part of the Liaodong Peninsula, the Chinese peninsula west of Korea, to Japan. The Liaodong Peninsula contained Port Arthur, a port city in which Russia was deeply interested (see below).
- China agreed to pay Japan a great deal of money (silver).
- Japan gained access to several treaty ports in China. By occupying treaty ports, Japan became a colonial power in China, just like the European nations that were already occupying treaty ports there.
- Japan and China agreed that Korea would remain independent.

The Triple Intervention

However, China and Japan were no longer the only nations interested in the Korean region. At the time, Russia was building its Trans-Siberian Railway to create easier access to the Pacific Ocean, and it needed a warm-water port in the east. Russia wanted Port Arthur, which lay on the Liadong Peninsula that Japan had just captured.

In order to reclaim Port Arthur for China, Russia formed an alliance with France and Germany. Shortly after Japan and China signed the Treaty of Shimonoseki in 1895, these three allies demanded that Japan return control of the Liaodong Peninsula to China. Their diplomatic bullying of Japan became known as the "Triple Intervention," and it succeeded in its goal of restoring Port Arthur to Chinese control.

The Triple Intervention also succeeded in making Japan an enemy of Russia. Japan went along with the Triple Intervention's demands because it had no other choice: Japan knew that it could not defend itself against the combined navies of Russia, France and Germany. Even so, the Japanese deeply resented the Russians' manipulations, and they resolved to be better prepared for their next confrontation with Russia.

The Russian-Japanese War (1904 – 1905)

Russia in Port Arthur

Russia had spent much of its history questing for a warm-water port city like Port Arthur. In 1859, Russia established the port city of Vladivostok in its frigid province of Siberia; but Vladivostok was only a northern cold-water port, closed by ice for much of the year. The Russians wanted a good warm-water port farther south, and they found one at Port Arthur, which lay on China's Liaodong Peninsula just west of Korea.

In 1898, Russia achieved a major goal when it succeeded in leasing Port Arthur from China. Russia also received permission to build the South Manchuria Railway across Chinese territory, connecting Port Arthur to Russia's Trans-Siberian Railway (see below). With railroad access to the excellent Port Arthur, Russia was ready to become a major player in the Pacific.

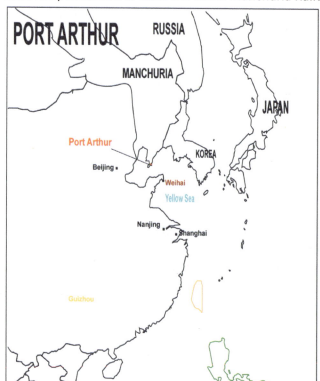

Negotiations with Russia

Japan, which had just returned the Liadong Peninsula to Chinese control because of the threat of the Triple Intervention, watched these developments nervously. The Japanese took a sour view of any powerful Russian presence in China, because they feared that it might lead to a Russian presence in nearby Korea and then an attack on Japan. In order to defend itself against that grim possibility, Japan sought a treaty with Russia that would guarantee Korea's independence. However, Japan was in a hurry: it was eager to guarantee Korea's independence before the Russians could complete the Trans-Siberian Railway, strengthening their hold on Manchuria and Port Arthur.

In its testy negotiations with Russia, Japan threatened to attack Port Arthur if Russia refused to guarantee Korea's independence. The two enemies' negotiations broke down when Russia's leader, Tsar

Nicholas II, failed to respond to Japan's requests quickly enough. Tsar Nicholas bided his time because (1) he knew that Russia would be stronger in East Asia after it completed the Trans-Siberian Railway, and (2) he refused to believe that tiny, backward Japan would dare to attack a major world power such as Russia.

Surprise Attack

Tsar Nicholas II was mistaken. On February 8, 1904, Japan launched a surprise attack on Russian forces at Port Arthur (see picture). Three hours later, when the battle was already well underway, Japan telegraphed its declaration of war to Russia. The surprise attack followed by a declaration of war was a tactic Japan would use again at Pearl Harbor, Hawaii in 1941 (see Chapter 26).

Port Arthur's many shore batteries (land-based cannon) made the port too difficult to capture by sea, so the Japanese later resorted to a ground invasion. Japanese troops landed in Korea, then moved overland to attack Port Arthur from the rear. Russia hurried to complete the last sections of the Trans-Siberian Railway so that it could send more troops from the west to defend Port Arthur; but Russia's reinforcements arrived too late. In December 1904, Port Arthur fell to the Japanese.

The Battle of Tsushima and the Treaty of Portsmouth

Months before Port Arthur fell, Tsar Nicholas II had dispatched another Russian fleet to the Far East. His fleet departed from the Baltic Sea in far northwest Europe, and had to sail all of the way around Africa to reach the Far East-- because Britain, an ally of Japan, controlled the shorter route through the Suez Canal. The long delay of the Baltic Sea fleet's arrival would turn out to be critical.

When Port Arthur fell in December 1904, Russia's Baltic Sea fleet was still far to the southwest, rounding the east African island of Madagascar. The fleet had been counting on making port at Port Arthur after it had raised Japan's blockade; but with Port Arthur in Japanese hands, it had nowhere left to go. The only East Asian port open to the fleet was Vladivostok, Siberia, Russia; and the closest route to Vladivostok lay nearby Japan.

When the tsar's fleet finally arrived near Japan in May 1905, months after the fall of Port Arthur, the Japanese were waiting for it. At the Battle of Tsushima, the Japanese fleet "crossed the Russian T": that is, the Japanese arrived ahead of the Russians and crossed their path, so that Japanese ships could train their many broadside guns on Russian ships, while the Russian ships could only fire their few forward guns. The Russians lost eight large battleships and about 5,000 men in the May 27-28, 1905 Battle of Tsushima, while the Japanese lost only a few small ships and just over 100 men. The Russo-Japanese War was over, and tiny Japan had laid low the vast, grand Russian Empire.

The unexpected results of the Russo-Japanese War affected both Russia and Japan, in opposite ways:

- The war wrecked the Russian navy and profoundly embarrassed the proud Russian Tsar Nicholas II. Weakened by his failures in the Russo-Japanese war, Tsar Nicholas II was forced to surrender some of his power in the Russian Revolution of 1905 - 1907 (see Chapter 18).
- By defeating Russia, Japan became a major world power, and began to dream of building a vast empire in Korea, China and Southeast Asia (see Chapter 26).

U.S. President Theodore Roosevelt volunteered to help negotiate the 1905 **Treaty of Portsmouth** that ended the Russo-Japanese War, and won a Nobel Peace Prize for his efforts.

Major Results of the Russian-Japanese War and the Treaty of Portsmouth:

1. Japan took over Port Arthur and the Russian-built railroad that connected Port Arthur to Manchuria.
2. Japan took over Russia's lease on the Chinese-owned South Manchuria Railway Zone.
3. Russia removed its troops from Manchuria and returned the region to Chinese control.
4. Russia abandoned its interest in Korea. Japan would annex (absorb) Korea five years later, in 1910.

WORLD GEOGRAPHY FOCUS

FASCINATING FACTS: The Trans-Siberian Railway

The Trans-Siberian Railway is a nearly 6,000-mile-long Russian railroad that crosses vast Siberia to connect Moscow in the west with Vladivostok in the east. Tsar Alexander III commissioned the Railway in 1891, hoping to improve access to his nation's interior and connect all of Russia to the Pacific Ocean.

The Trans-Siberian Railway crosses some of the world's coldest inhabited lands. Siberia became famous as a prison for Russia's convicts and exiles: Over the years, Russia's tsars sent countless criminals and political enemies to work camps across frozen Siberia, where enormous distances and extreme cold rendered escape all but impossible. Much of the miserable work of building the Trans-Siberian Railway was performed by these prisoners.

When the 1904-1905 Russian-Japanese War began, a section of the Trans-Siberian Railway near Irkutsk remained incomplete. In that region, the railway's route took a long turn around Lake Baikal, the world's largest and deepest freshwater lake. The Russians scrambled to complete the railway so that they could move troops from western Russia to Port Arthur; but the railway's single track meant that east-bound troop trains had to spend long hours waiting for west-bound returning trains to pass. The new Trans-Siberian Railway was too inefficient to supply a fast-moving war, and Port Arthur fell to Japan in December 1904.

MISSIONARY FOCUS

GIANTS OF THE FAITH: Hudson Taylor (1832 – 1905), Founder of the China Inland Mission

Hudson Taylor was a British Protestant missionary who served in China for 51 years. Taylor founded the China Inland Mission, the largest missionary organization in China before the Boxer Rebellion.

Hudson Taylor became a Christian believer when he was seventeen, and made his commitment to foreign missions in that same year. His interest in China became sharper in 1951, when China's Taiping Rebellion broke out: At the time, Britain's missionaries hoped that Hong Xiuquan's strange revolution was the beginning of a huge wave of Christian conversions in China. Taylor prepared himself to get involved in that wave by studying medicine in London. He also studied the Mandarin Chinese language, as well as the languages of Bible study and translation: Hebrew, Greek and Latin. Part of his work in China would be translating the Bible into several different Chinese dialects.

When Taylor arrived in Shanghai, China, he soon found that few Chinese were prepared to trust these strange Westerners who were so different from themselves. Unlike most European missionaries, who felt superior to the Chinese and kept themselves separate from them, Taylor tried to make himself more like the Chinese by adopting some of their customs. He proved how far he was willing to go by shaving his forehead and wearing his hair in a queue like a Han Chinese. When other missionaries challenged him about acting like a Chinese, he told them that "We should seek to make them Christians, not Englishmen."

When the Second Opium War ended in 1860, most of China became open to foreign missionaries for the first time. In 1865, while back in England on furlough, Taylor founded the China Inland Mission with the goal of spreading Christ's gospel to the interior of China, where no one had ever heard it. In funding his mission, Taylor was inspired by his friend George Muller (see Chapter 1), who never begged for money. The China Inland Mission had no fundraising program; it simply laid its needs before the Lord in prayer and accepted whatever funds the Lord's people donated.

The China Inland Mission became China's largest missionary organization before the Boxer Rebellion. As a result, it suffered the most when the Boxers began attacking Christians in 1898: 58 of Taylor's missionaries and 21 of their children died in Boxer attacks. After the Boxer Rebellion, when China was occupied by Western armies for about a year, some missionaries collected payments for lost lives and property damage caused by the Boxers. Taylor's mission was different: it imitated Christ by turning the other cheek and humbly refusing to accept any payments.

Because of Hudson Taylor and his China Inland Mission, China was home to about 600 Christian missionaries by 1900. After the Boxer Rebellion, that number quadrupled.

GIANTS OF THE FAITH: Lottie Moon (1840 – 1912)

Charlotte Digges "Lottie" Moon was born on a plantation near Charlottesville, Virginia ("Lottie" was a nickname for "Charlotte"). Lottie's parents held the belief, unusual in the 1850s, that daughters should be thoroughly educated; so they sent her to the Albemarle Female Institute, which was the female counterpart to Charlottesville's University of Virginia. Lottie became one of the first women in the South to receive a master's degree. She began to take her Christian faith seriously when she attended a revival at her school at the age of eighteen.

Lottie Moon followed her younger sister into Chinese mission work in 1873. She taught in a girls' school in Dengzhou, China, where she made friends with the local children by baking them cookies; but her real passion was for evangelism and church planting. She felt so tied down by teaching that she eventually abandoned it and moved into full-time church work in China's interior. At first, Lottie kept herself separate from the Chinese like the other missionaries did; but, like Hudson Taylor, she soon learned that the Chinese responded to her message far better if she looked and acted more like them.

Lottie was an excellent and prolific writer. Throughout her 39 years of ministry in China, she wrote letters and articles about mission work for her friends and sponsors in the Southern Baptist Foreign Mission Board. Among her topics:

- She asked the board to send more female missionaries, because she realized that only female missionaries were likely to reach Chinese women.
- She encouraged Southern Baptist women to establish missionary support groups in each local church back home in America. These groups still exist today, and they continue to collect a "Lottie Moon Offering" for mission work every year.
- She encouraged her fellow missionaries to take temporary furloughs back home so that they could recover their strength and live longer.

The years after the Boxer Rebellion were filled with poverty for China, which, in addition to its many other problems, owed its conquerors a great deal of money. Lottie Moon was so sensitive to that poverty that she shared the little food she had with her Chinese friends. She died of malnutrition in 1912.

U.S. GEOGRAPHY FOCUS

FASCINATING FACTS about MINNESOTA:

- <u>Statehood</u>: Minnesota became the 32nd US state on May 11, 1858.
- <u>Bordering states/bodies of water/countries</u>: Iowa, North Dakota, South Dakota, Wisconsin, Canada and Lake Superior
- <u>State capital</u>: St. Paul
- <u>Area</u>: 86,939 sq. mi (Ranks 12th in size)
- <u>Abbreviation</u>: MN
- <u>State nickname</u>: "Gopher State," "North Star State"
- <u>State bird</u>: Loon
- <u>State tree</u>: Red Pine
- <u>State flower</u>: Showy Lady's Slipper
- <u>State song</u>: *Hail Minnesota*
- <u>State Motto</u>: "The Star of the North"
- <u>Meaning of name</u>: "Cloudy water, " "white water" or sky water" (translated from Dakota language)
- <u>Historic places to visit in Minnesota</u>: The Mall of America, The St. Lawrence Seaway, Old Log Theater, The Minneapolis Sculpture Garden, American Swedish Institute, Laura Ingalls Wilder Museum, Paul Bunyan State Trail, Niagara Cave
- <u>Resources and Industries</u>: farming (corn, dairy, hogs, turkeys, wheat, soybeans, oats), food processing, iron mining, paper printing and publishing, tourism, metal fabrication

Laura Ingalls Wilder Home

Flag of Minnesota

- Minnesota adopted this flag in 1893.
- It has a royal blue field with Minnesota's state seal in the center.
- Surrounding the seal are 19 gold stars arranged in four groups of four and one group of three. These groups are arranged to form a five-point star around the seal. The large star at the top represents Minnesota itself.

Chapter 14

Western Pioneer Trails, Indian Wars in the American West

U.S. HISTORY FOCUS

WESTERN PIONEER TRAILS

Before the 1869 completion of the Transcontinental Railroad, American pioneers from the East who wanted to settle in the West had three options for their journey to the West:

1. They could take a long, expensive and risky sea journey around South America's Cape Horn;
2. They could take an equally risky sea journey that included a shortcut overland across Panama or Nicaragua; or
3. They could take an equally risky journey overland on one of the pioneer trails.

The pioneer trails began as trade routes for traders of fur or other goods, then began to improve as more and more pioneers used them to move west. The longest and best-known pioneer trail was the Oregon Trail.

The Oregon Country

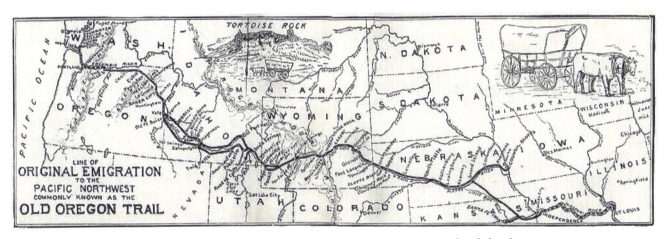

In the early 1800s, the Oregon Country was all of the North American land that lay

1. West of the Continental Divide,
2. North of Mexico's claim at the 42° parallel, and
3. South of Russia's claim at the 54° 40' parallel.

Both Britain and the U.S. claimed the Oregon Country. The Treaty of 1818 set the boundary between U.S. and British territory at the 49° parallel (Britain to the north, U.S. to the south); but it also set up a confusing situation in which both nations controlled the Oregon Country at the same time. The decades-long dispute over Oregon's boundaries became known as the Oregon Question. Militant Americans like President James Polk were eager to answer the Oregon Question by claiming all of the Oregon Country for the United States. They used the slogan "Fifty-four Forty or Fight!" to drum up support for their expansionist cause.

Britain's interest in the Oregon Country revolved around the Hudson's Bay Company, a British trading company that bought and sold furs. British, French and American fur traders blazed an overland trail from Missouri to Oregon so that they could move furs from America's interior to the Hudson Bay Company's trading posts on Oregon's Columbia River. But in the 1830s, European hat makers changed their hat linings from beaver fur to silk, and the formerly thriving North American fur trade began to collapse.

At the same time, American pioneers began to grow interested in settling the Oregon Country. In the 1840s, when the pioneers began to move into Oregon, the Oregon Question needed an answer. Two things made the negotiations between the British and the Americans easier:

1. The loss of the fur trade made the British less interested in the Oregon Country; and
2. The coming Mexican-American War made the Americans reluctant to fight a second war at the same time with the powerful British.

The 1846 Oregon Treaty finally settled the Oregon Question by establishing a permanent boundary between U.S. and British territories at the 49° parallel. Some former fur traders found work guiding the pioneers along their overland trail, which became known as the Oregon Trail.

The Oregon Trail

The Oregon Trail that carried those pioneers to the Oregon Country stretched for about 2,000 miles across the territories that would become Kansas, Nebraska, Wyoming, Idaho and Oregon. It began in the east at Missouri River towns like Independence, Missouri and Council Bluffs, Iowa; and it ended in the west at the town of Portland, at the junction of the Willamette and Columbia Rivers.

Travelers on the Oregon Trail began by following the Platte River valley west. In Nebraska, they passed Fort Kearny and Chimney Rock, an awesome spire of rock that stood over 300 feet above the plain (see picture). In Wyoming, they passed Fort Laramie and crossed the Continental Divide at the South Pass through the Rocky Mountains. In Idaho, they passed a lava formation called the Craters of the Moon and the Snake River's Shoshone Falls (see picture). They got their first sight of the lush, green lands they longed for when they descended from the mountains into Oregon's Grande Ronde Valley. Then they moved on to the fertile Willamette River valley in western Oregon, where most of them settled.

FASCINATING FACTS: Following the Trails

Traveling the Oregon Trail usually required about four to six months. Pioneers left the Missouri River area in the early spring to take advantage of the summer weather. Provisions along the trail were scarce and expensive, so most pioneers tried to carry all of the food they would need for the entire journey aboard ox-drawn wagons known as "prairie schooners." Each adult traveler needed about 300-500 pounds of food for the journey; the usual foods were bread, bacon and beans. In the trail's early days, the lack of good bridges and fords meant that the pioneers sometimes had to seal their wagons as best they could against water and float them across rivers. The trail's many other perils included Indian attacks, high mountains, bad weather and bad water (which led to diseases such as cholera).

The California Trail
The California Trail followed the Oregon Trail to Idaho, then turned southwest through Nevada toward California. When the California Trail's travelers arrived in western Nevada, they chose one of several Sierra Nevada Mountain passes to reach their destinations near the California coast. One of these passes was named the "Donner Pass" after the ill-fated Donner Party, a group of pioneers who had so much trouble on the trail during the winter of 1846 - 1847 that some of them became cannibals in order to survive a hard winter in the mountains.

The Bozeman Trail
A gold rush in Montana led to the creation of the Bozeman Trail, another offshoot of the Oregon Trail. The Bozeman Trail left the Oregon Trail in Wyoming to head northwest for Bozeman, Montana. Travelers used the Bozeman Trail for only about four years, from 1865 - 1869.

The Mormon Trail
The Mormon Trail was a third offshoot of the Oregon Trail. After the Mormon Church's founder, Joseph Smith, was attacked and killed in an Illinois jailhouse in 1844, the Mormons sought a homeland where they could practice their religion without being persecuted. Beginning in 1846-1847, Smith's successor Brigham Young led his people along the Mormon Trail to their new home in Utah. The Mormon Trail began in Nauvoo, Illinois, the Mormons' former home, then joined the Oregon Trail in Nebraska. It left the Oregon Trail in Wyoming to head southwest to Salt Lake City, Utah.

The Santa Fe Trail and the Fort Smith-Santa Fe Trail
The Santa Fe Trail was a separate, 1200-mile trail that led from Franklin, Missouri to Santa Fe, New Mexico. Because the Santa Fe Trail traveled through Comanche and Apache Indian country, its travelers were in more danger of Indian attack than travelers on the Oregon Trail were. The Santa Fe Trail was used more for trade than for settlement. Railroad companies laid tracks along its route in the 1870s.

The Fort Smith-Santa Fe Trail passed through Oklahoma to connect Fort Smith, Arkansas with Santa Fe.

AMAZING AMERICANS: Buffalo Soldiers

The Buffalo Soldiers were black soldiers who served in the U.S. Army after the Civil War. Comanche or Cheyenne Indians named them after the buffalo out of respect, probably because: (1) they were strong and tough, and (2) they had black, curly hair like the buffalo's. The U.S. Congress formed the first Buffalo Soldier unit, the U.S. 10th Cavalry Regiment, in 1866.

During the Indian Wars in the West, the Buffalo Soldiers escorted and protected settlers, cattle herds and railroad crews along the treacherous trails of the West. They also fought in the Indian Wars. About one fifth of the U.S. Army's cavalry troops were Buffalo Soldiers, and they fought in over 170 Indian War battles.

When Did Each State Become a State?

Each of the original Thirteen Colonies became an independent state when the United States declared its independence from Britain on July 4, 1776. All thirteen were part of a loose confederation under the Articles of Confederation from 1777-1786. Beginning in 1787, each of them formally became part of the United States of America when its state legislature ratified the new U.S. Constitution. The first of the thirteen to ratify the Constitution was Delaware, and the last was Rhode Island.

Most of the remaining 37 states became U.S. territories before they formally entered the Union as states. The 1787 Northwest Ordinance established that when a new territory contained 5,000 male voters, it could elect a legislature and become a recognized U.S. territory. After that, Article IV of the U.S. Constitution gave the U.S. Congress full power to decide what territories to admit to the Union as states. Most territories organized constitutional conventions and wrote constitutions for their proposed new states, then formally entered the Union when the U.S. Congress approved their constitutions. A few states followed slightly different paths to statehood.

#	STATE	DATE	ORIGINS
1	Delaware	Dec. 7, 1787	One of the Thirteen Colonies
2	Pennsylvania	Dec. 12, 1787	One of the Thirteen Colonies
3	New Jersey	Dec. 18, 1787	One of the Thirteen Colonies
4	Georgia	Jan. 2, 1788	One of the Thirteen Colonies
5	Connecticut	Jan. 9, 1788	One of the Thirteen Colonies
6	Massachusetts	Feb. 6, 1788	One of the Thirteen Colonies
7	Maryland	April 28, 1788	One of the Thirteen Colonies
8	South Carolina	May 23, 1788	One of the Thirteen Colonies
9	New Hampshire	June 21, 1788	One of the Thirteen Colonies
10	Virginia	June 25, 1788	One of the Thirteen Colonies
11	New York	July 26, 1788	One of the Thirteen Colonies
12	North Carolina	Nov. 12, 1789	One of the Thirteen Colonies
13	Rhode Island	May 29, 1790	One of the Thirteen Colonies
14	Vermont	Mar. 4, 1791	Formerly claimed by both New York and New Hampshire; <u>never a territory</u>
15	Kentucky	June 1, 1792	Formerly claimed by Virginia; <u>never a territory</u>
16	Tennessee	June 1, 1796	Formerly claimed by North Carolina; became the Southwest Territory, the first U.S. territory accepted into the Union as a state
17	Ohio	March 1, 1803	Part of the Northwest Territory
18	Louisiana	April 30, 1812	Formed from part of the Louisiana Purchase and the Spanish Cession of 1819; became the Territory of Orleans
19	Indiana	Dec. 11, 1816	Part of the Northwest Territory
20	Mississippi	Dec. 10, 1817	Formed from land claimed by Georgia and South Carolina, along with part of the Spanish Cession of 1819

21	Illinois	Dec. 3, 1818	Part of the Northwest Territory
22	Alabama	Dec. 14, 1819	Formed from land claimed by Georgia, along with part of the Spanish Cession of 1819; became part of the Mississippi Territory
23	Maine	Mar. 15, 1820	Formerly claimed by Massachusetts and known as the District of Maine; never a territory
24	Missouri	Aug. 10, 1821	Part of the Louisiana Purchase
25	Arkansas	June 15, 1836	Part of the Louisiana Purchase
26	Michigan	Jan. 26, 1837	Part of the Northwest Territory
27	Florida	Mar. 3, 1845	Ceded by/purchased from Spain in 1819
28	Texas	Dec. 29, 1845	Declared independence from Mexico to become the Republic of Texas; never a territory
29	Iowa	Dec. 28, 1846	Part of the Louisiana Purchase
30	Wisconsin	May 29, 1848	Part of the Northwest Territory
31	California	Sep. 9, 1850	Part of the Mexican Cession after the Mexican War, then directly admitted as a state; never a territory
32	Minnesota	May 11, 1858	Formed from parts of the Louisiana Purchase, the Northwest Territory and the British Cession of 1818
33	Oregon	Feb. 15, 1859	Part of the Oregon Territory
34	Kansas	Jan. 29, 1861	Part of the Louisiana Purchase
35	West Virginia	June 20, 1863	Divided from Virginia when the counties on the west side of the Allegheny Mountains refused to secede from the Union in 1861; never a territory
36	Nevada	Oct. 31, 1864	Part of the Mexican Cession after the Mexican War; became part of the Utah Territory
37	Nebraska	Mar. 1, 1867	Part of the Louisiana Purchase
38	Colorado	Aug. 1, 1876	Formed from parts of the Mexican Cession, Texas and the Louisiana Purchase, as well as the Spanish Cession of 1819
39	North Dakota	Nov. 2, 1889	Formed from parts of the Louisiana Purchase and the British Cession of 1818; became part of the Dakota Territory
40	South Dakota	Nov. 2, 1889	Formed from parts of the Louisiana Purchase and the British Cession of 1818; became part of the Dakota Territory
41	Montana	Nov. 8, 1889	Formed from parts of the Louisiana Purchase and the Oregon Territory
42	Washington	Nov. 11, 1889	Part of the Oregon Territory
43	Idaho	July 3, 1890	Part of the Oregon Territory
44	Wyoming	July 10, 1890	Formed from parts of the Louisiana Purchase, the Oregon Territory, Texas and the Mexican Cession
45	Utah	Jan. 4, 1896	Part of the Mexican Cession

46	Oklahoma	Nov. 16, 1907	Formed from the Oklahoma Territory and the Indian Territory, mostly land that had been set aside for Native American tribes
47	New Mexico	Jan. 6, 1912	Formed from parts of Texas, the Mexican Cession and the Gadsden Purchase
48	Arizona	Feb. 14, 1912	Formed from parts of the Mexican Cession and the Gadsden Purchase
49	Alaska	Jan. 3, 1959	Purchased from Russia in 1867; became the District of Alaska, then the Alaska Territory
50	Hawaii	Aug 21, 1959	Annexed in 1898; became Hawaii Territory

INDIAN WARS IN THE WEST

FASCINATING FACTS: The Indian Removal Act

In the early 1800s, five Indian tribes— Cherokee, Chickasaw, Creek, Choctaw and Seminole— still lived in the American southeast. These "Five Civilized Tribes" tried to adapt to the new European way of life by educating themselves and adopting European customs; but white Americans like President Andrew Jackson still viewed them as savages, and wanted to eject them from the southeast so that white settlers could take over their homelands.

In 1830, President Andrew Jackson signed the **Indian Removal Act**. The Indian Removal Act authorized Jackson to offer the Five Civilized Tribes new homes in districts west of the Mississippi River, districts that were reserved for American Indians. These were unsettled territories that would eventually become parts of Oklahoma and Kansas, and they became the first Indian Reservations. More than 40,000 members of the Five Civilized Tribes walked or rode the Trail of Tears to their new and poorer homes in Oklahoma (See Year 3, Chapter 29 for more on the Trail of Tears).

CHEROKEE   CHOCTAW   MUSCOGEE (CREEK)

CHICKASAW   SEMINOLE

Treaties with the American Indian Tribes

When the pioneers moved west of the Mississippi and began settling on the homelands of western Indians, the ideas of "Indian removal" and "reservations" continued. The U.S. Congress tried to keep Indians and white settlers separate with the **Indian Appropriations Act of 1851**, which set aside money so that the United States could buy land from the western tribes. Several tribes signed treaties in which they agreed to move onto Indian reservations in exchange for promises of money, schools, hospitals, food and other aid. Sometimes the U.S. Army used force, or the threat of force, to make the tribes sign these treaties. Plains Indians who had made their livings killing buffalo were expected to give up hunting and become farmers. But their reservation land was often poor farmland, so many of them ended up depending on government money for survival.

The signing of new treaties ended with the passage of the **Indian Appropriations Act of 1871**, when the United States stopped treating the tribes as nations and started treating each American Indian as an individual. Over the years, the government had found that some of its treaties weren't working, for several reasons. Among them:

1. Some tribes had more than one branch, and sometimes two or more branches claimed the same area. A treaty that removed one branch of an Indian tribe from an area did not necessarily remove all of the branches.
2. Some tribes had more than one chief, and not all of these chiefs agreed to sign their tribe's treaties.
3. White settlers felt that the treaties had set aside too much land for the Indians, and wanted to create smaller reservations for the America Indians so that whites could claim more land for themselves.

To get around these difficulties, the government put an end to the American Indian treaties. The last treaty with an entire tribe was the 1868 Treaty with the Nez Perce (see below). Instead of making more treaties, the government began setting aside farms for individual American Indians and their families.

Indian Wars

In order to enforce the treaties and keep Indians on their reservations, U.S. Army troops (including the Buffalo Soldiers) fought Indian wars all over the West with numerous tribes:

- On the Great Plains of the central United States (from modern-day Texas to Montana), they fought the Arapaho, Comanche, Cheyenne, Kiowa and several Sioux tribes;
- In the desert southwest of modern-day Arizona and New Mexico, they fought the Apache and Navajo tribes;
- In the Pacific northwest of modern-day Oregon, Washington, Idaho, Wyoming and Montana, they fought the Nez Perce tribe.

These are just a few of the many areas and tribes involved in the Indian wars. The last major Indian war ended in 1878 with the defeat of the Nez Perce; but the real end of the Indian wars came at the December, 1890 Battle of Wounded Knee, now better known as the Massacre at Wounded Knee.

AMAZING NATIVE AMERICANS: Crazy Horse (1842? – 1877) and the Battle of Little Bighorn

Crazy Horse was an Oglala Lakota Sioux from the area of modern-day South Dakota. His mother nicknamed him "Curly"; but at the age of 16, he took his father's name, "Crazy Horse," which literally meant "His Horse is Crazy."

Crazy Horse was part of the Sioux Indian Wars from their beginning to their end. In 1854, when he was probably about twelve, Crazy Horse witnessed some of the Sioux Wars' very first shots at the Grattan Massacre. The Grattan Massacre happened when a group of about 30 U.S. soldiers led by an eager, American Indian-hating lieutenant named John Grattan confronted a large Sioux village about a cow that someone had stolen from a white traveler on the Mormon Trail. During the confrontation, the situation grew tense, and a large number of Sioux warriors gathered around the soldiers in preparation for a fight. One of the nervous U.S. soldiers reportedly fired the first shot of the Indian Wars when he shot a Lakota Sioux chief named Conquering Bear in the back. As soon as the soldier fired, the Sioux warriors leapt to the attack and massacred all 30 soldiers.

As an adult, Crazy Horse fought in several major battles of the Sioux Wars, including:

- The December 21, 1866 Fetterman Massacre, in which Crazy Horse and a small band of warriors led eighty soldiers from Fort Phil Kearny, Wyoming out of the protection of their fort and into a pre-arranged ambush

by over 1,000 Sioux warriors, who were hidden behind a hill. The Sioux killed Captain Fetterman and all of his soldiers.
- The August 2, 1867 Wagon Box Fight, in which 31 U.S. soldiers armed with powerful, fast-firing new breech-loading rifles used the cover of a corral made from 14 wagon bodies to hold off a force of 1,000-2,000 Sioux warriors for an entire day until army reinforcements arrived to drive the warriors off.
- The June 17, 1876 Battle of Rosebud Creek, in which Crazy Horse temporarily defeated his enemy General George Crook, preventing Crook from combining his troops with the nearby troops of Lieutenant Colonel George Custer.
- The June 25-26, 1876 Battle of Little Bighorn, which included the final defeat and death of Lieutenant Colonel George Armstrong Custer at Custer's Last Stand.

FASCINATING FACTS: Custer's Last Stand

George Custer was a well-known Union army veteran of the Civil War who fought in the Battle of Gettysburg and numerous other battles. After General Lee's surrender at Appomattox, Union General Phil Sheridan honored Custer's gallant Civil War service by presenting him with a priceless gift: the table upon which Lee and Grant had signed their surrender agreement. After the Civil War, Custer went on to serve the U.S. Army in the Indian wars of the West.

In June 1876, Custer's small army was part of a larger army that had been assigned to

1. Hunt down the remaining Sioux and Cheyenne who still refused to abandon their way of life and go to live on their assigned reservation;
2. Defeat their warriors; and
3. Force all of the Sioux and Cheyenne onto their reservation. One of those Sioux warriors who refused to go to his reservation was Crazy Horse.

Lieutenant Colonel Custer's battle with Crazy Horse would be his last. On June 25, 1876, Custer found a large band of Sioux and Cheyenne camped near the Little Bighorn River in what is now Montana. The Sioux holy man Sitting Bull had called them there to discuss what they should do about the ever-growing demands of their white enemies. Custer was so eager for victory that he decided to attack without first learning how many enemy warriors he was facing.

As it turned out, the Sioux and Cheyenne had at least 5 - 10 times Custer's numbers. In the Battle of Little Bighorn, Crazy Horse and his warriors overwhelmed Custer's small army, killing Custer and about 200 other soldiers atop a hill that became known as "Last Stand Hill."

After the loss at Little Bighorn and the death of the popular Custer, the U.S. Army was more determined than ever to defeat the Sioux and the Cheyenne. By then, the loss of the buffalo herds had made it difficult for the Indians to continue their war. On May 6, 1877, less than one year after the Battle of Little Bighorn, Crazy Horse finally surrendered and moved onto the reservations the U.S. government had set aside for the Sioux and the Cheyenne (see picture).

A few months later, General Crook decided that an

inspiring warrior leader like Crazy Horse was too dangerous to keep on the reservation. Fearing that Crazy Horse might change his mind about living on the reservation and decide to lead another Sioux rebellion, Crook ordered him arrested and jailed. When a group of soldiers arrived to arrest Crazy Horse, he struggled with them, and one of them killed him with a bayonet.

AMAZING NATIVE AMERICANS: Geronimo (1829 – 1909)

Geronimo was an Apache from the area of modern-day New Mexico and Arizona. In 1858, when he was 29 years old, Geronimo returned from a trading expedition in Mexico to find that his wife, mother and three children had all been murdered by Mexican troops. Geronimo hated Mexicans for the rest of his life. His Mexican enemies gave him the name "Geronimo," perhaps because his repeated attacks caused them to call on the Catholic Saint Jerome ("Geronimo" in Spanish) for help.

Among Mexicans and white Americans, Geronimo was considered "the worst Indian who ever lived." He was notorious for raiding small Mexican and American settlements, stealing their supplies and killing their people. In Mexico, New Mexico, Arizona and Texas, Geronimo fought a guerrilla-style war that continued long after the last major Indian Wars of the West were over.

Among the Apache, Geronimo was an honored warrior hero. Like many such Indian heroes, he was believed to have special, mystical powers that protected him from bullets and allowed him to walk without leaving tracks. Geronimo became famous among his enemies for both abilities, whether they were mystical or not: he survived numerous bullet wounds, and he escaped from army search parties time after time. Once, army troops trapped Geronimo in a cave and set guards at its only known entrance, believing that they had trapped him at last. Somehow, he escaped them. No one has ever found another exit from that cave, which is still known as Geronimo's Cave.

An army that included 5,000 U.S. soldiers, 500 scouts and up to 3,000 Mexican soldiers finally tracked the elusive Geronimo down in 1882. Against overwhelming odds, he and a small band of followers escaped the army yet again. Outnumbered and worn down by constant pursuit, Geronimo finally surrendered in 1886. He spent the rest of his life as a prisoner of war in Florida and at Fort Sill, Oklahoma, where he died in 1909. Geronimo never returned to his beloved homeland in Arizona.

AMAZING NATIVE AMERICANS: Chief Joseph (1840 – 1904) and the Nez Perce Indians

The Nez Perce Indians lived in the Oregon Country near the Snake, Salmon and Bitterroot Rivers. The explorers of the 1804 - 1806 Lewis and Clark Expedition were the first American citizens to meet the Nez Perce. The name Nez Perce, which is French for "pierced nose," came from one of the expedition's interpreters, who mistook them for the Chinook Indians who lived farther west. The Chinooks did indeed pierce their noses, but the Nez Perce did not.

When the pioneers began to follow the Oregon Trail, the lives of the Nez Perce began to change. In 1855, the Nez Perce chiefs willingly signed a treaty that set aside for them a large reservation that included nearly all of

their native lands. But a steady stream of settlers continued to flow westward over the Oregon Trail, and those settlers cast hungry eyes on the land that they had promised to the Nez Perce.

In 1863, the Nez Perce were far less willing to sign the new treaty the U.S. government offered them, because that treaty set aside for them a new reservation that was only about one tenth the size of the first. Because the government used it to steal their land, this treaty became known among the Nez Perce as the Steal Treaty.

Because the Steal treaty offered money, schools and a hospital for their reservation, some of the Nez Perce agreed to sign it and move onto their new, smaller reservation. Some, however, did not. The Nez Perce who followed Chief Joseph the Elder refused to dishonor their past by leaving the graves of their ancestors behind. Joseph the Elder made his son, the future Chief Joseph, promise never to sell the ancestral lands upon which his people had lived and died.

Joseph replaced his father as Chief in 1871. Matters came to a head in 1877, when U.S. Army General O.O. Howard tried to force Chief Joseph's band of Nez Perce to abandon the graves of their ancestors and move onto their reservation. In response, Chief Joseph and other chiefs led about 800 Nez Perce on a 1,600-mile retreat toward safety in Canada, pursued by General Howard's 2,000 U.S. Army troops. Chief Joseph's cunning tactics against a superior foe brought his people within 40 miles of the Canadian border before the army finally cornered and defeated them. This is the speech that Joseph delivered at his surrender to General Howard in 1877:

"Tell General Howard that I know his heart. What he told me before I have in my heart. I am tired of fighting. Our chiefs are killed. Looking Glass is dead, Tu-hul-hil-sote is dead. The old men are all dead. It is the young men who now say yes or no. He who led the young men [Joseph's brother Alikut] is dead. It is cold and we have no blankets. The little children are freezing to death. My people— some of them have run away to the hills and have no blankets and no food. No one knows where they are— perhaps freezing to death. I want to have time to look for my children and see how many of them I can find. Maybe I shall find them among the dead. Hear me, my chiefs, my heart is sick and sad. From where the sun now stands I will fight no more against the white man."

After his capture, Joseph continued to fight for his people. In 1879, he traveled to Washington to appeal to the Americans' supposed love of freedom and equality for all, which to him did not seem to extend to the American Indians. He pleaded the Nez Perce case before President Rutherford Hayes, saying:

"We cannot hold our own with the white men as we are. We only ask an even chance to live as other men live. We ask to be recognized as men. We ask that the same law shall work alike on all men. If an Indian breaks the law, punish him by the law. If a white man breaks the law, punish him also.

Let me be a free man, free to travel, free to stop, free to work, free to trade where I choose, free to choose my own teachers, free to follow the religion of my fathers, free to talk, think and act for myself— and I will obey every law or submit to the penalty."

After Chief Joseph's final defeat, most of the Nez Perce remained on their reservation; but Chief Joseph was never allowed to rejoin them. The U.S. army feared that he might lead another rebellion, so it sent him to a separate reservation. He never returned to his homeland.

Other interesting facts and quotes from Chief Joseph:
- General O.O. Howard, who delivered the ultimatum to Chief Joseph that started his run for the Canada

> border, was the same O.O. Howard whom Confederate General Stonewall Jackson caught napping in his famous flank attack at the 1863 Civil War Battle of Chancellorsville (see Chapter 5).

- "I have carried a heavy load on my back ever since I was a boy. I realized then that we could not hold our own with the white men. We were like deer. They were like grizzly bears. We had small country. Their country was large. We were contented to let things remain as the Great Spirit Chief made them. They were not, and would change the rivers and mountains if they did not suit them."

- "If you pen an Indian up on a small spot of earth, and compel him to stay there, he will not be contented, nor will he grow and prosper."

The Ghost Dance

The **Ghost Dance** was a spiritual awakening that spread through a number of western Indian tribes in 1889 and 1890, after the western Indian wars were over and nearly all Indians were confined to their reservations. The Ghost Dance began among the Paiute Indians of Nevada, when a prophet named Wovoka shared his vision of all Indian peoples living at peace with the white man. Wovoka taught that if his people worked hard, lived moral lives and gave up some of their more savage traditions, then they could one day be free, live at peace with the white man and be reunited with their dead ancestors (the "ghosts" of the Ghost Dance).

To help bring all of this about, Wovoka began a series of ritual circle dances (see picture). Other tribes heard about Wovoka's vision, and the Ghost Dance began to spread from reservation to reservation.

However, not all of the western tribes interpreted Wovoka's vision in the same peaceful way. Among South Dakota's Lakota Sioux, there remained plenty of warriors who were willing to live in peace– but only after they had first destroyed their enemies. Some of the Sioux believed that Wovoka's Ghost Dance was a warrior dance that could give them strength for battle and protect them from bullets.

Sitting Bull (1831? – 1890)

The soldiers and Indian agents who guarded South Dakota's Great Sioux Reservation watched the ghost dancers with growing alarm, afraid that the Sioux were preparing to break out of their reservation and restart the Sioux Wars. In order to prevent this, they began to arrest the ghost dancers' leaders. They sent one group of American Indian police to arrest Sitting Bull, a Sioux holy man who had won fame during the Indian Wars (see picture). The arrest went badly. Sitting Bull struggled with the police, and some of his supporters started shooting. In the resulting chaos, Sitting Bull was killed.

The Battle/Massacre of Wounded Knee (December 29, 1890)

The Indian agents also ordered the arrest of a second Sioux chief named Big Foot, but Big Foot and his 350 Sioux followers had already left the reservation. On December 28, 1890, U.S. soldiers caught up with Big Foot and his followers and forced them to make camp near South Dakota's Wounded Knee Creek. The soldiers' mission was to arrest Big Foot, disarm the Sioux and return them to their reservation.

On the next day, December 29, the soldiers asked the Sioux to surrender their weapons. Some of them refused; and in the chaos, someone started shooting.

About 500 soldiers faced about 350 Sioux at the Battle of Wounded Knee. Of those Sioux, only about 120 were warriors; the rest were women and children. The soldiers used their modern weapons, including four rapid-fire, heavy horse-drawn guns, to mercilessly wipe out about 150 of the 350 Indians in the camp. Many of the dead were women and children. The Battle of Wounded Knee, now better known as the Massacre at Wounded Knee, was the last major armed fight of the Sioux Wars.

In some ways, the Ghost Dancers were similar to China's Boxers (see Chapter 13): because the American Indians were unable to overcome their enemies' superior technology, they tried to defeat them through spiritual warfare. When their last, best efforts failed, the last American Indians finally surrendered and gave in to the white man's demands. The Ghost Dance religion declined after the Battle of Wounded Knee, the Western American Indians' final defeat.

CRITICAL CONCEPTS: The Indian Wars had three endings:

1. The major battles ended with the 1877 defeat of the Nez Perce;
2. The guerrilla-style wars and raids ended with the 1886 capture of Geronimo; and
3. The Ghost Dance ended with the 1890 Battle/Massacre of Wounded Knee.

FASCINATING FACTS: Pueblos

Pueblos were the apartment-like homes and communities of the southwestern Pueblo tribe. Pueblo buildings usually had two or more floors, and pueblo dwellers used ladders to move between floors. Pueblo buildings could be home to several families; the average family's entire "apartment" within its pueblo was about 12 feet by 24 feet. Most pueblos had at least one 'kiva', an underground ceremonial room. Early pueblos were heated by fireplaces set in the center of their rooms, and had holes in their roofs to allow the smoke to escape. Later pueblos had corner fireplaces and chimneys.

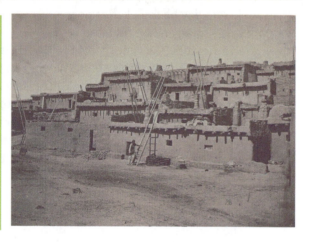

AMAZING AMERICANS: Buffalo Bill Cody (1846 – 1917)

"Buffalo Bill" Cody was a well-known symbol of the wild American West. At some time in his life, Buffalo Bill worked at nearly all of the jobs that went along with the wild West: fur trapping, cattle driving, gold prospecting, Pony Express riding, stagecoach driving, buffalo hunting, scouting and soldiering in the Indian Wars. He earned fame as a showman and actor in *Buffalo Bill Cody's Wild West Show*, which entertained excited audiences with demonstrations of life in the West.

William Frederick Cody was born into a Quaker family in Iowa. His father, Isaac Cody, was an abolitionist who moved his family to "Bloody Kansas" (see Chapter 4) so that he could speak out against slavery. At one anti-slavery meeting, Isaac made Kansas slave owners so angry that one of them attacked him with a knife. Isaac never recovered from his injuries, and he died when Bill was only eleven. In that same year, Bill took a job riding along with wagon trains so that he could help support his family. When he was fourteen, he took another job working for the short-lived Pony Express (see Chapter 8).

Bill served in the army twice, first as a wagon driver, then later as a scout in the Indian Wars. As a scout, one of his jobs was to hunt buffalo. Workers on the Kansas Pacific Railroad nicknamed him "Buffalo Bill" because he supplied them with buffalo meat. His bravery as a scout earned him a Congressional Medal of Honor in 1872.

In that same year, Bill appeared with his friend Texas Jack Omohundro as an actor in a show about the Wild West. From that time on, Bill usually spent his summers working in the West and his winters doing shows in the East. In 1883 he organized his own show, *Buffalo Bill Cody's Wild West,* near Omaha, Nebraska.

Buffalo Bill's show brought the American West to life. Bill had made a great number of friends during his career in the West, and many of these friends appeared in his show. The show usually began with horseback parade that included real cowboys, real Indian-fighting soldiers and real Indians like Sioux Chief Sitting Bull himself in full ceremonial dress. Some shows featured reenactments of Custer's Last Stand, stagecoach robberies or Indian attacks on wagon trains. One popular attraction of Buffalo Bill's show was a display of marksmanship by Annie Oakley, who could fire a rifle to split a playing card turned sideways from a distance of 90 feet, then pierce the card five more times before it hit the ground. The show ran for thirty years, ten of them in Europe; and it made "Buffalo Bill" one of the most recognized names in all of the world.

Later in life, Buffalo Bill used his fame to speak out in favor of women's rights and against the ill-treatment of American Indians, many of whom were his friends. He died of kidney failure in 1917.

HISTORIC HORSES: Sallie Gardner

Sallie Gardner was a racehorse that belonged to Leland Stanford, the California governor for whom Stanford University was named. Stanford commissioned an early photography experiment to prove that horses at full gallop actually raised all four hooves off of the ground at the same time.

The June 1878 experiment involved a series of twenty-four cameras lined up side-by-side on a racetrack. The cameras' shutter releases were all connected to silken strings that stretched across the track. When Sallie Gardner galloped past the row of cameras, she tripped each camera's shutter in succession, generating a series of 24 sequential pictures of Sallie in motion. Then the experimenters viewed the sequence on a zoopraxiscope, a device designed to display the images in rapid succession. The experiment worked: the images proved that Sallie Gardner did in fact raise all four hooves at once. More importantly, "Sallie Gardner at a Gallop" became one of the very first motion pictures of all time, and helped inspire Thomas Edison to invent the Kinetograph (an early motion picture camera) and the Kinetoscope (an early motion picture viewing device).

MISSIONARY FOCUS

GIANTS OF THE FAITH: Jonathan Goforth (1859 – 1936)

Jonathan Goforth was a Canadian Presbyterian missionary, one of the many missionaries who was inspired by the ministry of Hudson Taylor, founder of the China Inland Mission. Jonathan and his family were in China during the Boxer Rebellion, an uprising against foreigners that threatened the lives of all outsiders living in China, especially Christian missionaries. Jonathan was lightly wounded by a boxer attack, but he survived and returned to China in 1901.

Upon his return to China, Jonathan changed his tactics. After he witnessed a Christian revival in Korea, he grew determined to bring a similar revival to China; so he stopped living as a settled missionary and became a wandering evangelist. He was an inspiring speaker, full of passion for the Gospel, and his revival-style preaching helped convince thousands of Chinese to give their lives to the Lord. He served in China for 46 years. During those years he established thirty-one mission stations and trained more than sixty native Chinese pastors.

Interesting quote from Jonathan Goforth:
- "I love those that thunder out the Word. The Christian world is in a dead sleep. Nothing but a loud voice can awake them out of it."

U.S. GEOGRAPHY FOCUS

FASCINATING FACTS about OREGON:

- Statehood: Oregon became the 33rd US state on February 14, 1859.
- Bordering states/bodies of water: California, Idaho, Nevada, Washington State and the Pacific Ocean
- State capital: Salem
- Area: 98,381 sq. mi (Ranks 9th in size)
- Abbreviation: OR
- State nickname: "Beaver State"
- State bird: Western Meadowlark
- State tree: Douglas Fir
- State flower: Oregon Grape
- State song: *Oregon, My Oregon*
- State Motto: "She Flies With Her Own Wings"
- Meaning of name: unknown
- Historic Places to visit in Oregon: Crater Lake National Park, Klamath Falls, The Columbia River gorge, Sea Lion Caves, Heceta Head Lighthouse, International Rose Test Garden, Silver Falls State Park, The Carousel Museum, Fort Clatsop National Memorial, The Tillamook Naval Air Museum
- Resources and Industries: farming (wheat, cattle, vegetables, nursery stock, fruits and nuts, sheep), forestry and timber, paper products, electronics, tourism, mining (coal)

Crater Lake, Oregon

Flag of Oregon

- Oregon adopted this flag in 1925.
- It is the only state flag that has different designs for the front and the back.
- It uses only two colors, blue and gold.
- The shield on the front is outlined with 33 stars (the number of states in 1859).
- The eagle on the front represents the United States; the beaver on the back is the state animal.

Chapter 15

Big Business, the "Robber Barons"

MISSIONARY FOCUS

GIANTS OF THE FAITH: Billy Sunday (1862 – 1935)

Billy Sunday was born in Iowa in 1862, the grandson of poor German immigrants. Billy's father died in the Civil War. Because his mother could not afford to take care of him, Billy spent part of his childhood living in orphanages. He was supporting himself by the time he was 14 years old.

One of God's gifts to Billy was his speed: in his day, he was one of the fastest sprinters alive. He applied his speed to the game of baseball, where he used it to steal bases and make spectacular catches in the outfield. He played professional baseball from 1883-1891 on teams in Chicago, Pittsburgh and Philadelphia.

In 1886, Billy and some baseball teammates heard a presentation from a ministry team at Chicago's Pacific Garden Mission. A mission volunteer named Sarah Clarke led Billy to Christ, and he began to hear the Lord calling him to the ministry. In 1891, with baseball teams offering him $400 - $500 per month to play for them, he gave up his baseball career to take a job at the YMCA (Young Men's Christian Association) for $83 per month.

Billy's life as a traveling evangelist began as an apprentice to another evangelist, J. Wilbur Chapman. Billy served as Chapman's "advance man," arriving in town before his boss to make everything ready for the coming revival meetings. In 1896, when Chapman decided to leave the revival trail to become a church minister, Billy began to lead his own revivals.

Billy worked for years before he was finally successful enough to have an advance team like his mentor Chapman's. Later, his audiences surpassed Chapman's. Cities and towns that wanted to fight crime and promote clean living invited Billy to lead month-long tent revivals, where he preached against sin. Later, when Billy became more popular, they built temporary wooden "tabernacles" to contain his revival crowds. In order to control the dust and noise inside these tents and tabernacles, they spread sawdust on their floors. The people who answered Billy's altar calls and came to the stage for prayer were said to be "walking the sawdust trail." As many as 300,000 "trail hitters" walked the sawdust trail and devoted their lives to Christ at Billy's revivals.

Because he was an athlete, Billy Sunday became an athletic preacher. He stood on podiums to confront his audiences. He struck exaggerated poses and made wild gestures. He had to print his sermon notes in extra-large letters so that he could glimpse them as he ran past the podium on his frequent trips from one side of the stage to the other.

Billy's sermon topics were the fundamentals of sin and salvation. As part of the Temperance Movement (see Chapter 10), he often spoke out against nightclubs, bars and drinking, because he had seen drunkenness tear apart lives and families. The excitement he generated as he preached from city to city helped to pass the Eighteenth Amendment to the Constitution, which prohibited alcohol throughout the United States.

U.S. HISTORY FOCUS

STOCKS AND STOCK EXCHANGES

> **DEFINITIONS:**
> **Investors** are people, groups of people or businesses who have money and want to use that money to earn more money.
> **Stock** is the sum total of a company's wealth: its money, its goods, its buildings, its land and everything else it owns, along with its name, its reputation, its manufacturing secrets and other things that make it a valuable business. Companies issue stock certificates to represent "shares," or portions, of their stock.
> **Shares** are portions of a company's stock that are bought and sold on stock exchanges.
> **Stock Exchanges** are markets in which companies' stock certificates are bought and sold among stock brokers and investors.
> **Interest** is money paid for a loan. When investors deposit their money in banks, the banks pay interest on that money. The interest payments are usually a small percentage of the amount invested, paid monthly.

Some companies are private businesses owned by one person or a small group of people. But building a business is often expensive, especially when it requires major purchases such as land, factory buildings and heavy machinery. When a company needs more money than its private owners have (or are willing to risk), one way to get that money is to offer its stock for sale on a stock exchange. When it does, it becomes a publicly traded company.

Publicly traded companies have one major advantage over private ones: they have access to more money. Stock exchanges have plenty of investors, and all investors can examine each publicly traded company to decide if they want to invest their money by purchasing shares of its stock. That stock can be divided among a large group of investors so that no one has to invest too much. For example, a company can raise $1 million if the stock exchange can find 1,000 investors who are willing to invest only $1,000 each.

Publicly traded companies earn money for their investors in two main ways:

1. By prospering and increasing in value, so that their shares are worth more than their investors paid for them; and
2. By paying dividends, or portions of their profits, to their investors.

Unfortunately, publicly traded companies can also lose money for their investors by <u>failing</u> to prosper and <u>losing</u> value. If that happens, then their shares are worth less than their investors paid for them, and their investors lose money. Investing on a stock exchange can be risky. Investors are always seeking to "buy low and sell high," because they make money when they buy shares at a low price and sell them later at a higher price.

Some investors loan their money to banks in order to earn interest payments; but banks are investors themselves, and they always pay their lenders as little interest as possible. Investors who want to earn more than banks are willing to pay are often forced to take the risk of buying and selling shares on a stock exchange.

The New York Stock Exchange

The largest stock exchange in the world is the New York Stock Exchange (NYSE), which trades on Wall Street in lower Manhattan (one of the five boroughs of New York City). A group of 24 stock traders founded the forerunner of the NYSE in 1792, when they signed the Buttonwood Agreement under a Wall Street sycamore (buttonwood) tree. In 1817, their organization became the New York Stock & Exchange Board; and in 1863, it assumed its present name, the New York Stock Exchange.

FASCINATING FACTS: Wall Street

- Manhattan's Wall Street, the home of the New York Stock Exchange, was named for a literal wall. Wall Street was laid out behind a stockade built in 1685 to protect Manhattan's original Dutch settlers from Indian attacks.

- A Wall Street building named Federal Hall served as the USA's first capitol building under the Articles of Confederation (from 1777-1789). On April 30, 1789, President George Washington took his oath of office on Federal Hall's balcony before an audience gathered on Wall Street. The U.S. moved its capital from New York to Philadelphia in the following year, 1790.

- So much money changes hands on Wall Street that the street itself has become a world-renowned symbol of finance. The term **"Wall Street"** can refer to the New York Stock Exchange itself, or to New York's entire finance industry.

- An investor who believes that stock prices will rise is known as a **"bull"** (because of the bull's great strength and energy). When stock prices continue to rise for a long time, stocks are in a **"bull market."** Investors can make money easily in a bull market.

- An investor who believes that stock prices will fall is known as a **"bear"** (like a bear going into hibernation, who first grows fat and then falls asleep). When stock prices continue to fall for a long time, stocks are in a **"bear market."** It is difficult, but not impossible, for investors to make money in a bear market.

- Investors who hold a company's shares for a long time, expecting them to rise in value, are said to be "long" on that company.

- Investors who expect a company's shares to lose value and are therefore planning to sell them in a short time are said to be "short" on that company.

FASCINATING FACTS: Short Sales

It is possible to make money on a falling stock by using a risky tactic known as "short selling." In a short sale, an investor borrows shares from a broker and promises to return them before a set future date. Then he immediately sells them at today's price. In the future, when the price goes down, he buys shares at the new lower price and returns these to the broker to replace the ones he

borrowed. He gets to keep the difference between the two prices.

As an example, let us consider a short sale of the Acme Steam Car Company:

1. Today, shares of the thriving Acme Steam Car Company are selling for $10 apiece. Investor Wile E. looks into the future and sees that Acme's steam cars will soon be replaced by the new gas engine cars produced by the Acme Gas Car Company. Wile E. believes that shares of the Acme Steam Car Company will be worth far less in the future, so he decides to short sell Steam Car shares.
2. Wile E. borrows 100 shares of the Acme Steam Car Company from his stock broker and promises to return them in a month (He pays fee for this service).
3. Wile E. immediately sells his 100 borrowed shares for today's price of $10 apiece and pockets $1,000.
4. One month later, the first gas engine car appears and becomes an instant success. No one wants a steam car anymore, and the price of Acme Steam Car Company shares falls from $10 to $2 overnight.
5. Wile E. buys 100 of the Acme Steam Car Company's shares for $2 apiece, paying $200.
6. Wile E. returns these 100 shares to his broker, who has to accept them because they're the same as the ones he loaned to Wile E. (even though they're now worth much less).
7. Having taken in $1,000, but paid out only $200, investor Wile E. gets to keep $800 for himself! Furthermore, he has earned this $800 without spending any of his own money (except his broker's fee)!

Unfortunately for Wile E., there is another possible outcome. Suppose that the Acme Steam Car Company already knows about the new and wildly popular Acme Gas Car Company, and has made arrangements to buy the company before its cars can go on the market. If that happens, Acme Steam Car Company stock might rise to $20 instead of falling to $2. And if that happens, Wile E. will have to pay $2,000 to buy shares to replace the ones he borrowed. Instead of gaining $800, he will lose $1,000. Successful short selling depends on circumstances and timing, and it's a risky business.

Other interesting facts about short selling:
- Because short sellers tend to drive down market prices, making their profit from the misfortunes of others, some people consider them to be bad for the stock market. Short selling has occasionally been banned over the years.
- It is also possible to "sell a person short" – that is, to underestimate his or her abilities and to presume that he or she will never amount to anything. This expression comes from short sales.

FASCINATING FACTS: The Dow Jones Industrial Average

The Dow Jones Industrial Average (DJIA) is a stock price average that summarizes the stock market's daily value with a single number. It is a valuable tool for gauging the stock market's condition from day to day. When *Wall Street Journal* editor Charles Dow invented the DJIA in 1896, it was simply the average stock price of eleven large, important companies. Today the DJIA tracks thirty prominent companies, and the companies on its list change from time to time. The average is calculated by adding the prices of all thirty stocks and then multiplying that sum by the "Dow multiplier," a number which the company adjusts occasionally to keep the index consistent.

The Robber Barons and the Gilded Age

In every age, there have been people and businesses who have sought riches above all else. Here are some notable examples from Years 1, 2 and 3:

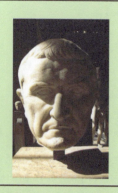	*Marcus Licinius Crassus* (115 BC? – 53 BC), part of Rome's First Triumvirate (along with Julius Caesar and Pompey). Crassus grew wealthy by seizing the property of political prisoners condemned to death by his friend Sulla. He also benefited from Rome's frequent fires by purchasing valuable land at bargain prices after an estate burned down. He was even accused of setting some of these fires. When Crassus' enemies captured him, they supposedly taunted him for his greed by making him swallow molten gold.
	*Genghis Khan* (1162? – 1227), Khan of the Mongol Empire that covered most of Asia and eastern Europe during the 1200s and 1300s. The Khans grew wealthy by demanding tribute payments from all of the many tribes and kingdoms they conquered. They cared little about who called himself prince of a kingdom, so long as he made his tribute payments on time.
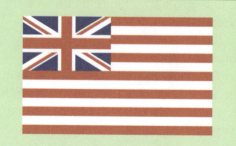	*The East India Company* (1600 – 1874), the company with a charter from the British king for trading in the Far East. The East India Company hired private armies to help it control nearly all of India and its wealth.

The Industrial Revolution of the 1800s made it possible for business people to build wealth faster than ever before. Modern factories enabled them to create more goods than before; and modern transportation enabled them to distribute their goods farther, faster and to more people than ever before.

As a result, the Industrial Age of the late 1800s and early 1900s produced more fabulously wealthy businessmen than any other age. This was especially true in the United States, where the government did little to regulate big businesses until the early 1900s. The wealthiest businessmen of the age made fantastic fortunes in railroads, steel, oil, real estate and banking. Among them were famous names like John Jacob Astor, Andrew Carnegie, Jay Gould, J.P. Morgan, John D. Rockefeller, Leland Stanford and Cornelius Vanderbilt.

These men (and others like them) became known as the "robber barons" because their wealth often came at the expense of millions of employees, many of whom worked long hours for low wages and lived in poverty. Author Mark Twain and others called the time of the robber barons "The Gilded Age," because the robber barons grew ever more rich, while their employees grew ever more poor. Because business was booming, the Gilded Age looked like a golden age from the outside; but a closer look revealed that its prosperity was as thin as gilding, the fine layer of gold on gold-plated jewelry. Underneath that thin layer of prosperity lay a thick mass of poverty and suffering.

BRILLIANT BUSINESSMEN

John D. Rockefeller (1839 – 1937)

In the years after the Civil War, John Davison Rockefeller took advantage of America's rapid westward growth and its growing need for oil to become perhaps the single wealthiest man who ever lived.

Rockefeller began his business career as a lowly grocery clerk. He had such a talent for business that he was able to co-found a business with a partner when he was only 20 years old. Around that time, refined crude oil (kerosene) was just beginning to replace whale oil as a fuel for lamps and stoves; so Rockefeller and his partner built an oil refinery in Cleveland, Ohio. In 1870, Rockefeller founded the Standard Oil Company; and by 1880, Standard Oil would become the United States' largest and, some would say, greediest oil company.

Standard Oil was well known for driving its competitors out of business. Rockefeller wanted to earn profit on his oil from the moment he pumped it out of the well until the moment his customers used it to fill their lamps. He bought oil wells and refineries. He bought his own rail tank cars, and built pipelines to move his oil from place to place. He even bought a network of tank wagons to deliver oil to individual homes and customers. Rockefeller wanted to "cut out the middlemen" (like railroad companies and local oil delivery companies) so that Standard Oil could keep all of its oil profits for itself. He also wanted to "corner the market" on oil, to control the entire oil supply so that everyone who wanted oil would be forced to buy from Standard Oil. With the market cornered and competition eliminated, Standard Oil could set oil prices higher and make even more money.

Trustbusting

Rockefeller built Standard Oil into the first "trust," a huge interstate corporation designed to corner markets and control prices. When Theodore Roosevelt became President, he began a series of "trust-busting" lawsuits against trusts like Standard Oil (see cartoon). Roosevelt was influenced by the stories of a journalist named Ida Tarbell, who wrote a long series of articles in *McClure's* magazine to expose Standard Oil's unfair business practices, including:

1. ***Corporate espionage***: spying on its competitors to learn their business plans in advance
2. ***Undercutting prices***: temporarily setting oil prices below what oil cost to produce, so that its smaller competitors, who had to match these prices, couldn't earn money
3. ***Secret price agreements***: secretly negotiating with railroad companies to make Standard Oil's transportation costs lower and everyone else's higher

Rockefeller's supporters called Ida Tarbell a "muckraker" and a sore loser because Rockefeller had driven her father out of the oil business; but she backed her accusations with hard, believable evidence, and the damage was done. In 1911, the Supreme Court of the United States agreed with President Roosevelt's antitrust lawsuit and broke up the Standard Oil Trust into 34 separate, smaller companies. Those companies were the forerunners of modern oil companies like ExxonMobil, Chevron and ConocoPhillips.

Like some of the other robber barons, Rockefeller spent his later years donating money through charities that he founded. He created his main charity, the Rockefeller Foundation, in 1913. The Rockefeller Foundation gave away hundreds of millions of dollars, primarily for education and medical research. Rockefeller's son, John D. Rockefeller Junior, managed much of his charity work.

John Junior also built New York City's Rockefeller Plaza, an immense office complex that covers a large area of central Manhattan near Times Square. One of Rockefeller Plaza's attractions is Radio City Music Hall, home of the well-known Rockette dancers, who are also named for Rockefeller.

J.P. Morgan (1837 – 1913)

John Pierpont Morgan was a highly successful New York banker, investor and finance manager. Morgan was a private businessman, not a government official; but on two separate occasions, U.S. presidents called on Morgan to use his many business contacts and his knowledge of banking to save the U.S. economy from near ruin.

The first occasion was in 1895, when the U.S. Treasury was running out of gold after the Panic of 1893. President Grover Cleveland asked Morgan to find gold to shore up the treasury. Morgan assembled a group of investors who were able to loan the U.S. a staggering amount of gold to keep the nation's treasury from going bankrupt.

On the second occasion, during the Panic of 1907, several major New York banks were in financial trouble. If so many important banks had all gone bankrupt at the same time, their losses might have spread throughout the entire U.S. economy and caused a major economic depression. In order to prevent this grim possibility, Morgan locked those bankers in a room in his New York mansion and forced them to agree on a strategy to stay out of bankruptcy. They agreed to loan one another money and to find new lines of credit from foreign banks. Morgan's tactics became the model for the new Federal Reserve System of banks, which was established in 1913.

J.P. Morgan's name is still honored in the world of New York finance. It appears today in the names of banking and investment companies such as JP Morgan Chase and Morgan Stanley.

Andrew Carnegie (1835 – 1919)

Andrew Carnegie rose from poverty as a weaver's son to become one of the wealthiest men in history. He was also a well-known philanthropist (charitable giver) who gave away hundreds of millions of dollars to his favorite causes.

Carnegie was born in Scotland in 1835, but immigrated to the United States with his parents in 1848. At age 12, he took a job in a cotton mill to help support his family, working 6 days per week, 12 hours per day. Despite this heavy workload, he somehow retained enough energy to read and educate himself. Later, he worked in a telegraph office, where his bosses took notice of his quick mind. Through his friendships with his bosses and other businessmen, he learned about a series of investments that helped make him rich. He earned his first $1 million by the time he reached his early 30s.

Carnegie earned the bulk of his wealth in the steel business, by founding or purchasing numerous companies that produced steel or supported steel production. In 1892, he merged several of these businesses to form the tremendously successful Carnegie Steel Company in Pittsburgh, Pennsylvania. Nine years later, in 1901, he sold

Carnegie Steel to J.P. Morgan so that Morgan could form U.S. Steel, the world's largest steel company. For his personal share of Carnegie Steel, Morgan paid Andrew Carnegie $225 million– a sum that would be worth nearly $6 billion in 2010 dollars.

Carnegie was also known for giving away his wealth, especially to fund public library buildings. He funded public libraries in nearly every state, giving away more than $45 million in the process. After he retired in 1901, he spent the rest of his life managing his charities.

In 1889, Carnegie published an essay called "The Gospel of Wealth" that revealed some of his thoughts about money and charity. Carnegie believed:

1. That certain people are born with extraordinary talent and ambition;
2. That in a free society, these gifted people will naturally rise to the top of the business world and grow wealthy;
3. That the wealthy should not leave their fortunes to their children, who are likely to waste them;
4. That instead, because these gifted people know best how to manage money, they should spend the last third of their lives managing their own charities and carefully giving away all of their money in the best possible way;
5. That these charities should not waste money on the daily needs of people too lazy to work for themselves;
6. That instead, these charities should help people educate themselves through literature and the arts, improving the human race.

Carnegie's name appears on numerous libraries, schools, foundations and awards that are still well-known. Among them:

- Carnegie Hall, a concert hall in New York City
- Carnegie-Mellon University, a university founded as the Carnegie Technical School in Pittsburgh
- The Carnegie Medal, awarded yearly for the United Kingdom's best children's book
- The Carnegie libraries, more than 2,500 libraries all over the U.S., the U.K. and elsewhere

FASCINATING FACTS: Scottish Tartan

Tartan is a multi-colored, patterned cloth. The woolen Scottish tartan that is used to make kilts is a national symbol of Scotland. During the 1700s, when England was trying to absorb Scotland into its empire, the English tried to destroy Scottish patriotism by banning Scottish tartan. Their effort only made the Scottish love their tartan more. Early in Scotland's history, each district of Scotland created its own unique pattern of tartan, because local weavers dyed their yarns using only the dyes that were made in their area. Later, certain tartan patterns came to belong to certain clans and institutions.

AMERICAN INVENTIONS, ACCIDENTAL AND OTHERWISE

The Accidental Invention of the Potato Chip

In 1853, George Crum was working as a chef in a Saratoga Lake, New York restaurant when a cranky dinner customer sent his French fries back to the kitchen, complaining that they were too thick and too soft. A frustrated George decided to err in the opposite direction and make French fries that were too thin and too crisp. He sliced his potatoes as thinly as possible, fried them in oil and then over-salted them. To his surprise, his cranky customer loved his paper-thin, salty fried potatoes. George called his new recipe "Saratoga Chips." They were such a hit that Crum was able to open his own restaurant featuring a basket of Saratoga Chips on every table.

Why Tires are Black

Until 1910, rubber tires were usually colored off-white, amber or tan because these were the colors of the rubber tree sap used in making rubber. But road dirt always made these light-colored tires appear dusty and dingy; so, in order to improve their tires' appearance, the B.F. Goodrich Company decided to make its tires black by adding carbon black pigment to their rubber.

As it turned out, adding carbon black had a second, unexpected result: Tires with carbon black lasted five times longer than tires without carbon black. Today's common black tires owe their color and durability to Goodrich's accidental discovery.

The Steam-Powered Motorcycle

Inventor Sylvester Roper built the first motorcycle in 1868. It was a steam-powered bicycle with wooden wheels and iron tires. Like a modern motorcycle, it had its throttle and brake controls on its handlebars.

Two things made Roper's steam motorcycle impractical:

1. It could only travel about 8 miles before it needed water added to make more steam, and
2. The steam boiler under the seat ran at about 300 degrees Fahrenheit, making for an uncomfortable ride.

Sylvester Roper toured fairs and circuses all over New England with his motorcycle until he was well into his 70s. He died in a crash while he was trying to set a new 40 mile per hour motorcycle speed record.

"Make Mine Moxie"

Moxie Cream Soda was one of America's first mass-produced soft drinks. Moxie came on the market in 1876 as a "patent medicine" that could supposedly cure everything from paralysis and anxiety to the common cold. Its curative powers were attributed to a rare "secret ingredient" derived from some mysterious South American plant. The makers of Moxie added soda water to their medicine to make it drinkable, and were surprised to find that it tasted good that way. By 1884, Moxie Cream Soda was available in bottles and at soda fountains. The company's catchy slogan was "Make Mine Moxie," and its spokesman, the "Moxie Man," helped sell its product. Now a person who is full of spirit and determination like the Moxie Man can be said to have "moxie."

Montgomery Ward's Catalog

Aaron Montgomery Ward was a businessman who saw an opportunity to "cut out the middleman" as John D. Rockefeller had cut out the oil business's middlemen. In Ward's case, the "middlemen" were country store owners who charged their country-dwelling customers high prices on goods shipped from faraway cities. Ward's idea was to mail these country people illustrated catalogs of goods so that they could order their goods directly from him and pick them up themselves at the nearest train station. In this way, they could buy their goods at the same prices city customers paid.

Ward had some difficulty getting his business off the ground, especially when his warehouse burned in the 1871 Great Chicago Fire (see below). The first Montgomery Ward catalog went out in August 1872, and advertised 163 items for sale. It was little more than a price list with ordering instructions. Country store owners, angry at Ward's attempt to cut them out of their business, sometimes publicly burned his catalogs. Nevertheless, Ward's business grew with the catalog, which began to include more and more items that country people couldn't find in stores anywhere near their homes.

By 1883, the Montgomery Ward catalog was about 240 pages long and listed about 10,000 items for sale. It was known as the "Wish Book," and country people eagerly awaited its arrival in the mail. In addition to the usual items like clothing and household goods, one could also buy unexpected items like boats and even whole house kits.

Ward's biggest competitors were Richard Sears and Alvah Roebuck, who founded Sears, Roebuck and Company in 1896. Sears often offered lower prices than Ward, but Ward argued that his goods were priced higher because they were of higher quality. Sears surpassed Montgomery Ward in yearly sales for the first time in 1900.

FASCINATING FACTS: The Real McCoy

A Canadian black named Elijah McCoy designed an oil cup to lubricate train wheels as they ran along the track. McCoy's oil cups worked better than any of his imitators' oil cups, so railroad men began checking to make sure that any rail cars they bought were fitted with "the real McCoy" oil cups and not some cheap imitation.

This is only one of many possible explanations for the origin of the phrase "the real McCoy," which means "genuine."

AMAZING AMERICANS: John Deere (1804 – 1886)

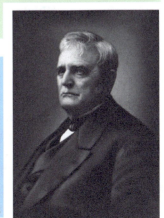

John Deere was a blacksmith who developed the polished moldboard plow, also known as the "self-scouring plow" and the "plow that broke the Plains." Deere & Company became one of the world's best-known farm equipment manufacturers.

Deere began his career as a Vermont blacksmith's apprentice, and became a blacksmith himself in 1825. Blacksmiths were plentiful in Vermont, but rare out West, where the pioneers were settling the Northwest Territory. When Deere had money troubles in Vermont, he decided to move to Illinois, where skilled blacksmiths could use their rare skills to earn more money.

Midwestern soils turned out to be different from Eastern soils: they contained a kind of sticky clay that stuck to farmers' cast iron plowshares, clogging them and bringing the teams that pulled them to a stop. Plowing Midwestern clay was slow and hard work with a cast iron plow, because the farmer was forced to stop often so that he could scrape the clay off of his plowshares.

Deere was an experienced metal polisher. When he saw the farmers' difficulties with the Midwestern soil, he figured out that a plowshare made of polished cast steel would move through Midwestern clay far more easily than one made of rough cast iron. Deere spent years developing the perfect shape for his moldboard plows. He sold his first cast steel plow in 1837, and it was a big success. Ten years later, he was selling about 1,000 plows per year.

Deere & Company had a long-standing reputation for quality, a reputation based in part on this well-known Deere quote:

"I will never put my name on a product that does not have in it the best that is in me."

Over the years, Deere made several innovations in the farm machinery business:

- He began to manufacture plows before his customers ordered them, so that (1) farmers could see them before they bought them, and (2) he could work efficiently and stay ahead of the demand. This was unusual in the early years of the Industrial Revolution.
- He mounted two or more plowshares on a single plow to make the first "gang plow," which enabled farmers to plow two or three times faster.
- He developed the first riding farm implement, the Hawkeye Riding Cultivator.

The 1871 Great Chicago Fire

The hot, dry summer of 1871 left Chicago parched and susceptible to fire. On October 8, 1871, a fire broke out in Patrick O'Leary's barn, perhaps after Mrs. Catherine O'Leary's cow kicked over a burning oil lantern. A combination of factors allowed the fire to spread out of control rapidly:

1. The city's firefighters reacted slowly because they were exhausted from fighting another fire the day before.
2. When the firefighters finally did respond to the fire, they first went in the wrong direction.
3. The supply of water for fighting fires was dangerously low.
4. A fierce southwest wind drove the flames and burning embers into the heart of the city.

Chicago was a city built of wood. Its builders followed no modern building codes, which have since been designed to block drafts between floors and slow the spread of flames. Chicago's tall, drafty wooden buildings acted like chimneys, drawing the flames upward from floor to floor. Houses, churches, factories and shops all burned like torches. The fire burned from Sunday night until Tuesday morning, when a heavy rain helped to quench it.

The costs of the Great Chicago Fire were enormous: it killed about 300 people, left over 100,000 people homeless and destroyed about $200 million worth of property. Chicago's homeless lived in tent villages until the city got back on its feet.

Other interesting facts about the Great Chicago Fire:

- Several sports teams, including the Chicago Fire professional soccer team and the Flames of the University of Illinois at Chicago, are named for the Great Chicago Fire.
- Christian evangelist Dwight L. Moody (founder of the Moody Bible Institute) lost his church in the fire; and Christian hymn writer Horatio Spafford (who wrote "It is Well with My Soul") lost his home in the fire.
- Montgomery Ward lost its warehouse in the fire.
- Three other large fires burned along Lake Michigan at the same time as the Great Chicago Fire. It is possible that Mrs. O'Leary's cow was blamed unfairly, and that a shower of burning meteors or some other ignition source sparked the series of fires along the lake that day.

FASCINATING FACTS: The 1906 San Francisco Earthquake

The 1906 San Francisco Earthquake was one of the worst natural disasters in the history of the United States. The earthquake struck at 5:12 am on Wednesday, April 18, 1906 and lasted for about one minute. Its epicenter was about 2 miles off the San Francisco coast. The quake was so powerful that the ground ruptured along about 300 miles of California's San Andreas Fault. Tremors were felt as far north as Oregon, as far south as Los Angeles and as far inland as Nevada. Over 3,000 people died in the quake and large fire that followed.

FASCINATING FACTS: Monopoly

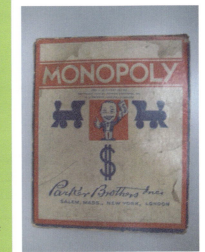

Monopoly, the popular Parker Brothers board game, was developed from an earlier game patented in 1904 by a Quaker woman named Elizabeth Magie. As a good Quaker, Magie disapproved of the way money-hungry landlords were able to use their wealth to capture even more wealth at the expense of the poor; so she invented "The Landlord's Game" to illustrate the many ways in which landlords could take advantage of their tenants. Beginning around 1910, a socialist economist named Scott Nearing used Magie's game to teach the evils of robber baron capitalism to his economics students at the University of Pennsylvania. Nearing's students helped to spread the game's popularity.

A man named Charles Darrow sold his own version of Monopoly to Parker Brothers in 1935. Darrow's version of the game was the opposite of Magie's: instead of insulting landlords, his game glorified them. The object of Darrow's game was to "corner the market" on real estate and charge opponents high rents until they couldn't afford to pay anymore. Monopoly was the perfect game for the Great Depression era of the 1930s, because it allowed the average poor person to pretend that he or she was a big-money dealmaker like Rockefeller, Morgan or Carnegie.

In order to protect its right to sell Monopoly exclusively– in other words, to secure its monopoly on Monopoly– Parker Brothers paid Elizabeth Magie $500 for her patent on "The Landlord's Game." Darrow, on the other hand, fared slightly better: he became a millionaire on royalty payments for the millions of Monopoly games Parker Brothers sold.

Other interesting facts about Monopoly:
- The top-hat wearing "Monopoly Man" (also known as "Rich Uncle Pennybags") who appears on the game's "Chance" and "Community Chest" cards may have been modeled after J.P. Morgan.

- Robber baron Andrew Carnegie didn't approve of "The Landlord's Game," nor of Scott Nearing's teachings against capitalism and the robber barons. Before Carnegie would agree to donate money to the University of Pennsylvania, he insisted that the university first fire Scott Nearing.

U.S. GEOGRAPHY FOCUS

FASCINATING FACTS about KANSAS:

- Statehood: Kansas became the 34th US state on January 29, 1861.
- Bordering states: Colorado, Missouri, Nebraska, Oklahoma
- State capital: Topeka
- Area: 82,277 sq. mi (Ranks 15th in size)
- Abbreviation: KS
- State nickname: "Sunflower State"
- State bird: Western Meadowlark
- State tree: Cottonwood
- State flower: Sunflower
- State song: *Home on the Range*
- State Motto: "To the stars through difficulties"
- Meaning of name: Named after the Indian tribe who lived in the area (Kansa, Konza or Kaw)
- Historic places to visit in Kansas: Rock Island Bridge, Maxwell Game Preserve, Lee Richardson Zoo, Greyhound Hall of Fame, Kansas Cosmosphere and Space Center, Garden of Eden in Lucas, Lake Afton Public Observatory, The Kansas Underground Salt Museum, Amelia Earhart Birthplace Museum, Kansas Barbed Wire Museum
- Resources and Industries: farming (cattle, hogs, corn, wheat and other grains, soybeans and sorghum), printing, aircraft and automobile manufacturing, gas and oil, food processing

Amelia Earhart Home

Flag of Kansas

- Kansas adopted this flag in 1927.
- The flag has a navy blue field with the state seal in the center and the state flower, a sunflower, at the top. The seal features Kansas farmland, covered wagons, Indians hunting bison, a farmer in a field and a log cabin.
- The seal's 34 stars mark the fact that Kansas was the 34th state.

Chapter 16

American Inventions, Persia, the Balkan Wars

U.S. HISTORY FOCUS

AMAZING AMERICANS: Henry Ford and the Model T

Henry Ford introduced the Ford Model T automobile in 1908. Ford was not the first to build a gasoline-engine automobile, but his Model T was remarkable in several ways:

- Ford created a moving assembly line to produce the Model T. Each new vehicle under construction moved from station to station down the assembly line. At each station, auto workers added a particular component or components: a transmission, a steering wheel, a windshield, a door, or any other part they were assigned. The assembly line improved manufacturing efficiency tremendously. Each worker performed his assigned task over and over, so he knew exactly what to do and could do it quickly. There was no need to move tools or parts along the line, since they could all be delivered to the station where they were needed and kept there. By 1914, Ford's assembly line could build a Model T in 93 minutes.

- The Model T was aimed at America's middle class, so it was far more affordable than other vehicles of its day. In 1909, it sold for $850, the equivalent of about $20,400 in 2010. By the 1920s, the efficiency of the assembly line had reduced its price to a paltry $290, the equivalent of about $3100 in 2010.

- New Model T owners often received instructions from mechanics when they took possession of their new vehicles. Early models had a hand crank for starting, and owners had to grip the crank properly or risk breaking their arms if the engine "kicked back." To avoid this kickback, mechanics instructed owners to "retard the spark" on the magneto (ignition system) while they were cranking the engine, then "advance the spark" after the engine caught and ran.

- The Model T had a planetary transmission. A planetary gear set consists of a central "sun" gear, two or more "planet" gears that rotate around it and an interior-toothed "ring" gear around the planet gears. Planetary sets are capable of producing a wide range of gear ratios, and Henry Ford was fond of them. Even the Model T's steering wheel used a planetary set to make steering easier.

- Drivers sometimes had to drive their Model Ts backwards!

This became necessary for two reasons: (1) On early Model Ts, the gasoline tank was positioned under the seat. When these cars climbed steep hills, the gas tank was beneath the engine, and gravity couldn't feed the engine gasoline. The easiest solution was to climb steep hills in reverse so that the gas tank would be above the engine! (2) The planetary transmission relied on friction bands, which wore out over time. On steep hills, a worn friction band could begin to slip, leaving the car motionless. Because the reverse band got so little use, it was usually less worn. So if a Model T's transmission bands were slipping, one could usually climb a hill in reverse, then turn around at the top of the hill and drive on!

- The flip side of the assembly line's efficiency was its resistance to change. Because changes in the model T meant major changes on the expensive assembly line, Ford resisted changes. This applied to color, as well: Henry Ford told his team that "Any customer can have a car painted any color that he wants so long as it is black."

- By 1918, half of America's cars were black Model T Fords. The company made more than 15 million Model Ts before retiring the model in 1927.

FASCINATING FACTS: A Presidential First

William McKinley was the first President to ride in a self-propelled automobile. He rode in a steam automobile first, then later in an electric car. An assassin killed McKinley years before the Model T appeared.

AMAZING AMERICANS: The Wright Brothers and the Wright Flyer

Brothers Wilbur Wright (1867 – 1912) and Orville Wright (1871 – 1948) were skilled craftsmen who owned a repair shop in Ohio. Their experience in working on everything from printing presses to bicycles to gasoline engines served them well over the years from 1899-1903, which they spent developing the world's first heavier-than-air aircraft, the *Wright Flyer*.

The Wright Brothers' success was the result of careful study, determination and hard work. Their ingenuity made them the best aeronautical engineers in the world of their day. Earlier engineers had learned that curved wings (airfoils) produced a lift force as they sped through the air, allowing gliders to remain aloft longer; but the Wright Brothers refined the airfoil, perfecting its shape and taking careful measurements of the lift force it produced in a wind tunnel they built themselves. The Wrights also accomplished several other firsts:

- They were the first to design an aircraft control system that could control all three angles of an aircraft's flight (roll, pitch and yaw).
- They were the first to add an engine to their glider successfully (they built their engine themselves in their Ohio bicycle shop).
- They were the first to create an aircraft propeller and to realize that it operated on the same mechanical principles as an airfoil.

The Wright Brothers chose Kitty Hawk, North Carolina as the site of their flight experiments because of the area's high prevailing winds and sandy soil. The wind provided extra lift for their airfoils; and the sandy soil softened their landings, which were often rather rough.

The Wrights' first glider, which they tested at Kitty Hawk in July-August 1901, was hardly better than those built by earlier engineers. Through the rest of that year and the beginning of the next, they built their wind tunnel and tested dozens of different airfoil shapes. Their new airfoils enabled them to build a far superior glider for testing at Kitty Hawk during the summer of 1902.

The gasoline-powered Wright Flyer of 1903 was based on the 1902 glider. A gasoline engine and two chain-driven propellers pulled the Wright Flyer through the air; and the Wrights steered it by warping its wings like a bird's. The Wright Brothers flew four successful test flights in their *Wright Flyer* on December 17, 1903.

On its first flight, piloted by Orville, the flyer traveled 120 feet in 12 seconds. The third, last and longest flight of the day covered 852 feet. After this flight, high winds flipped the flyer over several times, damaging it so severely that it never flew again. Despite its success, the Wright Flyer was so unstable in the air that the Wright Brothers went back to the drawing board for a major redesign before they built 1904's *Wright Flyer II*.

In 1905, Wilbur piloted yet another model, the *Wright Flyer III,* on a successful flight of nearly 25 miles, ending with a safe landing.

After the success of the *Wright Flyer III*, the brothers felt that their aircraft was ready to demonstrate and sell; so they shrouded their designs in secrecy in order to prevent others from stealing their work. Most people were unaware of their successes, and those who were aware of them were highly skeptical.

The Wrights spent the next two years improving their designs and negotiating with their likely buyers, the governments of America and Europe. By the time they finally demonstrated their newest designs for the governments of France and America in 1908, they were able to fly effortless circles and figure 8s all over the demonstration field. Everyone who witnessed these demonstration flights immediately renounced skepticism. The work of the Wrights had far surpassed that of any other aeronautical engineer, including Samuel Langley, who had received government money to develop a piloted flying machine that never flew.

WORLD HISTORY FOCUS

PERSIA

The Persian Empire
Like its neighbor Afghanistan, Persia (modern-day Iran) lies in the borderland between the West and the East. Over the centuries, Persia has changed hands several times, and has been dominated by Greeks, Arabs, Mongols and Turks as well as by native Persians.

The ancient Persian Empire (~550-330 BC) was the largest empire the world had yet seen. Persia's founding emperor, Cyrus the Great, united his empire with the kingdom of the Medes by defeating his grandfather, the Median King Astyages. Next, Cyrus conquered the Babylonian Empire by diverting the Tigris River and marching his army up its dry riverbed and into the city of Babylon (on the day when the Babylonian

Prince Belshazzar saw the "writing on the wall" in the Bible Book of Daniel, chapter 5). It was Cyrus of Persia who allowed the first Jews to return from Babylonian exile and to begin building their Second Temple in Jerusalem. Cyrus and his heirs built their Persian Empire until it included nearly all of the Ancient Near East: from Egypt in the southwest, north to Asia Minor and the Black Sea, and east to India's Indus River.

The Greeks in Babylon

All of that came to an end with the rise of the Greeks. As part of his campaign to conquer the entire known world, the Greek Alexander the Great defeated the last Persian Emperor, Darius III, in 330 BC. Then when Alexander died young in 323 BC, the Wars of the Diadochi divided his empire. One of Alexander's three great military commanders, General Seleucus, took control of the part of Alexander's empire that included Persia, and made it part of his new Seleucid Empire. Persia belonged to the Greek-speaking Seleucid Empire until Arsaces I of Parthia (a region in northern Persia) led a successful rebellion against the Seleucids.

The Return of the Persians

With the rise of the Parthians, Persia returned to the control of native Persians. The Parthian Empire controlled Persia from around 227 BC - 224 AD. Then another native Persian empire, the Sassanid Empire, replaced the Parthians. The Sassanid Empire, named for a Zoroastrian leader from southern Persia, ruled Persia from 224 - 651 AD. The Sassanids would be Persia's last non-Muslim rulers.

Islam in Persia

The rise of Islam began with the Prophet Muhammad's migration to Medina (the *Hegira*) in 622 AD. Islam united the Middle East's Arabs into a mighty, world-conquering Islamic Empire. In 651 AD, the Abbasid Caliphate of the new Islamic Empire conquered Persia's Sassanid Empire and brought the Islamic faith to Persia. In time, Islam thoroughly replaced Persia's native Zoroastrianism and other faiths.

Even though the Arabs' faith replaced the Persians' faith, however, the Arabs' culture did not replace Persia's culture. The Persians remembered their proud history, and did not allow the Arabs to absorb them.

Most Arabs were Sunni Muslims, but the Persians gravitated toward Shia Islam, and modern Iran is home to the world's largest concentration of Shia Muslims.

The Mongols and Tamerlane

During the 1200s, Persia suffered a devastating invasion by the Mongol heirs of Genghis Khan. During the 1300s, Persia suffered a second devastating invasion at the hands of Tamerlane (Timur), a descendant of both the Mongols and the Turks. Persia also suffered during the Black Plaque epidemic of the 1300s. These devastations claimed the lives of up to three fourths of Persia's population, and that population would not return to its previous level for several centuries.

Despite all of these troubles, Persia never became part of the Ottoman Empire, the world's dominant Islamic empire. Persia's Shah Ismail established the Safavid Dynasty, Persia's first thoroughly Shia Muslim Dynasty, in 1501. Persia remained distinct, independent and proud.

Persia versus Russia

During the 1700s, the growing Russian Empire began to eye Persia with interest. Persia possessed something that Russia had wanted almost from the beginning of its history under Rurik the Viking around 860 AD: access to the world's oceans through a good southern port. In Persia's case, those ports lay on the Persian Gulf. Only Persia's weakening Safavid Dynasty stood between the Russian Empire and the Persian Gulf. Russia's interest in Persian territory led to four Russo-Persian Wars, all of which Russia won:

The 1722 – 1723 Russo-Persian War (aka the Persian Campaign of Peter the Great): In 1722, Pashtun tribesmen from eastern Persia and Afghanistan overthrew the Safavid Dynasty. Russia's Emperor, Peter the Great, made use of the chaos in Persia to conquer several provinces in north Persia. Russia would return all of these provinces and make peace with Persia in 1735, just before the onset of one of the Russo-Turkish Wars between Russia and the Ottoman Empire.

The 1796 Russo-Persian War (aka the Persian Expedition of Catherine the Great): In 1794, Agha Muhammad Khan killed the last Zand Dynasty king and founded Persia's Qajar Dynasty. In 1796, Russia's other "great" emperor, Catherine the Great, took advantage of the political chaos in Persia to capture Azerbaijan and other north Persian territories. Before Russia could solidify its gains, Catherine the Great died, and Russia entered its own period of chaos under her weak successor, Tsar Paul I.

The 1804 – 1813 Russo-Persian War: Over about ten years of fighting, Russian Tsar Alexander I captured Azerbaijan once again and added parts of Georgia and Armenia to Russia's holdings.

The 1826 – 1828 Russo-Persian War: With encouragement from Britain, which had by now loaned Persia a great deal of money, Persia invaded and tried to retake the provinces it had lost in the previous war. Russia's superior weapons and tactics allowed it to retain Azerbaijan, Georgia and Armenia.

The Great Game, Again

During the mid-1800s, both Russia and Britain were interested in Persia. Russia wanted Persia for its access to the Persian Gulf and the Indian Ocean; while Britain wanted Persia so that it could oppose Russian expansion and protect its trade routes to and from British India. Later, Britain also wanted Persia's oil resources. These conflicts between Russia and Britain made Persia part of the same "Great Game" that threatened Afghanistan (see Chapter 3).

Having barely survived a century of wars against Russia, then suffered Russia's manipulations during the Great Game, Persia was eager to accept Britain's help against its enemy to the north. Two Persian shahs, Naser al-Din Shah Qajar and Mozaffar ad-Din Shah Qajar, borrowed a great deal of British money trying to prevent Russia from swallowing Persia during the Great Game.

INTERESTING INDIVIDUALS: Naser al-Din Shah Qajar (reigned 1848 – 1896)

Naser al-Din Shah, who rose to power in Persia in 1848, was the best-known shah of Persia's Qajar Dynasty. Naser was the first Persian Shah to visit Europe, and he became a great admirer of Europe's technology and culture. On his first European trip in 1873, Britain's Queen Victoria honored him with a knighthood (see picture). Back home in Persia, Naser tried to put European ideas into practice by modernizing Persia's postal service and creating school systems modeled after European ones. Naser also tried to make Persia less Islam-centered by taking power from Islamic religious leaders and bestowing it upon secular leaders.

Unfortunately, Naser's love for Europe did not prevent the European powers from dominating Persia. Naser borrowed a great deal money from European banks to finance his reform programs. His eagerness to accept British money forced him to give the British what they wanted, and Britain gained more and more control over Persia's affairs.

Nor did Naser's love for Europe bring him honor at home. Although Persia's empire had suffered several setbacks, there were still plenty of Persians who were proud of their nation and its culture, which they believed had been the equal of Rome's in its heyday. They felt that Naser's interest in European ideas dishonored Persia's proud history. One such Persian, Mirza Reza Kermani, assassinated Naser al-Din Shah at a prayer service in 1896.

Mozaffar ad-Din Shah Qajar (reigned 1896 – 1907)

Mozaffar ad-Din Shah became the Shah of Persia after the assassination of his father Naser. Mozaffar shared his father's interest in European ideas and European money. Like his father, he traveled in Europe and was fascinated by what he saw there. He was so excited about the new motion picture technology he saw in Europe that he ordered his staff to bring it to Persia immediately.

Mozaffar's travel expenses and purchases cost a great deal of money; and Persia already owed British bankers the large sums borrowed by his father Naser, as well as regular interest payments. In short, Persia's finances were a wreck. But instead of living within his means and reforming Persia's finances, Mozaffar made Persia's debt problem far worse by borrowing even more money, this time from Russian bankers.

It was during Mozaffar's reign that Britain began to take a major interest in Persia's oil resources.

FASCINATING FACTS: The D'Arcy Oil Concession

In 1901, a wealthy British miner named William Knox D'Arcy purchased the right to mine oil over nearly all of Persia. Geologists had told D'Arcy that there might be crude oil hidden beneath Persia's sands; but at the time, no one had struck oil there, and Persia contained not one functioning commercial oil well.

- <u>What D'Arcy Paid</u>: D'Arcy paid Mozaffar ad-Din Shah and the Persian government 20,000 British pounds and an equivalent amount of money in the form of stock in his oil exploration company. In addition, he promised Persia 16 percent (one sixth) of his company's profits, if any, each year.

- <u>What D'Arcy Received</u>: D'Arcy's company received exclusive mining rights all over Persia, with the exception of the five northern provinces that bordered Russia. This meant that D'Arcy's company alone had the right to search for oil, produce oil and even transport oil over most of Persia's more than 600,000-square-mile territory. According to the agreement, D'Arcy's oil mining rights were to remain in place for 60 years.

D'Arcy's company began searching for oil in 1903. D'Arcy poured most of his considerable personal wealth into the company; but for years, his search for oil met with only frustrating results.

Five years later, when D'Arcy was nearly bankrupt and ready to shut the company down, his explorers finally found enough oil to produce and sell. <u>After D'Arcy's explorers and geologists learned where to look, it became clear that Persia was simply brimming with valuable oil.</u>

In 1909, a group of wealthy British businessmen formed the Anglo-Persian Oil Company (APOC) to purchase D'Arcy's suddenly valuable Persian oil mining company. These businessmen immediately paid D'Arcy 2,000,000 British pounds for the Persian oil rights he had purchased from Mozaffar Shah-- fifty times the amount D'Arcy had paid the shah for them. The APOC soon began producing oil-- and oil profits-- at a remarkable rate.

Five years later, in 1914, the conflicts that led to World War I were brewing, and war was on the horizon. In that year, the British government moved to strengthen its hold on Persia's oil by purchasing 51 percent of the APOC's shares, becoming the company's controlling stockholder. The British government also won the APOC's promise that Britain's navy could buy oil from the APOC at a fixed price for the next 30 years. With these agreements in place, Persia became Britain's most important supplier of the all-important oil that it needed for national defense.

Other interesting facts about the D'Arcy Oil Concession:

- In later years, the APOC would become British Petroleum (BP), which is still one of the world's largest oil companies.

- The APOC's valuable Persian oil rights did not remain uncontested for long. When Persia's leaders realized how very much oil wealth they had sold for a song, they demanded more royalties' payments from the APOC. Negotiations over Persian oil money went on for decades, and the APOC made several large payments to the Persians to keep them happy and to keep the oil flowing.

- D'Arcy and the British have been criticized for paying Persia so little for oil rights that turned out to be so valuable. In D'Arcy's defense, one must remember that when he set out to find oil in Persia, there was no guarantee of success. When D'Arcy founded his oil company, he immediately invested 500,000 British pounds from his personal fortune, and he had to borrow even more before his explorers finally found large oil stores. The explorers worked under miserable conditions, beset by abundant insects, temperatures up to 120° F and plenty of hostile Persians. D'Arcy might just as easily have lost his entire investment. D'Arcy and his team succeeded through initiative, risk and perseverance. Britain could also argue that the Persians might never have found their oil without British help. Even so, the Persians successfully argued that because the oil came from their land, they deserved a greater share of the profits that it generated.

The Constitutional Revolution of 1906 and the Majles

The people of Persia finally grew so disgusted by their shahs' shameful admiration of Britain and Russia that they launched a revolution against Mozaffar Shah. The Constitutional Revolution of 1906 forced Mozaffar to surrender his absolute power as shah, and to adopt a constitution for Persia. The revolution also required Mozaffar to form an elected assembly of representatives known as the *Majles*, Persia's first elected government (see picture). Mozaffar ad-Din Shah died of a heart attack within days after he signed away much of the Persian shahs' power to the Majles.

Muhammad Ali Shah Qajar (reigned 1907 – 1909)

Muhammad Ali Shah Qajar was Mozaffar's son and successor. As Persia's crown prince before he became shah, Muhammad had strongly opposed his father's decision to sign the constitution that revolutionaries forced upon him in 1906; so when he became shah, he set out to eliminate the constitution and reclaim his full authority as Persia's all-powerful shah.

With backing from Russian soldiers, Muhammad Ali Shah used military force to try to dissolve the Majles. But the same revolutionaries who had defeated Mozaffar also defeated Muhammad; and in 1909, Mohammad was forced to leave Persia and flee into a life of exile with his Russian friends.

The End of the Great Game (1907)

During Mohammad Ali Shah's brief reign, Britain and Russia finally negotiated a treaty to bring an end to their rivalry in Persia and Afghanistan. The primary goal of their treaty was to bring an end to the Great Game so that Britain and Russia could team up against a new threat: the Triple Alliance of Germany, Austria-Hungary and Italy, which was soon to become their opponent in World War I.

In the Anglo-Russian Convention, signed in 1907, Britain and Russia finally ended the Great Game with these agreements:

- Persia would be divided into three zones: (1) A southern zone of British influence; (2) A northern zone of Russian influence; and (3) A neutral buffer zone between the two.
- Russia would consider Afghanistan a British protectorate, and would no longer interfere in Afghani affairs.

Britain and Russia established boundaries for these three zones and completed all of these agreements without ever bothering to ask the people of Persia or Afghanistan what they thought about them. Later, when the Persians and the Afghanis learned of the agreements, both had even greater reasons to resent British and Russian interference in their affairs.

Ahmad Shah Qajar (reigned 1909 – 1925) and World War I

Ahmad Shah Qajar was only eleven years old when his father Muhammad Ali Shah fled into exile in Russia. Young Ahmad Shah ruled with the help of a regent until he came of age in 1914. Ahmad and his regent restored the Majles, the Persian parliament that his father had tried to destroy.

During Ahmad's reign, Persia served as a battleground for the opposing armies of World War I. Russian and British forces fought in Persia to protect their oil resources from Germany and the Ottoman Empire. Persians watched from the sidelines as foreign armies overran their country and did whatever they pleased there.

Late in World War I, British forces tried to invade Russia from Persia as part of a failed attempt to reverse Russia's October Revolution of 1917 (see Chapter 18). As a result, Russia's new Bolshevik government stationed troops in Persia to defend itself against Britain long after World War I was over. For much of his reign, Ahmad ruled little of Persia outside his capital city of Tehran.

The Pahlavi Dynasty

Ahmad's weak government was easy prey for a revolution. In 1921, a Persian general named Reza Khan marched into Tehran with a small army and overthrew Ahmad Shah. Ahmad's efforts to fend off Reza Khan failed, and he finally fled into European exile in 1923. Ahmad technically remained Persia's shah until 1925, when Reza Khan replaced him and became Reza Shah Pahlavi.

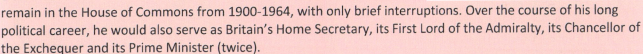

Ahmad was the last shah of the Qajar Dynasty. Reza Shah was the founder of the new Pahlavi Dynasty, which would hold power in Persia (Iran) until Ayatollah Ruhollah Khomeini's Islamic Revolution in 1979.

BRILLIANT BRITONS: Winston Churchill (1874 – 1965)

Winston Churchill was a British journalist, soldier and politician who came of age near the end of Britain's Victorian Era. Churchill's gifts of determination, courage and foresight helped guide his nation through the 20th Century's two world wars.

Churchill was the son of a wealthy and prominent British politician named Lord Randolph Churchill. As a young man, Churchill served in the British army in India, Sudan and South Africa. He earned extra money by working as a war correspondent, contributing newspaper articles from several of the vast British Empire's numerous battlefronts. After the Boers of South Africa captured Churchill during the Second Boer War, he became a British hero by escaping from their prison camp and traveling 300 miles to safety without being recaptured. His military heroism and his reputation as a writer earned him the recognition he needed to win election to Britain's Parliament.

After an unsuccessful run for Parliament in 1899, Churchill won election as a member of the House of Commons in 1900. He would remain in the House of Commons from 1900-1964, with only brief interruptions. Over the course of his long political career, he would also serve as Britain's Home Secretary, its First Lord of the Admiralty, its Chancellor of the Exchequer and its Prime Minister (twice).

Churchill comes into Persia's story because of his interest in oil. As First Lord of the Admiralty from 1911-1915, Churchill was responsible for Britain's proud navy. At the time, oil was only beginning to replace coal as a fuel for navy vessels, and naval engineers were only beginning to understand that oil contained about twice as much energy per unit weight as coal. Churchill was quick to see the advantages that oil-powered ships would have over coal-powered ones:

1. They could be built lighter and faster;
2. They needed refueling less often;
3. Refueling them caused much less strain on their crews;
4. They could be refueled at sea; and
5. They needed fewer crewmen to tend their engines.

Churchill was eager to convert Britain's navy from coal to oil and to secure an oil supply for Britain's defense. It was Churchill who urged Parliament to purchase 51% of the Anglo-Persian Oil Company's shares, making Britain the APOC's controlling stockholder so that Britain's all-important navy would always have a ready supply of oil (see the D'Arcy Oil Concession above).

Churchill lost his position as First Lord of the Admiralty during World War I, when Britain blamed him for the Allies' unexpected loss at the Battle of Gallipoli (Gallipoli is the peninsula that forms the northwest side of the Dardanelles Strait). Instead of hanging his head in shame, Churchill preserved his honor by resigning his government office and rejoining the army to serve his country in the trenches as a lieutenant colonel throughout the remainder of WWI. In the years between the two world wars, Churchill continued to insist on a strong defense for Britain, and was one of only a few who warned the Allies against allowing Germany's Fuhrer, Adolf Hitler, to rebuild Germany's military. He was also one of USSR-style communism's strongest opponents.

During World War II, when Germany threatened the British homeland, Britain turned to Churchill for leadership. Churchill replaced Neville Chamberlain as Prime Minister, then guided Britain through the Battle of Britain and the rest of World War II with bravery and determination. During the war years, Churchill made the most inspiring speeches of his life, and became one of the world's most respected leaders.

Surprisingly, Britain replaced its inspiring leader in 1945, the year in which World War II ended. He served as Prime Minister once again from 1953-1955, and died in 1965 at the age of 90.

Inspiring WWII quotes from Winston Churchill:
- "We shall defend our island, whatever the cost may be, we shall fight on the beaches, we shall fight on the landing grounds, we shall fight in the fields and in the streets, we shall fight in the hills; we shall never surrender."
- "Let us therefore brace ourselves to our duties, and so bear ourselves, that if the British Empire and its Commonwealth last for a thousand years, men will still say, 'This was their finest hour.'"
- "The gratitude of every home in our Island, in our Empire, and indeed throughout the world, except in the abodes of the guilty, goes out to the British airmen who, undaunted by odds, unwearied in their constant challenge and mortal danger, are turning the tide of the World War by their prowess and by their devotion. <u>Never in the field of human conflict was so much owed by so many to so few</u>." (After Britain's successful defense in the Battle of Britain)
- "Now this is not the end. It is not even the beginning of the end. But it is, perhaps, the end of the beginning." (After an Allied victory in North Africa)

THE BALKAN WARS

The Balkan Peninsula is a large European peninsula east of the Italian Peninsula that contains the nations of Albania, Bosnia, Bulgaria, Croatia, Greece, Macedonia, Montenegro, Romania and Serbia. During the Ancient and early Medieval ages, most of the Balkan Peninsula belonged to the Roman and Byzantine Empires. Later in the Medieval age, most of the Balkan Peninsula fell to the Ottoman Empire. From the 1453 Fall of Christian Constantinople through the Russo-Turkish War of 1877-1878, Ottoman Muslims dominated the Balkans. The Eastern Orthodox Christians who still lived in the Balkans lived

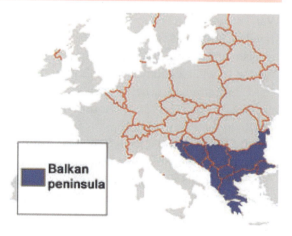

as second-class citizens under the Muslims, and often rebelled against their Muslim rulers (see Chapter 10).

By the late 1800s, the near-collapse of the Ottoman Empire had created a "power vacuum" in the Balkans, an absence of authority that allowed new authorities to dream of taking the Ottomans' place. Serbia and Greece had both won their independence from the Ottoman Empire during the 1830s. The Russo-Turkish War of 1877 - 1878 had left the Ottoman Empire barely hanging on to a divided Bulgaria (see Chapter 10). These three Balkan powers-- Bulgaria, Greece and Serbia-- were all ready to drive the Ottoman Empire out of the Balkans forever. Unfortunately, they were also jealous of one another: none of them wanted to see the others become too large and powerful.

From 1878 - 1914, the Balkan nations were the center of conflict in Europe. German Chancellor Otto von Bismarck, who left office in 1890, once predicted that the next great European war would begin in the Balkans. Bismarck was rarely wrong about such things.

A Brief Timeline of the Balkan Wars

1885: The Principality of Bulgaria and the province of Eastern Rumelia unite to form a much larger Bulgaria. Both Serbia and Greece feel threatened by Bulgaria's size, and Serbia declares war to claim part of Bulgaria's territory. Bulgaria defeats Serbia in the Serbo-Bulgarian War and retains its claim on all of its territories. The new, powerful Bulgaria considers itself the "Prussia of the Balkans," but it is still technically part of the Ottoman Empire under the terms of the 1878 Treaty of Berlin (which ended the Russo-Turkish War).

1908: The Young Turk Revolution (see Chapter 10) overthrows Sultan Abdulhamid II, and the Young Turks' Committee of Union and Progress (CUP) takes control of the Ottoman government. Three nations, one of them from outside the Balkan Peninsula, decide to take advantage of the chaos in the Ottoman government:

> **1908, October 5:** Bulgaria declares itself completely independent of the Ottoman Empire.

Picture by Antonio Piotrowski shows Bulgarians crossing the border into Serbia

> **1908, October 6:** Austria-Hungary formally annexes (absorbs) Bosnia, which it has supervised since 1878 under the Treaty of Berlin. Neighboring Serbia resents the annexation, but is forced to accept it temporarily.
> **1908, October:** Greece annexes the island of Crete, another Ottoman possession.

1908, October 8: Serbians who are angry over Austria-Hungary's annexation of Bosnia form a group known as *Narodna Odbrana*, "National Defense," and make plans to reclaim Bosnia for "Greater Serbia" (see below).

1912: Bulgaria, Greece, Serbia and Montenegro unite to form the Balkan League, an alliance they will use to claim the Ottoman Empire's last territories in the Balkans (Thrace, Macedonia and others).

1912: The First Balkan War, a war between the Balkan League and the Ottoman Empire, begins. The Balkan League defeats the Ottoman Empire in the First Balkan War.

1913, May: The **Treaty of London** ends the First Balkan War. The Ottoman Empire surrenders its claims to all territory northwest of a line drawn between the cities of Enos (on the Aegean Sea) and Midia (on the Black Sea). This line is dangerously close to the Ottoman capital at Constantinople (see map). The Ottoman Empire loses all of its territory on the Balkan Peninsula except for the little that lies southeast of the Enos-Midia Line.

After the First Balkan War and the Treaty of London:
- The Balkan League controls the entire Balkan Peninsula except for Bosnia (annexed by Austria-Hungary) and Albania (strongly Muslim).
- Bulgaria occupies Thrace.
- Greece occupies southern Macedonia.
- Serbia occupies northern Macedonia.
- The member nations of the Balkan League disagree about how to divide the large territories they have won in Thrace and Macedonia.

Early 1913: Bulgaria becomes unhappy with the division of territory at the end of the First Balkan War because it wants more territory in Macedonia. Bulgaria moves its armies into position to capture northern Macedonia (already occupied by Serbia) and southern Macedonia (already occupied by Greece).

1913, June: The Balkan League dissolves. Serbia and Greece form a new military alliance to oppose their former ally, Bulgaria, in Macedonia.

1913, June-August: The Second Balkan War, a war between the former allies of the Balkan League, begins. Serbia, Greece and Romania defeat Bulgaria in the Second Balkan War.

After the Second Balkan War and the Treaty of Bucharest:

- Serbia gains territory in northern Macedonia.
- Greece gains territory in southern Macedonia and eastern Thrace.
- Romania gains territory in northern Bulgaria.

1913-1914: Victorious Serbia returns its attention to Bosnia, which it hopes to claim from Austria-Hungary. Hatred between Serbia and Austria-Hungary approaches the boiling point.

FASCINATING FACTS: Greater Serbia

Tsar Dusan the Mighty founded the Serbian Empire on the Balkan Peninsula in 1346. At its peak around 1370, Serbia controlled the entire western half of the Balkan Peninsula, and was far larger than Bulgaria or Greece. Unfortunately, Christian Serbia was not far larger than its most powerful enemy, the Islamic Ottoman Empire. The Serbian Empire fell to the Ottomans at the Battle of Kosovo in 1389; and over the decades that followed, Serbia gradually became part of the Ottoman Empire. It would remain so for four centuries.

During the early 1800s, when the Ottoman Empire began to lose its grip on the Balkan Peninsula, the people of Serbia wanted to reclaim as much of their ancient empire's territory as possible-- even though much of that territory now belonged to the neighboring nations of Albania, Bosnia, Bulgaria, Greece and Montenegro. The movement to restore Serbia its former glory was known as "Greater Serbia."

Some of the Serbians who believed in a Greater Serbia worked with Serbia's ally, Russia, to gain as much territory as possible for Serbia through diplomatic negotiations. Others, however, formed secret paramilitary groups and tried to win territory in more violent ways. One violent paramilitary group, the Black Hand, was so angry at Austria-Hungary for annexing Bosnia in 1908 that it sent a group of assassins to attack Austria-Hungary's royal family.

1914, June 28: Serbian Gavrilo Princip (see picture), a member of the Black Hand, assassinates Arch-Duke Franz Ferdinand, heir to Austria-Hungary's throne, in Sarajevo, Bosnia.

In response, <u>Austria-Hungary declares war on Serbia</u> (with encouragement from Germany's Kaiser Wilhelm II). Serbia calls on its ally Russia for help, and Russia declares war on Austria-Hungary. In response, Austria-Hungary calls on its ally, Germany, for help, and Germany declares war on Russia. **Thus the assassination of Arch-Duke Franz Ferdinand activates a cascading series of alliances that touches off World War I** (see Chapter 17).

FASCINATING FACTS: The Airplanes of World War I

After the Wright Brothers successfully demonstrated and sold their aircraft designs in France and America in 1908, they spent years defending their aircraft patents in court. Their lawsuits consumed their attention, and American aircraft technology stagnated while America awaited the outcome of the Wrights' court wars.

The same was not true in Europe, where American patent law mattered less. European aircraft designs advanced rapidly, far surpassing the Wright designs within just a few years. By the time World War I began in 1914, Britain, France and Germany were all capable of producing highly useful military aircraft.

Early World War I aircraft served the same military purposes that hot-air balloons had served earlier: they spied out enemy troops' locations and numbers (reconnaissance). Because they had no other way to defend themselves, early military pilots carried handguns so that they could shoot at enemy pilots. Early pilots could also carry and drop light grenades or bombs on ground targets.

The next problem was to develop weapons and defenses for military aircraft. Pilots could mount rifles or machine guns in their aircraft, but they couldn't fire straight ahead without destroying their own propellers and shooting themselves down. A French pilot named Roland Garros became the first military pilot to shoot down ("kill") another aircraft after he bolted steel deflectors to his propeller to protect it from his own machine gun fire. Garros made four aircraft kills before he himself was shot down and killed in 1918.

The next major improvement came when German engineers used the aircraft engine's camshaft to time the aircraft's machine gun fire with the rotation of the propeller, so that when the pilot fired, the bullets flew between the fast-spinning propeller blades instead of into them.

Among the best-known aircraft models of World War I:

	The British-built *Sopwith Camel*, a powerful biplane equipped with a heavy rotary engine and two machine guns (Snoopy's plane).
	The Dutch/German-built *Fokker Eindecker*, a monoplane that scored so many kills that it became known as the *Fokker Scourge*.
	The French-built *Nieuport 11*, the biplane that outclassed the Eindecker and ended the Fokker Scourge.

INTERESTING INDIVIDUALS: The Red Baron

World War I's best-known pilot was the German ace Manfred von Richthofen, also known as the "Red Baron." The Red Baron's primary warplane was the *Fokker Dr.I* triplane, a more-advanced successor of the *Fokker Eindecker*. The Red Baron received credit for 80 kills, more than any other WWI pilot. He was so well respected on both sides of the war that when he was finally shot down on April 21, 1918, his enemies paid their respects to him in a memorial service.

U.S. GEOGRAPHY FOCUS

FASCINATING FACTS about NEVADA:

- Statehood: Nevada became the 36th US state on October 31, 1864.
- Bordering states: Arizona, California, Idaho, Oregon, Utah
- State capital: Carson City
- Area: 110,622 sq. mi (Ranks 7th in size)
- Abbreviation: NV

- State nickname: "Silver State," "Sagebrush State"
- State bird: Mountain Bluebird
- State tree: Single-Leaf Pinon (Bristlecone Pine)
- State flower: Sagebrush
- State song: *Home Means Nevada*
- State Motto: "All for Our Country "
- Meaning of name: from a Spanish word meaning "snowcapped"
- Historic places to visit in Nevada: The Reno Ice Pavilion, Las Vegas, Hoover Dam, The ghost town of Rhyolite, Berlin-Ichthyosaur State Park, The Virginia City steam train, Nevada Gambling Museum
- Resources and Industries: farming (cattle, sheep, dairy, potatoes, hay), tourism, mining (gold and silver), electric equipment, machinery

Hoover Dam by Ansel Adams

Flag of Nevada

- Nevada adopted this flag on March, 26, 1929 but revised it in 1991.
- The flag has a field of cobalt blue with sagebrush flowers and a banner in the upper left corner.
- The banner reads "BATTLE BORN" because Nevada's statehood came during the Civil War.

PRESIDENTIAL FOCUS

PRESIDENT #27 : William Howard Taft (1857 – 1930)	
In Office: March 4, 1909 – March 4, 1913	Political Party: Republican
Birthplace: Ohio	Nickname: "Big Bill"

President Theodore Roosevelt hand-selected William Howard Taft to replace him as President in the election of 1908. Taft's close association with Teddy Roosevelt led some to joke that the name "Taft" was really an acronym for "Take advice from Ted."

Taft was a lawyer whose main ambition was to enjoy a long career as a judge. His wife and parents, though, had higher ambitions for him. His first major political assignment came after the U.S. "liberated" the Philippines from Spanish rule in the 1898 Spanish-American War: after that war, President William McKinley appointed Taft as Governor General of the Philippines. At the time, the Filipinos were in revolt against the Americans because they felt that America's so-called "liberation" of the Philippines meant only that they now had American dictators instead of Spanish ones. Taft brought the violence in the Philippines under control by drafting a fair Philippine constitution (complete with its own bill of rights) and by treating the Filipinos fairly.

Taft's success in the Philippines won the admiration of President Roosevelt, who rewarded him by appointing him as his Secretary of War from 1904-1908. Roosevelt carefully groomed Taft as his successor, and vigorously supported Taft's Presidential campaign in the election of 1908.

Therefore Roosevelt was extremely disappointed when, as soon as he became President, Taft decided to reverse some of his famous mentor's decisions. President Taft tried to break up J.P. Morgan's U.S. Steel Company, a trust that Roosevelt had personally decided to leave untouched during the Panic of 1907. Taft also fired the chief forester of the United States, a personal friend of Roosevelt's who was responsible for the nature conservation efforts that were so close to Roosevelt's heart.

Roosevelt was so angry with Taft that he decided to run against Taft in the Presidential election of 1912. First, Roosevelt tried to win the Republican Party's nomination away from the sitting President Taft. When the Republican Party decided to ignore Roosevelt and re-nominate Taft anyway, Roosevelt formed his own political party, the Bull Moose Progressives, to oppose the Republicans. In the end, Taft and Roosevelt split the voters who usually voted Republican between them, and Democrat Woodrow Wilson defeated both of them to win the Presidency.

Other interesting facts about William Taft:
- Taft had a lifelong weight problem. At 6' 2" tall and up to 300 pounds, he was so large that he once got stuck in the White House bathtub. He later installed a special tub that was large enough for four.
- Taft played golf and tennis and loved watching baseball. He was also a good dancer.
- Taft generally hated politics, and considered the White House to be "the loneliest place in the world."
- Taft's lawyerly ambitions continued even after he served as President. When President Harding appointed him as Chief Justice of the Supreme Court in 1921, Taft became the first and so far the only person in history to serve as both President of the United States and Chief Justice of the United States Supreme Court.

Notable quotes from William Taft:
- "I love judges, and I love courts. They are my ideals, that typify on earth what we shall meet hereafter in heaven under a just God."
- "Don't write so that you can be understood, write so that you can't be misunderstood."

Chapter 17

Revolution in Mexico, World War I (Part I)

WORLD HISTORY FOCUS

MEXICO

WHAT HAS GONE BEFORE

Ancient Mexico

Through the Ancient and Medieval ages, the territory that is now Mexico was home to several Native American cultures and empires. The Olmecs lived in south central Mexico from about 1200-300 BC, and are best known for their colossal head statues (see Year 1, Chapter 15). Another native culture, the Maya, lived in parts of Mexico and northern South America at various times, and still survives there today.

The Aztecs

The last Native Americans to dominate Mexico were the Mexicas of the Aztec Empire. The Aztec Empire was an alliance of three powerful city-states that collected tribute payments from smaller cities and villages all over Mexico.

One of these city-states, Tenochtitlan, was built on the site of modern-day Mexico City. The Mexica Indians founded Tenochtitlan around 1325, and built the Aztec Empire around it over the next 100+ years. The Aztecs are best known for their pyramid-like temples (see picture) and for the human sacrifices that were part of their religious rituals. Aztec clerics sacrificed human beings by the tens of thousands, possibly because they believed that the shedding of human blood kept the sun moving across the sky.

The arrival of the Spanish explorers changed Mexico forever. *Conquistador* Hernan Cortes landed in Mexico in 1519. Aided by a deadly epidemic of smallpox among the Aztecs, Cortes quickly defeated Aztec Emperor Montezuma II and claimed Mexico for Spain. The Aztec Empire disappeared by 1521. Mexico City became the capital of New Spain, one of the huge Spanish Empire's four viceroyalties in the New World (a viceroyalty is a sub-kingdom ruled by a viceroy, or "substitute king").

Mexican Independence

The people of Mexico lived as second-class citizens under Spanish rule. Even Mexicans of pure Spanish descent held lower status than the *peninsulares*, those born on Europe's Iberian (Spanish) Peninsula. When Napoleon of France attacked Spain in 1808, the people of Mexico jumped at the chance to rebel against the Spanish government that had mistreated them for so long. Mexico began its revolution against Spanish control in 1810, under the leadership of Catholic priest Don Miguel Hidalgo y Costilla. After rebel leader Agustin de Iturbide captured Mexico City and deposed the Spanish governor in 1821, Spain finally recognized Mexico's independence. Agustin became the first and only emperor of the short-lived First Mexican Empire.

The United Mexican States

Almost immediately, a powerful Mexican general named Antonio Lopez de Santa Anna supported a revolution against the New Mexican Empire. In 1824, Mexico adopted a Republican constitution (with democratically elected representatives) and established the United Mexican States. Within a few years, however, Santa Anna led a revolution against his own government (which he had left in the hands of Vice President Farias) and changed the Mexican constitution by adding a set of amendments called the Seven Laws. The Seven Laws essentially replaced Mexico's Republican government with a military dictatorship under Santa Anna.

Conflicts with Texas and the United States

Texas refused to accept Santa Anna's dictatorship, and won independence from Mexico in the 1835-1836 Texas War for Independence. Texas was an independent republic for ten years before it became part of the United States in 1846. Then, after Santa Anna's loss in the 1846-1848 Mexican-American War (see picture), the United States forced Mexico to surrender its northern holdings in exchange for a payment of about 18 million dollars.

Between the Texas Cession, the Mexican Cession and the 1853 sale of the Gadsden Purchase to the U.S., Mexico lost about 900,000 square miles of territory. Mexico emerged from its conflicts with the U.S. with less than half of its previous territory. It was also burdened with heavy foreign war debts (See Year 3, Chapter 33 for a summary of Santa Anna's life and career).

MEXICO IN THE MODERN ERA

The Mexican Civil War (aka the Reform War, 1855 – 1861)

In 1855, Mexico finally got rid of the corrupt Santa Anna for the last time. Mexico adopted a new constitution in 1857, one that guaranteed the people of Mexico freedoms like the ones in the U.S. Bill of Rights: freedom of speech, freedom of the press and so on. The new constitution also promised better education for Mexico's children.

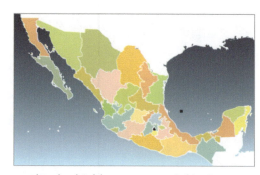

However, one of the new constitution's promised freedoms proved to be highly controversial in Roman Catholic Mexico: freedom of religion. Mexico's Catholic conservatives were used to a wealthy, powerful state church that operated its own courts and owned a great deal of property, just as the Catholic Church in Spain did. The new liberal, anti-Catholic constitution took away the Catholic Church's power to operate courts-- it brought all courts under the authority of the government and made every citizen equal under the law. It also gave

Mexico's new government the power to confiscate church property.

The Mexican Civil War, also known as the Reform War, was the Catholic conservatives' attempt to fight back against the anti-Catholic liberals. The conservatives wanted to take back their government from liberal leaders like Benito Juarez, who wrote the anti-Catholic laws that went into Mexico's 1857 constitution. From 1855-1861, conservatives rebelled against Mexico's new liberal government in cities all over Mexico. At first, the conservatives were successful: in 1857, they captured Mexico City, arrested Benito Juarez and tried to establish a new conservative government for Mexico.

After Juarez was released in 1858, he moved to Veracruz, an important port city on the Gulf of Mexico, and set up the liberal government there. The conservatives tried to capture Veracruz twice, and failed both times. These failures turned the tide of war against the conservatives, allowing the liberals to recapture Mexico City in early 1861. <u>Benito Juarez, the political hero of the Mexican Civil War, won election as President of Mexico in March 1861</u>.

The French in Mexico

In order to finance its last two miserable wars, the Mexican-American War and the Mexican Civil War, Mexico had borrowed a great deal of money from France, Spain and Britain. Mexico's finances were in such terrible shape that in 1861, President Juarez didn't have enough money to make any payments on his debt. France's Emperor Napoleon III took advantage of Mexico's desperate situation to launch an invasion.

<u>FASCINATING FACTS:</u> The French Invasion of Mexico, the Battle of Puebla and *Cinco de Mayo*

Cinco de Mayo means "5th of May" in Spanish. Cinco de Mayo is a Mexican holiday that commemorates a surprising Mexican military victory over the invading French at the 1862 Battle of Puebla (see picture).

In 1861, two miserable wars had left Mexico devastated and bankrupt. In order to finance its wars, Mexico had borrowed a great deal of money from France, England and Spain. When the Mexican Civil War ended in 1861, Mexico was in such a state of chaos that it couldn't collect enough tax money to meet its scheduled debt payments. With few other options open to him, Mexican President Benito Juarez decided to declare a two-year "moratorium" on all foreign debt payments. Juarez announced that Mexico would pay nothing at all against what Mexico owed for two solid years, but he promised to start making payments again when the two years were over.

Naturally, the Spanish, the English and the French all found this arrangement highly unsatisfactory. All three nations sent warships to Veracruz, Mexico to demand their money. The Spanish and the English never intended to invade Mexico, and both of them soon withdrew.

The French, however, had other plans. Emperor Napoleon III of France saw the chaotic situation in Mexico as a chance to expand his Second French Empire. Napoleon III's plan was to invade Mexico, overthrow its weak government and set up a new government that would owe its very existence to France. In this way, Mexico would become a French puppet. Napoleon III was well aware that the ongoing American Civil War had thoroughly diverted the attention of the United States from the situation in Mexico. He hoped to take advantage of the USA's distraction to conquer Mexico and gain a strong foothold in the Western Hemisphere.

On May 5, 1862, 5,000 ill-equipped Mexican soldiers defeated a much larger and better-trained French army at the Battle of Puebla (Puebla is a city that lies between Veracruz and Mexico City). Even though France eventually defeated Mexico, the victory at Puebla made Mexicans proud because of the French military's lofty reputation: Poor, run-down Mexico had defeated the world's finest army, if only for a time. Modern Mexicans, especially those who live near Puebla, celebrate Cinco de Mayo with decorations, food, music and dancing.

Maximilian I and the Second Mexican Empire

After an early loss at the Battle of Puebla, the French defeated President Juarez's government and captured Mexico City in 1863. The Catholic conservatives who had just lost the Mexican Civil War sided with the French against Juarez and the liberals. In 1864, France established a new government for Mexico, the Second Mexican Empire.

As emperor, Napoleon and the conservatives chose Ferdinand Maximilian Josef (see picture), an Austrian member of Europe's royal Hapsburg family. Mexico crowned its new Emperor Maximilian I of Mexico on June 10, 1864. At first, Mexico's Catholic conservatives supported Emperor Maximilian's takeover of Mexico wholeheartedly.

Soon after he came to power, however, Maximilian angered Mexican conservatives by turning away from the Catholic Church. Maximilian's government had much in common with the liberal government of former President Benito Juarez: he wanted to confiscate church property and eliminate church-run courts.

Emperor Maximilian's abandonment of the Catholic Church left him with few allies. Mexican conservatives turned against him because he behaved like the liberals they despised; while Mexican liberals had always hated him because he was a foreign invader. Furthermore, when the American Civil War ended in 1865, the United States began to take an interest in Mexican affairs again. Under the Monroe Doctrine, the U.S. did not allow Eastern Hemisphere nations to control Western Hemisphere ones; and after the Civil War, America was ready to enforce the Monroe Doctrine again.

For all of these reasons, Maximilian's reign was brief. The U.S. aided Mexico's liberals in their fight against Maximilian by "losing" caches of weapons in places where they knew the liberals would find them. In 1867, the same Mexican liberals who had defeated Mexican conservatives in the Mexican Civil War managed to overthrow Emperor Maximilian and expel the last of their French occupiers. Mexican President Benito Juarez returned to his former office, and the Second Mexican Empire came to an end.

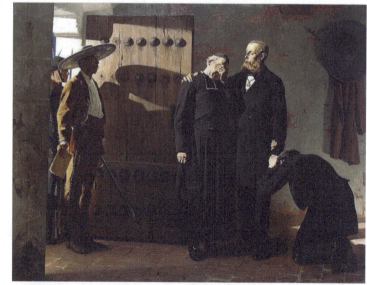

Despite loud protests from Europe's royal Hapsburg family and others, President Juarez and the Mexicans decided to punish Maximilian for invading Mexico by executing him. Juarez felt that the execution was necessary in order to demonstrate that Mexico would tolerate no more foreign dictators (picture shows the deposed Emperor Maximilian just before his execution).

The Porfiriato

President Juarez did not have long to enjoy his victory. In 1871, a popular Mexican general named Porfirio Diaz ran for president against Juarez. None of the presidential candidates won a majority in the popular (nationwide) election that year; so by law, the Mexican congress decided the result. Since the congress was full of Juarez' supporters, Juarez won re-election easily. Diaz protested that this was unfair, and that Juarez had already been president for too long.

Benito Juarez died of a heart attack in 1872. In 1876, Diaz ran for president against Juarez's successor, the former Chief Justice Lerdo, and lost again. Once again, Diaz and his supporters accused the president of election fraud; but this time, Diaz had enough support to launch a revolution against Lerdo's government. Diaz's revolution overthrew President Lerdo at the Battle of Tecoac in November, 1876. In early 1877, with Lerdo out of the way, Porfirio Diaz finally won election as Mexico's president. **His presidency was so long and notorious that it received its own name, the "Porfiriato."**

INTERESTING INDIVIDUALS: Jose de la Cruz Porfirio Diaz Mori (1830 – 1915)

Porfirio Diaz was a Mexican army general who became popular with the people of Mexico when he defeated the French invaders at the 1862 Battle of Puebla. After overthrowing President Lerdo in 1876, Diaz won election as Mexico's president in 1877. Porfirio Diaz would rule Mexico off and on for the next 35 years, from 1876-1911. Diaz's reign was not all bad: after more than 65 years of unrest, Diaz brought 35 years of relative peace, stability and prosperity to Mexico. Unfortunately, the methods he used to maintain that stability were the methods of a tyrant.

Diaz accused Mexico's previous presidents, Juarez and Lerdo, of cheating on presidential elections in order to remain in office longer. As a presidential candidate in 1872, 1876 and 1877, Diaz promised to end all of this cheating by remaining in office for only one four-year term. He kept this promise by not running for reelection in 1880, and allowing his chosen successor, Manuel Gonzalez, to become president in his place. Still, Diaz remained a powerful minister in Gonzalez' government.

In 1884, Diaz won the presidency again by claiming that Gonzalez was incompetent. By now, Diaz had decided that no one else could manage Mexico as well as he could. He abandoned his earlier promises about serving for a single term, and decided to remain in office for as long as possible. He accomplished this by several methods: (1) by cheating on elections and altering their results; (2) by amending Mexico's constitution to allow himself an unlimited number of presidential terms; and (3) by threatening, imprisoning and even murdering his potential opponents.

One of Diaz's goals as president was to restore his nation's stability after 65 years of revolution and unrest. To Diaz, Mexico's continual unrest proved that his young nation was not yet ready for democracy. He believed that Mexico needed strong, enlightened leadership until its backward, uneducated people could grow up enough to vote intelligently; and he believed that he alone was the man to provide that leadership. Mexico's economy, businesses and landowners all prospered under Diaz; but their prosperity usually came at the expense of millions of poor Mexicans, most of whom were so uneducated that they never had any opportunity to improve themselves.

In 1908, when he was nearly 78 years old, Diaz finally announced that Mexico was ready for democracy and a new president. A candidate named Francisco Madero campaigned against Diaz for the next presidential election, which was set for 1910. As a presidential candidate, Madero did what all candidates do: he criticized Diaz loudly. Despite what Diaz had recently said about democracy, he responded to Madero's criticism in his usual way: He jailed Madero, along with about 5,000 of his supporters, for criticizing Mexico's government. With his leading opponent in jail and his own people operating the polls, Diaz won the 1910 presidential election as easily as he had won the last six.

While he was free on bond, Diaz's opponent Madero fled to Texas. From his San Antonio exile, Madero declared the 1910 presidential election invalid and called for an armed revolution against Diaz. Madero's "Letter from Jail" became the spark that set off the 1910-1929 Mexican Revolution. Early in the Revolution, Diaz's support collapsed, and he fled to France in 1911. Diaz died in exile in 1915.

THE MEXICAN REVOLUTION

A Brief Timeline of the Mexican Revolution
1910, October 5: From his exile in San Antonio, Texas, USA, Francisco Madero publishes the "Letter from Jail"

declaring the presidential election of 1910 a fraud and calling for an armed revolution against Porfirio Diaz.
Late 1910 - Early 1911: Rebel leaders like Pancho Villa and Emilio Zapata begin to defeat Diaz's *federales* (federal army troops) and capture Mexican cities.
1911, May: Porfirio Diaz agrees to step down as Mexico's president. He departs for France, where he will die in 1915.

1911, November: Francisco Madero wins election as President of Mexico.
1911-1912: Before Madero can even assume office, he is criticized for failing to reform Mexico as he promised. Liberal reformers want Madero to confiscate land from big *hacienda* (ranch) owners and distribute it to the *peons* (poor) immediately, but Madero resists redistributing land so suddenly. More fighting erupts as revolutionary leaders Villa and Zapata turn against Madero.

1913, February 9-19: For **"Ten Tragic Days"** (*La Decena Tragica*), rebel forces battle government forces inside Mexico City (see picture). Before the conflict even begins, the rebels capture the city's arsenal, La Ciudadela, without firing a shot. President Madero chooses General Victoriana Huerta to lead the city's defense.
1913, February 20: At the end of the Ten Tragic Days, General Huerta (see picture) betrays Madero and has him arrested and imprisoned. General Huerta takes Madero's place as Mexico's president. Within two days, Madero dies under suspicious circumstances (Madero was almost certainly executed by Huerta's men).

1913-Early 1914: Huerta reveals himself as a harsh military dictator, worse than Porfirio Diaz, whom the Mexican Revolution was intended to overthrow. Rebel leaders Villa and Zapata oppose Huerta. So does U.S. President Woodrow Wilson, who sends U.S. naval forces to Mexico's port of Veracruz, pressuring Huerta to resign.
1914, July: Huerta resigns and flees into exile. Huerta's later attempts to re-enter Mexico fail, and he dies in 1916.

FASCINATING FACTS: Pancho Villa (1878 – 1923), Emiliano Zapata (1879 – 1919) and the Spirit of the Mexican Revolution

Pancho Villa and **Emiliano Zapata** were the two most powerful revolutionary generals of the Mexican Revolution. Villa led the revolution in the north, while Zapata led in the south. While their power lasted, Villa and Zapata ruled their regions of Mexico like almighty governors, printing money and negotiating with foreign powers like the United States. Early in the Mexican Revolution, the United States supported Villa and Zapata in their battles against Presidents Porfirio Diaz, Francisco Madero and Victoriano Huerta by giving them money and military supplies. Later, however, the U.S. turned against the revolutionaries and supported President Venustiano Carranza instead.

Villa and Zapata were the essence and the **spirit of the Mexican Revolution**. That spirit was profoundly opposed to two things: (1) wealthy landowners, and (2) any Mexican government that didn't want to take wealthy landowners' *haciendas* away from them and redistribute their land among the poor immediately. Even after a 65-year struggle for independence, Villa and Zapata believed, Mexico's poor were still held down by the same things that had held them down when Mexico was a Spanish colony:

1. Wealthy landowners had collected nearly all of Mexico's good farmland into large plantations called *haciendas*. The hacienda owners treated Mexico's poor *peons* like slaves, paying them the lowest possible wages and offering them no way to educate or improve themselves.
2. The Roman Catholic church, which still influenced Mexico's government and owned a great deal of land, favored its wealthy contributors over the poor.

As military governors, Villa and Zapata actually began robbing the hacienda owners of their land and distributing land to their soldiers and peons. When the new revolutionary President Francisco Madero disagreed with this idea, Villa and Zapata turned against him and fought on against both Madero and Huerta. Mexico's next president, Venustiano Carranza, defeated Villa in 1915 and Zapata in 1919.

1914, August: Venustiano Carranza (see picture) takes Huerta's place as Mexico's president. Rebel leaders Villa and Zapata oppose Carranza, for some of the same reasons that they turned against Madero; but Carranza has enough support (including support from U.S. President Woodrow Wilson) to remain president.

1916-1917: Carranza convenes a constitutional convention, which creates and adopts Mexico's new Constitution of 1917 (As of 2010, this constitution is still in place).

1920: Carranza decides that he will not run for reelection, and that his successor must not be a military general. Carranza's generals restart the Mexican Revolution and assassinate him.

1920-1924: Mexico enjoys a brief period of stability under President Alvaro Obregon (see picture), one of Carranza's generals.

1924: Plutarco Calles (see picture) succeeds Obregon as President of Mexico.

1926-1929: The Mexican Revolution continues with the *Cristero* War, an uprising of Catholics (*Cristeros*) who are angry because they feel (1) that the Constitution of 1917 has robbed the Catholic church of its power and influence, and (2) that atheists are taking over the government of Mexico.

1928: Former president Alvaro Obregon is elected to succeed Calles; but before he can take office, Obregon is assassinated by a *Cristero*. Calles retains control of Mexico as *Jefe Maximo* (supreme leader).

1929: The long Mexican Revolution finally ends as *Jefe Maximo* Calles forms the Institutional Revolutionary Party (PRI), an anti-Catholic, socialist political party that embodies the spirit of the Mexican Revolution. From 1929-2000, every Mexican president and most elected representatives will be members of the PRI.

FUN FACTS ABOUT MEXICO

- Mexico is the largest Spanish speaking country in the world.
- 90% of Mexico's people are Roman Catholics.
- Mexico's unit of currency is the peso.
- Mexico's flag has three colored stripes. The green stripe represents hope; the white stands for purity; and the red stands for the spilled blood of Mexico's national heroes.

- The border between Mexico and the United States is the second longest border in the world (the Canadian/United States border is the longest).
- The Aztecs built Tenochtitlan, which became Mexico City, on an island in a lake known as Lake Texcoco. Most of the lake has since been drained.
- Both chocolate and chili originated in Mexico.
- The red poinsettia flower is native to Mexico. It is named for the first U.S. ambassador to Mexico, Dr. Joel Poinsett.
- Mexican children do not receive their Christmas gifts Christmas Day. Instead, they receive them on January 6, the traditional anniversary of the Wise Men's visit to the baby Jesus.

FASCINATING FACTS: The Mexican Hat Dance

The *Jarabe Tapatio* ("Guadalajara Dance"), known in English as the "Mexican Hat Dance," is a Mexican dance tune that appeared at the outset of the Mexican Revolution around 1910. A well-known, standardized courtship dance that accompanies the tune appeared near the end of the Mexican Revolution. For a time, the Mexican government promoted the *Jarabe Tapatio* as Mexico's national folk dance.

FASCINATING FACTS: Papel Picado

Papel Picado is a Mexican art style that involves paper cutting. Mexican paper cutting began with the Aztecs, who produced a type of paper from tree bark and used it to create art depicting their gods and goddesses. When the Spanish colonized the Americas, they brought their knowledge of Chinese paper cutting art to Mexico. Chinese and Aztec paper cutting art merged into modern *papel picado*. *Papel picado* banners now appear in Mexico's streets at every national festival. They also appear at baptisms, weddings, holidays and funerals.

Modern *papel picado* makers cut standard designs from stacks of tissue paper using chisels and templates. They can create up to forty identical banners at the same time.

THE TITANIC

FASCINATING FACTS: The Sinking of RMS *Titanic*

When the RMS *Titanic* launched in 1912, it was the largest passenger ship in the world. The White Star Line, a British shipping and transportation company, built the *Titanic* and its two sister ships, the *Olympic* and the *Britannic*, in an effort to outclass its competitors and become the world's largest cruise line. The White Star Line paid 7,500,000 British pounds to build *Titanic* over the three years from 1909-1912.

By the standards of its day, *Titanic* was immense. It was 882 feet (268 meters) long, and its fully loaded weight was 46,328 tons. It could carry a maximum of 3,547 passengers and crew. The *Titanic* was propelled by steam from 29 boilers, which together consumed up to 825 tons of coal per day. Every stateroom was equipped with electric lights and heat. It even contained a heated swimming pool, a first for any sailing vessel. When its first passengers boarded in April 1912, *Titanic* was so new that its paint was still wet in some spots.

Titanic was also equipped with technology that was designed to make it safer: a series of 15 bulkheads that divided Titanic's lower hull into 16 separate, watertight compartments. If the hull was breached, allowing seawater to enter one or more of the compartments, the doors between the compartments could be sealed immediately to keep seawater from flooding all of the compartments at once. In this way the ship could continue to float, even if several of its compartments were flooded. However, there was a limit to the number of compartments that could be flooded before *Titanic* would begin to sink.

Titanic's captain was Edward John Smith, a Royal Navy reserve officer with 32 years' seniority at White Star Line. Smith moved to *Titanic* from her sister ship, the slightly older *Olympic*. Less than a year before *Titanic*'s launch, Smith had piloted the *Olympic* into a serious collision with the Royal Navy's HMS *Hawke*, costing the White Star Line a fortune in repairs and lost revenues. Nevertheless, he still enjoyed an excellent reputation among the White Star Line's wealthy customers; so when *Titanic* was ready to sail, Smith received the prestigious command.

On April 10, 1912, *Titanic* set sail from Southampton, England bound for New York City, New York carrying over 2,200 passengers and crew. Captain Smith pushed his ship's speed to its limit of about 25 miles per hour, steaming hard in order to impress the world with an early arrival in New York. Large icebergs were common in April; but even after he received several ice warnings, Smith didn't slow *Titanic* down.

At 11:40 PM on the clear, moonless night of April 14, the ship's lookouts spotted an iceberg dead ahead. Before *Titanic*'s inadequate rudder could complete a turn to avoid the berg, the ship struck underwater ice all along the starboard side of its hull. The collision tore a 300-foot-long gash in the hull, and *Titanic* began to ship water in five or six of its forward compartments. The bulkhead doors sealed immediately; but neither the doors nor the ship's pumps could prevent the flooding of the forward compartments, which were all open to the sea. As they filled with water, *Titanic*'s bow began to sink, and water began to flow over the bulkheads into even more compartments farther astern. It soon became apparent that *Titanic* would sink, and Captain Smith gave the order to load everyone into the ship's lifeboats.

Unfortunately, because its designers had considered it so unlikely to sink, *Titanic* didn't carry enough lifeboats to rescue everyone aboard. Chaos reigned on the main deck as people scurried to find a place on the inadequate lifeboats. The first lifeboat had a capacity of 65 persons, and could probably have carried even more; yet it launched with only 28 aboard. According to established protocol, women and children were to board lifeboats first; but a number of men boarded them anyway. A large number of women and children perished, most of them from the cheaper 2nd and 3rd class compartments. The lifeboats saved only about 700 passengers. More than 1,500 passengers remained aboard when the last lifeboat launched, and nearly all of them drowned or froze to death when *Titanic* went down.

At 2:10 AM, two and one half hours after the impact, *Titanic*'s water-laden bow nosed down into the deep, raising its unflooded stern high out of the water. The stress of lifting the heavy stern split *Titanic* from its main deck down to its keel. The stern collapsed back into the water and remained afloat temporarily, but the

heavy bow continued to drag the stern down by the unbroken keel. Both halves disappeared beneath the waves at 2:20 AM, two hours and 40 minutes after *Titanic* struck the iceberg.

WORLD WAR I, PART ONE

Casus Belli (The Reasons for the War)

The spark that ignited the fire of World War I was the assassination of Archduke Franz Ferdinand, heir to the throne of Austria-Hungary, by Serbian enemies of Austria-Hungary (see Chapter 16). The fuel that the fire burned, however, was a deeper matter. Dozens of factors contributed to the outbreak of World War I, and most of them had more to do with tensions between the European powers than with tensions in the Balkans. Among them:

- **The Rise of Germany:** By defeating France in the Franco-Prussian War of 1870-1871, the newly unified German Empire proved itself as a major European power. The French resented the Germans, not only for humiliating France by crowning their new emperor in the Palace of Versailles near German-occupied Paris, but also for continuing to hold the Alsace-Lorraine region of northeast France after that war. For their part, the British eyed the buildup of the German military with growing alarm.

- **Germany's von Schlieffen Plan:** Long before World War I, Germany was well aware of its precarious strategic position. Germany lay in the center of Europe with potential enemies on all sides, and it knew who those enemies were likely to be in the next war, whenever it came. Acting on the theory that the best defense is a good offense, a German strategist named Count von Schlieffen proposed that no matter how the next war began, Germany should immediately attack France. Von Schlieffen planned to use Germany's superior military speed to put France out of action within the first six weeks of the next war, and then use that same speed to transfer army operations eastward against Russia.

- **A Series of Alliances:** During the long struggle to maintain a balance of power in Europe, the European Powers created a series of mutual defense alliances:

    1. In the 1879 **Dual Alliance**, Germany and Austria-Hungary agreed to defend one another if Russia attacked either of them. When Italy joined the Dual Alliance in 1882, it became the **Triple Alliance**.
    2. In the 1892 **Franco-Russian Alliance**, France and Russia became allies when they agreed to help one another with loans and military assistance.
    3. In the 1904 **Entente Cordiale**, Britain and France ended their centuries of animosity to become military allies.
    4. In the 1907 **Anglo-Russian Entente**, Britain and Russia ended the "Great Game," their battle for control of Persia and Afghanistan, and became allies.

When the war began, each declaration of war triggered a defensive alliance, drawing another nation into the war— which in turn triggered another alliance. In this way, all of Europe was pulled into the war.

- **Germany's Kaiser Wilhelm II**: Kaiser Wilhelm II, the Emperor of Germany, helped instigate World War I by:

  - Supporting Austria-Hungary's declaration of war on Serbia after the assassination of his friend the archduke, essentially giving Austria-Hungary a "blank check" to attack Serbia and promising German support if there were consequences;
  - Building up Germany's military in preparation for the next war and promoting Prussian-style militarism;
  - Recklessly promoting Germany's racial and national pride, leading many Germans to believe that their nation was invincible.

A Brief Timeline of World War I, Part 1

1871: Prussia and the German states unite to form the German Empire.
1882: Austria-Hungary, Germany and Italy form the Triple Alliance, in which all promise to protect one another if any of them is attacked.

1888: Kaiser Wilhelm II rises to power as Germany's Emperor.

1905: Japan defeats Russia at Port Arthur and elsewhere in the Russo-Japanese War.
1908: Austria-Hungary formally annexes Bosnia, despite the objections of Serbia and others.
1912: In the First Balkan War, the Balkan League defeats the Ottoman Empire, winning independence for the entire Balkan Peninsula.

1913: Woodrow Wilson takes office as President of the United States.

1913: In the Second Balkan War, Serbia and Greece defeat Bulgaria and win more territory for themselves. The Balkan nations seek alliances with powerful empires for protection against their enemies. Serbia strengthens its alliance with Russia, while Bulgaria, which was once Russia's ally, seeks an alliance with Serbia's and Russia's enemy, Austria-Hungary. <u>Serbia turns its attention to recapturing Bosnia from Austria-Hungary.</u>

1914, June 28: Serbian assassin Gavrilo Princip shoots and kills Archduke Franz Ferdinand, heir to the throne of Austria-Hungary. The "July Crisis" over Austria-Hungary's reaction to the assassination begins.

> FASCINATING FACTS: Gavrilo Princip and the Black Hand
>
> The Black Hand was a secret group of militant Serbians who were bent upon recapturing Bosnia from Austria-Hungary (see Chapter 16). In 1914, members of the Black Hand decided to assassinate Archduke Franz Ferdinand, the heir to Austria-Hungary's throne, in an effort to terrorize Austria-Hungary and force it to meet their demands. The Black Hand's leaders may have hoped that Serbia's alliance with Russia would protect their nation from Austria-Hungary's inevitable, angry reaction.

The Black Hand planned its assassination attempt for Sarajevo, Bosnia, where the archduke was scheduled to be an honored guest at the opening of a new hospital on June 28. Gavrilo Princip was one of six Black Hand members chosen to carry out the assassination. Like the others, Princip was equipped with three weapons: a hand grenade, a revolver and a dose of cyanide that he could use to kill himself if he was captured.

As the archduke's open car passed by on the way to the hospital, one of the assassins tried to toss a hand grenade into it— and missed. The grenade exploded under a different car, wounding several people but missing the archduke entirely. Police and crowds immediately surrounded the archduke's car, making another assassination attempt impossible. Princip and the others quietly withdrew, and the archduke was safe for the moment.

Minutes later, the archduke decided to go to a hospital to check on the injured. Fatefully, his route took him directly past the café where Princip had gone to consider his next move. Even more fatefully, the car stopped right in front of the café. Princip took advantage of the opportunity and fired his revolver into the open car, killing both the archduke and his wife.

Police and crowds captured and subdued Princip immediately. He tried to commit suicide; but his dose of cyanide proved to be too weak or outdated to kill him, and he survived to stand trial. Because he was less than twenty years old, Austrian law did not allow the death penalty for him; so instead he received the maximum allowed sentence for someone his age, twenty years imprisonment. Confined to a filthy prison under miserable conditions, Princip died of tuberculosis four years later.

A furious Austria-Hungary blamed the assassination on Serbia, and presented Serbia with a list of demands that became known as the "July Ultimatum." When Serbia failed to meet all of its demands, Austria-Hungary recalled its ambassador from Serbia and declared war on Serbia on July 28, 1914.

July 28: Austria-Hungary declares war on Serbia.

July 31: Russia honors its alliance with Serbia by mobilizing troops to defend Serbia against Austria-Hungary.
August 1:
- Germany honors its alliance with Austria-Hungary by declaring war on Russia.
- France honors its alliance with Russia by mobilizing troops against Germany.
- Italy declares that it will remain neutral, despite its membership in the Triple Alliance, because its allies have not been attacked.
- The Ottoman Empire signs a secret alliance with Germany, entering the war on the side of the Triple Alliance.

August 3:
- Germany declares war on France.
- German troops invade Russia.

August 4:
- German troops move through neutral Belgium on their way to invade France.
- Britain protests the invasion of neutral Belgium and declares war on Germany.

August 6:
- Austria-Hungary declares war on Russia.
- Serbia declares war on Germany.

August 9: As a close ally of Serbia, Montenegro declares war on Germany.

August 11: France declares war on Austria-Hungary.
August 12: Britain declares war on Austria-Hungary.

August 14: Germany fights France and a small British Expeditionary Force (BEF) in the Battle of the Frontiers, which is really a series of four battles that includes the Battle of the Ardennes Forest. The Germans defeat the French and the British, forcing them to retreat to France's Marne River. On one single day, August 22, about 27,000 French soldiers die in the Battle of the Frontiers.

August 17: Russia's army invades Germany at Prussia.

August 18: The United States declares its neutrality.

August 23: Japan declares war on Germany. Japan's involvement in WWI is only in the Far East.

CRITICAL CONCEPTS: *At this point in the war, the web of alliances has entangled the following combatants:*

On the side of the Central Powers: Austria-Hungary, Bulgaria, Germany and the Ottoman Empire
On the side of the Allied Powers: Australia, Belgium, Britain, Canada, China, France, Greece, Japan, Montenegro, Russia, Serbia and South Africa

Before the war is over, alliances will entangle more than 30 nations in one way or another.

August 26: The German army achieves its greatest victory over Russia in the Battle of Tennenberg.
September 5: French and British troops rally to win the Battle of the Marne, halting the German invasion of France.
September 7: Germany defeats Russia in the Battle of the Masurian Lakes.
September 15: The combatants build their first trenches on the war's Western Front.

Definition: The Western Front and the Race to the Sea

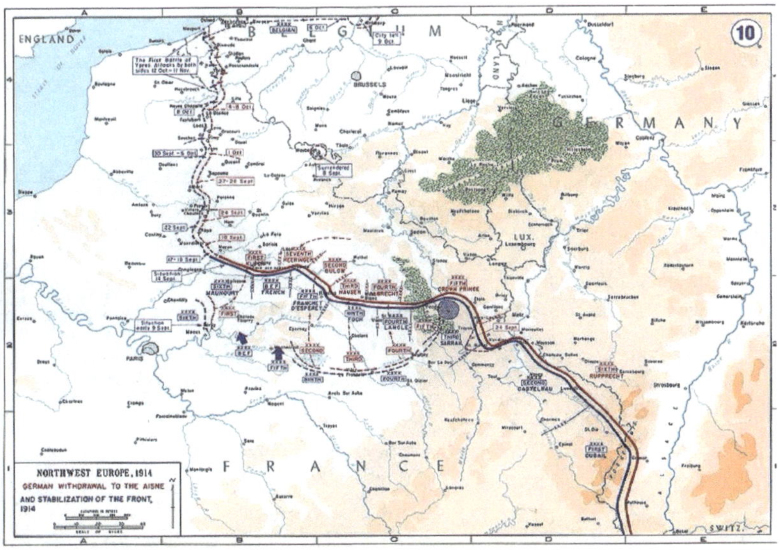

During World War I, the Western Front was the battle line between the armies of the Central Powers and the Allies to Germany's west, primarily France and Britain. Early in the war, after the Allies stopped the German advance at the Marne River, both Western Front armies continually tried to gain an advantage by moving northwest around their enemies' flanks. In this way, they soon extended their battle lines northwest until they reached the North Sea. This phase of the battle became known as the Race to the Sea.

When the Race to the Sea was over, both sides built defensive trenches along most of the now 200-mile-long Western Front (see map).

FASCINATING FACTS: Trench Warfare during World War I

Since ancient times, armies have built earthen defenses to protect themselves from attack. During World War I, new weapon technology made defensive trenches more important than ever before. Powerful weapons like machine guns and repeating rifles made it possible for small groups of defenders to mow down attackers by the dozens and hundreds. To protect themselves from these terrible weapons, WWI soldiers spent most of the war concealed in long lines of trenches. Since the warplanes of the day carried only limited weaponry, trenches were an excellent defense against everything except artillery fire.

The trenches of WWI were miserable places to live. Because they lacked natural drainage, they were often full of rainwater, rats and filth. Troops who stood guard in damp trenches through week after week often developed "trench foot," a serious foot infection that could lead to gangrene (tissue rot).

Although the trenches were an effective defense, they were weak on offense. In order to attack, soldiers had to climb up out of the trenches, exposing themselves to withering machine gun fire. Next, they tried to cross the "no man's land" between their own trenches and their enemies'. Often they had to stop to remove barbed wire or other barriers, which were designed to slow them down and expose them to machine gun fire longer. Even if they managed to capture an enemy trench, they soon came under fire from nearby enemy trenches. In this way, the war dragged on with heavy casualties for years with little movement on either side.

October 14: The first Canadian troops arrive to defend Britain. Recall that although Canada is an independent Dominion of the British Empire, it still shares Britain's king and is a close ally. Australia, too, is a Dominion, and will also come to Britain's aid.

November 2: Russia declares war on the Ottoman Empire. A few days later, the Ottoman Empire openly joins the Central Powers, and Britain and France declare war on the Ottoman Empire.

December 21: German warplanes conduct their first air raid on Britain (Recall that the Wright Brothers first demonstrated their airplane in Europe only in 1908).

December 25: The opposing armies lay down their weapons to join in a rendition of the Christmas hymn "Silent Night."

FASCINATING FACTS: The Christmas Truce

December 24, 1914 was a Christmas Eve marred by the bitter losses of five miserable months of war. On that night, French, British and Scottish soldiers standing guard in their trenches overheard singing from enemy trenches on the other side of the Western Front. They soon realized that their German counterparts were singing "Stille Nacht, Heilige Nacht," the German version of the Christmas hymn "Silent Night."

The English-speaking soldiers joined their voices with the Germans', and soon the song filled the air. Soldiers used their bayonets to raise candles above the trenches, creating a scene reminiscent of a church candlelight service. There were even Christmas trees in places. Some bold soldiers began to emerge from their trenches and venture into no man's land to trade gifts with the enemy (see picture). Some even played games of soccer in no man's land. The Christmas Truce was an unofficial, unapproved truce that ignored all of the usual rules of military conduct.

1915, January 31: German forces use tear gas against Russian forces in Poland.

FASCINATING FACTS: Poison Gas in World War I

A British Gas Bomb

An international treaty, the Hague Convention of 1899, banned the "use of projectiles the object of which is the diffusion of asphyxiating or deleterious gases." The Hague Convention's authors considered the use of poison gas cowardly and inhumane. Nevertheless, in their zeal to gain any possible advantage in war, both sides developed and used poison gases during World War I.

The Germans used tear gas for the first time on January 31, 1915. They fired it at their Russian enemies on the Eastern Front, but the freezing winter air temperature kept the liquid tear gas from vaporizing. The Russians couldn't inhale it, so no one was hurt.

Later experiments were more successful, and the armies began to add more chemical weapons to their arsenals. Among them:

1. Chlorine gas, which attacked the lungs and could kill in high concentrations;
2. Phosgene gas, which was mixed with chlorine to render it even more deadly; and
3. Mustard gas, which took enemies out of action by blistering the skin and irritating the eyes, throat and lungs.

Mustard gas became WWI's most notorious gas because the burns it inflicted caused so much suffering; but phosgene gas killed more soldiers.

Poison gas could cut both ways. One British gas attack caused 60,000 casualties on the British side when shifting winds drove the gas back at the attackers. Later in the war, both sides developed protective masks and suits to keep their soldiers safe from gas attacks. Poison gas probably killed about 100,000 soldiers during WWI.

May 7: A German submarine sinks a large British passenger ship called the *Lusitania,* killing 1,200 people. Over 100 of the dead are American citizens.

September 1: Germany agrees to stop sinking passenger ships without warning.
September 5: Russia's Tsar Nicholas II takes command of Russia's armies.

1916, February 10: Britain is forced to begin drafting young men to replenish its armies.
February 21: The Battle of Verdun begins.

> ### FASCINATING FACTS: The Battle of Verdun
>
> Verdun is a strategically important town on the Meuse River in northeast France. The Battle of Verdun was World War I's longest battle, and one of its costliest. In ten months of fighting, the French and the Germans suffered more than 350,000 casualties each (dead, wounded and missing). When the long battle finally ended, France claimed victory because it had successfully defended Verdun from Germany's onslaught. However, very little ground changed hands, so the battle was in some ways a stalemate.
>
> The French remember the Battle of Verdun as one of the very worst in all of their long history.

July 1: The Battle of Somme begins.

> ### FASCINATING FACTS: The Battle of the Somme
>
> The Somme is a region of northern France, named for the Somme River that runs through it. On July 1, 1816, British and French armies attacked the German army in the Somme in an effort to draw German troops and equipment away from the terrible Battle of Verdun.
>
> The Battle of the Somme would turn out to be even worse than the Battle of Verdun. The artillery barrage that started the attack failed to weaken the Germans' defenses very much. Therefore, when British and French infantrymen began charging across no man's land, plenty of German machine gunners remained in the trenches to mow them down. The British suffered nearly 60,000 casualties on the battle's first day alone. Total casualties on both sides reached well over 1 million. In the end, Britain and France claimed victory because they gained ground and forced the Germans to retreat about 7 miles.
>
> The British remember the Battle of the Somme as one of the very worst in all of their long history.

September 15: The British use armored tanks in combat for the first time.
November 7: Woodrow Wilson wins reelection as President of the United States by using the slogan "He Kept Us out of War" (check Chapter 18 to see whether the U.S. really stayed out of WWI).
December 7: David Lloyd George takes office as Prime Minister of Britain.
December 29: Russian nobles assassinate Tsar Nicholas' adviser and confidante, Rasputin.
1917, January 19: Germany sends its Mexican ambassador the Zimmerman Telegram (see Chapter 18).

WORLD WAR I TIMELINE CONTINUES IN CHAPTER 18

Other names for World War I	
The War to End All Wars	The Great War
The Big One	The War to Make the World Safe for Democracy
The War of the Nations	The First World War
The World War	

FASCINATING FACTS ABOUT WORLD WAR I

- *Soldier deaths:* Approximately 200 soldiers died for every hour of World War I, nearly 10 million total.
- Britain, France, Germany, Austria-Hungary and Russia each suffered more than 1 million soldier deaths. Germany suffered more than 2 million soldier deaths.
- About 70 million men and women participated in the war. About half of these, 35 million, were either killed, wounded or captured.
- During the war, a 1918 epidemic of Spanish Influenza killed even more people than the war itself. It was the most devastating epidemic in world history, and it killed about 51 million people worldwide.
- World War I was the first war that was fought on three continents (Europe, Asia and Africa).
- The United States' actual time in combat in World War I was only a little over seven months.
- During the war, a sitting United States President (Woodrow Wilson) visited a European nation for the first time.

U.S. HISTORY FOCUS

AMAZING AMERICAN: "Uncle Sam"

During the American Revolution, a recruit named Sam Wilson joined the U.S. Army at age 15. Sam survived the war, and went on to found a successful meat-packing business in Troy, New York in 1789. Mr. Wilson's friendly nickname was "Uncle Sam."

During the War of 1812, Sam Wilson's company supplied meat for the U.S. Army. Sam packed his army meat in special barrels stamped "US." When government meat inspectors visited Sam's meatpacking plant, they asked what the "US" stamp meant. A workman laughingly replied, "Uncle Sam!" Over the years, the nickname "Uncle Sam" became accepted far and wide as a symbol of the United States government.

During WWI, artist James Montgomery Flagg created a magazine poster entitled "What Are You Doing for Preparedness?" His portrait of a white-haired, bearded "Uncle Sam" in patriotic clothing became one of the best-known posters in the world. When the U.S. began recruiting soldiers for WWI in 1917 and 1918, it used Flagg's Uncle Sam on over four million posters with the slogan "I Want You for U.S. Army."

In 1961, the U. S. Congress officially recognized "Uncle Sam" Wilson as the forefather of America's national symbol, "Uncle Sam."

Other interesting facts about Uncle Sam:
- The "U.S. ARMY" label that appears on army uniforms is sometimes said to stand for "Uncle Sam Ain't Released Me Yet."
- U.S. can also stand for "Uncle Sugar," especially when someone is receiving checks from the U.S. government.

U.S. GEOGRAPHY FOCUS

FASCINATING FACTS about NEW MEXICO:

- Statehood: New Mexico became the 47th US state on January 6, 1912
- Bordering states/country: Arizona, Colorado, Oklahoma, Texas, Utah and Mexico
- State capital: Santa Fe
- Area: 121,589 sq. mi (Ranks 5th in size)
- Abbreviation: NM
- State nickname: "Land of Enchantment"
- State bird: Roadrunner
- State tree: Pinon Pine
- State flower: Yucca
- State song: *O, Fair New Mexico*
- State Motto: "It grows as it goes"
- Meaning of name: named for its southern neighbor, Mexico, of which it was once part
- Historic places to visit in New Mexico: Whole Enchilada Fiesta, Elephant Butte Reservoir, White Sands National Monument, Philmont Scout Ranch, Gila Wilderness, Santa Fe Opera, Deming duck races, Carlsbad Caverns
- Resources and Industries: farming (cattle, sheep, dairy, hay, nursery stock, grains, beans), tourism, mining (copper, gold, potash, silver, uranium, lead and zinc), petroleum and coal products, food processing, stone and glass products

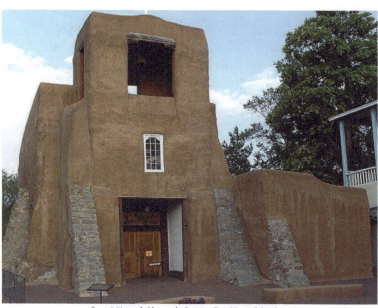

San Miguel Chapel, Santa Fe, New Mexico
The Oldest church structure in the United States

Flag of New Mexico
- New Mexico adopted this flag in 1920.
- Its colors are also the colors of Spain's flag.
- The symbol on the flag is ancient sun symbol called a *Zia*.
- The four rays on the *Zia* symbol represent the four directions, the four seasons, the four parts of the day and the four parts of life.

Chapter 18

Revolution in Russia, World War I (Part II)

WORLD HISTORY FOCUS

REVOLUTION AND CIVIL WAR IN RUSSIA
See Chapters 2 and 12 for background on Russia

A Brief Timeline of Russian History from 1850 – 1924

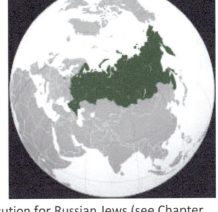

1853-1856: Russia's ambition to control the Black Sea suffers a setback in the Crimean War (see Chapter 2).
1855: Alexander II replaces his late father Nicholas I as Tsar of Russia.
1861: Tsar Alexander II frees Russia's serfs.
1867: U.S. Secretary of State William Seward purchases the Alaska Territory from Russia for $7.2 million.
1877-1878: In the Russo-Turkish War, fought on the Balkan Peninsula, Russia helps the nations of the Balkan Peninsula drive Russia's long-time enemy, the Ottoman Empire, out of the Balkans.
1881: Russian revolutionaries assassinate Tsar Alexander II. Alexander III takes his father's place as Tsar of Russia.
1882: Tsar Alexander III enacts the May Laws, initiating 30 years of persecution for Russian Jews (see Chapter 12).
1894: Alexander III dies. Nicholas II takes his father's place as Tsar of Russia.
1896: In the Khodynka Tragedy, peasants who have gathered in hopes of receiving inauguration presents from their new tsar are trampled to death in a stampede.

INTERESTING INDIVIDUALS: Tsar Nicholas II (1868 – 1918)

Tsar Nicholas II was the last Tsar of Russia and the last of the Romanov Dynasty. Nicholas II's reign was filled with tragedy from beginning to end; and at its end, the bottled-up anger of the Russian people exploded in a Revolution that destroyed Nicholas' empire, his family and his life.

Nicholas' early reign was marred by a series of tragedies, some of which were of his own making:

- The Khodynka Tragedy: After Nicholas' coronation ceremony in May, 1896, a large group of poor peasants gathered at Moscow's Khodynka Field, hoping to receive wedding gifts (primarily food) from their new tsar. When a rumor spread that there weren't enough gifts to go around, the crowd stampeded, trampling roughly 1,000 people to death. The Khodynka Tragedy highlighted the extreme poverty that drove Russia's peasants to desperation.

- The Russo-Japanese War of 1904-1905: After finally securing a warm-water port at Port Arthur (near Korea), Russia lost the port and most of its navy in a humiliating loss to Japan (see Chapter 13). Since Japan had only recently emerged from its backward seclusion, its ability to defeat the great Russian Empire highlighted Russia's military weakness.

Bloody Sunday: Members of the Imperial Guard

- <u>Russia's Bloody Sunday</u>: In 1905, Tsar Nicholas' troops gunned down roughly 1,000 mostly unarmed workers who were on strike in St. Petersburg. These workers were part of a much larger group of protesters who were trying to present Nicholas with a petition requesting better working conditions for Russia's poor laborers. Nicholas' willingness to turn his troops' guns on defenseless, impoverished citizens highlighted the tsars' lack of concern for Russia's common people.

Russia's Bloody Sunday was part of a larger 1905-1907 Russian Revolution, in which poorer Russians sought to take away some of the tsars' absolute power and establish a constitutional monarchy like the ones in the West. Nicholas' grandfather, Alexander II, had established the elected local councils known as zemstvos (see Chapter 12), but Russia still lacked an elected national council. In response to the 1905 Revolution, Tsar Nicholas II gave in to some of the revolutionaries' demands: in 1906, he surrendered some of his power to a national council known as the Duma, which adopted a new Russian constitution. However, Nicholas was careful to ensure that he could veto any decision the Duma made, and the Duma met only four times over the next ten years.

Nicholas receives much of the blame for entangling Russia in World War I. Tsar Nicholas II and Germany's Kaiser Wilhelm II were related both by blood and by marriage, and knew each other well. In a series of telegrams (written in English) now known as the "Willy-Nicky Correspondence," the two emperors repeatedly warned each other that their aggressive actions could only lead to war; but neither was willing to show weakness by backing down.

For the Russian people, World War I was by far the greatest tragedy of Nicholas II's reign. Russia was utterly unprepared to face Germany's modern military machinery. Russia's backward industry and transportation system were simply incapable of meeting the demands the war placed upon them. Russia had plenty of young men and could field an immense army; but it couldn't equip all of its troops with weapons, supply them all with ammunition or move them to wherever they were needed along WWI's 1,000-mile long Eastern Front. More than 1 million Russian soldiers died in WWI, while the Russian people suffered unimaginable poverty and hunger as they sacrificed their own needs to support the war effort. After Tsar Nicholas took personal command of Russia's forces in September 1915, he began to receive much of the blame for Russia's war losses and his people's suffering.

With revolution already in the air, such a high level of misery could not continue forever. In early 1917, Tsar Nicholas' armies began to abandon him. During the 1917's February Revolution, a special session of the

Duma demanded that Nicholas abdicate his throne; and without the support of his armies, Nicholas was powerless to refuse. Nicholas named his brother as his heir, then abdicated his throne on March 15, 1917. But Nicholas' brother never took the throne. Instead, the Duma replaced Nicholas' government with a provisional (temporary) government under Alexander Kerensky. Soon after Kerensky took office, he moved Nicholas and his family to the safety of a former governor's mansion, where they continued to live a wealthy lifestyle at the government's expense.

Unfortunately for the former Tsar Nicholas and his family, there was a second Russian revolution in 1917. Socialist/communist revolutionaries known as Bolsheviks, led by Vladimir Lenin, swept the Kerensky government away in the October Revolution of 1917. The Bolsheviks represented Russia's poor laborers, and they wanted the wealthy Romanovs to suffer as they themselves had suffered. They moved the Romanovs to far less glamorous accommodations and put them on soldiers' rations.

Finally, on July 17, 1918, the Bolsheviks executed the entire Romanov family: Nicholas, his wife Alexandra, his daughters Olga (age 22), Tatiana (21), Maria (19) and Anastasia (17), and his son Tsarevich Alexis (13).

1900: Vladimir Lenin joins the Russian Social Democratic Labor Party (RSDLP).
1903: The RSDLP divides into the Bolshevik and Menshevik factions. Lenin leads the Bolsheviks.
1904-1905: In the Russo-Japanese War, Japan humiliates Russia by driving the Russians out of their warm-water port at Port Arthur and destroying much of the Russian navy.
1905-1906: In the Russian Revolution of 1905, Russian revolutionaries seek Western-style reforms such as freedom of the press and a constitutional monarchy.

1905, January 22: On Russia's Bloody Sunday, Tsar Nicholas II's troops gun down unarmed workers who are on strike for better working conditions.

1905: Tsar Nicholas II's wife Alexandra first seeks Rasputin's help with her son's hemophilia. Rasputin becomes an important adviser to the Romanovs, but other Russian nobles will hate him.
1906: In response to the Russian Revolution of 1905, Tsar Nicholas II approves a Russian constitution and creates an elected national council known as the Duma.
1914, July: In the Willy-Nicky Correspondence, Kaiser Wilhelm II and Tsar Nicholas II exchange telegrams in a failed attempt to avoid World War I.

1914, August: WW I begins.

1915, September: With the war going poorly on the Eastern Front, Tsar Nicholas II takes personal command of Russia's armies. When the war continues to go poorly, he receives the blame.

1916, December 29: A group of Russian nobles assassinates Rasputin.

FASCINATING FACTS: Tsarevich Alexis and Hemophilia

A *tsarevich* is a tsar's son and a potential heir to his throne. Like most of Europe's royal families, the Romanovs were highly concerned with producing an heir and passing the tsar's power on to him when they were gone. Nicholas and his wife Alexandra had five children, but their first four were daughters. Only their fifth child, their son Alexis, was a potential heir to Russia's throne. Unfortunately, Alexis suffered from a severe form of hemophilia. One factor in the downfall of Tsar Nicholas II was the plan he and his wife undertook to rescue Tsarevich Alexis from his hemophilia.

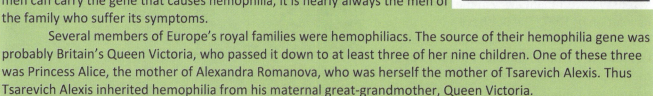

Hemophilia is a rare, hereditary blood disease that prevents the blood from coagulating (clotting) properly in response to an injury. Hemophiliacs' blood has difficulty forming strong scabs to seal off cuts. As a result, hemophiliacs can bleed for a long time from small injuries like simple cuts and bruises. Severe hemophiliacs can sicken and even die from injuries that would seem minor to non-hemophiliacs.

Women rarely suffer from hemophilia. Although both women and men can carry the gene that causes hemophilia, it is nearly always the men of the family who suffer its symptoms.

Several members of Europe's royal families were hemophiliacs. The source of their hemophilia gene was probably Britain's Queen Victoria, who passed it down to at least three of her nine children. One of these three was Princess Alice, the mother of Alexandra Romanova, who was herself the mother of Tsarevich Alexis. Thus Tsarevich Alexis inherited hemophilia from his maternal great-grandmother, Queen Victoria.

Young Alexis' hemophilia caused him a great deal of pain and suffering. Even minor injuries carried the threat of death for Alexis, and he nearly died several times as a child. His worried mother Alexandra left no stone unturned in her search for good care for her son. Alexandra's desperation left her open to the influence of the only man who seemed able to help Alexis, a strange faith healer named Rasputin.

INTERESTING INDIVIDUALS: Grigori Rasputin (1869 – 1916)

Grigori Rasputin was an Orthodox Christian from a peasant background who received at least some education at one or more monasteries. Despite the time he spent at monasteries, Rasputin was neither a priest nor a monk. Instead, he was a unique Christian mystic who gained a reputation as a faith healer. When Tsaritsa Alexandra grew increasingly desperate over her son Alexis' hemophilia, she called on the faith healer Rasputin in the hope that he could provide help where no one else could.

It worked. Somehow, Rasputin was able to help Alexis through more than one episode in which he was near death. Rasputin may have prevented doctors from administering poor treatments that would only have made Alexis worse; he may have had some instinctive medical knowledge that others lacked; or he may have called mystical powers to his aid somehow. However he did it, he was successful. The Romanovs became thoroughly convinced that Rasputin had saved their son's life more than once, and that he had mystical powers of healing and prophecy that would make him an excellent adviser in their government.

Others, however, were less convinced. While Rasputin was working his way into the Romanovs' confidence, his drunken and immoral lifestyle outside the castle was destroying the confidence of others. The undue influence that the immoral peasant Rasputin exerted over Russia's royal family made enemies for him among Russia's nobles and in Russia' Orthodox Christian Church.

As the miseries of World War I dragged on, Rasputin's enemies began to lay more of the blame for Russia's troubles at his feet. It was at least partly on Rasputin's advice that Tsar Nicholas decided to take direct command of Russian forces in World War I, with poor results. Tsaritsa Alexandra ran the government in her husband's absence, with equally poor results. With Nicholas gone, Alexandra relied on Rasputin's advice more heavily than ever; and some began to suspect the two of being romantically involved.

The nobles' resentment of Rasputin finally boiled over. A small group of Russian nobles, two of them relatives of the Romanovs, decided that Rasputin's inappropriate influence on the royal family made him a grave threat to the Russian empire, and decided to lure him into a trap and kill him. They murdered the mysterious Rasputin on December 16, 1916, and disposed of his body in an icy river, from which police later recovered it. Rumors of Rasputin's mystical powers continued to follow him even into the grave. Although the murderers were well known, the Russian police never prosecuted anyone for Rasputin's murder.

Rasputin's true importance to the Russian revolutions of 1917 remains shrouded in mystery. Some believe that the Tsar and his wife lost the Russian people's trust by relying too much on the advice of this strange mystic. Others suggest that revolution-minded peasants were fond of Rasputin, and resented their nobles for murdering their peasant-born hero. Either way, Rasputin's fall probably contributed to the fall of Tsar Nicholas, which came just three months after Rasputin's murder.

Early 1917: With the war going poorly and the Russian people suffering, Tsar Nicholas' troops begin to abandon him.

1917, February-March: In the February Revolution, a new provisional government under Alexander Kerensky forces Tsar Nicholas II to abdicate his throne. The centuries-long reign of Russia's tsars comes to an end.

FASCINATING FACTS: The Two Revolutions of 1917

By 1917, the revolution against Russia's tyrannical tsars had been brewing for decades. Would-be revolutionaries assassinated Tsar Alexander II in 1881, even after he took steps to limit his own power by freeing Russia's serfs and establishing Russia's first elected local councils (*zemstvos*). The tsars who followed Alexander II– his son Tsar Alexander III and his grandson Tsar Nicholas II– hated the revolutionaries for murdering Alexander II, and were determined to preserve their power and pass it on to their heirs, whatever the cost.

Revolution was slow to take hold in Russia, for a number of reasons:

- Since the time of Ivan the Terrible (1530-1584), the tsars had maintained secret police forces that protected the tsars' power by ferreting out political opponents and revolutionaries. The secret police pitted neighbor against neighbor and priest against confessor until most Russians were afraid to speak against the tsars for fear of arrest.

- The tsars censored Russia's press, forbidding its journalists and pamphleteers from publishing anything negative about their government. This made it difficult for revolutionaries to spread their pamphlets and other literature (recall how important Thomas Paine's pamphlet "Common Sense" was to the American Revolution-- no one could have read "Common Sense" if it had been written in Russia).

- The tsars diverted revolutionary anger by channeling it against the Jews. They blamed Russia's money problems on the Jews and organized pogroms against them so that the Jews would bear the brunt of the people's anger.

- Russia was vast, mostly rural, and technologically backward. Its transportation and communication systems were minimal, and many of its people were illiterate. These weaknesses made it difficult for many Russians even to hear about the revolution, or to learn more about it once they did hear.

It took the miseries of World War I to overcome these difficulties and tip the balance in the revolutionaries' favor. Because of the war, Russia's economy was collapsing, its debt was skyrocketing and its people were dying in record numbers. Productivity went down while prices went up, which meant that the goods needed to sustain life were both scarce and expensive. The Russian people's anger and desperation over the war led to two revolutions in 1917.

- The **February Revolution** forced Tsar Nicholas II to abdicate his throne and replaced his government with a provisional government under **Alexander Kerensky** (see picture). The revolutionaries were happy to see the tsar deposed, but were enraged when the Kerensky government declared its intention to continue the war the tsar had begun. The revolutionaries wanted to abandon the war effort and focus Russia's energy on recovering from the war's ravages. They spent the summer of 1917 in open revolt against the Kerensky government. In response, during 1917's July Days, Kerensky's troops opened fire on groups of revolutionaries who were peacefully demonstrating in Russia's streets. Kerensky had proved himself to be just as willing to use violence against his own people as Tsar Nicholas had been.

- As a result, Kerensky's government was short-lived. In 1917's second and more important revolution, the **October Revolution**, the Bolsheviks deposed Kerensky and sent him into exile. They replaced the Kerensky government with a group of local councils from all over Russia known as *soviets*. The soviets quickly elected a new national council under the guidance of Bolshevik leader **Vladimir Lenin** (see picture). This council's name and composition would change frequently over the next several years.

The Bolsheviks' first acts were to enact laws and decrees in support of their Marxist-Leninist ideals. These ideals were Lenin's special version of German philosopher Karl Marx's socialist philosophy of government (see below). Within days, the Bolsheviks:

- Passed a Decree on Peace that declared Russia's intention to withdraw from WWI;
- Passed a Decree on Land that abolished some private property, taking land from large landowners and "redistributing" it among peasant farmers;
- Took over management of Russian banks and bank accounts (as part of their program to abolish private property);
- Turned management of Russia's factories over to the local soviets (so that the government, not wealthy businessmen, could control factory production)
- Confiscated land, buildings and bank accounts that belonged to the Russian Orthodox Church (because Lenin and Marx despised religion and the church); and
- Declared that Russia would not repay the money it had borrowed from foreigners to finance WWI.

Vladimir Lenin sweeping away the capitalists

Lenin soon established a security force called the *Cheka* to enforce his will. Ironically, the Cheka was similar in form and function to the tsars' secret police force. The Cheka began imprisoning Lenin's political opponents almost immediately. Apparently, the communist revolution hadn't changed things as much as Lenin had promised it would.

The October Revolution succeeded in sweeping away the Kerensky government, but it failed to win the Bolsheviks uncontested power over Russia. The years that followed were filled with the chaos of the 1917-1922 Russian Civil War between the Red Army of the Bolsheviks and the White Army of their anti-Bolshevik opponents, who tried and failed to restore the Russian Empire. The Bolsheviks ultimately won that war and established the Union of Soviet Socialist Republics (USSR) in 1922.

1917, July: During the July Days, Kerensky's troops fire on a peaceful protest against the Kerensky government's plan to continue fighting World War I.

1917, October: In the October Revolution, Lenin and the Bolsheviks sweep away the Kerensky government and establish a new socialist government in Russia. The Bolsheviks declare Russia's intention to withdraw from WWI.

1918, March 3: In the *Treaty of Brest-Litovsk*, Russia withdraws from World War I after huge losses of territory. Russia cedes Finland, Latvia, Estonia, Lithuania, Belarus, Ukraine and part of Poland to Germany.

1918, July 17: The Bolsheviks assassinate the former Tsar Nicholas II and his entire family.

INTERESTING INQUIRIES: What about Anastasia?

Anastasia Romanova was the fourth child and the youngest daughter of Tsar Nicholas II and his wife Alexandra. Anastasia was an attractive and charming young lady, full of life and spirit. She was nearing adulthood in 1917 when the October Revolution brought about the rise of the Bolsheviks and the doom of the Romanovs. Anastasia died with her family in the following year at the hands of Bolshevik executioners.

Or did she?

According to the stories of the Romanovs' executioners, one or more of the Romanov girls survived their initial attacks. On their mother's instructions, each of the girls had apparently sewn family jewels into their clothing for safekeeping, and the hard gems may have temporarily shielded some of them from the executioners' bullets and bayonets. Nevertheless, all of them were severely wounded, if not killed; and after the smoke from the first attack cleared, the executioners returned to finish off all of their victims. Modern DNA tests on the Romanovs' remains have proved (to the satisfaction of most) that all of the Romanovs, including Anastasia, died together on that day in 1918.

After the execution, however, there began a rumor that Anastasia had somehow survived. In the years that followed, various women pretended to be the lost Anastasia and tried to claim her inheritance. None of these pretenders ever proved her claim. The persistent rumor about Anastasia's survival may have been rooted in little more than an unwillingness to accept the horrific fate of a lovely and vivacious young woman at the hands of her drunken, thuggish executioners.

1918, August 30: A female revolutionary from a competing political party shoots Lenin twice, but fails to kill him. Lenin suffers ill health from this attack for the rest of his life.

1918, September: The Bolsheviks begin a period of "Red Terror" in which they assassinate thousands of their political enemies.

DEFINITIONS: Communism and Socialism

Communism is a political philosophy which maintains that all property should be community property. The ultimate goal of communist philosophers like Lenin and Marx was supposedly to create an ideal communist society in which everyone shared everything equally. In that ideal communist society, all land, homes and possessions would belong to the community, and everyone in the community would share equally in both labor and the good things that their labor produced. There would be no wealthy factory owners and no poor wage laborers, no nobles and no peasants. Under ideal communism, everyone would be on an equal footing.

Socialism is a separate but similar political philosophy which maintains that all farms and factories (the "means of production") should be owned and operated by the government (society). Like communists, socialists aim to eliminate both extreme wealth and extreme poverty by distributing their society's wealth fairly and evenly. There are several varieties and degrees of socialism.

Lenin and Marx viewed socialism as a temporary step on the way to the ideal communist society. They wanted to use the power of the government to manage the transition between the unfair rule of the tsars and the ideal communism that was coming. They believed that after their socialist government distributed society's wealth fairly, then ideal communism could take over and thrive as communities learned to manage themselves.

INTERESTING INDIVIDUALS: Vladimir Ilyich Lenin (1870 – 1924)

Vladimir Lenin was the leader of the revolutionary Bolsheviks and the founder of the USSR. He was also the author and promoter of much of the communist/socialist philosophy that dominated Russia for 75 years, and still influences Russia today.

Lenin came from a family of revolutionaries. His parents were educators who taught their children to believe in equal rights for all. His older brother, a Marxist revolutionary, was executed for trying to assassinate Tsar Alexander III. Raised under these influences, Lenin became a radical whose goal was to eliminate Russia's oppressive tsars and replace them with a new socialist government.

Around 1900, Lenin joined the Russian Social Democratic Labor Party (RSDLP), a political party full of revolutionary socialists like himself. In 1903, the RSDLP divided into two major factions: the minority *menshinstvo,* or the Mensheviks, and the majority *bolshinstvo*, or the Bolsheviks. Lenin was the dominant figure among the Bolsheviks for the rest of his life. His revolutionary and criminal activities (he robbed a Tbilisi, Russia bank in 1907 in order to finance his revolutions) forced him to spend much of that life hiding in exile.

In 1917, Lenin emerged from hiding to become the leader of the October Revolution. Lenin and the Bolsheviks disbanded Kerensky's provisional government by taking over Moscow's Winter Palace and exiling Kerensky. The new Bolshevik government declared Russia's intention to withdraw from WWI, then began reorganizing Russia as a socialist nation. Nevertheless, the new government retained several familiar features from the old tsarist government Lenin hated so much:

1. Lenin censored any press articles that criticized the Bolsheviks;
2. Lenin established his own secret police force called the Cheka; and
3. During a period in 1918 known as the "Red Terror," Lenin ordered his Cheka to execute thousands of political enemies, including the Romanovs, without trials.

Not everyone yielded to the Bolsheviks. The Bolsheviks' Red Army spent the next several years battling the White Army for control of Russia in the **Russian Civil War**. When the Bolsheviks had trouble supplying the Red Army with food, they confiscated food from the very peasants they claimed to love and represent. When the peasants resisted, Lenin clamped down on them with harsh laws and violence. During the Russian Civil War, Lenin proved that he was just as capable of using violence against his own people to achieve his aims as Kerensky or the tsars were.

In the year after the October Revolution, Lenin survived two assassination attempts. The two bullet wounds he received in the second attack damaged his health for the rest of his life.

In 1922, ill health forced Lenin to allow his lieutenant **Josef Stalin** (see picture) to take his place at the head of the Bolsheviks (known by then as the Communist Party). Lenin went on to die of a stroke in 1924.

Other interesting facts about Vladimir Lenin:
- Both before and after Lenin's death, Russia's Communist Party praised him as a genius and a hero of the common man. When he died, the Party embalmed his remains and placed them on public display in a mausoleum in Moscow's Red Square so that his many admirers could pay their respects. His carefully preserved remains are still on display in Red Square as of 2010.
- Countless cities, towns and villages in Russia and the former Soviet Union have honored Lenin with a street name, a park, a building, a statue or even all four.

1918-1922: In the Russian Civil War, the Bolsheviks' Red Army battles the anti-Bolshevik White Army for control of Russia.

1922, April 3: With Lenin's help, Josef Stalin becomes General Secretary of the Central Committee of the Communist Party.

1922, December: The separate republics of the former Russian Empire unite to form the Union of Soviet Socialist Republics (The USSR, also known as the Soviet Union).

1924, January 21: Lenin dies.

THE USSR'S STORY CONTINUES IN CHAPTER 20

WORLD GEOGRAPHY FOCUS

FASCINATING FACTS: St. Petersburg

Like most good communists, Vladimir Lenin was an atheist. When Lenin took over Russia, one of his goals was to stamp out the Russian Orthodox Christianity that had dominated Russia for about ten centuries. Within about a year of the successful 1917 Bolshevik Revolution, the Bolsheviks had confiscated all of the church's buildings and properties in Russia.

Another of the Bolsheviks' anti-Christian tactics was to change the name of one of Russia's greatest cities, St. Petersburg. St. Petersburg was a port city on the Baltic Sea that had been founded in 1817 by Peter the Great. Its name honored Jesus Christ's Apostle Peter, and the Bolsheviks disliked the fact that the name constantly reminded Russians of Christianity. In 1924, they changed the city's name from St. Petersburg to Leningrad so that it would honor Lenin instead. The city restored its old name after the fall of the USSR in 1991.

Saint Isaac's Cathedral, St. Petersburg's largest Russian Orthodox cathedral. The Soviets stripped the cathedral of all of its treasures and turned it into a museum.

WORLD HISTORY FOCUS (continued)

WORLD WAR I, PART 2

A Brief Timeline of World War I, Part 2
1917, January 19: Germany's Secretary of Foreign Affairs sends the Zimmerman Telegram to its Mexican ambassador.

INTERESTING INQUIRY: Why did the United States enter World War I?

Several factors contributed to the United States' entry into World War I. Among them:

- <u>U.S. Ties to Britain</u>: The United States was tied to English-speaking Britain culturally, economically and militarily. The British portrayed the war as a fight to preserve freedom and democracy, and the Americans listened. Americans were concerned that if Britain fell to Germany, then the U.S. might also fall.

- <u>Distrust of Germany</u>: Americans were proud of their freedom and their free form of government. Americans distrusted Germany's Kaiser Wilhelm II, whom they saw as a trigger-happy, militant dictator.

- <u>The Sinking of the *Lusitania*</u>: Early in the war, German submarines (undersea boats or "u-boats") freely attacked any vessel that they believed might support Britain and her allies, including vessels that carried American passengers. A German u-boat sank Britain's RMS *Lusitania* on May 7, 1915. Among the nearly 1,200 dead were 128 American citizens.

- <u>The Attack on the *Sussex*</u>: After the U.S. expressed its outrage over the murders of its citizens aboard the *Lusitania*, another German u-boat torpedoed the British passenger ferry *Sussex* on March 24, 1916, killing or injuring 25 more Americans. In response, U.S. President Woodrow Wilson threatened to cut off diplomatic ties with Germany– a step down the path to war.

- <u>The Abdication of Russia's Tsar Nicholas II</u>: Freedom-loving Americans also distrusted Russia's dictatorial tsars, and didn't want to join any alliance that included Russia. They were more willing to join the Allies after Russia's Kerensky government forced Tsar Nicholas II to step down during Russia's 1917 February Revolution (see above).

- <u>The Zimmerman Telegram</u>

FASCINATING FACTS: The Zimmerman Telegram

Arthur Zimmerman was Germany's Secretary of Foreign Affairs during the early years of WWI. While Germany was at war, one of Zimmerman's jobs was to use his diplomatic connections to undermine his nation's enemies. Early in the war, he encouraged both Ireland and India to rebel against Britain. He also encouraged Russia's revolutionaries to rebel against the tsars.

When it began to seem likely that the U.S. would declare war on Germany, Zimmerman tried the same diplomatic stunt against his new enemy. In January, 1917, British cryptographers deciphered a coded telegram that Zimmerman had

sent to Germany's ambassador to Mexico. In the Zimmerman Telegram, Zimmerman ordered the ambassador to offer Mexico an alliance with Germany if the U.S. threatened to enter the war. He also instructed the ambassador to offer Mexico Germany's aid in recapturing the Mexican Cession of 1848 (California and much of the American Southwest, won in the 1848 Mexican-American War) in exchange for Mexico's aid against the U.S.

Britain presented the telegram to U.S. President Woodrow Wilson on February 24, 1917. When newspapers published the story of the telegram in March, Americans were outraged by Germany's underhanded tactics. The telegram confirmed Americans' worst fears about the threat of German armies on American soil.

The Zimmerman Telegram provided one of the final pushes that sent the U.S. over the brink into World War I. The entry of the U.S. was a major turning point in the war.

1917, February 24: Britain presents the decoded Zimmerman Telegram to U.S. President Woodrow Wilson.
1917, March: During Russia's February Revolution, the Kerensky government forces Tsar Nicholas II to abdicate his throne.
1917, April 2: President Woodrow Wilson asks the U.S. Congress to declare war on Germany in order to "make the world safe for democracy."

1917, April 6: The United States declares war on Germany.

Late in WWI, more than 30 nations were involved, including:

On the side of the Central Powers: Austria-Hungary, Bulgaria, Germany and the Ottoman Empire
On the side of the Allied Powers: Australia, Belgium, Britain, Canada, China, France, Greece, India, Italy, Japan, Montenegro, New Zealand, Portugal, Romania, Russia, Serbia, South Africa and the United States
Neutral Powers: Denmark, Norway, Spain, Sweden and Switzerland

1917, April-May: Wearied by bloody and unproductive offensives led by commanders who seem not to care how many soldiers they lose, French soldiers begin to mutiny.
1917, May 18: The United States passes the Selective Service Act so that it can draft soldiers by the tens of thousands.
1917, June: The first US troops arrive on the war's Western Front in France.
1917, October: Lenin and the Bolsheviks overthrow Russia's Kerensky government. The Russian Civil War begins.
1917, November 2: In the Balfour Declaration, named for the British prime minister, the British government declares its support for a Jewish state in Palestine (modern-day Israel, see Chapter 28).
1917, December 8: Britain captures Jerusalem from the Ottoman Empire.
1917, December: Russia and Germany sign an armistice (ceasefire) that lasts for about two months.
1918, January 8: Woodrow Wilson details his Fourteen Points in a speech to the U.S. Congress.

FASCINATING FACTS: The Fourteen Points

In a January 8, 1918 address to the U.S. Congress, President Woodrow Wilson detailed his idealistic vision for the post-World War I world. Because his speech covered fourteen main points, it became known as the Fourteen Points Speech. As the war neared its end, Wilson's Fourteen Points became the basis of negotiations with Germany, Austria-Hungary and the Ottoman Empire.

Broadly speaking, the Fourteen Points envisioned the end of the world's empires and their imperialist wars. Wilson wanted:

1. Germany to withdraw from France, Belgium and Russia;
2. The Ottoman Empire to withdraw from the southern Balkan Peninsula;
3. The Empire of Austria-Hungary to withdraw from the northern Balkan Peninsula (including Bosnia, where WWI began);
4. An end to the secret alliances that had drawn so much of the world into the war;
5. Arms reductions to make the whole world less apt for war; and
6. Free trade and free passage of all the world's oceans, seas and straits for everyone.

Woodrow Wilson addressing Congress

To enforce all of this, Wilson proposed a new international organization called the League of Nations. The League of Nations that Wilson envisioned would use diplomacy and international pressure to ensure that the nations of the world would no longer attack one another in an effort to conquer and control territory. Wilson wanted all nations, large or small, to be free and independent of large, grasping empires.

1918, March 3: In the Treaty of Brest-Litovsk, Russia withdraws from World War I after huge territorial losses. Russia cedes Finland, Latvia, Estonia, Lithuania, Belarus, Ukraine and part of Poland to Germany.

1918, March - July: Germany launches its Spring Offensive, a series of major offensives on five different fronts. Germany loses many soldiers, but gains little ground. When the Spring Offensive is over, Germany is right back where it started.

1918, July: Russia's Bolsheviks assassinate the Romanov family.

1918, August 8: In the Hundred Days Offensive, the Allies begin to break through German lines on the Western Front.

1918, August-October: A series of Allied victories in the Hundred Days Offensive begins to make it clear that Germany will lose the war.

1918, October: As hard-line German leaders continue to order offensives that are obviously doomed to fail, war-weary German military units begin to mutiny. The German Revolution against the Kaiser's German Empire begins.

1918, October: After a series of losses, the Empire of Austria-Hungary dissolves into several smaller, independent states. Among them: German Austria, Hungary, Czechoslovakia, Poland, Western Ukraine and the Balkan territory that will become Yugoslavia (which includes Bosnia, where WWI began).

1918, November 9 - 10: Germany adopts a new republican form of government based on a constitution written at Weimar, Germany. The Weimar Republic replaces the German Empire (although the German Revolution continues into 1919). Abandoned by his armies, Kaiser Wilhelm II flees into exile in the Netherlands.

1918, November 11: Major fighting in World War I officially ends on Armistice Day. The ceasefire is timed for the eleventh hour of the eleventh day of the eleventh month of 1918.

<u>1919</u>, **June 28:** The Treaty of Versailles defines the harsh terms of Germany's surrender (see Chapter 20).

FASCINATING FACTS: The Red Remembrance Poppy

Ever since World War I, the Red Remembrance Poppy has served as a reminder of soldiers who have made the ultimate sacrifice. The poppy's blood-red color is a sober symbol of the bloodshed in war.

During World War I, a Canadian army doctor named John McCrae served in the trenches near Flanders, Belgium. Flanders was the site of some of the war's heaviest fighting, and one of McCrae's closest friends died in battle there. Days after the battle, McCrae walked row after row of soldiers' graves in search of his friend's grave, but he never found it. Instead, he found thousands of red poppy flowers that were the first plants to spring up in the freshly turned earth of the graves.

McCrae saw the poppies as a tribute to his friend, and wrote this poem in honor of all those who died at Flanders:

In Flanders' Fields

In Flanders' fields the poppies blow
Between the crosses, row on row,
That mark our place: and in the sky
The larks, still bravely singing, fly
Scarce heard amid the guns below.

We are the dead. Short days ago
We lived, felt dawn, saw sunset glow,
Loved and were loved, and now we lie
In Flanders' fields.

Take up our quarrel with the foe;
To you from failing hands we throw
The torch; be yours to hold it high,
If ye break faith with us who die
We shall not sleep, though poppies grow
In Flanders' Fields.

—John McCrae, 1915

Today, members of the Commonwealth of Nations (mostly former Dominions of the British Empire) observe Remembrance Day each year on November 11, the anniversary of the armistice that ended WWI. On Remembrance Day, mourners often lay wreaths of red poppies on the graves of soldiers who died in battle.

FASCINATING FACTS: WWI Doughnuts

During World War I, volunteers from the Salvation Army traveled to France to try to ease the war's hardships for America's soldiers in any way they could. They wanted to provide good home-baked treats like cakes and pies, but their limited camp equipment made baking difficult.

Two volunteers named Helen Purviance and Margaret Sheldon hit upon the idea of making doughnuts for the troops. Soon these two "lassies" had hundreds of homesick American men lined up outside their kitchen tents, eagerly waiting for their chance to receive a fresh doughnut to remind them of home. Before the end of the war, the Salvation Army began distributing its popular doughnuts from "Doughnut Mobiles." The Red Cross continued the doughnut tradition during World War II.

Winnipeg the Bear and Winnie the Pooh

Winnipeg the Bear was a black bear cub from somewhere near Ontario, Canada. A Canadian cavalry lieutenant named Harry Colebourn purchased her for $20 as he traveled to Europe to fight in WWI. Colebourn's unit made the cub its unofficial mascot, and named her "Winnipeg" after the city in Manitoba, Canada. When the unit moved from England to France, Colebourn left "Winnie" at the London Zoo, where her tame and friendly ways made her a popular attraction. Winnie remained at the London Zoo until she died in 1934.

One of Winnie's fans at the London Zoo was a young English boy named Christopher Robin Milne. Winnie was so tame that Christopher was allowed to sit inside her cage with her. In the woods near Christopher's home lived another animal that Christopher loved, a swan he named Pooh.

In honor of these two favorite animals, Christopher changed the name of his stuffed toy bear from "Edward Bear" to "Winnie-the-Pooh."

Christopher's father, author A. A. Milne, made Winnie-the-Pooh and Christopher the central characters in a series of popular children's books based on his young son's prolific imagination. Milne published *Winnie-the-Pooh* in 1926, and *The House at Pooh Corner* in 1928. He set his stories in the Hundred-Acre Wood, which was based on a real wood near the Milne family's vacation home; and he based his other characters, including Kanga, Tigger and Eeyore, on real stuffed animals from Christopher's collection.

U.S. HISTORY FOCUS

FASCINATING FACTS: Rin-Tin-Tin

When American soldiers began arriving in France during the last year of World War I, French children gave them pairs of tiny dolls named "Rintintin" and "Nenette" to carry in their pockets for luck. After the Americans helped the French drive the Germans out of the Lorraine region of northeast France, an American soldier named Lee Duncan rescued a pair of week-old German Shepherd puppies from a bombed-out dog kennel.

Duncan decided to name the puppies Rintintin and Nenette after the dolls. Nenette soon died, but Rintintin survived and moved with Duncan to his home in Los Angeles, California.

Rin-Tin-Tin turned out to be a highly intelligent, trainable and powerful dog. He understood his master's commands instinctively, and he could scramble over a 12-foot high fence. Because he lived in Los Angeles, Duncan naturally sought to put "Rinty" to work in the film industry. In his first role, Rin-Tin-Tin played a wolf in a 1922 silent film produced by Warner Brothers. The film was one of Warner Brothers' first successes. Rin-Tin-Tin played in 26 films for Warner Brothers before he died in 1932.

AMAZING AMERICANS: Sergeant York (1887 – 1964)

Alvin York was perhaps the best-known American soldier of World War I. York's exceptional marksmanship and bravery in battle earned him the Congressional Medal of Honor, the United States' highest military award.

Before the war, York was a Tennessee Christian and a pacifist who wanted nothing to do with the war. However, when the Selective Service drafted York, he had little choice but to answer the call. While York was in training, his commanders convinced him that the Bible allowed Christians to fight when fighting was necessary.

During the fall 1918 Battle of Argonne Forest, 30 - 35 German machine gunners eliminated more than half of York's unit, including the sergeant in charge. Left in command of the unit, York ordered his men to remain under cover while he went out alone to find a way to outflank the machine gunners. When the machine gunners began to fire on him, York engaged them single-handedly. His remarkable, rapid-fire marksmanship enabled him to eliminate nearly all of the machine gunners and capture the rest, even though they had machine guns and he had only a rifle and a pistol. York later said: "A higher power than man power guided and watched over me and told me what to do."

FASCINATING FACTS: The Doughboys

"Doughboy" was an informal nickname for American soldiers, especially infantrymen, for about 100 years. Its origins are uncertain. Some believe that the nickname originated during the 1846-1848 Mexican-American War, when American infantrymen marched overland through dry, dusty Mexico until their uniforms were covered with a fine dust that made them look like unbaked dough. It is also possible that the dust gave them the color of the local adobe buildings, and that "doughboy" is an altered version of "adobe."

"Doughboy" was the most popular nickname for the American soldiers of World War I, and today the name applies especially to them. British soldiers may have picked up the nickname because the American uniforms' large buttons reminded them of the buttons on gingerbread men made of dough.

1917 U.S. Marine Poster

U.S. GEOGRAPHY FOCUS

FASCINATING FACTS about NEBRASKA:

- Nebraska has the only unicameral ("one-sided") legislature in all of the 50 states. All of the other states have legislatures with two houses, but Nebraska's has only one.
- Statehood: Nebraska became the 37th US state on March 1, 1867.
- Bordering states: Colorado, Iowa, Kansas, Missouri, South Dakota, Wyoming
- State capital: Lincoln
- Area: 77,354 sq. mi (Ranks 16th in the state)
- Abbreviation: NE
- State nickname: "Cornhusker State," "The Tree Planters' State"
- State bird: Western Meadowlark
- State tree: Cottonwood
- State flower: Goldenrod
- State song: *Beautiful Nebraska*
- State Motto: "Equality Before the Law"
- Meaning of name: an Indian word for the Platte River, which flows through Nebraska
- Historic places to visit in Nebraska: The Lied Jungle, Chimney Rock, Stuhr Museum, Chevyland USA, Kolache Festival, Union Pacific Railroad's museum, Hall of History Boys Town, Pioneer Village, Museum of the Fur Trade, Mitchell Pass
- Resources and Industries: farming (corn, wheat, cattle, hogs, sorghum, soybeans), food processing, machinery, printing and publishing

Mitchell Pass

Flag of Nebraska

- Nebraska adopted this flag in 1925. It is one of the newest state flags.
- The flag has a blue field with the gold-and-silver seal of Nebraska in its center.
- The banner on the seal bears the state motto, "Equality Before the Law."

PRESIDENTIAL FOCUS

PRESIDENT #28: Woodrow Wilson (1856 – 1924)	
In Office: March 4, 1913 – March 4, 1921	**Political Party:** Democratic
Birthplace: Virginia	**Nickname:** "The Professor"

Woodrow Wilson was both a lawyer and a college professor before he first won elected office as Governor of New Jersey. In the Presidential election of 1912, former Presidents Taft and Roosevelt divided the larger Republican vote between them, leaving Wilson to slip into office with the smaller, but united, Democratic vote (see Chapter 16).

Wilson's domestic program, which he called the "New Freedom," involved a strong central government and a strong Presidency. Wilson's Presidency saw the beginning of two major programs that still affect the daily life of every American: the **Federal Reserve Banking System** and the **U.S. Income Tax**.

Wilson also believed in strong war powers for the President. After Congress honored his request and declared war on Germany in April 1917, Wilson created a government Committee on Public Information whose task was to drum up American support for the war effort. He also signed the Espionage and Sedition Acts, which allowed him to imprison anyone who spoke against the war or his government. The Espionage and Sedition Acts took away the freedom of speech that the U.S. Constitution guaranteed to all American citizens, but Wilson believed that such laws were necessary to protect the war effort. U.S. government officials arrested about 1,500 Americans under the Espionage and Sedition Acts.

As the end of World War I approached, Wilson traveled to Europe and tried to persuade the other victorious Allies to include his Fourteen Points (see above) in the Treaty of Versailles that ended the war. However, the other Allies were more interested in punishing Germany and demanding retribution payments than in Wilson's grand vision for the post-war world. Wilson's biggest success at Versailles was securing Allied support for his new, visionary League of Nations.

When Wilson got back to the United States, though, he found that the League of Nations had little support at home. Wilson's Republican opponents resisted the League of Nations because they felt that it would take away America's sovereignty, its right to make decisions for itself. The United States never joined the League of Nations that President Wilson had envisioned and helped to create, even though other nations did.

In 1919, Wilson took a trip around the United States, delivering speeches in which he tried to convince reluctant Americans to join the League of Nations. This long and difficult trip damaged his health, and he suffered a stroke in late 1919. Wilson spent the rest of his Presidency in seclusion because of the effects of the stroke.

Other interesting facts about Woodrow Wilson:
- Wilson won the 1920 Nobel Peace Prize for his efforts in ending World War I.
- In order to help the Red Cross raise money during World War I, Wilson allowed sheep to graze on the White House lawn.
- Wilson was the first president to deliver an address to the entire nation by radio.
- The U.S. Daylight Savings Time program, designed to save energy during a time of war, began during Wilson's Presidency.
- He was born Thomas Woodrow Wilson, but dropped his first name when he graduated from Princeton University.
- Wilson was the first President with a Ph.D. degree, hence the nickname "Professor."
- Wilson's first wife, Ellen, died in 1914 during Wilson's first term in office. Fifteen months later, he married his second wife, a Washington widow named Edith Galt. Because the press criticized him for remarrying so soon, he didn't hold his wedding in the White House.

Notable quotes from Woodrow Wilson:
- "Liberty has never come from Government. Liberty has always come from the subjects of it. The history of liberty is a history of limitations of governmental power, not the increase of it."
- "There is no higher religion than human service. To work for the common good is the greatest creed."

Chapter 19

The Roaring Twenties, Independence for Ireland and India

U.S. HISTORY FOCUS

THE ROARING TWENTIES

For many Americans, the decade of the 1920s was a time of optimism and prosperity. World War I was behind them, and the United States had played a critical role in turning that war around. Because all of the fighting happened overseas, the U.S. didn't suffer the war's ravages as the nations of Europe did. The U.S. suffered a brief post-World War I Depression as businesses transitioned from the war-time economy (building tanks and artillery shells) to the peacetime economy (building cars and radios). After that, America's economy took flight and remained aloft until 1929.

Along with prosperity, the Roaring Twenties brought technological and cultural changes that had a lasting impact on all of the decades that followed.

Commercial Radio

The science of transmitting telegraph signals over the airwaves was called wireless telegraphy (or radiotelegraphy). The "radio" that Guglielmo Marconi patented in 1897 was actually a wireless telegraph. Later engineers pioneered the science of adding voice and other audio signals to wireless transmissions.

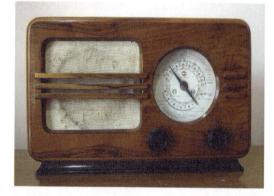

Canadian-born radio engineer Reginald Fessenden made what was probably the first audio AM radio transmission on Christmas Eve, 1906. On that night, Fessenden broadcast

1) a recording of a Handel largo,
2) himself playing the violin on "O Holy Night" and
3) a Christmas greeting with a scripture.

Commercial radio grew like wildfire through the Roaring Twenties. Pittsburgh, Pennsylvania's KDKA, the nation's first commercial radio station, opened in 1920. By 1922, most U.S. states had at least one radio station. Early radio programming included news, sports, music (the Grand Ole Opry, a weekly country music show, appeared in 1925), comedy (Amos & Andy, a popular comedy, appeared in 1928) and even dramas (radio soap operas).

From Silents to Talkies

Early film engineers had difficulty synchronizing sound with motion picture images, so early motion pictures were all silent. Most silent films were narrated by printed story boards that appeared on the screen periodically throughout the film, constantly interrupting the show. Silents tended to be highly unrealistic.

During the Roaring Twenties, engineers developed a system called Vitaphone for synchronizing sound with film. With Vitaphone, the sound was recorded on a vinyl record, not on the motion picture film itself. Each theatre that wanted to show Vitaphone features had to

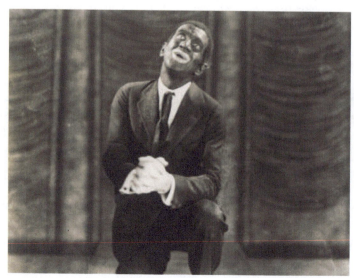

purchase special Vitaphone equipment, including a film projector that was mechanically linked to a record player. The theatre's projectionist had to align film and record carefully before starting the film projector and the record player at the same time. After that, if all went well, the motion pictures and the sound kept time with one another.

The first Vitaphone feature film was "The Jazz Singer," which starred a Lithuanian Jewish singer and entertainer named Al Jolson. The story of "The Jazz Singer" related the persecution of the Jews to the persecution of blacks, and Jolson performed parts of the film in blackface. "The Jazz Singer" premiered in New York City on October 6, 1927. With this premiere, motion pictures progressed from "silents" to "talkies" and from airy fantasy to bold realism.

Steamboat Willie

The first sound cartoon (an animated short film with sound) followed the first talkie less than a year later. Its name was "Steamboat Willie"; it starred Mickey Mouse; and it was directed, produced and voiced by a struggling cartoonist named Walt Disney. Steamboat Willie premiered on September 19, 1928 as a lead-in to a full-length feature film.

Flappers

The ratification of the 19th Amendment, which granted women the right to vote, came in 1920. Along with it came a shift in attitudes about women.

The modern, progressive women of the Roaring Twenties were known as "flappers." Flappers refused to accept the limits placed on them by conservative thinkers. They dressed in stylish clothes with short skirts. They cut their hair in non-traditional, bobbed styles and wore brightly-colored makeup. Unlike their conservative forebears, flappers felt free to smoke in public, drink in public and dance wild dances to jazz or swing music in public. Flappers drove their own cars, stayed up late at night and took risks that would have shocked their mothers.

The flappers challenged the traditional notion that a woman's highest ambitions should be to serve her husband and provide good, moral upbringings for her children. They wanted something different than tradition and responsibility, which they considered stifling. Like many people of the Roaring Twenties, they tended toward materialism. They wanted expensive dinners, dancing on the town, new clothes, a new car, a new radio, and a chance to see all of the latest films and shows. They wanted to go out and have some fun.

FASCINATING FACTS: Ernest Hemingway and the Lost Generation

The first page of author Ernest Hemingway's novel The Sun Also Rises contains this quote from his friend, author Gertrude Stein: "You are all a lost generation." Both Hemingway and Stein were members of the "Lost Generation," the generation of people who came of age around the time of World War I. The term "Lost Generation" can refer to more than one group of people:

1. In Britain and France, the Lost Generation sometimes refers to the generation of young men that was all but wiped out by World War I's ravages. So many young men died that their loss created a permanent gap in the population, a "Lost Generation" of Britons and Frenchmen.
2. In America, the Lost Generation sometimes refers to the generation

of young men who came of age during the war and whose life experiences the war shaped. Although America fought in World War I only briefly and suffered less damage than its Allies, America's young men did not emerge from the war unscathed. The horrors of war left them changed: they were generally more worldly, more cynical and more bitter than their fathers.
3. Most of all, the Lost Generation refers to a generation of American authors who lived and wrote during the Roaring Twenties, including Hemingway, Stein, poet T.S. Eliot, novelist F. Scott Fitzgerald and others. These authors were disillusioned by the war and by American life in general. Most were atheists who had given up on America's dominant Christian faith, and had become convinced that human life was meaningless and purposeless. Several of them left America and went to live in Paris, where atheism, cynicism and disillusionment were already in fashion.

AMAZING AMERICANS: Babe Ruth (1895 – 1948)

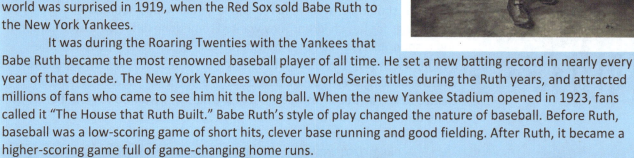

George Herman "Babe" Ruth wandered the streets of Baltimore, Maryland from an early age. In order to keep George out of trouble, his parents enrolled him at St. Mary's Industrial School for Boys, which was both a reform school and an orphanage. At St. Mary's, George's mentor Brother Matthias Boutlier taught him the game of baseball.

George signed a contract to play professional baseball with the Baltimore Orioles in 1914, when he was 19 years old. In order to sign the still-underage George, Orioles owner Jack Dunn had to become George's legal guardian until he was 21. When his teammates learned this, they nicknamed George "Jack Dunn's new babe." Baseball fans knew him as "Babe" Ruth for the rest of his life.

Ruth lasted just five months with the Orioles before Dunn traded him to the Boston Red Sox. During Ruth's five years with the Red Sox, he became one of baseball's biggest stars, first as a pitcher, then as an outfielder and a great hitter. Babe Ruth began to hit more home runs than any other batter before him. Therefore the baseball world was surprised in 1919, when the Red Sox sold Babe Ruth to the New York Yankees.

It was during the Roaring Twenties with the Yankees that Babe Ruth became the most renowned baseball player of all time. He set a new batting record in nearly every year of that decade. The New York Yankees won four World Series titles during the Ruth years, and attracted millions of fans who came to see him hit the long ball. When the new Yankee Stadium opened in 1923, fans called it "The House that Ruth Built." Babe Ruth's style of play changed the nature of baseball. Before Ruth, baseball was a low-scoring game of short hits, clever base running and good fielding. After Ruth, it became a higher-scoring game full of game-changing home runs.

Among Ruth's records:
- The record for consecutive scoreless innings as a pitcher, 29 2/3 innings. This record stood for 43 years.
- The record for the most home runs in a single season, 60 home runs. This record stood until 1961.
- The record for the most career regular season home runs, 714 home runs. This record stood until 1974.
- The record for the longest home run ever hit at Chicago's Wrigley Field.

THE STORY OF THE ROARING TWENTIES CONTINUES IN CHAPTER 21

WORLD HISTORY FOCUS

This week's world history lessons focus on two nations that sought and won independence from Britain: Ireland and India.

IRELAND

What Has Gone Before

The story of Ireland is often the story of Ireland's churches: Celtic Christian, Roman Catholic, Protestant and Anglican (Church of England). After Saint Patrick (and others) brought Christianity to Ireland's Celtic tribes around 430 AD, the Christian faith took a firm hold in Ireland. The native Irish grew fiercely loyal to the Roman Catholic Church and to its popes.

The first English king to claim lordship over Ireland was King John, son of King Henry II and brother of King Richard I the Lionheart. Henry II gave his son John Ireland as a gift in 1177; but after John became king in his own right, he barely managed to retain control over England itself, let alone Ireland. Through most of the Middle Ages, England maintained control of a shrinking portion of Ireland known as **the Pale**, centered around the city of Dublin on Ireland's east coast ("pale" can mean "fence.") The growing areas of Ireland beyond English control were said to be "beyond the Pale," part of a wild, uncontrolled territory.

The Pale had dwindled to a small fraction of Ireland's territory by the time King Henry VIII ascended England's throne in 1509 (red area on map). Henry VIII knew that the areas of Ireland beyond the Pale had been used to launch wars and rebellions the English mainland, so he decided to bring Ireland firmly under English control. This decision touched off a series of bloody wars and rebellions all over Ireland that lasted for about 75 years, through the reigns of Henry's successors King Edward VI, Queen Mary I and Queen Elizabeth I. **It was only during the reign of King James I**, who reigned over England, Scotland and Ireland from 1603-1625 (and over Scotland alone before then), that the **English finally subdued all of Ireland**.

The Plantations

During the long battle for control of Ireland, the victorious English began to take conquered lands from the native Irish and give it to settlers from England, Scotland and Wales. Two classes of Englishmen received these Irish lands:

1) **undertakers**, who undertook contracts to import loyal Englishmen to work and defend their new lands; and
2) **servitors**, English soldiers who fought to subdue Ireland.

England's plan was to import enough settlers to push out the native Irish and replace them with loyal English subjects. Like Edward VI, Elizabeth I and James I, most of these settlers were Protestants. These resettled, redistributed portions of Ireland became known as the Plantations.

The best-known Plantation was Northern Ireland's Ulster Plantation. England's plan to replace the Irish with the English succeeded best in Ulster. So many Protestants from England and Scotland settled in Ulster that it became the only territory in Ireland with a Protestant majority. The remainder of Ireland remained staunchly Roman Catholic, even after the Church of Ireland, Ireland's official state church, weakened the Roman Catholic Church by confiscating most of its considerable property in Ireland.

Catholic Rebellions and the Penal Laws

The Catholics did not give up Ireland without a fight. In the Irish Rebellion of 1641 and the Eleven Years' War that followed, Ireland's Catholics temporarily won back their island and formed the new government of Confederate Ireland. All of this fighting took place while England's King Charles I battled to save his throne during the English Civil War. Charles lost his throne, and his head, in 1649; and England became a kingless

Commonwealth during the Oliver Cromwell years (1649-1660; See Year 3, Chapter 9). Although the Catholics controlled Ireland for a time, Cromwell swiftly re-conquered them, and distributed even more of their land to English settlers. After Cromwell died, England restored the monarchy under Charles I's son, King Charles II.

Catholicism made one more brief comeback during the reign of Charles II's brother and successor, King James II. When James II's Italian wife gave birth to a Catholic heir in 1688, England's Protestants began to fear the rise of another Catholic dynasty. To prevent this, they invited William of Orange, husband of James II's daughter Mary Stuart, to take James II's place as their king. In the 1688 Glorious Revolution, James II obligingly fled to France without even offering William of Orange a fight. With James gone and William and Mary safely in power, Parliament made it illegal

(1) for any Catholic to become England's king, or
(2) for any English king to marry a Catholic.

In 1689, James II turned up in Ireland, where the Catholic natives appreciated their Catholic king; but William soon defeated James in the Williamite War, and James fled once again.

Throughout all of this, Ireland's English rulers punished Ireland's Catholics with a series of Penal Laws. Beginning in 1607, Irish Catholics could not hold public office or serve in the military. Other Penal Laws confiscated Catholic lands: By the early 1700s, only 7% of Ireland's territory was in Catholic hands. Through the 1700s and on, poor Catholic farmers worked on farms that were owned by absentee Protestant landlords, some of whom had never even set foot in Ireland.

FASCINATING FACTS: The Irish Rebellion of 1798 and the Act of Union

In 1791, Irishmen inspired by the recent American and French Revolutions formed a revolutionary group called the Society of United Irishmen. This society led a struggle for Irish religious freedom and independence from Britain in the **Irish Rebellion of 1798**. This was not another Catholic uprising-- the society included Protestants, Catholics and Anglicans. Instead, it was an effort to recapture Ireland's government and establish an independent Ireland— Irish "home rule." Unfortunately, the rebellion had the opposite of its intended result: Britain quickly controlled the rebellion, then sought to prevent further rebellions by folding Ireland into Britain.

The 1801 **Act of Union** accomplished this. **The Act of Union abolished Ireland's parliament and rolled Ireland into a new kingdom, the United Kingdom of Great Britain and Ireland.** Ireland's elected representatives became members of Britain's parliament instead of their own. Britain's King George III became King of Great Britain and Ireland.

The new United Kingdom added the red, x-shaped Cross of Saint Patrick to the background of its flag, creating the flag of the United Kingdom (the "Union Jack") in its modern form.

Ireland in the Modern Era

The Plantation system and the Penal Laws continued to affect land ownership in Ireland for centuries. Throughout the early 1800s, most of Ireland's farms remained in the hands of wealthy absentee English landlords. Most of these landlords cared little for the farms or for the poor Irish who worked them; they cared only for the income they generated. That income came from the grains and beef those farms produced. Absentee landlords wanted nothing to interfere with their farms' grain or beef output, because anything that did so would also interfere with their income. For this reason, Ireland's poor Catholic tenant farmers didn't eat grain and beef. Instead they ate potatoes, which they raised for themselves on small garden plots they rented from their landlords. Potatoes were the only crops they could raise on such tiny plots that would feed an entire family.

In 1845, Ireland's poor tenant farmers began to find sickly spots on the leaves of their potato plants.

FASCINATING FACTS: The Potato Blight and the Great Irish Famine (1845 – 1850)

Potato Blight is a fungus-like disease that affects potato plants, leaving the potatoes they produce rotten and useless. Potato Blight gained a foothold in Ireland in 1845, perhaps after it was carried in with loads of bat and gull guano fertilizer collected from islands all over the world. The Potato Blight epidemic destroyed about half of Ireland's potato crop in 1845, and about two thirds in 1846. It damaged Ireland's potatoes so badly that potato yields took several years to return to normal.

Early in 1846, great numbers of poor Irish tenant farmers and their families began starving in the Great Irish Famine. The Potato Blight had quickly destroyed their primary source of food. Famines are fairly common throughout history; they have occurred from Bible times to modern times, usually caused by natural disasters such as persistent drought or swarming locusts.

But this famine was unusual, because in the Great Irish Famine, Ireland's tenant farmers starved in a land full of food.

It was a question of ownership. The blight didn't affect other Irish crops like wheat and oats, which remained plentiful through the blight years; but those crops were set aside for the absentee landlords. The tenant farmers didn't own those crops, and therefore couldn't eat them, even though their own labor had raised them and harvested them. Ireland continued to export food, even as the very people who had produced that food starved to death. Most absentee landlords didn't give their tenants food from their stores because doing so would have reduced the landlords' income. The British government was reluctant to send food because it feared that gifts of food would make Irish farmers lazy and dependent, unwilling to work. The government was also unwilling to send money to Ireland, because it feared that Irish revolutionaries would use that money for weapons instead of food. So Ireland's poor tenant farmers and their families continued to starve, surrounded by food that they dared not touch.

The Great Famine was a turning point in Irish history. The famine killed about 1 million Irish men, women and children, and forced another 1 million to leave Ireland forever. It reduced Ireland's population by an enormous 20-25 percent. It created an "Irish Diaspora," a world-wide scattering of the Irish similar to the scattering of the Jews (many Irish emigrated to the United States). The famine also highlighted the British government's lack of concern for its Irish citizens, whom it seemed to view as members of a lower class. Some even accused the British government of attempted genocide (race-killing), saying that it failed to help the hungry Irish because it wanted them exterminated.

The Struggle for Home Rule

Irish Home Rule was the idea that Ireland should be governed by the Irish, not by the British Parliament in faraway London. From the 1880s through 1914 (when World War I began), three Irish Home Rule bills appeared before Britain's Parliament.

The Home Rule bills' strongest opponent was Parliament's House of Lords, which held veto power over the House of Commons until 1911. The Lords were extremely reluctant to grant Home Rule for Ireland, because they feared that it might lead to Home Rule for nearby Scotland or Wales. In the Lords' view, Home Rule had the potential to fragment and destroy the United Kingdom.

The Home Rule bills' strongest supporter was a British prime minister named William Gladstone.

BRILLIANT BRITONS: William Gladstone (1809 – 1898)

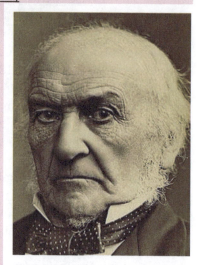

William Ewart Gladstone was a British Prime Minister who took the cause of Ireland to heart. For much of his career, Gladstone was a leader of Britain's Liberal Party, which opposed the Conservative Party favored by the Queen. In Gladstone's day, a "liberal" was one who supported rights and freedoms like those outlined in the US Constitution's Bill of Rights (freedom of the press, freedom of religion, freedom of speech and the like); while a "conservative" was one who supported the power of Britain's monarchy and nobility. As a believer in equal rights, Gladstone became the most important champion of Home Rule for Ireland.

Gladstone served as Prime Minister four separate times, more than any other prime minister in history. During his third and fourth terms as prime minister, he introduced Home Rule bills for Ireland. The first, in 1886, was defeated in the House of Commons. The second, in 1893, was vetoed by the House of Lords.

Although Gladstone failed to enact Home Rule, he did succeed in passing several laws that favored Irish liberty, including:

1. A series of Irish Land Acts that made it easier for tenant farmers to purchase land from their landlords. Eventually, the Land Acts ended the era of absentee landlords.
2. The Irish Church Act of 1869, which disestablished the Church of Ireland so that it was no longer Ireland's state church. Disestablishment meant religious freedom for Irish Catholics, who would no longer be forced to pay tithes to a Protestant church they despised. (Those who opposed the disestablishment of state churches like Ireland's believed in "antidisestablishmentarianism." At 28 letters, antidisestablishmentarianism is the longest non-technical word in the English language.)

With Gladstone's help, Ireland made long strides in the direction of Home Rule and liberty.

Northern Ireland

Despite William Gladstone's efforts, not everyone in Ireland wanted Home Rule. The Plantation system had changed Ireland. In six counties of Northern Ireland's Ulster region, Britain had succeeded in replacing many of Ireland's native Catholics with Protestants of English and Scottish ancestry. The people of Northern Ireland were more loyal to Britain than to Ireland. Northern Ireland resisted Home Rule because it feared what might happen to it if Ireland's large Catholic majority ever gained control. Furthermore, Northern Ireland's huge industrial center at Belfast depended on trade with Britain, and didn't want to do anything that might disrupt that trade.

Irish Patriotism

This placed Northern Ireland at odds with the rest of Ireland, which wanted Home Rule very much. During the late 1800s and early 1900s, patriotic groups sprang up all over Ireland. Among them:

1. The **Irish Republican Brotherhood** (IRB), founded on St. Patrick's Day, 1858 to promote a constitutional Republic of Ireland that would be free of Britain's monarchs.
2. *Sinn Fein* (Gaelic for "we ourselves"), founded in 1905 to promote an independent Irish legislature.
3. The **Irish Volunteers**, the military wing of the IRB, founded in 1913.

Sinn Fein and the others got their wish in 1914, when the Third Irish Home Rule Bill finally passed in Britain's Parliament. Unfortunately, it passed in the very same year when World War I threatened. Soon after that war broke out, the British Parliament shelved the Home Rule Bill so that it could focus on the war. Parliament planned to revisit Home Rule as soon as the brief, easy matter of World War I came to a close.

The Easter Rising (1916) and the Irish Declaration of Independence (1919)

But Home Rule didn't wait for the end of World War I, which turned out to be neither brief nor easy. The IRB saw the war as an opportunity to strike while Britain's attention was elsewhere. It also had encouragement and promises of aid from German Foreign Minister Zimmerman, the same man whose Zimmerman Telegram to Mexico would help bring the U.S. into World War I (see Chapter 18).

During Easter Week, 1916, members of the Irish Volunteers and other patriotic groups staged the **Easter Rising**, a rebellion in which they sought to take over Dublin. The rebels established a base at Dublin's post office building and tried to capture Dublin Castle (see picture), the seat of British government in Ireland. The rebellion quickly failed because the rebels were few in number, ill-equipped and poorly led. British troops were able to quell the Easter Rising in less than a week.

The aftermath of the Easter Rising turned out to be more important than the Rising itself. After British officials had regained control, they responded to the Rising with harsh punishments.

They arrested about 3,500 people whom they believed to be connected to the rebellion, whether or not they had actually participated in it. This included members of Sinn Fein, which at the time was a peaceful organization that had had nothing to do with the rebellion. Fifteen rebels faced British firing squads. Among them was a rebel leader named James Connolly, whose war wounds were so bad that he had to be carried in on a stretcher and strapped to a chair for his execution. Connolly's pitiful condition didn't stop the British from executing him.

Irish anger over Britain's harsh treatment of the rebels accomplished what the Easter Rising could not. The Irish grew sympathetic to Sinn Fein, and began to swell its ranks. Sinn Fein began to promote the IRB's idea of republican government for Ireland, independent and free of Britain's monarchs.

In 1918's Parliamentary election, nearly all of Ireland's newly elected members of Parliament came from the suddenly popular Sinn Fein. These members of Parliament decided not to go to London to meet with Britain's Parliament. Instead they established a new, independent Irish Assembly (*Dail Eireann* in Gaelic) in Dublin. On January 21, 1919, the Irish Assembly adopted the Irish Declaration of Independence from British rule.

The Irish War of Independence (1919 – 1921) and the Anglo-Irish Treaty

Britain, of course, refused to recognize Ireland's independence; and so did nearly every other nation on earth. In the Irish War of Independence, Ireland struggled to maintain the independence it had claimed. The new Irish Republican Army, led by Sinn Fein and IRB member Michael Collins, conducted guerrilla-style raids against British forces for more than two years, pushing the British government in Ireland to the brink of collapse. Despite its successes, the IRA itself was also near collapse from lack of ammunition and supplies by July, 1921.

In that month, Britain suddenly and unexpectedly offered a truce and a treaty. The **Anglo-Irish Treaty** offered Ireland something that Home Rule advocates had wanted since the 1801 Act of Union: an independent Irish Parliament that would meet in Dublin, Ireland's capital. Under the terms of the Anglo-Irish Treaty:

- The new Irish Free State would become a Dominion of the British Crown similar to the Dominions of Canada and Australia, with an independent Parliament.
- Britain's monarch would remain Ireland's official head of state, just as in the other Dominions. Ireland's governor-general would report to Britain's monarch.
- Members of Ireland's Parliament would swear allegiance to Britain's monarch.
- Northern Ireland (six counties of Ulster Province) would have the option to withdraw from the treaty and remain part of the United Kingdom of Great Britain and Ireland.

Both Parliaments, Britain's and Ireland's, ratified the Anglo-Irish Treaty by early 1922.

Northern Ireland immediately exercised its right under the treaty to withdraw from the Irish Free State and to remain part of the United Kingdom. The remainder of Ireland established a provisional government that would become the Irish Free State.

The Irish Free State and the Irish Civil War (1922 – 1923)

Although the Anglo-Irish Treaty represented an enormous victory for Irish independence, nearly half of the IRA found it to be an unacceptable compromise. They had fought for an independent republic, not for a constitutional monarchy that remained under Britain's thumb. They hated Britain for its harsh handlings of the Easter Rising and the War of Independence, and they could not imagine swearing allegiance to Britain's hated king.

As a result, the IRA split into two halves, one half that favored the Anglo-Irish Treaty and one half that opposed the treaty. These two halves began to battle one another in a year-long Irish Civil War.

If anything, the Irish Civil War was bloodier than the War of Independence. The very IRA members who had hated Britain for its outrageous crimes now committed outrageous crimes of their own– not against the British, but against their own former allies in the IRA. One important casualty of the Irish Civil War was IRA leader Michael Collins.

INTERESTING INDIVIDUALS: Michael Collins (1890 – 1922)

Michael Collins was a freedom fighter who fought with the Irish Volunteers at Dublin's post office building in 1916's Easter Rising. Three years later, Collins helped lead the IRA through the successful Irish War of Independence. His cleverly organized, guerrilla-style attacks pressured the British government in Ireland until it could no longer function, forcing Britain to meet Ireland's demand for more independence in the 1921 Anglo-Irish Treaty.

Collins was part of the Irish delegation that helped negotiate the Anglo-Irish Treaty. He saw the treaty as a major victory for the IRA, even if it didn't guarantee full independence for Ireland. In approving the treaty's terms, Collins adopted a long-term view: He believed that the treaty was a step down the path toward freedom, and that it would win Ireland the "freedom to achieve freedom" even if it didn't meet all of the IRA's demands right away.

However, Collins was well aware that the treaty's terms would be unacceptable to a large part of the militant, embittered IRA, which demanded nothing short of full independence from Britain. After signing the treaty, Collins remarked, "I have signed my own death warrant."

His prophecy came true. Early in the Irish Civil War, Collins traveled to Ireland's County Cork to try to negotiate peace with the anti-Treaty wing of the IRA. On August 22, 1922, members of that wing ambushed Collins' vehicle. He died in the gun battle that followed the ambush, and didn't live to see the free Ireland for which he gave his life.

The Irish Civil War ended in May, 1923, with the surrender of the IRA's anti-Treaty wing. **The Irish Free State was a Dominion of the British Crown from 1923-1937.**

The Republic of Ireland

Michael Collins' long-term view of the Anglo-Irish Treaty turned out to be correct: Ireland became more and more independent over the years to come. In 1937, a new Constitution of Ireland removed the office of the governor-general, which had reported to Britain's king, and replaced it with a President of Ireland. The constitution also changed the name of the Irish Free State to simply "Ireland." This new Ireland was no longer a Dominion of the British Crown.

In 1949, Ireland declared itself a fully independent republic and severed all ties with Britain.

In doing so, it abandoned its membership in the British Commonwealth (now the Commonwealth of Nations). As of 2010, Ireland remains an entirely independent republic.

In that same year, Britain declared that Ulster (Northern Ireland) would be a permanent part of the United Kingdom of Britain and Ireland; and so it remains. Some in Ireland still hold out hope for a peaceful reunion with Northern Ireland someday.

FUN FACTS ON IRELAND

- Some Irish Catholics believe that their patron Saint Patrick will judge them on Judgment Day.
- A common tradition on an Irish child's birthday is to hold the child upside down and bump his head lightly on the floor, once for every year of his age.
- Irish castles were known for their "murder holes." These were holes that allowed defenders to drop heavy stones or hot oil on the heads of any attackers who stood near the gates (see picture).

Common Irish Plays on Words:
- "Not backwards in coming forwards": describes one who is not shy
- "No flies on him": describes one who is not easily deceived
- "A tongue that would clip a hedge": describes one who is a gossip
- "Come for a day and stay for a week": used when a guest has overstayed his welcome

Common Irish Proverbs and Sayings:
- "It's easy to halve the potato when there is love."
- "Do not take the thatch from your own roof to buy slates for another man's house."
- "A goose never voted for an early Christmas."
- "God is good, but never dance in a small boat."
- "Get down on your knees and thank God you are still on your feet."
- "What butter and whiskey won't cure, there's no cure for."

FASCINATING FACTS: The Shamrock

The shamrock, a three-leaved clover, is the best-known symbol of Ireland. According to legend, the shamrock was sacred to Ireland's ancient Druids because of its three leaves (three was a magical number to the Celts). When St. Patrick arrived in Ireland in the 400s, he combated the Druidic religion by using the three-leaved shamrock to illustrate the Christian concept of the Trinity (God in Three Persons— Father, Son and Holy Spirit). During Ireland's struggle for Home Rule, the shamrock became a symbol of rebellion, and those who wore it risked hanging.

INDIA

The British Raj

The British East India Company, a publicly traded business with a charter from the British government, acted as a government over much of India for over 100 years. After the 1857 Sepoy Rebellion (see Chapter 1), the British government dissolved the East India Company and took over the government of India. The British established a new government office, the India Office, to administer India, and set a British Viceroy ("substitute king") in charge of Indian affairs. The era of the British government's control over India was known as the British *Raj* (*raj* means "reign"). The British Parliament's Royal Titles Act of 1876 allowed Queen Victoria to take the title "Empress of India," and India became known as the "Indian Empire" or "British India."

Through most of the British Raj, a small cadre of about 1,000 - 1,200 British officials was responsible for governing tens of millions of native Indians. The British maintained well-defined racial lines between themselves and the native Indians: the British were the masters, while the Indians were their servants.

During the late 1800s, the Indians began to wonder why they were always the ones waving the fans, while the British were always the ones sitting on the porch swings and taking the breeze.

The Indian National Congress

Slowly, groups of educated Indians began to seek more self-government for India. During the Raj, the British appointed the members of all legislative (law-making) councils, and they rarely appointed native Indians. In 1885, a collection of Indian and British reformers founded the Indian National Congress with the objective of providing more native Indians a chance to serve on their own legislative councils.

In response to pressure from the Indian National Congress (among other things), the Raj government passed the Indian Councils Act of 1909. This new law allowed elections for some government councils, and it also allowed certain classes of native Indians to be elected to those councils. The Councils Act was a major victory for the Indian National Congress.

However, by 1909, the Congress's aims had grown more bold: it was now seeking to make India a semi-independent Dominion of the British Crown like the Dominions of Canada and Australia.

India During World War I: The Hindu-German Conspiracy

World War I tested India's loyalties. Parts of India remained loyal to Britain and provided soldiers, manpower and supplies for Britain's defense (see picture). Other parts, especially the troubled areas of Bengal and Punjab, saw the war as an opportunity to rebel while Britain's attention was elsewhere.

Britain's primary enemy, Germany, encouraged this rebellion as much as possible. Germany's efforts to destabilize India during World War I became known as the Hindu-German Conspiracy. Punjabi Indians of the Ghadar Party, who had emigrated overseas to the United States and Canada, also encouraged the rebellion. The Raj government managed to contain all of these conspiracies through the war years.

After the war, the Raj government passed the unpopular Rowlatt Act so that it could continue to root out and prosecute the members of the Hindu-German Conspiracy under martial (wartime) law. It used military tribunals (military courts with special wartime powers) to try, convict and execute every rebel it could find who was involved in the Hindu-German Conspiracy.

The Amritsar Massacre (April 13, 1919)

The Punjabis reacted to the Rowlatt Act with protests and violence. Publicly, they demonstrated in the streets. Secretly, they cut telegraph lines, damaged railroad tracks and burned British-owned buildings.

The British tried to control these protests by enforcing martial law. More than once, British troops fired into crowds to disperse protesters. After violent protests at Amritsar, Punjab on April 10, 1919, the local British government banned public gatherings of more than four people.

The Punjabis ignored the ban on public gatherings, if in fact they ever even heard about it. On April 13, 10,000 - 15,000 of them gathered near the Amritsar Temple for a festival known as *Vaisakhi*. *Vaisakhi* was an ancient harvest festival that Punjabis of all faiths had celebrated for centuries, and many of its celebrants that year probably had no idea that the British had declared their gathering illegal.

British Brigadier General Reginald Dyer (see picture) decided to enforce the ban on public gatherings in the most brutal way imaginable.

Without issuing warnings to the crowd of any kind, Dyer led rifle-armed troops into the *Vaisakhi* gathering and opened fired on the celebrants.

His troops fired more than 1,600 rounds and killed about 400 - 1,000 people. More were injured or killed as the crowd stampeded, trying to escape the soldiers' bullets. The Amritsar Massacre highlighted the sad fact that Britain's Raj government tended to value the lives of its Indian subjects very little.

When news of the Amritsar Massacre spread, it enraged Indians from all over India, not just in Punjab. It was an attack on Indian people of all three major Indian faiths (Hindu, Muslim and Sikh), and Indians of all faiths responded.

Mohandas Gandhi

Mohandas Gandhi was a prominent member of the Indian National Congress who led the protest against the Rowlatt Act. After the Amritsar Massacre, some members of the Congress resorted to violence against the British Raj, but Gandhi suggested a different means of protest.

DEFINITIONS: Swaraj and Satyagraha

Swaraj means "independence" and "self-government." In Gandhi's understanding, it also meant self-reliance, self-sufficiency and non-reliance on British manufactured goods and technology. Gandhi was aware that Indians increased their reliance on Britain when they purchased British machine-manufactured goods such as thread and cloth. Gandhi's response was *swaraj*, completely self-reliance, which he achieved by spinning his own thread and weaving his own cloth.

Satyagraha is a blend of Sanskrit words which, taken together, mean "holding firmly to the truth." Gandhi also called it "truth-force," "love-force" and the "force that is born of truth and love and non-violence." *Satyagraha* was the notion that India's protest against British rule was so plainly just and proper that it did not need to be defended with violence. By persistent, non-violent resistance to British outrages, Gandhi's followers would shame Britain into recognizing the obvious truth that Indians were capable of governing themselves, and should have the right to do so.

INTERESTING INDIVIDUALS: Mohandas Gandhi (1869 – 1948)

Mohandas Gandhi was a prominent leader of the Indian National Congress, the primary organization in the fight for Indian independence. From about 1920 until his assassination in 1948, Gandhi supplied the leadership in both thought and deed that guided India toward independence from Britain. Indians consider Gandhi the Father of Indian independence.

Gandhi was a native of India who had the privilege of studying in England and earning a law degree there. In 1893, he moved to another part of the British Empire, South Africa. There Gandhi experienced British racism against Indians and blacks first-hand. In response, he became an activist for Indian rights and organized his first protests against harsh British rule.

Gandhi returned to India in 1915 and remained there for the rest of his life. As a leader and sometimes President of the Indian National Congress, he led India's protests against British rule. Unlike some other leaders, though, Gandhi insisted that these protests should be non-violent. Gandhi promoted *satyagraha*, the idea that a truly just person should not need to defend his views with violence. He believed that the cause of Indian *swaraj*, or independence, was so obviously just that the world could not help but see Britain's injustice in opposing it.

Gandhi's insistence on *swaraj* and *satyagraha* took several famous forms:

- **Non-cooperation:** Gandhi encouraged his followers to simply refuse to cooperate when the British made unreasonable demands. When the British tried to disperse gatherings, Gandhi's followers gathered anyway. When the British levied harsh taxes, Gandhi's followers simply refused to pay. India's vast population made it difficult for the British to force everyone to go along with its many rules. In 1930, when the British levied a high tax on salt, Gandhi led a 240-mile "March to the Sea" to protest the tax. When he reached the sea, he made his own sea salt in order to avoid paying the tax. The march became such a vast spectacle that it earned Gandhi an invitation to a "Round Table Conference" in London, where he tried to negotiate more freedoms for Indians.

- **Boycotts:** Gandhi encouraged his followers to avoid purchasing British manufactured goods like cotton cloth. Instead, he taught them to spin their own thread, weave their own cloth, make their own clothes and become completely self-reliant. In order to prove that Indian ways were just as good as British ones, he abandoned the garb of a British attorney and took to wearing a traditional Indian loincloth. He wore this humble garment even in the presence of India's viceroy and other high officials.

- **Hunger strikes:** Gandhi's hunger strikes took advantage of his personal popularity. When Gandhi was in prison, or when different factions of the Indian National Congress refused to agree, Gandhi refused to eat until his opponents gave in. No one wanted to be responsible for allowing the great Gandhi to starve to death, so his hunger strikes became a great incentive to compromise.

Gandhi during a Salt March

Gandhi's decades-long, principled stand on non-violence made him India's most honored figure. Late in his life, the Indian people knew him by two titles of great respect: *Mahatma*, "great soul," and *Bapu*, "father."

Not everyone shared this respect. Some Hindus felt that Gandhi's insistence on complete non-violence had rendered Hinduism incapable of achieving its goals, and that Gandhi surrendered to the demands of India's Muslims too easily. One such Hindu assassinated Mohandas Gandhi on January 30, 1948, mere months after India finally achieved Gandhi's dream of independence from Britain.

Interesting quotes from Mohandas Gandhi:
- "An eye for an eye only ends up making the whole world blind."
- "I am prepared to die, but there is no cause for which I am prepared to kill."
- "I like your Christ, I do not like your Christians. Your Christians are so unlike your Christ."

Independence

The Indian National Congress officially declared independence for India in 1930; but Britain, of course, refused to recognize it. The 1935 Government of India Act granted more self-government, especially local self-government, for India.

Indian independence had to wait yet again during the World War II years of 1939-1945, when Britain desperately needed Indian military aid. Some Indian military units mutinied against their British commanders during the war. **Gandhi also opposed India's participation in the war, saying that it was unfair that India should fight to preserve democracy for Britain while Britain continued to deny democracy for India.**

The end of British domination in India finally arrived in 1947, after WWII, with the passage of the Indian Independence Act. Under its terms, effective August 15, 1947:

1. The Indian Empire would be partitioned into two Dominions, India (mostly Hindu) and Pakistan (mostly Muslim).
2. India and Pakistan would be Dominions of the British Crown and would retain the British monarch as their official heads of state.
3. India and Pakistan would be members of the British Commonwealth, but would be free to leave the Commonwealth if they chose.
4. Britain would no longer be responsible for governing any part of the former Indian Empire.

SEE CHAPTER 27 FOR THE PARTITION OF INDIA

FUN FACTS ON INDIA

- India has more post offices than any other nation in the world.
- The game of chess originated in India.
- India's national bird is the peacock.
- An Indian holds the current world record for "most worms eaten": 200 earthworms in 30 seconds.

INTERESTING INDIVIDUALS: Rudyard Kipling (1865 – 1936)

Rudyard Kipling was a British author and poet who was born in Bombay, India. Although he spent most of his life elsewhere, Kipling never forgot his origins in India, and his writing included a great number of stories about India. Kipling authored works of every sort, from imaginative children's novels like *The Jungle Book* to reflective poetry like *Gunga Din* to political commentary like *The White Man's Burden*. His success earned him the Nobel Prize for Literature in 1907.

Kipling lived and wrote when the British Empire was at the height of its power. He traveled and lived all over that Empire, and some of his writings highlighted the Empire's overreaching misdeeds. Kipling's poetry contributed to the Empire's growing conscience and called it to repentance:

> Far-called our navies melt away—
> On dune and headland sinks the fire—
> Lo, all our pomp of yesterday
> Is one with Nineveh and Tyre!
> Judge of the Nations, spare us yet,
> Lest we forget—lest we forget!
>
> If, drunk with sight of power, we loose
> Wild tongues that have not Thee in awe—
> Such boastings as the Gentiles use,
> Or lesser breeds without the Law—
> Lord God of Hosts, be with us yet,
> Lest we forget—lest we forget!

– from Kipling's poem "Recessional"

Selected works from Rudyard Kipling:
Mandalay (1890); *Gunga Din* (1890); *The Jungle Book* (1894); *The Second Jungle Book* (1895); *If--* (1895); *Captains Courageous* (1897); *Recessional* (1897); *The White Man's Burden* (1899); *Kim* (1901); *Just So Stories* (1902)

MISSIONARY FOCUS

GIANTS OF THE FAITH: Sundar Singh (1889 – 1929)

Sundar Singh was a member of a wealthy Sikh family from the Punjab province of northern India. Sundar attended an English school, so he was aware of Christianity; but as a young Sikh, he was not fond of Christians.

When Sundar's beloved mother died in 1904, Sundar blamed God. He purchased a Bible, the holy book of the Christians he hated, and proceeded to burn it page by page. Then he decided to commit suicide. As he bathed himself in preparation for his suicide ritual, he asked aloud for God to reveal Himself and swore that if God didn't, he would commit suicide that very night.

God answered. Before dawn, Sundar received a vision of Christ that filled him with peace and understanding. Sundar could not convince his family of the truth of his vision, so he began living in communities of Christians. He became a baptized Christian on his sixteenth birthday.

Unlike many other Indian converts to Christianity, Sundar never adopted European-style clothing and speech. He received training in an Anglican seminary, but gave it up after less than a year. For the rest of his life, he remained distinctly Indian, and his Christianity had an Indian, Eastern mystical flavor. Sundar's faith was more concerned with meditation, Christian service and missionary work than it was with church services and robes. When he traveled in the West, he criticized the style of Christianity he found there. He believed that the people of the East sought God more diligently than those of the West, even though they sought Him in all the wrong ways.

Sundar traveled all over India, Afghanistan and south Asia on foot, sharing the gospel as he went. He traveled so widely and frequently that people called him "the Apostle with the Bleeding Feet." He made several summer sojourns to Tibet, some 900 miles from his home. On one such sojourn in 1929, Sundar simply disappeared. The story of what happened to him remains unknown.

Interesting quotes from Sundar Singh:
- "He was searching for me before I sought Him. Christ whom I had never expected came to me. I was praying, 'If there be a God, reveal Thyself'...I was praying to Hindu gods and incarnations. But when He came there was no anger in His face, even though I had burnt the Bible three days before. None of you have ever destroyed Scripture like me. He is such a wonderful, loving, living Saviour..."
- "A newborn child has to cry, for only in this way will his lungs expand. A doctor once told me of a child who could not breathe when it was born. In order to make it breathe the doctor gave it a slight blow. The mother must have thought the doctor cruel. But he was really doing the kindest thing possible. As with newborn children the lungs are contracted, so are our spiritual lungs. But through suffering God strikes us in love. Then our lungs expand and we can breathe and pray."
- "While sitting on the bank of a river one day, I picked up a solid round stone from the water and broke it open. It was perfectly dry in spite of the fact that it had been immersed in water for centuries. The same is true of many people in the Western world. For centuries they have been surrounded by Christianity; they live immersed in the waters of its benefits. And yet it has not penetrated their hearts; they do not love it. The fault is not in Christianity, but in men's hearts, which have been hardened by materialism and intellectualism."

GIANTS OF THE FAITH: Amy Carmichael (1867 – 1951)

Amy Carmichael was born to devout Presbyterians in Northern Ireland. In 1887, Amy heard the great leader of the China Inland Mission, Hudson Taylor, deliver a speech about missionary life in China. Taylor's speech convinced Amy that she was called to be a foreign missionary, and she found her life's work in India.

Despite frequent bouts with ill health, Amy Carmichael served the Lord in India for fifty-six consecutive years without taking a single furlough. She made her home in Tamil Nadu, near India's southern tip. Tamil Nadu's Hindu priests often supported themselves by selling young girls into lives of prostitution. Amy organized the Dohnavur Fellowship, a church that became a sanctuary for such girls and rescued them from that miserable fate. After one such rescue, she was nearly jailed for kidnapping. Amy also produced 35 published works about Christianity and mission life.

Amy spent the last 20 years of her life bedridden after she was injured in a fall. She died in 1951 at the age of 83. Her grave is inscribed only with the word Amma ("Mommy" in Tamil).

U.S. GEOGRAPHY FOCUS

FASCINATING FACTS about COLORADO:

- <u>Statehood</u>: Colorado became the 38th US state on August 1, 1876.
- <u>Bordering states</u>: Arizona, Kansas, Nebraska, New Mexico, Oklahoma, Utah, Wyoming
- <u>State capital</u>: Denver
- <u>Area</u>: 104,094 sq. mi (Ranks 8th in size)
- <u>Abbreviation</u>: CO
- <u>State nickname</u>: "Centennial State"
- <u>State bird</u>: Lark Bunting
- <u>State tree</u>: Colorado Blue Mountain Spruce
- <u>State flower</u>: Rocky Mountain Columbine
- <u>State song</u>: *Where the Columbines Grow*
- <u>State Motto</u>: "Nothing Without Providence"
- <u>Meaning of name</u>: Colorado is Spanish for "red." The name refers to the Colorado River, which has a muddy red color.
- <u>Historic places to visit in Colorado</u>: The Durango & Silverton Narrow Gauge Railroad, the Western Stock show, Great Sand Dunes National Monument, Pikes Peak, Mesa Verde, The Kit Carson County Carousel, Glenwood Springs, Florissant Fossil Beds National Monument, Buffalo Bill Grave and Museum, Tiny Town Railroad, Cave Of The Winds, Garden Of The Gods
- <u>Resources and Industries</u>: farming (wheat, dairy, corn, hay, cattle, sheep, hogs, fruits and vegetables), mining (gold, silver, uranium), tourism, oil, manufacturing, food processing, transportation.

Balance Rock in Garden of the Gods

Flag of Colorado

- Colorado adopted this flag on June 5, 1911.
- The flag's field has three horizontal stripes of equal width, two outer blue ones and one central white one.
- In the center of the stripes is a red C (for Colorado) filled with a yellow disc that represents the sun.
- The blue on the flag represents the sky; the red represents the earth; the yellow represents the sun; and the white represents the snow on Colorado's many snow-capped mountains.

PRESIDENTIAL FOCUS

PRESIDENT #29: Warren G Harding (1865 – 1923)	
In Office: March 4, 1921 – August 2, 1923	**Political Party:** Republican
Birthplace: Ohio	**Nickname:** "Winnie"

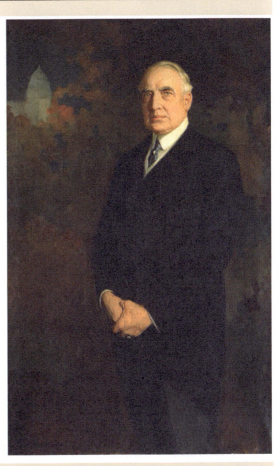

Warren Gamaliel Harding was a U.S. Senator from Ohio who won election to the Presidency in a landslide. Harding took office at the beginning of the Roaring Twenties, when America's economy was recovering from World War I and unemployment was falling rapidly. He was a charismatic President and an excellent speechmaker, and his popularity lasted throughout his brief administration.

Unfortunately, some members of that administration were corrupt. Before Harding took office, Congress had set aside some untapped oil reserves for the navy at a place called Teapot Dome, Wyoming. Harding's Interior Secretary, Albert Fall, leased Teapot Dome's oil fields to some friends in the oil business. In exchange, Fall secretly received a low-interest loan and other gifts. These payoffs lined Fall's pockets and made him a wealthy man, until the change in his lifestyle made investigators suspicious. After a well-publicized investigation by Montana Senator Thomas Walsh, the Teapot Dome Scandal became one of the most notorious political scandals in American history.

But the scandal and the damage it caused to Harding's reputation both came after Harding's death. Warren G. Harding died of a heart attack or a stroke in 1923, while he was on a nationwide speaking tour to reconnect with the American people.

Other interesting facts about Warren G. Harding:
- Harding played poker twice a week, and once gambled away some White House china.
- Harding wore size fourteen shoes.
- Harding was the first President who rode in a car at his inauguration.

Notable quotes from Warren G Harding:
- "America's present need is not heroics but healing; not nostrums but normalcy; not revolution but restoration."
- "Only solitary men know the full joys of friendship. Others have their family; but to a solitary and an exile his friends are everything."

Chapter 20

The Treaty of Versailles, the USSR under Stalin

U.S. HISTORY FOCUS

AMAZING AMERICANS: Amelia Earhart (1897 – 1937?)

Amelia Earhart was among the world's first female pilots. Earhart took her first flying lesson in January 1921, and bought her first airplane six months later. She set her first flying record, the women's altitude record, in 1922. In 1923, she became the sixteenth woman in the world to receive a pilot's license. When her family fell on hard times, however, she had to sell her airplane.

Even without an airplane, Earhart managed to remain an active pilot, and wrote a number of newspaper articles that promoted women's flying. Her enthusiasm drew the notice of a group of publicists who wanted to sponsor a sensational event: the world's first transatlantic flight with a woman aboard. On June 17, 1928, she became the first woman ever to fly across the Atlantic Ocean– but only as a passenger, not as a pilot. This success earned her fame on both sides of the Atlantic and a tickertape parade in New York City.

In the dawning age of radio, film and world travel, it was easier than ever to convert fame into money. These new technologies made it possible to sell big news stories to growing audiences around the world, and each audience enthusiastically paid for the privilege of hearing and reading these stories. Publicity firms and newspapers sponsored inspiring figures like Amelia Earhart to create the next big event that would sell more newspapers (and more advertising) than ever before. Amelia was the perfect figure for this sort of publicity: she was attractive, vivacious, daring, successful, and willing to promote herself by writing books about her life and adventures. Her fame allowed her to promote air travel for the companies that would become Transworld Airlines (TWA) and Northeast Airlines. It also enabled her to have friendships with famous people like First Lady Eleanor Roosevelt– which boosted her fame all the more.

Soon Earhart was setting records as a pilot, not as a passenger. **In August 1928, she became the first woman to fly solo across North America. And on May 20, 1932, she became only the second person in the world– of either gender– to fly solo across the Atlantic Ocean** (Charles Lindbergh was the first, see Chapter 23). For this feat of daring, she earned the Distinguished Flying Cross in America and the Legion of Honor in France. Her continued interest in long-distance flights led her to conceive what she regarded as the ultimate long-distance test: a flight around the world near the equator.

Earhart bought a new airplane for the journey, a twin-engine Lockheed Electra. She also hired an experienced navigator, Fred Noonan, to help her find her way across the wide oceans. She departed from Miami, Florida on June 1, 1937, headed east. She crossed the Atlantic Ocean, Africa, India and Southeast Asia before she arrived at the large Island of New Guinea on June 29. Three days later, on July 2, 1937, Earhart and Noonan took off for the trip's greatest challenge: the 7,000-mile journey across the Pacific Ocean toward San Francisco and home.

They never made it home. Poor weather and clouds made it difficult for Earhart and Noonan to find their next scheduled stop, tiny Howland island in the central Pacific near the equator. Despite help from three U.S. ships, all burning every light they possessed to guide the way, the flyers missed the island. The ships could hear Earhart broadcasting on her radio, but she seemed unable to hear their replies. They finally lost touch with her.

Presumably, Earhart ran out of fuel and went down in the ocean. Some held out hope that she had somehow managed to land on some uncharted island. President Roosevelt ordered an extensive search that eventually cost the United States $4 million, but it did no good: the searchers turned up no trace of Amelia Earhart, Fred Noonan or their Lockheed Electra.

AMAZING AMERICANS: Gertrude Ederle (1905 – 2003)

Publicists also sponsored athletes, providing them with money that allowed them to do things no one had ever done before. A newspaper sponsored Olympic gold medalist Gertrude Ederle, a long distance swimmer, to train for another big event. In 1925, when she was 20 years old, Ederle became the first woman to swim across the English Channel. She managed the 35-mile trip from Cap Gris Nez, France (near Calais) to Kingsdown, Kent, England (near the cliffs of Dover) in 14 1/2 hours. Her time for the crossing was almost 2 hours faster than the men's record at the time. Ederle's feat earned her a New York City tickertape parade like Amelia Earhart's.

WORLD HISTORY FOCUS

THE TREATY OF VERSAILLES

The armistice that ended World War I came into effect at 11 AM on November 11, 1918 – on the eleventh hour of the eleventh day of the eleventh month. However, the 11/11 armistice was only a laying down of arms: it ended the shooting, but it was not a real peace treaty. Over the months that followed the armistice, the victorious Allied Powers dictated separate terms of peace for Germany, for the Empire of Austria-Hungary and for the Ottoman Empire. The results were five major treaties:

- The 1919 **Treaty of Saint Germain**, which dissolved the Empire of Austria-Hungary. Its terms forced the new Republic of Austria to recognize the independence of Hungary, Poland, Czechoslovakia and the territory that would become Yugoslavia (see below).
- The 1920 **Treaty of Trianon**, which established the greatly reduced borders of the new Republic of Hungary. Its harsh terms cost Hungary several major cities and cut it off from the sea.
- The 1920 **Treaty of Sevres** and the 1923 **Treaty of Lausanne**, which partitioned the former Ottoman Empire. The Treaty of Lausanne brought an end to the Ottoman Empire; that empire's remnant became the new Republic of Turkey. Turkey gave up the former Ottoman Empire's territory in Egypt, Sudan, Syria, Iraq, Greece, Bulgaria and elsewhere.
- The 1919 **Treaty of Versailles**, which established the terms of Germany's surrender.

The Treaty of Versailles

Versailles was the palace and seat of government of France's extravagant "Sun King," Louis XIV (reigned 1643 -1715). The palace lies about 12 miles southwest of Paris. In the 1870-1871 Franco-Prussian War, the then newly-established German Empire had humiliated France by

1. occupying Paris,
2. forcing France to pay war reparations,
3. claiming the Alsace-Lorraine region, and

4. crowning its first emperor at the Palace of Versailles.

At the end of World War I in 1918, France and Britain were ready to return the Germans' 1871 favor by humiliating Germany with another harsh peace treaty, also negotiated at Versailles.

The primary negotiators of the Treaty of Versailles were known as the "**Big Four.**" All had different priorities going into the negotiations, and none came out with everything he wanted. From left to right in the illustration, they were:

- **David Lloyd George**, Prime Minister of Great Britain. Britain wanted reparations payments— great sums of money to pay the costs of the war and to provide for the needs of the many widows and orphans the war created. Britain also wanted to punish Germany, but not too harshly: there was great danger that if the treaty's punishments made Germany too weak, then communist Russia might absorb Germany. Britain also wanted to preserve its own overseas empire; so Britain opposed Woodrow Wilson's anti-empire Fourteen Points (see Chapter 18).

- **Vittorio Orlando**, Prime Minister of Italy. Italy had come into the war late and had fought primarily against Austria-Hungary, so Italy received little of what it demanded at Versailles. When Prime Minister Orlando realized that Italy wouldn't receive all of the territory it demanded, he walked out of the peace conference, and the Big Four became the Big Three for a time.

- **Georges Clemenceau**, Prime Minister of France. As the war's primary battleground, France had suffered WWI's ravages more than any other nation. France wanted 1) large reparations payments, 2) sections of German territory (including Germany's Rhineland and Alsace-Lorraine regions, see below), and 3) strict limits on the size of Germany's army so that Germany couldn't attack France again.

- **Woodrow Wilson**, President of the United States. Wilson wanted to use the Treaty of Versailles to bring the world into line with the vision of his Fourteen Points. Essentially, this meant the end of large empires. Wilson wanted 1) arms reductions, 2) free trade on free oceans, seas and straits, 3) home rule for every race and nation that sought it, and 4) an end to the secret alliances that had started World War I in the first place. To oversee all of this, Wilson wanted a new League of Nations with the power to enforce his vision. As Wilson envisioned it, the League of Nations would be a governing world body that could call on the armies of its member nations to end wars before they began (see below).

Both France and Britain received much of what they wanted from the treaty, especially in the area of war reparations payments. This is a partial list of the terms of the Treaty of Versailles, signed on June 28, 1919, five years to the day after the assassination of Archduke Ferdinand (see Chapter 17):

- **Germany and the other Central Powers accepted full responsibility for causing the war, and hence accepted responsibility for paying the war's costs.**
- Germany accepted limits on the size and capabilities of its military.
- Germany agreed not to import or export weapons.
- Germany agreed not to manufacture tanks, military aircraft, submarines or poison gas.
- Germany agreed to pay enormous war reparations: a total of over $30 billion, the equivalent of about $400 billion in 2010. Parts of these reparations would be paid in goods like coal and steel.
- **In order to reassure France, Germany's Rhineland region (on its border with France) would be occupied by Allied troops for fifteen years.**

- Germany agreed to surrender a number of territories (see below).
- The Big Four agreed to found the League of Nations (see below).

The Germans did not agree that the war's blame and costs should rest entirely upon their shoulders, and considered these terms far too harsh. Nevertheless, with their armies defeated and the German Revolution in progress, they lacked the means to refuse, and were forced to accept the treaty.

The heavy financial burdens the Treaty of Versailles placed on Germany's new Weimar Republic led to extremely high inflation and a near-collapse of its economy in the early 1920s. World War I's outcome and the Treaty of Versailles left Germans bitter, angry, and increasingly eager for revenge (see Chapter 24).

Under the terms of the Treaty of Versailles, borders shifted on all sides of Germany:

- France gained the Alsace-Lorraine territory on its German border.
- Belgium, Denmark and Czechoslovakia all gained territories on their German borders.
- Poland gained West Prussia and other territories on its German border. East Prussia remained part of Germany, but was cut off from the rest of Germany by Polish West Prussia. This arrangement gave Poland access to the Baltic Sea.
- Germany lost all of the territory it had gained from Russia in the 1918 Treaty of Brest-Litovsk. Parts of this territory went to Poland and to the Baltic nations of Lithuania, Latvia and Estonia.
- Germany lost its overseas territories (primarily in Africa) to the new League of Nations.

DISPUTED DOMAINS: The Alsace-Lorraine

The Alsace-Lorraine is a territory that lies along the traditional borders between Germany and France. The Alsatian part of the territory lies on the west bank of the Rhine River (opposite Germany on the east bank), and the Lorraine part lies to the north along the Moselle River. The region's largest city is Strasbourg. The Alsace-Lorraine is blessed with iron ore and coal in abundance.

Iron and coal were exactly what Germany needed to become Europe's industrial and military giant (recall German Chancellor Bismarck's statement about "blood and iron" from Chapter 7). Because of that, the new German Empire claimed the Alsace-Lorraine after its victory over France in the Franco-Prussian War of 1870-1871. Over the years from 1871-1918, Germany built enough mines and iron processing facilities to make the Alsace-Lorraine a crucial part of the German Empire's industry— especially its war industry.

The French resented the loss of their territory, and wanted it back. Therefore, after Germany lost WWI, the Treaty of Versailles restored the Alsace-Lorraine to victorious France. This meant that France also claimed all of the region's German-built mines and other facilities. The Alsace-Lorraine that France reclaimed after WWI was worth a great deal more than the one it had lost in 1871.

The loss of so much wealth and resources was a sore blow to Germany; so now it was the Germans who resented the loss of their territory. Germany reclaimed the Alsace-Lorraine one more time, when it invaded and occupied France from 1940-1944 during World War II. After World War II, the Alsace-Lorraine again returned to French control, where it remains today.

DISPUTED DOMAINS: Yugoslavia

One result of the 1919 Treaty of Saint-Germain, which dissolved the Empire of Austria-Hungary, was the creation of a short-lived state called the "State of Slovenes, Croats and Serbs." This was the state that became known as *Yugoslavia*, which means "land of the southern Slavs."

The creation of Yugoslavia was an attempt to follow President Wilson's Fourteen Points: Wilson wanted home rule and independence for any nationality or ethnic group that sought them. Yugoslavia was intended to be a "pan-Slavic" state, a new and independent state that would unite all Slavic peoples and restore their right of self-government after the centuries they had spent under the control of outside empires (Byzantine, Ottoman and Austria-Hungary).

Unfortunately, pan-Slavism turned out to be no more than an idealistic vision. In reality, there was no such thing as pan-Slavism. The people of the new Yugoslavia were loyal to their traditional nationalities and faiths, not to the new, artificially-created Yugoslavia. Wilson wanted them to become Yugoslavians; but instead, they remained loyal Bosnians, Croatians, Kosovars, Macedonians, Montenegrins, Serbs and Slovenes.

For a time, outside forces continued to hold Yugoslavia together. During World War II, the Central Powers controlled and divided Yugoslavia. After that war, Yugoslavia fell under the influence of communism: it became the Socialist Federal Republic of Yugoslavia and followed communist leader Marshal Tito until his death in 1980.

The 1991 breakup of the USSR was a major failure for the communist vision. As soon as the USSR dissolved, several formerly communist states began to demand their independence. The republics that made up Yugoslavia began to demand their independence even before the USSR dissolved. **Today Yugoslavia no longer exists, and its former territory belongs to seven independent states: Bosnia, Croatia, Kosovo, Macedonia, Montenegro, Serbia and Slovenia.**

FASCINATING FACTS: The League of Nations

LEAGUE OF NATIONS

SOCIETE DES NATIONS

The Treaty of Versailles created the new League of Nations as a place for international diplomacy (friendly negotiation). The League's purpose was to mediate (negotiate) international disagreements, and so to prevent wars before they could begin. When a rogue nation threatened war against another nation, the League could take three steps:

1. It could issue stern warnings and resolutions to the rogue nation;
2. It could impose economic sanctions on the rogue nation, refusing to trade with it; and

3. It could ask its member nations to combine their armies in a coalition and use military force against the rogue nation.

The combined disapproval of the many nations in the League carried a great deal of weight. Rogue nations were much more likely to obey the demands of a large, powerful League of Nations than they were to obey the demands of any one nation.

However, the League had several weaknesses. The first was ironic:

The United States, whose President Woodrow Wilson had proposed the League in the first place, refused to join the League.

The U.S. Congress was wary that the League might commit American troops to action without Congress's permission. They saw the League as a violation of U.S. sovereignty, its right to make its own decisions without outside interference. Woodrow Wilson worked so hard promoting the League– to no avail– that he ruined his already weakened health, and died soon after he left office. Without the United States, which was becoming the world's largest economy and most powerful nation, the League was much weaker than it might have been.

Another weakness was a lack of courage and determination among the League's member nations. It was one thing to issue a warning to a rogue nation (step 1 above), but it was quite another to voluntarily give up profitable trade (step 2), or to raise and fund an army to enforce the League's will (step 3).

In 1932, when Japan invaded China's Manchuria region (see Chapter 32), the League of Nations demanded that Japan withdraw from China (step 1). Japan refused, then withdrew its membership in the League. The League's next step should have been step to impose economic sanctions against Japan (step 2); but instead, none of the League's member nations were ready to go this far, so the League simply dropped the matter. Japan continued to occupy Manchuria, proving that the League of Nations was weak and ineffective.

The real test of the League of Nations came in the years leading up to World War II, when Adolf Hitler began to build up Germany's military in direct violation of the Treaty of Versailles. When Hitler's warlike actions went unpunished, it became obvious that the League had failed in its purpose. The League held no regular meetings after 1938, and formally dissolved in 1946.

There are two common views of the League of Nations' place in history:

- One view is that President Wilson's vision was right, and that if everyone had followed his plan properly, then the world would have seen no more major wars. World War II and subsequent wars never would have happened if the League had taken the proper steps according to its charter and if its member nations had backed the League up with economic sanctions and military intervention.
- The other view is that Wilson's vision required the United States to surrender its sovereignty when it joined the League. According to this view, the League was a "world government" that set itself above national governments, robbing them of their right to manage their own affairs. The League allowed small nations with corrupt governments to band together and control larger, stronger nations. The League's opponents viewed joining the League as an act of treason against the United States.

THE UNION OF SOVIET SOCIALIST REPUBLICS (USSR)

The Russian Empire Becomes the USSR

The two Russian revolutions of 1917, the February Revolution and the October Revolution, brought an end to the tsars and the Russian Empire (see Chapter 18). The Bolsheviks established a new government based on a collection of *soviets*, or councils, all under the leadership of the Bolshevik Party and Vladimir Lenin.

Not everyone yielded to the Bolsheviks. The Bolsheviks' Red Army spent the next several years battling the anti-Bolshevik White Army for control of Russia in the Russian Civil War. It was not until December 1922 that the Russian Civil War ended and the separate republics of the former Russian Empire united to form the Union of Soviet Socialist Republics (USSR).

USSR after WW II   RUSSIA IN 2012

During the Russian Civil War, assassination attempts destroyed Lenin's health. For the last six years of his life, Lenin suffered ill effects from bullet wounds he received in 1918. He died in 1924, less than two years after he achieved his dream of founding a socialist state in Russia.

In 1922, Lenin helped his protégé Josef Stalin become the Bolsheviks' highest official, the General Secretary of the Central Committee of the Communist Party. Near the end of his life, Lenin began to regret choosing Stalin as his successor. Lenin's doubts were justified, for the worst was yet to come: Josef Stalin would turn out to be one of history's deadliest dictators.

The New Economic Policy and the Five Year Plans

Both Lenin and Stalin were deeply interested in spreading socialism and communism throughout the new USSR. Both wanted to stamp out capitalism, the Western-style economic system under which businesses operated purely for money and profit. They believed that profit led to greed, that greed led to wealth, and that wealthy people ruined their society by forcing the poor to work for pitiful wages. They wanted to replace the society capitalism had created with a new, ideal communist society. Their plan was to create a classless society in which no one was rich or poor, a society in which everyone shared food, goods, property and labor equally.

After the October Revolution, Lenin's first steps as Russia's new leader (see picture) were to take control of nearly all of Russia's banks and businesses. During the Russian Civil War that followed the October Revolution, communist party officials took charge of factories and confiscated nearly all products and farm produce for the state.

Lenin's new USSR was strictly socialist: the government owned and controlled every bank and business, and was on its way to owning every farm.

Naturally, not everyone was fond of this policy. Business owners had worked hard to build their businesses, and didn't want to give them up to the government. Farms and factories began producing less under socialism, because the Russian people lost all of their reasons to work hard. Why would anyone bother to work extra hard when the benefits of that hard work all went to the government?

After the Russian Civil War, Lenin began to believe that he had brought strict socialism on too quickly, so he backed off a bit. Under the New Economic Policy, he relaxed his strict socialism and allowed small businesses and farms to keep more of what they earned. Farms and factories began producing more again as the Russian people regained their reasons to work hard. Lenin believed that the Russian people only needed more education to see the benefits of communism. The more they learned, he believed, the more they would understand that communism was the best way to create a classless society. The New Economic Policy, with its temporarily relaxed socialism, was only a small setback on Lenin's path to the ideal communist society.

Stalin saw things differently. **In the late 1920s, Stalin reversed the late Lenin's lenient New Economic Policy and replaced it with the first Five Year Plan.** Stalin wanted his first Five Year Plan to accomplish two things:
1. He wanted to modernize the USSR and make it a great industrial nation equal to Germany or the United States.
2. He also wanted to complete the USSR's conversion to socialism and to prove that socialism was superior to capitalism.

The first Five Year Plan was an industrial plan that included lists of goals for the all-important steel industry and other industries. It was also a plan to advance socialism by "collectivizing" of all of the USSR's farms. **Stalin planned to force every farmer to donate his land to a government-owned collective, eliminating private ownership of farms.**

Stalin's collectivization of farms led to a terrible famine in 1932-1933.

FASCINATING FACTS: The *Holodomor* ("Killing by Hunger")

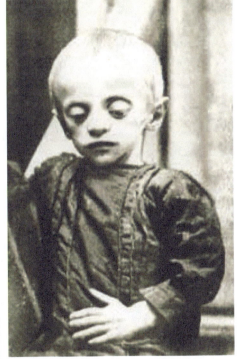

The *Holodomor* was a terrible Soviet famine that took place in Stalin's USSR in 1932 - 1933. The famine was centered in Ukraine, the rich-soiled southern republic that traditionally raised much of Russia's food. Like the Irish tenant farmers of the 1840s Potato Blight, the farmers of Ukraine were left to starve in a land full of food.

As good socialists on their way to creating the ideal communist society, both Lenin and Stalin wanted to convert private businesses to government-owned businesses. This included farms. They believed that farming would become more efficient and productive if farmers stopped working on their privately-owned farms and began to work together on large "collective farms" owned by the government. Stalin found it difficult to get this idea across to the Ukraine's well-established farmers, known as *kulaks*, who were understandably reluctant to give up their hard-won property merely to satisfy the mad notions of distant men who knew nothing of farming.

However, Stalin had the power to enforce his will, whether it was mad or not. He sent communist officials to each Ukrainian village, and these officials forced farmers and villagers to attend long meetings at which communist party members extolled the virtues of communism and collective farming. The *kulaks* came under heavy pressure to join the collective farms and to hand their land over to the government. Those *kulaks* who refused often disappeared to Siberia, like the later victims of the Great Purge.

The USSR's new collective farms failed for several reasons:

- **Stalin's Five Year Plans**: In order to modernize the USSR's industry and economy, Stalin regularly announced five year plans that outlined the progress he expected in the coming years. These plans came with production quotas for various items, including grains like wheat and oats. Stalin wanted to prove that communism was superior to capitalism, so he wanted to see farm production improve every year. Unfortunately, when his communist party began to interfere with the *kulaks*, farm production actually went down, not up. In order to meet Stalin's constant demands for rising crop yields, USSR officials had to confiscate the grain that normally would have gone to feed the farmers who raised it. Stalin's men watched carefully to ensure that no farmer held back grain for himself or his family. As a result, Ukrainian farmers starved while Stalin sold their grain overseas to impress the world with communism's big success.

- **Lost Agricultural Skill**: Along with farm ownership came farming skill. The Ukraine's *kulaks* knew how to operate their farms, and when Stalin killed them or sent them to Siberia, he lost a great deal of farming experience and know-how. The communist officials he placed in charge of his new collective farms often knew nothing of farming.

- **Dead Livestock**: Some angry *kulaks* killed their animals before they went to Siberia so that their communist oppressors couldn't use them. The resulting shortage of animals set Ukrainian farming back for years.

- **Lost Sense of Ownership**: People who were forced to work on collective farms simply didn't work as hard as people working their own land. This was a common failing under socialism and communism: Since extra work didn't earn extra pay, there was no reason to do extra work. Joining a collective reduced the incentive to work, and increased the incentive to let someone else do the work.

Uncounted millions of Ukrainians died in the *Holodomor* because of incompetent communist meddling.

Despite the glaring testimony of millions of corpses, Stalin managed to deny that any famine ever took place. While he lived, Stalin's expert propaganda allowed him to deny truths that were obvious to all. His government-owned newspapers simply ignored the dead, and neither the rest of the nation nor the world learned much about the *Holodomor* for decades. After Stalin's death, however, his successor Nikita Khrushchev denounced him as an evil dictator, and the USSR slowly began to admit that some of its official history was inaccurate.

With dead numbering in the millions, the *Holodomor* ranks among history's very worst tragedies.

DEFINITION: **Propaganda** is highly biased (one-sided) speech or writing that is designed to convince the public of something that may or may not be true. Stalin was an excellent propagandist who used words to convince the USSR's people of all sorts of things that were untrue:

- Stalin used propaganda to claim that his personal enemies were really enemies of the people who wanted to defeat the communist revolution and return to capitalism.
- He used propaganda to convince his people that all Western capitalists were liars who wanted to destroy the communist revolution and return the USSR's people to the slavery they had known under the tsars.
- He also used propaganda to alter history: for years, the USSR claimed that the *Holodomor* never happened.

Most people heard only the news Stalin allowed them to hear, and had little way of knowing that their leader, who spoke of the glorious communist revolution in such glowing terms, was really lying to them in order to control them and keep them on his side.

DASTARDLY DICTATORS: Joseph Vissarianovich Stalin (1879 – 1953)

Joseph Stalin came from a peasant family that lived in Russia's Balkan province of Georgia (east of the Black Sea). "Stalin," which comes from the Russian word for steel, was not his true family name; instead, it was a name he chose for himself after he became a revolutionary. Although the young not-yet-Stalin attended a Georgian Orthodox Christian seminary for a time, he was more interested in the writings of Karl Marx and Vladimir Lenin than in religious matters. Stalin joined Lenin's Bolshevik Party in 1903.

As a Bolshevik (communist) revolutionary and an outlaw, Stalin:

1. wrote and distributed propaganda against the tsars;
2. organized protests against the tsars;
3. encouraged labor strikes and other acts of rebellion against the tsars; and
4. committed robberies to pay for all of these revolutionary activities.

The tsars' officials supposedly arrested Stalin and banished him to Siberia no fewer than seven times; but somehow, he earned release or escaped each time.

In 1917, Stalin returned from his last Siberian imprisonment to take over the writing and publishing of *Pravda*, the Bolshevik Party's official newspaper. When Lenin returned from exile in that same year, the year of the October Revolution, Stalin and *Pravda* became Lenin's most important means of reaching out to the Russian people and spreading his communist ideas.

As Lenin rose in power and influence, he lifted Stalin along with him. During the Russian Civil War that followed the October Revolution, Lenin made Stalin part of his five-member *Politburo* (executive committee) and a military leader. And in 1922, Lenin helped Stalin win election as General Secretary of the Communist Party's Central Committee.

As both a military leader and a communist leader, Stalin began to show his true, murderous colors. He was quick to execute his enemies, and quick to burn any village that aided his enemies. He often directed his harsh attacks against the same poor, laboring underclass that the communists claimed to defend. As brutal as Lenin himself was, Stalin's excessive violence shocked even him. Late in his life, Lenin began to criticize Stalin.

However, Lenin's health was failing. For the last two years of Lenin's life, his poor health confined him to the Gorki estate near Moscow. Stalin was able to limit the number of people who were allowed to visit the dying former leader. When Stalin learned that Lenin's last writings recommended removing Stalin as General Secretary, he hid those writings from the public. Stalin's experience with propaganda at *Pravda* made him a master at controlling what the public read and thought, so he had no trouble keeping his position as General Secretary after Lenin died.

THE GREAT PURGE: The next stain on Stalin's already filthy career was the 1936-1938 *Great Purge* (or *Great Terror*). The Great Purge was a murderous rampage in which Stalin eliminated everyone who criticized him and everyone who might have a chance to take his place as leader of the USSR. No one was safe during the Great Purge; secret police watched anyone and everyone carefully for any sign of anti-communist activities. Poets, teachers, politicians and anyone else who dared to speak ill of Stalin were all in danger of arrest. Many of the very Bolsheviks who had helped Stalin in his rise to power suddenly found themselves

1. arrested,
2. accused of being an "enemy of the people,"
3. subjected to show trials with predetermined outcomes, and then
4. executed or exiled to Siberia.

Stalin's expert propaganda convinced the public that he was murdering all of these victims in order to destroy the enemies of communism. All of these deaths, he assured the public, were necessary to ensure the success of the communist revolution and the creation of an ideal communist utopia in the USSR. At the end of the Great Purge, Stalin used propaganda once again: he blamed the Great Purge's excessive violence on his hand-selected chief of secret police, Nicolai Yezhov, and ordered Yezhov's execution as well. In the eyes of Stalin's devoted followers, Yezhov, not Stalin, received the blame for the Great Purge.

Stalin remained in power throughout the World War II years. Before the war began in 1939, Stalin and Hitler signed the Molotov-Ribbentrop Pact, in which the USSR and Germany each agreed not to intervene if the other went to war. In this deal, the two devils decided how they would divide northern and eastern Europe: Stalin would invade and conquer eastern Poland, Finland, Lithuania, Latvia and Estonia, while Hitler would invade and conquer western Poland (caption in the "Rendezvous" cartoon by David Low reads: 'Hitler: "The scum of the earth I believe." Stalin: "The bloody assassin of the workers I presume."')

If Stalin and Hitler had remained friendly, who knows what might have happened? Fortunately, fascists and communists hated one another. **In a world-altering blunder, Hitler broke the Molotov-Ribbentrop Pact and turned against Stalin in 1941** (see Chapter 25). Hitler's attack on the USSR opened up a whole new front of World War II, the miserable Eastern Front. In response, Stalin and the USSR joined the Allies in their fight against Hitler.

At first, Hitler's elite army pushed deep into USSR territory. With his inferior army pushed to its limit by elite German forces, <u>Stalin threatened to execute any USSR army officer who retreated or surrendered. Thus Stalin's army was trapped between the terror of Hitler and the terror of mad, murderous Stalin</u>. The suffering of Soviet and German troops during the frozen standoffs at the Battles of Stalingrad and Moscow was beyond endurance. In the end, Hitler failed to conquer Russia just as Napoleon had failed before him. Stalin drove the Germans back out of the USSR and eventually captured Germany's capital, Berlin. Ironically, the dictatorial Stalin emerged from World War II as one of the victorious Allies who had fought to preserve freedom and democracy.

Under Stalin, however, the people of Eastern Europe would have neither freedom nor democracy. In conferences at Yalta (on the Crimean Peninsula) and Potsdam (in occupied Germany), Stalin convinced his western Allies that the USSR should be allowed to retain the territories it had occupied late in the war. Poland, Czechoslovakia, Hungary, Bulgaria, Romania, Albania and others all fell behind the "Iron Curtain" of Soviet-influenced communism (see Chapter 27). Stalin remained firmly in power until he died of a brain hemorrhage on March 5, 1953.

FASCINATING FACTS: The Gulag

"Gulag" is a Russian acronym for the Russian words that translate as "Chief Administration of Corrective Labor Camps and Colonies." The *Gulag* was the Stalinist government agency in charge of prison and forced labor camps. Most of the Gulag's prison camps were located in Russia's Siberia province, where frozen climate and vast distances rendered escape all but impossible. The Gulag also established forced labor camps near large work projects such as railroads, canals and subways.

The Russian practice of imprisoning political enemies in Siberia began under the tsars, and Stalin himself was supposedly imprisoned there seven times; but the tsars were mere amateurs compared to Stalin. The tsars imprisoned enemies by the hundreds, but Stalin imprisoned them by the hundreds of thousands. **In his zeal to promote communism, Stalin empowered communist party officials to imprison anyone who expressed skepticism about his communist government**:

- When a businessman resisted the government takeover of his business, he went to Siberia.
- When a *kulak* resisted joining a collective farm, he went to Siberia.
- When an urchin made a wisecrack about the failures of communism, he too went to Siberia.
- The secret police even opened citizens' personal letters and used them to weed out Stalin's critics.
- Anyone who fell afoul of a communist party official could be sent to Siberia, often without trial: the secret police established three-man councils called *troikas* with the power to convict and imprison offenders.

Conditions in the Gulag were miserable. The climate was frigid, the labor was back-breaking, and the food was scarce. Gulag prison guards took pleasure in making life miserable for the inmates, and in shooting those who attempted escape. Countless inmates never left the Gulag alive.

Russian author Alexander Solzhenitsyn told the Gulag's story in a long book entitled *The Gulag Archipelago*. Solzhenitsyn went to the Gulag in 1945 for criticizing (in a personal letter) Stalin's handling of World War II, and remained there until 1953. *The Gulag Archipelago* began revealing the miseries of Gulag life to Western readers when it was published in 1973, but the book was banned in the USSR until 1989.

FASCINATING FACTS: Faberge Eggs

Moscow Kremlin Egg   Madonna Lily Egg   Equestrian Egg   Peter the Great Egg

Russian Orthodox Christianity dominated Russia for nearly 1,000 years. Orthodox Christianity became popular in Russia around 990 AD, when Vladimir the Great held a mass baptism for the entire city of Kiev; and it remained popular until the rise of the Bolsheviks in 1917. Russian Orthodox Christians had a deep appreciation for art and design. They loved elegant church buildings with graceful, domed roofs, and they also appreciated the beautiful icons and objects that decorated these churches.

Tsar Alexander III was no exception. In 1885, Alexander Romanov commissioned jeweler Peter Faberge to create a particularly beautiful and extravagant work of the jeweler's art, a special Easter egg for his wife Maria. Faberge's first royal egg, nicknamed the "Hen Egg," opened to reveal a golden yolk and a ruby-eyed hen. Then the hen itself opened to reveal a tiny replica of Russia's royal crown. Later, the tsars allowed the House of Faberge to create royal eggs in any design it wished, with one proviso: they must always contain a surprise. In order to please the tsars, Faberge designed most of his eggs to depict honored events or themes from Russian history.

Faberge continued to create elaborate eggs for the royal Romanovs for as long as they remained in power, finishing a total of fifty. Forty-two of these Faberge Eggs survive. In 1917-1918, the Bolsheviks nationalized Faberge's jewelry company, and the Faberge family fled the country.

U. S. GEOGRAPHY FOCUS

FASCINATING FACTS about WASHINGTON:

- Statehood: Washington became the 42nd state on November 11, 1889.
- Bordering states/countries/bodies of water: Idaho, Oregon, Canada, Puget Sound and the Pacific Ocean
- State capital: Olympia
- Area: 71,362 sq. mi (Ranks 18th in size)
- Abbreviation: WA
- State nickname: "The Evergreen State"
- State bird: Willow Goldfinch
- State tree: Western Hemlock
- State flower: Coast Rhododendron
- State song: *Washington, My Home*
- State Motto: "By and By"
- Meaning of name: named for the first President of the United States, George Washington
- Historic places to visit in Washington: Mt. Rainier and the Cascade Range, Olympic National Park, Cape Flattery, Governor Albert D. Rossellini Bridge, San Juan Island National Historic Park, World Kite Museum, Northwest African American Museum, Whale Watching In Westport
- Resources and Industries: farming (raspberries, hops, apples, cherries, pears, grapes, nuts, cattle, wheat, seafood), tourism, computer software, papermaking and forestry, manufacturing, hydroelectric power

Washington State's Governor's Mansion

Flag of Washington

- Washington adopted this flag in 1923.
- Its field is dark green, and the state seal in the middle bears the image of George Washington.
- Washington's flag is the only U.S. state flag that has a green field.
- It is also the only US state flag that features an American president.

Chapter 21

The Roaring Twenties (Part II), Italy, Egyptian Independence

U.S. HISTORY FOCUS

THE ROARING TWENTIES (continued from Chapter 19)

Swing Dancing

The 1920s was a time of celebration, and jazz lovers celebrated with a series of popular new dances. The Charleston, the Lindy Hop (named for aviator Charles Lindbergh), the Foxtrot and the Shimmy all started during the 1910s or 1920s. Jazz lovers also celebrated with dance marathons, long contests in which couples danced for hours and days on end in order to win money, fame or other prizes. One dance marathon lasted for three weeks.

The Greatest Thing since Sliced Bread!

Before the 1920s, bakers sold bread in whole loaves, unsliced. An Iowa inventor named Otto Rohwedder invented a whole-loaf electric bread slicer in 1924, and by 1928, sliced bread was all the rage. Sliced bread allowed children to make their own sandwiches without having to use sharp knives to cut the bread.

The children's sandwich of choice was peanut butter and jelly. Peanut butter was inexpensive, and jelly made the sandwiches sweet. During the Great Depression of the 1930s, peanut butter sandwiches were an important staple food for poor children.

There She Is!

1921 was the year of the first Miss America beauty contest, which was held in Atlantic City, New Jersey. Margaret Gorman of Washington D.C. became the first Miss America. The Miss America pageant was closed to "colored" women, and no Black women entered until 1970.

King Tut's Tomb

A British Egyptologist and artist named Howard Carter discovered the tomb of Pharaoh Tutankhamen on November 26, 1922. Carter found the tomb buried under tons of rubble in the Valley of the Kings near the ancient city of Thebes, Egypt's capital during the New Kingdom era. Pharaoh Tutankhamen was the young son and heir of Akhenaten, Egypt's only monotheist pharaoh. His tomb was special because it was almost entirely unmolested by the ancient grave robbers who had plundered so many other tombs.

WORLD HISTORY FOCUS

> This week's lesson covers **nationalists** who wanted to restore independence to two large, formerly great nations that had lost their independence: Italy and Egypt.
>
> **A nationalist is a patriot who wants his nation to be independent, united and proud.**
>
> - Before World War I, nationalists in **Italy** cast out the foreign empires of Austria, France and Spain to restore Italy's unity and independence.
> - After World War I, nationalists in **Egypt** cast out the British Empire to restore Egypt's independence.
>
> The age of foreign empires was ending, and nationalists all over the world were seeking independence.

ITALY

WHAT HAS GONE BEFORE

Italy in the Medieval Age

After the Western Roman Empire disintegrated in 476 AD, the Italian Peninsula fell into disunity. Throughout the Medieval Age and into the Early Modern Era, Italy had no united government. Instead, it lay divided into separate city-states and kingdoms with constantly shifting names, rulers and boundaries. Capua, Florence, Genoa, Lombardy, Salerno, Sicily, Tuscany, Venice and Verona were just a few of Italy's many city-states and kingdoms of the Medieval Age. Powerful outsiders— including France and Spain to the west and Austria to the north— invaded and controlled Italy's border regions. And one powerful insider— the Roman Catholic Church, led by the Pope from the Holy See in Rome— controlled central Italy after the Donation of Pepin gave the popes control over the Papal States in 754 - 756.

The Napoleonic Kingdom of Italy and the Congress of Vienna

During the Early Modern era, Emperor Napoleon Bonaparte sought to absorb Italy into the French Empire (along with all the rest of Europe). In northern Italy, he established the **Napoleonic Kingdom of Italy** with himself as King and his adopted son as Viceroy. Farther south, he occupied Rome, banished the Pope, and confiscated a great deal of Italian artwork. When Napoleon was at the height of his power around 1810, his French Empire dominated most of Italy. The era of Napoleon brought Italian unity of a sort, but French domination wasn't precisely the sort of unity Italian nationalists had in mind.

All of Napoleon's efforts came to nothing after his defeat at the Battle of Leipzig in 1814. The Sixth Coalition (Austria, Britain, Prussia, Russia, Spain and others) went on to occupy Paris, and Napoleon's marshals forced him to abdicate his throne. In the aftermath of the Napoleonic Wars, the **Congress of Vienna** reestablished Europe's boundary lines, restoring Italy to its former, divided state— with several changes.

After the Congress of Vienna, the Italian Peninsula lay divided between:

1. the Kingdom of the Two Sicilies (Sicily Island and southern Italy);

2. the Papal States (Rome and central Italy);
3. Tuscany (north of the Papal States);
4. Sardinia-Piedmont (Sardinia Island and northwest Italy);
5. Lombardy-Venice (north and northeast Italy); and
6. several smaller kingdoms and city-states, including Parma, Modena, Lucca and San Marino.

Most of these states were controlled or heavily influenced by larger empires from outside Italy: The Austrian Empire claimed Lombardy-Venice, and controlled Tuscany; while Spain controlled the Kingdom of the Two Sicilies. The popes continued to control the Papal States. Only the Kingdom of Sardinia-Piedmont, ruled by the royal House of Savoy, was relatively independent. It was this independence that made Sardinia-Piedmont and the House of Savoy important in the coming movement to unite all of Italy.

<u>IL RISORGIMENTO</u> ("The Resurgence")

The Carbonari and the Holy Alliance

The movement to unite Italy began even before Napoleon's demise, with the formation of a revolutionary group known as the **Carbonari**.

The Carbonari were a secret society with a secret membership. They were organized in distinct "cells" for maximum secrecy, and the members of one Carbonari cell might not know the members of another cell. **To introduce themselves to one another, they used secret signs or secret handshakes taught only to the Carbonari**. They also used secret initiation rites, and required new "apprentice" members to train for at least six months before they could become "masters."

Secrecy was an absolute necessity for the Carbonari, because in 1815, the empires of Russia, Austria and Prussia banded together in a three-way Holy Alliance to crush rebellions wherever they sprang up. By 1818, Britain and France had joined the Holy Alliance. The Holy Alliance was designed to defend monarchies and empires, and to save European royalty from the sort of revolutionary commoners that had risen up and assassinated King Louis XVI during the French Revolution.

The Empire of Austria was particularly interested in controlling Italy. Austrian troops helped to defeat the Carbonari's early attempts at revolution in the Two Sicilies, Sardinia and elsewhere.

Young Italy

The successor to the Carbonari was **Young Italy** (*La Giovine Italia*), a new revolutionary group founded by a Carbonari member named **Giuseppe Mazzini** (see picture). Young Italy was only one of several revolutionary groups with similar names and goals: Young Europe, Young America, and the Young Turks all shared some of Young Italy's ideas. These "young" revolutionaries were tired of empires, tired of despotic (cruel and absolute) monarchies, and tired of the Catholic popes that supported these monarchies.

Young Italy was another secret society like the Carbonari, but with a different set of requirements: Its members were required to

1) be under forty years of age,
2) own a rifle and at least 50 rounds of ammunition, and
3) own a dagger.

Like the Carbonari, Young Italy opposed empires and foreign despots; but Young Italy also had a second, more specific goal: it wanted to unify all of Italy into one free and independent republic.

Like the Carbonari, Young Italy had a rough beginning. Its first revolution attempt, in 1834, was discovered before it could begin, and a dozen Young Italy members were executed. Mazzini himself was tried *in absentia* and sentenced to death, but the royals never caught him. Mazzini lived in exile for most of the next 15 years, writing articles and letters to promote Young Italy and the revolution.

The Revolutions of 1848 and the First Italian War of Independence

1848 was a year of revolutions, not only in Italy, but also in several other European nations. France, Germany, Austria and Italy all faced revolutions in 1848 from members of organizations like Young Italy and Young Europe, who were tired of despotic monarchs. None of the revolutions was well organized, and none succeeded in unseating any emperors or kings.

In Italy's, the **Revolution of 1848** (see picture) had some important results. In the northern Kingdom of Sardinia-Piedmont, the revolution forced King Charles Albert to adopt a constitution for the first time, changing his government from an absolute monarchy to a constitutional monarchy with a two-house parliament. And when several north Italian cities rebelled against Austrian rule, Charles Albert tried to capitalize on their rebellion by attacking the Austrian armies in those cities.

Charles Albert's attempts to capture northern Italy from Austria were part of the 1848-1849 **First Italian War of Independence**, a revolution that spread through much of Italy before Austria and France brought Italy back under control. Charles Albert may not have been pursuing Italian unity and independence, but he was at least resisting foreign domination of Italy at the hands of Austria.

King Charles Albert lost the war, and his crown, in 1849. After Austria defeated his army at the Battle of Novara, Charles Albert abdicated (gave up) his throne and left Italy for a life in exile. Charles Albert's son and heir, Victor Emmanuel II, took his father's place as King of Sardinia-Piedmont.

Restoring Unity to Italy (the *Risorgimento*) and the Second War of Italian Independence

King Victor Emmanuel II became the symbol of Italian independence that his father was not. Together with his new Prime Minister, Count Camillo di Cavour, Victor Emanuel built Sardinia-Piedmont into a new Kingdom of Italy that encompassed the entire Italian Peninsula.

All of this didn't happen overnight. First, Victor Emanuel earned favor with France's Napoleon III by assisting France in the 1853-1856 Crimean War. Then he used his good relationship with Napoleon III to make a helpful arrangement: Napoleon III agreed to help Victor Emanuel eject the Austrians from northern Italy if Victor Emanuel would transfer the territories of Nice and Savoy to France.

This arrangement only half succeeded. In the 1859 **Second Italian War of Independence**, Sardinia-Piedmont won control of Lombardy and Tuscany, but not of Venetia farther east. Then in 1860, heroic Italian

commander Giuseppe Garibaldi captured the Kingdom of the Two Sicilies with a famous force that started out with only 1,000 troops (*Il Mille*).

INTERESTING ITALIANS: Giuseppe Garibaldi (1807 – 1882)

Giuseppe Garibaldi was the great military hero of the fight for Italian unity. Garibaldi was a swashbuckling, red-shirt-and-cape-wearing freedom fighter who led revolutionary battles on two continents over the course of four decades. His personal charisma drew young men to his side and helped turn the tide for the ***Risorgimento***.

As a young man, Garibaldi was a member of both the **Carbonari** and **Young Italy**. Like Mazzini, he was condemned to death in absentia for his part in Young Italy's first attempt at revolution in 1834; and like Mazzini, he escaped and lived in exile for years. For Garibaldi, that exile was in South America, where he joined revolutions in Brazil and Uruguay. It was in Brazil that he met his wife Anita, who bore him four children and fought beside him until the day she died.

Garibaldi returned to Italy for the **Revolution of 1848** and fought to support a new Italian republic Mazzini was trying to establish in Rome. Rome was the capital of the Papal States, and the Pope was forced to flee Rome when Mazzini and Garibaldi's revolutionaries took over the city. However, after the Pope reached safety in Gaeta, he called on his old Catholic-church-loving ally France for aid. At the time, the French army was one of the world's finest. Garibaldi held the French off for a time; but in 1849, he had to flee Italy once again. His wife Anita died during Garibaldi's retreat from Rome.

Garibaldi's greatest victory came during the **Second War of Italian Independence**. In May 1860, he led a 1,000-strong force of northern Italians, the red-shirted *Il Mille*, against the Neapolitan forces defending Sicily ("Neapolitan" means "of the city of Naples," and Naples was the capital of the Kingdom of the Two Sicilies). So many Sicilian rebels swelled Garibaldi's ranks that he was able to conquer the entire island. Then he moved on and conquered the part of the kingdom that lay on the Italian mainland. For a time, Garibaldi ruled the conquered Kingdom of the Two Sicilies.

But Garibaldi had neither royal blood nor the desire to be king. In September, Garibaldi met Sardinia-Piedmont's King Victor Emanuel for the famous "Handshake of Teano" and handed over his conquered Kingdom of the Two Sicilies to him. King Victor Emanuel would soon reign over a newly reunited Italy.

The Kingdom of Italy and the Third War of Italian Independence

In the following year, 1861, Garibaldi's Two Sicilies held a plebiscite (a referendum, or a free democratic vote) to decide whether or not to unite with Victor Emanuel's Kingdom of Sardinia-Piedmont (which now included Lombardy and Tuscany as well). The proposed new **Kingdom of Italy** would be a constitutional monarchy, and would use the same constitution King Victor's father Charles Albert had granted during the Revolution of 1848. This constitution, known as the *Statuto Albertino*, granted its kings a great deal of power, and it was certainly not the kind of republican constitution that Young Italy's Mazzini wanted. It did, however, include representation for Italy's people in its two-chamber parliament: the people would elect representatives to the lower house, while the king would appoint the members of the upper house.

This was enough for Italy's revolutionaries. Garibaldi was content to hand the Two Sicilies over to King

Victor Emanuel at the "Handshake of Teano," on the road between Rome and Naples (see picture). The people of the Two Sicilies soon voted to unite with Sardinia-Piedmont.

The new kingdom officially came into being on March 17, 1861. The Kingdom of Italy wasn't everything Young Italy had wanted, but it was at least an independent and (nearly) united Italy.

The job of unifying Italy wasn't quite finished in 1861, because two important areas still remained under foreign control: Austria still held Venice, and France still helped the popes defend the last vestiges of the Papal States.

The militant German state of Prussia helped the new Kingdom of Italy sort out these last details. In the 1866 **Third War of Italian independence**, Italy allied with Prussia to drive the Austrians out of Venetia at last. And in 1870, the Franco-Prussian War drew France's attention away from its defense of the remaining Papal States, and the **Kingdom of Italy finally captured Rome**.

After enduring for 1100 years in one form or another, the Papal States came to their final end; and the Kingdom of Italy moved its seat of government into Italy's ancient capital, the city of Rome. The *Risorgimento*, which had begun with the Carbonari around 1810, ended in 1870 with a united and independent Italy.

THE RISE OF FASCISM

Italy Joins the Triple Alliance

After *Il Risorgimento*, Italy's goals changed. Victor Emanuel's son and successor, King Umberto I (see picture), concerned himself less with Italian unity and more with the creation of an Italian Empire. Umberto wanted to expand Italy by adding more territories on the Balkan Peninsula, across the Adriatic Sea; at the time, those territories were only loosely held by the crumbling Ottoman Empire, the "Sick Man of Europe" (see Chapter 10). He also wanted to build Italy's wealth by colonizing Ethiopia and Libya. Italy was preparing to join the Scramble for Africa (see Chapter 11); but before it did, Umberto wanted to join a defensive alliance to protect his nation from outside attack while its armies were away invading Africa.

In 1882, the Kingdom of Italy joined with the German Empire and Italy's former enemy, the Empire of Austria-Hungary, to form the **Triple Alliance**.

FASCINATING FACTS: The Triple Alliance

The Triple Alliance was a mutual defense agreement in which each of the three members agreed to defend the others if any of them came under attack. Ironically, the nation that had just spent 60 years stamping out imperialism was now joining an organization designed to preserve and enlarge empires.

Italy's alliance with Austria-Hungary did not sit well with all Italians. Some nationalists still believed that Italy's unity was incomplete, and that territories like Austrian-held Dalmatia (on the opposite coast of the Adriatic Sea) rightfully belonged to Italy. Furthermore, Umberto was an unpopular king, and some believed that he oppressed poor Italians as much as the Austrians had. King Umberto I became one of the heads of state who was assassinated by anarchists around the turn of the 20th Century (U.S. President William McKinley was another).

Italy During World War I

Umberto I's son and successor was King Victor Emanuel III. When World War I broke out in 1914, Germany and Austria-Hungary expected Victor Emanuel to act on Italy's agreement and join in the defense of the Triple Alliance.

By 1914, however, that alliance was no longer to Italy's advantage. Turning against the alliance made more sense: By turning against the Triple Alliance, Italy could hope to gain Austrian-held territories to the north, territories Italy's nationalists still wanted. Then the Ottoman Empire joined the war on the side of the Triple Alliance, giving Italy even more reason to turn against the Alliance: if the Allies defeated the Triple Alliance, then Italy could also hope to gain Ottoman-held territories on the Balkan Peninsula.

FASCINATING FACTS: The London Pact

Italy had one more reason to turn against the Triple Alliance: encouragement from Britain. Britain's diplomats worked busily in Italy, Egypt and elsewhere to make sure that the Triple Alliance had as little support as possible. In April 1915, less than a year after the war broke out, Italy and Britain signed the secret London Pact, in which Italy agreed to declare war on Austria-Hungary and Germany in exchange for control of a long list of territories after the war. Italy's nationalists saw World War I as a chance to reclaim the *irredenta*, Austrian- and Ottoman-held territories that the nationalists believed rightfully belonged to Italy.

A Miserable War

World War I was nearly as miserable for Italy as it was for Britain and Germany. From 1915-1917, Italy made little or no progress in its invasion of Austria-Hungary, and suffered terrible losses for no gain. However, Italy's efforts did relieve pressure on the rest of the Allies by drawing German and Austrian forces away from the Western Front.

In late 1918, as Austria-Hungary began to crumble, Italy finally broke through Austria's lines. Italian armies were able to occupy much of the Austrian territory Italy wanted to claim before the November 11 armistice ended the war.

Italia - Classe 1888 soldati della I Guerra mondiale

Disappointment at Versailles

Therefore the Italians were bitterly disappointed with the 1919 Treaty of Versailles, which didn't allow them to keep those hard-won territories. The Allies had several reasons for denying Italy's territorial desires:

1. Italy was a former ally of militant Germany and Austria-Hungary, the two empires that bore the blame (in the world's eyes, if not in their own) for starting the war. France and Britain considered Italy untrustworthy.
2. Italy had delayed declaring war on Austria for nearly a year, and did not declare war on Germany until 1916. France and Britain had lost countless soldiers early in the war while they waited for Italy to come to their aid.
3. Italy's territorial desires clashed with U.S. President Woodrow Wilson's Fourteen Points plan, which was to allow as many territories as possible to decide their own national loyalties after the war.

But what about the **London Pact**, in which the British promised those territories to Italy? <u>The Allies chose to ignore it</u>. World War I had turned out to be far longer and far worse than anyone had expected, and the entry of the United States and so many other nations altered prior agreements. Britain had not won the war on its own, and therefore could not honor the London Pact on its own. President Wilson's goal was to eliminate empires, not to help Italy build a new one.

> In the end, Italy gained only a fraction of the *irredenta* territories it had hoped to reclaim. Needless to say, the Allies' decision was highly unpopular with Italy's nationalists.

The Rise of Fascism and the March on Rome

The Italian leaders who stood by while Italy lost all of that territory were also unpopular. Italy's Prime Minister Vittorio Orlando, who was present at Versailles for most of the negotiations, resigned his post five days before the signing of the Treaty of Versailles. Discontent with Italy's government soon led to the rise of a new political party, Benito Mussolini's Fascist Party.

DEFINITIONS: Fascism and the Blackshirts

The **Fasces** was a symbol of the ancient Roman Empire, akin to a modern-day national flag. The Roman Fasces was a cylindrical bundle of birch rods with an axe head emerging from the center. The bound rods symbolized the strength that comes from unity, and the axe head signified dominion and the power to decide life or death.

In the Italian language, *fasces* came to mean "bundle" (like the bundle of birch rods) or "league." Soon after World War I, Benito Mussolini founded the *Fasci di Combattimento* ("Combat League") to promote his political aims:

1. A strong and united Italy that would reclaim its lost territories (the *irredenta*);
2. Extreme national pride;
3. Militarism;
4. An all-powerful government that would manage Italy's affairs properly; and
5. Strict censorship and repression (control) of political enemies.

The Combat League was a collection of militia units that became known as the **"Blackshirts."** The Blackshirts modeled their uniforms after the *Arditi*, elite units of the Italian military. The Blackshirts had no real legal authority; but in Mussolini's eyes, they were necessary to maintain order when the Italian government failed to do so. Mussolini used the Blackshirts to end strikes by labor unions, which he hated. By 1921, Mussolini transformed the Combat League into a political party, the **National Fascist Party**, and the new party began supporting candidates in Italy's elections.

During World War II, **"fascism"** came into the English language as a term for any government that resembled Mussolini's or Adolf Hitler's. "Fascism" can refer to extreme national pride or racist pride. It can refer to totalitarianism, government by an absolute dictator who promotes nationalist pride and racism. It can also refer to attacking political enemies by using highly biased propaganda. When one person calls another a "fascist," he is comparing that person to Mussolini or Hitler. Such comparisons are rarely intended as compliments.

Mussolini took advantage of the Italian people's disappointment with their government to take control of Italy. During the week of October 22-28, 1922, Mussolini's Fascist Party organized a **March on Rome**. Mussolini remained behind in Naples, perhaps because he feared arrest. When the Fascists arrived in Rome, they demanded that King Victor Emanuel III fire the prime minister of his government and replace him with Mussolini.

For some reason, the King agreed. He certainly had the power to refuse: the King's armies far outnumbered the Blackshirt squads that were taking up key military positions all over the country. But the King didn't want to start a civil war, so he refused to call out his armies. The King may have sympathized with Mussolini's goals, or he may merely have preferred the Fascists to Italy's other major political parties. Whatever his motives, **on October 28, 1922, King Victor Emanuel III elevated Benito Mussolini to the post of Italian Prime Minister**.

In light of what followed, most people would agree that this was a mistake.

DASTARDLY DICTATORS: Benito Mussolini (*Il Duce*, 1883 – 1945)

Benito Mussolini was a soldier and politician who rose to power as Italy's Prime Minister and ruled Italy as a dictator, even though Italy still had a king. Mussolini created Italian Fascism and became its dominant figure.

Mussolini's parents named him for Mexican revolutionary Benito Juarez (see Chapter 17). Like his namesake, Mussolini would become a successful revolutionary. A talented scholar and writer, Mussolini studied the writings of socialist, atheist political philosophers like Karl Marx and Friedrich Nietzsche. He wrote and edited for Italy's leading socialist newspaper, *Avanti!*, and became a prominent Italian socialist.

Mussolini on the March to Rome

However, Mussolini broke with the socialists over World War I. Italy's Socialist Party opposed Italy's involvement in the war, but Mussolini joined the Italian nationalists who wanted to reclaim the *irredenta*. World War I marked a major shift for Mussolini: he abandoned the socialists, who supposedly fought to eliminate class distinctions and elevate the poor, and instead joined the militant nationalists, who fought for national pride.

After World War I, Mussolini formed the Blackshirts, a collection of militia groups that would develop into the National Fascist Party (Adolf Hitler's Brownshirts were modeled on Mussolini's Blackshirts). In 1921, 36 of Mussolini's Fascist Party members won election to government councils. Mussolini became the Fascist Party's *Il Duce,* "the Boss."

World War I left Italy's economy in chaos and its government deeply in debt. Poverty was everywhere, and labor strikes became common. Mussolini hated labor unions and their strikes because they interfered with strong, authoritarian government. During a widespread general strike in 1922, Mussolini and the Fascists decided to take advantage of the chaos with a March on Rome to highlight the government's incompetence. When the Fascists arrived in Rome, they demanded the Prime Minister's job for Mussolini, and King Victor Emanuel III complied.

As prime minister, Mussolini set about recreating the Italian government as a dictatorship. Through the **Acerbo Law**, he made certain that Fascist party members could gain a 2/3 majority in the parliament by winning just 25% of the popular vote. This Fascist majority meant that the King couldn't remove Mussolini as Prime Minister. With that assurance in place, Mussolini proceeded to turn Italy into a police state. His Blackshirts ruled the streets under martial law. He assumed personal control of several government ministries, and his government took over the operations of Italy's formerly private industries. He personally chose the nation's newspaper editors and censored what they published. He banned all other political parties in 1928.

As an authoritarian dictator, Mussolini was the natural ally of other authoritarians like Spain's General Franco and Germany's Chancellor Hitler. Just before World War II broke out, Mussolini allied with Hitler in the Pact of Steel, in which Italy and Germany agreed to cooperate with one another and to defend one another. Hitler also encouraged Mussolini to adopt a German-written Manifesto of Race that stripped Italian Jews of their citizenship.

But Italy's military was not prepared for the war that Hitler unleashed. During World War II, Mussolini tried to build his empire in the Balkans and in North Africa, but Italy's military and industry simply weren't up to the task. The war was so disastrous for Italy that Mussolini's supporters quickly deserted him. By July, 1943, the Allies were preparing to invade Sicily and launch a major offensive against Italy in World War II's Italian Campaign. As Allied bombs began to fall on Rome, King Victor Emanuel dismissed Mussolini as Prime Minister and had him arrested. The King's government of southern Italy ended up turning against Germany and fighting with the Allies for the remainder of the war.

Hitler wasn't finished with Mussolini. In September, 1943, German paratroopers rescued Mussolini from the mountaintop resort where the King had imprisoned him. With Hitler's backing, Mussolini established the new Italian Social Republic in northern Italy to oppose the King's forces in southern Italy. But Mussolini seemed to understand what Hitler didn't: that Fascism was finished.

When the western Allies invaded Germany near the end of World War II in 1944, they spared Mussolini for a time by invading through France (at Normandy) instead of Italy. In April 1945, as Germany began to collapse, Mussolini and his mistress tried to flee Italy and take refuge in neutral Switzerland. They never made it. A band of Italian "partisans" (the King's soldiers) caught Mussolini and executed him on April 27-28, 1945.

FASCINATING FACTS: What About the Trains?

The popular saying that "Mussolini made the trains run on time" may have come from the March on Rome. Mussolini didn't lead the March on Rome personally, but remained behind in Naples. When the March reached Rome and the King agreed to the Fascists' demands, Mussolini wasn't there. The King sent Mussolini a telegram requesting his presence so that he could make him Prime Minister, and Mussolini boarded a train. Supposedly, Mussolini told this train's conductor that it was absolutely essential for his train to arrive "on time."

Most people use this phrase to comment on Mussolini's government, not on this one train ride. Some interpret it positively, suggesting that even though Mussolini was a repressive dictator, at least his methods led to an efficient government that "made the trains run on time." Others interpret it sarcastically, suggesting that no amount of railroad efficiency could possibly justify Mussolini's brutal repression of his enemies.

WORLD GEOGRAPHY FOCUS

FASCINATING FACTS: Vatican City

In 1870, the conclusion of the *Risorgimento* brought about the end of central Italy's Papal States. Rome became the capital of King Victor Emanuel II's government, and the popes lost their authority over Rome and the surrounding territories. Nevertheless, the popes had to remain in Rome as the chief priests of Rome's Holy See. Pope Pius IX said that he felt like a prisoner in Rome after the Italian government took over the city. 1870 was the first year of a 50-year feud between the Italian government and the popes.

Ironically, it was the atheistic Benito Mussolini who brought an end to that feud. Although *Il Duce* was no Roman Catholic, he appreciated the popes' enormous influence over hundreds of millions of Catholics worldwide. He decided to seek favor with those Catholics by making the popes happy.

In the 1929 *Lateran Treaty*, Mussolini created an independent state for the popes within the City of Rome called the **"State of Vatican City."** Within Vatican City's walls, the popes would rule just like secular kings. Vatican City became the Catholic Church's inviolate enclave, where no other authority could command.

Interesting facts about Vatican City:
- Its area is about 110 acres. About half of this area is covered with gardens.
- Its population is about 800.

- The members of the popes' small guard unit, the Pontifical Swiss Guard, are recruited from Switzerland.
- Its many buildings include churches, palaces, museums and a vast library containing the church's very oldest Christian manuscripts.
- St. Peter's Basilica, Catholicism's holiest church, lies on St. Peter's Square within Vatican City.
- The Sistine Chapel, which includes Michelangelo's best-known paintings on its grand ceiling, lies inside the popes' Apostolic Palace, near St. Peter's Square.

FASCINATING FACTS: Black Smoke, White Smoke

Whenever a pope dies, the Roman Catholic Church's College of Cardinals meets in the Sistine Chapel to elect the next pope. The selection process is secretive. The cardinals spend time in prayer before and during their meetings, and rules prohibit them from discussing the selection of the pope with the outside world. The politics of man are not supposed to enter their thoughts; the new pope is supposed to be God's choice, not man's.

Despite all of this solemn secrecy, Roman Catholics around the world still want to know what's going on inside the Sistine Chapel. In order to appease them, the cardinals provide tantalizing hints using the smoke emanating from the Sistine Chapel's chimney. Throughout their deliberations, they burn chemicals to create black smoke. When they've made their decision, the cardinals bind together all of their ballots and notes and throw them into the fire, together with a chemical that creates white smoke. When the outside world sees the white smoke, it knows that the voting is over. Soon after the white smoke appears, the chief cardinal emerges to announce "*Habemus papam*!" ("We have a pope!").

EGYPT
(Continued from Chapter 2)

FROM OTTOMAN EMPIRE TO BRITISH EMPIRE

The Khedivate of Egypt

Egypt's Muhammad Ali Pasha won near-independence from the Ottoman Empire in 1840 (see Chapter 2). Throughout the 1800s, however, Egypt remained part of the struggling Ottoman Empire and continued to make tribute payments to the Ottoman sultans. By increasing those tribute payments, Ismail Pasha became the first Egyptian *wali* (governor) whom the Ottoman sultans officially allowed to claim the title *Khedive*, or "Lord," of Egypt.

Khedive Ismail and his son and successor, Khedive Tewfik, were friendly with Europeans in general, and with the British in particular. Both grew up in European schools, and sometimes considered themselves more European than

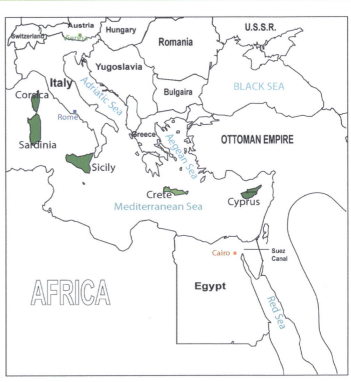

African. Their loyalty to the Ottoman Empire was minimal. Like the Persian shahs of the late 1800s, they wanted to modernize their nation with the help of Western technology and Western investment money (see Chapter 16). And like the shahs, they faced rebellions at home from nationalists who resented foreign interference in their affairs.

The British Take Over

Unfortunately, Egypt's economy could not keep up with its khedives' spending. Khedive Ismail (see picture) spent so much money buying shares of the Suez Canal Company and pursuing war against Ethiopia that his government was unable to make its debt payments. These debts, financed largely by British bankers, resulted in a gradual British takeover of Egypt:

1. In 1875, Ismail sold Egypt's shares of the Suez Canal Company to the British government. The price he received, about 4 million British pounds, was nowhere near enough to cover his debts.
2. In 1878, Britain took over part of Ismail's government so that Britain could manage Egypt's finances (and recover the money its bankers had loaned). Nationalist Egyptians believed that Ismail was far too friendly with Britain, and were furious that he had surrendered control of Egypt so easily. Under the leadership of Ahmed Urabi, the nationalists rebelled against Ismail.
3. In 1879, at the urging of the British, Ottoman Sultan Abdulhamid II deposed Ismail and made Ismail's son, Tewfik, Khedive of Egypt. The British protected Khedive Tewfik from the Urabi Rebellion, even as Urabi took control over most of Egypt.
4. In the 1882 Battle of Tel el-Kebir, a British expeditionary force defeated the Urabi Rebellion. **British troops began a long-term occupation of Egypt** in order to 1) maintain control over the Suez Canal and 2) insure that Egypt would repay its debts.

Khedive Tewfik (see picture at left) died suddenly at the age of 39, leaving his 17-year-old son Abbas to become Khedive Abbas II in 1889. Abbas II (see picture at right) inherited a British-occupied Egypt. But the new Khedive was less friendly with the British than his predecessors had been, and more supportive of the nationalists who wanted the British out of Egypt. The British eyed Abbas II warily.

The 1914 outbreak of World War I was a crisis for Britain. The Ottoman Empire joined the Central Powers against Britain and her Allies, and Egypt was still at least loosely aligned with the Ottomans. The British feared that if a rebellious Egypt turned against them in the middle of a desperate war, they might lose the all-important Suez Canal and all of their investments in Egypt.

The Sultanate of Egypt

As it happened, Abbas II was near Constantinople recovering from an assassination attempt when WWI broke out. The British took advantage of this opportunity to rearrange matters in Egypt.

In late 1914, Great Britain accused Abbas II of turning against them and siding with the Ottomans. For this, they deposed him.

They also declared that Egypt would no longer be part of the Ottoman Empire. In the place of the Khedivate of Egypt, they established the new Sultanate of Egypt and made it a Protectorate of Great Britain.

Egypt was no longer a part of the Ottoman Empire. Hussein Kamel, Abbas II's uncle, became Egypt's first sultan. Three years later, Sultan Kamel died, and his brother Ahmed Fuad took his place as Sultan of Egypt.

THE QUEST FOR INDEPENDENCE

The *Wafd* and the Egyptian Revolution of 1919

As soon as WWI ended, the issue of Egyptian independence resurfaced. In late 1918, Egyptian nationalists led by Saad Zaghloul formed a *Wafd* ("Delegation") to demand the end of British occupation. Saad and his delegation wanted to make these demands in London and at Versailles, where the Treaty of Versailles was being negotiated and where the Allies were deciding major changes of territory all over Europe. Britain refused to allow this. When the *Wafd* continued to protest, the British exiled Saad and his delegation on the Island of Malta in the middle of the Mediterranean Sea.

The Egyptian people didn't take kindly to the banishment of their nationalist heroes. Throughout the spring and summer of 1919, nationalist Egyptians demonstrated against British occupation and rioted in the streets (the picture is of Egyptian Muslim women demonstrating in the streets). The British tried to suppress the Egyptian Revolution of 1919 using the same violent methods they would later use in India (see Chapter 19), but the riots continued.

Independence and the Kingdom of Egypt

So the British resorted to diplomacy. Over the next two years, negotiations alternated with riots as the British hammered out an agreement with the *Wafd* that led to independence for Egypt.

> On February 28, 1922, Britain formally granted Egypt its independence. **Egypt became an independent constitutional monarchy with a king and a parliament of its own**.

Sultan Fuad changed his title and became King Fuad. The new Parliament began work on Egypt's new constitution, which it would adopt in 1923.

Most members of Egypt's new Parliament were also members of Saad Zaghloul's *Wafd* Party. As the leaders of the Revolution and of the negotiations for independence, *Wafd* Party members had become Egypt's most popular and powerful politicians. In the decades to come, Egypt's King Fuad and his successor King Farouk would battle the *Wafd* Party for control of Egypt.

They would also battle Britain.

> **Although formal independence was a big step, it did not stop the British occupation of Egypt.**

Britain did not agree to withdraw its troops until it signed the Anglo-Egyptian Treaty of 1936; and even after that agreement, British troops continued to control the Suez Canal Zone until the Suez Crisis in 1956.

> ### FASCINATING FACTS: The Fez
>
> A *fez* is a cylindrical, flat-topped, tasseled hat made of red felt. The hat took its name from the city of Fez in Morocco, North Africa, where it first appeared. It is also known as a tarboosh. The Fez became common attire for Muslim men during the era of the Ottoman Empire.

MISSIONARY FOCUS

GIANTS OF THE FAITH: Lillian Trasher (1887 – 1961)

Lillian Trasher was a Pentecostal Christian from Georgia, USA. In 1910, two weeks before she was to be married, she attended a presentation by a missionary to India. As soon as she heard the missionary speak, she knew that the Lord was calling her to overseas missions as well. When she discussed the Lord's call with her fiancé, she found that he was unwilling to join her; so she broke off their engagement. As she continually asked the Lord in prayer where to go, she was struck by this verse:

"I have seen, I have seen the affliction of my people which is in Egypt, and I have heard their groaning, and am come down to deliver them. And now come, I will send you into Egypt." –Acts 7:34

In that same year, Lillian and her sister sailed for Egypt. She had no money other than what she had earned by selling her meager possessions, and no long-term plans for financial support. Her only plan was to trust the Lord to meet her needs and to show her what to do. The Lord led her to Asyut, Egypt, about 200 miles south of Cairo on the Nile River.

Soon after Lillian arrived in Asyut, she was called to the bedside of the dying mother of a young child. After the mother died, Lillian learned that the baby's grandmother intended to throw the unwanted orphan into the Nile River. Lillian couldn't allow that. Instead, she took the child in herself. That child, a baby girl Lillian named Fareida, was the first of thousands of orphans Lillian would shelter at Asyut's Lillian Trasher Orphanage.

Because she still lacked any outside financial support, Lillian was forced to ride around on a donkey begging food from her neighbors to feed her orphans. More than once, her requests brought her more orphans instead of food. She never turned a child away. The people of Asyut knew her as the "Lady on a Donkey" or the "Mother of the Nile."

In 1914, her work caught the attention of the mission-minded Assemblies of God churches in the USA, and they began to support her work. Her orphanage grew to house 50, then 300, then finally 1,200 orphans and widows near the end of her life. During the USA's Great Depression, her American support dried up for a time, but God continued to provide and Lillian's orphanage continued to increase in size.

Lillian Trasher served the Lord in Egypt for fifty years. She died in 1961, but her orphanage still operates today.

U.S. GEOGRAPHY FOCUS

FASCINATING FACTS about MONTANA:

- Statehood: Montana became the 41st US state on November 8, 1889.
- Bordering states/country: Idaho, North Dakota, South Dakota, Wyoming and Canada
- State capital: Helena
- Area: 147,040 sq. mi (Ranks 4th in size)
- Abbreviation: MT
- State nickname: "Treasure State"
- State bird: Western Meadowlark
- State tree: Ponderosa Pine
- State flower: Bitterroot
- State song: *Montana*
- State Motto: "Gold and Silver"
- Meaning of name: from the Spanish word for "mountainous"
- Historic places to visit in Montana: Glacier National Park, the Rocky Mountains, Rocky Mountain Front Eagle Migration Area, Bowdoin National Wildlife Refuge, Flathead Lake, Yellowstone National Park, Glacier National Park, National Bison Range, Charles M. Russell Museum Complex, Museum of the Rockies, Little Bighorn Battlefield National Monument
- Resources and Industries: farming (sugar beets, cattle, wheat, barley), mining (gold, silver, copper and coal), oil, forestry and paper making, food processing, tourism

Pompeys Pillar National Monument in Montana

Flag of Montana
- Montana adopted this flag in 1905.
- The flag has a blue field with the state seal in the center and "MONTANA" written in bold yellow letters across the top.
- The state seal features (1) the state motto (*Oro et Plata*, "Gold and Silver"), (2) a mountain lake scene, and (3) a pick, shovel and plow to represent mining and farming.

Chapter 22

Nationalism and Communism in China, Japan in Manchuria

WORLD HISTORY FOCUS

NATIONALISM AND COMMUNISM IN CHINA
(See Chapter 13 for China's Collisions with the West)

The Qing Dynasty After the Boxer Rebellion

After China's humiliating defeat at the hands of the Western powers in the 1898 - 1900 Boxer Rebellion, Empress Dowager Cixi remained in power by giving in to the Western powers' demands. Among other things, she allowed Chinese students to receive Western educations overseas again, and she banned the archaic Chinese practice of foot binding.

These efforts preserved Cixi's personal rule, but not her dynasty's. Cixi had manipulated the Qing emperors quietly, from "behind the curtain," for over forty years; and the weakened Qing Dynasty was finally suffocating in her grasp.

In 1898, Cixi had placed her nephew, the Guangxu Emperor, under house arrest for trying to reform the Qing government without her permission (in the Hundred Days' Reform). He was still under house arrest in 1908, when Cixi's health began to fail. **One day before Cixi died, the Guangxu Emperor also mysteriously died.** No one knows who killed him, but one popular theory is that Cixi ordered his murder in a final act of revenge so that he could never reclaim his throne. Before she died, Cixi named the Guangxu Emperor's not-quite-3-year-old nephew, Puyi, as the Qing Dynasty's next emperor. Because Puyi was underage, a regent would rule in his place.

After Cixi's death in 1908, China was ripe for revolution. The Qing Dynasty teetered on the brink of collapse because

1. It lacked a strong emperor,
2. It was a minority Manchu dynasty in a majority Han China, and
3. The dynasty's many failures had convinced most Chinese that it had lost the "Mandate of Heaven," or the right to rule China by virtue of its moral superiority.

The Chinese Revolution of 1911 (aká the Xinhai Revolution or the Sichuan Revolution)

Revolution had already been brewing in China since around 1894, when a revolutionary named Sun Yat-sen established the Revive China Society. Sun Yat-sen and his followers wanted to eject the Manchu Qings, restore China's majority Han government and establish a representative republic in China. In 1905, the Revive China Society combined with other revolutionary groups to form the **Tongmenghui** (aka the Revolutionary Alliance), a secret revolutionary society that recruited soldiers from within the Qing Dynasty's armies.

The spark for the **Chinese Revolution** came in May

1911, when the Qing government announced that it was taking over (nationalizing) all of China's railroads. Two of those railroads, including the one that ran through the Province of Sichuan, were funded by private investors. These investors stood to lose all of their investment money if the government confiscated their railroads; so they established the Sichuan Railroad Protection Society to resist the government takeover of their property.

The Qing governor of Sichuan Province responded to the Sichuan Railroad Protection Society's protests by arresting its leader and making membership in the Society illegal. The governor expected the Society to respond to his decisive action by surrendering meekly; but instead, the Society staged a large, angry protest against the arrests of its leaders. Faced with a large crowd of protesters, the governor decided to assert his authority even more forcefully. This time, he ordered his troops to fire their weapons into the crowd. His attack killed several Railroad Protection Society demonstrators– which only escalated the public's anger against the Qing government even more.

The *Tongmenghui* took advantage of that anger: *Tongmenghui* leaders used public outrage over the killings to inspire a general revolution against the Qing Dynasty. As the revolution spread, the *Tongmenghui* encouraged all of the southern Chinese provinces around Sichuan to vent their anger by declaring independence from the Qing government.

One by one, they began to do so. **By late 1911, every Chinese province south of the Yangtze River had declared independence from the Qing Dynasty government, and was at least loosely part of the *Tongmenghui*'s new Republic of China.** The president of that republic, which came into being on January 1, 1912, was Sun Yat-sen.

INTERESTING INDIVIDUALS: Sun Yat-sen (1866 – 1925)

Sun Yat-sen was a medical doctor and a highly respected leader of the Chinese Revolution of 1911. Dr. Sun promoted the overthrow of the Qing Dynasty and created the philosophy that underpinned the new Republic of China. Chinese people on both Taiwan and the mainland remember him as the "Father of the Nation."

As a young man, Sun was dismayed by the Chinese people's dependence upon opium and by China's weakness against the foreigners who occupied its "treaty ports." While living in Hawaii, he received training in the modern schools of the West, and learned to admire what the West had achieved. **Sun wanted the Chinese people to have what the people of the West had: representative government, liberty and modern technology. However, Sun was also a strong Chinese nationalist: He wanted China to remain independent and protected against foreign occupation.**

In 1894, Dr. Sun founded the Revive China Society to promote a Han-led republican government in China. A year later, the Revive China Society attempted a military coup to overthrow the Qings. When the coup failed, Dr. Sun became a wanted man in China, and had to leave his home for a life in exile. For the next 15 years, he lived overseas in Japan, England and the USA, trying to promote a revolution against the Qings and a new government for China. Over time, he developed the Three Principles of the People that he hoped would guide that new government:

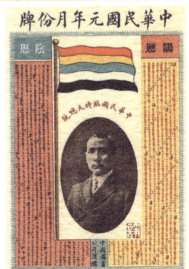

1) *Minzu*, Chinese nationalism that would unite all Chinese and make China independent of foreign empires;
2) *Minquan*, a government with democratically elected representatives; and
3) *Minsheng*, a new form of Chinese socialism which would ensure that every Chinese worker could find a job and support himself and his family.

During the Chinese Revolution of 1911, Sun Yat-sen returned to China and quickly won election as President of the new Republic of China (picture commemorates Sun Yat-sen as

President). At the time, this new Republic controlled southern China only loosely, and northern China not at all. President Sun held office only briefly: In order to strengthen the Republic and overthrow the Qing Dynasty at last, Dr. Sun sacrificed his position as President and turned the Republic over to Yuan Shikai, the Qing government's Prime Minister. Yuan Shikai took Dr. Sun's place as president, turned against the Qing Dynasty and forced the six-year-old Emperor Puyi to abdicate his throne in early 1912.

Unfortunately, Yuan Shikai turned out to be little better than the Qing Dynasty he replaced. When Yuan declared himself Emperor in 1915, Dr. Sun and most of China turned against him. China fell into a time of chaos known as the Chinese Warlord Era: part of the Qing Dynastys' former army, the Beiyang Army, governed in the north, while former Beiyang generals became regional warlords over the provinces of the south.

Still fighting for his vision of a republican government for China, Dr. Sun set up his own military government in the southern province of Guangdong. By now, he was convinced that the only hope for a republican government in China was for his military government to march into the North and overthrow the Beiyang Army and the other warlords. In preparation for this "Northern Expedition," he established a military school in the Guangdong Province city of Guangzhou (Canton). His school's commandant was an experienced soldier named Chiang Kai-shek.

Dr. Sun spent the rest of his life building up his forces and planning his Northern Expedition, but he didn't live to see the expedition through. His health turned against him, and he died of liver cancer in 1925.

Dr. Sun's Three Principles of the People are immortalized in the national anthem of the Republic of China, which still governs modern-day Taiwan.

The Kuomintang (KMT) and the Chinese Warlord Era

After Sun Yat-sen turned leadership of the Republic of China over to Yuan Shikai (see picture), his *Tongmenghui* combined with other revolutionary groups to form a new political party known as the **Kuomintang (KMT)**. The KMT's purpose was to support good candidates for election to the Republic's new national legislature. The KMT won a majority of the seats in that legislature's first national election in late 1912.

Unfortunately, Yuan Shikai paid little attention to the new legislature's demands. He dismissed the legislature in 1914, then declared himself Emperor in 1915. He also outlawed membership in the KMT, and most KMT members had to run for their lives. While Yuan Shikai lived, KMT members remained in exile overseas or in treaty ports like Shanghai, where Yuan Shikai's law didn't apply.

Yuan Shikai died in 1916, and his former generals became warlords all over a divided China. **This time of chaos in China, from 1916 - 1928, became known as the Chinese Warlord Era.**

In 1920, Sun Yat-sen managed to revive the KMT in southern China's Guangdong Province. He established a military government in the city of Guangzhou (Canton). There, Dr. Sun laid his plans to overthrow the warlords and the remnants of dead Yuan Shikai's government in northern China (the Beiyang government). He opened a military school where he trained the KMT's army, preparing it for a "Northern Expedition" to unseat the warlords. But before he could bring his Northern Expedition plans to fruition, Sun Yat-sen died of liver cancer in 1925.

It was during Sun Yat-sen's last years that China's northern neighbor, the USSR, began to sow the seeds of USSR-style communism in China.

FASCINATING FACTS: The Comintern (Communist International)

In 1919, while the Bolshevik Party was transforming the former Russian Empire into the new USSR, communist leaders were divided on an important issue. Vladimir Lenin and others believed that their communist revolution would soon fall to attacks from Western capitalist nations unless they immediately promoted similar communist revolutions in nations all over the world. Josef Stalin leaned toward the opposite view, that they should focus on perfecting communism in the USSR before they moved on to other nations.

While Lenin lived, his view prevailed. In 1919, communists from around the world gathered in Moscow for the first meeting of the Communist International, also known as the *Comintern*. The Comintern was assigned the task of promoting communist revolutions worldwide.

Lenin was aware of Sun Yat-sen, and believed that Dr. Sun's *Minsheng* socialism was similar to his own socialist/communist philosophy. In 1923, Comintern agents moved into China on a mission to remake the Kuomintang (KMT) as a new Chinese Communist Party.

As the head of Dr. Sun's military school and the leader of his army, Chiang Kai-shek was able to overcome other contenders to become the new leader of the KMT after Dr. Sun's death. Chiang Kai-shek was neither a communist nor a socialist, but rather a strong Chinese nationalist.

INTERESTING INDIVIDUAL: Chiang Kai-shek (1887 – 1975) and the Northern Expedition

Chiang Kai-shek was Sun Yat-sen's successor as leader of the Kuomintang. Chiang led the Northern Expedition and reunited China in 1926 - 1928, only to see his beloved China and the Kuomintang divided yet again in a battle between nationalists (like himself) and Russian-influenced communists (like Mao Tse-tung).

Young Chiang Kai-shek was attending a Japanese military school in 1907 when exiled Chinese revolutionaries won him over to the cause of the Chinese Revolution. As a member of the Kuomintang, Chiang won special favor with Sun Yat-sen by rescuing him from an assassination attempt in 1923. Dr. Sun hired Chiang as commandant of the Whampoa Military Academy, the soldiers' school he established to prepare for the Northern Expedition.

Soon after the Comintern began advising and supplying the Kuomintang in 1923, Dr. Sun sent Chiang to Russia to see what he could learn from Russian military and political advisers. Chiang admired the Russian military, but quickly decided that communism would not do for China. **For the rest of his life, he opposed China's growing Communist Party**. Nevertheless, the Kuomintang needed all of the help it could get, so Chiang accepted USSR and Comintern aid to supply the Northern Expedition.

THE NORTHERN EXPEDITION:

The Northern Expedition began in July, 1926. **In less than a year, Chiang's Kuomintang army swept through China and defeated most of its warlord enemies. Almost immediately, however, Chiang began having trouble with communist members of the KMT, who were trained and heavily influenced by the Comintern.** When the communists moved into a conquered province, they immediately acted on their Comintern training by "nationalizing" farms and businesses, bringing them under communist party control. Against Chiang's will, the KMT's mission to reunite China was turning into a communist revolution.

When he was unable to control the communists, Chiang decided to eliminate them. In April 1927, Chiang ordered a major purge of the KMT's Chinese communists, especially those in the treaty port of Shanghai (picture shows communist prisoners being rounded up by the KMT).

The KMT called Chiang's communist purge the "Great Purge," but communists called it the "Shanghai Massacre" or the "White Terror." Chiang rounded up and either imprisoned or killed a great number of his former allies, the Chinese communists. His brutal methods left the KMT ashamed and divided. Some KMT members were angry with Chiang over the purge, and formed a new and separate branch of the KMT. However, when Chiang's KMT enemies learned that the Russian-led communists were planning to take over their branch of the KMT, they reunited with Chiang.

Reunited or not, the KMT was powerless to prevent the Japanese invasions of China in the years before World War II. As Chiang's KMT grew weaker, it grew more vulnerable to the communist attacks that came after that war.

** See Chapter 29 for more on Chiang Kai-shek **

The Chinese Civil War (1927 – 1949)

Chiang Kai-shek's 1927 Great Purge was only the beginning of a long-running war between Chiang's KMT nationalists and Russian-influenced Chinese communists. This war was called the **Chinese Civil War**, and Chiang's primary communist opponent was Mao Tse-tung (see Chapter 29 for more on Mao Tse-tung).

Mao's strategy for rebuilding the Communist Party after the Great Purge was to retreat to the rural areas of southeast China, where he would educate Chinese peasants in communism and build a new communist nation. With help from the USSR, Mao succeeded in winning the hearts of the Chinese peasants. In 1931, Mao was able to establish the new Chinese Soviet Republic (CSR), a small collection of communist Chinese provinces.

The Encirclement Campaigns

Mao's communist communities grew and thrived– that is, until their success drew the attention of the communist-hating Chiang Kai-shek. Even before Mao founded the CSR in 1931, Chiang launched a series of **encirclement campaigns** to wipe out Mao's communist guerrilla armies. Chiang's first four encirclement campaigns all failed, largely because Chiang had trouble organizing his armies.

Chiang's Fifth Encirclement Campaign was more successful. In 1933 - 1934, Chiang sent an overwhelming force against the Chinese Soviet Republic. Mao's losses were so great that they threatened the very existence of Chinese communism. In order to save communism, Mao was forced to lead the loyal communists who remained in a long, grueling retreat known as the **Long March**.

FASCINATING FACTS: The Long March (1934 – 1935)

When Chiang Kai-shek's Fifth Encirclement campaign threatened to annihilate the Chinese Soviet Republic, Mao Tse-tung led the surviving remnants of his armies on an epic retreat to escape Chiang's relentless attacks. This retreat became known as the Long March.

The facts of the Long March are shrouded in Mao's dishonest communist propaganda. No one knows how long the march was, or just what route the marchers took, or how many people marched, or how many marchers abandoned Mao along the way. According to the simplified version of Mao's story, about 100,000 people began the march. These brave men, women and children traveled about 8,000 miles in 370 days, carrying heavy loads across impossible terrain under grueling weather conditions. Many of them froze to death, or suffocated in the frigid temperatures and thin air of high mountain passes, or drowned in some of the many rivers that barred their passage. When the marchers arrived at their destination in the far northwest reaches of China, only about 5,000 of the original 100,000 marchers remained.

Mao's critics doubt his version of events. They suggest that the march was only about half as long as Mao claimed. They also note that

1. Mao himself was reportedly carried on a chair through much of the march, and that
2. although tens of thousands of communist peasants died on the march, no senior communist party leaders died.

Of course, Mao's critics might also have reason to be dishonest about the facts of the Long March. Whatever the facts were, Mao somehow turned the Long March into a propaganda victory for Chinese communism. Even though the march decimated Mao's following, Mao claimed that the successful conclusion of the march proved that the Chinese people could survive anything. Whenever Mao asked his followers to make some difficult sacrifice, he reminded them of the Long March, and told them that no trial could be greater than the one they had already endured.

The Long March turned out to be a strategic victory as well as a propaganda victory. By retreating so far and for so long, Mao's communists gained the time and distance they needed to escape from Chiang Kai-shek's relentless attacks. When they reached their destination in the North, Mao was able to rebuild his communist following quickly.

INTERESTING INDIVIDUALS: Emperor Puyi, the "Last Emperor" (1905 – 1967)

Emperor Puyi was the last Qing Dynasty emperor and the last true Emperor of China.

Puyi was a great nephew of Empress Dowager Cixi and a nephew of the Guangxu Emperor. In 1908, when the Empress Dowager's death was upon her, she chose Puyi to be China's next emperor. Reportedly, Cixi cemented Puyi's place as emperor by ordering the murder of her nephew, the Guangxu Emperor, just before she died. Puyi was 2 years and 10 months old when he took his uncle's place as emperor.

The young emperor Puyi lived in the emperor's palace at the Forbidden City in Beijing, where his caretakers guarded him closely and treated him as if he were a god. Grown men "kowtowed" to him, groveling and averting their eyes in his royal presence. When he was 17, he chose a bride and a concubine from a set of pictures, without ever meeting any of the pictured women beforehand.

Long before Puyi was 17, however, the Chinese Revolution of 1911 put an end to the Qing Dynasty. Yuan Shikai deposed Puyi as emperor in 1912, when he was still only six years old. Puyi remained in the Forbidden City through most of the Chinese Warlord Era-- until 1924, when one of China's many warlords forced him to leave.

It was then that Puyi began his relationship with China's enemy, Japan. Puyi moved from the Forbidden City to the Japanese embassy in Beijing, then to the Japanese section of Tianjin, one of China's treaty ports. During these years, the still-young Puyi sought Japan's help in getting his throne back. The Japanese found a use for Puyi: in 1931, when they invaded Chinese Manchuria and remade it as Japanese Manchukuo (see below), they made Puyi the "puppet emperor" of their new territory. The Chinese viewed Puyi as a traitor for siding with the invader Japan, and would have assassinated him if they could; but the Japanese protected him.

Near the end of World War II, though, the Japanese were no longer in a position to protect anyone. When the USSR invaded Manchukuo near the end of that war, the Soviets captured Puyi and imprisoned him. He only escaped punishment as a traitor by claiming that the Japanese had forced him to do their bidding. After China's communist revolution, communist leader Mao Tse-tung brought Puyi back to China and "reeducated" him as a good communist. The newly humble Puyi even worked as a lowly gardener in order to remain in the communists' good graces. He died of heart disease in 1967.

In 1937, China's nationalists and communists temporarily set aside their differences and combined forces in an effort to fight off a common enemy, imperial Japan.

<u>JAPAN IN MANCHURIA</u>

The Growing Japanese Empire

All the while China was struggling to remain united and independent, its neighbor Japan was thriving and expanding its empire. Japan's primary target areas for expansion were

1. the Korean Peninsula and
2. the mainland adjacent to Korea, known as Manchuria.

Manchuria was traditionally part of China, and was the home of the Manchu Qing Dynasty that had ruled China since 1644. However, in the late 1800s, the Russian Empire had become important in Manchuria. The Russians signed a lease with China that granted them a warm-water harbor at Port Arthur, just west of the Korean Peninsula; and then they built railroads through Manchuria to connect their new Trans-Siberian Railway to Port Arthur (see Chapter 13).

Japan had already defeated China in the 1894-1895 First Chinese-Japanese War, fought mainly on the Korean Peninsula. After Japan also defeated Russia in the 1904-1905 Russian-Japanese War, Korea officially became part of Japan's "sphere of influence," and Japan took over Russia's lease of the South Manchuria Railway Zone. Then, in 1910, **Japan officially annexed Korea**.

When the Chinese Revolution erupted in 1911, Japan was ready to move beyond Korea and into Manchuria.

The Twenty-One Demands

In 1915, the same year in which Yuan Shikai declared himself Emperor of China, Japan signaled its aggressiveness by sending China a list of Twenty-One Demands. These demands included:

1. More Japanese control of Manchuria and the South Manchuria Railway Zone.
2. More Japanese control of China's Shandong Province, which lay on China's east coast south of Manchuria.
3. More Japanese control of eastern Inner Mongolia, which lay beyond Manchuria to the west.

Japan also wanted to place Japanese officials within the Chinese government, but this outrageous demand was not part of the final treaty.

China had been weakened by its internal battles, and had little choice but to agree to Japan's terms. The revised list of thirteen demands became an official treaty in May, 1915.

FASCINATING FACTS: The Manchurian Incident (aka the Mukden Incident) and the Invasion of Manchuria

In the years after World War I, the League of Nations and other powers kept a watchful eye on greedy empires like Japan's. In 1922, Japanese empire-builders were disappointed when the League demanded that Japan return the Shandong Province to Chinese control. To the empire-builders, this was progress in the wrong direction. With the League of Nations keeping watch, Japan knew that it would need a good excuse if it was to take over the highly desirable Manchuria, with its plentiful resources and good farmland. The group of Japanese soldiers who carried out the Manchurian Incident provided their nation with just such an excuse.

On September 18, 1931, Japanese soldiers placed explosives near a section of the South Manchurian Railway that they were supposed to be guarding. No one knows who ordered them to do so. Some blame the soldiers themselves, claiming that they were part of a plot to expand Japan's empire without their government's permission. Others believe that Emperor Hirohito and the Japanese government knew all about the bombing plan, and authorized it beforehand.

The soldiers planted the bomb far enough from the tracks to insure that it would do little damage— it was, after all, Japan's railway— but near enough to cause a scene. On the night of September 18, they set the bomb off. The damage was minimal. The explosion injured no one, and damaged no trains. The damage to the rails was not even sufficient to derail the next train that passed through (the picture depicts undamaged rails with only a small railroad tie fragment lying beside the tracks).

Nevertheless, the Japanese treated the explosion like a major international incident. On the morning after the bombing, Japanese forces opened fire on nearby Chinese forces in retaliation for their supposed destruction of Japan's railway. The Chinese offered little resistance, and the Japanese began to capture more and more Manchurian territory.

If Emperor Hirohito did in fact know nothing of the Manchurian Incident before it happened, he certainly did nothing to stop what followed.

The Manchurian Incident became Japan's pretext (excuse) for a full-scale invasion and occupation of Manchuria. The Japanese completed their occupation of Manchuria in early 1932.

Manchukuo and the Lytton Report

Next, the Japanese needed a strategy to make their occupation permanent without drawing the anger of the League of Nations (which had been established after WWI to prevent empire-building of precisely this sort). They hit upon the idea of establishing a new state, **Manchukuo**, in occupied Manchuria. On paper, Manchukuo would be independent; but in reality, Manchukuo would be a puppet state with a government owned and operated entirely by Japan.

In order to make the new state Manchukuo legitimate in the eyes of the Chinese, Japan rolled out its big surprise: Manchukuo's ruler would be none other than China's last Qing Dynasty emperor, the deposed Emperor Puyi! After the warlords ejected Puyi from the Forbidden City in 1924, Puyi lived in the Japanese portion of the Chinese "treaty port" city of Tianjin. He was eager to return to his throne, and believed that the Japanese might help him do so. Therefore he was disappointed when he discovered that the Japanese wanted him in Manchukuo only as a figurehead, and not as a truly independent emperor.

Japan's puppet state strategy did not deceive the League of Nations, nor did the figurehead Puyi deceive the Chinese. In early 1932, the League sent Britain's Earl of Lytton to investigate Japan's invasion and occupation of Manchuria. **The Lytton Report** did not accuse Japan of bombing the South Manchurian Railway (in the Manchurian Incident), but it did blame Japan for the invasion that followed. In 1933, when the Lytton Report formally accused Japan of deliberately attacking and occupying Manchuria, Japan withdrew its membership in the League of Nations.

> **Japan continued to occupy Manchuria, and the League of Nations did nothing more to stop the occupation.**

The resources Japan gained by occupying Manchuria were vital to their military buildup in the years leading up to World War II. Without Manchuria, Japan would probably have been too weak to consider attacking the United States navy at Pearl Harbor, Hawaii on December 7, 1941.

The Second Chinese-Japanese War (1937 – 1945)

Japanese troops continued to harass China up and down China's east coast. Their harassment finally led to a declaration of all-out war between China and Japan in 1937. This Second Chinese-Japanese War continued throughout World War II, and would not end until World War II also ended in 1945.

FASCINATING FACTS: The Abacus

The abacus is an Asian calculating tool. There are many kinds of abaci, but the common Chinese abacus has two decks of beads: an upper deck, or "heaven deck," and a lower deck, or "earth deck."

An abacus bead only registers a value when it is pushed toward the center bar that divides the two decks; all other beads register zero. Place value on an abacus is just like place value in digital numbers: the first row of beads on the right represents ones, the second row represents tens, the third row represents hundreds, and so on. Heaven deck beads represent the digit "5," while earth deck beads represent the digit "1." For example: to represent the number 6, one would go to the far right row and move one heaven deck bead and one earth deck bead toward the center bar: 5 + 1 = 6. To represent the number 70, one would go to the second row and move one heaven deck bead and two earth deck beads toward the center bar: 50 + 20 = 70. The abacus in the illustration registers the number 37, 925.

The operations of addition, subtraction, multiplication and division with an abacus are all similar to the same operations with pencil and paper. The abacus user tends to calculate more quickly because he doesn't need to write the numbers down. With deft fingers and minds, abacus users can perform some calculations more quickly than electronic calculator users.

MISSIONARY FOCUS

GIANTS OF THE FAITH: Eric Liddell (1902 – 1945)

Eric Liddell was the son of English missionaries who served in China. He spent most of his youth in English boarding schools, and rarely saw his parents. Eric's parents served in China during the Boxer Rebellion, when angry Chinese "boxers" attacked Westerners living in China. About two hundred foreign missionaries and thirty thousand Chinese Christians were killed in the Boxer Rebellion.

Eric was an excellent runner, and in 1924, he qualified to represent Britain in the Olympic Games. He was scheduled to run the 100 meter sprint, but was dismayed to learn that its final was scheduled for a Sunday.

Running on a Sunday was against Eric's strict beliefs about keeping the Sabbath, so he disqualified himself from the 100 meter final. Britain's hope for a medal was dashed, and Britons back home criticized and mocked Eric for being so rigid.

Eric's coaches scheduled him to run in the 400 meter race instead. The 400 meter race was a different race, requiring a different style of running than the 100 meter, and Eric hadn't trained to run it. Therefore Eric's critics were stunned when he not only won the 400 meter race and earned a gold medal for Britain, but also broke the world record in the process. For this success, Eric was dubbed the "Flying Scotsman."

Eighteen months after the Olympics, Liddell went to China as a missionary and lived among the Chinese through the turmoil of the 1930s. During World War II, China became too dangerous for Eric's family, so he sent his pregnant wife and two young girls to Canada while he remained in China with his brother. When the Japanese captured their region of China, Eric and his brother were placed under house arrest. In 1943, Eric was moved to an internment camp for foreigners. Eric's cheerful attitude helped to maintain order under very difficult circumstances in a miserable camp. Eric Liddell died of a brain tumor on February 21, 1945, five months before the end of the war liberated his prison camp.

The film "Chariots of Fire" relates the story of Eric's success in the Olympic Games.

GIANTS OF THE FAITH: Gladys Aylward (1902 – 1970)

Gladys Aylward was an English Christian who wanted to be a missionary to China. As a young woman, Gladys applied to join Hudson Taylor's China Inland Mission, but she couldn't pass the organization's rigorous tests. However, when Gladys was 30, she discovered that an aging missionary named Jeannie Lawson was looking for a younger assistant to carry on her work in China. Gladys couldn't afford to make the trip to China in the usual way, by ship. Instead, she packed her passport, her Bible, and a little bit of money and set off for China over land. She took the Trans-Siberian Railway all the way to Vladivostok, USSR, then used a combination of boats, trains, mules and her own feet to cover the rest of the long distance to inland China (red dot on map).

Gladys and Jeannie operated an inn that provided food and shelter for Chinese merchant caravans. While travelers stayed at the inn, Gladys and Jeannie shared the Gospel and Bible stories with them. When the elderly Jeannie died, Gladys remained in China to continue her ministry. When she learned that there were a large number of unwanted children in her area, she expanded her ministry to care for them. She also provided medical care for Chinese soldiers who were wounded during the Chinese-Japanese War that began in 1937. The Chinese began to call Gladys *Ai-weh-deh*, "Virtuous One."

By 1940, the dangers of that war began to make Gladys' area unsafe for her and her orphans. When this happened, Gladys decided to lead her one hundred orphans on a 100-mile trek across a mountain range, on foot, to safety in another province (Gladys was not afraid of long journeys!). When they got there, Gladys continued her ministry in the new location. She built a church, visited prisoners, cared for the sick and shared the Gospel with whomever would listen.

When the Chinese Communist Party took control of China in 1947, the communists' hostility to Christians forced Gladys to leave China. She spent ten years in England, then returned to Taiwan (the Republic of China, founded on Taiwan by China's Nationalists) in 1958 to open another orphanage.

In 1958, Hollywood produced a film about Gladys' life called "The Inn of the Sixth Happiness."

U.S. HISTORY FOCUS

AMAZING AMERICANS: Eleanor Roosevelt (1884 – 1962)

As the wife of President Franklin D. Roosevelt, Anna Eleanor Roosevelt was the First Lady of the United States from 1933-1945. She was also the niece of President Theodore Roosevelt.

Although Eleanor was born into a wealthy New York family, her childhood was troubled. She lost both her mother and her father within a two-year period: Her mother died of diphtheria when Eleanor was eight; and her father, an alcoholic who spent time in a sanitarium (mental hospital), died when Eleanor was nine. Young Eleanor had to live with her grandmother until she reached boarding school age.

Eleanor was attending a young ladies' finishing school near London, England in 1901 when her uncle, Theodore Roosevelt, took over as President of the United States (after the assassination of President McKinley). After she returned to the United States, she drew the romantic interest of Franklin Delano Roosevelt, her father's fifth cousin (her own fifth cousin one generation removed). Franklin began courting Eleanor in 1903, and married her in 1905. At their wedding ceremony, Eleanor's Uncle Theodore gave away the bride. The two branches of New York's Roosevelt family– the Oyster Bay, Republican Roosevelts (led by Theodore) and the Hyde Park, Democratic Roosevelts (soon to be led by Franklin)– were becoming a sort of American royalty.

- In 1918 Eleanor learned that Franklin, by now the father of her six children, was carrying on an extramarital affair with her secretary. The affair ruined their marriage. Franklin and Eleanor remained married, but their relationship after the affair was more like a business partnership than a marriage. Because the reporters of the day were discreet (kept secrets), most people didn't know about the affair, and it didn't affect Franklin's political career.

After polio paralyzed Franklin's legs in 1921, Eleanor became his spokesman and partner in politics. Eleanor was popular with women voters, who had only recently gained the right to vote, and Franklin benefited from her popularity. Eleanor's aid was instrumental in getting Franklin over his illness and into the White House.

From 1935 to 1962, Eleanor wrote a syndicated newspaper column called "My Day." This short column appeared six days per week, fifty-two weeks per year, for twenty-seven years. In "My Day," Eleanor shared so many of her personal experiences in the White House that millions of readers came to admire her as they might admire a personal friend. Her column helped her to remain popular and influential long after Franklin died in 1945. She also used her column to advocate for her favorite causes.

Eleanor was an early advocate of women's rights, black rights and human rights in general. She held press conferences in the White House exclusively for women reporters, and encouraged women to take voting seriously. When the Tuskegee Airmen became the U.S. Army's first black pilots during World War II, Eleanor showed her support by riding in one of their airplanes. Later in life, Eleanor advocated for human rights by working with President Kennedy's Peace Corps and with the United Nations. She remained an important figure in Democratic politics until she died in 1962.

U.S. GEOGRAPHY FOCUS

	NORTH DAKOTA	SOUTH DAKOTA
Statehood:	November 2, 1889 (39th/40th state)	November 2, 1889 (39th/40th state)
Bordering states/country:	Minnesota, Montana, South Dakota, Canada	Iowa, Minnesota, Montana, Nebraska, North Dakota, Wyoming
State capital:	Bismarck	Pierre
Area:	70,700 sq. mi (Ranks 19th in size)	77,116 sq. mi (Ranks 17th in size)
Abbreviation:	ND	SD
Nickname:	"Peace Garden State"	"Mount Rushmore State"
State bird:	Western Meadowlark	Ring-necked Pheasant
State tree:	American Elm	White Spruce
State flower:	Wild Prairie Rose	Pasque flower
State song:	*North Dakota Hymn*	*Hail, South Dakota*
Motto"	" Liberty and union, now and forever, one and inseparable"	"Under God the people rule"
Meaning of name:	Named after the Dakota Indians	Named after the Dakota Indians
Historic places to visit:	Theodore Roosevelt National Park, North Dakota badlands, Writing Rock State Historic Site, Devils Lake, Dakota Dinosaur Museum, The Lone Tree Wildlife Management Area, Sitting Bull Burial State Historic Site, Ellendale's Opera House, Killdeer Mountain Roundup Rodeo, Paul Broste Rock Museum, Turtle Racing Championship, The International Peace Garden	Mount Rushmore, Deadwood, Custer State Park, Jewel Cave, Wind Cave, The Crazy Horse mountain, Badlands National Park, Sage Creek Wilderness, Harney Peak, Black Hills Classic Motorcycle Rally, The Mammoth Site of Hot Springs, The Pioneer Auto Museum, Art B. Thomas Hershell-Spillman Carousel, The George S. Mickelson Trail, The Silent Guide Monument, Mato Paha "Sacred Mountain"
Resources and Industries	farming (wheat, rye, barley, oats, sunflowers, dairy, sugar beets, cattle), mining (lignite, coal), oil, electric power generation, food processing, tourism	farming (cattle, hogs, wheat, soybeans, dairy, corn), mining (gold), food products, machinery and lumber, tourism

State flag:		
Flag information:	Adopted in 1911. The flag has a dark blue field with a bald eagle (representing the U.S.) on the front. The eagle is protected by a red, white and blue shield with 13 stars and 13 stripes. There are also 13 gold stars above the eagle. All of the 13s represent the U.S.' original 13 colonies.	Adopted in 1963. The flag has a field of sky blue with the state seal in its center. The seal is surrounded by golden sunrays and the words "South Dakota" and "The Mount Rushmore State."

FASCINATING FACTS: Mount Rushmore

Mount Rushmore National Memorial is a huge sculpture carved into the southeast face of Mount Rushmore, a granite mountain near Keystone, South Dakota. The sculpture commemorates four U.S. Presidents: George Washington, Thomas Jefferson, Theodore Roosevelt and Abraham Lincoln. The Memorial's chief sculptor, John Gutzon Borglum, envisioned it as a monument to America's "Manifest Destiny," the idea that a nation as free and good as the United States must surely be destined by God to overspread the North American continent and beyond. Borglum believed that each of these Presidents played a part in Manifest Destiny:  Washington secured America's independence, Jefferson acquired the Louisiana Purchase, Lincoln held the Union together during the Civil War, and Roosevelt expanded America's empire overseas during the Spanish-American War.

The work at Mount Rushmore began in 1927, while Calvin Coolidge was President. Coolidge vacationed in South Dakota that year, and gave the dedication speech for the Memorial. The work proceeded in stages: Washington's sculpture was dedicated in 1934, Jefferson's in 1936, Lincoln's in 1937, and Roosevelt's in 1939. The sculpture is actually incomplete, according to its sculptor's vision. Borglum's original design included monuments to the Louisiana Purchase, the Declaration of Independence, the Constitution and more; but the project ran out of money before he could add all of these things. Borglum died in March 1941, and his son declared the project complete a few months later.

Other interesting facts about Mount Rushmore:
- Sculptor Gutzon Borglum had already worked on the Confederate Memorial Carving at Stone Mountain, Georgia when he was chosen to design Mount Rushmore. That project also ran into financial problems, and lay incomplete until 1972, more than 100 years after the Civil War.
- Borglum originally intended to place Jefferson on Washington's right. After the work began, however, workers uncovered huge cracks in the mountain that made that site too unstable for sculpting. They had to dynamite Jefferson off of Washington's right and move him to Washington's left.

PRESIDENTIAL FOCUS

PRESIDENT #30: Calvin Coolidge (1872 – 1933)	
In Office: August 2, 1923 – March 4, 1929	**Political Party:** Republican
Birthplace: Vermont	**Nickname:** "Silent Cal"

Calvin Coolidge was the Governor of Massachusetts when he won election as Warren Harding's vice president. When Harding died of a heart attack or a stroke in 1923, Coolidge took his place as President. Coolidge's own father, a notary public, administered the new President's oath of office at the family home in Vermont.

As a New England Puritan and a Calvinist Christian, (his full name was John Calvin Coolidge), Coolidge wasn't stained by the scandals that had plagued the Harding administration. He earned a reputation for openness and honesty by holding an average of two press conferences per week. The public trusted him, and he won reelection easily in 1924.

Coolidge was less active than previous Presidents like Roosevelt and Wilson, who believed in a strong Presidency. Coolidge believed in limited government, less regulation and lower taxes. He also believed in hard work and personal responsibility. He reduced taxes on incomes and inheritances, freeing up more money for investments. The U.S. economy soared during Coolidge's Roaring Twenties Presidency. He also vetoed farm relief programs because he didn't believe that the government should meddle in private business. Modern-day conservatives give Coolidge credit for helping the U.S. economy to thrive during his Presidency. Modern-day liberals blame him for leaving too much money in the hands of the wealthy, creating the conditions that led to the Stock Market Crash of 1929 and the Great Depression within a year after he left office.

Coolidge had a mixed record on civil rights. He signed the Indian Citizenship Act, which extended full U.S. citizenship to all American Indians for the first time (until 1924, many Indians were still considered to be citizens of their various tribal nations). But he also signed the Immigration Act of 1924, which discriminated against Eastern Europeans and Italians who wanted to immigrate to the United States (see Chapter 9).

Other interesting facts about Calvin Coolidge:
- Coolidge was the only President born on July 4th, Independence Day (both Thomas Jefferson and John Adams died on Independence Day).
- He signed the bill that created the Mount Rushmore Commission in 1925.
- He installed a mechanical exercise horse in the White House, and used it quite a bit.
- While Coolidge was in office, his 16-year-old son died of an infection.
- He earned a reputation as a tightwad by serving only ice water at his many White House dinner parties.
- Poet Dorothy Parker told Coolidge at a dinner party that she had bet someone that she would be able to get "Silent Cal" to say more than two words to her. "Silent Cal" responded with exactly two words: "You lose."

Notable quotes from Calvin Coolidge:
- "We do not need more intellectual power, we need more spiritual power. We do not need more of the things that are seen, we need more of the things that are unseen."
- "Industry, thrift and self-control are not sought because they create wealth, but because they create character."

Chapter 23

The Great Depression

U.S. HISTORY FOCUS

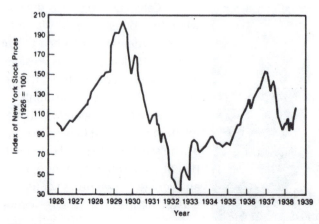

Margin Buying in the Roaring Twenties

The Roaring Twenties was a decade of prosperity and growth in the United States. Thanks to President Calvin Coolidge, income and inheritance taxes were low, so investors had extra money to invest. The most popular place to invest that money was on the New York Stock Exchange, where steadily rising stock prices (a "bull market") promised high rates of return on investments.

In order to take advantage of the steadily rising stock prices of the Twenties, some investors made deals with stock brokers that allowed them to purchase stocks "on the margin." Margin buyers purchased stocks by paying 10-20% of the stock price (the "margin") from their own pockets and borrowing the other 80-90% from a broker or a bank. These large loans allowed margin buyers to own up to ten times as much stock as they could have owned with just their own limited investment money. Margin buyers became the legal owners of the stocks they purchased on the margin, and could buy or sell them as they chose; but they also had to repay their 90% loans, and the stock itself was the collateral (security or assurance) for those loans.

MARGIN BUYING REWARDS: Margin buying had its rewards. If the stock's price went up, margin buyers reaped the increase as if they owned 100% of the stock. Of course, there were expenses: brokers and banks made money from their margin-buying clients by charging fees and interest for their services. But if the stock's price continued to rise steadily, as most stocks did during the Twenties, those expenses were a minor annoyance. High-rolling margin buyers tended to overlook such expenses as long as their investments continued to earn money.

MARGIN BUYING RISKS: On the other hand, margin buying also had its risks. If the stock's price went down, any losses came out of the margin buyer's 10%, not out of the bank's 90%-- it was after all his investment, not the bank's. If the price went down as much as 10%, one of two things happened:

1. If the margin buyer believed that his stock's price would continue to go down, he sold the stock at its new, lower price and used the money to pay off his 90% loan. In doing so, he lost his entire 10% investment and walked away from his investment with nothing. Even though the stock was still worth 90% of its original price, none of that money belonged to the margin buyer; it was all borrowed money that belonged to the bank.

2. If the margin buyer still believed that his stock's price would rise in the future, the margin buyer tried to save his investment by forking over more money. Now that the stock's price was lower, the collateral for the 90% loan was worth less, and the bank wanted more collateral to cover its loan. Therefore, if the margin buyer wanted to keep his stock, he had to provide that collateral by paying his bank another 10% of the stock's price. This payment assured the bank that it wouldn't lose money (banks never want to lose money). Paying extra money to save a losing investment was called "meeting a margin call."

Men like Commerce Secretary (and soon to be President) Herbert Hoover were well aware of risky stock trading tactics like margin buying, and were concerned that too much margin buying might cause heavy losses if stocks prices started to go down instead of up. If stock prices went down too fast, margin buyers wouldn't have enough money to meet their margin calls, and the banks that loaned the margin buyers money would lose money along with them.

FASCINATING FACTS: Ticker Tape Parades and the Canyon of Heroes

Ticker tape was the thin, rolled paper that the New York Stock Exchange used to record stock trades. Every time a stock changed hands, machines recorded the sale on ticker tape. Before the advent of computers, Wall Street investors and brokers used ticker tape by the mile, and there was always plenty of it on hand around New York's financial district.

During the dedication of New York Harbor's Statue of Liberty in 1886, someone decided that ticker tape would make good confetti for the celebration. After that, New York City began to host noisy, messy ticker tape parades with miles of ticker tape confetti for popular heroes like Charles Lindbergh and Amelia Earhart. The site of the ticker tape parades in lower Manhattan's financial district is known as the "Canyon of Heroes."

The Roaring Twenties Cease to Roar

The economic exuberance of the Roaring Twenties was doomed to end. During the late 1920s, highly efficient factories built by businesses with plenty of investment money began to produce more goods than they could sell ("overproduction"). By 1929, new orders for factory goods like cars, radios and washing machines all began to slow down, yet factories continued to produce these goods in record numbers.

As a result, goods began to pile up in warehouses and on store shelves. In an effort to sell these excess goods, factories and stores tried to entice buyers by lowering their prices ("deflation"). As prices began to fall, businesses began to lose money, and the people who invested in those businesses began to lose confidence in the value of those businesses' stocks.

INTERESTING INQUIRY: What determines a stock's value?

Simply put, a stock's value is whatever some buyer will pay for it on the day its owner offers it for sale. That value can remain fairly steady, or it can fluctuate daily. Sometimes a stock's value fluctuates because of changing business conditions: a business's product might become obsolete, or competitors might win away a business's customers. Sometimes, however, a stock's value fluctuates mainly because of investors' changing attitudes.

Several factors determine a business's value. Some of them are "hard assets": its money, its goods, its buildings, its land and every other material object it owns. And some of them are "soft assets": its name, its reputation, its manufacturing secrets and everything else that improves its ability to earn money.

In a steady economy, the value of hard assets remains fairly steady, because they can always be sold for a fair price. But the value of soft assets goes up or down according to investors' attitudes about the business. If investors are confident that a business will earn money, they value its stock highly. If they believe that a business may lose money, they value its stock far less. Even in a steady economy, a stock's value is heavily influenced by investors' confidence in the business that issues the stock.

As deflation set in in the late 1920s, most investors' confidence turned to doubt. Stock values declined as investors began to doubt the ability of any business, even a previously solid business, to earn money. As the economy began to weaken, even hard assets became difficult to sell, because no one wanted to buy them. This robbed stocks of even more value. In 1929, stock prices began to fluctuate dramatically as investors' attitudes about stock values changed from exuberance to panic.

FASCINATING FACTS: Panic Selling

New York Stock Exchange after the 1929 crash

Stock brokers on the busy New York Stock Exchange operate by executing orders from their customers. The simplest orders are market orders, which include buy orders and sell orders. A buy order instructs the broker to buy a stock at the market price (the lowest price some seller will offer); while a sell order instructs the broker to sell at today's market price (the highest price some buyer will pay). Stock prices remain fairly stable as long as sellers can find buyers who are willing to pay an agreeable price.

Panic Selling happens when no one wants to buy a stock at any price. When investors lose confidence in the value of a stock, they may decide to sell it before its price can fall too far. If every investor decides to sell the same stock at the same time, then none of them can find buyers. The brokers who are selling the stock are forced to lower their prices dramatically until they finally find a buyer. The stock's price plummets, destroying in a matter of minutes all of the value that has taken years of hard work to acquire.

As other investors watch stock prices falling far and fast, they may begin to fear that they will lose their entire investment if they don't sell right away; so they may issue more sell orders. If there are still no buyers, stock prices fall still further. Panic selling can destroy a stock's entire value in a matter of hours.

DEFINITION: The Great Depression

The Great Depression was a long period of time when many Americans lost their jobs and had severe money troubles. It was an era of poverty and hunger in the United States. The Great Depression began with the Stock Market Crash of 1929 and lasted throughout the 1930s. It finally ended in the early 1940s, when the United States began to increase its production of war materials in preparation for World War II.

The Stock Market Crash of 1929

The Dow Jones Industrial Average (see Chapter 15) reached an all-time high of 381 points on September 3, 1929. For the rest of September, stocks declined; but in early October, they began to rise again. Investors' confidence was shaky, but they continued to buy stocks because none of them wanted to be left out when stock prices started to rise again. Margin buyers borrowed money so that they could buy stocks at these new, lower prices, then get rich when stock prices soared to new highs (they hoped).

Unfortunately for the margin buyers, the rest of October brought another steep decline in stock prices and a major loss of investor confidence. The stock slide culminated in three dark days in late October:

October 24, 1929, "Black Thursday": Early in the day, an enormous number of sell orders started a round of panic selling. So many investors sold their stocks that the NYSE's stock ticker fell far behind in its job of recording the day's sales. Prices fell rapidly. From an opening of 306, the DJIA fell 34 points to a low of 272. Stocks lost 11% of their entire value in a single morning, and were down 29% from their September peak.

Late in the day, a group of five large banks tried to reverse the market's slide by pooling together about $100 million and using it to buy stocks. Their calm confidence brought investors back into the market, and the DJIA revived to close at 299, down only 7 points for the day.

October 28, 1929, "Black Monday": After a calm Friday and a weekend break, the NYSE opened with another round of panic selling. No bankers intervened this time. From an opening of 301, the DJIA fell 44 points to a low of 257 and then closed at 260. Stocks lost 14 % of their value in a single day, and were down 32% from their September peak.

Outside the New York Stock Exchange after Black Tuesday Crash

October 29, 1929, "Black Tuesday": As soon as the NYSE opened, the panic selling resumed. The DJIA fell to a low of 212 before closing at 230. Stocks lost another 11% of their value in a single day, and were down almost 40% from their September peak.

Although these three **"black"** days were filled with financial drama, they were really only the beginning of the stock market's Great Depression slide. October, 1929 was the first month of a long, deep decline (or "bear market") that lasted for almost three years. The DJIA reached its ultimate low on July 8, 1932, when it closed at just 41 points– down 89% from its September 3, 1929 peak. **An investment that was worth $100 at that peak was worth just $11 in 1932.** The Dow Jones Industrial Average did not return to its pre-Depression high of 381 until November, 1954– 25 years after the crash.

Losses of that size were large enough to affect even the wealthiest of businesses, the nation's banks.

FASCINATING FACTS: Bank Runs

Banks are in the business of making loans: loans to businesses, loans to investors, loans to homeowners, loans to college students, and loans to car buyers, among other types. Banks earn money by charging interest and fees on these loans. The money that banks loan comes from their account customers, people who open savings accounts, checking accounts or investment accounts and keep most of their money in the bank.

Banks are able to use a portion of their customers' money to make loans because they know from experience that their account customers will leave most of their money in the bank, and will usually withdraw only as much as they need. Banks don't keep all of their customers' money on hand; they invest it. They loan much of it to their loan customers, and keep on hand only enough to cover their account customers' daily withdrawal needs. This system works fine as long as customers trust their bank. So long as account customers are confident that they can get their money out of the bank when they need it, they generally pay little attention to the bank's other business.

During the Great Depression, banks came under a great deal of strain. When businesses failed, they couldn't repay their business loans. When homeowners lost their jobs, they couldn't keep up with their mortgage payments. When investors who had purchased stocks on the margin lost money, banks lost money too. Banks lose money when loans go bad; and during the Great Depression, far too many loans went bad at once. Like other businesses, banks began to struggle under the weight of their losses; and watchful bank customers began to lose confidence in their banks.

When too many customers lost confidence in a bank at once, the result was a Bank Run (or a Run on the Bank). A bank run usually started with a rumor, true or otherwise, that a certain bank didn't have enough money to cover its account customers' withdrawals. Customers who heard such rumors immediately rushed to the bank to claim their money. They knew that if the bank ran out of money, the last customers to arrive wouldn't get anything from the bank; and they didn't want to be part of that unfortunate crowd.

Bank runs tended to become self-fulfilling prophecies. As more customers arrived to claim their money, the teller lines stretched outside the bank's doors. Bystanders began to wonder why so many people were standing around the bank, and soon the rumor of the bank's failure spread far and wide– which brought even more customers to the bank to claim their money (see picture). Eventually, the bank's money ran out, and the bank had to close its doors. Customers who arrived at the bank too late, or not at all, stood to lose part or all of the money they had saved there.

From Crash to Depression

The Stock Market Crash of 1929 was an early symptom of an economic illness that would spread around the nation. Failing businesses led to unemployment, and unemployment led to poverty. Falling prices led to lower wages and a lower standard of living. Continued unemployment and poverty led to hunger and homelessness.

FASCINATING FACTS: Soup Kitchens and Bread Lines

As the Great Depression worsened, more and more people found themselves unable to buy food, and America's streets filled with hungry people. In response, churches and other charitable groups established kitchens that served soup and/or bread to help hungry people survive. Some charged 5 cents per meal to help cover expenses, and some offered free meals.

Prohibition-era gangster Al Capone established a soup kitchen in Chicago to help improve his tawdry image.

FASCINATING FACTS: Hoovervilles

Hoovervilles were villages of makeshift shelters that grew up on the outskirts of cities all over the United States during the Great Depression. Hoovervilles sprang up on riverbanks or around railroad tracks near cities where their residents hoped to find work. These villages took their name from President Herbert Hoover, who presided over the early years of the Great Depression and thus received much of the blame for its miseries. Hooverville residents built their shanties and shacks by the dozens and hundreds from whatever scraps of discarded lumber, tin or cardboard they could find.

The impoverished people of the Great Depression wound up in Hoovervilles for a number of reasons. Among them:

- *Mortgage Foreclosures:* People who lost their jobs during the Great Depression had trouble making the mortgage payments on the loans they had taken out to purchase their homes. When homeowners missed their mortgage payments for a number of months, banks could foreclose the mortgage and sell the home in order to recover their loan money. Such foreclosures left the impoverished homeowners homeless and landless, so they were forced to move out of their homes and build makeshift shelters on land they did not own.

- *Day Laborers:* As Depression-era families' financial situations grew desperate, one or more family members (such as the father and/or the eldest son) often struck out in search of work that would help support the family. Such people often hopped aboard a freight train when no one was looking and traveled to a different area of the country where the Depression was less severe. Even if they didn't manage to find full-time jobs, they might still hope to find temporary work as day laborers on a farm or a construction project. While they waited for their luck to improve, they lived in a temporary shelter in a Hooverville.

The residents of Hoovervilles sometimes pooled the little food they had managed to gather in a community dish known as a "Mulligan Stew."

FASCINATING FACTS: Foreclosure Sales and Penny Auctions

When economic times are hard, they are usually doubly hard for farmers. Operating a small farm often involves borrowing. Farmers take out loans for land, for farm buildings, for equipment, for seed and for fertilizer. Even in good economic times, small farms are often in debt every year from planting time until harvest time.

The years of the Great Depression were not good economic times. Low food prices cut into farmers' earnings, and poor weather reduced their crop yields. In a time when farmers already had no more than they needed, the Depression left them with even less.

When farmers fell behind on their loan payments, the foreclosure process began. First came a series of notices warning farmers to make their loan payments or suffer the consequences. Then came a final notice informing them that their bank was foreclosing their loan for failure to pay. The bank's next step was to set a date for an auction, a farm foreclosure auction at which it planned to sell everything the farmer had used as collateral for his loan: his equipment, his land, his buildings and even his crops.

Some farmers accepted this fate meekly, and left their farms to seek a living elsewhere while the bank sold everything they owned. Others did not.

At some farm auctions, local farmers protected their unfortunate neighbors from foreclosing banks by showing up to bid at their foreclosure auctions. All of the farmers got together before the bidding began and decided on a strategy. When their neighbor's plow went on the auction block, one farmer bought it for a penny and gave it back to him. When his wife's cook stove went on the auction block, another farmer bought it for a penny and gave it back to her. As long as the farm community worked together, it could control the sale price of each item. Such auctions became known as "Penny Auctions."

Of course, penny auctions only worked if there were no bidders from outside the local farm community to outbid these penny bidders. Local farmers took care of this problem by intimidating or threatening outside buyers. No buyer or bank agent wanted to outbid a penny bidder if doing so might earn him a beating from a group of burly farmers.

Banks soon caught on to the penny auction tactic. They learned to protect themselves from losses at would-be penny auctions by asking for police protection at foreclosure auctions or by setting high minimum bids for each item.

MORE FASCINATING FACTS ABOUT THE GREAT DEPRESSION

- The Great Depression was part of a worldwide economic depression, but that Depression lasted longer in the United States than anywhere else. It began with the **Stock Market Crash of 1929**, lasted throughout the 1930s, and finally ended in the early 1940s, when the United States began to increase its production of war materials in preparation for World War II.
- The Dow Jones Industrial Average did not return to its pre-Depression high of 381 until November, 1954– 25 years after the crash.
- During the worst years of the Great Depression, 25% of the U.S. workforce was unemployed. Another 25% of the workforce suffered wage cuts or lower work hours.
- The Empire State Building, the Chrysler Building, and Rockefeller Center (all in New York City) were all Great Depression-era building projects. The Golden Gate Bridge (in San Francisco) was also a Great Depression-era building project.
- This verse from "Brother, Can You Spare a Dime?", a popular American song from the Great Depression era, captures the spirit of the hard-working Americans who built a great nation, only to find themselves begging for money when there was no more work to be found:

> Once I built a railroad, I made it run, made it race against time.
> Once I built a railroad; now it's done. Brother, can you spare a dime?
> Once I built a tower, up to the sun, brick, and rivet, and lime;
> Once I built a tower, now it's done. Brother, can you spare a dime?

The New Deal

The fact that the Presidential election of 1932 fell during the lowest point of the Great Depression made it difficult for the incumbent (sitting) President, Herbert Hoover, to win votes. Hoover's election opponent and most of America's voters placed the blame for the nation's many troubles squarely on Hoover's shoulders.

The new President, Franklin D. Roosevelt, promised to turn the economy around with a set of new government programs and policies designed to provide "relief, recovery and reform." Campaign flyers, posters, murals, buttons and speeches all promised the public a *New Deal* when President Roosevelt caught hold of the country's reins.

. William Gropper's "Construction of a Dam" (1939) mural

The Hundred Days

But the New Deal was not some grand recovery strategy that Roosevelt developed before taking office. Rather, it was a change in attitude about the role of government in American life. Earlier Presidents like Coolidge and Hoover believed that the U.S. Constitution granted the federal government limited powers. Franklin Roosevelt acknowledged no limits on his power. He met with the U.S. Congress every day for the first 100 days of his administration, and during those Hundred Days, the Congress passed every act and regulation Roosevelt and his "brain trust" (a collection of reputedly brilliant advisers) proposed.

Fireside Chats

President Roosevelt was a great communicator. Other Presidents had addressed the nation via radio, but Roosevelt made his addresses personal. During his twelve years in office, he delivered thirty radio addresses known as fireside chats, well-crafted speeches broadcast nationwide complete with the sound of a crackling fire in the background. The fireside chats were intended to make listeners feel as if the President was a guest in their home, seated in a chair beside their fire. In his fireside chats, Roosevelt clearly and patiently explained what his New Deal government was doing to solve the nation's problems.

When Roosevelt first took office, the banking crisis caused by the bank runs had closed the nation's banks. In his first fireside chat, the new President tried to calm the fears that led to bank runs by carefully explaining that banks invest their money and don't keep all of it on hand in cash. The American people responded to Roosevelt's calm, friendly manner: when the banks reopened a few days later under new rules, bank runs were less common.

The communication skills Roosevelt displayed in his fireside chats made him one of the most popular Presidents of all time. Even when his policies failed to have their intended effect, a lot of Americans remained convinced that Roosevelt was a good man with a difficult job who was at least trying to do the right thing.

FASCINATING FACTS: Alphabet Soup

The New Deal is best remembered for the dizzying number of government programs it created. Some were intended to provide jobs for the unemployed; some were intended to fund and construct large public works projects; and some were intended to provide relief (government aid) to American citizens whom the Depression had left in poverty. Nearly every New Deal program had its three-letter acronym, so the many programs combined to make up a sort of "alphabet soup." Among the most memorable New Deal programs:

***PWA**, Public Works Administration:*

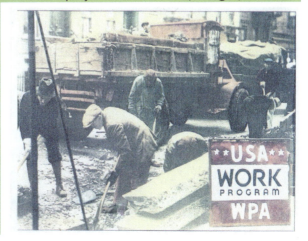

The PWA distributed government money for large public works projects such as dams, bridges, schools and hospitals. The PWA hired contractors to build such well-known projects as Washington state's Grand Coulee Dam (the largest hydro-electric dam in the U.S.), the Lincoln Tunnel (a tunnel under the Hudson River that connects New Jersey with Manhattan), and the Overseas Highway (which connects the Florida Keys to mainland Florida). In funding these projects, the PWA put millions of unemployed Americans to work. It also helped private businesses by boosting the demand for materials like concrete and steel.

***WPA**, Works Progress Administration:*

The WPA also worked on large public works projects, but in a different way: WPA employees worked directly for the government, not for private contractors. Because the WPA built less challenging projects and used unskilled labor, its workers gained a reputation for laziness. The WPA's critics claimed that its acronym really stood for "We Piddle Around."

CCC, *Civilian Conservation Corps*:
The CCC was a jobs program with two special focuses:

1. it hired only unmarried young men between the ages of 18 and 25; and
2. its projects were intended to conserve America's natural resources. Among other things, the CCC built national parks and planted trees in deforested areas.

TVA, *Tennessee Valley Authority (still in existence)*:
The TVA was an enormous government project designed to provide relief to one of America's poorest regions, the Tennessee Valley. The TVA's primary task was to build hydroelectric dams and power transmission lines to provide electric power to rural areas that had never had it before. It also built enormous flood and erosion control projects to keep the area's farmland from flooding and washing away. In order to do all of this, it had to take over a great deal of land that would be flooded by its dams.

SSA, *Social Security Administration (still in existence)*:
The SSA's purpose was to provide relief payments to the people hardest hit by the Depression: the elderly, widows, orphans and the disabled. These payments were funded by a new tax on workers' wages (the FICA, or Federal Insurance Contributions Act, tax). The SSA was also designed to help create jobs by allowing older workers to retire from the workforce, opening up jobs for younger workers who were unemployed.

FDIC, *Federal Deposit Insurance Corporation (still in existence)*:
The FDIC guaranteed bank customers that if their bank failed, they could still retrieve their money from the FDIC (within limits). This insurance policy was designed to restore the American people's confidence in their banks and prevent bank runs, which still continued even after Roosevelt's famous first fireside chat.

NRA, *National Recovery Administration*:
The NRA's goals were

1. to bring cut-throat competition between big businesses under control, and
2. to advance the rights of workers who joined labor unions.

For big industries like coal and steel, the NRA tried to establish workers' guarantees such as a minimum hourly wage and a maximum number of work hours per week. It also tried to fix prices for these industries' products. The NRA's designers believed that fixed prices would leave big businesses with fewer reasons to overwork their workers and undercut their competitors' prices.

FASCINATING FACTS: "Black Monday" and Packing the Supreme Court

The U.S. Constitution grants the federal government limited powers, and lists them specifically ("enumerates" them). The Tenth Amendment to the Constitution says that every power that the Constitution does not grant to the federal government automatically belongs to the states or to the citizens.

When the New Deal began, the federal government suddenly started doing a great number of things it had

never done before-- taxing workers and sending their money to retirees, setting wages, fixing market prices and so on. Some conservatives believed that Roosevelt's New Deal programs violated the Constitution, and they were willing to challenge these programs' constitutionality in the U.S. Supreme Court.

The New Deal program that offended conservatives most was the NRA (National Recovery Administration). Because the NRA had so much power to govern big business by negotiating labor contracts and fixing prices, it acted almost like a fourth branch of government. Several businesses sued the NRA, arguing that the Constitution did not allow Congress and the President to set up an unelected agency with such broad powers.

The courts agreed. In 1935, the U.S. Supreme Court turned against the New Deal and declared the act that had created the NRA unconstitutional. This was only one of three major Court decisions that went against President Roosevelt and the New Deal on "Black Monday," May 27, 1935. Roosevelt took these Black Monday losses personally. He railed against the "old men" of the court, whom he nicknamed the "nine buzzards on a bench."

In response, Roosevelt decided to try to "pack the court." The law did not allow him to remove justices from the Supreme Court, but it also didn't limit the number of justices seated in the Court. Roosevelt believed that if he appointed a few more sympathetic justices to the Court, then he would have enough votes to win close decisions and save his New Deal programs.

So Roosevelt proposed the Judicial Procedures Reform Bill of 1937. This new law would allow the President to appoint up to six additional Supreme Court justices, one for each justice on the court over 70 years 6 months in age. Roosevelt even tried to sell his plan directly to the American people in one of his famous "fireside chats," But instead of defending the New Deal, Roosevelt tried to tell the public that the Court's elderly, overworked justices needed some fresh young justices to relieve their excessive caseload.

Roosevelt's effort to pack the court failed. His judicial "reform" bill never passed, and the public trusted him a little bit less after he tried to deceive them about the real reason why he wanted to pack the court.

Keynesian Economics and High Taxes

John Maynard Keynes was a British economist whose ideas had a heavy influence on Franklin Roosevelt and his "brain trust." Before Keynes, most economists believed that economic recessions were part of a normal business cycle, and that they would correct themselves without help from governments. Keynes taught the opposite: he believed that governments should take major steps to even out the natural highs and lows of business cycle and keep recessions from turning into depressions.

These steps involved, primarily, spending money. Keynes taught that when the demand for goods and services declined during a recession, governments should boost that demand by spending money on needed projects. Higher government spending would take the place of sagging private spending and keep workers employed while the recession lasted. Roosevelt's PWA, WPA, CCC and TVA were all efforts to boost demand through government spending. The SSA was, in part, an effort to boost demand by giving the elderly money to spend. The ideas behind all of these programs came from Keynesian economic theory.

One side effect of all of this government spending was high taxes. Before Roosevelt even took office, President Hoover raised taxes on high incomes from 25% to 63%. Under the Revenue Act of 1936, Roosevelt boosted the highest tax rate to 79%. According to this tax schedule, a person who earned $5,000,000 in 1936 kept just $1,050,000 for himself, and paid $3,950,000 to the government. Later, these tax rates rose even higher.

FASCINATING FACTS: Marbles

During the Great Depression, most families couldn't afford luxuries like expensive toys. The only gift some families could afford for their children was a small collection of marbles.

The game of Marbles has been around since ancient times. The most common marbles game involves trying to knock opponents' marbles out of a ring drawn on the ground. Early players made their "marbles" out of round stones, nuts, or fruit pits. Later, potters made marbles out of fired clay. The first glass marbles came from Germany in the 1800s.

To make things more interesting, some players raised the stakes of their games by gambling for the marbles themselves. The loser of a marbles game might also lose a treasured "aggie," "oxblood" or "cat's eye" marble.

AMAZING AMERICANS: Charles Lindbergh (1902 – 1974) and the Lindbergh Baby

Charles Lindbergh began his flying career as a wing walker and a parachutist for a "barnstormer," a pilot who made a living by performing stunts for crowds and offering airplane rides from makeshift runways in farmers' pastures. After he bought his own airplane, Lindbergh became a barnstormer himself. Later, Lindbergh flew for the U.S. Army Air Service.

He was still a member of the Army reserve when, in pursuit of a $25,000 prize, he undertook the first solo flight across the Atlantic Ocean. The nearly unknown Charles Lindbergh became an American hero on May 20-21, 1927, when he flew a single-engine plane he named *Spirit of St. Louis* nonstop from Long Island, New York to Paris, France. Lindbergh's courageous, pioneering trip earned him the Congressional Medal of Honor and the nicknames "Lucky Lindy" and "The Lone Eagle." Soon after he finished the trip, he published a popular book about his life and adventures that helped make him a lifelong celebrity.

The success of Lindbergh's flight helped transform the public's opinion about flying. Before Lindbergh, flying meant barnstorming stunts and joy rides. After Lindbergh, it meant air mail and safe public transportation.

Through no fault of his own, Lindbergh's success led to tragedy for his family. On March 1, 1932, kidnappers abducted Lindbergh's 20-month-old son Charles Jr. from the second floor of his New Jersey home. The kidnappers left a note demanding a $50,000 ransom payment for the child's return. Because of Lindbergh's fame, newspapers referred to the kidnapping of the Lindbergh baby as the "Crime of the Century."

Lindbergh negotiated with his son's kidnappers through an intermediary, who told him that the child was alive and was being held captive on a boat. He paid the ransom and received instructions about how to reclaim his son, only to find that the kidnappers had lied to him: the child was not where they had said he would be. Sadly, in April, a delivery driver found the child's remains in some woods along a road, just a short drive from the Lindberghs' home. After this discovery, it was clear that the kidnappers had never intended to return the child alive.

Suspicion for the kidnapping and murder fell on a number of possible conspirators. A British house servant of the Lindberghs', Violet Sharp, committed suicide after investigators questioned her three times; but she may have done so only because she feared a fourth grilling from cruel, heavy-handed police investigators. Two years after the kidnapping, those investigators caught a man named Bruno Hauptman spending some of the bills Lindbergh had used to make the ransom payment. Hauptman was tried, convicted and executed for kidnapping and murder; but he never confessed, and he never revealed any more details about the crime.

WANTED
INFORMATION AS TO THE WHEREABOUTS OF

CHAS. A. LINDBERGH, Jr.
OF HOPEWELL, N. J.

SON OF COL. CHAS. A. LINDBERGH
World-Famous Aviator

This child was kidnaped from his home in Hopewell, N. J., between 8 and 10 p. m. on Tuesday, March 1, 1932.

DESCRIPTION:
Age, 20 months   Hair, blond, curly
Weight, 27 to 30 lbs.   Eyes, dark blue
Height, 29 inches   Complexion, light
Deep dimple in center of chin
Dressed in one-piece coverall night suit

ADDRESS ALL COMMUNICATIONS TO
COL. H. N. SCHWARZKOPF, TRENTON, N. J., or
COL. CHAS. A. LINDBERGH, HOPEWELL, N. J.
ALL COMMUNICATIONS WILL BE TREATED IN CONFIDENCE

March 11, 1932
COL. H. NORMAN SCHWARZKOPF
Supt. New Jersey State Police, Trenton, N. J.

FASCINATING FACTS: *War of the Worlds*

On October 30 (Halloween), 1938, actor and filmmaker Orson Welles presented a radio drama about a fictitious invasion from Mars. As his script, Welles used an adaptation of science fiction author H.G. Wells' novel *War of the Worlds*. The format of the radio program allowed Welles and his cast to read their script for 40 minutes, uninterrupted by commercials, in a style that sounded just like a series of news bulletins. The broadcast sounded so realistic that some listeners were convinced that it was a real news report, and called their local police stations to warn them that an actual Martian invasion was taking place.

U.S. GEOGRAPHY FOCUS

FASCINATING FACTS: The Dust Bowl

Not all of America's Depression-era problems were economic ones. The 1930s included some of the hottest and driest years on record, and this bad weather led to serious problems for the farmers of the Midwest.

In the late 1800s, as new railroads made the West accessible and the threat of hostile Indians diminished, settlers quickly filled up the Midwest. The buffalo that had roamed the plains soon disappeared. Long cattle drives ceased as barbed-wire fences divided the vast prairie into homesteads and crop farms. Millions of acres of prairie came under tillage for the first time as John Deere's steel plowshares broke the plains (see Chapter 8).

Unfortunately, not all of the plains were suitable for crop farming. The High Plains region that encompassed parts of Oklahoma, Kansas, Texas and Colorado was normally very dry, too dry for crops. For a few unusually wet years in the 1920s, the new farms of the High Plains produced bumper crops. But in 1933, the dry years returned.

The drought of 1933 - 1935 was an ecological (environmental) crisis for the High Plains region. The prairie grass that fed the buffalo had also served to hold the prairie's rich topsoil in place. Now it was gone, plowed under to make room for crops; and when the drought began, the parched topsoil quickly turned to dust and began to blow in the High Plains' ever-present wind. Huge dust storms began to attack farms and towns all over the region. The High Plains region was becoming a Dust Bowl.

The Dust Bowl storms' fine, heavy dust penetrated everywhere. It choked livestock to death and ruined farm machinery. It collapsed ceilings and roofs with its weight. It also blinded travelers: Farmers caught outside during dust storms couldn't find their way from their barns to their houses. Car and truck drivers couldn't see their roads. The overwhelming dust even caused a lung disease called "dust pneumonia." Great clouds of

dust containing thousands of tons of topsoil flew all over the region, and remnants of these clouds sometimes reached as far east as New York and Washington DC.

The drought and the dust storms combined to take away everything the farmers of the High Plains had. Hard times forced many of them to leave their farms forever. Great numbers of them migrated to California to find work on farms, but these "Okies" (displaced farmers from Oklahoma) were not always welcome there. John Steinbeck chronicled the sad experiences of one fictitious Okie family, the Joads, in a Pulitzer Prize winning Depression-era novel called *The Grapes of Wrath*.

Route 66

When the Joads and the other Okies traveled to California, they followed what John Steinbeck called the "Mother Road," U.S. Route 66. Route 66 was a 2,450-mile-long U.S. Highway that began in Chicago, Illinois and ended in Los Angeles, California. Along the way, it passed through Missouri, Kansas, Oklahoma, Texas, New Mexico and Arizona.

Before **Route 66** opened in 1926, most of the small towns of the West had no access to a major thoroughfare. After the road opened, those towns began to benefit from cross-country car and truck traffic that brought customers to their restaurants and hotels. Because Route 66 connected the main streets of so many towns of the West, it became known as the "Main Street of America."

Route 66 put towns like Glenrio, Texas, which straddled the Texas/New Mexico border, on the map. As the halfway point between Chicago and Los Angeles, Glenrio became a popular stop for travelers. Hollywood filmmakers filmed their version of Steinbeck's *The Grapes of Wrath* in and around tiny Glenrio. Later, though, when President Eisenhower's new Interstate Highway System bypassed Glenrio, travelers no longer stopped there, and it became a ghost town.

PRESIDENTIAL FOCUS

PRESIDENT #31: Herbert Hoover (1874 – 1964)	
In Office: March 4, 1929 – March 4, 1933	**Political Party:** Republican
Birthplace: Iowa	**Nickname:** "Grand Old Man"

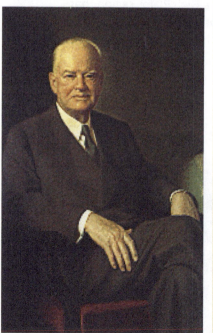

Herbert Hoover was a Stanford University-educated geologist who traveled the world as a mining consultant in search of the best sites for mines. Good work made Hoover wealthy, and he became a millionaire by the age of 40. He entered government life as the director of President Wilson's Food Administration during World War I. He held a cabinet-level position as Secretary of Commerce under Presidents Harding and Coolidge before he won election to the Presidency in 1928.

Like his predecessor, President Coolidge, Hoover believed in limited government. Before the Great Depression began, Hoover was well aware that America's poor farmers were in trouble; but he was unwilling to tackle the economy's problems by creating new government agencies and powers. Liberal lawmakers wanted Hoover to create an agency to distribute farm "subsidies," which were direct payments to hurting farmers from government funds; but that was Roosevelt's way, not Hoover's. Instead, Hoover established a farm council that encouraged farmers to plan their plantings together, voluntarily, in an effort to prevent overproduction of certain under-priced crops.

The Great Depression destroyed Hoover's previously excellent reputation with the American people. The U.S. economy lost 1.5 million jobs in November-December 1929, and matters only continued to get worse. The stock market reached its lowest point, and unemployment reached its highest point, just months before the 1932 Presidential election. The economy's problems were certainly not all Hoover's fault; but to America's voters, it seemed that he had not done enough as President to fix them. His opponent, Franklin Roosevelt, easily convinced the nation that Hoover was the wrong choice for a second term as President in 1932.

Other interesting facts about Herbert Hoover:
- While Hoover directed President Wilson's Food Administration, his name became a household word: to "Hooverize" meant to use food efficiently so that more food could go to support Europe during WWI.
- Hoover did not take a salary as President, but instead donated all of his earnings to charity.
- He exercised by tossing a medicine ball for 30 minutes each day.
- His son had two pet alligators that sometimes wandered around the White House.
- "The Star Spangled Banner" became the U.S. national anthem during Hoover's Presidency.

Notable quotes from Herbert Hoover:
- "Peace is not made at the council table or by treaties, but in the hearts of men."
- "It is a paradox that every dictator has climbed to power on the ladder of free speech. Immediately on attaining power each dictator has suppressed all free speech except his own."
- "Older men declare war. But it is the youth that must fight and die."

Chapter 24

The Spanish Civil War, Germany's Weimar Republic and the Rise of Hitler

WORLD HISTORY FOCUS

SPAIN

What Has Gone Before

Ancient philosophers held that the Pillars of Hercules bounding the Straits of Gibraltar marked the ends of the earth. In their illustrations, they engraved the Pillars with the words "Ne Plus Ultra" to indicate that there was "nothing more outside" the Mediterranean Sea.

When King Charles V of Spain built Spain's great empire in the New World, he defied that ancient wisdom. Charles playfully adopted "Plus Ultra" as his motto to demonstrate that there was indeed more, much more, outside the Pillars of Hercules. For three centuries, from about 1500 - 1800, much of Spain's wealth came from its New World colonies.

Back home in Europe, however, the Spanish Empire suffered a series of defeats that marked a long decline in Spanish power:

- England's defeat of the Spanish Armada in 1588 signaled the coming end of Spain's domination of the world's oceans.
- In 1648, when the Peace of Westphalia ended Europe's Thirty Years' War, Spain lost much of its territory in central Europe's Holy Roman Empire.
- In 1713, when the Treaty of Utrecht ended the War of Spanish Succession, Spain lost its territories in Italy and the Netherlands to Austria.

From about 1648 - 1800, the Spanish Empire was shrinking, but it still retained its vast holdings in the New World.

In the early 1800s, even those holdings began to escape Spain's grasp, largely due to Spain's troubles with Emperor Napoleon of France. Napoleon took away most of Spain's North American holdings when he forced Spain to return the Louisiana Territory to France in 1800 (Napoleon sold the territory to the U.S. in 1803). And in 1808, Napoleon invaded Spain and deposed King Ferdinand VII, hoping to replace the king with his brother Joseph Bonaparte. Napoleon's meddling temporarily destroyed Spain's government, leaving Spain's South American and island colonies to fend for themselves with temporary governments called *juntas*. These semi-independent colonies soon broke apart in a series of Spanish-American Wars of Independence.

By 1830, out of all of Spain's formerly enormous New World holdings, it retained only the islands of Cuba and Puerto Rico. Spain lost even these, and Southeast Asia's Philippine Islands as well, in the 1898 Spanish-American War (see Chapter 12).

King Ferdinand VII and Queen Isabella II

Napoleon's interference left Spain divided against itself. When King Ferdinand VII returned to the Spanish throne in 1814, he found that Spain had changed. The juntas that had fought off Napoleon had written the new Constitution of 1812 for Spain, a constitution that placed strict limits on the returning king's power.

Ferdinand would suffer no limits on his power. He arrested the constitution's biggest supporters, and

insisted on his own autocratic and arbitrary rule. In the 1820-1823 Liberal Triennium, Spanish revolutionaries restored the Constitution of 1812 for three years; but a French army sent to preserve Spain's monarchy restored Ferdinand to his throne once more. When Ferdinand returned, he avenged himself on the revolutionaries mercilessly. Few Spaniards mourned when Ferdinand died in 1833.

His daughter, Queen Isabella II, fared no better. Because Ferdinand had no sons, succession law demanded that he hand his throne down to a male heir, his brother Carlos. Instead, Ferdinand passed a new law that made his two-year-old daughter Isabella his heir. Ferdinand's wife, Maria Cristina, served as Isabella's regent for the first seven years of her reign. Ferdinand's maneuver set up another civil war, the First Carlist War, between the supporters of Carlos and the supporters of Maria Cristina. Two more Carlist Wars marred Isabella's reign, and she abdicated her throne after Spain's so-called Glorious Revolution in 1868. Isabella lived the rest of her life as an exile in Paris.

"Glorious" was hardly the proper word to describe what happened next.

King Amadeo I and the First Spanish Republic

After two years of near-anarchy, Spain's legislature, the Cortes, elected a new king from a different European royal family. King Amadeo I was the second son of Victor Emmanuel II, the Italian king who unified Italy under his reign in 1859-1870 (see Chapter 21). King Amadeo knew little about Spain, and was completely unprepared for Spain's wide assortment of warring factions. He reigned for only three tortured years, from 1870-1873; and at the end of his reign, he declared chaotic, war-torn Spain to be simply "ungovernable."

At the time, Amadeo may have been right. Spain's next government, the **First Spanish Republic**, elected four different Presidents in less than two years. The chaotic First Spanish Republic came to an end when a prominent Spanish general decided to throw the army's support behind Spain's traditional royal family. His choice as king was Isabella's son and heir, Alfonso.

INTERESTING INQUIRY: Why was Spain "Ungovernable"?

When King Amadeo I said that Spain was "ungovernable," he meant that there seemed to be nothing his government could do to soothe the nation's chaos. Several long-standing conflicts combined to make Spain more chaotic than its European neighbors:

1. *Carlists versus Cristinos:* The *Carlists*, who supported Ferdinand VII's brother Carlos for the kingship, were royalists who believed in an absolute monarchy in the hands of a king chosen by God and approved by the pope in Rome. The *Cristinos*, who supported the late King Ferdinand's wife Maria Cristina and daughter Isabella II, believed in a constitutional monarchy like Britain's.
2. *Monarchists versus Republicans:* The Monarchists believed that Spain needed a strong king, while the Republicans wanted to elect their own representatives in a free republic.
3. *Catholics versus Secularists:* Strict Roman Catholics believed that God and the Catholic Church should guide their government, while secularists resisted surrendering their government to priests and bishops whom they didn't trust.
4. *Rich versus Poor:* Spanish society was divided into two well-defined classes, rich and poor, and it was almost impossible to move from one class to the other. The poor resented the charmed lives of the rich, who were not subject to the military draft or repressed under martial law imposed by Spain's dictatorial kings.

The Restoration of the Monarchy

Alfonso returned from the exile he had shared with his mother Isabella to take his place as King Alfonso XII of Spain. He proved to be far more popular than his mother had been, and he dealt his mother's rival Carlos and his Carlist supporters their final defeat. Unfortunately for Spain, Alfonso XII died of tuberculosis in 1885, just ten years after he took the throne.

Alfonso XII's son and heir, Alfonso XIII, had not even been born when his father died. He took his late father's place as king as soon as he was born on May 17, 1886. Alfonso XIII's mother, Queen Maria Christina, served as his regent until he turned 16 in 1902.

FASCINATING FACTS: The Khamsa Amulet

Khamsa is the number "five" in the Arabic language. The Khamsa (Hamsa) amulet is the "good luck hand," also known as the "Hand of Fatima" or the "Hand of Miriam." Both Jews and Muslims wear Khamsa amulets, for two related purposes: Open-fingered amulets ward off the "evil eye" (often depicted on the amulet), and closed-fingered ones gather good luck. Khamsas appear all over the Middle East and North Africa, especially in Morocco.

For Muslims, the Khamsa amulet represents the hand of Fatima, their Prophet Mohammed's favorite daughter; and it also represents the Five Pillars of Islam. For Jews, the amulet represents the hand of Miriam, Moses' sister; and it also represents the five books of the Torah.

Spanish Morocco and the Rif War

Like all of the other European powers, Spain joined the Scramble for Africa. Spain's portion of Africa lay just across the Strait of Gibraltar from mainland Spain, in northern Morocco. In the 1912 Treaty of Fez, Spanish Morocco became a protectorate of Spain, while the rest of Morocco fell to France. The Spanish operated iron mines in Spanish Morocco's Rif Mountain region, which included *Jebel Musa*, the other "Pillar of Hercules" opposite the Rock of Gibraltar.

In September 1921, the Berber Muslims of Rif declared independence from Spain and established the new Republic of Rif. Even after Spain got help from France, it had a great deal of trouble controlling the Rif rebellion and reestablishing control of **Spanish Morocco**. The Republic of Rif came to an end in 1926, but not before the **Rif War** cost the Spanish a great number of lives and a great deal of embarrassment.

In an "ungovernable" nation like Spain, the embarrassment of the Rif War was enough to reignite the smoldering embers of discord into a roaring flame. The conflict was the same as it had been before the Restoration of the monarchy: **conservatives** (including the military) backed the king, while **liberals** hoped to remove the king and establish a second Spanish republic.

From 1923-1930, Spain was essentially a military dictatorship under Prime Minister Miguel Primo de Rivera, one of the generals who fought in Morocco.

INTERESTING INDIVIDUALS: Miguel Primo de Rivera (1870 – 1930)

Miguel Primo de Rivera was an officer in the Spanish army who gained experience in the Spanish-American War, World War I and the Rif War. During the Rif War in 1921, the Spanish army suffered a disastrous loss at the Battle of Annual in northeast Morocco. An invading Spanish unit drove deep into enemy territory, and the army of Rif managed to cut off the unit's retreat and destroy it. The Cortes (legislature) blamed the catastrophe on the military's incompetence, and ordered an investigation.

Rivera and the military took the opposite view: they blamed the Cortes, not only for the disaster at Annual, but also for Spain's continuing problems with poverty and chaos. In 1923, Rivera and the military suspended Spain's constitution and established what they said would be temporary martial law. Rivera expected martial law to last for a matter of months, only until new elections could replace the selfish and incompetent members of the Cortes with true Spanish patriots. Instead, it lasted for seven years.

King Alfonso supported Rivera by naming him prime minister, and Rivera did not overthrow the king. Nevertheless, Rivera ruled Spain as a dictator for those seven years, using the same methods other dictators used: censorship of the press and imprisonment of political enemies. Rivera presided over a brief economic boom, part of the same boom that lifted the economy worldwide after World War I. When the boom ended in the late 1920s, Rivera began to lose his grip. In January, 1930, when the army turned against him, he resigned as prime minister. He departed for retirement in Paris, where he died two months later.

The Second Spanish Republic

When the army turned against Miguel Primo de Rivera, it also turned against his supporter, King Alfonso XIII. Spain was once again tiring of its monarchy, and there was more support for a new Spanish republic. In the elections of 1931, candidates who supported the republic won a large majority, and King Alfonso was forced to leave the country. For the next 10 years, he continued to claim his place as Spain's king, even though Spain no longer had a king.

For in April 1931, those elected republicans established the new **Second Spanish Republic**. By adopting the new Constitution of 1931, the Republic restored freedom of speech and halted the dictator Rivera's censorship of the press. In a more controversial move, it also established the Republic's authority over the Catholic Church.

The Popular Front and the Nationalists

Even after the establishment of the Second Spanish Republic, the battle between monarchists and republicans continued. The old divisions between Catholic and Secularist, Rich and Poor still remained. To complicate matters, there were also new reasons for division: During the 1930s, **communists** from the USSR and the Comintern (see Chapter 22) and **Fascists** from Italy and Germany (see Chapter 21) began to take a special interest in Spain's affairs.

In order to boost their chances of winning elections, Spain's many factions united into two main political parties:

1. The **Popular (People's) Front**, which supported the free republic, was a coalition of secularist republicans, labor unions, socialists and communists. The Comintern supported the Popular Front because it hoped that the Spanish Republic would become a socialist republic like the USSR.
2. The **Nationalist Party** supported a return to the monarchy and the church. Fascists from Germany and Italy supported the Nationalists because they represented strong government and dictatorial control.

Violence and Assassinations

The years of the Second Spanish Republic were filled with street demonstrations and violence. Militant, church-hating communists began to take over the Popular Front, burning churches and murdering Catholic priests. Nationalists feared a communist takeover that would bring an end to traditional, church-loving Spain. When the Nationalists failed to win majorities in Spain's elections, they began to consider how they might overthrow the republic through force.

Flag of the Falanges

In July 1936, Nationalists from the *Falange* (Phalanx), a fascist group led by Miguel Primo de Rivera's son, assassinated a popular member of the Socialist Party named Jose Castillo. Members of the Popular Front responded by assassinating a nationalist named Jose Calvo Sotelo.

Nationalist members of the military took advantage of the chaos surrounding the assassinations to launch a *coup d'etat* (military takeover) against the Popular Front government.

The leader of the *coup* was General Francisco Franco.

INTERESTING INDIVIDUALS: General Francisco Franco (1892 – 1975) and the Spanish Civil War

Francisco Franco was an experienced army officer and a commander of the Spanish Foreign Legion, an elite unit that was formed to maintain control of Spanish Morocco. He was also a member of an old military family with ties to Spain's royal family. Franco led the Nationalist forces during the Spanish Civil War.

In July 1936, when the Nationalists' coup d'etat attempt began, Franco's forces quickly seized control of about one third of the Spanish mainland and then marched on Madrid. But the Popular Front rallied to defend Madrid, and Franco's assault transformed from a quick coup into a 3-year siege. Franco's plans for a quick coup failed, and the much longer **Spanish Civil War** began.

Bolstered by a great deal of aid from Italy and Germany, Franco's forces came out on top of that war. Madrid finally fell in late March, 1939, and its fall brought an end to the Spanish Civil War. Franco and the Nationalists ousted the Popular Front and took control of Spain.

By the end of the Spanish Civil War, Franco had unified his supporters into one political party, outlawed all other parties and assumed the title *Jefe del Estado* ("head of state"). He would retain that title, with some added embellishments, until his death in 1975.

Franco was not gracious in victory. In order to seal his hold on power and crush any opposition, his regime executed as many as 200,000 Popular Front supporters immediately after the Spanish Civil War. He also resumed strict control of Spain's newspapers, and was quick to imprison or deport his political opponents throughout his long reign. All Spaniards soon learned that it was unwise to disagree publicly with General Franco.

Germany's support for Franco did not earn his allegiance. **Spain remained neutral during World War II, as it had during World War I.** Spain was even a haven (safe shelter) for Jews escaping from German-held France during World War II: despite Hitler's urging, Franco did not establish anti-Jewish laws like Germany's and Italy's. As a good nationalist, Franco kept Spain's Catholics happy by supporting the Catholic Church.

In 1947, Franco re-established Spain's monarchy, but did not name any monarch. He continued to live in the king's palace and to wear the king's military uniform. For all intents and purposes, he was Spain's king; but he never assumed that title, possibly because he was a royalist who respected royal blood and knew that there was no royal blood in his veins. When Franco's end drew near in 1969, he named Juan Carlos de Bourbon, a grandson of King Alfonso XIII, as Spain's next king. General Franco died in 1975.

FASCINATING FACTS: The Red Terror and the White Terror

THE RED TERROR: General Franco wasn't the Spanish Civil War's only executioner. Communist members of the Popular Front, known as "reds" because of their connection to the USSR's Red army, were strongly opposed to Catholicism (and to religion in general). In the Red Terror before and during the war, the Popular Front's "reds" murdered about 1 in 5 of Spain's Catholic priests and nuns. They also murdered tens of thousands of their Nationalist Party political enemies who were caught on the wrong side of the lines before and during the war.

THE WHITE TERROR: Not to be outdone, Franco and the Nationalist Party responded with a far larger White Terror of their own. The Nationalists hated the communists, whom they felt were trying to destroy the Catholic Church and ruin traditional Spain. Where the Popular Front murdered tens of thousands, the Nationalists murdered hundreds of thousands. Most were Franco's political enemies or enemies of the Catholic Church. White Terror executions continued long after the end of the Spanish Civil War.

Wherever Nationalist armies held sway, the church revived. **Today Spain remains about 95% Catholic.**

FASCINATING FACTS: The Mystique of the Spanish Civil War

Several wars have been called "the first modern war," but the Spanish Civil War was "modern" in a new sense: it was the first major war of the radio age. Through the magic of radio, the war drew up-to-the-minute attention from people all over the world. Hearing the sounds of the war from on-the-spot reporters made the war more real to listeners. Both sides also used the radio to spread their propaganda in order to encourage their friends and demoralize their enemies.

Other details also contributed to the special mystique of the Spanish Civil War:

Communism versus Fascism:
The Spanish Civil War was an early battleground between the Communism of Stalin and the Fascism of Hitler and Mussolini. Stalin and Hitler tested their new tanks, warplanes and bombs on the battlefields of the Spanish Civil War, practicing for the far larger World War II that was to come.

Communism versus Conservatism:
The free peoples of the West didn't know which side to support. The Spanish Civil War was an early battle in the war between communist-leaning Western progressives and church-supporting Western conservatives:
- Western socialists, communists, progressives and labor union supporters tended to support the communists of the Popular Front. They were interested in communism because of its promise to create a classless, equal society by taking property from the wealthy and redistributing it to the poor.
- Traditional conservatives were alarmed by the potential spread of communism, which they feared would destroy their liberty; and they were also alarmed by the Popular Front's attacks on priests and Catholic churches. For these reasons, they tended to support General Franco and the Nationalists. Unfortunately, this choice placed them on the side of brutal Fascists like Hitler and Mussolini. With both sides killing indiscriminately, it was difficult to decide who the good guys were. In supporting Franco, the conservatives of the West hoped that they had chosen the lesser of two evils.

FASCINATING FACTS: Hemingway and Orwell in the Spanish Civil War

Two well-known Western authors, Ernest Hemingway and George Orwell, were directly involved in the Spanish Civil War. Hemingway reported on the war from Madrid while the city was under siege. Like most progressives, he favored the Popular Front. His novel *For Whom the Bell Tolls* is based on the Spanish Civil War.

As a young man, George Orwell actually fought for the Popular Front because he sympathized with the labor unions it represented. However, Orwell was no friend of communism later in life: two of his works, *Animal Farm* and *1984,* clearly warn of the dangers of Stalinism.

FASCINATING FACTS: Picasso's *Guernica*

Guernica is an impressionist painting by Spanish artist Pablo Picasso. The painting depicts, in Picasso's unique way, the destruction that took place in the town of Guernica, Spain during the Spanish Civil War.

On April 26, 1937, twenty-eight German warplanes bombed Guernica for two solid hours. Their attack was intended to support General Franco and to terrorize supporters of the Popular Front. In addition to leveling the town, the Guernica bombing raid killed at least several hundred people and injured many more. The majority of its victims were women and children who were not involved in the fighting in any way.

Picasso, who was living in Paris, had received a commission to create a mural for the 1937 Paris World's Fair. When he heard about the destruction of Guernica, he abandoned his original idea for the mural and instead painted *Guernica* on May 1, 1937.

FASCINATING FACTS: The Spanish Siesta

A *siesta* is a mid-day break. The siesta's name comes from the Latin words *hora sexto*, or "sixth hour." In the days before clocks, people marked the time of day by noting the number of hours after sunrise; thus, the sixth hour fell around mid-day. For Spanish farmers who lived in hot climates, the siesta was a chance to avoid working outside through the hottest part of the day. A traditional siesta might last two or more hours, beginning with a large meal and ending with a long nap.

GERMANY'S WEIMAR REPUBLIC

Germany After World War I

Near the end of World War I in late 1918, the German military began to collapse (see Chapter 18). Even when all was clearly lost, some generals refused to capitulate, so their units mutinied against them. On November 9, 1918, Kaiser Wilhelm II began to understand that he could no longer count on the loyalty of his military, so he fled into exile in the Netherlands. In the German Revolution of 1918-1919, the Kaiser's imperial government gave way, and a new republican government appeared. The Weimar Republic (blue area on map), named for the German city of Weimar, formally adopted a new

German constitution at the end of the German Revolution in August 1919. That constitution guaranteed German citizens elected representatives in Parliament and civil rights like free speech and freedom of the press.

Patriotic Germans had difficulty living with the war's bitter outcome. Unwilling to accept the fact that their proud military had suffered defeat, they blamed their loss on the liberals who had opposed the war from the beginning-- the same liberals who formed the Weimar government.

FASCINATING FACTS: The Stab-in-the-Back Legend

Even when all was clearly lost, some German generals refused to capitulate, and continued to order offensives that were doomed to fail. At the end of a long, miserable war, those German troops who had managed to survive were unwilling to spend their lives in pursuit of their generals' mad, impossible dreams; so they began to mutiny. As those generals lost control of their units, they complained bitterly that their government was not supporting them.

German patriots agreed. They reasoned that because their proud military could not have been defeated, it must have been "stabbed in the back" by the liberal republicans who formed the Weimar Republic. These nationalists blamed anyone who could be accused of having loyalties outside Germany:

1) Communists and Marxists, who were suspected of loyalty to Russia's Bolsheviks;
2) Catholics, who were suspected of loyalty to the Pope; and especially
3) Jews, whose exclusive faith made them outsiders wherever they lived.

During the 1930s, Adolf Hitler's National Socialist (Nazi) Party made great use of the *Stab-in-the-back Legend*. Hitler convinced the German people that their army had never truly been defeated, and would not be defeated in the next war.

Hyperinflation in the Weimar Republic

The Treaty of Versailles placed burdens on the German economy that proved impossible to bear. Before World War I, much of Germany's industry had been devoted to producing weapons. The treaty placed heavy limits on weapons production, so nearly every German who worked in the weapons industry had to change jobs. The treaty also cost Germany important industrial territories like the Alsace-Lorraine, which Germany ceded to France (see Chapter 20). Furthermore, the treaty placed the blame for the war squarely on Germany's shoulders, and the victorious Allies insisted on huge war reparations payments.

By 1923, the Weimar Republic couldn't come up with the money for these payments.

The Republic's response was simply to print more of its currency, the paper mark. Since the Allies would accept only gold marks or foreign currency, the Republic couldn't use its paper marks to pay the Allies; but it could still use them inside Germany. When it was unable to collect all of the money it needed through taxes or borrowing, the Weimar Republic began to print paper marks by the truckload, then by the boxcar load in an effort to fund its government activities. The printing of so much paper money led first to inflation, then to hyperinflation.

CRITICAL CONCEPTS: Inflation

Inflation can happen for complicated reasons, but the simplest explanation is this: when too much money is chasing too few goods, each unit of money is worth less. The German economy produced a limited amount of goods and services, but the Weimar Republic printed a nearly unlimited number of paper marks to pay for them. Suddenly there were hundreds of millions of paper marks available to pay for the same limited number of items. There were more paper marks per item, so prices went up.

FASCINATING FACTS: Hyperinflation in the Weimar Republic

The tales of hyperinflation in the Weimar Republic would be funny if they didn't represent so much misery:

- One-mark notes became so worthless that Germans used them to paper their walls (see picture) or as note paper.
- Germans carried huge bundles of nearly worthless paper marks to their banks in wheelbarrows to exchange them for larger notes.
- Prices rose so quickly that merchants had to raise prices several times each day in order to avoid losing money.
- Anyone who received a paycheck immediately rushed to buy groceries before prices could rise any higher.
- The post office printed stamps worth millions and even billions of paper marks.
- The Republic began printing paper mark notes in such huge denominations as 50 million, 100 million and even 1 billion or more.
- As of November 1, 1923, Germans were paying these outrageous food prices: 3 billion paper marks for a pound of bread, 36 billion paper marks for a pound of meat, and 4 billion paper marks for a glass of beer. At these prices, an evening meal for 3-4 people cost more than 50 billion paper marks.

The Weimar Republic finally got its hyperinflation under control by issuing a new currency called the *rentenmark*, which was loosely tied to the price of gold. In 1924, one *rentenmark* was worth 1 trillion of the old paper marks.

Hyperinflation understandably caused a great number of Germans to be unhappy with their Weimar government. In the 1930s, Adolf Hitler exploited that unhappiness to take control of Germany's government as the Weimar Republic's chancellor.

THE RISE OF HITLER

DASTARDLY DICTATORS: Adolf Hitler (1889 – 1945)

Adolf Hitler was born into a poor peasant family in northern Austria, near the German border. His father, Alois Hitler, was an Austrian customs official who was strongly loyal to Austria. Alois wanted Adolf to follow in his footsteps with the Austrian government, but Adolf wanted to study the arts and become a painter or an architect. When Alois insisted on sending his son to technical school anyway, Adolf performed poorly. The young man who would grow up to be Germany's dictator never even finished high school. Father and son seldom agreed, and Alois beat Adolf frequently. Possibly for this reason, Adolf turned against his father's country and loudly proclaimed his love for all things German. Adolf was a proud German patriot and nationalist for the rest of his life.

Hitler was living in Munich, Bavaria, Germany when World War I broke out in 1914. Because he was still an Austrian citizen, he had to beg permission to serve in the Bavarian army. Even though he served Germany throughout the war, he would not become an official German citizen until 1932— the same year in which he became Germany's chancellor.

Although Hitler apparently served his army officers bravely, he never rose above the rank of corporal. Near the end of the war, a mustard gas attack temporarily robbed Hitler of his vision. The blinded Hitler fumed, powerless, as Germany's lines gave way and its military units began to mutiny. Unable to believe that his beloved German army could ever be defeated, Hitler became a strong believer in the Stab-in-the back Legend (see above).

Hitler was still an army corporal when his commander sent him to observe a meeting of a new political party called the German Workers' Party.

The National Socialist German Workers' Party

A German nationalist named Anton Drexler founded the German Workers' Party in 1919, shortly after the end of World War I. Drexler wanted to create a political party that spoke for Germany's common people, whom he believed to be patriotic nationalists like himself. The German army sent Corporal Adolf Hitler to check up on the party at one of its small meetings in a Munich beer hall.

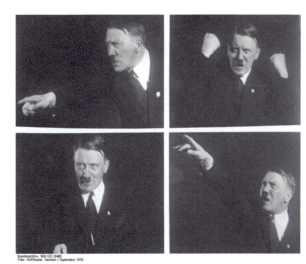

Hitler was supposed to be observing the party's meeting, but instead he became so involved in the political talk that he got into a loud argument. Hitler's speech-making skills and bold opinions impressed Drexler so much that he invited Hitler to join the party. Shortly thereafter, Hitler left the army and began practicing his speechmaking as a full-fledged member of the German Workers' Party.

On February 24, 1920, the German Workers' Party changed its name to the **National Socialist German Workers' Party**, often abbreviated as the National Socialist Party or the **Nazi Party**. On that same day, Hitler outlined the Nazis' beliefs and demands in a speech before about 2,000 people, his largest audience yet. These twenty-five beliefs came in a few broad categories:

Nationalism: The Nazis believed that true Germans were members of the strongest and finest race on earth. Therefore, they believed that Germans deserved a greater Germany. They wanted to break the Treaty of Versailles, take back Germany's lost territories and restore Germany's damaged pride.

Socialism: The Nazis wanted their government to control all of Germany's major industries, especially those that served the military. They also wanted to confiscate the land, money and inheritances of the wealthy and use that wealth to promote a strong German state.

Anti-Semitism: The Nazis wanted to solve the "Jewish Problem"-- the conundrum over what to do about Germany's Jewish minority. They believed that the Jews had used their wealth to control the capitalist Western nations that fought Germany in WWI, and they also believed that German Jews had led the liberal republicans that "stabbed German troops in the back" and cost Germany the war.

Over the years that followed, Hitler preached these principles of Nazism to ever-increasing crowds. He became the Chairman of the Nazi Party on July 28, 1921.

FASCINATING FACTS: The *Sturmabteilung (SA),* aka the Brownshirts

The *Sturmabteilung,* or "Storm Troopers," was a paramilitary group that supported Hitler and the Nazis (Paramilitary groups carry weapons and perform some soldierly duties, but are not official units of a nation's military). The German people knew the storm troopers by their uniforms, and nicknamed them **"Brownshirts."**

The Brownshirts' early duties involved maintaining order at Hitler's frequent speeches, which were often held at the large beer halls where Germans liked to gather in the evenings. If anyone in the beer hall disagreed with Hitler or heckled him, the Brownshirts beat him up and threw him out. The Brownshirts also intimidated Hitler's political enemies, such as the communists, by appearing at their rallies and demonstrating against them loudly and violently. Later, after President Hindenburg granted Hitler emergency powers under the Reichstag Fire Decree, the Brownshirts received the power to open citizens' mail and monitor their telephone conversations in an effort to hunt down Hitler's enemies. Their brutal intimidation tactics helped Hitler immeasurably in his rise to absolute power.

The Beer Hall Putsch and Imprisonment

Putsch is the German word for a *coup d'etat*, or a quick military takeover of the government. With the aid of his Brownshirts, Hitler and his Nazis made one early attempt to overthrow the Weimar government. This attempt, known as the **Beer Hall Putsch**, came in late 1923, when the Weimar Republic's hyperinflation was at its peak (see above).

On November 8, 1923, Hitler and his Brownshirts surrounded a Munich beer hall called the *Burgerbraukeller*, where about 3,000 Germans were gathered to hear an important German official deliver a political speech. Hitler planned to use his great speechmaking skills to convince both the official and his audience to join the *putsch*. While the Brownshirts trained a machine gun on the hall's doors, Hitler burst inside, fired a single shot into the air and announced that the Nazis were taking over the German government. While his helpers, including now-infamous lieutenants Rudolf Hess and Herman Goring, held the official at gunpoint, Hitler quickly charmed his audience into joining the Nazis and supporting their government takeover. The power of Hitler's silver tongue seemed almost magical.

But Hitler's plans didn't account for the German army. On the next day, Hitler led about 2,000 men in a march on Munich's Defense Ministry, but they were unprepared for battle. After a brief skirmish with soldiers who were still loyal to the Weimar government, Hitler was wounded, captured and charged with high treason.

Despite the serious charge against him, Hitler's only punishments were a fine and eight months in prison. His judges were sympathetic to his cause, and gave him a light sentence. Hitler used his trial to gain national attention for himself and his strong opinions; and he used his time in prison to write a political manifesto and autobiography called *Mein Kampf*.

FASCINATING FACTS: *Mein Kampf*

Hitler originally wanted to title his manifesto *Four and a Half Years of Struggle against Lies, Stupidity and Cowardice*, but settled for the more palatable title *Mein Kampf* ("My Struggle"). In the 27 chapters of *Mein Kampf*, Adolf Hitler detailed his strong political opinions and told the German people how he had arrived at them. Hitler dictated *Mein Kampf* to his personal assistant Rudolf Hess while he languished in prison after the failed Beer Hall Putsch. The book was a blend of autobiography, personal political manifesto, and Nazi propaganda. It explained, in part, how Hitler had come to hate the Jews and to believe that Jewish treason lay at the heart of Germany's difficulties. It also foreshadowed much of what would happen during Hitler's coming dictatorship, such as his invasions of Czechoslovakia, Poland and Russia and his attempt to exterminate the Jewish race.

Building the Nazi Party

The Beer Hall Putsch taught Hitler that if he was to take over the German government, he would have to do it by legal means. He spent the next several years focusing on Nazi Party activities like promoting his ideas, sponsoring candidates and winning elections. During these years, the rest of Hitler's now-infamous cadre of lieutenants joined him in the Nazi Party: Adolf Eichmann, Joseph Goebbels, Heinrich Himmler, Reinhard Heydrich, Rudolf Hoess, Joseph Mengele, and many others.

The onset of the Great Depression in 1929 gave the Nazis another boost. After several years of relative stability, the Weimar Republic's economy suddenly went into a tailspin (along with the rest of the world's economies). Hitler and the Nazis blamed Germany's troubles on the political parties in power, and plenty of Germans agreed.

Hitler as Chancellor

==The Nazis never won a majority in the German parliament, and Hitler never won election as Germany's president==.

However, in an election in late 1932, the Nazis did win more seats in parliament than any other party. This was enough to convince the elderly President Hindenburg, against his will, to appoint Hitler as his government's chancellor, or highest official. **On January 30, 1933, Hitler became the head of the German government**. As chancellor, he was second in rank only to the President, whose duties were more ceremonial than practical.

In order to achieve his dream of becoming Germany's dictator, Hitler needed one more boost.

The Reichstag Fire Decree

That boost came in the form of the 1933 Reichstag Fire. On February 27, 1933, a suspicious fire gutted the Reichstag, the building in Berlin where Germany's parliament met. The police blamed the fire on a lone communist, who confessed to the crime under torture (and was later executed).

The Reichstag On Fire

Hitler seized upon the fire as a political opportunity. On the day after the fire, he declared that the destruction of the Reichstag was proof that the country was on the verge of a communist takeover. The situation was so dire, Hitler exclaimed, that President Hindenburg should immediately grant him "emergency powers" so that he could root out Germany's villainous communists and nip the nascent rebellion in the bud.

In the Reichstag Fire Decree, passed on February 28, 1933, President Hindenburg did just that. **From the moment Hindenburg signed the Decree, the Nazis had the power to take away German citizens' civil rights**. They could read citizens' mail and monitor their phone conversations. They could imprison citizens without trial. They could censor citizens' speech and control the press. Hitler claimed that he needed these "emergency powers" to deal with the immediate crisis of the communist revolution, but in fact the Nazis retained these powers until their downfall at the end of World War II.

The Enabling Act

Despite his chancellorship and his emergency powers under the Reichstag Fire Decree, there remained one obstacle in Hitler's path to a fully legal dictatorship: Germany's parliament. Hitler paved his path around the obstacle of Parliament with a new law called the *Enabling Act*.

> The Enabling Act granted Germany's chancellor the power to make laws, even laws that contradicted Germany's constitution, without approval from Parliament.

Proposing such an act was a bold step, even for Hitler. Any parliament that passed the Enabling Act would essentially be handing over all of its power to the chancellor and rendering itself powerless-- essentially voting itself out of existence. However, Hitler's power was already nearly complete. His Brownshirts roamed the streets of Berlin, intimidating citizens and imprisoning his political enemies. Through a combination of bullying and political maneuvering, Hitler was able to collect enough votes to pass the Enabling Act on March 23, 1933.

A year later, when President Hindenburg died, Hitler merged the offices of chancellor and president into a single new office.

> In 1934, Adolf Hitler became the first and only **Fuhrer**, Germany's Chancellor, President and undisputed dictator.

FASCINATING FACTS: The Night of the Long Knives (June 30 - July 2, 1934)

After Hitler won legitimate power as Germany's chancellor, his Brownshirts became more of an embarrassment than an asset. While the Nazi Party was in the minority, the Brownshirts provided the muscle Hitler needed to intimidate his political enemies and spread his propaganda. Their threatening presence even helped Hitler bully the parliament into passing the Enabling Act. But their activities also included a great deal of illegal street violence and murder.

When Hitler took charge of the government, he was suddenly responsible for maintaining law and order in Germany. This posed a problem for the new chancellor, because the 3-million-strong throng of Brownshirted thugs shouting his name in the streets actually represented the very opposite of law and order. Furthermore, the Brownshirts' leader, Ernst Rohm (see picture), had ambitions of taking over Germany's legitimate military, the *Reichswehr*. The *Reichswehr* hated Rohm and the paramilitary Brownshirts; but as Fuhrer, Hitler needed strong support and agreement from the *Reichswehr*.

For these reasons, Hitler demonstrated his characteristic cruelty and ruthlessness by turning against the very people who had helped him to achieve power. From June 30 - July 2, 1934, Hitler conducted a murderous purge of the Brownshirts that became known as the *Night of the Long Knives*. Two of Hitler's now-infamous paramilitary and police units, the SS and the Gestapo, carried out the purge. They offered Rohm a chance to commit suicide; and when he refused, they shot him to death on Hitler's orders. Dozens of others also died in the purge. On the day after the purge, Hitler brazenly passed a law declaring the murders of Rohm and the others legal, after the fact, because he claimed that they were necessary to prevent the overthrow of the German government.

The Brownshirts continued to exist, but they became a shadow of their former selves as their members scattered or were drafted into legitimate army units.

INTERESTING INDIVIDUALS: The *Hitler Jugend* (Hitler Youth)

The *Hitler Jugend*, or "Hitler Youth," began in 1922 as an arm of the Brownshirts set aside for boys too young to participate in street violence.

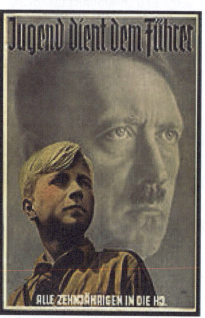

Hitler used the Hitler Youth organization to indoctrinate German boys in his core beliefs and political opinions, which then became theirs as well. Hitler youths learned to believe that theirs was a superior race and that they should devote their all to the advancement of a proud Germany. They also prepared themselves for military life by learning such basic soldiers' skills as marching, map reading, trench digging, marksmanship, bayonet combat and even the handling of explosives.

By 1930, Hitler's youth program included four distinct organizations: the *Jungmadel* (Young Girls) for girls 10-14; the *Bund Deutscher Madel* (League of German Girls) for girls 14-18; the *Deutsches Jungvolk* (Young German People) for boys 10-14; and the *Hitler Jugend* (Hitler Youth) for boys 14-18. Membership in one of these groups was more or less mandatory by 1939. For each group, Hitler's propaganda writers created magazines and posters designed to appeal particularly to its age and interests. Each group learned to love Germany and to look down on other, inferior nations. Each group also learned to love the German race and to view the Jews with suspicion and hatred.

Many members of the Hitler Youth graduated directly into the SS, the paramilitary squad that replaced the Brownshirts as the primary workers of Hitler's evil will. During World War II, Hitler Youth members of ever younger ages were drafted into military service.

FASCINATING FACTS: The Swastika

The *swastika* is a cross with four arms of equal length, all bent at right angles. The Nazis adopted the swastika as their symbol because it was associated with the Aryans, an ancient race from which the Germans were supposedly descended.

However, the swastika was in wide use long before the Nazis adopted it. The Indian religions of Hinduism, Buddhism and Jainism all used the swastika (some Indian peoples also claim descent from the Aryans). They and

others used it as a symbol of life, the sun, power, or good luck. The early pilots of the 1920s, including Charles Lindbergh, painted the swastika on their planes for luck (in their dangerous profession, they had special need of luck).

After the brutal Nazis adopted the swastika, it lost its appeal as a good luck charm. Today, German law forbids the use of the swastika.

FASCINATING FACTS: Hitler's Views on Women

Before Hitler came to power, the German women of the liberal 1920s worked outside the home in all sorts of jobs. Hitler took a more conservative view of women; he believed that their place was in the home. When the pressures of World War II began to overwhelm Germany, Hitler was forced to change his mind and allow women to return to the work force. Until then, however, he believed that women served one primary purpose: to produce and raise good, racially pure German children to populate the vast territories he planned to conquer for Germany.

Hitler promoted German marriages by passing a Law for the Encouragement of Marriage. This law entitled young German couples to a very nice government loan,

Eva Braun and Hitler

roughly equivalent to a family's average annual income. The more children they raised, the less of this loan they eventually had to repay: one-child families repaid 75%; two-child families repaid 50%; three-child families repaid 25%; and four-child families repaid nothing at all. There were also medals for child-birthing: four children earned women a bronze medal, six children earned a silver medal, and eight children earned a gold medal.

As for Hitler himself, he never married until just before his death. Hitler and his long-time mistress, Eva Braun, were married for less than two days before they committed suicide together in Hitler's Berlin *Fuhrerbunker* at the end of World War II.

MISSIONARY FOCUS

GIANTS OF THE FAITH: C. S. Lewis (1898 – 1963)

Clive Staples Lewis was born in Belfast, Northern Ireland (part of Great Britain) in 1898. He didn't like the name "Clive," and his family and friends called him "Jack." Jack's mother died when he was ten years old, and he found comfort in reading and writing. In 1916, he won a scholarship to Oxford University; but before his studies were complete, World War I intervened, and he enlisted in the British army. After Jack had served for five months on the Western Front, a British artillery shell fell short of its intended target and wounded him. When he recovered from his wounds, he returned to Oxford to earn degrees in Greek, Latin, Philosophy, Ancient History and English. He went on to become an Oxford "Don," or gentleman professor.

While he was in his teens, Jack Lewis became an atheist. He became interested in Christianity again through the works of authors like George MacDonald (*Phantastes*) and G.K. Chesterton (*The Everlasting Man*). Oxford friends like J.R.R. Tolkien, author of *The Lord of the Rings*, also helped convince Jack to convert from atheism to Christianity in 1931. Ironically, this former atheist later became one of the most successful Christian authors of the 20th Century.

Over the years from 1949 - 1954, Lewis wrote a series of Christian children's novels called *The Chronicles of Narnia*. The series included seven imaginative books: *The Lion, the Witch and the Wardrobe*, *Prince Caspian*, *The Voyage of the Dawn Treader*, *The Silver Chair*, *The Horse and His Boy*, *The Magician's Nephew* and *The Last Battle*. The Narnia stories were allegories in which a lion named Aslan represented Christ, a white witch represented Satan (or one of his devils), and child characters learned to overcome their sinful natures by doing battle against evil. The Narnia series became Lewis's most popular work; it sold well over 100 million copies and was translated into forty-one languages.

Lewis also wrote several other great Christian works, including:

- *Out of the Silent Planet*, *Perelandra*, and *That Hideous Strength*: a Christian "space trilogy" that laid out most of Lewis' Christian theology in stories that took place on Mars, Venus and Earth
- *The Great Divorce*: a depiction of Lewis' vision of heaven and hell
- *The Screwtape Letters*: a fancied correspondence between demons bent on destroying Christians' faith
- *Till We Have Faces*: a Christian re-imagining of the mythical story of Cupid and Psyche
- *Mere Christianity*: a collection of lectures and essays on Christian apologetics

In 1952, Jack Lewis met Joy Davidman Gresham, another former atheist who had converted to Christianity. Joy was an American poetess and mother of two who had separated from her husband and was living in England. She later divorced. Joy wanted to remain in England, where her children were attending school; but her travel visa was expiring, and she was about to be deported. To make matters worse, she discovered that she had bone cancer. In order to help her avoid deportation, Jack Lewis married Joy Davidman in a civil ceremony in 1956.

Either before or after this first ceremony, the couple discovered that they truly loved one another, and had a second, religious marriage ceremony beside Joy's hospital bed in 1957. Joy's cancer took her life in 1960. Lewis related his feelings about this bereavement in a book titled *A Grief Observed*. He died in 1963 at the age of sixty-four.

U. S. GEOGRAPHY FOCUS

FASCINATING FACTS about OKLAHOMA:

- Statehood: Oklahoma became the 46th US state on November 16, 1907.
- Bordering states: Arkansas, Colorado, Kansas, Missouri, New Mexico, Texas
- State capital: Oklahoma City
- Area: 69,898 sq. mi (Ranks 20th in size)
- Abbreviation: OK
- State nickname: "Sooner State"
- State bird: Scissor-tailed Flycatcher
- State tree: Redbud
- State flower: Mistletoe
- State song: *Oklahoma!* (from the musical play by Rodgers and Hammerstein)
- State Motto: "Labor Conquers All Things"
- Meaning of name: from an Indian word meaning "Red people"
- Historic places to visit in Oklahoma: Crystal Bridge at the Myriad Botanical gardens, Turner Falls Park, Anadarko, National Cowboy Hall of Fame, World Championship Cow Chip Throw, Jenks - Antique Capital of the World, Spiro Mounds, Ponca City's Centennial Plaza, National Lighter Museum, Chickasaw National Recreation Area
- Resources and Industries: farming (cattle, wheat, peanuts, cotton, poultry, dairy), oil, natural gas and mineral mining, transportation equipment, rubber and plastics, food processing

Pioneer Woman Statue, Ponca City, Oklahoma

Flag of Oklahoma
- Oklahoma adopted this flag on April 2, 1925.
- It has a sky blue field, the name "OKLAHOMA" in white letters, and the traditional battle shield of an Osage Indian warrior.
- The shield is crossed by two symbols of peace, a peace pipe and an olive branch.

PRESIDENTIAL FOCUS

PRESIDENT #32: Franklin D. Roosevelt (1882 – 1945)		
In Office: March 4, 1933 – April 12, 1945		**Political Party:** Democratic
Birthplace: New York		**Nickname:** "FDR"

Franklin Roosevelt won election as President in 1932, just as the economy of the Great Depression reached its lowest depths. He won by promising Americans a "New Deal" and assuring them that the Roosevelt administration would not ignore their problems as the Hoover administration had. Roosevelt's New Deal changed the complexion of the U.S. government and the Presidency forever. Before Roosevelt, most Presidents believed that the Constitution placed heavy limits on their power; but Roosevelt acknowledged few, if any, limits on his power. He believed that his government could and should do whatever it took to combat the Great Depression, even if some of its acts violated the U.S. Constitution. When the Supreme Court declared some of the New Deal's programs unconstitutional, Roosevelt tried (and failed) to "pack the court" by adding justices who would vote in the New Deal's favor.

Roosevelt was a great speaker who regularly communicated with the American people through radio messages he called "fireside chats." In these chats, he offered patient explanations of America's problems and the actions he took to solve them. Even when the New Deal's many programs failed to lift America out of its Depression, FDR's fireside chats kept most Americans convinced that their President was at least trying to do the right thing. His other great communication asset was his popular wife Eleanor, whom many Americans came to view as a personal friend as they read her daily newspaper column, "My Day."

President George Washington established a precedent that no President, however popular, should hold office for more than two four-year terms. However, when World War II threatened America's security at the end of President Roosevelt's second term, he decided to run for an unprecedented third term. After guiding the United States through most of World War II, he died in office (of a stroke) on April 12, 1945. His death came less than three months after his inauguration to an unprecedented *fourth* term, and only weeks before the Allies' victory in Europe.

Other interesting facts about Franklin Roosevelt:
- FDR was of the "Hyde Park," Democratic Party Roosevelts, while his cousin Teddy Roosevelt was of the "Oyster Bay," Republican Party Roosevelts.
- A bout with polio cost FDR the use of his legs when he was 39 years old. When FDR spoke before an audience, he was usually seated behind a podium so that his audience wouldn't think less of him when they saw his wheelchair and his polio-damaged legs.
- FDR was the first President to fly in an airplane and the first to appear on television.
- FDR was the only U.S. President who won election to four terms. Two years after he died, the U.S. Congress passed the 22nd Amendment to limit Presidents to two terms.

Notable quotes from Franklin Roosevelt:
- "True individual freedom cannot exist without economic security and independence. People who are hungry and out of a job are the stuff of which dictatorships are made."
- "Human kindness has never weakened the stamina or softened the fiber of a free people. A nation does not have to be cruel to be tough."

Chapter 25

World War II (Part I), The Holocaust

WORLD HISTORY FOCUS

WORLD WAR II (PART I)

Casus Belli for World War II in Europe

In some ways, World War II in Europe was a continuation of World War I, and the **Treaty of Versailles** was little more than a truce that maintained a fragile peace for the 20 years between the end of World War I in 1919 and the beginning of World War II in 1939. According to this view, the flawed Treaty of Versailles made World War II inevitable: it was at once too heavy-handed and too lenient. On one hand, the heavy reparations payments it levied angered belligerent Germans until they demanded war. On the other hand, it left Germany largely intact, capable of rebuilding a strong military and rising up to challenge its neighbors once more.

In other ways, World War II was a separate war, driven by the newly powerful forces of **communism** and **fascism**. Stalin and the Comintern promoted communist revolutions in China and Spain, and hoped to spread their philosophy of strictly enforced "equality" around the world. Hitler and Mussolini sought to build empires based on race-proud, nation-proud, militaristic fascism. There was nothing new about empire-building; but Hitler's fanatical pride of race brought a new flavor to his imperialism. Hitler fought for *lebensraum*, "living space," for Germans; and had he succeeded, he would happily have exterminated the "inferior" races of each new territory he conquered so that he could replace them with citizens of good, loyal German stock. This plan was already well underway before the Allies managed to stop him in 1945.

CRITICAL CONCEPTS: Decoding the Nazis

A short list of terms, definitions and abbreviations from Nazi Germany:

Gestapo: *Geheime Staats Polizei*, "Secret State Police." The Gestapo spied out and arrested Hitler's enemies, especially the Jews.
Heer: The German army.
Kriegsmarine: The German navy.
Luftwaffe: "air weapon," the German air force.
Panzers: German tanks. A Panzer division was an updated version of the old-fashioned horse cavalry, a fast-moving army division equipped with tanks instead of horses.
SS: *Schutzstaffel*, or "Protection Squadron." The SS was a paramilitary group that handled special tasks such as providing Hitler's personal protection, spreading Hitler's propaganda and operating Hitler's concentration camps.
Waffen-SS: The armed wing of the SS. Waffen-SS units often fought like regular army units; but as members of Hitler's special police force, they were never part of the *wehrmacht*.
Wehrmacht: The combined forces of the German military: army, navy and air force.

A Brief Timeline of World War II in Europe, Part I

In the years leading up to World War II, Hitler's Germany made a series of bold moves to reclaim territories it had lost after World War I. Each of these moves violated the Treaty of Versailles. Theoretically, the League of Nations had the power to enforce the Treaty of Versailles; but in reality, the League was powerless if its member nations were unwilling to enforce its demands.

1935: Germany declares that it will no longer obey the restrictions the Treaty of Versailles placed on its military, and begins rebuilding its forces openly. The League of Nations protests, but none of its member nations act on this protest.

1936, March 7: Germany reoccupies the Rhineland, the territory east of the Rhine River on the border between France and Germany (opposite the Alsace-Lorraine).

After World War I, France insisted that the Allies occupy the Rhineland to create a buffer between France and Germany. Allied troops withdrew from the Rhineland in 1930, but it remained a demilitarized zone (no German troops allowed) under the Treaty of Versailles-- that is, until Germany violated the Treaty.

1938, March 12: Germany takes over the government of Austria in the *Anschluss*.

INTOLERABLE INVASIONS: The Anschluss

Anschluss is a German word for "connection." The *Anschluss* was Germany's "connection" with Austria, in which German troops invaded Austria, occupied it and absorbed it into the German Empire. Some Austrians were willing participants in the *Anschluss*, and some were not.

Austria was a German-speaking nation and a natural ally of Germany, but it had never been part of the German Empire formed in 1871. Instead, it was part of the Empire of Austria-Hungary, which was dissolved at the end of WWI. After that war, some Austrians wanted to unite their new republic with Germany's, but the Treaty of Versailles demanded that they remain separate because their union would have made Germany larger and stronger.

Hitler resented this restriction, as he resented most of the Treaty of Versailles' restrictions. One of his first goals was to bring all German-speaking peoples under one German government, especially the people of his native Austria. In 1934 the Austrian Nazi Party, which Hitler controlled through a German Nazi leader known as a ***gauleiter***, actually assassinated one Austrian chancellor who opposed unifying Austria with Germany.

The next Chancellor, Kurt Schuschnigg, also opposed unification. At a meeting on the issue in Berchtesgaden, Germany, Hitler presented Schuschnigg with a long list of demands and threatened his personal safety. In response, Schuschnigg decided to appeal to the Austrian people: he scheduled a nationwide popular vote ("plebiscite" or referendum) on the issue of unification for March 12, 1938. Even though plenty of Austrians supported unification with Germany, Schuschnigg was fairly certain that a majority of Austrians still supported an independent Austria, and that Hitler would lose the popular vote.

Hitler must have thought so too, because he didn't wait for the referendum. Instead, he sent German troops into Austria on March 12 to take control of Austria's government. Austria formally united with Germany that same day. On April 2, 200,000 cheering Austrians gathered in Vienna (Austria's capital) to greet their "liberator" Hitler. In order to confirm his popularity, Hitler rescheduled the popular vote on unification for April

10. The presence of German soldiers and Nazi Party members at the polling places may have influenced the vote: Over 99% of Austria's voters supported unification with Germany.

The events of the *Anschluss* form the background for the popular musical "The Sound of Music."

1938, March - September: Hitler presses Czechoslovakia to surrender control of the Sudetenland, the western, German-speaking portion of its territory.

1938, September 29: In the Munich Agreement, Britain, France and Italy agree to allow Germany to claim the Sudetenland from Czechoslovakia. The government of Czechoslovakia is not consulted.

FASCINATING FACTS: Neville Chamberlain (1869 – 1940) and Appeasement

Neville Chamberlain was the Prime Minister of the United Kingdom from 1937 - 1940. During the years leading up to World War II, Chamberlain and others tried to deal with Hitler's bold aggression through ***appeasement***— that is, they tried to satisfy Hitler by giving him what he demanded, even when his demands violated the Treaty of Versailles, and then hoping that he wouldn't make more demands. Two of the Hitler demands that Chamberlain and his fellow appeasers met were Austria and Czechoslovakia.

Chamberlain was inclined to appease Hitler, rather than confront him militarily, for several reasons:

- Chamberlain and other Britons believed that the Treaty of Versailles had been too hard on Germany, and were ready to relax some of its demands in exchange for peace.
- The financial strain of the Great Depression, combined with the war debt left over from WWI, had left the British government poorer. Few British leaders wanted to add more financial burdens by financing an expensive altercation with Germany.
- In 1938, the misery-filled memory of WWI was still fresh, and few Britons held any desire for another war with Germany.
- Chamberlain was more interested in domestic (internal, home-related) affairs than in international affairs, and he wanted the Hitler problem to go away.
- In 1938, no one yet knew just how far Hitler was willing to go in pursuit of his mad dreams.

When Germany overran Austria in the *Anschluss*, Chamberlain and the appeasers did little more than protest. Their failure to act emboldened Hitler's plans for Czechoslovakia.

Czechoslovakia was similar to Austria in one way: the Sudetenland was home to millions of German-descended people, and Hitler demanded the right to reclaim their land for Germany. In another way, however, Czechoslovakia was completely different: unlike Austria, Czechoslovakia had the industry and the military strength to defend itself, and was prepared to do so if it could find any allies to help.

It found none. Chamberlain traveled to Germany three times in 1938 to negotiate the Czechoslovakia situation with Hitler:

September 15: On Chamberlain's first trip, Hitler agreed that Germany would annex (take over) the Sudetenland only if the Sudetenland's people voted to unite with Germany in a popular vote. Chamberlain emerged from this meeting believing that he could preserve peace in Europe by merely convincing Czechoslovakia to hold a popular vote on the issue of surrendering the Sudetenland to Germany.

September 22: On Chamberlain's second trip, Hitler announced that his earlier demands were no longer sufficient. Now Hitler wanted to occupy the Sudetenland immediately, and hinted that he wanted parts of

Poland and Hungary as well. Chamberlain emerged from this meeting alarmed by Hitler's hunger for more territory, but still determined to preserve the peace.

September 29-30: On Chamberlain's last trip, now known as the *Munich Conference*, he surrendered the Sudetenland in exchange for Hitler's glib promise that he would not try to claim any more European territories. The Czech government agreed to withdraw from the Sudetenland. Any Czech living in the Sudetenland who did not want to live under German rule would have to move out on the following day, October 1, and would not be allowed to take anything with him (Hitler didn't want anything of value to escape his grasp).

<u>FASCINATING FACTS:</u> The Anglo-German Agreement

Before he left the Munich Conference, Chamberlain asked Hitler to sign a short "Anglo-German Agreement" in which England and Germany agreed to avoid war between them. Fresh from his triumph over the Sudetenland, Hitler quickly agreed. When Germany's Foreign Minister Ribbentrop questioned Hitler about the agreement, Hitler responded that Ribbentrop was not to worry: "That piece of paper is of no further significance whatever."

Chamberlain, on the other hand, treated the agreement as the most significant thing to come out of the Munich Conference. To Chamberlain, that short document guaranteed peace for Britain, and that was what mattered. Back home in England, he waved the agreement in the air and announced that he had honorably negotiated "peace for our time." Men like future Prime Minister Winston Churchill, who had warned against appeasing Hitler, doubted that Chamberlain had achieved either "honor" or "peace."

1938, October 1: With Prime Minister Chamberlain's permission, Germany takes over Czechoslovakia's Sudetenland region.

1939, March 15: In violation of the agreement at the Munich Conference, German troops take control of what remains of divided Czechoslovakia.

1939, May 22: Germany and Italy sign the **Pact of Steel**, formally known as the "Pact of Friendship and Alliance between Germany and Italy."

In the **Pact of Steel**, Hitler and Mussolini agreed to work together and to defend each other if either was attacked. The Pact of Steel formed the "Rome-Berlin Axis"; Germany, Italy and their allies would become known as the "Axis Powers."

1939, August 23: Germany and the USSR sign the *Molotov-Ribbentrop Pact*, formally known as the "Treaty of Non-Aggression between Germany and the USSR."

In the **Molotov-Ribbentrop Pact**, Hitler and Stalin publicly agreed to remain neutral if either of them was attacked. They also agreed, secretly, to divide Eastern Europe into two "spheres of influence," a western sphere for Germany and an eastern sphere for the USSR. They were essentially dividing Poland, which lay between them and which they both planned to invade very soon.

1939, September 1: Germany invades western Poland.

1939, September 2: Britain and France demand that German forces withdraw from Poland within one day. Italy declares itself neutral. In doing so, Italy fails to honor the Pact of Steel, just as it had failed to honor the Triple Alliance at the outset of WWI.

> **1939, September 3:** When Germany fails to withdraw, **Britain and France declare war on Germany**. British India and the Dominions of Australia and New Zealand all follow suit within hours.

1939, September 16: The USSR invades eastern Poland.

1939, September 19: Germany and the USSR complete their separate takeovers of Poland, meeting at Brest-Litovsk (where Germany and Russia had negotiated Russia's withdrawal from WWI; see picture).

1939, October 10: The last Polish forces surrender. With his goals in Poland accomplished, Hitler makes an offer of peace to Britain and France, but both refuse.

INTOLERABLE INVASIONS: The Gleiwitz Incident and the Invasion of Poland

Germany's invasion of Poland marked the real beginning of World War II. The attack began one week after Germany and the USSR signed the Molotov-Ribbentrop Pact (see above).

Hitler's pretext (excuse) for the invasion of Poland was a "false flag" operation called the Gleiwitz Incident. In a false flag operation, an aggressor disguises some of his own troops as enemy troops and uses them to launch a harmless attack on himself. Then he blames the attack on his enemy and pretends to be outraged. The cagy Hitler used false flag operations in Austria and Czechoslovakia as well as in Poland. In all three cases, he constantly claimed that good people of German descent were being oppressed by foreign governments, and needed his help.

In the Gleiwitz Incident, troops from Hitler's paramilitary SS captured a radio station in Gleiwitz, Germany, near the Polish border, and used it to broadcast anti-German propaganda. Hitler blamed the attack on German-hating Poles from across the border, and used it to justify the full-scale invasion of Poland that he had already been planning for months.

That invasion began on September 1, 1939, the day after the Gleiwitz Incident. Hitler's attack was designed to isolate, surround and destroy as many units of the Polish army as possible. It was also designed to kill as many "racially inferior" Poles as possible-- the real purpose of the invasion was to capture *lebensraum*, "living space," for people of good German stock.

When the invasion began, the overmatched Polish army retreated to the east and hoped for assistance from its promised allies, Britain and France. The undoing of that strategy come on September 16, when the USSR invaded Poland from the east. Faced with overwhelming opposition, the Poles were forced to surrender before any western aid could arrive. The German army and the USSR's Red army met at Brest-Litovsk, the same city where Germany and Russia had negotiated Russia's withdrawal from WWI in late 1917. For the duration of the war, Poland's government lived in exile, and portions of the Polish navy and air force aided Britain in the Battle of Britain and elsewhere.

1940, April 9-10: Germany invades and conquers Norway, establishing a puppet government under Norwegian defense minister Vidkun Quisling. The word "quisling" will enter the English language as a synonym for "traitor."

1940, May 10: Germany launches a massive invasion all across Western Europe. France, Belgium, the Netherlands and Luxembourg all come under attack. Britain's Prime Minister Chamberlain loses the confidence of the British Parliament, and resigns. Winston Churchill becomes Britain's new prime minister.

INTOLERABLE INVASIONS: The Maginot Line and the Battle of France

After World War I, France eyed its belligerent neighbor to the northeast warily. In the years between the two world wars (the "interbellum"), France carefully fortified its border with Germany by creating a series of bunkers, forts, tank obstacles and other defenses called the **Maginot Line** (named for French Defense Minister Andre Maginot). The French praised the Maginot Line as an impregnable defense against German aggression.

Unfortunately for the French, Minister Maginot's line was best suited to fight the First World War, not the second. The new German army was far faster and better equipped than the one that had assailed France in World War I. There was a radio inside each of Germany's numerous Panzer tanks, allowing the Germans to coordinate their attacks far better than before; and the German *Luftwaffe's* (air force's) *Stuka* bombers filled the skies (see picture). The long, defensive trench battles of World War I were a thing of the past: a defensive trench was of little use against a dive-bombing warplane.

In the **Battle of France**, the German response to the Maginot Line was simply to go around it. German troops attacked France by first passing through Belgium and Luxembourg, where France's defenses were light. As in Poland, the German tactic was to punch through French lines quickly, surround French army units and destroy them (some called this tactic *blitzkrieg*, or "lightning war"). Most of the Maginot Line's dearly-bought defenses were useless once the Germans were on the French side of the line.

Germany's conquest of France required only a week longer than its conquest of Poland. Less than six weeks after the invasion began, German troops captured Paris (see picture) and received France's surrender at Compiegne Forest. Surviving members of the French government fled to exile in Britain, where they established the government of "Free France" under General Charles de Gaulle. Through the rest of the war, de Gaulle tried to inspire the French to resist their Nazi occupiers.

Those who remained behind in France tried a different tactic with the Nazis: cooperation. In the central France city of Vichy, just south of the line of German occupation, Germany allowed France to establish a new government under French Marshal Philippe Petain. Petain was angry at his British allies, both for failing to provide more warplanes to defend France and for ordering the evacuation at Dunkirk (see below). Petain had no love for the Germans, but he also believed that Britain had abandoned its ally France in its hour of need. Britain's Prime Minister Churchill urged Petain to continue to fight a guerrilla war against German occupiers, but Petain chose instead to surrender.

Petain's "**Vichy France**" helped Germany battle the Allies in North Africa, and it also allowed its police force to help the German SS round up Jews to send to the Holocaust (see below). After the war, the restored government of France sentenced Marshal Petain to death as a traitor, but ended up commuting his sentence to life in prison.

1940, May 15: The Netherlands surrenders to Germany.
1940, May 25: With northern France overrun by German forces, British and French forces retreat to a

beachhead at Dunkirk, France.
1940, May 28: Belgium surrenders to Germany.
1940, May 26 - June 3: In Operation Dynamo, Britain and France evacuate the 330,000 troops trapped in Dunkirk to safety across the English Channel.

FASCINATING FACTS: The Evacuation of Dunkirk

Early in the Battle of France, the British Expeditionary Force (BEF) joined units of the French army in northern France to defend France's border with Belgium. When the battle began on May 10, the BEF was as surprised as everyone else by the speed with which the Germans penetrated their lines and moved around them. Less than three weeks later, the Germans surrounded the BEF on three sides and pushed it toward the sea. In desperation, British commanders ordered an immediate evacuation by ship across the English Channel. They named the mission **"Operation Dynamo"** because they prepared its plans in a dynamo (electric generator) room in the basement of Dover Castle, on the British side of the Channel.

Operation Dynamo was no easy mission. There were about 330,000 British and French troops to move, and there were no berths at Dunkirk to accommodate deep-water troop ships. This meant that there was no way for the evacuees to board such large ships, save by swimming. In order to get their men out, the British needed smaller boats that could ply the shallow waters near the beach at Dunkirk.

So the British put out a plea for every merchant boat, fishing boat or pleasure boat available that might conceivably cross the 25-mile-wide English Channel and rescue some soldiers. About 800 such small vessels responded. Piloted by both military and civilian boatmen, the "little ships of Dunkirk" crossed the Channel to Dunkirk, moved as close to shore as their drafts allowed, and loaded the soldiers aboard. Then they ferried them out to larger troopships, which carried them across the Channel to Britain and (relative) safety.

As romantic as it was, the legendary success of the "little ships" would have turned to failure quickly without the help of the British Royal Air Force (RAF). Although the German army had ordered a temporary halt after three weeks of hard action, the *Luftwaffe* (German air force) had not. Brave RAF pilots served to keep most of the evacuees safe from the *Luftwaffe* for the nine days it took Operation Dynamo to evacuate those 330,000 men.

1940, June 10: Italy declares war on France and Britain.
1940, June 14: The Germans capture France's capital city of Paris.
1940, June 22: France surrenders to Germany at Compiegne Forest. Britain becomes the last western European power left standing against the German onslaught.
1940, July 1: With Paris and northern France under German occupation, France establishes a new government at the city of Vichy. France's Vichy government, led by French Marshal Petain, will cooperate with Germany through the rest of the war. After the war, some of its leaders will be executed as traitors.

FASCINATING FACTS: The French Surrender at Compiegne Forest

After Germany won the Battle of France, Adolf Hitler was in the mood to settle an old score. Hitler had never gotten over Germany's defeat in World War I, and believed that France and its Allies could never have defeated Germany if the Jews and the Communists had not "stabbed German troops in the back" at the end of that war (see Chapter 24). Therefore when Germany's turn at victory came at the end of the Battle of France, Hitler took every opportunity to savor the moment.

Hitler demonstrated his sense of history by choosing Compiegne Forest as the site of the armistice negotiations. Compiegne was the place where France had dictated its armistice terms to Germany at the end of World War I. During the years between the wars, the French had built a large memorial park around the site of Germany's surrender. This memorial included several monuments, including one that enclosed the very rail car in which France's Marshal Foch had accepted Germany's surrender in 1918. The tables were about to be turned.

When Hitler's men arrived at the memorial park, they moved that rail car to the very spot where it had sat for the first armistice 22 years before. Then Hitler sat in Marshal Foch's seat while he watched the French sign the new armistice. Finally, he ordered all of the monuments destroyed and the entire memorial park razed. One of the things the Germans destroyed was a monument that depicted an eagle (the symbol of Germany) lying dead, pierced by an upright French sword (see picture).

With these symbolic gestures at Compiegne, Hitler felt that he had demonstrated German superiority, set the historical record straight and erased a stain from Germany's proud history.

1940, June 30 - July 1: In preparation for an invasion of Britain, Germany captures all of the islands in the English Channel between France and Britain.
1940, July 10: The Battle of Britain begins with air attacks against ships in the English Channel. Hitler plans to first control the Channel, then launch an invasion force across the Channel into Britain.
1940, August 26: British warplanes bomb Berlin, Germany's capital, for the first time.
1940, August 30: In the London Blitz, the Germans retaliate for the Berlin bombing with heavy bombing raids on London.
1940, September 17: Britain's successful air defense forces Hitler to postpone the German invasion of Britain for the last time. Britain will continue to suffer bombing raids, but is no longer in daily danger of immediate invasion.

DESPERATE DEFENSES: The Battle of Britain

The Battle of Britain was Britain's struggle to survive the German onslaught that had just overwhelmed its neighbor and ally, France. It was also the struggle to save the last free nation in Europe. Some of Britain's darkest days, as well as some of its finest hours, came in the Battle of Britain.

In its favor, Britain had two defenses that France lacked: the English Channel and the British navy. These defenses forced Hitler to attack in a certain way, for these reasons:

1. Hitler could not hope to launch a ground invasion against Britain without first controlling the English Channel, because his defenseless troop ships would be vulnerable to attack by sea or by air from the moment they set sail across the Channel.
2. Hitler could not hope to control the English Channel without first neutralizing the British navy, which was still larger and stronger than Germany's.
3. Hitler could not hope to neutralize the British navy without first destroying the Royal Air Force (RAF), because RAF fighter planes defended the British navy from Hitler's Stuka dive bombers.

For all of these reasons, Germany's target in the Battle of Britain was the British Royal Air Force (RAF).

At the outset of the Battle of Britain, all of the *Luftwaffe*'s might and energy was focused on the destruction of the RAF.

The RAF rose to the challenge. In air-to-air combat, the British pilots who were defending their homeland always managed to give better than they got. Their warplanes were equal to the *Luftwaffe*'s, and their skills were perhaps a bit better. The RAF also had two advantages:

1. its warplanes were closer to their airstrips, so that they usually had an advantage in fuel; and
2. British ground-based radars helped the RAF locate enemy squadrons while they were still crossing the English Channel, so that they could attack *Luftwaffe* bombers before they reached their targets.

The *Luftwaffe* shifted its strategy several times: it tried focusing on

1. destroying British warplanes in the air,
2. destroying ground-based radar installations, and
3. destroying airstrips and the airplane hangars where the RAF repaired and equipped its warplanes.

Each time, the RAF managed to fight the *Luftwaffe* off.

Later, the Luftwaffe resorted to terror bombings of cities all over Britain, especially London. These attacks often came at night, when darkness made it harder for the RAF to find and destroy *Luftwaffe* bombers. On night attacks, Luftwaffe bombers could be guided to their targets by a city's lights. To prevent this, British officials ordered "blackouts," which required every home and business to cover its windows tightly with black curtains so that no light could escape. The people of London began to hear air raid sirens nightly. Families sent their children to the country for safety; while in the city, ordinary citizens donned gas masks and took cover in basement bomb shelters. A single German bomber crew could rouse an entire city from slumber and force its people to spend hours cowering in their assigned shelter. Fear and lack of sleep made Londoners irritable and miserable.

The RAF's stiff defense of Britain forced Hitler to postpone his planned ground invasion again and again. By mid-September, 1940, Hitler finally determined that he wouldn't be able to invade Britain that year. Reluctantly, he turned his attention elsewhere. British Prime Minister Winston Churchill thanked the valiant RAF for saving Britain from the Nazis with these words:

"Never in the field of human conflict has so much been owed by so many to so few."

1940, September 27: Germany, Italy and Japan sign the Tripartite Pact.
Throughout 1941: Germany, Italy and Britain battle for control of their colonies in North Africa.

1941, June 22: Hitler launches the world-changing Operation Barbarossa, a massive invasion of the formerly neutral USSR.

1941, June 22: On that same day, the USSR declares war on Germany and joins the Allies in the fight against the Axis Powers.

FASCINATING FACTS: Operation Barbarossa and the Eastern Front

Germany's invasion of the USSR marked the opening of a whole new theater of World War II, the *Eastern Front*. It also had one other immediate affect: it caused the formerly "neutral" USSR, which had actually cooperated with Germany in the invasion of Poland, to switch sides and join the war on the side of Britain and the Allies.

Hitler had always intended to confront the USSR someday, for several reasons:

- Hitler hated communists, and blamed them (in part) for Germany's loss in WWI.
- Hitler believed that the Slavic peoples who populated Russia were racially inferior to Germans (Aryans). Germans needed *lebensraum*, "living space," and Hitler planned to get it by exterminating the inferior Slavs and filling their conquered land with people of good German stock.
- Germany needed more resources to pursue its war against the West, and the USSR had them: highly productive farmland in the Ukraine, and bountiful oilfields in Baku (Azerbaijan).
- Hitler believed that by conquering the USSR, he could eliminate the threat in the east and focus all of his resources on conquering the West.

Hitler also held the USSR's military in low esteem. He believed that it had been so weakened by Stalin's Great Purge (see Chapter 20) that it would prove to be leaderless and incompetent, and that the mighty German army would roll over the USSR as quickly as it had rolled over Norway, Belgium and France. This mistaken belief would cost the Germans dearly. Because of it, Hitler's officers planned for a short war, and weren't prepared for the long, miserable mess that **Operation Barbarossa** and later Eastern Front battles turned out to be.

At first, the Nazis were successful, and their Panzer tank divisions drove deep into Soviet territory. They defeated Russian defenses, caused terrible casualties among the Russians, and captured important targets all along the new Eastern Front.

Soon, however, they found that the "Blitzkrieg" tactics that had served them so well in France weren't as effective in the USSR. Russia was too vast. The fast-moving Panzers advanced too far ahead of the supply lines that kept them stocked with fuel, ammunition and food. Before their slower units could move forward, the Russians closed in behind the Panzers, cutting them off from their sources of supply. With their overland supply lines cut, the Panzers could receive supplies only by air. In the late-1942 **Battle of Stalingrad**, the Luftwaffe carried thousands of tons of supplies to cut-off Panzer divisions. Unfortunately, the Panzers needed not thousands, but tens of thousands of tons of supplies.

There was also the cold-- bitter, unendurable cold. In planning for their short, summer war, the Nazis had not accounted for the cold, or provided the extra clothing, fuel and other supplies it demanded. As the season turned, the ill-prepared, cut-off German soldiers endured unimaginable suffering in the frigid winter air around Russian cities like Moscow and Stalingrad.

It was on the **Eastern Front** of World War II that Hitler's mad racial hatred reached its highest expression. The Eastern Front saw mass deportations and the creation of "concentration camps" to house the deported. It saw mass executions and mass burials in common graves. It even saw attempts to exterminate entire races and populations, especially Hitler's most hated enemies, the Jews.

At the height of his power, which he achieved in 1941, Hitler controlled all of the territory in blue on the map at right.

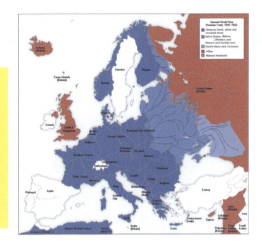

At this point in the war, the major nations involved are:

On the side of the Axis Powers: Germany, Japan, Italy, Hungary, Romania and Bulgaria

On the side of the Allies: Britain (along with its Commonwealth of Britain nations Australia, British India, Canada, New Zealand and South Africa), Free France, Poland, Belgium, Denmark, Luxembourg, the Netherlands, Norway, Greece, Yugoslavia and the USSR

WORLD WAR II TIMELINE CONTINUES IN CHAPTER 26

THE HOLOCAUST

A "holocaust" is the utter destruction wrought by a raging fire. "**The Holocaust**" is the term historians use for the destruction wrought by the fire of Adolf Hitler's extreme hatred for one particular race, the Jewish people.

Anti-Semitism, or racial hatred for the Jews, began long before Hitler's time. From the days of Abraham, Moses and Joshua, religious Jews maintained a strict separation between themselves and the other races and nations that surrounded them. The Jews insisted that there was only one God, and refused to acknowledge any other gods. They also believed that as descendants of Abraham, they were the children of a special promise that God had made to them alone.

The Jews' refusal to mingle caused their neighbors to resent their stubborn pride; and their insistence on monotheism got them into trouble with the law. The Bible books of Esther and Daniel both tell of the troubles Jews had with foreign governments when they refused to bow down to their rulers as gods. In 70 AD, the Romans destroyed the Jews' Second Temple in Jerusalem for the same reasons. In the process, the Romans also destroyed the last remnants of the Jewish nation in Israel, scattering the Jews who survived in a Diaspora that would carry them all over the world.

In Europe, the Jews were set apart from their neighbors in new ways. Their predominantly Christian neighbors attacked them with new accusations:

- **"Christ Killers":** Some of their Christian neighbors condemned the Jews for "killing Christ" by asking the Romans to crucify Him. In calling the Jews "Christ killers," Christians called down on them the same curse that the Jews in the Book of Matthew called down on themselves when they begged Pilate to crucify Christ (see Matthew 27:25, "His blood is on us and our children").

- **"Blood Libel":** Others accused the Jews of using the blood of Christian children in their ritual sacrifices. Such false accusations are called "blood libel."

- **Usury:** For centuries, the Catholic Church forbade its members to charge interest on loans; but those Catholics' Jewish neighbors charged interest happily. Poor Christians resented Jewish bankers and businessmen for their shrewd tactics and great wealth.

Hitler took these accusations against the Jews still farther:

1. He accused wealthy Jewish capitalists of controlling the Western capitalist nations that had opposed Germany in World War I.
2. He accused Jewish communists of stabbing the German army in the back at the end of that same war (see Chapter 24).
3. He believed that Jewish communists also controlled the Bolsheviks, who had overrun Russia in 1917 and who were now Germany's enemies.
4. He believed that the Jews' stubborn insistence on remaining separate made them disloyal to Germany.

In Hitler's mind, Germany had few problems that didn't originate with the Jews. Both before and during World War II, Hitler began to cast around for the "**Final Solution**" to the "**Jewish Question**" that had plagued Europe for centuries. His solution involved forcing Jews into "**ghettos**," deporting them *en masse*, confining them to forced labor and concentration camps, and ultimately exterminating as many Jews as possible.

A Brief Timeline of the Holocaust

1933, March 22: Hitler's Nazi Party opens *Konzentrationslager Dachau,* its first concentration camp for political enemies. Dachau will be the second camp liberated by Western armies at the end of WW II. Note that Hitler had just been named Chancellor of Germany in January 1933.

1933, April 1: The Nazis stage a boycott of all Jewish shops and businesses, encouraging Germans to buy only from loyal Germans, not from Jews.

1933, May 10: Nazi propaganda director Joseph Goebbels encourages German university students to burn books by "Jewish intellectuals" like Albert Einstein.

Inspection at Dachau by Himmler in 1936

1933, September 29: The Nazis prohibit Jews from owning land.
1935, September 15: The Nuremburg Race Laws deprive German Jews of their citizenship.

FASCINATING FACTS: The Nuremburg Race Laws

Nowhere are Hitler's mad theories on race more plain than in the **Nuremburg Race Laws**. The very names of these laws tell the full tale of Hitler's extreme racial pride and hatred for the Jews:

- *The Laws for the Protection of German Blood and German Honor*: Among other things, these laws 1) forbade Jews to marry Germans; 2) forbade Jews to employ German women under 45 years old as housekeepers; and 3) forbade Jews to fly the German flag (but encouraged them to fly Jewish flags to mark themselves as Jews).

- *The Law for the Protection of the Genetic Health of the German People*: This law required anyone who wished to marry to submit to a medical examination to make sure he or she wasn't carrying any genetic diseases. Only if Germans' genes were certified pure did they receive certificates of "fitness to marry."

Around 1936: Hitler temporarily relaxes his crackdown on Jews to avoid disapproval from the many foreigners who travel to Berlin, Germany for the 1936 Olympic Games.
1938, July 23: The Nazis require all Jews over the age of 15 to apply for Jewish identity cards.

1938, July 25: The Nazis forbid Jewish doctors to practice medicine.
1938, August 17: The Nazis require Jews to change their names on all official documents: all Jewish women must add "Sarah" to their names, and all Jewish men must add "Israel" to their names.
1938, September 27: The Nazis forbid Jewish lawyers to practice law.
1938 October 5: The Nazis require all Jewish passports to be stamped with a large red "J."
1938, November 9-10: *Kristallnacht*.

FASCINATING FACTS: Kristallnacht

In October 1938, the Nazis rounded up about 17,000 Polish Jews who had been living in Germany and tried to deport them to Poland. Poland refused to accept these Jews, leaving them to live as unwanted, homeless beggars near the Germany/Poland border for months. On Nov 7, 1938 Herschel Grynszpan (see picture), the 17-year-old son of one of these deported Jews, took his revenge on the Nazis by shooting Ernst vom Rath, a German diplomat stationed in Paris. Rath died of his wounds on November 9. The Nazis responded to the murder of their diplomat with a long night of terror attacks against Jews and Jewish businesses. Their attack came on *Kristallnacht*, German for "night of broken glass."

On *Kristallnacht*, the Nazis released all of the pent-up hatred that years of their anti-Semitic propaganda had created in the German people. They coordinated attacks that destroyed thousands of Jewish businesses and homes (their glass storefronts and windows provided *Kristallnacht*'s "broken glass"). They burned about 200 synagogues and sent about 25,000 Jewish men to concentration camps. About 90 Jews died on *Kristallnacht*. The Nazis refused to allow any of the businesses destroyed on *Kristallnacht* to re-open.

Two days after *Kristallnacht*, the Nazis fined Germany's Jews one billion marks for all of the damage they had supposedly caused. Because Grynszpan had used a gun to murder vom Rath, the Nazis also used the incident to justify confiscating the weapons of every German Jew.

1939, February 21: The Nazis make it illegal for Jews to own objects made of precious gold and silver.
1939, April 30: Jews lose their right to rent homes from German owners, and are forced to move into Jewish-owned properties.
1939, May: Both Cuba and the United States refuse to receive Jewish refugees attempting to escape from Germany aboard the MS *St. Louis*.

FASCINATING FACTS: The Voyage of the MS *St. Louis*

Not all German Jews were content to sit and watch while the Nazis took away their rights one by one: some of them tried to escape the Nazis by seeking asylum overseas. On May 13, 1939, the German passenger liner MS ***St. Louis*** embarked on a journey from Hamburg, Germany to Havana, Cuba, where the 930 Jewish refugees aboard hoped to find safety with friends and relatives who were already living in Cuba.

Unfortunately, the Cuban government was friendly with the Nazis. Before the *St. Louis* arrived in Havana, the Cubans revoked nearly all of the refugees' entry visas, and admitted only 29 refugees into Cuba. The refugees turned to the nearby United States for help, **but the U.S. refused to admit any of them at all**: it had already reached its immigration quota for the year. Canada also refused to intervene. With nowhere left to go, the St. Louis sailed back to Europe, arriving at Antwerp, Belgium on June 17, 1939.

Eventually, the 901 refugees who remained were divided between Britain, France, Belgium and the

Netherlands. They believed that they were safe from Hitler-- that is, until the following year, when Hitler captured France, Belgium and the Netherlands, all within a few weeks. About 250 of the *St. Louis* refugees died in the Holocaust by war's end.

1939, July 4: The Nazis forbid Jews to hold government jobs of any kind.
1939, September 23: The Nazis forbid Jews to own radios.

1939, November 23: With Poland occupied by Germany, the Nazis require Polish Jews over the age of 10 to wear yellow "stars of David."

1940, February 12: The Nazis begin to deport German Jews to occupied Poland.
1940, October 16: The Nazis establish a Jewish "ghetto" in Warsaw, Poland to house hundreds of thousands of Polish and (later) German Jews.
1940, November 16: The Nazis seal off the Warsaw ghetto with barbed wire-topped walls.

FASCINATING FACTS: The Warsaw Ghetto

A "ghetto" is a poor neighborhood of a city. Even before World War II, the Jews who lived in European cities often chose to isolate themselves in sections known as "Jewish quarters" or "Jewish ghettos." During WWII, those unfortunate Jews who lived in German-occupied territories no longer had any choice in the matter: The Nazis enforced the Jews' isolation by rounding them up and confining them to Jewish ghettos. Then the Nazis "sealed" certain ghettos by walling off the streets that connected them to the rest of the city. Armed guards controlled access to the ghettos' gates, locking the Jews inside.

As home to Europe's largest population of Jews, Poland was also home to Europe's largest and most densely populated Jewish ghettos. The Polish cities of Krakow, Lviv, Lodz and Zamosk all had large ghettos. The largest ghetto of all was at Poland's capital city of Warsaw, where up to 400,000 Jews at a time were crammed into the infamous *Warsaw Ghetto*. The average room in the Warsaw Ghetto's buildings housed about nine Jews. The Nazis didn't want to waste food on Jews they were planning to murder anyway, so they severely restricted the amount of food entering the ghetto. Warsaw Ghetto Jews received only about one tenth of the food they needed to remain healthy and strong. As a result, their health failed, and they suffered and died in the ghetto by the tens of thousands.

The Nazis' "**Final Solution**," their effort to exterminate every European Jew, began in earnest in early 1942. It was then that the Nazis began to "**liquidate**" Jewish ghettos by rounding up those Jews who had survived and sending them to extermination camps like Auschwitz-Birkenau and Belzec. Warsaw Ghetto Jews often met their deaths at the nearby extermination camp known as Treblinka.

Because the Nazis had forbidden Jews to own radios, Warsaw Ghetto Jews received little news of what was happening to their people. Most of them expected to be relocated to labor camps where they would work to support the Nazi war effort; they had difficulty believing that the Nazis would simply murder them when there was so much work for them to do.

When the awful truth finally became clear to them-- when they realized that the Nazis intended to murder them all-- the Jews of the Warsaw Ghetto began to resist. In early 1943, when the Nazis began to round up more Jews for more trips to Treblinka, the Jews fought back. Because they had few weapons and little ammunition, their resistance didn't last long. In April 1943, the Nazis attacked the Warsaw Ghetto and began demolishing it, building by building, block by block, leveling more than one square mile of the city of Warsaw. In the process, they rounded up or killed every Jew they could catch.

1941, July 31: The Nazis officially begin preparations for the "Final Solution," their attempt to exterminate all Jews in German-held territories.
1941, September 3: The Nazis conduct their first test of Zyklon-B, the poison gas they will use to eliminate Jews in the "gas chambers" of their new extermination camp at Auschwitz.
1941, December 8: Chelmno, the first extermination camp in Poland, begins the gruesome work of killing large numbers of Jews all at once.
1941, December 12: Another passenger ship carrying Jewish refugees tries to escape the Nazis.

FASCINATING FACTS: The *Struma*

Jews were subject to the "Final Solution" in every nation where the Nazis held sway. One group of Jewish refugees from eastern Europe sought to escape the "Final Solution" by chartering a Black Sea passenger ship from Romania to Palestine (the home of ancient Israel), where they hoped to find shelter and build new lives. Only a few of them had valid entry visas for Palestine when they left Romania.

The ship they chartered, sight unseen, was the SS *Struma*. Most of the *Struma*'s 790 passengers paid dearly for their tickets to Palestine. Therefore when they first saw the *Struma*, they were unpleasantly surprised to learn that it was a small, aging ship in appalling condition: Its sleeping quarters were so cramped that passengers could not sit up in them, and its only power source was an engine that had been salvaged from an underwater wreck.

The *Struma* embarked from Constanta, Romania on December 12, 1941. Its water-fouled engine failed before it got very far, and tugboats were required to tow the *Struma* to nearby Istanbul, Turkey, across the Black Sea from Romania. There, its passengers waited aboard ship while the Turks and the British tried to decide what to do with them (the British had been in charge of Palestine, the Struma's destination, since the end of World War I). The British authorities didn't want to upset Palestine's Arab majority by admitting too many Jews, so they allowed only the passengers with valid entry visas to disembark and continue their journey to Palestine overland.

The rest of the passengers remained aboard. Britain refused to admit them to Palestine; Romania refused to allow them to return there; and Turkey refused to allow them off of the ship. After more than two months, the Turks washed their hands of the problem by simply ordering the Struma out of Istanbul's harbor and towing it out to sea. On February 23, 1942, the Turks abandoned the *Struma* in the Black Sea. The ship's engine failed yet again, despite weeks of repair attempts. With over 700 Jewish passengers still aboard, the Struma drifted, helpless, about 10 miles north of Istanbul.

On the next day, a violent explosion rocked the *Struma*. The heavily damaged *Struma* immediately sank to the bottom of the Black Sea, killing everyone aboard except one. The lone survivor, found drifting amid the wreckage, was unable to explain the explosion. Decades later, a historian examining war records from the USSR theorized that a Soviet submarine had torpedoed the Struma as part of the USSR's efforts to prevent supplies from reaching its enemy Germany.

The sad end of so many desperate Jewish refugees aboard the *Struma* shamed many Britons. After the war, that shame helped goad Britain into supporting the creation of a new Jewish homeland in Palestine.

1942, January: Zyklon-B poison gas becomes the Nazis' murder weapon of choice at Auschwitz (see picture).
1942, Spring - Summer: Auschwitz begins "processing" (exterminating) Jews from territories all over Nazi-occupied Europe.
1942, July 23: A new extermination camp called Treblinka opens in Poland, northeast of Warsaw.

FASCINATING FACTS: The Breakout at Treblinka

Treblinka was an extermination camp northeast of Warsaw, Poland. Treblinka's Nazis were responsible for the murders of more than 800,000 Jews. On Aug 2, 1943, seven hundred Jewish prisoners launched an attempt to escape from Treblinka. Of those seven hundred, only about two hundred escaped; the rest died fighting. Their rebellion damaged the camp so badly that it brought an end to exterminations at Treblinka. There were also breakout attempts, with varying degrees of success, at Auschwitz, Belzek, Sobibor and other extermination camps.

1943, Jan 29: The Nazis order the extermination of gypsies (Roma) as well as Jews.
1943, May: SS Dr. Josef Mengele, the demented conductor of cruel medical experiments on human subjects, arrives at Auschwitz.
1943, May 19: The Nazis announce that their capital city of Berlin is *Judenfrei* (free of Jews).
1943, June 11: The SS orders the extermination of all Jews living in ghettos in Poland.
1943, October: The Danish Underground helps transport over 7,000 Danish Jews to safety from the Nazis.

DELIGHTFUL DANES: Ellen Nielsen

Ellen Nielsen lived in German-occupied Denmark during World War II. She lost her husband in 1941, so she supported her six children by buying fish from fishermen and selling it at market. In 1943, two Jewish boys approached Ellen and asked her to help them escape the Nazis. She hid the boys in her home until she could find some trusted fishermen friends to carry them across the *Kattegat*, the strait that separates Denmark from Sweden.

The Danish Underground, a secret organization that was trying to help Danish Jews, found out about Ellen's rescue of the Jewish boys. Over the following weeks, the Danish Underground used Ellen's home and help to send more than one hundred Jewish refugees to Sweden.

Unfortunately, the Nazis caught wind of her operation. In December 1944, the Nazis caught Ellen, arrested her, tortured her and sent her to the Ravensbruck concentration camp in Germany. At Ravensbruck, the Nazis condemned Ellen to death and placed her in the line leading to the gas chambers three separate times. Twice, she was able to save herself by bribing a guard with goodies from parcels sent by a Danish relief organization. The third time, she had run out of bribes, so she simply waited in line to die like everyone else.

At the last moment, Nazi guards approached to tell her that there was a new agreement between Germany and Sweden: from that moment on, Danish prisoners would be shipped to Sweden and held there. Ellen Nielsen went to Sweden, where she remained in prison until war's end. Then she was released to return safely to Denmark.

Female prisoners selected to go with the Swedish Red Cross

1944, July 24: Soviet troops invading German-occupied Poland from the east liberate the first German extermination camp.
1944, Aug 4: The Gestapo arrests Anne Frank and her family in Amsterdam, Holland.

INTERESTING INDIVIDUALS: Anne Frank (1929 – 1945)

Anne Frank was one of the more than one million Jewish children whom the Nazis killed during the Holocaust. Anne was born in Frankfurt, Germany. When the Nazis came to power in the 1930s, Anne's family moved to Amsterdam, Netherlands, hoping to escape. Unfortunately, the German army overran the Netherlands in May 1940; and in 1942, the Nazis began deporting Dutch Jews to Poland's extermination camps. When the Nazis summoned Anne's sister Margot to a labor camp, Anne's father Otto decided to act.

In July 1942, the Frank family and four other Dutch Jews went into hiding from the Nazis in a secret apartment behind the office of their family-owned business. The entrance to their well-concealed apartment was hidden behind a bookcase in the business's office. Non-Jewish friends smuggled in food and supplies for the Franks at great risk to their own lives. The Franks and their friends lived there for two years in silent fear, constantly aware of the danger of detection. Anne kept a personal record of her time in hiding in her diary.

Eventually, someone tipped off the Nazis. On August 4, 1944, the Gestapo discovered the Franks' hiding place. They arrested Anne, her family and her friends, and sent them all to Auschwitz.

The time the Franks bought by hiding was not quite enough to save their lives. They all narrowly missed going to Auschwitz's gas chambers as soon as they arrived. The Nazis stopped using Auschwitz's gas chambers for mass killings later that year; but even so, conditions at Auschwitz remained unspeakably miserable, with prisoners dying daily of starvation and disease. Anne's mother and father remained in Auschwitz, separated by the Nazis, while Anne and her sister Margot were moved to the labor camp at Bergen-Belsen. Sadly, both sisters died of typhus in March 1945, just a few weeks before the Allies liberated their camp. Their mother also died in Auschwitz before liberation. Only their father left Auschwitz alive.

After the war, Anne's father published her diary as *The Diary of a Young Girl*.

1944, August 6: The last Jewish ghetto in Poland, the one at Lodz, is "liquidated": the SS empties the ghetto and sends 60,000 Jews to Auschwitz.
1944, October 30: The Nazis conduct the last mass execution in the gas chambers at Auschwitz.
1944, November 25: The Nazis try to cover their tracks at Auschwitz by destroying the ovens where they had burned the bodies of murdered Jews.
1945, January 27: The invading USSR reaches Auschwitz and liberates it.

FASCINATING FACTS: Death Marches

Late in World War II, when the tide of the war began to turn unmistakably against Germany, the Nazis who had slaughtered millions of Jews began to wonder what would happen to them when the outside world learned of their mad, genocidal misdeeds. They were well aware that they were guilty of war crimes, and they knew that war criminals were often punished with swift executions. Frightened by this possibility, they tried to cover their tracks by destroying the evidence against them.

Of course, the worst possible evidence of Nazi war crimes was the testimony of a surviving extermination camp prisoner who had witnessed those crimes. For this reason, the Nazis tried to ensure that few such witnesses would survive the war. As the USSR's army approached the extermination camp at Auschwitz, the Nazis dynamited their cremation ovens and evacuated the camp, leading their remaining prisoners on long marches to escape the invaders. About 60,000 Auschwitz prisoners left the camp on foot, bound for destinations farther behind German lines. Most of them were already weak with hunger and disease, and were in no condition to set out on a long march. The Nazis shot anyone who was too weak to continue.

The Nazis conducted many other such *death marches* during the winter of 1944-1945, some of them just days before Germany's surrender. They did not intend for their marchers to survive, and few of them did.

FASCINATING FACTS: The Star of David Badge

The origins of the Star of David are uncertain. One folk tale reports that the Star of David is modeled after the shield of the young Israelite warrior David, the slayer of the Philistine giant Goliath who would later become Israel's king. In order to save valuable metal, David's shield was supposedly made of leather stretched across the simplest metal frame that would support a round shield: the two overlapping triangles of the Star of David. It is also possible that each of the Star of David's twelve angles represents one of Israel's twelve tribes.

At various times and places during the Medieval Age, both Christian and Muslim authorities forced Jews to identify themselves by wearing Star of David badges. During World War II, the Star of David became a sad symbol of the Holocaust when the Nazis forced Jews to wear the yellow Star of David Badge.

MISSIONARY FOCUS

GIANTS OF THE FAITH: Corrie ten Boom (1892 – 1983)

Corrie ten Boom and her family were Dutchmen involved in the Dutch resistance movement against the Netherlands' Nazi occupiers during WWII. Unlike some so-called "Christians," the ten Booms didn't condemn the Jews as "Christ-killers." Instead, they saw them as they are portrayed in the Old Testament: as God's chosen people, the ones through whom the blessings of Christ came, even if they all didn't believe that Christ was the Messiah. The ten Booms exemplified Christian faith in action. They sheltered young Jews who were summoned to forced labor camps, concealed Jews in their own home and created a network of other Dutchmen who were willing to house Jewish refugees. Corrie used her connections with the local government to find the extra ration cards that allowed her to buy food for her refugees.

In order to hide all of their Jewish house guests, the ten Booms built a secret room inside Corrie's bedroom at the top of the house. This room was only the size of a closet, and the refugees had to crawl through a cupboard to reach it. After the war, Corrie wrote a book about her WWII experiences called *The Secret Room*.

On February 28, 1944, the Gestapo raided the ten Boom home. Six hidden Jews in the secret room went undiscovered, but the Nazis arrested Corrie and her entire family. Corrie's father died ten days after the arrest.

Female Prisoners at Ravensbruck

Corrie and her sister Betsie were sent to the Ravensbruck concentration camp in Germany, where Betsie died in December 1944. Surprisingly, the Nazis released Corrie on New Year's Eve, December 31, 1944. She later learned that her release was the result of a clerical error, and she credited that "error" to God's plan for her life.

After the war, that plan involved writing, speaking and travel. Corrie wrote more than 20 books on Christian topics, but her favorite topic was forgiveness— even for her Nazi persecutors.

Chapter 26

World War II (Part II)

WORLD HISTORY FOCUS

WORLD WAR II (PART II)

U.S. Involvement in World War II

When the Nazis invaded Western Europe in 1940, the United States made every effort to remain neutral. Most Americans saw the war in Europe as a European problem, and had no appetite whatsoever for another bloody European war. Early in the war, the U.S. required Britain to pay in cash (gold or gold-backed currency) for every scrap of war material it bought from the U.S. This policy allowed the U.S. to help its ailing economy by selling weapons to Britain, while at the same time remaining safely neutral in the eyes of a belligerent Germany.

However, the freedom-loving United States could not continue forever to ignore a fascist-driven World War that threatened to destroy every free government in Europe. One of the reasons the U.S. had entered the First World War was that a threat to freedom in Europe was a threat to freedom everywhere. This threat was doubly obvious in late 1940, when the Nazis occupied France and came so close to occupying Britain as well. President Franklin Roosevelt was eager to help Britain remain free from the Nazis, and he finally found a way to do so.

FASCINATING FACTS: The Lend-Lease Act

In March 1941, President Roosevelt signed the Lend-Lease Act, a law that allowed the U.S. to "lend" war material to Britain and her allies. Through the Lend-Lease Act, the U.S. began providing warships, battle tanks, trucks, warplanes and other war materials to Britain, France, the USSR and China. Before the war was over, the value of these goods would add up to about $50 billion (the equivalent of almost $750 billion in 2010). Although these goods were theoretically provided as "loans," few of them were ever repaid. In a radio address, President Roosevelt encouraged Congress to pass the Lend-Lease Act so that the United States could become the world's "Arsenal of Democracy." This declaration did not escape the notice of Germany, Italy, or their new ally Japan.

When the U.S. began openly providing warships and tanks to the Allies without payment, it could no longer claim that it had not chosen sides. The passage of the Lend-Lease Act was the unofficial end of U.S. neutrality in World War II. The official end of U.S. neutrality, however, would have to wait until late 1941.

THE PACIFIC WAR

Casus Belli for World War II in the Pacific

The causes for war in the Pacific Theater of World War II were simpler than the causes for the war in Europe: the Pacific War was an old-fashioned case of empire-building. Japan wanted to build its empire by expanding into China, Vietnam, the Dutch East Indies and other islands of Southeast Asia. In doing so, Japan would gain the same advantages that European nations gained when they built their empires in the Scramble for

Africa: it would have access to more resources and bigger markets. Japan needed more oil, more iron and more rubber to build its growing industries. It also needed more people to buy all of the goods that those growing industries produced.

Japan's empire-building began in earnest when it annexed Korea in 1910 (see Chapter 22). Its next target for expansion was China: Japan controlled sections of the "treaty ports" all along China's east coast (as did Britain, France, Germany, the U.S. and others, see Chapter 13), and it wanted to expand those holdings. Japan's next major move was the 1931 Manchurian Incident, a "false flag" operation that allowed it to take over Chinese Manchuria and set up the puppet government of Manchukuo under deposed Chinese Qing Emperor Puyi (see Chapter 22). In 1937, Japan's constant demands for more Chinese territory developed into the full-blown Chinese-Japanese War.

Japan in French Indochina (Vietnam)

To China's south lay French Indochina (modern-day Vietnam, Cambodia and Laos), which had been a colony of France since the 1880s. The next step in Japan's empire-building enterprise was its invasion of French Indochina.

During the Chinese-Japanese War, China had difficulty bringing in foreign supplies through its own ports because the Japanese navy blockaded those ports. The Chinese got around this problem by landing supplies at the Indochina port of Haiphong, then carrying them through Indochina and into China

Japanese troops entering Saigon

by rail. The supplies that came through Indochina kept China's armies on their feet so that they could continue their war against the invading Japanese.

The Japanese wanted to put a stop to this; so, in September 1940, Japan invaded French Indochina and took control of its ports and railroads, closing down China's supply line. At the time, the Nazis had just conquered and occupied France's homeland, and the new government of Vichy France (see Chapter 25) was powerless to prevent the invasion. Instead of resisting, Vichy France cooperated with Japan; so the Japanese invasion of French Indochina required only a few days.

> In that same month, Japan signed the Tripartite Pact that made it a part of the Axis Powers already fighting World War II in Europe.

The U.S. Reaction

The United States signaled its disapproval of this invasion with a series of embargos (trade restrictions) against Japan. The embargo that hurt Japan the most was the embargo on oil sales: at the time, Japan purchased most of its oil from the U.S., and the embargo meant that the U.S. cut off oil sales to Japan entirely. Oil was an absolute necessity for Japan's war effort. Japan asked the U.S. to lift its embargo, but President Roosevelt refused to negotiate unless Japan first withdrew from China, a U.S. ally. That proposal didn't fit Japan's plans at all.

Because of the embargo, Japan was forced to seek other sources of oil. The sources they desired lay to the southwest, at valuable ports in the Dutch East Indies and at British-held Singapore. But those ports were European colonies, and the Japanese knew that the world would not fail to take notice if they suddenly attacked and conquered more European colonies. The war in Europe had the Europeans thoroughly distracted, unable to respond; but there was still the United States.

The Japanese began to believe that the United States was the most formidable obstacle between them and their empire-building goals in Southeast Asia. Therefore, in 1941, they conceived a plan to attack the U.S. Navy and eliminate U.S. power in the Pacific so that they could build their empire as much as they pleased there.

A Brief Timeline of World War II in the Pacific

1940, September: Japan invades French Indochina.
1941, March 11: President Roosevelt signs the Lend-Lease Act that allows the U.S. to "lend" war equipment to the Allies.
1941, July: The U.S. freezes Japan's assets in U.S. banks and announces an oil embargo against Japan.
1941, November 26: A strike force with six aircraft carriers sails out of northern Japan on a heading for Hawaii. On this same day, U.S. Secretary of State Hull delivers the Japanese ambassador a note demanding Japan's withdrawal from French Indochina and China. Japan refuses, and stiffens its resolve to attack the U.S. Navy.

1941, December 7: Japan declares war on the United States, Britain and the Netherlands (singling out the Netherlands because Japan plans to conquer the Dutch East Indies).
1941, December 7: Before the U.S. even receives Japan's declaration of war, warplanes from Japan's 6-carrier strike force attack the U.S. naval base at Pearl Harbor, Hawaii.
1941, December 8: The United States and Britain declare war on Japan.

FASCINATING FACTS: The Bombing of Pearl Harbor

Pearl Harbor is an important U.S. naval base on the island of Oahu, Hawaii. It is a shallow-water "lagoon harbor" with only a narrow opening to the sea, so its waters are usually more calm than the waters of open harbors. In 1940, President Roosevelt moved the U.S. Navy's main base in the Pacific from its old location at San Diego, California to Pearl Harbor. This move put the navy closer to the action in Southeast Asia, and closer to conflict with Japan.

Japan's attack on Pearl Harbor was designed to knock the U.S. Navy out of the Pacific War before that war even began.

The Japanese wanted to defeat and demoralize the Navy by eliminating its proud battleships and warplanes; and they wanted to terrorize the American people, whom they knew were already reluctant to join the war. They knew that a successful attack would raise in Americans' minds the specter of Japanese warships marauding along the United States' peaceful west coast. They believed that one quick, decisive blow might convince the Americans to withdraw their forces from Southeast Asia, leaving the Japanese free and clear to expand into that area as much as they liked.

Japan launched its attack from six aircraft carriers positioned more than 100 miles northwest of Hawaii. Japanese warplanes carried out the entire attack. The first wave of 183 warplanes struck Pearl Harbor at 7:55 AM on December 7, 1941. The second wave of 170 struck one hour later. The entire attack lasted only 90 minutes. In those 90 minutes, Japanese bombs struck eight U.S. battleships, sending four of them-- the *Arizona*, the *California*, the *Oklahoma* and the *West Virginia*-- to the bottom of the shallow harbor. The destruction of the *Arizona* (see picture) was particularly horrific-- a shell struck the huge battleship's forward magazine, exploding about 1 million pounds of gunpowder stored there. The *Arizona* sank within minutes. About half of the nearly 2,400 servicemen who died in the attack on Pearl Harbor were aboard the *Arizona*. The attack also destroyed or damaged about 10 smaller ships and two airfields.

Unfortunately for the Japanese, their successful attack on Pearl Harbor had the opposite of its intended effect. Instead of being intimidated, most Americans were outraged by what they considered an underhanded "sneak attack," carried out even as Japan pretended to negotiate for peace. They were also horrified at the loss of so many brave young servicemen, most of whom burned to death or drowned before they even got a chance to defend themselves. Japan, America decided, was a treacherous nation, not to be trusted.

In a speech to the American people on the day after the attack, President Roosevelt referred to that treachery when he described December 7, 1941 as **"a date that will live in infamy."**

The attack on Pearl Harbor changed American public opinion from strongly anti-war to strongly pro-war almost overnight. It also caused many Americans to loathe all Japanese; this loathing would soon lead the American government to confine American citizens of Japanese descent in concentration camps.

CRITICAL CONCEPTS: What the Japanese Missed at Pearl Harbor

Shortly after the attack on Pearl Harbor, President Roosevelt placed Admiral Chester Nimitz in command of the Navy's Pacific Fleet. Nimitz arrived at Pearl Harbor on Christmas Eve, December 24, 1941. The mood there was gloomy, but Nimitz was optimistic-- his experience and wisdom enabled him to see what others missed. After Nimitz toured the harbor by boat, he pointed out three critical errors that the Japanese had made:

1. ***They missed the dry-docks***: Although the Japanese pummeled U.S. battleships, they completely ignored the dry-docks a short distance away. With these dry-docks intact, the Navy would be able to raise several of its damaged ships from the shallow depths of Pearl Harbor and begin repairs immediately.
2. ***They missed the fuel***: The Navy stockpiled nearly all of the fuel for the entire Pacific Fleet in above-ground tanks just five miles from Pearl Harbor. A single bomb from a single Japanese bomber might have destroyed that entire fuel supply, leaving the Pacific Fleet helpless for months. The Japanese ignored those fuel tanks, leaving the Navy with plenty of fuel.
3. ***They missed most of the sailors***: Because the attack came on a Sunday, there were far fewer men aboard those damaged and destroyed battleships than there would have been on any other day of the week. Nimitz estimated that the Navy might have lost ten times as many men had the attack come on a weekday.

Nimitz believed that if the Japanese had corrected any one of these three mistakes, they might have delayed U.S. entry into the war by one or two years. Instead, the Navy was back on its feet and nearing full recovery in about two months.

1941, December 8: Nine hours after the attack on Pearl Harbor, Japan makes its first attacks on the U.S.-protected Philippine Islands.

1941, December 11: Acting on the Tripartite Pact, Germany and Italy declare war on the United States. The U.S. declares war on them as well.

1942, January 7: Japan begins its siege of Bataan, a peninsula on the Philippine island of Luzon that forms the west side of Manila Bay. U.S. and Filipino troops have retreated to Bataan for their final defense of the Philippines.

1942, January 11: Japan invades the Dutch East Indies.
1942, February 22: President Roosevelt orders General MacArthur out of the Philippines, essentially giving the Philippines up for lost.
1942, March 12: General MacArthur escapes from Corregidor Island in the Philippines' Manila Bay. When he arrives in Australia, he announces, **"I came from Bataan, and I shall return."**
1942, April 9: About 70,000 American and Filipino defenders of the Bataan Peninsula surrender to the Japanese.
1942, April 10: The Bataan Death March begins.

FASCINATING FACTS: The Bataan Death March

Nine hours after the Japanese attacked Pearl Harbor on December 7, 1941, they also attacked American and Filipino forces on Southeast Asia's Philippine Islands. Despite several hours' warning, U.S. General Douglas MacArthur and his men were as unprepared for an attack as the men of Pearl Harbor were. MacArthur's air force was nearly destroyed in the first wave of the attack, and he received little support from the Navy. His inexperienced ground troops were left largely on their own against a well-prepared Japanese invasion force.

In mid-December, MacArthur activated a pre-war defensive plan that called for his forces to retreat to Luzon Island's Bataan Peninsula and prepare to defend against a siege. Bataan was a defensible peninsula protected by Manila Bay to the east, the South China Sea to the west and mountainous terrain to the north. MacArthur's forces defended themselves well at Bataan, but they couldn't sustain themselves forever without outside supplies. The surprised U.S. military was only beginning to prepare for the war, and could send no help

on such short notice. When it became clear that Bataan would fall, President Roosevelt ordered MacArthur out of the Philippines because he didn't want the Japanese to take the valuable MacArthur prisoner. MacArthur left the Philippines reluctantly, vowing to return. The (roughly) 75,000 troops he left behind on Bataan surrendered on April 9, falling prisoner to the Japanese. The more heavily-armed forces on Corregidor Island, at the entrance to Manila Bay, held out against the Japanese for one more month before they, too, surrendered.

The lack of food and supplies had taken its toll on the besieged American and Filipino forces.

When Bataan surrendered, the Japanese suddenly had more than 75,000 famished and diseased prisoners of war (POWs) on their hands.

The Japanese wanted these POWs out of Bataan as quickly as possible so that they could continue their assault on Corregidor Island; but they didn't have nearly enough trucks to move so many men. So they decided to march them north, about 65 miles, to a new POW camp they would set up at Camp O'Donnell, beyond Bataan.

The Japanese were not kind in victory. The troops in charge of the march taunted and tortured their defeated enemies, mocking them for their surrender (Japanese troops considered surrender dishonorable, and preferred death to surrender). They also did not allow for their POWs' depleted physical condition. They denied their prisoners food and water, and they executed those who fell out of the march, unable to continue. They also executed hundreds of POWs for no reason at all. The death rate on the Bataan Death March is estimated at about 1 in 4, which means that about 18,000 - 20,000 Allied POWs who should have been protected by the law of war instead died as a result of animalistic Japanese brutality. The Bataan Death March gave Americans one more reason to view the Japanese as barbarians.

1942, April 18: In the "Doolittle Raid," the United States attacks the Japanese home islands for the first time at Tokyo, Japan.

> FASCINATING FACTS: The Doolittle Raid (April 18, 1942)
>
> After Pearl Harbor, the U.S. Navy needed a way to strike back at the Japanese, for two reasons: to let worried Americans know that America was not defeated, and to let overconfident Japanese know that Japan was not invincible. Unfortunately, the U.S. Navy was not yet the equal of the Japanese navy: it was only beginning to build the hundreds of warships and warplanes it would need to challenge Japan in Southeast Asia. With only 3 aircraft carriers in the Pacific to defend America's west coast, the Navy did not dare send a carrier strike force anywhere near Japan for fear that it might be destroyed.
>
> The Doolittle Raid was the Navy's answer to this problem. First, the Navy transferred two of its carriers from the Atlantic to the Pacific (by way of the Panama Canal). One of them was the USS *Hornet*, which was carrying 16 warplanes of a type no carrier had ever launched before: the Army Air Force B-25 bomber. Experiments proved that a good pilot could just barely manage to launch a B-25 from the *Hornet*'s roughly 800-foot-long flight deck. The B-25 could travel farther without refueling than the usual carrier-based bombers, and this extra range was crucial: it would allow the *Hornet* to attack Japan's home islands from a distance of roughly 500 miles, far beyond the usual maximum carrier attack range of about 200 miles. The plan for the Doolittle Raid, named for lead pilot Lieutenant Colonel Jimmy Doolittle (see picture), was to launch those 16 B-25s as soon as the *Hornet* came within 500 miles of Japan. The B-25s would bomb Tokyo and other Japanese cities, then use the last of their fuel to land in U.S.-friendly China. The *Hornet* strike force would withdraw to Pearl Harbor before the enemy even knew what had happened.
>
>
>
> Unfortunately, a Japanese scout ship spotted the *Hornet* when it was still at the very limit of the B-25s' range. The *Hornet*'s commander had to assume that the scout had alerted the Japanese to his presence, so he launched the B-25s from 650 miles out and immediately began steaming back to Pearl Harbor. **Those extra 150 miles would turn out to be crucial: All of the B-25s reached their targets over Japan, and all but one successfully dropped their bombs; but not one B-25 managed a safe landing as planned on a Chinese airfield.** Every flight crew except one ran out of fuel, and either crash landed or ditched their aircraft at sea.
>
> Most of the Doolittle Raid's pilots and crews parachuted to safety and soon returned home (with Chinese help). **However, eight men fell prisoner to the Japanese, and the Japanese executed three of them after a mock trial.** One more died of starvation and disease in a Japanese POW camp. Only four survived the war; one of these was future Christian missionary Jacob DeShazer (see below). The only B-25 that managed to land safely chose to land in the USSR. The USSR was closer, but politically problematic: the USSR was not at war with Japan in 1942. That crew had to bribe a smuggler in order to escape the USSR.
>
> Lieutenant Colonel Doolittle thought that the raid had gone rather badly, and expected to be court-martialed for losing every single plane involved in his mission. Instead, the Army Air Force honored him with a promotion for boosting American spirits with a successful strike on Japan.
>
> For over one year, President Roosevelt refused to say how the U.S. had launched the B-25s of the Doolittle Raid, and teased the Japanese by saying that they had come from Shangri-La (a fictional utopia from the 1933 novel *Lost Horizon*, supposedly located high in the Himalayan Mountains of Tibet).

1942, May 6: The island of Corregidor in the Philippines' Manila Bay falls to the Japanese. The fall of Corregidor completes the Japanese conquest of the Philippine Islands.

1942, May 4-8: U.S. and Japanese aircraft carriers fight the Battle of the Coral Sea (near the Solomon Islands). One U.S. carrier, the *Lexington*, is so badly damaged that its crew is forced to open its scuttle valves and sink it.

FASCINATING FACTS: Aircraft Carrier Warfare

Warplanes are extremely powerful and fearsome weapons, but most of them have one major limitation: their range is limited by the amount of fuel they can carry. Between WWI and WWII, the world's largest navies developed a new way to take advantage of the rapidly improving warplanes and missiles they were developing: They moved them within range of their targets using oceangoing airbases known as aircraft carriers.

Carrier tactics in the Pacific War were a new kind of warfare. Carriers enabled Japan to launch a sneak attack on Pearl Harbor from over 100 miles away, without ever alerting the U.S. Navy's heavy battleships to their presence. Carriers allowed the Navy to launch bombers over Japan in the Doolittle Raid, even after the U.S. had lost all of its ground-based airstrips in Southeast Asia. The Battle of the Coral Sea was fought entirely by carrier-based warplanes; Japanese and American carriers never came close enough to see one another.

Typical WW II aircraft carriers could carry about 90 warplanes. They stored some of these planes on their lower decks (hangar decks), and shuttled them up to their flight decks using elevators. Although these flight decks were about 800 feet long, they were still not long enough for most planes to take off and land on them without assistance. Carriers turned to face the wind whenever they launched to help their planes take the best advantage of the wind's lift; and they used steam-powered catapults to help their planes get up to speed swiftly. They used tail hooks to slow the planes down on landings. Landing on a carrier was no easy task. Carrier flight decks were moving targets, constantly shifting with the waves.

WWII aircraft carriers carried three basic types of warplanes:

Fighters: Fighters performed combat air patrol (CAP) by flying high above their carrier group and descending upon any attacking enemy bombers to shoot them down before they could bomb their carriers. Fighters also protected their own bombers on attack runs.

Level Bombers (Torpedo Bombers): Level bombers carried a single heavy, motorized torpedo, which propelled itself toward the target once the bomber dropped it into the water.

Dive Bombers: Dive bombers dove almost straight down upon their targets, then released their bombs and pulled out of the dive at the last moment.

1942, June 4-5: In a major turning point of the Pacific War, the U.S. Navy defeats the Japanese navy in the Battle of Midway.

FASCINATING FACTS: The Battle of Midway

Midway Island is a small group of islands in the Pacific Ocean, about "midway" between North America and Asia. It lies about 1300 miles northwest of Hawaii. Midway was home to a U.S. naval base that included airfields and plenty of fuel storage, and it was highly important to the defense of America's west coast. In early 1942, the Japanese conceived a secret plan to capture Midway in an effort to extend their territory and defend against more attacks like the Doolittle Raid.

Unknown to the Japanese, their "secret" plan was no secret. **Shortly before the attack came, American code experts broke the primary code the Japanese used to scramble their messages.** By decoding intercepted radio transmissions, those code experts were able to inform Admiral Nimitz that Midway was Japan's next target, and to tell him how many ships were coming and how they were arranged. Even though the Japanese would have four carriers to Nimitz's three, his advantage in information made the difference-- the Japanese never knew how many carriers they were fighting, and never found two of the three American carriers.

Even so, the American victory was not achieved without a great deal of sacrifice. The first three squadrons of American bombers that arrived at the Japanese carriers had no fighters along to protect them, and Japanese fighters from the carriers' CAP destroyed nearly all of them. However, this meant that when the next two squadrons of American bombers arrived, the Japanese CAP was out of position-- it had descended to destroy those first three squadrons, and could no longer defend its carriers. In a matter of minutes, those two squadrons set three Japanese carriers ablaze and out of commission. All three later sank, scuttled by their crews to keep them out of American hands. Later in the day, American bombers found and destroyed the fourth Japanese carrier. In response, the Japanese managed to find and damage just one American carrier, the USS *Yorktown*. Even the *Yorktown* might have been salvaged; except that on the next day, a Japanese submarine spotted the damaged, listing carrier and torpedoed it, sending it to the ocean floor.

The Battle of Midway was a turning point in the Pacific War. The Japanese carrier fleet was crippled, and would launch no more attacks anywhere near America's west coast. The important victory at Midway gave the U.S. Navy time in which to build its fleet for the future.

1942, August 7: The Allies launch their first major ground offensive in the Pacific War when U.S. Marines and others land on Guadalcanal Island (in the Solomon Islands). They capture a Japanese airstrip, then hold it against repeated Japanese assaults. This is the first in a series of islands captured in Admiral Chester Nimitz's "island-hopping" campaign, which is designed to push the Japanese back and give the Allies control over military bases closer to Japan.

1943-1944: The U.S. Navy builds the many aircraft carriers and warplanes it will need to challenge Japan in Southeast Asia. The Navy began the war with 8 large carriers. During these two years, it will build 14 more.

1943-1944: Allied submarines destroy hundreds of Japanese merchant ships, cutting off Japan's access to oil and other vital supplies. Early in 1945, the Japanese will essentially run out of oil.

1943-1944: The Allies' "island hopping" campaign recaptures several earlier Japanese conquests, forcing the Japanese to retreat to their home islands.

1944, June 19-20: The U.S. Navy overwhelms the Japanese navy in the Battle of the Philippine Sea near the Mariana Islands. Japan loses so many warplanes and pilots that for the remainder of the war, its aircraft carriers are nearly useless.

1944, October 20: General Douglas MacArthur keeps his promise to return to the Philippines when he lands on the island of Leyte. The Allied campaign to recapture the Philippines begins. Some Japanese will continue to fight on the Philippines for the remainder of the war (and even beyond).

1944, October 23-26: The U.S. Navy all but eliminates the Japanese navy in the Battle of Leyte Gulf (in the Philippines). For the remainder of the war, many Japanese ships will remain in Japanese ports because they have no fuel. Japanese warplanes attack as kamikazes for the first time.

FASCINATING FACTS: Kamikazes

Carrier-based aircraft pilots are highly trained specialists in Warcraft. It is no easy matter to strike an enemy warship with a bomb; from high in the air, even the largest ships appear as small targets, easy to miss. By 1944, the Japanese had lost most of the trained pilots who had the skills and experience necessary to score hits on enemy warships, and they were having difficulty training more. So they altered their pilot training program, and began to teach a new tactic called a *kamikaze attack*. Kamikaze attacks gave inexperienced pilots a better chance to win honor by scoring a hit, but they also involved a rather important sacrifice on the pilots' part.

Kamikaze attacks were suicide attacks that sacrificed both pilot and plane. Kamikazes loaded their warplanes with explosives and fuel, then intentionally crashed them into Allied warships. Kamikaze aircraft were like manned missiles, guided to their targets by suicidal Japanese pilots who never meant to return home.

The idea of suicide appealed to some. By 1944, the war had turned against Japan, and Allied forces were island-hopping their way toward Japan's home islands; defeat was all but certain. The profound Japanese sense of honor and shame made it extremely difficult for their warriors to accept defeat. Traditional Japanese *samurai* warriors preferred suicide to defeat. When defeat was upon them, they often asked their comrades to kill them so that their enemies wouldn't get the chance; or they used the ritual of *seppuku* (*hara-kiri*) to end their lives by their own hands in the most painful way imaginable.

The first Japanese squadron that had been openly trained for kamikaze duty struck in the October, 1944 Battle of Leyte Gulf. Kamikazes were also important in the Battle of Okinawa, closer to Japan's home islands. **Japanese warriors' refusal to accept defeat would have great bearing on the way the Pacific War ended.**

Late 1944: The Allies begin using captured islands as bases for B-29 bomber raids on Japan's home islands, including raids on their capital city of Tokyo.

1945, February 19 - March 26: The U.S. Navy and Marines attack and capture Iwo Jima.

FASCINATING FACTS: The Battle of Iwo Jima

Iwo Jima was a small, well-defended island 650 miles south of Tokyo, Japan. It held an airbase, heavy artillery and 22,000 soldiers protected by well-built fortifications. As the Allies prepared to attack Japan's home islands, they could not afford to bypass such a potent enemy base. The U.S. Navy began its attack on February 19, 1945 with a crushing battleship attack on Iwo Jima's Mt. Suribachi, but most of the dug-in Japanese defenders survived this. The U.S. Marines suffered terrible losses as they landed on Iwo Jima's beaches under heavy fire. They needed more than a month to root out Iwo Jima's last defenders, many of whom preferred suicide to the dishonor of surrender.

The Battle of Iwo Jima was immortalized by a famous photograph of six Marines raising an American flag atop Iwo Jima's Mount Suribachi on the fifth day of the battle. The photograph won a Pulitzer Prize, and became the basis for the Marine Corps War Memorial in Arlington, VA (see photo). The U.S. Marine Corps honors the Marines who fought on Iwo Jima most highly.

1945, April 1 - June 22: Allied forces attack and capture Okinawa, a group of islands that lies about 950 miles southwest of Tokyo and only 340 miles from the southernmost of Japan's four main islands.

The Japanese defense at Okinawa is even stiffer than at Iwo Jima, and losses on both sides are even heavier. Kamikaze attacks cause more damage to Navy warships in the Battle of Okinawa than in any other battle. As U.S. Army and Marine forces overrun Okinawa, many in the Japanese military commit suicide to avoid surrender. Japan's emperor encourages civilians on Okinawa to kill themselves to avoid capture, and also to avoid what the military promises will be torture at the hands of the Allies.

1945, August 6: U.S. forces devastate the city of Hiroshima, Japan with the world's first atomic bomb attack.

1945, August 8: The USSR declares war on Japan and invades Manchukuo (Chinese Manchuria, which has been occupied by Japan since the Manchurian Incident in 1931).

1945, August 9: U.S. forces drop a second atomic bomb on Nagasaki, Japan.

FASCINATING FACTS: The Atomic Bomb Attacks on Hiroshima and Nagasaki

In October 1939, about one month after Germany invaded Poland to begin WWII, Albert Einstein and a group of prominent physicists informed President Roosevelt of a dire possibility: that Germany might soon be able to build an extremely powerful new type of explosive by creating a chain reaction in uranium. Roosevelt decided that America must beat the Germans to the punch. His determination created the Manhattan Project, a huge American research agency that developed the world's first atomic bombs. The Manhattan Project developed two types of atomic bombs before the end of WWII: a simple uranium-based bomb and a far more complex plutonium-based bomb. The Project's scientists considered the uranium bomb's success so certain that they did not go to the expense of testing it. The plutonium bomb had its first successful test on July 16, 1945.

President Roosevelt died of a stroke on April 12, 1945, before the Allies achieved final victory on either of WWII's fronts. It fell to his successor, President Truman, to decide what to do with the Manhattan Project's research. The bloody battles of Iwo Jima and Okinawa proved to Truman that the Japanese would never surrender unless he struck them an overwhelming blow, and he was reluctant to sacrifice more American marines, soldiers and sailors to strike that blow. Truman made the difficult decision to use the Manhattan Project's atomic weapons on Japan's home islands.

The task of dropping the bombs fell to the U.S. Army Air Forces' 393d Bomb Squadron, which flew B-29 Superfortress bombers modified specifically for the task. The first bombing was set for August 6, 1945, about two weeks after the final capture of Okinawa. USAAF Colonel Paul Tibbets dropped the first atomic bomb, a uranium bomb codenamed "Little Boy," from a B-29 he named "Enola Gay" after his mother. Its target was **Hiroshima**, an industrial port city in southern Japan full of important military targets. Three days later, on August 9, USAAF Major Charles Sweeney dropped the second atomic bomb, a plutonium bomb codenamed "Fat Man." Its target was

Nagasaki, a port city where Japan built many of its warships.

The destructive power of those two atomic bombs was nearly unimaginable. Each of them killed tens of thousands of people instantly, and injured tens of thousands more. Many of those injured would later die, horribly, as their internal organs succumbed to the effects of radiation poisoning. Each explosion laid waste of a huge portion of its target city, and also poisoned the city's ground, food and water with "fallout" (material made dangerously radioactive by the atomic explosion). The bombs did not distinguish between soldiers and civilians; women and children suffered and died alongside soldiers and sailors.

Horrible though they were, the atomic bombs accomplished their task: by August 10, Japan determined to surrender. In a radio speech to the nation on August 15, Emperor Hirohito explained the reasons for his reluctant decision:

"... the enemy has begun to employ a new and most cruel bomb, the power of which to do damage is, indeed, incalculable, taking the toll of many innocent lives. Should we continue to fight, not only would it result in an ultimate collapse and obliteration of the Japanese nation, but also it would lead to the total extinction of human civilization."

1945, August 14: Japan surrenders to the Allies.

1945, September 2: The Japanese sign their formal surrender agreement aboard the battleship USS *Missouri* in Tokyo Bay. September 2nd becomes known as "Victory in Japan Day," or "V-J Day".

CRITICAL CONCEPTS: Why did Truman Decide to Use Atomic Weapons?

President Truman's decision to use devastating atomic weapons of mass destruction has been controversial ever since he made it. As both President of the United States and Commander in Chief of the U.S. military, Truman had to weigh humanitarian issues against the needs of his nation and his fighting force.

Humanitarian Issues:
- Some feel that the use of atomic weapons of mass destruction is inhumanly cruel, and cannot be justified for any reason. Tens of thousands of victims-- man and woman, adult and child, guilty and innocent-- are all wiped out in seconds. Others linger in agony as unseen radiation attacks their bodies.
- Some feel that attacks should focus only on military targets and avoid civilians. Weapons of mass destruction are "scorched earth," "total war" weapons that attack civilian as well as military targets; they don't discriminate.
- Some fear that the unchecked use of atomic weapons could devastate the earth and wipe out the entire human race.
- Some accused Truman of racism, and said that while he was comfortable slaughtering the obviously foreign Japanese, he would never have used atomic weapons on white Europeans.

Truman's Arguments:
- The Japanese refused to surrender. Their profound sense of honor and shame made them prefer suicide to surrender. Truman felt that he needed to strike an overwhelming blow to force the Japanese into surrender.
- Using atomic bombs instead of invasions to force the Japanese to surrender would save the lives of tens of thousands of American troops, who were Truman's primary responsibility.
- The conquests of Iwo Jima and Okinawa had already killed well over 100,000 Japanese soldiers, as well as uncounted civilians. An atomic bomb would not kill any more Japanese than these attacks had already killed. Furthermore, an invasion of Japan's main islands could well prove to be far more costly than even the invasion of Okinawa.
- Truman saw little difference between using one large atomic bomb and using thousands of smaller conventional bombs, as the Allies had done in German cities like Dresden and Hamburg and also in Tokyo (At the time, doctors and scientists knew little or nothing about radiation sickness).

FASCINATING FACTS: Origami Cranes

Japanese legend teaches that the beautiful and magical Japanese Crane may grant a wish to anyone who folds 1,000 origami (folded paper) cranes. In 1977, an American author named Eleanor Coerr wrote a true story about a young Japanese girl who badly needed the Japanese Cranes to grant her wish and save her life. Coerr's book was entitled *Sadako and the Thousand Paper Cranes.*

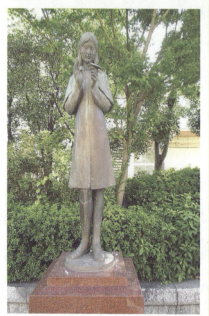

Sadako Sasaki was living with her parents in Hiroshima, Japan on August 6, 1945 when the U.S. Army Air Force dropped the world's first atomic bomb there. The blast instantly killed tens of thousands of Japanese; but many thousands more died later of radiation burns or of diseases caused by radiation. At the time, scientists knew little about the ways that radiation attacks the human body. Hiroshima would teach the whole world about the dangers of radiation.

Japanese who received high doses of radiation from the blast often died within hours or days. Others suffered longer and died later, often from cancers caused by radiation. In those who received lower doses of radiation, like Sadako, those cancers sometimes took years to develop. Sadako was only two years old when the bomb struck, but she was twelve when the lingering effects of the radiation caused her to develop leukemia, a cancer of the blood. A friend brought origami squares to Sadako's hospital bed so that she could fold 1,000 cranes and win the cranes' blessing; but the legend of the cranes failed Sadako, and she died of leukemia.

FASCINATING FACTS: The Lookout Air Raids and Fire Balloons

After the Battle of Midway, the Japanese no longer had enough aircraft carriers to strike anywhere near the United States without abandoning the defense of their homeland. In desperation, they tried some unusual means of attack.

The Lookout Air Raids:

On September 9, 1943, a floatplane launched from a Japanese submarine operating off America's west coast dropped two incendiary bombs on Oregon's Mount Emily. This was the first and only time an enemy aircraft succeeded in dropping bombs on targets in the continental United States. The bombs' purpose was to start a forest fire and strike terror in the hearts of Americans. However, the Lookout Air Raid failed: fire lookouts quickly spotted the fire, and favorable weather kept it from spreading. The Japanese tried again on September 29, and again failed to start a significant fire.

Fire Balloons:

From November 1944 - April 1945, Japan launched over 9,000 fire balloons (see picture) toward the United States and Canada. These were large hydrogen balloons carrying incendiary (fire-starting) or anti-personnel bombs. They were launched from Japan in the hope that the prevailing winds of the jet stream would carry them all the way across the Pacific Ocean and over North America. Most of them never arrived-- only 300 were ever found, and even those didn't succeed in creating fires and fear as the Japanese intended. They were, however, responsible for one tragedy: In Oregon, a woman and five children on a picnic were killed when they got too close to a fire balloon that had landed in the woods.

FASCINATING FACTS: Japanese-American Internment Camps

Japan's surprise bombing of Pearl Harbor at the beginning of the Pacific War taught many Americans to hate and distrust the Japanese as a race. The possibility of a Japanese attack on America's west coast made the west coast a potential war zone, and the U.S. military didn't want traitors living in its war zone. President Roosevelt decided to protect Americans from any more potential Japanese treachery by "interning" (imprisoning) over 100,000 American Japanese living on America's west coast into "War Relocation Camps." The government chose these prisoners purely on the basis of their race: anyone with even a single Japanese great-great grandparent could be sent to the internment camps, even if every other ancestor was a loyal American. Some of the prisoners were Japanese citizens living in America, but some were American citizens. Many of them protested that they were loyal Americans, and even sued the government in the U.S. Supreme Court.

In December 1944 the U.S. Supreme Court ruled that, while the government had the power to intern suspected traitors, it would have to release all loyal American citizens from its internment camps. The government repealed its internment order in January 1945, and Japanese Americans returned to their west coast homes.

INTERESTING INDIVIDUALS FROM THE PACIFIC WAR: Hirohito, Tojo and Yamamoto

Emperor Hirohito (1901-1989): Hirohito was the grandson of Japan's Meiji Emperor, the emperor who presided over the opening of Japan during the Meiji Restoration (see Chapter 9). Hirohito became Japan's crown prince as a fifteen-year-old in 1916, and ascended the Chrysanthemum Throne when his father died in 1926.

For all of the centuries before World War II, the Japanese viewed their tennos (emperors) as godlike beings too holy to be concerned with the mundane business of mere mortals. As the heads of Japan's Shinto religion, the tennos concerned themselves with loftier matters than the management of Japan's daily affairs. In public meetings with Japanese government officials, the tennos almost never spoke, because they were too exalted to be dragged into niggling arguments with lesser beings.

This lofty position saved Hirohito from prosecution as a war criminal at the end of World War II. Because Hirohito supposedly wasn't involved in the decision to make war on the West, the Allies blamed Japan's WW II atrocities-- the surprise attack at Pearl Harbor, the Bataan Death March and others-- on government officials and military officers like Prime Minister Hideki Tojo, not on Hirohito. Instead of prosecuting Hirohito, the Allies used his help to maintain control of Japan after the war. Hirohito became Japan's "first democrat," a model for the new, peace-loving Japanese citizens of the post-WW II years.

Hirohito had a lifelong fascination with the West. In 1975, when he was 74 years old, Hirohito paid a visit to his old enemy the United States. On a 15-day tour, the Emperor met President Gerald Ford and actors John Wayne and Charlton Heston. He also toured Disneyland, where he met Mickey Mouse and Snow White's Seven Dwarves in person and received a Mickey Mouse watch as a gift. He died in 1989 after a long illness.

Hideki Tojo (1884 – 1948): As Prime Minister of Japan from 1941 - 1944, Hideki Tojo led Japan to war against the United States and personally approved several Japanese atrocities: the surprise attack on Pearl Harbor, the murders of prisoners of war and many others.

After Japan surrendered, Tojo tried to commit suicide by shooting himself in the chest, but missed his heart. Allied doctors saved his life with an emergency surgery. While Tojo was recovering in the hospital, an Allied dentist made him a new set of dentures. Drilled into those dentures in Morse Code were the words "Remember Pearl Harbor."

Having rescued Tojo from death, the Allies put him on trial for war crimes and executed him in 1948.

Isoruko Yamomoto (1884 – 1945): Admiral Yamamoto became Japan's most esteemed naval officer by planning and carrying out Japan's successful surprise attack on Pearl Harbor. He lost part of his luster after he lost the 1942 Battle of Midway.

After the Allies gained an island foothold at Guadalcanal, the Solomon Islands in 1943, they intercepted a radio transmission that listed details of an inspection tour Yamamoto was making in the area. President Roosevelt ordered his military to "get Yamamoto." The Allies killed Yamamoto on April 18, 1943 by intercepting his transport plane and shooting it out of the sky.

WORLD WAR II IN EUROPE
(Continued from Chapter 25)

CRITICAL CONCEPTS: A Short Who's Who of the Nazi Party

As bad as Hitler was, even he could not perpetrate so much evil without help. A great number of Hitler's lieutenants earned reputations nearly as black as his. Some of them were tried at the Nuremburg Trials, a series of war crimes tribunals held in late 1945 - 1946. Here are just a few of Hitler's most notorious lieutenants and their fates:

Adolf Eichmann: Eichmann was an SS officer who managed the transportation of Jews from all over Europe to the extermination camps of the Holocaust. Israeli foreign service agents (the Mossad) found Eichmann hiding in Argentina years after the war. Israel tried, convicted and hanged him for his crimes.

Joseph Goebbels: Before the war, Goebbels was a propaganda expert who wrote much of the Nazis' anti-Jewish literature. He organized boycotts against Jewish merchants and orchestrated attacks like *Kristallnacht*. Before Hitler shot himself near the end of the war, he named Goebbels Germany's Chancellor (he also named Admiral Karl Donitz President). Goebbels and his wife killed all of their six children with morphine and cyanide before taking their own lives at the end of the war.

	**Herman Goering:** Goering was the commander-in-chief of the *Luftwaffe*, Germany's air force, and one of Hitler's most trusted lieutenants early in the war. After the war, Goering was convicted of war crimes at the Nuremburg Trials and sentenced to death. He committed suicide with cyanide on the night before he was to be hanged.
	**Rudolf Hess:** Hess was Hitler's personal assistant during his rise to power. He idolized Hitler, and wrote down Hitler's manifesto *Mein Kampf* as Hitler dictated it while he was in prison after the Beer Hall Putsch. After Hitler became Germany's Fuhrer, Hess was Hitler's Deputy Fuhrer. In late 1941, Hess apparently went mad and flew to Scotland in an unauthorized attempt to negotiate peace with Britain. The British captured him and imprisoned him in the Tower of London. At the Nuremburg Trials, Hess received a punishment of life in prison.
	**Reinhard Heydrich:** Heydrich rose to power in the Nazi Party by learning secrets about Hitler's enemies and using them for blackmail. These secrets helped Hitler destroy his former allies, the Brownshirts, on the Night of the Long Knives. As head of the Gestapo and other Nazi secret police groups, Heydrich was a master at rooting out Hitler's enemies through spying, wiretapping and opening personal mail. He was trying to root out the Nazis' enemies in Czechoslovakia when Czechoslovakian agents assassinated him in 1942.
	**Heinrich Himmler:** As the leader of the SS, Himmler was personally responsible for the operations of the Holocaust. It was Himmler (along with Hitler) who insisted that all Jews must be exterminated, not merely repressed, robbed and deported. He ordered the liquidations of the Jewish ghettos. He personally visited the extermination camps, oversaw their operations and made suggestions for their "improvement." Himmler committed suicide with cyanide before the Nuremburg Trials.
	**Rudolf Hoess:** Hoess was the commandant of Auschwitz, the Holocaust's most notorious extermination camp. Hoess personally built, perfected and supervised Auschwitz's extermination equipment and techniques. On trial in Poland after the war, Hoess confessed to personally supervising the murders of 2,500,000 people and starving another 500,000. Poland executed him by hanging in 1947.
	**Joseph Mengele:** Dr. Mengele was a doctor who performed twisted, unspeakably cruel medical experiments on concentration camp prisoners at Auschwitz. His nickname was "The Angel of Death." Mengele escaped to South America after the war and was never captured.

FASCINATING FACTS: Nazi Plunder

Most murderers are also thieves, and the Nazis were no exceptions. Before and during World War II, the Nazis needed a great deal of wealth, for two reasons: to fund their hideously expensive war effort, and to satisfy the personal greed of individual Nazis. They acquired some of this wealth by systematically plundering the people and nations they conquered.

Their first victims were the Jews. In early 1939, shortly after *Kristallnacht*, the Nazis confiscated much of the German Jews' considerable wealth by making it illegal for Jews to own gold or silver. After the war began, they confiscated Jews' homes and nearly all of their possessions by forcing them into ghettos all over Eastern Europe. When the "Final Solution" of the Holocaust began, Nazi exterminators stole their victims' jewelry and searched their clothing for any gold or gems they might have stitched into the linings for safekeeping. They even extracted the gold from their victims' teeth. The fate of much of this "Nazi gold" remains unknown.

The Nazis were also notorious art thieves. They confiscated classic art from private homes and museums all over Europe. Some of it went into storage until Hitler could open the *Fuhrermuseum*, a grand new art museum he planned to build in Berlin. Some of it went into the private collection of Hermann Goering, commander of the *Luftwaffe* and Hitler's favorite lieutenant. Some of it was sold at auction for money to fund the war effort; and some of it disappeared into the light fingers of greedy Nazis all along the chain of command.

A Brief Timeline of World War II in Europe, Part II

1940, June 10: Italy declares war on Britain and France and casts its eye upon their holdings in North Africa.
1940, June 14: The North African Campaign begins. Britain attacks Italian territories in Libya, and Italy attacks British territories in Egypt.
1941, May 24: The German battleship *Bismarck* sinks the British battleship *Hood*.
1941, May 27: The British Royal Navy retaliates by sinking the *Bismarck*.

FASCINATING FACTS: The *Hood* and the *Bismarck*

Throughout the spring of 1941, the British Royal Navy warily awaited the arrival in the Atlantic of a new German battleship called the **Bismarck**. As the heaviest battleship of its time, the *Bismarck* was the pride of Germany's *Kriegsmarine*. Britain's pride was the Battleship **Hood**, a powerful beauty of a warship finished near the end of the First World War. The *Hood* was faster than the *Bismarck*, but its armor was far lighter. In its contest with the *Bismarck*, the *Hood*'s light armor would prove to be its undoing.

Bismarck

In May 1941, the *Kriegsmarine* ordered the *Bismarck* into the Atlantic Ocean on a mission to destroy and disrupt the shipping that was keeping Britain supplied with war material. The Royal Navy assigned the *Hood* to blockade the Strait of Denmark (between Greenland and Iceland) and prevent the *Bismarck* from escaping into the open sea. A newer British battleship called the *Prince of Wales* accompanied the *Hood*, while the German battleship *Prinz Eugen* accompanied the *Bismarck*.

The four battleships met on May 24, 1941. Both sides fired rapidly, but the *Bismarck* and the *Prinz Eugen* were the first to score hits. A large shell from the *Bismarck* penetrated the *Hood*'s deck and detonated inside one of her powder magazines. A colossal explosion tore through the *Hood*'s hull, sinking the proud battleship within minutes. Only 3 of the 1,419 men aboard survived.

However, the *Bismarck* did not emerge from the encounter unscathed: The *Prince of Wales* managed to damage the *Bismarck* before breaking off its attack. The *Bismarck* was forced to seek repairs in the nearest friendly territory, German-occupied France. Before it could get there, the Royal Navy found it once again. On May 26, torpedo bombers launched from a British aircraft carrier damaged the *Bismarck*'s steering so badly that it could only travel in circles. And on May 27, two British battleships caught up with the crippled *Bismarck* and sent it to the bottom of the Atlantic. Only about 115 of the 2,200 men aboard survived.

Hood

1941, June 22: Hitler launches Operation Barbarossa, a massive invasion of the formerly neutral USSR.

1941, June 22: On that same day, the USSR declares war on Germany and joins the Allies in the fight against the Axis Powers.

1941, September: The Siege of Leningrad, the USSR's second largest city, begins. This siege will last until 1944, when the USSR's Red Army will finally relieve Leningrad. Over the course of this years-long siege, more than half a million Russians will starve or freeze to death for want of food and fuel.

1941, September: Germany captures the Ukraine region of the USSR. Ukraine has been one of Hitler's primary objectives because its farms produce so much food. The Nazis plunder the Ukraine of its riches, and even haul off quantities of its famously black, fertile topsoil for use in German gardens.

1941, October: The Battle of Moscow, the USSR's capital and largest city, begins. Germany will lose the Battle of Moscow: winter weather and stiff Russian resistance will force the Germans into their first major retreat of the war by January 1942.

1941, December 7: Japan declares war on the United States, Britain and the Netherlands (singling out the Netherlands because it plans to conquer the Dutch East Indies).

1941, December 8: The United States and Britain declare war on Japan.

1941, December 11: Acting on the Tripartite Pact, Germany and Italy declare war on the United States. The U.S. declares war on them as well.

At this point in the war, the major nations involved are:

On the side of the Axis Powers: Germany, Japan, Italy, Hungary, Romania and Bulgaria

On the side of the Allies: United States, China, Britain (along with its Commonwealth of Britain nations Australia, British India, Canada, New Zealand and South Africa), Free France, Poland, Belgium, Denmark, Luxembourg, the Netherlands, Norway, Greece, Yugoslavia and the USSR

1942, Summer: Germany drives down the USSR's Don and Volga Rivers in an effort to capture the oil fields around the Sea of Azov and the Caspian Sea.

1942, September 13: The Germans finally surround Stalingrad, a Volga River city they have been approaching for months. The Battle of Stalingrad begins.

<u>FASCINATING FACTS</u>: The Battle of Stalingrad

Stalingrad (modern-day Volgograd) was a major USSR manufacturing center that lay along the banks of the Volga River, on the steppes (grassy plains) northeast of the Sea of Azov and northwest of the Caspian Sea. The city was a gateway to the oil-rich region near the Caspian Sea that Hitler sought to capture from the USSR. During the frigid winter of 1942-1943, luckless Stalingrad became the site of one of the ugliest and coldest battles of all time.

The battle began in September, 1942 with a heavy *Luftwaffe* bombing that left much of Stalingrad in ruins. Nazi Panzer divisions followed close behind, and eventually surrounded the city. Instead of abandoning the city, however, the USSR's Red Army chose to use it as a battlefield. In the confined streets of Stalingrad, tanks were sometimes less effective than rifles and grenades. The Red Army held its own against better-equipped German forces in a long, miserable guerrilla battle that stretched deep into winter.

The Red Army's breakthrough came when it managed to encircle about 250,000 soldiers of Germany's Sixth Army, cutting them off from supply. Because the Germans still controlled two airfields, the *Luftwaffe* was able to airlift thousands of tons of supplies to its cut-off army; but the operations of such a large army required not thousands, but tens of thousands of tons of supplies. As its supplies dwindled, the men of the Sixth Army began to starve and freeze to death.

Neither Hitler nor Stalin would allow his army to retreat; so both armies continued to endure conditions that were beyond endurance.

Germans and Russians alike struggled to survive that terribly cold winter of 1942 - 1943 with little clothing, little shelter and little fuel.

Near the end of January, the Germans gave up hope that the reinforcing armies Hitler kept promising them would ever arrive, and decided to surrender. Only about 91,000 of Germany's 250,000 trapped troops survived to become prisoners of war at Stalingrad. **After their surrender, a furious Hitler ordered a national day of mourning in Germany-- not for the tens of thousands of Germans who had died fighting for their country, but for the shame the survivors had brought upon Germany by surrendering.**

The USSR's hard-won victory at Stalingrad turned the tide of the European war's Eastern Front. Germany would win no more campaigns in the USSR, and the Red Army would begin to chase the Germans back into Poland and beyond.

1942, November 5: The Second Battle of El Alamein, an Egyptian port city west of Alexandria, ends with an Allied victory. This is considered the turning point of the North African Campaign.
1943, Spring: The Allies drive the last German and Italian units out of North Africa, ending the North African Campaign. The Allies begin planning an attack on Italy.
1943, July 10: The Allies' Italian Campaign begins with an invasion of the island of Sicily.
1943, July 24: King Victor Emmanuel III and his Parliament remove Italy's Prime Minister/Fascist Dictator Mussolini from office. Italy's government begins to disintegrate.

1943, September 3: The Allies invade mainland Italy. The King's government, which controls southern Italy, signs an armistice (ceasefire) with the Allies.

1943, September 10: The German army seizes control of Rome and northern Italy.
1943, September 12: German paratroopers rescue Mussolini from captivity and help him establish a new government, the Italian Social Republic, in northern Italy.

1943, October 13: The King's government of southern Italy declares war on its former ally Germany (northern Italy remains in German hands).

1944, January 6: Nearly a year after their victory at Stalingrad, Russian troops finally drive the Germans back out of the USSR and into Poland.

1944, June 6: On "D-Day," the Allies begin their invasion of France.

FASCINATING FACTS: D-Day (June 6, 1944) and the Invasion of Normandy

By early 1944, the Western Allies had dealt the Axis Powers several defeats: they had beaten back German attempts to conquer Britain and North Africa, and they had invaded and held southern Italy. However, they had yet to win back any of the western European territories that Germany had conquered in 1939 and 1940. France, Belgium, Luxembourg, the Netherlands, Norway and Denmark all remained in German hands, occupied and well-defended by German troops.

If the Allies were ever to defeat Germany, they would have to invade Western Europe. Nor did they have the luxury of waiting for Germany to surrender; for the USSR was already beginning to capture German territory in the east. The freedom-loving Allies trusted the USSR's socialist/communists little more than they trusted Hitler, and they could not allow Stalin to overrun and control Western Europe after he swallowed Germany. They had two options for their invasion of Germany: a Mediterranean Sea-based invasion by way of Italy, or a Britain-based invasion by way of France. **They chose France.**

Their plan, codenamed "Operation Neptune," was to cross the English Channel and land on the coast of Normandy, France. Operation Neptune divided the 50-mile-long Norman coast into five separate "beaches," each with its own landing force: **American troops would land on the western beaches, code named Utah Beach and Omaha Beach; while British and Canadian troops would land on the eastern beaches, code named Gold Beach, Juno Beach and Sword Beach.** More than 150,000 troops would land on these five beaches when Operation Neptune began on "D-Day," June 6, 1944. In addition to these, more than 13,000 paratroopers would land behind enemy lines and try to strike the beaches' German defenders from the rear. All of this would be accomplished with help from about 5,000 boats, 800 airplanes and 30,000 trucks. After the landing, the Allies would set up defenses to protect their new beachhead, then proceed to land the tanks, trucks, artillery and other equipment they would need to push on into Germany.

Unfortunately, their enemies were ready for them. By 1944, Germany had occupied Normandy for four years, plenty of time in which to build shore defenses. Some of the beaches were defended by high bluffs full of well-protected machine gun nests and artillery. The beaches themselves were rigged with tank traps, barbed wire and other obstacles to slow down the Allies' landing and keep them on the beach, within easy reach of German machine guns and artillery. The Allies suffered losses on every beach, but the worst losses were on Omaha, Gold and Utah. **About 5,000 American troops sacrificed their lives on Omaha Beach in the early hours of D-Day.**

The invasion of Normandy was terribly costly, but successful. With the beachhead at Normandy firmly in their grasp, the Allies were ready to begin building their forces in France for a final push into Germany.

FASCINATING FACTS: Parachutes and Paratroopers

Military *parachutes* provide safe landings for *paratroopers*, airborne soldiers who jump out of perfectly good airplanes. The earliest parachutes, built during the Medieval age, all used metal or wooden frames to retain their shape. The first foldable silk parachutes arrived in the late 1700s.

The military first used parachutes to allow hot air balloonists to jump down from their balloons. Airborne artillery spotters (scouts) would rise into the air aboard their hot air balloons, spy out targets for their artillery, then use their parachutes to jump to safety before the enemy could destroy their balloons.

The first parachute jump from an airplane came in 1911, about eight years after the Wright brothers made their first successful flight. During World War I, German Luftwaffe officers were reluctant to issue parachutes to their pilots because they feared that, as soon as their warplanes took their first hits, their pilots would bail out to save themselves instead of trying to save the plane.

The USSR was the first nation to develop the idea of using parachutes to drop entire units of parachute-borne soldiers behind enemy lines. Germany created its first parachute regiment in 1935, then used paratroopers for the first time in the *Anschluss*, their 1938 takeover of Austria. The United States created its first Army Airborne platoon in 1940; and by 1944, the year of the D-Day Normandy invasion, the U.S. Army had several airborne units. Here are two:

101st Airborne Division: the Screaming Eagles

The 101st Airborne Division has a screaming eagle as its emblem because, like the American eagle, its paratroopers swoop down from above to attack their prey. On D-day, the Screaming Eagles landed behind enemy lines near Utah Beach. Their mission was to attack the Germans' beach defenses from behind so that the troops arriving on the beach by boat would have an easier time landing.

Unfortunately, as the 101's paratroop-carrying planes approached the French coast, fog and antiaircraft guns forced some of them to break formation and scatter. Anti-aircraft guns destroyed several troop planes before or during their paratroops' jumps. Paratroopers were also extremely vulnerable to enemy fire while they were descending to the ground in their parachutes, helpless to maneuver. Many of the 101's paratroopers missed their targeted "drop zones," and ended up scattered over a wide area. It took time for the scattered units to find one another and unite to form effective fighting forces. Despite these difficulties, the Screaming Eagles accomplished most of their D-day missions and helped secure the beachhead at Utah Beach.

11th Airborne Division: the Angels

The 11th Airborne Division fought in the Pacific War, primarily in the Philippines. The paratroopers of the 11th earned their nickname, "The Angels," by rescuing over 2,100 American, British and Dutch civilians from a prison camp at Los Banos, the Philippines, only hours before their Japanese prison guards were scheduled to kill them. The Raid at Los Banos was one of the most successful military rescues of all time. Sadly, the Japanese took revenge for the raid by murdering about 1,500 Filipinos who lived in villages near Los Banos, and who had helped the Angels find Los Banos in the dark and complete their mission.

1944, July 20: Operation Valkyrie, a German reserve officers' plot to assassinate Hitler and take over the German government, fails.

FASCINATING FACTS: Operation Valkyrie

Operation Valkyrie began as a legitimate wartime plan to use Germany's reserve army, the *Ersatzheer*, to maintain order inside Germany. In the event of an emergency such as the death of the Fuhrer, Operation Valkyrie instructed the *Ersatzheer* to mobilize its troops in certain key areas of the Fatherland and maintain control of the government. Late in the war, a group of *Ersatzheer* officers tried to use the already-existing plans for Operation Valkyrie as part of a plot to assassinate Hitler and take over the German government.

Operation Valkyrie's key figure was Colonel Claus von Stauffenberg, a veteran army officer who had served on the Western Front, on the Eastern Front and in North Africa. He was assigned to the *Ersatzheer* only because he was recovering from wounds he had received in North Africa. Like Hitler, Von Stauffenberg was a patriot who longed to see the German Empire restored to its former glory. Germany's early successes against Poland and France had led von Stauffenberg and others to believe that Hitler was a military genius.

After Germany began to suffer losses, however, Hitler became an indecisive, erratic and often irrational military leader. By 1944, his mad refusals to surrender were beginning to destroy the German army. Men like von Stauffenberg wanted to put a stop to the war and negotiate peace with the Allies before the USSR could overrun Germany. They sought to depose Hitler, take over his government and rescue the army from his growing madness. Operation Valkyrie gave them the outlines of a plan for doing so; but because *Wehrmacht* members were required to swear oaths of personal loyalty to Hitler, the only way to release them from their oaths and take over the government was to assassinate Hitler.

Von Stauffenberg believed that his best hope for taking over the government lay in killing Hitler and his top lieutenants Goering and Himmler all at once. He aborted his first two planned assassination attempts because not all three men were present in the same room at the same time. On the day of his third attempt, July 20, 1944, he decided to go ahead with the assassination of Hitler whether the other two were present or not.

Von Stauffenberg planned his attack for a conference room where Hitler was scheduled to appear for a war planning session. He waited until Hitler and his officers started their conference, then planted a briefcase containing a time bomb under the conference table and left the room. After he left, it is believed, one of the men around the conference table pushed the briefcase behind one of the table's heavy legs. When the bomb exploded, the heavy table leg saved Hitler from the blast, and he escaped the attack with no worse injury than a damaged eardrum.

Von Stauffenberg heard the explosion from outside the building, and assumed that he had succeeded in killing Hitler. He flew to Berlin, announced that Hitler was dead, and tried to put Operation Valkyrie into effect. Unfortunately, his takeover plan fell apart as soon as everyone realized that Hitler was still alive. Von Stauffenberg and his co-conspirators were all arrested and executed on the next day, July 21, 1944.

1944, August 25: The Allies liberate Paris, France from its German occupiers.
1944, December 16-27: In the Battle of the Bulge, fought in the Ardennes region of Belgium, Luxembourg and France, the German army proves that it is still strong.

FASCINATING FACTS: The Battle of the Bulge and the Malmedy Massacre

The **Battle of the Bulge** came during the Allies' drive to liberate Western Europe from the occupying German army. In the winter of 1944-1945, as the Allies broke out of their D-Day beachhead and drove deeper into France and Belgium, the German army made one last attempt to break through the Allies' lines and cut off their supplies. Much of the battle took place in the thick forests of the Ardennes region of Belgium. Early German successes drove the Allies back far enough to cause a noticeable "bulge" in the Allies' defensive lines, and the battle takes its name from that bulge. With the help of reinforcements from U.S. General George Patton's Third Army, the Allies recovered and drove the Germans back. For American troops, the Battle of the Bulge was the largest and bloodiest battle of World War II.

Early in the Battle of the Bulge, German army units suddenly broke through the Allied lines and caught American troops by surprise. One group of about 150 American troops near Malmedy, Belgium found itself trapped in the sights of German SS tanks, and was forced to surrender. The SS troops were in a hurry, and didn't want to be burdened by prisoners of war; so they simply gathered their American prisoners in a field and machine gunned them. Only about 43 of the prisoners escaped the SS assault and survived to tell the tale. When word of the Malmedy Massacre spread, some American army units ordered their soldiers to shoot all German SS troops on sight.

1945, April 12: President Roosevelt dies. Vice President Harry Truman takes his place as President.

1945, April 21: Russian troops reach the outskirts of Berlin.
1945, April 28: Italian "partisans" (troops who support the King's government of southern Italy) capture and kill Italy's former dictator, Mussolini.

1945, April 30: Germany's Fuhrer, Adolf Hitler, commits suicide. Before he dies, he appoints Grand Admiral Karl Donitz as Germany's new President and Joseph Goebbels as Chancellor.

1945, May 2: German troops in northern Italy surrender.
1945, May 7 - 8: All German armies surrender unconditionally to the Allies.

1945, May 8: The Germans sign their formal surrender agreement at Rheims, France. May 8 becomes known as "Victory in Europe Day," or "V-E Day."

INTERESTING INDIVIDUALS: Erwin Rommel (1891 – 1944)

Erwin Rommel was a highly skilled and honored German battle general. Early in the war, Rommel led some of the lightning-fast Panzer attacks that captured France so quickly. During the North African campaign, Rommel's battle skills earned him a fearsome reputation among his Allied opponents, who called him the **"Desert Fox."**

Rommel was a loyal German, **but he was not a loyal Nazi**. Unlike other German generals, Rommel refused to allow his units to participate in the reckless slaughter of innocents and Jews. Late in the war, Rommel came to believe that Hitler had gone mad, and his friends convinced him to join the growing plot to overthrow Hitler. The Nazis learned of Rommel's involvement in the plot after the failure of Operation Valkyrie. Hitler didn't want to damage his army's morale by trying and executing its best-loved general, so he offered Rommel the chance to commit suicide instead. In order to save his family, Rommel accepted Hitler's offer and committed suicide with a Nazi-supplied cyanide capsule on October 14, 1944.

AMAZING AMERICANS: George S. Patton, Jr. (1885 – 1945)

American General George Patton commanded tank units and armies all over the Western Front. Patton was an inspiring and colorful leader, but he was also outspoken, opinionated and headstrong. His troops honored him for his battle skills, and believed that they had a better chance of surviving the war with him in command; but they also learned not to expect any coddling from George Patton.

One of the many colorful stories attached to Patton's name is the "slapping incident." After his victory in Sicily, Italy, Patton was visiting wounded soldiers in an army hospital when he encountered a shell-shocked infantry private. When he asked the private how he had been wounded, the private responded that he was "nervous" and couldn't "take it." Patton slapped him with his gloves, threw him out of the tent, kicked him in the seat and threatened to send him back to the battlefront. For this, General Eisenhower (America's most senior general and the supreme Allied commander in Europe) temporarily relieved Patton of his command.

Eisenhower was able to use Patton's absence to his advantage. While Eisenhower was planning his Britain-based invasion of Normandy, he left Patton behind in Sicily. The Germans expected Eisenhower to use the highly successful Patton to lead any major attack, so they assumed that when the invasion of Western Europe came, Patton would lead it from Italy. The Germans' respect for Patton meant that there were fewer German troops in place to defend Normandy on D-Day.

Eisenhower reinstated Patton to command after D-Day. Patton proved his worth yet again when he and his 3rd Army helped save the day in the Battle of the Bulge. He summarized his opinion of that German advance with these words: **"...this time the Kraut's stuck his head in the meat grinder, and I've got hold of the handle."**

Patton in Sicily

After successfully dodging bullets and bombs throughout his military career, Patton ironically died of wounds he received in a peacetime traffic accident in December, 1945.

> ### FASCINATING FACTS: Japanese in the American Military
>
> Surprisingly, there was one U.S. Army unit in Western Europe that was composed entirely of Japanese-Americans: The 442nd Regimental Combat Team. Most of the volunteer soldiers of the 442nd came from Hawaii, where the government did not intern Japanese Americans because there were too many of them. The army deliberately excluded the 442nd from action in the Pacific War because of uncertainty about Japanese-Americans' loyalties. Instead, the army assigned the 442nd to campaigns in Italy, France and Germany, where it fought bravely and successfully. Twenty-one Japanese-American soldiers of the 442nd earned the United States' highest military award, the Congressional Medal of Honor, for their service on the Western Front.

MISSIONARY FOCUS

> ### GIANTS OF THE FAITH: Jacob DeShazer (1912 – 2008)
>
>
>
> Jacob DeShazer was a bombardier aboard one of the B-25 bombers that attacked Japan in the April 18, 1942 Doolittle Raid. All of the Doolittle Raid's bombers ran out of fuel before they could reach safe runways in China. When Jacob's B-25 ran out of fuel, everyone aboard had to abandon the aircraft and parachute out over a part of China that was held by the Japanese. On the next day, the Japanese caught Jacob and seven other Americans of the Doolittle Raid and made them all prisoners of war. The Japanese tried and executed three of the prisoners, and starvation and disease took a fourth.
>
> As for Jacob and the others, they remained prisoners until the end of the war. Jacob spent 40 months as a Japanese POW, 34 of them in solitary confinement. About a year before the end of the war, a prison guard allowed Jacob to have a Bible for about three weeks. During those three weeks, the Lord used Scripture to teach Jacob about forgiveness. Before he read that Bible, Jacob's heart was filled with hatred for the Japanese who had attacked his nation so ruthlessly; but after he read it, that hatred was replaced with forgiveness and pity for the Japanese, most of whom had never heard the Gospel of Jesus Christ. Jacob vowed to return to Japan and bring them that Gospel.
>
> Jacob's release came on August 20, 1945, when American paratroopers liberated his POW camp. After the war, he attended a Christian college, then returned to Japan as a Christian missionary just as he had promised. He served there for 30 years, preaching a message of forgiveness and salvation. He even built a church in one of the towns he had bombed during the Doolittle Raid. During Jacob's years in Japan, he met Mitsuo Fuchida, the Japanese pilot who had led the first wave of bomber attacks on Pearl Harbor in 1941. Jacob's Christian witness helped convert Fuchida to Christianity, and Fuchida became a missionary as well.

Chapter 27

Dividing Germany, Dividing India

WORLD HISTORY FOCUS

DIVIDING GERMANY

The "Big Three" Conferences

During World War II, the leaders of the "Big Three" Allies-- **The United States, Britain and the USSR**-- met at three major conferences to make decisions about the conduct of the war. The agreements they reached at these conferences would affect life in Eastern Europe and elsewhere for the next 50 years and beyond.

The Tehran Conference (November 28 – December 1, 1943)
Participants: General Secretary Stalin, President Roosevelt, Prime Minister Churchill

The Big Three held their first meeting at Tehran, Iran in late 1943 to plan the future of the war. At this point in the war:

1. Stalin and his Red Army had won the Battle of Stalingrad and had nearly chased the Germans out of the USSR; and
2. the western Allies had captured southern Italy and were considering what to do next.

President Roosevelt realized that the victorious Stalin was in a position to capture all of Germany and perhaps Western Europe as well, and was eager to reach an agreement that would prevent that.

At the Tehran Conference, the Big Three decided (among other things):

- That the western Allies would invade German-occupied France in May 1944 (they actually did so on D-Day, June 6, 1944).
- That they would form a new organization for international cooperation called the United Nations.
- That Stalin and the USSR would be allowed to retain eastern Poland after the war.

At Tehran, for the first time, Stalin demanded and received the western Allies' permission to retain territory in eastern Europe-- territory that Hitler had promised him in the Molotov-Ribbentrop Pact a week before the war began, when Germany and the USSR divided Poland between them.

The Yalta Conference (February 4 – 11, 1945)
Participants: Prime Minister Churchill, President Roosevelt, General Secretary Stalin

The Big Three held their second meeting at Yalta, a city on the Crimean Peninsula in the Black Sea. Stalin insisted on holding the conference at Yalta for his own convenience, and most of the agreements the Big Three reached there suited Stalin's convenience as well.

At Yalta, Stalin pressed and extended his demands for control of more territory after the war. He repeated his demand that eastern Poland must remain in the hands of the USSR as a buffer against future invasions. He also made demands on Chinese territory, including the Russian-built railways in Japanese-occupied Manchuria and the port city of Port Arthur.

Prime Minister Churchill was extremely reluctant to meet Stalin's demands. Churchill hated communism-- when the Bolsheviks overthrew Russia's tsars in 1917, Churchill had said that **communism should be "strangled in its infancy"--** and he didn't want to see communist influence flowing over the map of Eastern Europe like a "Red amoeba."

President Roosevelt was less leery of Stalin, and also felt that the western Allies needed Stalin's help:

1. FDR believed that the new United Nations would have the power to prevent Stalin from annexing any more territory after the war (just as President Wilson believed in the League of Nations at the end of World War I).
2. FDR wanted Stalin's help in overcoming Japan, which remained unbeaten at the time of the Yalta Conference.
3. FDR had no interest in picking a fight with Stalin in Germany, where the USSR already had a much larger army than the western Allies had.

Roosevelt believed (or convinced himself) that if he gave Stalin what he wanted, then Stalin would help the western Allies restore freedom and democracy to Western Europe. Roosevelt was also weary, and therefore more inclined to give in to Stalin: By February 1945, Roosevelt was visibly ill (see picture), and many at the conference guessed that he was a dying man. He would die two months later, on April 12, 1945.

At the Yalta Conference, the Big Three decided (among other things):

- That the USSR would join the western Allies in the fight against Japan within 3 months after the end of the war in Europe.
- That after the Allies received Germany's unconditional surrender, they would divide Germany into zones of occupation.
- That the Allies would hunt down and try Nazi war criminals.
- That Stalin would retain eastern Poland, but would allow a more democratic form of government there.
- That the remainder of Poland, the part that Germany had conquered, would gain territory from Germany after the war to compensate it for the loss of eastern Poland.
- That this new Poland would have a democratic form of government.
- That the Allies would liberate the nations that had been conquered by the Nazis and return them all to democratic self-government.

CRITICAL CONCEPTS: Western Betrayals, the Iron Curtain and Operation Unthinkable

The ink on the agreement at Yalta was hardly dry before the western Allies began to realize that their trust in Stalin was misplaced. **Stalin never intended to support free elections in any part of Poland, and he never did.** As Churchill had feared, Stalin was bent on bringing all of Eastern Europe under his dictatorial control.

Eastern Europe was about to be caught in the firm grasp of USSR-style socialism/communism, and the western Allies were doing nothing to stop it.

In the eyes of eastern European freedom fighters, Yalta was only one of several Western Betrayals of Eastern Europe. Before the war, the West had failed to prevent Hitler from annexing Austria and Czechoslovakia. When the war began, the West had failed to send its armies to defend Poland against Hitler's invasion. Now, as the war ended, the West was failing to restore free government to Poland, and allowing Stalin to replace Hitler's dictatorship with his own.

Because the West failed to act against Stalin, several eastern European nations-- Albania, Bulgaria, Czechoslovakia, Hungary, Poland and Romania among them-- would fall under communist governments and become part of the "Soviet Bloc" or the "Communist Bloc" of nations.

By late 1945, Churchill and others were already describing the veil of secrecy that began to surround these newly communist nations as an **Iron Curtain**.

Not all Westerners wanted to allow this betrayal. Before the end of the war, Prime Minister Churchill ordered the creation of "Operation Unthinkable," a plan of attack in case the western Allies decided to drive the USSR back out of Germany and Poland. American General George Patton and others thought that war with the USSR was probably unavoidable, and were ready to get on with it immediately after V-E Day. However, by 1945, the western Allies were tired of war, and leery of picking a fight with a much larger Soviet army. They were also afraid that the USSR might ally itself with the still-unbeaten Japan. In order to avoid a confrontation with the USSR, they chose the compromises-- or **"Western Betrayals"**-- of Yalta.

The Potsdam Conference (July 16 – August 2, 1945) and the Potsdam Declaration
Participants: Prime Minister Churchill/ Prime Minister Attlee (pictured), President Truman, General Secretary Stalin

The final "Big Three" conference was at Potsdam, near Berlin, Germany (Potsdam was the traditional home of Germany's emperors). Several important changes had taken place in the months between Yalta and Potsdam:

1. Germany had surrendered to the Allies on V-E Day;
2. President Roosevelt had died, and President Truman had taken his place;
3. elections in Britain were in the process of removing Prime Minister Churchill and replacing him with Prime Minister Clement Attlee; and
4. the Manhattan Project had succeeded in building and testing the world's first atomic bombs.

Photo # USA C-1860 "Big Three" & Foreign Ministers at Potsdam, ca. July 1945

President Truman used the Potsdam Conference to issue a demand for Japan's surrender. In the Potsdam Declaration, Truman and the Allies demanded that the Japanese withdraw to their home islands, lay down their arms and replace their imperialist government with a more democratic one (among other things). When the Japanese refused to do any of these things, Truman ordered his Army Air Force to drop the atomic bombs that had just become available (see Chapter 26). Truman mentioned the new weapon to Stalin at Potsdam, but Stalin already knew about it through his spies.

FASCINATING FACTS: Dividing Germany

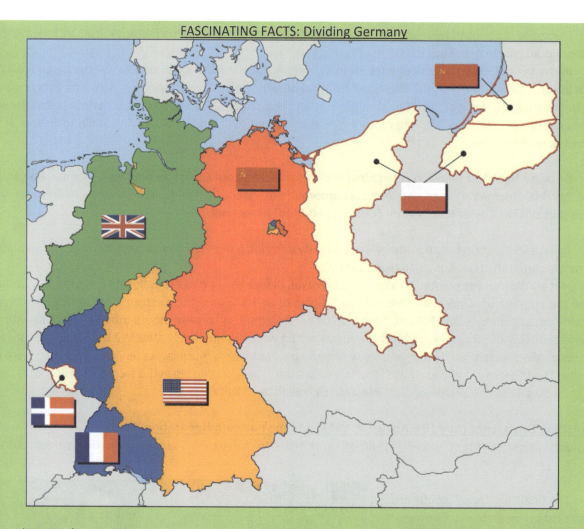

The Potsdam Conference also produced a more detailed agreement on how to deal with post-war Germany:

- It divided Germany into four zones, one each for the USA (orange), Britain (green), France (blue) and the USSR (red).

- It also divided Germany's capital, Berlin (see picture at right), into four zones, even though Berlin lay entirely inside the USSR's zone of occupation. The division of Berlin would later lead to two well-known western Allies/USSR standoffs over Berlin, the Berlin Blockade and Airlift and the Berlin Wall (see Chapter 31).

- It placed limits on Germany's economy. Germany's heavy industry, which had produced so much of its war equipment, was to be dismantled. Germany's new economy was to focus on agriculture and light industry; no warships, tanks or warplanes would be allowed. The Allies would approve all of German's industrial research to make sure that the Germans weren't trying to build new weapons.

- It forced Germany to pay war reparations to the USSR, Britain and France. The USSR collected some of those reparations payments in the form of forced labor: they used German labor teams to help rebuild USSR cities and industry that the war had destroyed.

- Potsdam also produced an agreement on Poland: Stalin and the USSR retained eastern Poland, while the new Poland received territory from Germany to the west and north (light yellow area on map above). The communist government Stalin had established in eastern Poland remained in place, and the Polish freedom fighters who had fought at the Allies' side throughout the war were forced to return home to a communist-dominated Poland.

The United Nations

The purpose of the League of Nations had been to prevent another war like World War I. The advent of World War II made it rather obvious that the League had failed in that purpose, and most of its member nations abandoned it before World War II even began.

The League's replacement, the United Nations, grew out of the alliance between the Allies of World War II. Before the United States even entered the war, Roosevelt and Churchill met to agree on the principles of that alliance, which were similar to the League's:

- Neither the U.S. nor Britain would seek to add territory through the war, and the people of every territory would be allowed to choose their own governments after the war.
- The U.S. and Britain would work for free trade and open seas.
- The U.S. and Britain would work for freedom, democracy, and human rights.
- The U.S. and Britain would work to limit the number of weapons in the world.

United Nations, New York

The principles of this agreement, known as the Atlantic Charter, became the principles of the United Nations. The newly chartered **United Nations** held its first meeting in London in early 1946. It moved into its completed Manhattan, New York headquarters in 1952. The United Nations contained 51 member nations when it began.

Like the League of Nations before it, the UN's power is limited because its member nations often fail to back up its decisions with economic sanctions and military force. One other feature of the UN's charter severely limits its capabilities: five member nations hold veto (Latin for "I forbid") powers over the UN's important Security Council. The five most powerful nations in the world-- the USA, the USSR, Britain, France and China-- all refused to sign the UN's charter unless they retained the right to veto UN decisions. All by itself, any one of them can block any important UN decision.

The Marshall Plan and the Truman Doctrine

After serving as the U.S. Army Chief of Staff throughout WWII, General George Marshall became President Truman's Secretary of State. As Secretary of State, Marshall proposed a plan to use United States money to rebuild the war-ruined economies of the nations of Western Europe. That plan became known as the Marshall Plan.

Western Europe was in trouble after the war. The war had destroyed so many factories and facilities that its economies had difficulty getting back on their feet. Many of its people were starving. Meanwhile, communists from the USSR were busily trying to convince down-on-their-luck Europeans that communism held the answers to all of their problems. General Marshall and others began to believe that if aid did not arrive soon, war-ravaged nations like Italy, France and Belgium might fall under the influence of communism just as Eastern Europe had.

General George Marshall

Marshall's plan was to alleviate Western Europe's suffering and rebuild its economies with large amounts of American cash. Over the course of four years, from 1948 - 1952, the Marshall Plan distributed about $13 billion to about 16 countries. This was on top of about $12 billion the U.S. had already donated under other programs. Those $25 billion would be worth about $225 billion in 2010 dollars.

The first payments went to Greece and Turkey, which President Truman believed would rapidly fall to the communists without aid. Britain and France received the most Marshall Plan aid; and in third place-- surprisingly-- was Germany. The Marshall Plan's European administrators came to believe that Europe could not rebuild its economy without also rebuilding Germany's. Even so, they took great care to ensure that Germany could not use its aid funds to build weapons.

One nation bitterly opposed the Marshall Plan: the USSR. The USSR's communists saw the Marshall Plan as an attempt to spread U.S. influence all over Western Europe. They angrily accused the U.S. of "imperialism" (empire-building), and refused to take any aid from their former ally. **The Marshall Plan's aid to Greece and Turkey was the first use of the Truman Doctrine, which said that the U.S. would help Greece and Turkey in their struggle to resist outside communist influence.** Truman's declaration of support for Greece and Turkey was part of the long struggle against communist expansion known as the "Cold War" (see Chapter 31).

INTERESTING INDIVIDUALS: Ernie Pyle

Ernie Pyle was a journalist who traveled with American troops on every front of World War II. Pyle filed colorful battlefield reports from North Africa, Italy, France and even the Pacific Theater. His reports appeared in about 300 syndicated newspapers all over the United States. During WWII, Ernie Pyle served as the eyes of the American public. He told not of generals' deeds and strategies, but of the experiences of the common soldier. He told how common soldiers fought, how they lived and how they died. **Tragically, Pyle himself suffered a soldier's fate: a Japanese soldier shot him to death while he was reporting on the Battle of Okinawa.**

This is an excerpt from Pyle's description of a beach in Normandy, France, on the day after D-Day:

"... Ashore, facing us, were more enemy troops than we had in our assault waves. The advantages were all theirs, the disadvantages all ours. The Germans were dug into positions that they had been working on for months, although these were not yet all complete. A one-hundred-foot bluff a couple of hundred yards back from the beach had great concrete gun emplacements built right into the hilltop. These opened to the sides instead of to the front, thus making it very hard for naval fire from the sea to reach them. They could shoot parallel with the beach and cover every foot of it for miles with artillery fire.

'Then they had hidden machine-gun nests on the forward slopes, with crossfire taking in every inch of the beach. These nests were connected by networks of trenches, so that the German gunners could move about without exposing themselves.

'Throughout the length of the beach, running zigzag a couple of hundred yards back from the shoreline, was an immense V-shaped ditch fifteen feet deep. Nothing could cross it, not even men on foot, until fills had been made."

Ernie Pyle sharing a cigarette on Okinawa

DIVIDING INDIA
*** see Chapter 19 for India's Struggle for Independence ***

The All-India Muslim League

British India's dominant religion was Hinduism; about 4 out of 5 Indians were Hindus. However, British India was also home to a great number of Muslims, and certain areas of India had large Muslim majorities.

The Indian National Congress (see Chapter 19) contained a Hindu majority, and its leader, Mohandas Gandhi, was India's most prominent Hindu. Early in the struggle for Indian independence, some of India's many Muslims began to feel that the mostly Hindu Indian National Congress didn't represent them very well. In 1906, those Muslims formed a new organization to represent their interests in the fight for Indian independence: the All-India Muslim League.

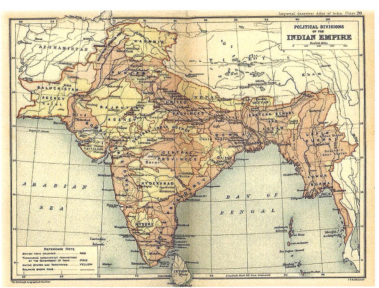

Map of the British Indian Empire from the 1909 Imperial Gazetteer of India

Mohandas Gandhi worked hard to bring India's Muslims back into the Indian National Congress. Gandhi wanted the new, independent India to be a secular state with freedom for all religions. But Gandhi didn't speak for the All-India Muslim League, which grew to resent him more and more. As time went on, the differences between Hindus and Muslims only grew wider:

- Muslims didn't approve of Gandhi's insistence on non-violent resistance to Britain; they wanted to fight for independence in their own way.
- Muslims wanted Muslim leaders like Muhammad Ali Jinnah to represent them; they didn't want Gandhi speaking for them.
- Muslims didn't want Hindu representatives creating laws for areas of India that contained Muslim majorities.

The Pakistan Resolution

Eventually, the Muslim League came to believe that the differences between Hindus and Muslims were so great that they could not live together under the same government. In the 1940 Pakistan Resolution, the Muslim League announced that its demands had changed, and that it no longer wanted fair representation for Muslims in an independent India. Instead, it wanted a separate Muslim state in India, independent of both Britain and Hindu India.

Name Origin: Pakistan

The name the Muslims chose for their new state, "Pakistan," blended the names of several regions in northwest India, including Punjab, Afghan and Kashmir.

The Cabinet Mission and Direct Action Day

Matters in India came to a head at the end of World War II. The war had drained Britain's treasury, and had also left the British people with little appetite for more overseas adventures. As a charter member of the United Nations, Britain was ready to obey one of the UN's founding principles and allow its former colonies independent home rule. In 1946, Britain sent a delegation called the Cabinet Mission to India with two plans for the government of the new Dominion of India. The first, the "**May 16th Plan**," called for the creation of Muslim-majority provinces within a united India. The second, the "**June 16th Plan**," called for new government that would eventually divide British India into two states: Hindu-majority India and Muslim-majority Pakistan.

Gandhi and the Indian National Congress rejected both plans. Gandhi wanted India to be united, not divided; he wanted no divisions based on religion. The Muslim League, on the other hand, wanted a divided India very much. Muslims wanted a guarantee that India's Hindus could never dominate its Muslims; and no plan that didn't create a separate state for Muslims could provide such a guarantee. The Muslim League came to believe that even under the June 16th Plan, India's Hindu majority would change the rules and continue to dominate Muslims.

FASCINATING FACTS: Direct Action Day

In August 1946, Muslim League leader Muhammad Ali Jinnah declared that India's Muslims would take "direct action" to demand a separate Muslim state. Jinnah may have intended nothing more than Muslim labor strikes and street demonstrations, but what he got was a deadly riot. **On Direct Action Day, August 16, 1946, Hindu and Muslim mobs rioted in the streets of Calcutta, the largest city in India's eastern Bengal Province.** Thousands of Indians died on Direct Action Day, and hundreds of thousands were injured. The riots spread to other Muslim areas in the west, and the violence continued for several months.

Independence and Partition

That violence gave the British even more reason to hurry up with their partition plan. The Indian Independence Act passed Britain's Parliament on July 18, 1947. Pakistan declared its independence on August 14, and India followed suit on August 15. Under the terms of the Indian Independence Act:

British India would be partitioned into two Dominions, **India** (mostly Hindu) and **Pakistan** (mostly Muslim). The new Pakistan would be divided into two "enclaves," or separate regions:

1. **West Pakistan**, centered around the western part of the province of Punjab, and
2. **East Pakistan**, centered around the eastern part of the province of Bengal. Between Muslim West Pakistan and East Pakistan would lie a broad stretch of Hindu India.

- India and Pakistan would be Dominions of the British Crown and would retain the British monarch as their official heads of state.
- India and Pakistan would be members of the British Commonwealth, but would be free to leave the Commonwealth if they chose.
- Britain would no longer be responsible for governing any part of the former Indian Empire.

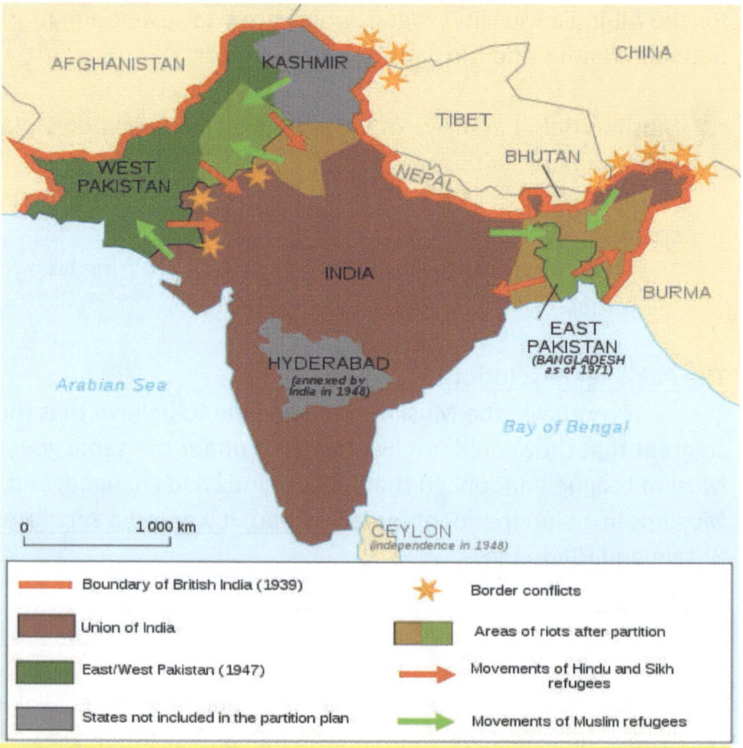

Migrations, Violence and Homelessness

What followed the partition was chaos even worse than before. Neither Hindus nor Muslims wanted to live in any territory dominated by the other faith, especially with all of the riots that had been going on; so, as soon as the new borders between India and Pakistan became known, people began to migrate. More than 7 million Hindus and Sikhs left homes that were suddenly part of Muslim Pakistan, and moved to India. More than 7 million Muslims left homes in Hindu India and moved to Pakistan. Suddenly there were more than 14 million homeless people on the roads between India and the two Pakistans, all of them desperate to find new homes and new ways to support themselves.

Along those roads, they clashed with one another. Muslims battled Hindus, Hindus battled Muslims, and Sikhs battled both. The worst violence happened in the northwestern region of British India known as Punjab, which the partition divided into Pakistani (Muslim) Punjab and Indian (Hindu) Punjab. The partition of Punjab also divided the homeland of India's Sikhs, most of whom moved into Indian Punjab. No one knows how many people died in the chaos and violence that broke out during those mass migrations between India and the two Pakistans, but the guesses range from 200,000 to as many as 1,000,000.

Kashmir and the Princely States

Not all Indian territory was part of British India. Since before the days of the East India Company, there had been semi-independent regions of India known as "Princely States," each governed by a *maharajah* or ruler of its own. Under British India, these Princely States were never truly independent; their princes remained in power only because Britain allowed them to, and they had little control over their external affairs.

Since Britain had never controlled the Princely States entirely, its partition plan didn't include a plan for their territories. Instead, each of the Princely States would have to make a decision: each could join India, join Pakistan, or remain independent.

FASCINATING FACTS: Kashmir

One particularly large and precious Princely State was Kashmir-Jammu, which lay in northern India on its borders with China and the new West Pakistan. Kashmir-Jammu was home to the Kashmir Valley, which India's Moghul Dynasty emperor Jahangir had described as a "heaven on earth." The Kashmir Valley was lush, beautiful, productive and highly valuable. The new governments of India and Pakistan both cast greedy eyes upon Kashmir as soon as the partition took effect in 1947.

When the partition came, the maharajah of Kashmir could not make up his mind which way to go. Parts of Kashmir had Muslim majorities, and other parts had Hindu majorities. In the years since the Partition, India and Pakistan have fought four wars, and three of them have involved Kashmir:

- ***The First Kashmir War (or the Indo-Pakistani War of 1947):*** Shortly after the partition in 1947, Pakistani troops invaded Kashmir and tried to claim it for Pakistan. Kashmir's maharajah asked India for help, and India responded with a counter-invasion. The two sides fought to a standstill at a UN-negotiated ceasefire line that divided Kashmir: India controlled the southeast, including the valuable Kashmir Valley; while Pakistan controlled the northwest. That ceasefire line formed the temporary border between Indian Kashmir and Pakistani Kashmir, and became known as the "Line of Control."

- **The Second Kashmir War (or the Indo-Pakistani War of 1965):** In 1965, Pakistan sent disguised soldiers across the border into Indian-held Kashmir to try to stir up a rebellion against Indian rule there. India fought back. The two sides fought for about six weeks before each returned to its own side of the Line of Control.

- **The Kargil War (or the Indo-Pakistani War of 1999):** The 1999 Kargil War was a replay of the Second Kashmir War, named for the Kargil district of Kashmir. Once again Pakistan sent disguised soldiers over the Line of Control; once again India fought back; and once again neither side gained any territory.

As of 2010, Kashmir remains disputed territory. The Line of Control still serves as the temporary border between Indian Kashmir (purple area on the map) and Pakistani Kashmir (green area on the map). To complicate matters even further, Kashmir's neighbor China claims a portion of Kashmir that lies on the Pakistani side of the Line of Control (yellow area on the map). Pakistan conceded that territory to China in 1963; but India, which also claims it, did not.

The Bangladesh Liberation War and the Indo-Pakistani War of 1971

The distance that separated East Pakistan from West Pakistan caused problems, especially for East Pakistan (see green areas on the map). East Pakistan had more people and paid more taxes than West Pakistan, but West Pakistan dominated Pakistan's government and received more government services. Both of Pakistan's capitals (first Karachi, then Islamabad) lay in West Pakistan, as did its military headquarters and most of its armies. West Pakistanis tended to regard the Bengali race of East Pakistan as inferior to the Punjabi and Pashtun races of West Pakistan. For these and many other reasons, East Pakistanis began to demand independence from West Pakistan.

In March 1971, West Pakistan sent troops into East Pakistan to root out the leaders of the independence movement there. The extreme violence of those troops' methods proved to East Pakistanis that West Pakistanis looked down on them, and led to more demands for independence.

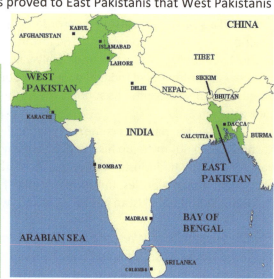

FASCINATING FACTS: Bangladesh

On March 25, 1971, East Pakistan formally declared itself independent of West Pakistan and renamed itself Bangladesh ("Nation of Bengal"). Bangladesh's declaration of independence was the beginning of the Bangladesh Liberation War.

When the Bangladesh Liberation War began, millions of refugees streamed into India from Bangladesh, trying to escape the violence. India was forced to send troops to its border with Bangladesh, both to maintain order in the refugee camps and to defend itself in case the war spilled over the border.

Bangladesh might not have survived its liberation war without help from India. India didn't participate in the war directly at first; but it did support Bangladesh with military equipment and supplies, and it allowed Bangladesh to train its troops in refugee camps on the Indian side of the border. With Indian assistance, the revolutionaries of Bangladesh were able to hold their own against better-trained and better-equipped troops from West Pakistan.

When West Pakistan began to fear that India would join the war on Bangladesh's side, it decided to strike India first. On December 3, 1971, Pakistan suddenly launched a surprise attack on 11 Indian airfields. This attack was supposed to wreck India's air force, stun the Indian government and prevent India from joining the war; but instead, it angered India into declaring war on Pakistan.

India's entry into the war quickly overwhelmed Pakistan. The Bangladesh Liberation War and the Indo-Pakistani War of 1971 ran side-by-side for less than two weeks, and both ended with Pakistan's surrender on December 16.

Results of the Bangladesh Liberation War:
- East Pakistan won its independence and became Bangladesh.
- West Pakistan, which had lost its separate, eastern territory, became simply Pakistan.

FASCINATING FACTS: The Sikhs and Operation Blue Star

In a nation as populous as India, even a small minority may represent millions of people. One such minority is the Sikhs. India's Sikhs believe in one god and follow the teachings of ten spiritual leaders known as "gurus." The tenth guru, who died in 1708, declared that he would be the last human guru, and that after his death, Sikhs would follow a religious text that contained the teachings of the ten gurus. That text became the last of the Sikh gurus, and is called the *Guru Garath Sahib*.

Sikhs are also well-known for wearing the "five K" symbols that remind them of their faith and make them stand out:

1. *Kesh*: Sikhs do not shave their hair, beards or mustaches because hair is a gift from God. They usually wrap their long hair inside a turban.
2. *Kanga*: Sikhs wear a wooden comb under their turbans to keep their long hair neat.
3. *Kara*: Sikhs wear a round iron bracelet that reminds them of their vows.
4. *Kirpan*: Sikhs carry a dagger that they may use to defend the weak and helpless.
5. *Kachehra*: Sikhs wear special undergarments to remind them of their vows.

The Sikhs' traditional homeland lies in the Punjab region of India and Pakistan. The 1947 partition of India divided Punjab between India and West Pakistan, and many Sikhs chose to migrate from West Pakistani Punjab to Indian Punjab. During the mass migrations that followed the partition of India, the worst violence happened in Punjab. Indian Punjab is home to the Sikhs' most important holy site, the Golden Temple in the city of Amritsar.

Like the Muslims, the Sikhs sought a homeland of their own during the 1947 partition of India. India's first Prime Minister, Jawaharlal Nehru, promised the Sikhs a homeland in India Punjab, but India only delivered part of what Nehru promised. During the 1980s, a group of Sikhs began carrying out guerrilla attacks against Hindus in an effort to force India to keep its promise of an independent Sikh homeland. According to the Indian government, these Sikh guerrillas used their holy Golden Temple at Amritsar as a base of operations because Indian police were forbidden to enter the Golden Temple.

In 1984, Indian Prime Minister Indira Gandhi decided that she could no longer allow the Sikhs to use their Golden Temple as a base of operations for criminal terrorism. Prime Minister Gandhi ordered her army to enter the Golden Temple, eliminate the Sikh radicals and restore order to Indian Punjab. Gandhi's attack on the Golden Temple was codenamed Operation Blue Star. The successful Operation Blue Star killed hundreds of Sikhs and destroyed part of the Golden Temple, including its important Sikh library, in its effort to defeat the Sikh guerrillas.

Sikhs denied that there had been any Sikh guerrillas in the Golden Temple, and considered Operation Blue Star an attack on their religious faith.

INTERESTING INDIVIDUALS: The Assassination of Indira Gandhi (1917 – 1984)

Indira Nehru was the only child of Jawaharlal Nehru, an important figure in the struggle for Indian independence who became the first prime minister of independent India. Like Mohandas Gandhi and other Indians who fought for independence, Jawaharlal spent a good bit of time in prison for speaking out against the government of British India. Indira helped her father by leading the "Monkey Brigade," a group of unnoticed children ("monkeys") who spied on the police and tried to warn men like Jawaharlal when the police were coming to arrest them. Indira took the last name "Gandhi" when she married a man named Feroze Gandhi in 1942. Neither she nor her husband was related to Mohandas Gandhi, the father of Indian independence.

When Jawaharlal died in 1964, the next prime minister appointed Indira to his cabinet. Two years later, when that prime minister died, Indira won election as India's third prime minister. **Indira Gandhi was the first woman in the world to win election as the head of a democratically elected government.** She served as India's prime minister from 1966 - 1977 and again from 1980 - 1984, and was the most important figure in India's government for almost twenty years.

Like other Indian leaders, Indira Gandhi used Sikh bodyguards. Sikhs follow a warrior tradition that makes them about 10 times more likely to volunteer for military service than other Indians. For centuries, Indian princes and maharajahs used highly skilled Sikh warriors as their personal bodyguards. After India gained its independence, Sikhs naturally took on the job of protecting India's prime ministers.

Indira was still using her Sikh bodyguards in 1984, when she ordered the Operation Blue Star attack that killed hundreds of Sikhs and damaged their Golden Temple. Friends warned her that Operation Blue Star might make her Sikh bodyguards angry enough to turn against her; but she knew her bodyguards personally, and believed that she could still trust them to honor their vow to protect her.

She misplaced her trust. On October 31, 1984, as Indira was walking through a garden at the prime minister's residence on her way to an interview, two of her Sikh bodyguards turned on her and shot her to death.

A Brief Timeline of More Recent Events in India and Pakistan

- In 1959, India allowed the Dalai Lama, the spiritual leader of Tibet, to set up a Tibetan government in exile in India. This angered China, which had always considered Tibet to be a part of China. China's anger over the Dalai Lama worsened a long-running border dispute with India in the Himalayas, and China and India fought a brief war over their border in 1962.

- In 1974, India became a nuclear power when it successfully tested its first nuclear weapon. Pakistan became a nuclear power in 1998.
- In 1984, a faulty tank at a Union Carbide chemical plant in Bhopal, India leaked poisonous pesticide gas that killed about 3,000 people and injured 500,000 or more.

FASCINATING FACTS: Rangoli

Rangoli are colorful works of art that often adorn the floors of Indian homes. Indians use Rangoli for luck, to honor their families or to welcome the gods into their homes during festivals.

According to Indian legend, the first Rangoli came out of the grief of an ancient Indian king. The young son of that king's high priest died suddenly, leaving both men stricken with grief. When the lord of the universe,

Brahma, saw the king's grief, he decided to help him. Brahma told the king to create a likeness of the boy on a wall so that Brahma could breathe life into the likeness and bring the boy back to life. The likeness the king created was the first Rangoli.

Because they illustrate the impermanence of life, Rangoli are not permanent. Many Rangoli are created on Indian floors only for festival times, and then cleared away when the festivals are over. Traditional Rangoli are often outlined with chalk, then filled in with colored flour, rice grains or powdered chalk. Some artists insist on an unbroken outside line to keep evil spirits out. Rangoli designs are usually symmetrical, and often represent objects from nature.

FASCINATING FACTS: Kabaddi

Kabaddi is a sport that south Asians have played for nearly 4000 years. The ancient armies of India may have developed the game of Kabaddi to boost the reflexes and self-defense skills of their soldiers.

A simple version of kabaddi:

A game of kabaddi requires no equipment other than an open field and two teams of at least seven players each. A line divides the playing field in half. Seven players from each team take the field, and the two teams take turns playing offense and defense.

To begin each play, a raider from the offensive team takes a deep breath, then starts repeating "kabaddi, kabaddi, kabaddi..." over and over while he runs across the line into the defensive team's territory. Then he tries to tag one or more players on the defensive team and run back to the safety of the other side before the defense can tag him back. The catch is that the defensive players must hold hands. If the defenders break hand contact to chase him, the offense scores. If the defenders fail to tag him before he returns to his side of the line, the offense scores. However, if the raider takes a breath before he makes it back to his side of the field, or if the defense tags him, the defense scores.

There is one further complication: After the raider tags a defender, one runner from the defensive team may break his handhold and chase him. Every player must act as his offense's raider at least once. Play ends when one team reaches 21 points.

MISSIONARY FOCUS

GIANTS OF THE FAITH: Ida S. Scudder (1870 – 1960)

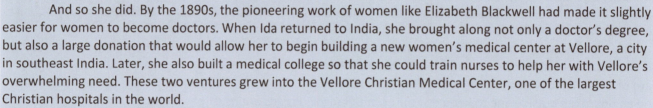

Ida Scudder was an American medical missionary from a family of medical missionaries. Born in India to a doctor/missionary father, Ida experienced India's poverty first-hand. As a result, Ida had little interest in medical missions when she was young. What Ida really wanted was to return to America, marry a wealthy man and live a life of ease and privilege.

It took the Holy Spirit to change Ida's mind. One night as Ida was preparing to return to America for college, three Indian men came to her father's house, one at a time, each seeking help for women who were dying in childbirth. One was a Muslim, two were Hindus, and not one of the three would allow a male doctor to see his wife. They wanted Ida to come and help their women; but Ida was as yet untrained, and had no medical help to offer.

On the next day, Ida found out that all three women had died. Then and there, she decided that the next time an Indian woman needed help, she would not be so powerless to help them. She vowed to become a medical doctor like her father and return to India so that she could help women in need.

And so she did. By the 1890s, the pioneering work of women like Elizabeth Blackwell had made it slightly easier for women to become doctors. When Ida returned to India, she brought along not only a doctor's degree, but also a large donation that would allow her to begin building a new women's medical center at Vellore, a city in southeast India. Later, she also built a medical college so that she could train nurses to help her with Vellore's overwhelming need. These two ventures grew into the Vellore Christian Medical Center, one of the largest Christian hospitals in the world.

For the rest of her life, Ida Scudder saw as many as 500 patients per day when she wasn't busy raising money for her hospital. She never married her wealthy man, but she did manage to convince several wealthy men to make large donations to her hospital. She died in India at the age of 89.

GIANTS OF THE FAITH: Mother Teresa (1910 – 1997)
Photo courtesy of Wikimedia-Commons User Túrelio, Creative Commons BY-SA 2.0-de

Mother Teresa, now also known as "Blessed Teresa of Calcutta," was born under the name Agnes Gonxha Bojaxhiu in the Macedonia region of the Ottoman Empire. When Agnes took her vows as a Roman Catholic nun, she adopted the name "Teresa" in honor of Therese of Lisieux, the patron saint of missionaries. This was fitting, because Sister Teresa had set her heart upon becoming a missionary in the Bengal region of British India. Bengal was one of the poorest regions on earth, desperately in need of missionary aid. Teresa was in Bengal for the Partition of 1947, which divided Bengal into Indian Bengal (in the west) and Pakistani Bengal (in the east). Teresa's life of ministry centered on the city of Calcutta, which lay in Indian Bengal.

Like many nuns, Teresa began her career as a teacher. She taught at St. Mary's High School in Calcutta for 20 years, working among the more privileged citizens of Calcutta who could afford to send their children to an English-speaking Catholic school. However, the terrible poverty Teresa saw around Calcutta weighed heavily on her heart; so, in 1948, she left St. Mary's to devote herself to relieving the poor in the slums of Calcutta. In that year, Teresa founded an open-air school for homeless children.

In 1950, Teresa received permission from the Catholic Church to establish a new order of nuns known as the "Missionaries of Charity." As the head of her order, Sister Teresa became known as Mother Teresa. The goal of the Missionaries of Charity was to care for the poorest of the poor. Mother Teresa and her fellow nuns took homeless, dying Indians off of the streets of Calcutta and brought them into a converted Hindu temple she named the "Home of the Pure Heart." There the nuns either nursed them back to health or ministered to them as they died.

In 1965, the Catholic Church allowed Mother Teresa to expand the Missionaries of Charity outside India. Over the next 30 years, the Missionaries of Charity opened more than 600 mission centers for the relief of the poor in more than 120 nations. Mother Teresa's constant concern for the poor won her admirers all over the world: she received the Nobel Peace Prize in 1979, and a Presidential Medal of Freedom from U.S. President Ronald Reagan in 1985.

U. S. GEOGRAPHY FOCUS

FASCINATING FACTS about IDAHO:

- Statehood: Idaho became the 43rd US state on July 3, 1890.
- Bordering states: Montana, Nevada, Oregon, Utah, Washington, Wyoming and Canada
- State capital: Boise
- Area: 83,570 sq. mi (Ranks 14th in size)
- Abbreviation: ID
- State nickname: "Gem State"
- State bird: Mountain Bluebird
- State tree: Western White Pine
- State flower: Syringa
- State song: *Here We Have Idaho*
- State Motto: "May it Endure Forever (It Is Forever)"
- Meaning of name: unknown
- Historic places to visit in Idaho: Hell's Canyon, Shoshone Falls, Mount Borah, Salmon River Mountains, Moon National Monument, Trinity Mountain, Eastern Idaho State Fair, Bruneau Dunes State Park, Bruneau Canyon Overlook, Lava Hot Springs, Birds of Prey Natural Area, Soda Springs, National Old Time Fiddlers Contest, Anderson Dam, Heaven's Gate Lookout
- Resources and Industries: farming (potatoes, wheat, sugar beets, barley, dairy, cattle, sheep), forestry and logging, mining (silver, lead, zinc, gold), machinery, chemical products, paper products, tourism

Shoshone Falls in Idaho

Flag of Idaho

- Idaho adopted this flag in 1907.
- It has a blue field with the state seal in its center and the words "State of Idaho" on a banner below the seal.
- The man on the state seal is a miner, and the woman represents liberty, equality and justice.

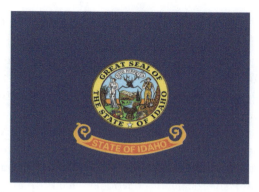

PRESIDENTIAL FOCUS

PRESIDENT #33: Harry S. Truman (1884 – 1972)	
In Office: April 12, 1945 – January 20, 1953	**Political Party:** Democratic
Birthplace: Missouri	**Nickname:** "Man of Independence"

Harry S. Truman was a U.S. Senator from Missouri who rose to the Vice Presidency as President Franklin Roosevelt's running mate in 1944. FDR died in office on April 12, 1945, leaving the new President Truman to serve most of the four-year Presidential term that FDR had won in the election of 1944. Truman represented the U.S. at the "Big Three" conference in Potsdam, and made the difficult decision to drop the world's first atomic bombs on Hiroshima and Nagasaki, Japan. He did so because he believed that Japan would never surrender unless the Allies struck some overwhelming blow, and because he believed that a full-scale invasion of Japan would cost the lives of more than 100,000 American soldiers.

Truman was also responsible for the "Truman Doctrine," which committed the United States to helping Greece and Turkey when they were struggling against communist takeovers. The Truman Doctrine helped lead the U.S. into the Korean War, fought to keep South Korea from falling to the communists of North Korea. However, the Truman Doctrine failed to prevent China from falling to communism in 1949. China entered the Korean War on the side of North Korea in late 1950, fighting the American forces defending South Korea to a standstill. When Truman decided not to pursue the war farther, some American Republicans accused Truman and his Democratic Party of being too "soft on communism."

Truman decided not to seek reelection in 1952. He lived on for 19 years after his Presidency, and died in his hometown of Independence, Missouri.

Other interesting facts about President Harry Truman:

- Truman loved playing cards, playing horseshoes and playing the piano.
- Truman's middle initial stood for nothing: he had no middle name.
- The vote for Truman's reelection in 1948 was so close that the Chicago Tribune newspaper actually printed an early edition with the headline "Dewey Defeats Truman" (Republican Thomas Dewey was Truman's opponent).

Notable quotes from Harry S. Truman:

- "America was not built on fear. America was built on courage, on imagination and an unbeatable determination to do the job at hand."
- "The atom bomb was no 'great decision.' It was merely another powerful weapon in the arsenal of righteousness."
- "In reading the lives of great men, I found that the first victory they won was over themselves... self-discipline with all of them came first."

Chapter 28

Israel, Egypt and the Suez Crisis

WORLD HISTORY FOCUS

ISRAEL

A Brief Timeline of Israel

2000 BC - 1500 BC: The era of the Hebrew Patriarchs Abraham, Isaac and Jacob (Israel).
1360-1085 BC: The era of the Judges.
1051 BC: The reign of Saul, Israel's first king, begins.
1004 BC: The reign of David, Israel's greatest king, begins.
971 BC: The reign of Solomon, the last king to rule a united Kingdom of Israel, begins.
931 BC: Israel divides into two kingdoms, the northern kingdom of Israel and the southern kingdom of Judah.
721 BC: The northern kingdom of Israel falls to the Assyrian Empire.
587 BC: The southern kingdom of Judah falls to the Babylonian Empire; the Babylonians destroy Solomon's Temple in Jerusalem.
559 - 530 BC: Cyrus the Great reigns over the Persian Empire. During his reign, Cyrus allows the Hebrew exiles to return to Israel and build the Second Temple.
332 BC: Alexander the Great overwhelms the Persian Empire and conquers the land of Israel (along with everything else). By now, the region is better known by the name "Palestine," derived from the name of Israel's enemies the Philistines.
166-160 BC: In the Maccabean Revolt, the Hebrews succeed in reestablishing a semi-independent Israel under the Seleucid Empire (one of the remnants of Alexander the Great's empire).
63 BC: Roman General Pompey captures Jerusalem and brings Palestine under Roman rule.
19 BC: Hoping to curry favor with the Jews, the Roman client king and would-be Jew Herod begins a decades-long restoration of the Second Temple around this time.

6 BC: Jesus Christ of Nazareth is born.

66 AD: The Jews rebel against Roman rule.
70 AD: The Romans defeat the Jewish rebellion and utterly destroy the Second Temple. The Jews scatter far and wide.
313 - 636 AD: The Byzantine Empire rules Palestine.
636 - 1099 AD: Arab Muslims rule Palestine. During this time, Muslims build the Dome of the Rock on the former site of the Temple.
1099 - 1291: Christians and Arabs struggle for control of Palestine during the Crusades.
1291 - 1516: The Muslim Mamluk Dynasty rules Palestine.
1517 - 1917: The Muslim Ottoman Empire rules Palestine.
1917: At the end of World War I, Britain defeats the Ottoman Empire and occupies Palestine.
1947: The United Nations votes to partition British Palestine into separate Arab and Jewish states.

The Ottomans surrendering Jerusalem to the British

425

1948, May 14: The UN partition plan goes into effect. Israel becomes an independent nation again for the first time in nearly 1,000 years.

DEFINITIONS

Zion: "Zion" is the Biblical name for one of the hills of Jerusalem, the capital of ancient Israel. The name "Zion" can refer to all of Jerusalem, or even all of Israel; but to Jews and Christians, it can also refer to God's holy kingdom on earth or in heaven.
Zionism: "Zionism" is a political movement that seeks to establish a permanent national home for the Jewish people in their ancient homeland of Israel, part of the larger territory known as Palestine.

SEE CHAPTER 25 FOR A DISCUSSION OF ANTI-SEMITISM AND THE HOLOCAUST

The Zionist Organization

Long before Hitler proposed his "Final Solution" to the "Jewish Problem" of what to do with Europe's Jews, one group of Jews proposed a far different solution. In 1897, a Hungarian Jew named Theodore Herzl (see picture) founded the Zionist Organization with the goal of creating a national home for the Jewish people in their ancient homeland of Israel.

Although the Jews had not held political power in Palestine since the Romans sacked Jerusalem in 70 AD, there were still Jews living in Palestine. Herzl and the Zionists wanted to boost Palestine's Jewish population through immigration (which they called *Aliyah*, Hebrew for "ascension"), then create some form of Jewish self-government in some part of Palestine. In the early 1900s, thousands of Zionist Jews began migrating to Palestine and purchasing land there, hoping to rebuild a Jewish homeland in their ancient Promised Land.

When Herzl formed the Zionist Organization, Palestine was part of the crumbling Ottoman Empire. The Ottoman sultans allowed the Jews some authority under the *millet* system (see Chapter 10), but Jews remained second-class citizens. As long as the Ottomans remained in control, Arab Muslims dominated Palestine.

The British Mandate for Palestine

During World War I, the Ottoman Empire fought on the losing side with the Central Powers (Germany, Austria-Hungary and Bulgaria). When the Ottoman Empire dissolved at the end of the war, Britain and France took over responsibility for governing all of the former Ottoman territory that lay in the circle surrounded by Turkey, Russia, Persia (Iran), Arabia, Egypt and the Mediterranean Sea. The British were no strangers to the Middle East: They already had interests in both Egypt (see Chapter 21) and Persia (see Chapter 16), and had fought in the Middle Eastern Theater of World War I to protect those interests.

In 1922, the League of Nations authorized Britain to govern Palestine under the British Mandate for Palestine. **For the next 26 years, Britain would have a great deal to do with the fate of Palestine.** Both Jews and Arabs knew that the British Mandate for Palestine was temporary, and both hoped to build nations of their own in Palestine when the Mandate ended. Therefore both sought help from the British.

The British had won World War I's Middle Eastern Theater with help from both Palestinian Arabs and Palestinian Jews, and had made promises to both in exchange for that help.

- Their promise to the Jews came in the 1917 Balfour Declaration, in which British Foreign Secretary Arthur Balfour declared Britain's support for a Jewish homeland in Palestine.
- Their promise to the Arabs came in the 1915 - 1916 letters that Sir Henry McMahon, the British High Commissioner for Egypt, wrote to Hussein bin Ali, the Sharif of Mecca.

Both Jews and Arabs expected Britain to honor its promises and to help them establish new nations in Palestine after World War I.

The Great Arab Revolt

When Adolf Hitler came to power in Germany in 1934, more Jews than ever sought to flee Europe and move to Palestine. Many of them succeeded, and Palestine became home to hundreds of thousands of Jews. Palestine's Arabs hated Jews nearly as much as Hitler's Germans did, and were not at all happy to see Palestine filling with Jews.

In 1936, Palestine's Arabs began a long, violent series of riots and attacks to protest both Jewish immigration and British rule. Palestine's Jews already had their own security force, the *Haganah* (Hebrew for "defense," see picture), established in 1920 to help the British police defend the Jews against Arab violence. Now a second, more radical force, the *Irgun*, began to attack militant Arabs. The militant Jews of the Irgun believed that they could succeed in establishing a Jewish state in Palestine only by matching the Arabs' violence. The *Haganah* and the *Irgun* would form the core of Israel's army when the time came to fight for Jewish independence.

Haganah Troops on Parade

TRAGIC TRUTH: British Limits on Immigration to Palestine

Britain's response to the Arabs' protests was to appease the Arabs by limiting the number of Jews it would allow into Palestine. Beginning in 1940, Britain agreed to allow no more than 15,000 Jewish immigrants into Palestine each year, a fraction of the number that wanted to come.

Unfortunately, **Britain's new limits on Jewish immigration arrived at precisely the time when Hitler's invasion of Poland began driving even more Jews out of Europe.** These limits left Europe's Jews with almost nowhere to hide from Hitler's Holocaust. The *Struma* incident (see Chapter 25) was only one example of a time when Britain's limits on Jewish immigration to Palestine cost fleeing Jews their lives. After the war, Britain continued to deport Jews who had survived the Holocaust and were trying to move into Palestine without permission.

FASCINATING FACTS: The *Aliyah Bet* Ships

Aliyah, Hebrew for "ascension," was the word Zionists used to describe immigration to Palestine. *Aliyah Aleph* ("Ascension A") described legal immigration, the migration of Jews who received valid entry visas from Britain during the British Mandate for Palestine. *Aliyah Bet* ("Ascension B") described a second kind of immigration: illegal immigration.

Aliyah Bet ships sailed before, during and after World War II in an effort to save Jews fleeing from the Nazis' Holocaust. The ill-fated *Struma* (see Chapter 25) was an *Aliyah Bet* ship. After World War II, Palestine's Zionist Jews traveled through Europe searching for Jews who had managed to survive Hitler's Holocaust. When they found them, usually in "displaced persons" camps, they invited them to move to Palestine and start new lives there. Unfortunately, the severe limits the British had imposed on Jewish immigration to Palestine were still in effect; so the Zionists tried to bring more Jews into Palestine illegally aboard the *Aliyah Bet* ships.

No one knows how many of the Aliyah Bet ships made it through, or how many Jews they brought to Palestine. The still-strong British navy caught up with many of the ships before they got anywhere near the harbors of Palestine. The British sent some of the ships' passengers to prison camps on the nearby British colony island of Cyprus, and only released them when the British Mandate for Palestine ended in 1948. Others they returned to Europe.

One well-known *Aliyah Bet* ship was the *Exodus 1947*, a decrepit passenger ship that set sail from France with more than 4,500 Jewish refugees and Holocaust survivors aboard. Because none of these refugees held valid entry visas, the British refused to allow any of them into Palestine. They transferred all of the refugees onto safer ships, then sent them back to France. When France refused to accept them, the British took them back to the British-controlled section of post-war Germany.

Germany was the last place on earth those refugees wanted to go, and British soldiers had to beat the resisting refugees and drag them off of the ships by force when they arrived there. In light of all the Jews' sufferings during WWII, the British people were ashamed to learn that their soldiers were beating pitiful Jewish Holocaust survivors into submission. The *Exodus 1947* gave the British one more good reason to want out of Palestine.

FASCINATING FACTS: The United Nations Partition Plan

After World War II, governing Palestine became an increasingly thankless task for the British, and they were eager to be finished with it. Nevertheless, they were still leery of offending Palestine's Arabs, so they continued their stiff opposition of Jewish immigration until the end of their Mandate.

On November 29, 1947, the General Assembly of the United Nations voted to accept a partition plan that divided all of Palestine west of the Jordan River into two separate states, one for Jews and one for Arabs. Because Palestine was still home to many more Arabs than Jews, the plan meant that thousands of Arabs would have to leave their homes if they wanted to live in the Arab state. However, the plan didn't force anyone to leave: Arabs could remain in their homes inside the Jewish state if they chose to.

The partition was not particularly favorable to Palestine's Jews. It did not grant the Jews their beloved city of Jerusalem-- Jerusalem lay entirely within one of the Arab sections, and was to be governed by the UN. Nor did the partition even grant the Jews a road to the all-important Jerusalem through Jewish-held territory. Nevertheless, most Jews accepted the partition gladly because they knew that it might be their only chance to have a homeland of their own.

Independence for Israel

The Arabs, on the other hand, rejected the partition plan outright, and refused even to discuss it. They regarded the partition plan as a theft of Arab lands, and were determined to defeat it. Civil war broke out in Palestine on the very next day after the UN accepted the partition plan. This civil war continued through the end of the British Mandate for Palestine, which Britain scheduled for May 15, 1948.

On May 14, 1948, Israel officially declared its independence, and the new nation of Israel was born.

On that day, the civil war between Palestinian Arabs and Palestinian Jews gave way to a new war. This was only the first of several Arab-Israeli wars that threatened Israel's survival.

The Arab-Israeli War of 1948

When Israel declared its independence, the civil war of 1947-1948 merged into the Arab-Israeli War of 1948. In this new war, neighboring Arab nations invaded Israel in an effort to strangle the new nation in its infancy.

Israel's neighbors Egypt, Syria, Lebanon and Jordan invaded from all sides.

Zionist mortar team outside Zafzaf in October 1948

Somehow, Israel survived. The new government drafted every able-bodied Jewish citizen, male or female, into its defense forces. It also received a great deal of financial aid from wealthy Jews all over the world who wanted to prevent the very real possibility of a second Holocaust. The *Haganah* and the *Irgun* banded together for Israel's defense. With help, Israel was able not only to hold off the Arab invaders, but also to conquer much of the Palestinian territory that the partition had set aside for Arabs. In 1949, Israel emerged from the war victorious, and signed armistice agreements with all four of its neighbors.

Results of the Arab-Israeli War of 1948:

- Israel controlled all of Palestine west of the Jordan River except for the West Bank and the Gaza Strip. Its new territory included the western part of the all-important Jerusalem. Israel's new borders with its Arab neighbors became known as the "green line."
- Jordan occupied the "West Bank," a territory on the west bank of the Jordan River that included East Jerusalem.
- Egypt occupied the "Gaza Strip," a strip of land on Palestine's southwest coast that bordered Egypt.
- Palestine's Arabs, who would have had a nation of their own under the UN partition plan, ended up with no nation at all, and became refugees.

FASCINATING FACTS: The Palestinian Exodus of 1948

During the Arab-Israeli War of 1948, Israel conquered a great deal of territory that the 1947 UN partition had set aside for Palestine's Arabs. As soon as their territory fell into Israeli hands, those Palestinian Arabs fled for Arab-controlled regions like the West Bank, Gaza, Jordan, Syria and Lebanon. More than 700,000 Palestinian Arabs became refugees, losing both their homes and their means of supporting themselves.

There is little agreement about why so many Arabs became refugees:

- Israel's supporters argue that no one forced the refugees to leave their homes, and that most of them did so only because they hated Jews and didn't want to live under a Jewish government.
- The Arabs' supporters argue that the refugees fled for their lives in fear of Israeli violence, and that Israel forced them out of the country to make more room for Jews.

At the 1949 Lausanne Conference after the war, Israel offered to allow 100,000 refugees to return to Israel in exchange for a peace agreement, but the Arabs rejected the offer. As of 2010, there were nearly 5 million Arabs who still claimed to be refugees or the descendants of refugees from the Arab-Israeli War of 1948. Many of them still live in poverty, and still hope to return to their homeland someday to reclaim what they and their families lost.

The Six Day War (1967):

By May 1967, constant clashes at Israel's borders had strained relations between Israel and its Arab neighbors to the breaking point. Egypt had stationed most of its army in the Sinai Peninsula, just across its border with Israel, and Israel believed that Egypt was preparing for an invasion. Arab forces were gathering on Israel's borders with Syria and Jordan as well.

Instead of waiting for the Arabs to strike, Israel made the aggressive decision to strike first.

On the morning of June 5, 1967, Israel's air force launched a surprise attack that destroyed nearly every warplane that Egypt owned before Egypt even knew the war had begun. Later that same day, Israel destroyed the air forces of Syria and Jordan as well. Over the six days from June 5 - 10, Israeli tanks and troops overran the Sinai Peninsula, the Gaza Strip, the West Bank and the Golan Heights, defeating the Arabs on all fronts at the same time within less than a week.

Destroyed Egyptian aircraft

Results of the 1967 Six-Day War:
- Israel occupied the Gaza Strip and the Sinai Peninsula. The Sinai, a triangular peninsula between Egypt and Israel, contained enough oil resources to produce all of the energy Israel needed.
- Israel occupied the West Bank, including East Jerusalem. Along with East Jerusalem and the West Bank came access to Jewish holy sites like the Wailing Wall that the Arabs had not allowed the Jews to use for years.
- Israel captured the Golan Heights, a strategic high ground on its northeast border with Syria. Control of the Golan Heights helped Israel to defend itself from Syrian artillery attacks.

The Yom Kippur War (1973):

After the Six Day War, Egypt and Syria were eager to reclaim their lost territory. The Yom Kippur War began on October 6, 1973, when **Egypt and Syria simultaneously launched surprise attacks on Israel.** They planned their attack for the Jewish holy day of Yom Kippur (the "Day of Atonement"), when they hoped to catch

Israel's defenses napping. Egypt invaded the Sinai Peninsula by crossing temporary bridges built over the Suez Canal (see picture), while Syria crossed Israel's northeast border and invaded the Golan Heights.

The Arab nations caught Israel by surprise, and drove deep into Israeli territory. Within a few days, however, Israel's defenses recovered and drove the Arabs back far beyond their borders. Israeli troops were within 100 kilometers of Egypt's capital, Cairo, when the war ended with a ceasefire on October 25. After the ceasefire, Israel withdrew within its 1967 borders; **no territory changed hands in the Yom Kippur War**.

However, the ceasefire didn't quite finish the war: the USSR, which supported the Arabs with money and weapons, accused Israel of violating the ceasefire, and threatened to enter the war on the Arabs' side. The USA, which supported Israel with money and weapons, threatened to enter the war on Israel's side. For a few days in late October, 1973, the world's two nuclear superpowers came near the brink of war over Egypt, Syria and Israel. Fortunately for the world, they both backed down.

Results of the 1973 Yom Kippur War:
- After this latest defeat, Egypt abandoned the idea of full-scale military assaults on Israel, and instead sought to recover the Sinai Peninsula through negotiation.
- The Arab members of the Organization of Petroleum Exporting Countries (OPEC) took revenge on the United States for its support of Israel by stopping oil shipments to the U.S. and Western Europe in late 1973. Their oil embargo caused a major gasoline shortage, which in turn caused long lines at gasoline stations all over the U.S. until OPEC lifted the embargo in 1974.

The Camp David Peace Accords and the Egypt-Israel Peace Treaty

In 1978, U.S. President Jimmy Carter invited the leaders of Egypt and Israel to the United States to negotiate a peace treaty between their two nations. Prime Minister Menachem Begin represented Israel, and President Anwar Sadat represented Egypt. The three leaders met at **Camp David**, a Presidential retreat near Thurmont, Maryland, to create a compromise that would allow Egypt and Israel to live side by side in peace.

In the Camp David Peace Accords, Israel offered to exchange **land for peace.** Israel offered Egypt the return of the Sinai Peninsula with its valuable resources. In exchange, Egypt offered Israel a peaceful neighbor that would no longer threaten to invade every few years. In the **Egypt-Israel Peace Treaty**, signed after Camp David in 1979, Israel agreed to withdraw from the Sinai Peninsula and return it to Egypt's control. Egypt agreed to sell Israel crude oil from the Sinai for its refineries and to keep waterways on both sides of the Sinai open for Israel's trade vessels.

Begin, Carter and Sadat from left to right

> ***Results of the 1979 Egypt-Israel Peace Treaty:***
> - Israel returned the Sinai Peninsula, which it had held since the Six-Day War of 1967, to Egypt.
> - Egypt made peace with Israel, and Israel had semi-friendly relations with one of its Arab neighbors for the first time since its birth in 1948.

The Fates of the West Bank and the Gaza Strip

The Camp David Accords were less successful in dealing with two other areas of Arab-Israeli conflict, the West Bank and the Gaza Strip. Israel had held both of these areas since the Six-Day War of 1967; but it had never annexed them (absorbed them into Israel), for several reasons:

1. The West Bank and the Gaza Strip were partitioned to the Arabs in 1947 for a reason: they were home to a great number of Arabs, and few Jews. Israel could not eject the Arabs without creating another mass exodus like the one in 1948; and it could not give the Arabs Israeli citizenship and grant them voting rights without allowing a lot of Israel-hating Arab representatives into its government.
2. Israel hoped to exchange part of the West Bank for peace with Syria and Jordan, just as it had exchanged the Sinai Peninsula for peace with Egypt.
3. The United Nations strongly opposed annexations; it supported self-government for the people of every region. Israel could not annex the West Bank and Gaza without inviting the wrath of the United Nations.

At Camp David, Israel agreed to withdraw its troops from the West Bank and Gaza and to allow the two regions to create independent governments for themselves within five years. Unfortunately, Israel has never felt safe doing so.

The fledgling governments of both regions, the West Bank and Gaza, have always been dominated by Arab terrorist groups like the PLO (Palestinian Liberation Organization) and *Hamas*, groups that openly admit that they want to see Israel destroyed and every Jew dead. Israel has been unwilling to surrender control of the West Bank and Gaza to governments that refuse to acknowledge Israel's right to exist.

For their part, the Arabs still resent Israel for forcing the Palestinian refugees out of their homes in 1948 - 1949, and hope to return those refugees to their homes someday. For these reasons, the West Bank and Gaza have remained firmly under the control of Israel's military.

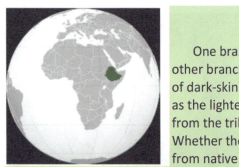

FASCINATING FACTS: Beta Israel

One branch of Father Abraham's Jewish family tree is quite different from every other branch. For centuries, the east African nation of Ethiopia was home to a race of dark-skinned people who read the Torah and lived according to Jewish law, just as the lighter-skinned Jews of Israel did. These "Beta Israel" Jews claimed descent from the tribe of Dan, one of the ten lost tribes of Israel's northern kingdom. Whether they were in fact descended from Dan, or whether they were descended from native Ethiopians who converted to Judaism, no one knows. Whatever their descent, they remained faithful to Judaism for centuries with little or no outside help.

As the Jews' national homeland, Israel has a "Law of Return" that guarantees Jews all over the world the right to immigrate to Israel if they choose to. Although some Jews doubted the Beta Israel Jews' origins, prominent Israeli rabbis agreed that they were Jews as real as any. Therefore in 1984, when famine and crises in Ethiopia put the

Beta Israel Jews in danger, Israel began a covert operation called "Operation Moses" to airlift some of them to Israel. More airlifts followed, and tens of thousands of Beta Israel Jews immigrated to Israel. By the early 1990s, few Beta Israel Jews remained in Ethiopia.

FASCINATING FACTS: *Tzedakah* Boxes

Tzedakah is a Hebrew word for "charity," and charity is an important part of the Jewish faith. To remind themselves of their duty to give charity, some Jews keep decorated donation boxes known as *tzedakah* boxes in their homes. These *tzedakah* boxes sit next to the *Shabbat* (Sabbath) candles to remind everyone that *tzedakah* is part of *Shabbat*. It is traditional to give *tzedakah* just before the lighting of the *Shabbat* candles on Friday evening.

FASCINATING FACTS: The Dreidel Game

A dreidel is a four-sided spinning top used in a very old Jewish children's gambling game. According to legend, during the time of the Maccabees (around 170 BC), the Greek King Antiochus tried to stamp out Judaism by banning Jewish worship and the study of the Torah. Jews who wanted to worship and study Torah anyway posted children outside their meeting places as lookouts. These lookout children needed an excuse to stay in the same place for a long time; so they played the dreidel game while they watched for soldiers, ready to warn the older Jews inside if the soldiers came too close.

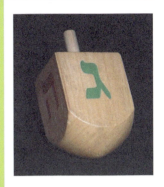

Directions for the dreidel game:
- Each player begins the game with about 15 pennies.
- At the beginning of a round, each player puts one penny into the "pot."
- The first player spins the dreidel and moves according to the letter of the Hebrew alphabet that lands face up:
    - נ (Nun, or nothing): the player does nothing
    - ג (Gimel, or everything): the player takes the entire pot
    - ה (Hey, or half): the player takes half of the pot
    - ש (Shin, or give): the player adds another penny to the pot
- When any player is out of pennies, he or she is out of the game. The game ends when one player has won all of the pennies.

FUN FACTS ABOUT ISRAEL

- Israel contains more scientists per unit of its population than any other nation in the world.
- Israeli engineers invented both cell phones and voice mail.
- Israel's unit of money is the shekel. Paper shekels are printed in both Hebrew and Braille so that the blind can read them too.
- The entire land of Israel stretches only about 290 miles from north to south and 85 miles from west to east at its widest point. With slightly less than 8,000 square miles of area, Israel is larger than only three individual U.S. states: Connecticut, Delaware and Rhode Island.

EGYPT AND THE SUEZ CRISIS
see Chapter 21 for a discussion of Egyptian Independence

King Farouk

Egypt declared independence from Britain in 1922. The Sultanate of Egypt that the British had founded at the beginning of World War I gave way to the new, independent Kingdom of Egypt. Sultan Fuad changed his title from "Sultan" to "King" and became the modern era's first Egyptian king. When King Fuad died in 1936, he passed his throne on to his 16-year-old son, Farouk (see picture).

King Farouk turned out to be a weak, spoiled king who made the mistake of angering everyone who might have supported him. He angered his Egyptian subjects by spending their money lavishly on himself: he loved to indulge himself by purchasing extravagant fancies like red sports cars, antique weapons and rare coins. And he angered his British supporters by failing to support Britain during World War II, even though much of the North African Campaign was fought on his doorstep. After WWII, King Farouk had few friends left, and he was ripe for overthrow.

Gamel Nasser and the Free Officers Movement

Farouk's overthrow would come from a group of nationalist Egyptian army officers called the Free Officers Movement. The Free Officers wanted to create a strong, proud and independent Egypt. They hated the

British, hated Israel and hated King Farouk. Farouk's self-indulgence and weakness disgusted them, and they were ready to replace their weak king with a strong leader who would expel the British and make Egypt truly independent of foreign control.

The leader of the Free Officers' leader was Gamal Abdel Nasser (see picture), an army officer who was tired of seeing Egypt humiliated. Nasser resented the fact that even though Egypt had supposedly been independent since 1922, British troops still controlled the Suez Canal. He was also part of the Arab army that lost Palestine to Israel in 1948, and he considered the Arabs' defeat a disgrace. Shortly after he returned from the Arab-Israeli War of 1948, Nasser began building the Free Officers Movement by approaching army officers he trusted and quietly inviting them to join the coming revolution. Although Nasser kept the movement as secret as possible, Farouk's government nearly discovered it more than once.

The Cairo Fire and the Egyptian Revolution of 1952

The spark for Nasser's revolution came from the direction of the all-important Suez Canal. On January 25, 1952, the British troops protecting the canal zone chased some criminals who had attacked British shipping into a police station in Ismailia, home of the Suez Canal Authority. The Ismailia police were sympathetic to the criminals, and refused to release them to the British. So the British attacked the police station, killing about 50 police officers in the process.

Cairo Fire

On the next day, angry Egyptians poured into the streets of Cairo, Egypt's capital, to demand that King Farouk declare war on Britain for attacking the policemen. Their protests erupted into riots and chaos. King Farouk's police force was so angry over the incident in Ismailia that it refused to intervene. Unknown arsonists started fires in British-owned buildings, and the fires spread because the city's fire department also refused to respond.

The Cairo Fire was the beginning of the end for King Farouk's government.

By mid-year, Nasser and his Free Officers felt ready to launch their *coup d'etat* against Farouk; so, on July 23, 1952, the Egyptian Revolution of 1952 began when the Free Officers Movement took over the government of Egypt. By then, most of the army had abandoned Farouk in favor of the Free Officers, so there was little resistance to their *coup*. Within a few days, the Free Officers deposed Farouk and sent him into exile in Italy.

The Free Officers formed a Revolutionary Command Council (RCC) to govern Egypt until they could form a more permanent government. Over the next few years, that government took on several different forms:

Muhammad Naguib (left) and Gamal Nasser (right)

1. From July 1952 - June 1953, Egypt remained a constitutional monarchy under the kingship of Farouk's infant son, Fouad II.
2. In June 1953, the RCC deposed Fouad II and created an Egyptian republic under President Muhammad Naguib, the highest-ranking member of the Free Officers Movement.
3. On November 14, 1954, Gamal Nasser placed President Naguib under house arrest and took his place as Egypt's president.
4. In 1956, Nasser produced a new republican constitution for Egypt and won election as Egypt's president. He also held elections for the republic's new parliament.

After four years of revolutionary governments, Egypt emerged in 1956 as a proud constitutional republic with Gamal Nasser as its highly popular, freely elected president. Furthermore, Nasser finally succeeded in ejecting the British from the Suez Canal Zone: **the last British occupiers left Egypt on June 18, 1956.** Egypt was at last truly independent.

The Aswan Dam

After World War II, the U.S. was at odds with its former Allies Britain and France over their continued control of the Middle East. Americans were angry because the British were always trying to protect their investments in the Middle East by appeasing the Arabs at the expense of the Jews. Britain angered Americans by refusing to allow more Jews to immigrate to Palestine; and it angered them further by continuing to support King Fouad, whom the U.S. viewed as a British puppet. Against Britain's wishes, the government of the United States supported Nasser's revolution.

However, Nasser also had a second supporter: the USSR. After Nasser came to power as president, he struck a deal with the USSR that allowed him to replace his British-supplied weapons with USSR-supplied ones. Nasser also granted Egypt's official recognition to the new communist government of mainland China, against America's will. **America refused to support Nasser's friendship with communists, whether they were Russian or Chinese.** Therefore, on July 19, 1956, the United States withdrew its support for the international funding of the Aswan Dam.

FASCINATING FACTS: The Aswan High Dam

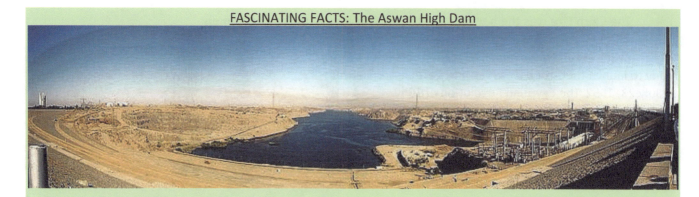

Egyptian agriculture lives or dies by the Nile River. Since ancient times, Egyptian farmers have irrigated their fields with the waters of the Nile. The Nile has also enriched their farms' sandy soil by carrying loamy silt downriver from central Africa. Unfortunately, the Nile can be a curse as well as a blessing: during wet years, it can rise up out of its banks and erase an entire growing season's crops in a matter of hours.

In order to make the Nile more predictable and safe, engineers proposed to dam the Nile near the city of Aswan in southern Egypt. The dams were designed to control seasonal flooding and to store more of the Nile's water for irrigation. Egypt's British occupiers finished their first dam, the Aswan Low Dam, in 1902. When the Nile continued to flood despite their dam, they raised the Low Dam's height twice-- once in 1912, and again in 1933. When this third project failed to control the Nile's floods, British engineers proposed to build a second dam farther upriver. This far larger dam would be called the Aswan High Dam.

President Nasser took over Egypt before the British could begin work on the Aswan High Dam. Nasser wanted to give Egypt's poor farmers a boost, and he believed that the Aswan High Dam was the right way to do it. Unfortunately, the project was far too large and complex for Egypt to build without outside help. In 1956, the project got caught up in the politics of the Suez Crisis (see below). When the U.S. and Britain refused to provide loans for the dam project, President Nasser turned to the USSR for funding. The Soviets wanted to strengthen their friendships with the Arabs, so they provided the loans and some of the engineering know-how necessary to build the project. With Soviet help, Egypt finished the Aswan High Dam in 1970. The finished dam included a sculpted monument to Soviet-Arab cooperation.

Other interesting facts about the Aswan Dam:
- The dam is about 2.4 miles long and 364 feet high. It took 10 years to build and cost well over $1 billion.
- The reservoir of water that backs up behind the dam is named Lake Nasser after Egypt's President Nasser. It extends about 340 miles up the Nile, and covers an area of about 2,000 square miles.
- The dam also includes a large hydroelectric power generation station that provides electric power to areas of Egypt that had never had it before.

The Suez Crisis

Nasser saw the loss of funding for the Aswan Dam as the only the latest in a long series of attacks on Egypt's independence. Finding himself strapped for cash, Nasser decided to tap a different source of wealth: **He nationalized the Suez Canal, bringing it firmly under Egyptian control for the first time since it opened in 1869** (picture shows the Suez Canal in February 1934). Claiming that Egypt would pay the Suez Canal Company's shareholders fair market value, Nasser simply took control of the canal's operations and all of the money they generated.

Nasser's move was exactly the sort of thing that Britain and France feared, and the very reason why Britain had stationed troops in the Suez Canal Zone for more than 80 years. Nasser was a popular, inspiring figure who wanted to unite all Arab peoples and create a United Arab Republic. If such a figure formed an alliance

The Suez Canal in February 1934

with the Soviet Union, Britain and France feared, it might mean the end of all of their colonies in the Middle East and North Africa.

FASCINATING FACTS: Operation Musketeer

Britain and France wanted to retake the canal zone immediately, but they weren't sure that they could count on America's support for a direct invasion by French and British troops. So they decided to involve a third nation, one that could count on America's support: Israel. Israel, too, was concerned about Nasser and all of the USSR-made weapons he was importing. Israel wanted to defuse the growing Arab threat on its southern border-- a threat that it feared could lead to a second Holocaust if Israel ever dropped its guard.

Britain and France presented Israel with a rather devious plan: they proposed that Israel should invade the Sinai Peninsula for the purposes of its own defense, which had only a little to do with the Suez Canal. That way, no one would assume that Israel was fighting for the Suez Canal. After Israel had pushed its way to the Canal, they proposed, British and French troops would rush to the rescue and put a stop to the war, like teachers breaking up a schoolyard brawl. This would provide Britain and France with an excellent excuse to station troops around the Suez Canal and retake control of its operations, which was what they wanted to do in the first place. The conspirators named their three-way plan "Operation Musketeer" after the Alexander Dumas novel *The Three Musketeers*.

Destroyed Egyptian Tanks

Operation Musketeer began according to its plan:

1. On October 29, 1956, Israel invaded the Sinai Peninsula and pushed its way toward the Suez Canal. Israel's troops pushed through the Sinai with little difficulty.
2. On October 30, Britain and France played their assigned role by calling on both Egypt and Israel to cease fire. Neither side responded-- Egypt didn't respond because it was under attack from Israel, and Israel didn't respond because it was playing out its own assigned role in Operation Musketeer.
3. On October 31, British and French forces began their own invasion of the Suez Canal Zone.

Militarily, Operation Musketeer was a big success. Egypt proved completely incapable of defending its Canal, and would have been utterly defeated within a week. Politically, however, Operation Musketeer was a failure. The United States did not support the invasion, even though Israel was involved; and the United Nations soon forced all of the troops involved to withdraw. No territory changed hands in the Suez Crisis, and Egypt retained control of the Suez Canal.

The Suez Crisis did have other important results:

- The victorious Gamal Nasser emerged as the hero of the Arab world. His eminent stature enabled him to form a union with Syria called the United Arab Republic (UAR) and become the foremost leader of the Arab world. However, the UAR was short-lived, and Egypt's defeat at the hands of Israel in the 1967 Six-Day War diminished Nasser's luster.

- Britain and France were thoroughly embarrassed, so much so that Britain's Prime Minister Anthony Eden resigned in disgrace. The age of African and Middle Eastern colonialism, which had begun with the Scramble for Africa and the Great Game in Persia and Afghanistan, was drawing to a close. More and more African and Arab nations would declare their independence in the coming years.

INTERESTING INDIVIDUALS: Anwar Sadat (1918 – 1981)

When the Free Officers Movement took control of Egypt during the Egyptian Revolution of 1952, one of the Free Officers made a nationwide radio announcement listing Egypt's many grievances against the weak and self-indulgent King Fouad. The voice Egyptians heard over their radios was that of Anwar Sadat.

Sadat was a high-ranking member of the Free Officers Movement who became President Nasser's second-in-command. In 1964, Sadat won election as Egypt's vice president; and when President Nasser died of a heart attack in 1970, Sadat took his place as President of Egypt.

At first, Sadat followed Nasser's strongly anti-Israel opinions and vowed to recapture the Sinai Peninsula by force. Sadat felt that Egypt could never restore its pride if it didn't avenge its defeat in the 1967 Six-Day War. It was Sadat who launched the 1973 Yom Kippur War, with help from Egypt's ally Syria.

After Egypt lost the Yom Kippur War, however, Sadat changed his mind about Israel. He decided that Egypt might never defeat Israel militarily, and he began to pursue peace with Israel so that Egypt could focus on its many other needs. In 1977, he personally visited Israel and spoke before Israel's parliament, the *Knesset*. And in 1978, Sadat joined U.S. President Jimmy Carter and Israeli Prime Minister Menachem Begin at the Camp David Peace Accords.

There, he helped negotiate the 1979 Egypt-Israel Peace Treaty, the very first peace treaty between Arabs and Israelis. Sadat paid for that treaty with his life.

Egypt's more radical Muslims believed that Sadat had shamed Egypt by giving in to the Israelis, and wanted the Islamic faith to be more central to Egypt's government. These Muslims decided that Sadat must die for his crimes; so, a Muslim cleric named Omar Abdel-Rahman issued a *fatwa*, or an execution order, for Anwar Sadat.

On October 6, 1981, Sadat was scheduled to deliver a speech at a victory rally in honor of Egypt's success at the beginning of the Yom Kippur War. Even though Egypt ended up losing that war, it still honored the anniversary of its invasion of Israel every year on October 6th. As Sadat stood up to speak, radical Muslims attacked his podium with grenades and automatic rifles. Anwar Sadat and 11 other people died in the attack.

Omar Abdel-Rahman, also known as the "Blind Sheikh," would later be involved in planning the 1993 bombing of New York City's World Trade Center.

MISSIONARY FOCUS

GIANTS OF THE FAITH: C. T. Studd (1860 – 1931), Founder of World Evangelization for Christ

Charles Thomas Studd was an English Protestant missionary who was among the many missionaries inspired by Hudson Taylor, founder of the China Inland Mission. He was one of seven Cambridge University-educated British Christians who joined the China Inland Mission in 1885 as the "Cambridge Seven." The fact that Studd was one of the best-known cricket players in the British Empire added a great deal to the Cambridge Seven's fame. The willingness of seven such bright and promising young men to devote their lives to missionary work in China drew a great deal of attention to the China Inland Mission, and helped it to grow.

Like George Mueller (see Chapter 1), C. T. Studd believed in waiting for God to provide for his ministry's financial needs. While Studd was in China from 1885 - 1894, his father died, and Studd received an inheritance of about 29,000 British pounds. Instead of keeping the money for himself, he donated it: 5,000 pounds to the Moody Bible Institute; 5,000 pounds to

George Mueller's ministry and orphanages; 5,000 pounds to the Salvation Army; 5,000 pounds to Minister George Holland, who had helped convert his father to Christianity; and another 5,000 pounds to the China Inland Mission. This left him with about 4,000 pounds. When he talked to his fiancée about the rest of the money, she reminded him that the Lord had told the rich young man to sell everything he had and give the money to the poor (Matthew 19:16-22); so Studd decided to give away the last of the money and start his married life with nothing. The Lord provided for all of his family's needs through more than 30 years of married life.

Most of the Cambridge Seven remained in China, but Studd's life's work was in Africa. After he first traveled to Africa in 1910, he became determined to set up mission stations all over Africa's interior that would carry the Gospel of Jesus Christ to the natives. The mission stations Studd founded formed the foundation of the Heart of Africa mission, which later became World Evangelization for Christ (WEC International).

U.S. GEOGRAPHY FOCUS

FASCINATING FACTS about WYOMING:

- Statehood: Wyoming became the 44th US state on July 10, 1890.
- Bordering states: Colorado, Montana, Nebraska, South Dakota, Utah, Idaho
- State capital: Cheyenne
- Area: 97,814 sq. mi (Ranks 10th in size)
- Abbreviation: WY
- State nickname: "Equality State"
- State bird: Western Meadowlark
- State tree: Cottonwood
- State flower: Indian Paintbrush
- State song: "Wyoming"
- State Motto: "Equal Rights"
- Meaning of name: Named after the Indian word that means "great plain"
- Historic places to visit in Wyoming: Yellowstone National Park, Grand Teton National Park, Devils Tower, Museum of the Old West and Old Trail Town, Washakie Museum, Tate Geological Museum, Fort Laramie, Fossil Butte National Monument
- Resources and Industries: farming (cattle, sugar beets hay, wheat, sheep) mining (coal, uranium) chemical products, lumber and wood, natural gas, oil, tourism

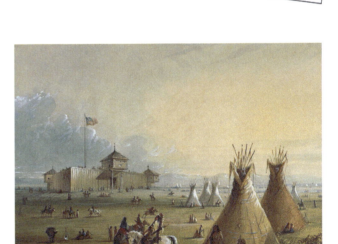

The first Fort Laramie prior to 1840 by Alfred Jacob Miller

Flag of Wyoming
- Wyoming adopted this flag on March 4, 1917
- The flag is blue with a red and white border
- It features the silhouette of an American Bison branded with the state seal
- The state's motto on the seal, "Equal Rights," is being held by a woman standing between two men who represent ranchers and miners.
- Wyoming was the first state to allow women to vote.

PRESIDENTIAL FOCUS

PRESIDENT #34: Dwight D. Eisenhower (1890 – 1969)	
In Office: January 20, 1953 – January 20, 1961	**Political Party:** Republican
Birthplace: Texas	**Nickname:** "Ike"

Dwight Eisenhower was a West Point graduate who spent the years between the two world wars as an aide to important army officers like John J. Pershing and Douglas MacArthur. He earned promotion to brigadier general (one star) just two months before the Japanese attack on Pearl Harbor brought the U.S. into WW II, so he was nowhere near the army's top ranks when the war began. However, General George Marshall (later the author of the Marshall Plan) noticed Eisenhower's talent for planning large operations, and promoted him rapidly. Eisenhower planned and executed all of the Allies' major operations in the European Theater of WW II, from North Africa to Italy to D-Day and Normandy. He earned his fourth star in December 1944; and in December 1945, he became one of the few American generals in history to earn a fifth star as a General of the Army.

After the war, Eisenhower succeeded General Marshall as Army Chief of Staff, then became President of Columbia University in New York City. As the hero of World War II, he was an obvious candidate for the Presidency, and both Democrats and Republicans asked him to run. But President Truman's conduct of the Cold War and the Korean War had turned Eisenhower against Truman, and he decided to run as a Republican. He easily defeated his Democratic Party opponent, Adlai Stevenson, in the elections of 1952 and 1956.

Eisenhower negotiated an end to the Korean War within the first year of his Presidency. The Eisenhower years were a time of post-war prosperity and optimism, but they were darkened by the ongoing Cold War and the threat of communism that continued to spread out from the USSR and China. In order to meet that threat, President Eisenhower announced the "Eisenhower Doctrine," which said that the U.S. would offer financial and military aid to any nation that felt threatened by communism. That doctrine helped lead the U.S. into confrontations with communists in Vietnam and elsewhere.

Other interesting facts about President Eisenhower:
- The U.S. began building its Interstate Highway System during Eisenhower's term.
- Eisenhower was the first President of all 50 states.
- His slogan during his Presidential elections was "I Like Ike."
- Ike's vice president for all eight years of his Presidency was Richard Nixon.
- The phrase "under God" was added to the Pledge of Allegiance during Eisenhower's term.
- Ike's favorite dessert was prune whip.
- Ike was the first President to appear on color television.
- Ike carried three coins in his pocket at all times for luck.

Notable quotes from President Eisenhower:
- "Without God, there could be no American form of Government, nor an American way of life. Recognition of the Supreme Being is the first -- the most basic -- expression of Americanism. Thus the Founding Fathers saw it, and thus, with God's help, it will continue to be."
- "The clearest way to show what the rule of law means to us in everyday life is to recall what has happened when there is no rule of law."

Chapter 29

Communism in China, the Korean War

WORLD HISTORY FOCUS

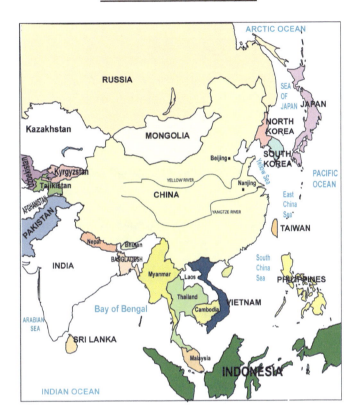

COMMUNISM IN CHINA
Continued from Chapter 22

China During World War II

When the Second Chinese-Japanese War began in 1937, the Kuomintang (KMT or Nationalist Party, led by Chiang Kai-shek) and the Communist Party of China (CPC, led by Mao Tse-tung) temporarily set aside their differences and united against their common foe, Japan. When Japan attacked the U.S. Navy at Pearl Harbor in 1941, the Second Chinese-Japanese War merged into World War II. Chiang Kai-shek was certain that the U.S. would eventually defeat Japan, so China joined the Allies and declared war on Germany and Italy as well as Japan.

In some ways, China was more of a burden to the Allies than a blessing. Years of war had destroyed most of China's already-limited ability to manufacture weapons. Because Japan controlled the ports all over southeast Asia (including China's), most of the war material the Allies supplied to China had to come from British India by way of an airlift over the Himalaya mountain range (which transport pilots called "the Hump"). That burdensome requirement placed severe limits on how much material the Allies could send.

Nor could the Allies convince Chiang Kai-shek to help them by sending Chinese armies against the Japanese in places like Burma and Vietnam. This was partly because Chiang's hands were full. Chiang's strained relationship with the communists meant that the KMT bore the brunt of Japan's attacks. Chiang's KMT army lost many of its best soldiers holding off the 1.5 million Japanese soldiers who occupied China's coastlands. China's primary contribution to the Allies was to keep those Japanese soldiers occupied so that Japan couldn't use them against the Allies elsewhere. Chiang's plan was to wait for the U.S. to overwhelm Japan, then drive the Japanese occupiers out of China after Japan was already beaten.

Communism Takes Over in China

After the war, the KMT and the CPC resumed the Chinese Civil War that had begun during the 1927 Northern Expedition, when Chiang turned on the communists. It was a struggle for control of China; and in that struggle, the KMT continually lost ground. Mao's communist philosophy was popular with the Chinese people: they liked the communist idea of stripping wealthy landowners of their farms and redistributing their land to the poor. Mao promised China's impoverished peasants more prosperity than most of them had ever imagined. As more and more Chinese defected to the CPC, Mao's communists gained ground, and Chiang's KMT became less and less popular.

The End of the Chinese Civil War

1949 was the year in which everything unraveled for the KMT. After dealing the KMT a major defeat in the formerly Japanese-held Manchuria, the CPC People's Liberation Army began capturing lightly defended cities all over northern China. Most of China's people had already been converted to communist beliefs by Mao's ubiquitous propaganda, and were ready to abandon the KMT and join the CPC.

As the communists advanced, Chiang retreated southward from his northern capital at Nanjing. His KMT armies withdrew to two southern provinces, Guangdong and Sichuan, for their last stand. Guangdong fell to the communists first. When the CPC laid siege to Sichuan as well, the battle was lost.

Chiang and the KMT fled to the airport at Chengdu, Sichuan's capital, then escaped by air to the large Chinese island of Taiwan.

FASCINATING FACTS: The Republic of China

Chiang set up the government of the Republic of China in his new capital at Taipei, Taiwan. Despite his crushing defeat at the hands of the communists, Chiang continued to insist that the Republic of China was the rightful government of all of China. For the rest of his life, Chiang laid plans to recapture mainland China from the communists and restore his government there.

None of those plans ever came to fruition. Chiang never set foot on mainland China again.

The People's Republic of China

Meanwhile, Mao Tse-tung was busy setting up a new communist government for China. On October 1, 1949, shortly before the communists' final victory over the nationalists, Mao proclaimed the foundation of the new **People's Republic of China**. The proclamation came from Tiananmen Square, adjacent to the old Qing emperors' Forbidden City in Beijing (Peking). In his proclamation, Mao named himself as Chairman of the Central People's Government and of the People's Revolutionary Military Commission. He also declared that the People's Republic of China was China's only legitimate government, and invited foreign governments to recognize his government formally. The People's Republic of China was Mao's to govern.

DASTARDLY DICTATORS: Mao Tse-tung (1893 – 1976)

Mao Tse-tung began his working career as an assistant librarian at the University of Peking. While Mao worked at the University, he read literature and attended lectures that sparked his interest in communism. Mao attended the first meeting of the Communist Party of China (CPC) in 1921, and he helped shape and steer the CPC from its very beginning.

It was Mao Tse-tung who realized that any effective revolution in China would have to begin with its rural peasants, not with its industrial workers. In other countries, labor unions and labor strikes were the key to revolution; but in China, where most of the population lived in the countryside and not in cities, peasants were the key. Mao was the CPC's propaganda expert, and his persistent teaching convinced China's hundreds of millions of peasants that communism would bring them more prosperity than they had ever believed possible.

Mao and his communists joined Chiang Kai-shek and the KMT (Nationalist Party) on the Northern Expedition to overthrow the warlords that ruled China after the fall of the Qing Dynasty. During the Northern Expedition, the communists began their USSR/Comintern-inspired takeovers of farms and businesses. Communism wasn't what Chiang had in mind, so he turned against the communists and tried to overcome them as he had overcome most of the warlords. In response, Mao led his followers on the difficult Long March to escape Chiang, then used his expert propaganda to rebuild his following in the north (see Chapter 22). The Second Chinese-Japanese War and World War II cost Chiang's KMT army most of its best soldiers, making it easier for the communists to defeat the KMT and proclaim the new People's Republic of China in 1949.

Mao was Communist China's foremost idea man, and Maoist philosophy guided the transformation of China into a purely communist state. Mao published essays and books by the score, and what he wrote touched the hearts of the Chinese people. In theory, Mao wanted a "classless" society in which there would be no "exploiters"-- people who used their wealth to enslave the poor. In Mao's communist utopia, everyone would work together and share everything equally. No one would set himself above anyone else; everyone would sacrifice himself for the sake of the community and a greater China. All Chinese would eat the same (often in communal cafeterias), dress the same (often in a communist-approved uniform called the "Mao Suit"), and share the same lot in life.

In pursuit of this utopia, Mao was prepared to be ruthless. He spoke casually of the killings that would

be necessary to eliminate everyone who opposed his communist revolution. He sent execution squads out into the provinces to root out anti-communists. He praised these squads for killing thousands of people, and encouraged them to kill still more. No one knows how many people died in Mao's program to cleanse China of all anti-communist feeling, but Mao himself freely admitted eliminating 700,000 political enemies in the early days of the People's Republic of China. One of his five-year plans, the "Great Leap Forward" (see below), was responsible for tens of millions of deaths. <u>Mao Tse-tung ranks alongside Stalin and Hitler as one of history's most prolific killers</u>.

Despite this legacy of murder, the People's Republic of China still honors Mao as the heroic leader of its communist revolution, just as Russia still honors Vladimir Lenin. When Mao died in 1976, China placed his remains on public display in an elaborate mausoleum in Beijing's Tiananmen Square.

Interesting quotes from Mao Tse-tung:
- "Communism is not love. Communism is a hammer which we use to crush the enemy."
- "Political power grows out of the barrel of a gun."

FASCINATING FACTS: Mao's Tactics against Anti-Communists

Mao hated disunity and dissent; he wanted every single Chinese citizen to unite behind his communist ideas. Naturally, some people resisted, so Mao developed a number of ingenious tactics to promote the Communist Party and root out anti-communist feeling:

- **The Campaign to Suppress Counter-Revolutionaries:** This was Mao's campaign to kill KMT members who still lived in mainland China, along with everyone else who resisted communism. This campaign included quotas for mass killings in various regions of China. Mao based these quotas, not on how many anti-communists lived in each region, but on a percentage of each region's population. Communist killing squads obediently filled Mao's killing quotas whether their victims were anti-communist or not.

- **Struggle Sessions:** Struggle sessions were public meetings in which Mao's communists accused their victims of anti-communist "crimes against the people" and then tortured and humiliated them in front of the entire community. Mao used struggle sessions against groups of people he hated, such as (1) landowners who resisted donating their farms to the collective and (2) college professors who taught against his ideas. Struggle sessions took advantage of the Chinese people's profound sense of honor and shame: no Chinese person wanted to be humiliated in public.

- **Re-education through Labor:** Although Mao first learned about communism at a university, he hated university intellectuals, and believed that China's peasants had much to teach them. When Mao's communists accused intellectuals of holding anti-communist beliefs, they often sent them to distant, rural farm labor camps where peasant life could "re-educate" them.

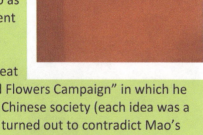

- **The Little Red Book:** The "Little Red Book" was a red-covered book full of quotations from the beloved Chairman Mao. Among other things, its quotations encouraged the Chinese to be selfless and to sacrifice themselves for the good of China and the Communist Party. The communists printed more than 1 billion copies of the Little Red Book. They distributed them to as many Chinese as possible so that they could carry them wherever they went and use them to study the great Mao's teachings.

- **The Hundred Flowers Campaign:** When Mao was ready to launch the "Great Leap Forward" (see below), he began with a program called the "Hundred Flowers Campaign" in which he asked the Chinese people to come forward with their ideas for improving Chinese society (each idea was a "flower" with the potential to beautify China). When some of these ideas turned out to contradict Mao's own, he identified the people who proposed those ideas and punished or killed them.

The Great Leap Forward (1957 – 1961)

Communist China and the USSR habitually set progress goals for their nations in the form of "5-year plans." The Great Leap Forward was one such 5-year plan. Mao launched the Great Leap Forward in 1957 with the primary goals of (1) increasing steel production and (2) forcing all of China's private farms into collective farms.

Steel Production:

Mao wanted to modernize and industrialize his technologically backward China, and he believed that steel production was the key to improving China's industry. Unfortunately, Mao knew next to nothing about steel production. When Mao saw a demonstration of a backyard steel smelting furnace, he assumed that everyone should be able to make steel in his backyard, and that steel-making was a simple matter. So Mao established steel production quotas for organizations of all kinds. Farms, villages, schools and even hospitals all struggled to meet Mao's steel quotas. Farmers, villagers, teachers and doctors had to set aside their usual tasks or work late into the night in order to tend their smelting furnaces.

Smelting Furnaces

Unfortunately for Mao, steel production was *not* a simple matter. Quality steel production requires an excellent fuel such as coal or coke to produce the high-temperature fires that steel-making needs. It also requires careful control of the metal's purity and temperature. Mao's backyard smelting furnaces proved to be practically worthless, and did little or nothing to boost China's steel production. Later, when Mao learned the truth of this, he refused to abandon the program because he didn't want to deflate his people's "revolutionary spirit."

Collective Farms:

Like Lenin and Stalin, Mao believed that farms would be more productive when they were all organized into collectives under the control of the communist state. The communists united farms and villages into communes of about 5,000 people each. Members of these communes gave up all of their property rights-- their farms and homes belonged to the state. Communist Party life replaced family life; everyone in the commune worked together and ate in the communal dining hall. Parents essentially gave up their children; the commune's children lived

A propaganda poster of a commune

together in a children's barracks, and were raised and educated by Communist Party teachers. This helped insure that the next generation of Chinese citizens would be less resistant to communism.

Unfortunately, as Lenin discovered in the USSR, collectivization did not necessarily improve farming efficiency. Mao knew no more of farming than he did of steel production, and his communists managed China's farms very poorly. During the Great Leap Forward, China's grain production actually went down, not up. Despite this, China sold much of the grain that should have gone to feed its people, for two reasons:

(1) to prove that the Great Leap Forward was working, and
(2) to make money with which to boost steel production.

The Great Chinese Famine:
The communists' ignorant meddling with farm production combined with dry weather to produce one of the worst famines of all time, the Great Chinese Famine. Anywhere from 15 to 45 million Chinese died in the tragedy of the Great Chinese Famine of 1958 - 1961.

FASCINATING FACTS: The Great Sparrow Campaign and the Law of Unintended Consequences

The Law of Unintended Consequences says that when governments make rules to control things that they don't fully understand, there will be bad unforeseen consequences that the governments didn't intend. The communist policies of the Great Leap Forward had several consequences that were not only unintended, but also deadly.

The Great Sparrow Campaign:
Mao noticed that China's ubiquitous sparrows were eating far too much of the people's grain, so he decided to eliminate them. He encouraged the children of China to attack sparrows wherever they found them. Schoolchildren killed sparrows with slingshots, beat cooking pans to frighten sparrows off or chased sparrows to the point of exhaustion and death. China's tens of millions of determined children were able to make a major dent in the sparrow population.

Mao learned too late that sparrows eat insects as well as grain. In the years that followed the Great Sparrow Campaign, vast swarms of locusts that would ordinarily have fallen prey to the sparrows were able to descend on China's crops unhindered. The locusts ate thousands of times more grain than the poor sparrows ever would have. Locust swarms combined with bad weather and other bad communist ideas to create the Great Chinese Famine.

Steel Quotas:
Mao established steel quotas for farmers and schoolchildren who had no idea how to produce steel. In their zest to meet Mao's quotas, such people took desperate measures: farmers sometimes melted down their farm tools, and schoolchildren sometimes melted down their families' pots and pans. Thus Mao's quotas had the opposite of their intended effect: since these items had to be replaced, China had less steel, not more.

The many failures of the Great Leap Forward damaged Mao's lofty reputation. Other communist leaders like Deng Xiaoping stepped forward to repair the damage, and Mao voluntarily stepped down from his post as manager of the day-to-day operations of the government.

The Cultural Revolution (1966 – 1976)

Since Mao had fallen out of favor with powerful members of the Communist Party of China, he decided to use his popularity with China's youth to attack the Party itself. In the Cultural Revolution, launched in 1966, Mao called on China's youth to purify themselves and cleanse China of all anti-communist thoughts and feelings. Declaring that a crisis was at hand, Mao shut down schools and formed selected Chinese youths into a new organization called the Red Guards.

FASCINATING FACTS: The Red Guards

Mao's Red Guards were young Chinese who had grown up when Mao was at the height of his power. Trained in communist schools by communist teachers, they were intensely loyal to Mao and eager to attack anything they perceived as anti-communist or anti-Mao. Mao encouraged his Red Guards to cleanse China of old, pre-communist thought by attacking the "Four Old Things": old customs, old culture, old habits and old ideas. In the name of Mao, the Red Guards rampaged through China destroying old art, old temples and shrines, and anything else that reminded them of China's pre-communist culture.

Intellectuals and college professors became a special target of the Red Guards. Mao had always hated intellectuals, whom he saw as the preservers and guardians of the old pre-communist culture (They also had an annoying habit of pointing out the flaws in Mao's plans). Mao taught the Red Guards that their teachers were part of a privileged class, and that this privileged class desired power over them. To complete the communist revolution, he said, the Red Guards must eliminate classes and make everyone in China equal.

Mao had little difficulty in turning children against their teachers. Anyone whom the Red Guards deemed to have a superior attitude could be denounced as an enemy of the Communist Party, subjected to a struggle session and forced to make a confession known as a "self-criticism." The Red Guards accused their teachers of teaching anti-communist philosophy, then tortured them in struggle sessions or sent them to "re-education through labor" camps in the far-off countryside.

In the Red Guards, Mao had unleashed a force that even he could not control. For several months, the Chinese people lived or died by the whims of overzealous, unrestrained children. Then the Red Guards began to divide into groups that attacked each other over differences of opinion. Mao finally had to use the army to subdue the Red Guards and end the program.

"Down to the Countryside"

Mao continued his war on intellectualism with one of his last Cultural Revolution programs, "Down to the Countryside." Continuing the idea of "Re-education through Labor," Mao ordered city-dwellers to relocate to the countryside where they would learn proper communist thought from Mao's beloved Chinese peasants. For years, these exiles from China's cities lived in poverty in far-flung provinces of China, where they dug irrigation ditches, cut bamboo or planted rice. Many of them never returned to their home cities until Mao died and the Cultural Revolution finally ended in 1976.

China's next leader, Deng Xiaoping, said that the Cultural Revolution had created a "lost generation" of Chinese people who had missed their chance to attend college and receive a better education.

INTERESTING INDIVIDUALS: Deng Xiaoping

Deng Xiaoping was a high-ranking member of the Communist Party who fell victim to the Cultural Revolution. In 1969, the Communist Party accused Deng of anti-Maoist beliefs and sent him to work in a tractor factory. He later returned to the Party as a "rehabilitated" communist, but the Party continued to view Deng with suspicion until Mao's death in 1976.

After Mao died, Deng was able to convince the Party that Mao's Cultural Revolution had been a mistake. Deng understood that Mao's overenthusiastic mismanagement had led to a great deal of poverty and suffering, so he sought to reform Chinese communism. He led the Communist Party away from Mao's absolute insistence on communist principles, especially in the areas of education and business. Mao had hated and distrusted highly educated intellectuals, but Deng encouraged young Chinese to go abroad and learn Western technology at Western universities. When they returned with heads full of technical knowledge,

China began to enjoy far more economic prosperity. Under Deng, intellectuals and businessmen became more free to prosper and grow wealthy without the constant fear of being denounced as anti-communists and sent to cut bamboo in the countryside.

However, Deng's relaxation of certain communist principles did not mean that he was granting his people freedom of speech. In 1989, the year in which communist governments in Eastern Europe began to collapse, hundreds or thousands of young Chinese gathered in Beijing's Tiananmen Square to protest the many ways in which communism restricted their freedom. Deng's army used live ammunition to disperse the protesters, killing an unknown number of them. The Chinese were free to pursue wealth under Deng Xiaoping, but they were not free to raise objections against their government.

Interesting quotes from Deng Xiaoping:
- "Poverty is not socialism. To be rich is glorious."
- "Reform is China's second revolution."

DISPUTED DOMAINS: Hong Kong and Macau

Hong Kong is a wealthy port city-state on the South China Sea. Part of Hong Kong lies on Hong Kong Island just off the Chinese coast, and part of it lies in mainland China. Hong Kong became a British colony after China lost the First Opium War to Britain in 1842. It remained a British colony until 1997, except during the WW II years, when it was occupied by Japan.

The Chinese Revolution of 1949 left Hong Kong untouched. Its connection to Britain protected it from the communists, and it continued to prosper even as the People's Republic of China struggled through the poverty and famine of the Mao years. For decades, Hong Kong's people resisted the idea of being annexed into China because they didn't want to share China's communism or its poverty.

In 1984, Britain and China reached a compromise on Hong Kong. Under the terms of that compromise, Hong Kong became part of the People's Republic of China in 1997, but only under a special condition: that Hong Kong could retain its own local government and laws for at least 50 years, until 2047.

Just southwest of Hong Kong lies Macau, another port city-state that was a colony of Portugal from the 1500s through 1999. In 1999, Macau became part of the People's Republic of China; but like Hong Kong, Macau retains its own local government and laws.

DISPUTED DOMAINS: Taiwan and the Chinese-American Mutual Defense Treaty

Taiwan is a large island that lies about 100 miles east of mainland China. When the communists defeated the nationalist Kuomintang in late 1949, Chiang Kai-shek flew to Taiwan and set up his government in Taiwan's capital city of Taipei. For more than two decades, Chiang continued to claim that his government, the Republic of China, was the only legitimate government of all China.

Plenty of people agreed. During the Cold War years, the United States and other Western governments refused to recognize the communist government of the People's Republic of China (PRC), and hoped that the Republic of China (ROC) would regain its strength and return to govern mainland China someday. In 1955, the United States and the ROC ratified the Chinese-American Mutual Defense Treaty, in which each agreed to defend the other in case of attack. Signed in the aftermath of the Korean War, this treaty was intended to keep the ROC safe from a possible communist invasion.

As time went on and mainland China grew more thoroughly communist, hope began to fade that the

ROC would ever return to mainland China. In 1971, the United Nations voted to expel the ROC's representatives to the U.N. and to accept representatives from the PRC instead. The United States recognized the PRC as China's legitimate government in 1979; and in 1980, President Jimmy Carter withdrew the U.S. from the Chinese-American Mutual Defense Treaty, eliminating Taiwan's primary defense against the PRC.

As of 2010, Taiwan remains free of the PRC. The United States is under no treaty obligation to defend Taiwan if the PRC should invade, but might still choose to do so.

FASCINATING FACTS: China's "One-Child" Policy

China is the most populous nation on earth, and has been so for a very long time. China's communist leaders believe that much of China's poverty problem can be traced to overpopulation. Therefore, in 1979, Deng Xiaoping's government tried to limit the growth of China's population by creating a family planning policy called the One-Child Policy. That policy is still in effect as of 2010.

The One-Child Policy restricts certain Chinese families to at most one child. The Communist Party enforces this policy very strictly. Each province has government officials who are responsible to make sure that no family violates the one-child policy. Large Chinese companies are required to hire entire staffs to enforce the policy on their many employees. Those who violate the one-child policy face fines, forced abortions, or even forced sterilizations. China even enforces this rule on Chinese citizens who live abroad; and if citizens living abroad violate it, the Communist Party may threaten those citizens' family members who are living back home in China.

China's one-child policy brings harsh government regulation and control into the most private area of family life. The policy is so strict that in some cases, families who have lost a child are not allowed to have another, and must remain childless for life. It has also led to an unbalanced population: since Chinese families traditionally value sons more than daughters, many families abort or abandon their infant girls in the hope that the next child to come along will be a boy.

FASCINATING FACTS: Chinese Yo-Yos

A real Chinese yo-yo is not like the modern carnival toy that is made of curled paper wrapped around a stick. The true Chinese yo-yo is a Ming Dynasty-era invention that consists of two wheels connected by an axle. The user holds a string taut between two sticks of bamboo, and the yoyo's axle rides on the string as it spins. The yoyo's wheels may be hollow with openings that make them whistle as they spin; such yoyos are known as "empty bells." Empty bell experts perform Chinese yoyo tricks to entertain crowds during Chinese festivals.

THE KOREAN WAR

Japan After World War II

Japan formally surrendered to the Allies on V-J Day, August 15, 1945. On that same day, President Truman appointed General Douglas MacArthur as Japan's military governor, giving MacArthur authority over all four of Japan's main islands and most of its island territories.

This arrangement was quite different from the one in Europe, where the Allies had divided Germany into four zones of occupation (one each for the USA, the USSR, Britain and France). The USSR had already occupied eastern Germany before V-E Day, and had a much larger army in Europe than the western Allies had; but the USSR had delayed entering the Pacific War, and barely contributed to the Allies' victory over Japan. The victory over Japan was mostly an American victory, and America dictated the terms of Japan's surrender.

> CRITICAL CONCEPTS: The Constitution of Japan
>
> General MacArthur's staff wrote a new constitution for Japan that transformed the former empire into a constitutional monarchy. Under Japan's new constitution, adopted in 1947, the emperor became a mere figurehead. The real power lay with Japan's new parliament and prime minister. The United States and Japan made peace in the 1952 San Francisco Peace Treaty, and Japan became independent once more.
>
> However, Japan's constitution included an important limitation on that independence: it did not allow Japan to maintain an army, navy or air force, and forbade Japan to settle its disputes with other nations through warfare. In this way, the Allies sought to ensure that Japan would never attack its neighbors again.

Korea Under Occupation

There was one important area of Japan's former empire where General MacArthur had no authority: northern Korea. Japan had annexed all of Korea in 1910, and Korea had been a Japanese colony ever since. When the USSR entered the Pacific War on August 9, 1945, Soviet troops immediately attacked Japanese forces in northern Korea as part of the Allied plan to force Japan to surrender. By prior agreement with the western Allies, Soviet troops halted their invasion at the line of 38° north latitude, which divided Korea roughly in half, north from south. The USSR occupied Korea north of the 38th Parallel, while United States troops arrived to occupy Korea south of the 38th Parallel in the weeks that followed.

Communism in Korea

Almost immediately, the US and the USSR began to bicker over Korea. The USSR naturally believed that Korea should have a communist government, while the US wanted to establish a democratic republic there. The US was already beginning to understand that Stalin had misled President Roosevelt at the Yalta Conference, and that the USSR intended to capture as much territory for communism as it possibly could. The US didn't want Korea to fall to communism in the same way that eastern Germany and Poland were already falling.

The Koreans themselves were as divided as the Chinese were. As in China, the battle was between Korea's communists and its nationalists. Korea's communists were heavily influenced by communists from China and the USSR. As for Korea's nationalists, they were bitter over the last 35 years of Japanese occupation. They wanted the new Korea to be united and free of all outside influences, whether from the US or the USSR.

Elections

In 1948, the United Nations called for elections to determine Korea's new government. The USSR was unwilling to allow free elections, because it couldn't be sure that the results would favor communism; so it refused to allow the UN to supervise elections in Soviet-occupied northern Korea. In response, the UN decided to hold a separate election in southern Korea, where it was free to supervise as it pleased. The communists boycotted the UN's election in southern Korea, claiming that it was an effort to divide Korea in two. With no communists participating, that election easily produced an anti-communist, republican, nationalist government.

The inauguration ceremony for the government of the Republic of Korea

> Korea's new nationalist president, Syngman Rhee, immediately outlawed communism in southern Korea and began rounding up and killing communists. Rhee's murderous rampages embarrassed the United States, which had strongly supported the nationalists in southern Korea's election.

As for northern Korea's communists, led by Kim Il-sung, they were imitating Mao Tse-tung by killing anyone and everyone in the north who opposed communism.

Both the USSR and the US withdrew from Korea in 1948 - 1949, leaving Korea divided: North Korea was in the hands of a communist government under Kim Il-sung, while South Korea was in the hands of a nationalist government under Syngman Rhee.

In 1950, Kim Il-sung and his communists launched the Korean War to destroy Rhee's nationalist government and unite the two Koreas, North and South, under a communist government.

A Brief Timeline of the Korean War (1950 – 1953)

1950, June 25: The North Korean People's Army (NKPA) crosses the 38th parallel into South Korea. The NKPA is heavily armed with modern Russian tanks, while the Republic of Korea (ROK, the government of South Korea) is lightly armed and completely unprepared.

1950, June 27: The United Nations commits itself to repel North Korea's invasion, and appoints U.S. General Douglas MacArthur to lead its forces. The UN coalition to defeat North Korea will eventually include troops from more than 16 nations, including the US, Britain, France, Australia, Canada and the Philippines.

1950, June 28: The NKPA captures Seoul, the capital of South Korea.

1950, July 5: UN forces battle North Korean forces for the first time, and lose.

1950, August 4: ROK and UN forces are driven back into a small corner of Korea surrounding Pusan, a large port city on Korea's southeast coast. Within the "Pusan Perimeter," they prepare to make their last stand against the NKPA's attempt to drive them out of Korea.

1950, September 15: UN forces make a surprise landing at the Korean port city of Incheon.

FASCINATING FACTS: The Incheon Invasion

Incheon is a port on the west coast of the Korean Peninsula, not far from Seoul, Korea's capital. Early in the war, the NKPA's attacks nearly drove ROK and UN forces out of Korea entirely. South Korea's defenders were left with only a small corner of the Korean Peninsula near Pusan, an area known as the Pusan Perimeter. In an effort to turn the tide of the war, General MacArthur proposed a daring amphibious (sea and land) invasion behind enemy lines. He chose to invade enemy territory at Incheon because it was close to Seoul, and an invasion there would help the South Koreans recapture their capital.

The invasion was a big success. The NKPA had few troops in place anywhere near Incheon to repel the landing. MacArthur's forces were able to secure the beach, build temporary pontoon docks and quickly begin landing troops and equipment. The landing at Incheon put ROK and UN troops in place behind enemy lines, where they could encircle NKPA armies and defeat them. They drove the NKPA out of Seoul and dramatically reversed the course of the war.

Unfortunately for MacArthur, the success of the Incheon invasion also had one other important result: it drew the attention of the Chinese. When ROK and UN forces crossed the 38th Parallel and threatened to capture all of North Korea, China decided to intervene in the Korean War. Mao Tse-tung did not want to see communism losing ground, especially so close to China; and he also did not want the UN to score a victory that might lead the West to believe that China was defenseless. China would enter the war just a few weeks after the Incheon invasion.

1950, September 29: The success of the Incheon invasion **reverses the war** so completely that UN forces recapture Seoul.

1950, October 9: UN forces cross the 38th parallel on a UN-approved mission to conquer North Korea and reunite the two Koreas.

1950 October 19: UN forces capture Pyongyang, the capital of North Korea. Despite warnings from the Chinese, General MacArthur continues to pursue the North Koreans far north of the 38th Parallel.

1950, October 19: Chinese forces secretly cross the Yalu River into North Korea.

1950, October 25 - November 1: Communist China enters the war and wins major victories over UN forces in the First Phase Offensive.

1950, November 24: General MacArthur launches a new offensive in North Korea which he says will win the war and have some of his troops "home by Christmas."

1950, November 25 - 30: China's Second Phase Offensive overwhelms UN forces, who are forced to retreat back across the 38th Parallel.

1951, January 4: In the **second major reversal** of the war, China and the NKPA recapture Seoul, South Korea.

1951, February 21: The UN's Operation Killer pushes China and the NKPA back across the 38th parallel.

1951, March 18: In the **third major reversal** of the war, UN forces recapture Seoul yet again.

1951, April 11: President Truman relieves General MacArthur of his command, and Lt. Gen Matthew Ridgway takes MacArthur's place as commander of UN forces. Ridgway's strategy will be more defensive than offensive.

AMAZING AMERICANS: Douglas MacArthur (1880 – 1964)

General Douglas MacArthur was one of World War II's best-known and most-decorated American military officers. He was the son of General Arthur MacArthur, the first American military governor of the Philippines (see Chapter 12). Both MacArthurs received the Congressional Medal of Honor, America's highest military award.

Douglas MacArthur's birth year, 1880, made him just the right age to play prominent roles in both WWI and WWII. He was also the U.S. Army's Chief of Staff during the early years of the Great Depression. In 1935, when the Philippines became semi-independent of the United States for the first time since the Philippine-American War (1899 - 1902), the new president of the Philippines asked MacArthur to help him build and train his army. With President Roosevelt's permission, MacArthur became the Field Marshal of the Philippine Army.

MacArthur retired in 1937, but was still in the Philippines in 1941 when the Japanese attacked the U.S. Navy at Pearl Harbor. When Japan invaded the Philippines in the Pacific War, Roosevelt ordered MacArthur out, and MacArthur made his famous vow to return someday ("I shall return"). Near the end of the Pacific War, he kept that vow, wading ashore at the Philippine island of Leyte on his way to drive the Japanese back out of the Philippines. It was MacArthur who accepted Japan's final surrender aboard the USS *Missouri* on V-J Day at the end of the Pacific War. After the war, MacArthur became Japan's military governor.

When the Korean War broke out, MacArthur was the senior military commander in the far east and the logical choice to command UN forces in the defense of South Korea. He had already promised South Korea's president, Syngman Rhee, that he would defend South Korea "as I would California." MacArthur saw Korea as the front line of the battle between communism and freedom, and he believed that a loss to the communists in Korea would lead to more losses in Europe. He wanted to pursue the Korean War aggressively, even if it meant confronting China, a far larger enemy.

President Truman had other ideas. Truman feared that if China and/or the USSR entered the Korean War, it might mean the end of the United Nations and the beginning of another world war. MacArthur considered Truman's position "appeasement," similar to British Prime Minister Neville Chamberlain's appeasement of Hitler before WWII, and he criticized the President for it publicly.

When MacArthur continued to press for aggressive action in North Korea, threatening China, Truman decided to relieve him of his command and replace him with General Matthew Ridgway, whose views were more in line with Truman's. President Truman's decision to fire the highly decorated hero of WWII shocked the military, the Congress and the American people.

When MacArthur returned to the United States, he appeared before Congress to explain himself and to deliver his farewell address. MacArthur told a cheering Congress that the US should fight the war to win, and that victory over North Korea would be impossible if UN troops were not allowed to attack China as well as North Korea.

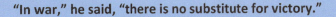

"In war," he said, "there is no substitute for victory."

The appeasement of China and the USSR, he said, would only lead to a far larger war in the future. MacArthur didn't believe in the United Nations formula for peace; instead, he believed in defeating communism and replacing communist governments with new governments that would be friendly to democracy. He believed that the new, U.S.-friendly governments of the Philippines and Japan were excellent examples of the way this could work. However, neither President Truman nor his successor, President Eisenhower, wanted to pursue the war in Korea any farther; so General MacArthur retired, and the Korean War ended in a stalemate.

1951, June 1: The two sides reach a stalemate at the **"Kansas Line"** just north of the 38th Parallel. Armistice Talks begin in June.

FASCINATING FACTS: Armistice Talks and Stalemate Battles

After June 1951, neither China and the NKPA nor the UN and the ROK launched any more major offensives. The war entered a cycle of

(1) armistice (ceasefire without a peace treaty) talks, followed by
(2) breakdown of the armistice talks, followed by
(3) bloody battles fought to a stalemate, followed by
(4) new armistice talks.

This cycle went on for two years, until it finally ended with an armistice agreement in July 1953. The armistice talks, which often took place at Panmunjom, Korea, usually broke down over two major issues:

1. **Prisoners of War (POWs):** China and North Korea wanted all of their soldiers who had been captured by the other side to be returned to communism; while South Korea and the UN wanted to give these prisoners of war the option of living in freedom under a democratic republic.

2. ***Nationalism:*** The nationalists of South Korea wanted to see Korea reunited, and were unwilling to let the war end with Korea divided between North and South.

During those two years of stalemate, the two sides fought several colorfully-named battles. These battles are remembered not only for their names, but also for the sacrifices of the many men who suffered and died to defend their countries. Among them:

The Battle of Bloody Ridge	The Battle of Heartbreak Ridge
The Battle of Old Baldy	The Battle of Pork Chop Hill

1952, November: General Dwight Eisenhower wins election as President of the U.S. In fulfillment of a campaign promise, Eisenhower travels to Korea to seek an agreement on how to end the war.

1953, July 27: The Korean Armistice Agreement ends the Korean War. The Military Demarcation Line becomes the accepted border between North Korea and South Korea.

FASCINATING FACTS: Korea's Demilitarized Zone (DMZ)

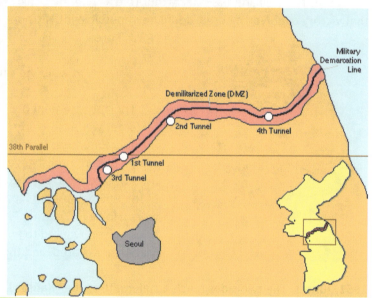

The last two years of the Korean War were a stalemate in which neither side gained or lost very much ground. During that time, the two sides established defensive lines along a battlefront that stretched all the way across the Korean Peninsula, a distance of about 150 miles.

In the Korean Armistice Agreement, both sides agreed to withdraw 2 kilometers behind the front lines, wherever they were on the day the armistice was signed. The front lines as of July 27, 1953 became the Military Demarcation Line that formed the border between North Korea and South Korea. That line crosses the original border, the 38th Parallel, at an angle from east-northeast to west-southwest. The 4-kilometer-wide "no man's land" centered on that line became Korea's Demilitarized Zone (DMZ). The DMZ is a buffer zone designed to prevent violent incidents that might result from angry soldiers brandishing weapons at one another across the border. Only a limited number of soldiers are allowed to patrol inside the DMZ at any one time, and they may carry only limited weaponry.

As of 2010, both the Military Demarcation Line and the DMZ still stand exactly where they stood in 1953. There have been several violent incidents inside the DMZ that have nearly led to a rekindling of the Korean War-- which, after all, has never truly ended, because the two sides have never signed a peace treaty. Both sides still patrol the DMZ carefully, and U.S. troops remain in South Korea to demonstrate that the U.S. is still committed to South Korea's defense.

FASCINATING FACTS ABOUT KOREA

- Korea's nickname is "The Land of the Morning Calm."
- Korea's primary religion is Buddhism, and one of the favorite Buddhist symbols there is the swastika. Koreans associate the swastika with peace and harmony, not with Germany's Nazi Party.

- Koreans relish making a loud 'hhuucchhkkkk' sound and spitting.
- Koreans become extremely offended when someone blows his nose at the table.
- Modern Korean taxis are color-coded: different colored taxis indicate different prices.
- North Korea has tried to tunnel underneath the DMZ no fewer than four times, but South Korean patrols have discovered each tunnel before the North Koreans could complete it.
- North Korea has built lavish-looking apartment buildings on its side of the DMZ so that the South Koreans will believe that North Korea is prosperous. When one studies these "apartments" through binoculars, it becomes clear that they are only unfinished shells, and that no one lives in them. Such buildings are examples of "Potemkin Villages," named for a Russian government official who may have pulled the same sort of stunt to trick Empress Catherine the Great.

FASCINATING FACTS: *Ssireum*, or Korean wrestling

Ssireum is the oldest traditional Korean sport. The two wrestlers wear belts that wrap around their waists and then down around their right thighs, giving their opponent two handles to grasp. Just before the match, the two wrestlers kneel in front of one other in a sandy pit. Each grasps his opponent's thigh belt with his left hand and his opponent's waist belt with his right. When the referee says "go," they climb to their feet, keeping their grasps on their opponent's belts, and wrestle that way until one of them forces the other to touch the ground with any part of his body above the knee.

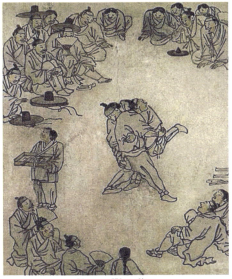

Korean Wrestling

MISSIONARY FOCUS

GIANTS OF THE FAITH: Robert Jermain Thomas (1839 – 1866)

Robert Jermain Thomas was a Welsh Christian missionary with a gift for languages. When Robert decided to become a missionary to China, he was able to learn Mandarin Chinese, a very difficult language, within just a few months. He set out for China as a newlywed, but his wife died soon after they arrived there.

In Robert's time, Korea was known as the "Hermit Kingdom" because it had very little contact with foreigners. Korea was as closed to traders as Japan had been before 1854 (see Chapter 9). Korea was home to a small Catholic community, but the Korean authorities did not approve of Christianity. To own a Bible in Korea was a crime punishable by death.

In 1865, Robert met two Korean traders who told him about a massacre of 8,000 Korean Catholics. The traders' story saddened the missionary, but he believed that he knew what Korea needed: the Word of God. Robert began to travel to Korea disguised as a Korean, distributing Bibles and preaching the Gospel. Each of these visits to Korea carried the risk of capture and an ugly death.

In 1866, when Robert was twenty-seven years old, he traveled to Korea on yet another mission to distribute Bibles. This time he went as a translator aboard an American trading ship. At the time, Korea was still closed to American trade. Korean soldiers warned the unwelcome traders' ship away, but they continued on their course until the soldiers managed to set fire to their ship. As the ship's passengers and crew fled the fire and tried to reach the shore, the Koreans began killing them.

Robert remained on the deck of the burning ship, throwing his Bibles one by one to the Koreans who were standing on the shore. When the fire began to singe his clothes, driving him off of the ship, he leapt to the shore and offered his last Bible to a Korean soldier. That soldier killed Robert with his lance.

The Koreans who were standing on the shores that day recovered many of Robert's Bibles. As a people accustomed to poverty, the Koreans had learned to waste nothing, so they used the pages of these Bibles to paper their walls. Later, as some of them began to read this unique wallpaper, the Spirit of the Lord began to move in their hearts. Robert's ministry helped pave the way for the coming Christian revival in Korea, and proved the truth of Isaiah 55:10-11:

"As the rain and the snow come down from heaven, and do not return to it without watering the earth and making it bud and flourish, so that it yields seed for the sower and bread for the eater, so is my word that goes out from my mouth: It will not return to me empty, but will accomplish what I desire and achieve the purpose for which I sent it."

GIANTS OF THE FAITH: Isobel Miller Kuhn (1901 – 1957)

Isobel Kuhn was a Canadian Protestant missionary, one of the many missionaries who was inspired by the ministry of Hudson Taylor, founder of the China Inland Mission. Isobel studied at Chicago's Moody Bible Institute, then traveled to China as a missionary and the wife of John Kuhn.

The area of China where the Kuhns ministered was a particularly difficult one. Isobel and John went to live among the Lisu people of China's Yunnan Province, on the border with Thailand. The Lisu were a small group of particularly poor Chinese border folk who had never had any contact with Christians before. When Isobel learned that the Lisu did almost nothing during the rainy season, she founded a Rainy Season Bible School to take advantage of their down time. Her ministry helped convince many of the Lisu to give their lives to Christ, and it also trained native Lisu missionaries who spread the Word of the Lord to many more of the Lisu people.

Interesting quote from Isobel Kuhn:
- "When I get to heaven they aren't going to see much of me but my heels, for I'll be hanging over the golden wall keeping an eye on the Lisu church!"

A Lisu woman

U.S. GEOGRAPHY FOCUS

FASCINATING FACTS about UTAH:

- Statehood: Utah became the 45th US state on January 4, 1896
- Bordering states: Arizona, Colorado, Idaho, Nevada, New Mexico, Wyoming
- State capital: Salt Lake City
- Area: 84,899 sq. mi (Ranks 13th in size)
- Abbreviation: UT
- State nickname: "Beehive State"
- State bird: Sea Gull
- State tree: Blue Spruce
- State flower: Sego Lily
- State song: Utah, We Love Thee
- State Motto: "Industry"

- Meaning of name: Utah is named after the Ute Indians
- Historic places to visit in Utah: The Great Salt Lake, Dinosaur National Monument, Bryce Canyon National Park, Arches National Park, Golden Spike National Historic Site, Rainbow Bridge, Grand Staircase-Escalante, Timpanogos Cave National Monument, The Bonneville Salt Flats
- Resources and Industries: farming (cattle, dairy, hay, turkeys, sheep) mining (gold, silver, copper, iron ore, lead, uranium, beryllium, coal) food products, steel, electronic equipment, machinery, aerospace, tourism (skiing)

Delicate Arch in Arches National Park

Flag of Utah
- Utah adopted this flag on December 21, 1913
- The flag is blue with the state seal in the center of the flag.
- The date 1847 on the seal represents the year Brigham Young led the first Mormon pioneers into the state.
- The date 1896 represents the year that Utah became a state.

Chapter 30

South and Central America, South Africa

HIGHLIGHT ON WORLD HISTORY

This chapter briefly covers nations on the continents of South America, Central America and Africa, most of which were colonies of European nations before they gained independence.

SOUTH AMERICA

Argentina	Capital: Buenos Aires

Like most nations of South and Central America, Argentina became a colony of Spain when Spain's *conquistadors* conquered most of the New World. Argentina was part of a viceroyalty (a large group of territories ruled by a Spanish governor) that also included most of modern-day Bolivia, Paraguay and Uruguay. Argentina won independence from Spain in a long series of revolutionary and civil wars that began in 1810.

Over the years, Argentina became a wealthy nation, but most of its riches remained in the hands of a small group of wealthy people. During the 1940s, a new president took power in Argentina by claiming to stand up to those wealthy people for the sake of Argentina's poor laborers.

INTERESTING INDIVIDUALS: Juan Peron (1895 – 1974) and Eva Peron (1919 – 1952)

Juan Peron was an Argentine army officer who helped to overthrow Argentina's conservative government in the Argentine Revolution of 1943 (a quick *coup d'etat*). After the *coup*, Peron became Argentina's new Minister of Labor. By fighting for the rights of workers against the big industries that sometimes mistreated them, Peron quickly became the hero of Argentina's labor unions. In rousing speeches, he criticized his own government for its failure to stand up to big businesses and demand more money for poor laborers. Peron's willingness to fight for workers' rights made him extremely popular with Argentina's poor. Another thing that made Peron popular with the poor was his girlfriend, a young actress named Eva Duarte. The lovely, charming Eva was also known for her concern for the poor.

In 1945, Peron's criticisms of the government angered his anti-labor enemies in the government so much that they forced him to resign his office, arrested him and imprisoned him. In response, Eva Duarte joined with Argentina's labor unions to defend Peron by organizing a series of huge public protests at Buenos Aires' *Plaza de la Mayo*. Argentina's poor came out by the tens of thousands to support Juan and Eva and to protest Juan's arrest. These embarrassing protests forced the government to release Peron after just a few days' captivity. Juan and Eva married later that year. The whole affair made the couple so enormously popular that Juan easily won election as President of Argentina in the following year, 1946. With Eva's help, he would also win a second term as president in 1951.

Only later did the Argentines discover that Juan Peron was not quite as wonderful as he seemed. Peron had openly admired Italy's fascist dictator, the late Benito Mussolini; and like Mussolini, Peron controlled his nation's newspapers and told them what to print. He also imprisoned his political enemies for speaking out against him (as they had imprisoned him). He showed sympathy for the Nazis by making Argentina one end of the "ratline" that Hitler lieutenants like Eichmann and Mengele used to scurry to safety at the end of WW II. The anti-communists of the Cold War (see Chapter 31) viewed Peron as a communist sympathizer who supported USSR-friendly figures like Egypt's Gamal Nasser and Cuba's Fidel Castro.

Peron also had problems with personal morality. After Eva died of cancer in 1952, Peron began to show his true colors by carrying on a love affair with a 13-year-old girl. He also legalized divorce and prostitution, much to the chagrin of his many Roman Catholic supporters. Like Spain's Popular Front before the Spanish Civil War (see Chapter 24), Peron was leading Argentina away from the Catholic Church and toward atheism and communism. As a result, the Pope excommunicated Juan Peron from the Roman Catholic Church on June 15, 1955.

On the next day, Peron was holding a rally for his supporters on the Plaza de la Mayo when Argentine warplanes suddenly flew over the Plaza and dropped bombs on the rally, killing over 350 people. The attack was the beginning of a military *coup d'etat* that soon overthrew Peron. The defeated Peron ran for his life and spent the next 18 years in exile, mostly in Venezuela. During those 18 years, the Catholic church-loving conservatives who overthrew Peron took over his government and did everything in their power to destroy his reputation.

They failed. Argentina's poor continued to believe that Peron had done more for them than anyone else ever had, and his popularity with them remained as strong as ever. When Peron returned to Argentina in 1973, he won election as president yet again. By this time, however, his health was failing, and he died in office in 1974.

Bolivia	Capital: Sucre

Bolivia was a colony of Spain that won its independence in 1825 during the Spanish American Wars of Independence. It was named for Simon Bolivar, a leader in those wars (see Year Three). Bolivia lost its one port city and its access to the mineral-rich Atacama Desert in the 1879 - 1884 War of the Pacific (see Chapter 6).

FASCINATING FACTS: Lake Titicaca

Lake Titicaca, South America's largest mountain lake, lies

on the border between Bolivia and Peru. At about 12,500 feet above sea level, Titicaca is the highest lake in the world that is open to commercial shipping. Its shape on the map is said to resemble that of a puma chasing a rabbit.

Brazil	Capital: Brasilia

Brazil was a colony of Portugal, not of Spain. It is by far the largest nation in South America, both by area and by population. Brazil was an independent empire from 1822 - 1899, then became an independent republic (see Chapter 6).

FASCINATING FACTS: The "Christ the Redeemer" Statue

High above the Brazilian city of Rio de Janeiro stands a mountain known as Corcovado; and high above Corcovado stands "Christ the Redeemer," the world's largest statue of Jesus Christ. Completed in 1931, the statue stands 130 feet tall, and its outstretched arms reach nearly 100 feet wide. The statue is considered one of the Seven Wonders of the Modern World.

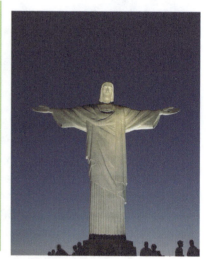

Chile	Capital: Santiago

Chile was a colony of Spain that won its independence in 1818. Chile won control of the mineral-rich Atacama Desert from Bolivia in the 1879 - 1884 War of the Pacific (see Chapter 6). It is one of South America's most prosperous nations.

Colombia	Capital: Bogota

While Colombia was a colony of Spain, it belonged to the northern South America Viceroyalty of Gran Colombia, along with Ecuador, Venezuela and Panama. When Colombia gained its independence from Spain in 1822, it joined those neighbors to form the Republic of Gran Colombia. Venezuela and Ecuador withdrew from the republic by 1830, but Panama remained part of Colombia until 1903 (see below). Modern-day Colombia is well known for its illegal cocaine cartels and wealthy drug lords.

FASCINATING FABLE: El Dorado

El Dorado is Spanish for "the golden one." The best-known legend of El Dorado refers to a lost city of gold that the gold-hungry Spanish conquistadors and others sought and never found. The earliest-known legend of El Dorado, though, refers not to a city, but to a man.

According to this legend, El Dorado was a *Zipa*, a chief of a South American native tribe called the *Muisca*. In one of the *Muisca*'s tribal ceremonies, a new *Zipa* would coat his entire body with gold dust and then dive into Lake Guatavita,

a crater-shaped mountain lake in what is now Colombia. After he did so, the rest of the Muisca would throw more golden objects into the Lake as offerings. The Spanish theorized that, after all of these offerings, Lake Guatavita ought to be simply full of gold, if they could only get to it. They made two attempts to drain the lake in the 1500s, but the little gold they discovered was not enough to pay them for their efforts.

Ecuador	Capital: Quito

Ecuador gained its independence from Spain in 1822. It joined Colombia, Panama and Venezuela in the Republic of Gran Colombia, then withdrew from that republic in 1830. Ecuador is South America's second largest producer of crude oil (behind Venezuela).

French Guiana	Capital: Cayenne

As of 2010, French Guiana remains an overseas "department" or province of France. French Guiana has never voted for independence from France, so it has South America's only non-independent government.

During the 1700s, the French established plantations in French Guiana and sent African slaves there to raise "cayenne pepper" (named for French Guiana's capital) and other crops. When France outlawed slavery in 1848, French Guiana's freed slaves moved to the colony's interior and built villages of their own. These freed slaves became known as "maroons" because they were marooned in French Guiana, unable to return to their native Africa.

FASCINATING FACTS: Devil's Island

Near the coast of French Guiana lies Devil's Island, which the French used as a prison from about 1780 - 1952. Devil's Island was where the French authorities sent people whom they never wanted to see again, including political prisoners and hardened criminals; it was a notoriously miserable prison. The well-known novel *Papillon* describes what author Henri Charriere claimed was a successful breakout from the prison on Devil's Island.

Guyana	Capital: Georgetown

Guyana, formerly known as British Guiana, was a colony of Britain that became independent in 1966. It is still a member of the Commonwealth of Nations, along with many other former British colonies such as Canada and Australia.

FASCINATING FACTS: JONESTOWN

In 1978, Guyana became famous as the home of "Jonestown," a cult colony of about 900 people that was founded by a California communist named Jim Jones.

A U.S. congressman from California named Leo Ryan traveled to Guyana to inspect Jonestown and make sure that Jones' communist cult wasn't holding any California citizens against their will. When Congressman Ryan arrived, several Jonestown colonists took advantage of his visit by stepping forward and announcing that they wanted to leave the colony under his protection.

As Ryan made arrangements to airlift these defectors out of Jonestown, Jim Jones began to worry about what they might reveal about his colony when they got back to California. Jones decided to kill these traitorous defectors, and Congressman Ryan, before they could reveal any of his ugly secrets. As Ryan's two small planeloads of people taxied down the runway to escape Jonestown, members of Jim Jones' security team attacked the planes and shot several people to death, including Congressman Ryan.

Jim Jones knew the revenge the United States would take on his colony for murdering a sitting congressman; so, later that day, Jones convinced the members of his cult to join him in a mass suicide by drinking Flavor-Aid laced with cyanide. Almost every member of the colony died.

Paraguay	Capital: Asuncion

Paraguay became independent of Spain in 1811. Paraguay's first dictator, Dr. Jose Gaspar Rodriguez de Francia, tried to build his nation into a utopia; but his successors involved Paraguay in the disastrous War of the Triple Alliance that nearly wiped out its male population (see Chapter 6).

Peru	Capital: Lima

Peru was a colony of Spain that won its independence in 1824 during the Spanish American Wars of Independence. Peru joined Bolivia against Chile in the 1879 - 1884 War of the Pacific, and lost (see Chapter 6).

FASCINATING FACTS: Machu Picchu

Machu Picchu is a remnant of a village or estate that the Incan people built around 1400 - 1450 AD. It lies on a high mountain ridge in Peru, 8,000 feet above sea level. Macchu Picchu is unusual because the Spanish conquistadors never discovered it in their rabid search for gold; unlike most Incan sites, it survived their pillage of South America unscathed. Machu Picchu remained unknown to all but local Peruvians until 1911, when a Yale University professor named Hiram Bingham rediscovered it and published a book about it. After that, it became a popular tourist attraction.

Suriname	Capital: Paramaribo

Suriname, formerly known as Dutch Guiana, was a colony of the Netherlands until 1975, when it became independent. The Netherlands operated slave plantations in Suriname until the Dutch abolished slavery in 1863.

Uruguay	Capital: Montevideo

Uruguay was part of a Spanish viceroyalty that also included Argentina, Bolivia and Paraguay. When Argentina gained independence from Spain in 1811, Uruguay wanted to become independent of Argentina, but Argentina refused. Uruguay declared independence anyway, and Argentina viewed it as a rogue eastern province. Therefore Argentina was willing to look the other way in 1820, when Brazil invaded Uruguay and annexed it in 1822.

However, Uruguay's independence movement was not quite finished. In 1825, a group of 33 Uruguayan patriots (the Thirty-three "Orientals" or Easterners) landed near Montevideo and declared Uruguay's independence once again. By then, Argentina had changed its mind, and it battled Brazil for control of Uruguay. In the 1828 Treaty of Montevideo, Brazil and Argentina agreed to grant Uruguay its long-sought independence.

Venezuela	Capital: Caracas

Venezuela gained its independence from Spain in 1821 in the Spanish Wars of Independence. It joined Colombia, Panama and Ecuador in the Republic of Gran Colombia, then withdrew from that republic in 1830. Venezuela is South America's largest producer of crude oil.

FASCINATING FACTS: Angel Falls

Venezuela is home to the highest waterfall in the world, Angel Falls. The waters of Angel Falls plunge nearly 3200 feet straight down a mountain cliff. The fall is so far that even during the wet season, when the river above the falls carries more water, much of the falling water dissipates as mist before it can reach the small river at the base of the mountain.

CENTRAL AMERICA

Belize	Capital: Belmopan

Belize was a colony of Britain, and was known as British Honduras. The British administered British Honduras from their colony on the island of Jamaica, and imported African slaves there to cut valuable Honduran mahogany wood. Belize became self-governing in 1964, and fully independent in 1981.

However, Britain still maintains a small naval squadron in Belize to protect Belize from Guatemala, which has never recognized Belize's independence. As of 2010, Guatemala still considers Belize to be a part of Guatemala.

Costa Rica	Capital: San Jose

Costa Rica was a colony of Spain that became part of the short-lived First Mexican Empire after Mexico declared independence from Spain in 1821 (see Chapter 17). The First Mexican Empire broke up with Santa Anna's overthrow of Emperor Agustin in 1823, so the states of Central America tried to form a separate union of their own. Costa Rica became part of the Federal Republic of Central America, a union that also included El Salvador, Guatemala, Honduras and Nicaragua. The Federal Republic of Central America's capital was at Guatemala City, Guatemala.

The Federal Republic of Central America lasted only until 1838 - 1840, when its bickering states began to withdraw their memberships. Costa Rica declared full independence in 1838.

El Salvador	Capital: San Salvador

El Salvador was another colony of Spain that became independent after the Federal Republic of Central America broke up.

FASCINATING FACTS: The Salvadoran Civil War

During the 1980s, a group of communist guerrillas from the Farabundo Mari National Liberation Front (FMLN) tried to overthrow El Salvador's government in the Salvadoran Civil War. These guerrillas received support from the Sandinistas, the communist political party that controlled the government of nearby Nicaragua. Before the end of the Cold War in 1989 - 1991, U.S. President Ronald Reagan was extremely concerned about the spread of communism in Central America. However, when the Salvadoran Civil War ended in 1992, the Cold War was over, and the communist FMLN became one of El Salvador's leading political parties.

Guatemala	Capital: Guatemala City

Guatemala was another colony of Spain that became independent after the Federal Republic of Central America broke up.

FASCINATING FACTS: Banana Republics

Around 1900, the government of Guatemala began to accept gifts and bribes from the United Fruit Company (now part of Chiquita Brands), a major producer of bananas and other fruits. Because of these bribes, the government of Guatemala was willing to allow the United Fruit Company to do as it pleased in Guatemala. What pleased the United Fruit Company was to overwork its Guatemalan laborers and pay them extremely low wages. Thus Guatemala became one of the original "banana republics," which were known for corrupt governments and backward economies capable of producing nothing beyond their native fruits.

| Honduras | Capital: Tegucigalpa |

Honduras was another colony of Spain that became independent after the Federal Republic of Central America broke up.

During the 1980s, Honduras served as a base for U.S.-supported Contra rebels who were battling the communist Sandinistas in neighboring Nicaragua (see below).

INTERESTING INDIVIDUALS: William Walker (1824 – 1860)

William Walker was an American "filibuster" or "freebooter," a man who wanted to use mercenary armies to conquer territory in Mexico and Central America. He was also a firm believer in the American doctrine of Manifest Destiny. Like many Southerners of his day, Walker believed that if the United States did not soon take firm control of the untamed, loosely claimed territories in Mexico and Central America, then some other nation would. Walker's plan was to take this matter into his own hands by first establishing U.S.-friendly territories in Mexico and Central America, then building them into republics that the U.S. could annex (just as the U.S. had annexed Texas).

In 1855, a civil war divided Nicaragua between two political parties. The leader of the smaller party was aware of Walker's filibustering plans, so he invited Walker to come to Nicaragua and provide military assistance. With help from local troops and mercenaries, Walker was able to defeat Nicaragua's larger political party and declare himself Nicaragua's head of state. He even won formal recognition for his new government of Nicaragua from U.S. President Franklin Pierce in 1856.

In order to win the approval of slaveholding Southerners, Walker legalized slavery in Nicaragua. Legalizing slavery cut both ways, though: Americans north of the Mason Dixon line had no interest in adding Nicaragua to the United States as a slave state, and abolitionists were angry with President Pierce for formally recognizing Walker's slaveholding Nicaraguan government.

Unfortunately for Walker, Central America was not as untamed and unclaimed as he had thought: The government of Costa Rica assembled an army to drive Walker out of Nicaragua before he could conquer any more Central American territory. The Costa Ricans made short work of Walker's small band of mercenaries, and Walker was forced to surrender and return to the United States.

Three years later, when Walker tried to return to Central America, British authorities captured him and turned him over to Honduras to be prosecuted as a pirate. The Hondurans executed the 36-year-old Walker on September 12, 1860.

| Nicaragua | Capital: Managua |

Nicaragua was another colony of Spain that became independent after the Federal Republic of Central America broke up.

FASCINATING FACTS: The Iran-Contra Scandal

During the 1980s, U.S. President Ronald Reagan announced the "Reagan Doctrine," which said that the US would oppose the USSR's efforts to establish communist governments all over the world. Reagan believed that the communist USSR was trying to establish another foothold for communism in Nicaragua like the one it already had in Cuba. To combat this, Reagan's administration provided financial and military support to Nicaraguan rebels known as the Contras, who were trying to overthrow Nicaragua's communist-supported Sandinista government.

In 1982, the U.S. Congress outlawed aid to the Contras for this purpose; but certain members of Reagan's administration continued to supply the Contras with aid anyway, illegally. This illegal aid money came from selling weapons to Iran, which was also illegal at the time. In 1986, the highly embarrassing "Iran-Contra Scandal" came to light and the illegal aid to the Contras stopped.

Panama	Capital: Panama City

Panama gained its independence from Spain in 1821 in the Spanish Wars of Independence and joined Colombia, Ecuador and Venezuela in the Republic of Gran Colombia. Ecuador and Venezuela withdrew from the republic in 1830, but Panama remained part of Colombia.

In 1903, U.S. President Theodore Roosevelt used a bit of "gunboat diplomacy" to help Panama declare independence from Colombia so that the U.S. could gain control of the Panama Canal Zone (see Chapter 12). The U.S. returned control of the Panama Canal Zone to Panama in 2000.

In 1989, US President George H. W. Bush ordered an invasion of Panama to depose its dictator Manuel Noriega, whom he accused of trafficking in drugs, laundering money and interfering with Panama's elections. Noriega was in jail in the US for drug trafficking until 2010, when he went to jail in France for money laundering.

AFRICA

The Scramble for Africa of 1880 – 1914 divided most of the African continent between the powerful nations of Western Europe (see Chapter 11). Most modern-day African nations were once colonies of European nations like Britain, Belgium, France, Germany, Italy, the Netherlands, Portugal and Spain (two exceptions are Ethiopia and Liberia).

World War I was the beginning of the end for the age of European empires. At the end of that war, U.S. President Woodrow Wilson's Fourteen Points declared that all nations that sought independence should have it. Later, after World War II, the new United Nations frowned upon the idea of empire-building.

Most African nations won their independence during the years from 1960 - 1975. In several of those newly independent nations, chaos erupted because their former European controllers were no longer there to police the violence between warring African tribes. Africa also saw wars between communists and anti-communists and wars between Muslims and non-Muslims.

Democratic Republic of the Congo	Capital: Kinshasa

The Congo Free State and Belgian Congo

The Democratic Republic of the Congo is also called the DRC or Congo-Kinshasa to distinguish it from its western neighbor, the similarly-named Republic of the Congo. Both nations' names come from the Congo River, the long, mighty central African river that flows through their midst. Much of Africa's densest, most untamed jungle lies within the vast DRC, and that jungle teems with exotic animals like gorillas and hippopotami.

During the Scramble for Africa, Belgium's King Leopold II colonized south central Africa and organized his colony as the Congo Free State. The Congo Free State became King Leopold's personal property. Like the English absentee landlords who had once controlled Ireland's far-off farms, Leopold's only concern for his far-off property was the money it could generate for him. Leopold's *Force Publique* army forced the natives of the Congo Free State to collect rubber tree sap for him in order to make him rich. His soldiers made examples of any natives who didn't work hard enough to suit him by cutting off their hands (see Chapter 11).

In 1908, Belgium's parliament put a stop to its king's shameful treatment of African natives by taking over the management of King Leopold's personal colony and making it a colony of Belgium. The Congo Free State became the Belgian Congo. Although conditions improved after the parliament took over, Belgians continued to treat the Africans of the Congo as second-class citizens.

Patrice Lumumba and the First Republic of the Congo

During the 1950s, a Congolese native named Patrice Lumumba founded an independence movement in the Belgian Congo. When Belgium finally answered Lumumba's demands and granted its colony independence in 1960, the Belgian Congo became the First Republic of the Congo.

On the First Republic of the Congo's Independence Day, June 30, 1960, the newly elected Prime Minister Lumumba told Belgium's proud king that "We are no longer your monkeys."

As soon as the Congo gained its independence, the African soldiers of the Congolese army began to rebel against their Belgian officers. As the new nation fell into chaos, two provinces seceded from the Congo and tried to set up independent governments of their own. The United Nations sent troops to restore order in the Congo; but Prime Minister Lumumba was unhappy with the UN troops because they were there only to prevent a civil war, not to prevent the rebel provinces from seceding. In order to hold the Congo together, Lumumba sought help from a powerful ally: the communist USSR.

Lumumba's friendship with the USSR drew the attention of the United States Central Intelligence Agency (CIA), which was trying to keep the USSR's communism from spreading. The CIA tried to keep communism out of Africa by encouraging the chief of staff of the Congolese army, Joseph Mobutu, to replace the communist-leaning Lumumba. In late 1960, with help from the CIA, Mobutu placed Lumumba under house arrest. <u>When Lumumba escaped in January 1961, Mobutu's men recaptured him and murdered him.</u>

INTERESTING INDIVIDUALS: Dag Hammarskjöld

Dag Hammarskjöld was a Swede who served as Secretary General of the United Nations from 1953 - 1961. In 1961, Hammarskjöld traveled to the Congo to try to negotiate a ceasefire between UN troops and rebel troops in one of the Congo's provinces. While he was en route, his plane crashed, and the general secretary died. No one knows what caused the crash, but some witnesses believed that a missile had shot the plane out of the sky.

Joseph Mobutu and Zaire

In 1965, Joseph Mobutu dissolved the elected government of the Congo and assumed control as the nation's new dictator. In 1971, he renamed his nation with the more African name "Zaire." He also took a more African name for himself, "Mobutu Sese Seko," which meant "the all-powerful warrior who goes from victory to victory." Mobutu assumed such lofty titles as "Savior of the People" and invited the people of Zaire to praise him. The nightly news in the Congo began with an image of Mobutu descending from the clouds like a mighty angel or a god. He outlawed all other political parties in Zaire but his own, and held presidential elections in which he was the only candidate.

With foreign aid money from the United States, Mobutu bought lavish homes and fleets of expensive cars for himself. He also chartered the Concorde, an extremely expensive, French-built supersonic transport airplane, for special trips. Nearly all of the billions of dollars of foreign aid money the U.S. sent to Zaire went to support the extravagant lifestyles of Mobutu, his family and his favorites. The United States continued to support Mobutu for one reason: because he hated communism, and would allow Zaire to have nothing to do with the USSR.

Mobutu remained in power in Zaire until 1997, when a rebellion forced him to flee the country. The rebels who ousted Mobutu renamed their nation "the Democratic Republic of the Congo."

Republic of the Congo	**Capital: Brazzaville**

The Republic of the Congo became a colony of France during the 1880s Scramble for Africa. It gained independence from France in 1960, just before its eastern neighbor the DRC gained independence from Belgium. The Republic of the Congo's capital, Brazzaville, lies just across the Congo River from the DRC's capital, Kinshasa.

Somalia	**Capital: Mogadishu**

Somalia lies in the "Horn of Africa," the pointed eastern peninsula that juts out beneath west Asia's Arabian Peninsula. During the Scramble for Africa, Britain established the colony of British Somaliland near

Somalia's northern coast, while Italy established the colony of Italian Somaliland near the southern coast. A united Somalia gained its independence in 1960.

The Somali Civil War and Famine

In January 1991, a group of Muslim warlords overthrew Somalia's government. Afterwards, these warlords couldn't agree about which of them would lead Somalia, so they began fighting among themselves. Their battles were the beginning of the Somali Civil War, which is still going on as of 2010.

The civil war destroyed Somalia's agriculture and created a famine in Somalia. Wealthier nations tried to send food to relieve the famine, but almost none of the food reached the hungry. Instead, the warlords captured the food shipments and sold them for money, which they used to buy more weapons for their civil war.

The United Nations and Operation Restore Hope

In 1992, the United Nations sent troops to defend the food shipments and ensure that they reached the hungry people who needed them. This project was called "Operation Restore Hope," and it was so successful that the UN decided to expand its mission in Somalia. Beginning in 1993, the UN troops' new mission would be to restore peace to Somalia and recreate a unified, peaceful, democratic government there.

Most of Somalia's warlords agreed to meet with the UN and negotiate peace. One, however, did not. A Muslim general named Muhammad Farrah Aidid resented the presence of UN troops in Somalia, and showed his resentment by attacking and killing 24 UN/Pakistani peacekeeping troops.

General Aidid's attack made him a wanted man, and the UN began hunting him. On July 12, 1993, spies reported that Aidid might be hiding in a certain building in Mogadishu, Somalia's capital. UN/United States troops acted on this information by launching a raid against that building and killing everyone inside. Unfortunately, their spies were either mistaken or deliberately deceitful: Aidid was not in the building; and instead of killing Aidid, the raid ended up killing about 60 civilians, many of them innocents.

Black Hawk Down

That failed raid turned the Somali public against the UN and the United States. Three months later, on October 3, 1993, UN/U.S. forces attempted another raid against Aidid's top lieutenants. Somalis poured into the streets to resist the Americans, hindering their raid. One of the Somalis used a rocket-propelled grenade to shoot down an American Black Hawk model helicopter. While the Americans were trying to rescue the survivors among the downed Black Hawk's crew, the Somalis shot down a second Black Hawk. In all, 18 American soldiers died in the Black Hawk Down incident. The Somalis celebrated the deaths of those 18 soldiers by dragging their remains through the streets of Mogadishu.

Six months later, the U.S. withdrew all of its forces from Somalia. The UN withdrew entirely in 1995. As of 2010, the Somali Civil War is still going on, and Somalia has no united government.

South Africa	Capital: Pretoria

After the 1899 - 1902 Boer War, the four British colonies of South Africa (Cape Colony, Natal, Transvaal and Orange Free State) united to form the Union of South Africa (see Chapter 11). Although Britain had defeated the Boers, South Africa was still home to a great many of their Afrikaner descendants. The language of these Afrikaners was *Afrikaans*, a dialect of the Dutch language.

For most of the 20th Century, South Africa's minority white population faced a problem: How could whites retain their superior wealth and status in a nation where blacks far outnumbered whites? To solve this problem, they developed a system of race laws called Apartheid.

FASCINATING FACTS: Apartheid and the African National Congress

Apartheid is Afrikaans for "apartness" or "separation." South Africa's Apartheid system was a collection of race laws designed to keep whites separate from and superior to blacks. Apartheid officially began in 1948, when the Afrikaner National Party won more seats than any other party in South Africa's parliament.

Under Apartheid, the National Party government assigned every citizen to one of four racial classes: white, black, "colored" or (later) Asian. Then it began to approve racist laws that legalized the racism that had already been part of South African culture since Europeans first moved there during the 1500s. These laws assigned blacks and "coloreds" separate areas for their homes and separate areas in which to operate businesses. "Pass laws" required blacks to carry government-issued passes whenever they ventured into the areas set aside for whites. Apartheid laws demanded separation between the races in every government department, service and facility: blacks and whites had separate schools, separate buses, separate parks and separate beaches.

Set against the Apartheid government was the African National Congress (ANC), a group of mostly black South Africans who protested racist laws. The African National Congress was similar to the Indian National Congress led by Mohandas Gandhi: its purpose was to demand justice and equal rights for native Africans from the Europeans who colonized and ruled their homeland. The ANC's protests against Apartheid took both nonviolent and violent forms.

A Brief Timeline of Apartheid and Resistance in South Africa

1909: The South Africa Act, an act of the British Parliament, unites the colonies of South Africa into the Union of South Africa. The Union of South Africa becomes a Dominion of the British Empire, similar to Canada and Australia.

1912: Black South Africans form the **African National Congress** (ANC) to protest their mistreatment at the hands of the white government. Over the years, parts of the ANC will practice nonviolent resistance like that of India's Mohandas Gandhi (who lived in South Africa from 1893 - 1915), while other parts will take up arms and resist Apartheid violently.

1913: South Africa's parliament passes the **Native Lands Act**, which outlines the specific areas of South Africa in which blacks may legally own land. Despite the fact that blacks make up 80% of the population, under the Native Lands Act they are allowed to own or purchase land in only 7% of South Africa's territory. 93% of South Africa is reserved strictly for whites.

1914: South Africa's Afrikaners (descendants of the Boers) establish the **National Party** to promote Afrikaner culture. Part of that culture is the insistence on slavery or near-slavery for blacks.

1948: The National Party wins more seats in parliament than any other party, allowing it to seat its first pro-Apartheid prime minister.

1950: Parliament passes the **Population Registration Act**, which requires every South African over 18 to carry an identification card indicating his or her race. The three main races are white, black and "colored" (mixed). Since some families include people from more than one of these categories, this means that some families will be divided by race.

1950: Parliament passes the **Group Areas Act**, which sets aside certain areas of South Africa's cities for each race.

1951: Parliament passes the **Bantu Authorities Act**, which establishes separate government agencies for blacks and whites.

1953: Parliament passes the **Preservation of Separate Amenities Act**, which allows the government to create separate facilities for blacks and whites. These separate facilities include public beaches, post offices, parks and even park benches.

1955: South Africa's government forces blacks out of Sophiatown, a black section of Johannesburg, and into a new black settlement called Soweto (for <u>So</u>uth <u>W</u>estern <u>T</u>ownships). Sophiatown is bulldozed, and a new white settlement is built in its place. This is only one of the many times when the Apartheid government relocates blacks against their will.

1960, March 21: In the **Sharpeville Massacre**, armed police crackdown on unarmed blacks who are protesting the "pass laws" that require them to carry passes identifying their race wherever they go. The police kill more than 60 protesters in the Sharpeville Massacre. Concerned about further protests, Parliament bans the African National Congress and declares a state of emergency for five months. During this time, police jail thousands of members of the ANC without trial.

1960: As a result of the Sharpeville Massacre, **Nelson Mandela** and other members of the ANC conclude that peaceful resistance to the Apartheid government will never win equal rights for blacks; so they decide to resist Apartheid through acts of sabotage and violence.

1961, May 31: The National Party fulfills one of its long-term goals when South Africa becomes a republic (instead of a constitutional monarchy with the British monarch as its head of state). The new republic leaves the Commonwealth of Nations, cutting most of its ties to Britain.

1962: Police arrest and imprison Nelson Mandela, leader of a militant wing of the ANC called the "Spear of the Nation."

1964: Mandela, who is already in prison, receives a life sentence for acts of sabotage and treason against the government of South Africa.

1970: Parliament passes the **Black Homelands Citizenship Act**, which says that South Africa's blacks are not citizens of South Africa, but rather of the "Bantustans" set aside for black African races. Blacks lose their South African citizenship, and will need passports to leave their "Bantustans" and enter white-controlled South Africa-- as if they are entering a foreign nation.

FASCINATING FACTS: Bantustans

The *Bantu* are a group of African tribes that live all over southern Africa; while the suffix *stan* means "land" in Persian. Thus *Bantustan* means "land of the Bantus."

By 1970, the Apartheid government was tired of dealing with the ANC's constant protests; but it was still unwilling to grant South Africa's blacks the voting rights, property rights and human rights they demanded. The government's solution was to make the separation of the races even more complete. Beginning in 1970, the Apartheid government tried to establish ten separate homelands, or "Bantustans," for ten different Bantu tribes that lived inside South Africa. Its goal was to relocate all of South Africa's blacks inside the Bantustans so that whites could have the rest of South Africa to themselves. Eventually, the government hoped to grant each of the Bantustans an independent government and wash its hands of the ANC.

In support of this plan, the Apartheid government relocated millions of blacks from their former homes in white South Africa to new homes in the Bantustans. Unfortunately for the government, the Bantustans were never as successful as it had hoped: The businesses of South Africa depended on their black workers, and the Bantustans were too far from these businesses to allow black workers to commute back and forth to work every day. The complete relocation of blacks would have destroyed South Africa's economy; so the Bantustan relocation program stopped long before it achieved its goal of complete separation of the races.

1976, June 16 - 17: The black students of Soweto riot against their oppressive government.

FASCINATING FACTS: The Soweto Uprising

Soweto is an abbreviation for "South Western Townships." Soweto was a township of Johannesburg, South Africa that the Apartheid government set aside for blacks relocated from other parts of the city.

In 1974, the Apartheid government passed a law that required public schools to teach certain subjects in the Afrikaans language (the language of the Afrikaners, the chief promoters of Apartheid). Most South African blacks resented Afrikaners, and didn't want to study their language. Instead, they wanted to study English, which was far more useful as an international language; and they wanted to study their native Bantu languages as well. The students' anger over the new law simmered for more than a year.

On June 16, 1976, the students of Soweto's schools held a large protest against the Apartheid government. The students marched through the streets of Soweto, carrying signs and chanting slogans.

When the students encountered the police, their protest became violent. None of the students held any weapon more powerful than a rock, but the police responded to their rocks with guns. The police crackdown killed an unknown number of protesters, some of them children.

Although the police managed to control the riots and restore order to Soweto, the Soweto Uprising was the beginning of the end for the Apartheid government. When the rest of the world saw that the government of South Africa was willing to attack and kill children in order to enforce its racist laws, the world turned against Apartheid. Governments around the world organized boycotts against South African businesses. Investors sold all of their shares in the stocks of South Africa's businesses, causing them to lose value. The intense international pressure eventually forced the Apartheid government to give in and repeal its Apartheid laws.

1980s: Governments around the world pressure South Africa to end Apartheid by launching an international boycott against South African businesses.

1990, February 2: The Apartheid government lifts its ban on the ANC and repeals some of its race laws.

1990, February 11: The Apartheid government releases Nelson Mandela from prison.

1990 - 1993: South Africa yields to international pressure and repeals its remaining Apartheid laws.

1994: Nelson Mandela wins election as President of South Africa. South Africa rejoins the Commonwealth of Nations.

INTERESTING INDIVIDUALS: Nelson Mandela (1918 – 2013)

Rolihlahla Nelson Mandela's first name means "troublemaker." The little boy whose parents gave him that fitting name would grow up to make a great deal of trouble for South Africa's Apartheid government.

Nelson Mandela was an attorney who joined the African National Congress in 1944 to help promote equal rights for South Africa's black citizens. At first, Mandela's protests against Apartheid were non-violent. However, the 1960 Sharpeville Massacre convinced Mandela that nonviolent protests would never persuade the National Party to grant blacks their rights; so, in 1961, he helped to found a more militant wing of the ANC known as the "Spear of the Nation." As leader of the Spear of the Nation, Mandela began conducting a bombing campaign against Apartheid government buildings. The goal of the bombings was not to kill or injure Afrikaners, but to damage their government's operations enough to force them to negotiate with the ANC. Mandela's bombing teams usually struck at night so that no one would be hurt; but even so, the bombings were still extremely dangerous.

The police caught up with Mandela in 1962, and the courts sentenced him to five years' hard labor. In 1963, while he was serving this sentence, the police arrested several other members of the banned ANC for plotting to overthrow the government. Since Mandela had been part of their group, the government tried him for treason alongside these new captives. On June 12, 1964, South Africa sentenced Mandela to life in prison for treason against the state.

While Mandela was in prison, he took correspondence courses and taught other prisoners. The prisoners' "school" inside his island prison became known informally as "Mandela University." Over the years, Mandela became the most prominent of the many ANC leaders who were spending most of their adult lives in the Apartheid government's prisons. People around the world heard Mandela's name and story; and his many supporters began to call on the South African government to release Mandela and end Apartheid.

More than once, South Africa's government offered to release Mandela if he would agree to abandon violent protests against Apartheid. Mandela always refused. As people around the world grew more aware of the wrongs of Apartheid, Mandela recognized that his continued imprisonment was the best weapon he had against the Apartheid government. The longer he remained in prison, the more his supporters would protest against Apartheid. The ANC had yet to achieve its goal of equal rights for all, and Mandela refused to sacrifice that goal just to win his personal freedom.

Finally, the international pressure on South Africa had its effect. On February 2, 1990, the government lifted its ban on the ANC; and on February 11, Mandela became a free man for the first time in 28 years. As the returning leader of the ANC, Mandela negotiated with the government until it granted every citizen the right to vote in the next election. In 1994, the year of the first truly free and all-inclusive elections in South African history, Nelson Mandela won election as South Africa's first black president.

Fun Facts on South Africa

- South Africa is home to a large percentage of the world's known supply of diamonds, platinum and gold.
- Not all penguins live in Antarctica: the Black-footed Penguin is native to South Africa. Its call sounds a bit like a donkey's braying.

MORE FASCINATING FACTS about the African Continent

- Africa is the second largest continent (after Asia), but Africa's coastline is shorter than any other continent's because it lacks the other continents' jagged outlines.
- Africa is home to more than 50 nations. Its largest nation by area is Algeria, and its smallest by area is Seychelles. Its largest nation by population is Nigeria, and its smallest by population is, once again, Seychelles.
- Tatouine is a city in the southern part of Tunisia, a nation in northern Africa. The deserts around Tatouine became the sets for the first *Star Wars* movie, "A New Hope," which first appeared on Movie Theater screens in 1978. "Tatooine" became the name of Luke Skywalker's fictional two-sunned, desert home planet.

FASCINATING FACTS: Kente Cloth

Kente is a colorful cloth woven in long strips with geometric designs and bright colors. Strips of *kente* cloth are fastened together to create clothes, blankets and other items. *Kente* cloth originated in the West African nation of Ghana, where it was once reserved for royalty.

There are about 300 distinct *kente* patterns, and most of them are named after proverbs, famous people or historical events. To the person who understands these patterns, an item made of *kente* can tell a tale. To an item's creator, that tale is often more important than the way the item looks or the purpose it may serve. Different colors have different meanings in *kente* cloth:

Yellow: life, royalty, wealth
Red: bloodshed, politics, death
Blue: peacefulness, holiness
Gold: royalty, wealth, spiritual purity
Black: aging, spiritual energy
Silver: joy, purity, serenity

Pink: gentleness
Maroon: mother earth, healing
Green: good health, newness, harvest
White: purification, healing, joy
Grey: ash, sinfulness
Purple: earth (usually worn by women)

MISSIONARY FOCUS

GIANTS OF THE FAITH: The Auca Missionaries

Jim Elliot   Nate Saint   Ed McCully   Peter Fleming   Roger Youderian

In 1955, a team of five Christian missionaries banded together to carry the Gospel of Jesus Christ to the Auca Indians of Ecuador. These missionaries' names were Jim Elliot, Nate Saint, Ed McCully, Peter Fleming and Roger Youderian. The Aucas were one of the few people groups in the world that survived into the 20th Century with no contact with the modern world. They had almost no technology beyond the making of spears and reed huts, and had never heard of the Bible.

The five missionaries were fascinated with the Aucas, but they needed a way to make contact with them without frightening them off. So they devised a clever way to lower gifts to the Aucas in a bucket dangling from an airplane in flight. By flying in a circle over the Aucas' camp and using a rope to lower his bucket gradually, pilot Nate Saint was able to suspend the Aucas' gifts directly in front of them at chest level. Although the bucket was still suspended from the plane, it hardly moved at all as Saint flew in circles above it. The missionaries sent the Aucas gifts in the bucket for thirteen weeks, getting to know them gradually before they finally felt ready to meet the Aucas in person.

On January 3, 1956, all five missionaries landed together along a river near the Aucas' village. They set up their camp and waited. Three days later, they met three Auca Indians, a young couple and an older woman who was acting as the couple's chaperone. They gave the Aucas food and took the young man for an airplane ride. When the Aucas left, the missionaries felt good about their first meeting.

Two days later, at around noon, a party of ten angry Aucas arrived at the missionaries' beach. They had met the young Auca couple alone in the jungle, without their chaperone, and they were angry with the couple. In order to deflect their anger, the young man claimed that the missionaries had molested the young woman, and that the two of them were only alone because he had been helping her escape the missionaries. When the enraged Aucas arrived at the beach, they were ready to kill the missionaries. They distracted the missionaries in order to separate them, then attacked them all with spears.

Although the missionaries owned guns, they did not use them. They had agreed beforehand that the mission of saving the Aucas was more important than their lives, and that they mustn't endanger that mission by shooting at the Aucas. The Auca spearmen killed all five missionaries.

What man intends for evil, the Lord can turn to good. A short time later, Jim Elliot's wife Elisabeth and Nate Saint's sister Rachel went to live among the Aucas. They made friends with them and shared the Gospel with them, and some of them became Christians. Over the years, the five Auca missionaries' sacrifice has inspired many other missionaries to commit their lives to sharing the Gospel.

U.S. GEOGRAPHY FOCUS

FASCINATING FACTS about ARIZONA:

- <u>Statehood</u>: Arizona became the 48th US state on February 14, 1912
- <u>Bordering states/countries</u>: California, Colorado, Nevada, New Mexico, Utah, Mexico
- <u>State capital</u>: Phoenix
- <u>Area</u>: 113,990 sq. mi (Ranks 6th in size)
- <u>Abbreviation</u>: AZ
- <u>State nickname</u>: "Grand Canyon State"
- <u>State bird</u>: Cactus Wren
- <u>State tree</u>: Paloverde
- <u>State flower</u>: Saguaro Cactus Blossom
- <u>State song</u>: Arizona March Song
- <u>State Motto</u>: "God Enriches"
- <u>Meaning of name</u>: The origin of Arizona is not known. Some possibilities include an Aztec meaning "silver-bearing" or a Pima Indian word meaning "little spring."
- <u>Historic places to visit in Arizona</u>: The Grand Canyon, Petrified Forest National Park, Painted Desert, Monument Valley, Meteor Crater, Canyon Diablo, Hoover Dam, Roosevelt Dam, Glen Canyon Dam, Tombstone, The Biosphere II, Havasu Canyon, Grand Canyon Caves, Lake Powell/Rainbow Bridge, Sunset Crater, Sedona Oak Creek Canyon, Salt River Canyon, Superstition Mountains, Picacho Peak State Park, Saguaro National Park, Chiricahua National Monument

Arizona State Capital - Photo by Jeff Dean

- <u>Resources and Industries</u>: farming (cattle, grain, cotton, dairy, lettuce, hay) mining (copper, gold, silver), transportation, machinery, printing, tourism

Flag of Arizona

- Arizona adopted this flag on February 17, 1917.
- It features 13 rays of red and gold on the top half of the flag. The 13 rays represent the 13 original colonies.
- The star on the flag is the color of copper to represent Arizona's copper-mining industry.
- The bottom half of the flag is the same blue color that is on the United States flag.

Chapter 31

The Cold War, Cuba, the Nuclear Arms Race, the Space Race

U.S. AND WORLD HISTORY FOCUS

THE COLD WAR

FASCINATING FACTS: The Cold War

United States Navy F-4 Phantom II intercepts a Soviet Tupolev Tu-95 D aircraft in the early 1970s

A "cold war" is a conflict that stops just short of becoming a "hot war," or a shooting war. The 20th Century Cold War was the long conflict between the Communist Bloc (the USSR and its satellites) and the West (the USA and its allies) that almost, but not quite, led to an all-out hot war between two nuclear-armed superpowers.

Theoretically, the Cold War was a war between two idealistic political philosophies:
1. Communists saw the Cold War as a battle to save the workers of the world from rich capitalists who wanted to defeat the workers' communist revolution and re-enslave them.
2. The West saw the Cold War as a battle to preserve freedom and democracy from ambitious communist dictators like the USSR's Josef Stalin and China's Mao Tse-tung, men who wanted to bring the entire world under the influence of communism.

In practice, however, neither side stuck to its idealist philosophy very strictly:
1. Although Stalin and his successors claimed to support the ideals of communism (such as a classless society and equality for all), they were actually ruthless dictators who enslaved their people far more thoroughly than Russia's hated tsars ever had.
2. In its effort to prevent the spread of communism, the USA supported nationalists like China's Chiang Kai-shek and South Korea's Syngman Rhee. These leaders' murderous attacks on the communists who opposed them hardly reflected the highest ideals of freedom and democracy (such as freedom of speech and the right to a fair trial).

Although the Cold War never developed into all-out war between the USA and the USSR, it was still a long and deadly conflict. These are some of the many conflicts that were part of the Cold War:

• The Division of Germany (1946 - 1949)	• The Communist Takeover of Cuba (1956 - 1959)
• The Berlin Airlift (1948 - 1949)	• The Cuban Missile Crisis (1962)
• The Korean War (1950 - 1953)	• The Nuclear Arms Race (1945 -)
• The Suez Crisis (1956)	• The Space Race (1957 - 1969)
• The Vietnam War (1955 - 1975)	• The USSR's War in Afghanistan (1979 - 1989)

FASCINATING FACTS: The Iron Curtain

The Iron Curtain was the line of separation between the communist-controlled countries of Eastern Europe and the free democracies of the West. Between 1945 - 1949, the USSR helped create communist governments in nearly every nation of Eastern Europe. Some became part of the USSR (the Union of Soviet Socialist Republics) as "SSRs" (Soviet Socialist Republics). The fifteen SSRs were:

Russia	Ukraine	Lithuania	Belarus
Latvia	Kazakhstan	Estonia	Azerbaijan
Georgia	Tajikistan	Moldova	Kyrgyzstan
Armenia	Turkmenistan	Uzbekistan	

Others became "satellite states," communist nations with governments controlled by the USSR. These included:

| Albania | Hungary | Bulgaria | Poland |
| Czechoslovakia | Romania | East Germany | |

Yugoslavia remained independent, although its dictator, Marshal Tito, was a communist/socialist and a friend of Stalin's until 1948. After 1948, Tito became one of the founders of the <u>Non-Aligned Movement</u>, a group of nations that supposedly refused to take sides in the Cold War conflict between East and West.

The Division of Germany

During the final weeks of World War II in Europe, the western Allies invaded Germany from the west, while the USSR continued to invade from the east. The USSR fought to conquer Germany's capital in the Battle of Berlin; while the western Allies pursued German armies far into eastern Germany, meeting their eastern ally the USSR at a line known as the "Line of Contact." This line lay well inside the territory that the USSR hoped to occupy after the war. In the Potsdam Conference (see Chapter 27), the Big Three Allies met to decide exactly which part of Germany each of them would occupy.

The Cold War distrust between the western Allies and the USSR was already growing, and it was far from certain that the western Allies would agree to withdraw from the Line of Contact. Some Allied leaders, including Winston Churchill, believed that the western Allies might be wise to start a new war against the USSR as soon as they had defeated the Germans. It was Churchill who ordered the creation of "Operation Unthinkable," a plan to drive the USSR back inside the borders it had before its 1939 invasion of eastern Poland at the beginning of WW II. However, Churchill's time as Prime Minister of Britain was running out: midway through the Potsdam Conference, new election results from Britain came in, and Clement Attlee replaced Churchill as Prime Minister. Britain and its new prime minister were more than ready for the war to be over; so Operation Unthinkable remained on the shelf.

At Potsdam, the two sides agreed to an exchange: the western Allies agreed to withdraw west of the Line of Contact to their western occupation zones; while the USSR agreed to allow the western Allies to occupy the western part of Berlin, Germany's capital. By 1949, the division of Germany was complete:

- The western Allies' three zones of occupation united to become the Federal Republic of Germany (FRG), or West Germany; West Germany's capital was Bonn.
- The USSR's zone of occupation became the German Democratic Republic (GDR), or East Germany; East Germany's capital was East Berlin. East Germany became one of several "satellite nations" of the USSR: its government was firmly under USSR control.

Berlin

The situation of Berlin was unique: Berlin lay well inside USSR-controlled East Germany, about 100 miles from West Germany. Like Germany itself, the city of Berlin was divided at first into four occupation zones; but the western Allies soon combined their three zones to form a united West Berlin. The USSR, of course, retained control of East Berlin. The problem was that no one wanted to live in East Berlin.

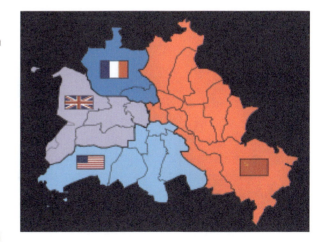

After four years of war, the Russians and the Germans were bitter enemies. At the end of the war, German soldiers had done everything they could to surrender to the western Allies instead of the USSR. The USSR's occupation of East Germany was far more harsh and brutal than the western Allies' occupation of West Germany. No German wanted to live under Russian occupation; nearly all Germans preferred the West to the East.

In Berlin, the contrast between West and East was even more obvious. The people of East Berlin and East Germany had only to look across the border to see that the people of West Berlin were more free, more prosperous and more happy than they were. West Berlin was like a thorn in the paw of the Russian bear, clear proof that life under communism wasn't nearly as wonderful as Lenin and Stalin had claimed it would be.

The Berlin Blockade

The war was hardly over before Stalin began scheming to drive the western Allies out of their zones of occupation. Stalin's goal was to reunite all of Germany under a single communist government. His plan was simple: he would choke off supplies to the Allied zones of occupation, both in West Germany and in the city of Berlin. Since East Germany was home to most of Germany's farms, the Allied zones of occupation would starve unless the western Allies constantly supplied them with food. Stalin didn't believe that they would be willing to do so, especially in West Berlin.

He was mistaken. In June 1948, when Stalin's Berlin Blockade cut off shipments of supplies to Berlin by both rail and water, the western Allies proved their loyalty to free West Berlin by supplying the city through the only means left open to them: by air.

FASCINATING FACTS: The Berlin Airlift

The Berlin Blockade began on June 24, 1948, when the USSR began turning away all of the trains and river barges that usually carried supplies from West Germany into West Berlin. On the following day, the USSR cut West Berlin off from its East German sources of supply as well. Stalin hoped that the Berlin Blockade would work like a military siege, starving the West Berliners until the western Allies were forced to abandon West Berlin to communism.

Instead of giving up, however, the western Allies decided to supply West Berlin by air. This was no easy undertaking. The 2 million people of West Berlin would require a total of about 5,000 tons of supplies per day in order to remain healthy and warm. This would require an incredible 1,500 flights per day back and forth between West Germany and West Berlin. But by 1948, the western Allies had sent most of their soldiers home, so there weren't enough planes or pilots available to carry so many supplies.

Despite these difficulties, within one month, the western Allies' cargo planes were carrying in 4,500 tons per day of coal, oil, milk, bread, vegetables and meat-- everything the West Berliners needed to survive, although their diet was a bit sparse. Just three years before, the West Berliners and the western Allies had been bitter enemies. Now, the West Berliners were depending upon the western Allies for their every need. They watched anxiously for the cargo planes to arrive, and helped unload the planes in exchange for payments of extra rations. The loyalty that the Allies showed to West Berlin during the Berlin Airlift formed a long-standing bond of friendship between the West Berliners and the western Allies.

The USSR did not interfere with the Berlin Airlift (very much) for two reasons:

1. Because the Soviets were certain that the Berlin Airlift would fail (after all, the *Luftwaffe*'s airlift had failed to save Germany's Eighth Army during the Battle of Stalingrad); and
2. Because in order to stop the airlift, they would have had to attack cargo planes that obviously posed no threat to them. To do so would have been an act of war, and the USSR was not ready to go to war over West Berlin.

On Easter Sunday, 1949, the cargo planes of the Berlin Airlift delivered almost 13,000 tons of coal to West Berlin within a single 24-hour period. The success of the "Easter Parade" proved to the USSR that the Allies could continue airlifting supplies into West Berlin for as long as they liked. The defeated USSR finally gave in and lifted the Berlin Blockade on May 12, 1949.

> ### FASCINATING FACTS: Operation Little Vittles
>
> Gail Halvorsen was one of many pilots who flew the cargo planes of the Berlin Airlift. One day during the Airlift, Gail met some German children at the airport in Berlin and decided to make them happy by giving them some chewing gum. He wanted to do more for them, so he made them a promise: when he flew in the next day, he would "wiggle" the wings of his cargo plane to let them know which one was his, then drop a small parachute with more candy for them. This arrangement worked just fine, and soon the children began to refer to Gail as "Uncle Wiggly Wings." Other pilots approved of Gail's idea, and soon began joining in on the candy drops, which became known as "Operation Little Vittles." Later, children in the U.S. began donating their own candy for Operation Little Vittles.

The Berlin Wall

For more than ten years after the failed Berlin Blockade, West Berlin continued to thrive, while East Berlin continued to decay. West Berlin shone like a beacon of freedom in the dingy gloom of East German communism, an ever-present lure to the poor souls whom geography had doomed to live on the communist side of the border. In desperation, many of those poor souls sought to change that doom by sneaking across that border into freedom on the other side.

West Berlin was an ideal escape route for those who wanted to escape communism. East German police found it impossible to patrol its many streets and alleyways constantly; there were simply too many paths of escape. The USSR's new leader, Nikita Khrushchev, began to fear that all of his best and brightest young minds would use West Berlin as an escape corridor to reach the West and freedom. The USSR threatened to take over the city more than once, but the western Allies continued to insist that West Berlin must remain free.

In desperation, Khrushchev decided to try to block any more escapes by building a long wall around West Berlin.

> ### FASCINATING FACTS: The Berlin Wall
>
> On August 13, 1961, East Germany closed its border with West Berlin and began building a wall around the free city. Much of the Berlin Wall's 87-mile length began as a hastily-strung wire fence reinforced by road barriers and police patrols. Within a few years, however, the East Germans replaced most of the fencing with a high concrete wall.
>
> In its final form, the Berlin Wall was a continuous 12-foot high solid concrete barrier topped with a smooth pipe that was difficult for would-be climbers to grasp. To guard against those who sought to climb it anyway, the wall also included other barriers:
>
>
>
> - The "Death Strip," a wide, sand-covered no-man's land on the East German side of the wall which made it easier for East German police to see and shoot anyone who approached the wall;
> - Trenches that prevented would-be escapees from driving their vehicles anywhere near the wall;
> - Trained attack dogs on long leashes that allowed them to reach wide areas of the Death Strip; and
> - Sharp spikes that prevented would-be escapees from jumping off of balconies anywhere near the Death Strip.

East Germany used similar barriers (without the concrete wall) along its entire 860-mile-long border with West Germany. These barriers were most effective: there were far fewer escapes with the Berlin Wall and the border fence in place. Those who did try to escape were forced to use creative transportation devices such as hot air balloons. As many as 5,000 people made successful escapes from East to West during the 28 years of the Berlin Wall's existence; but these were far fewer than the uncounted tens of thousands who escaped before it was built.

The USSR and East Germany explained the need for the Berlin Wall by saying that they were in the midst of a communist revolution. In time, they argued, communism would build a beautiful new society on the eastern side of the wall, a classless society that would be free of fascist Nazis and war-mongering Western capitalists. Anyone who sought to escape East Germany, they said, was a traitor to his people, selfishly trading a world-changing revolution for a few worldly comforts offered by greedy, dishonest capitalists.

For their part, the western Allies fought long and hard to preserve the people of West Berlin from the constant threat of a communist takeover.

Two U.S. Presidents made famous speeches in West Berlin, one near the beginning of the Berlin Wall's life, the other near its end:

- In 1963, U.S. President John F. Kennedy traveled to West Berlin to promise the West's undying loyalty to West Berlin by exclaiming "*Ich bin ein Berliner*," "I am a citizen of Berlin."

- In 1987, President Ronald Reagan traveled to the Wall's Brandenburg Gate to proclaim that communism had failed and freedom had won. He challenged USSR leader Mikhail Gorbachev to come to Berlin, open the Brandenburg Gate and "tear down this wall."

Two years later, soon after President Reagan left office, the USSR loosened its grip on its satellite nations in Eastern Europe. As the iron curtain began to collapse, East Germans gathered at the Berlin Wall on the night of November 9, 1989 to demand that its guards open the gates. When the crowds near the gates began to grow, confused gate guards waited on the telephone for their equally confused superiors to decide what to do. Finally, they decided to open the gates, and the people of Berlin traveled freely between the two halves of their city for the first time in 28 years. Berliners mocked the wall, the symbol of their captivity, by standing, celebrating, dancing and even juggling (see picture) on its top. In the days that followed, the reunified city of Berlin tore down the Berlin Wall, leaving only a few sections standing as memorials.

CUBA
see Chapter 12 for a discussion of Cuba and the Spanish-American War

Cuba After the Spanish American War

After the United States defeated Spain in the 1898 Spanish-American War, it could have annexed (absorbed) Cuba. It did not. Before that war even began, the U.S. Congress insisted (in the Teller Amendment) that the U.S. must not annex Cuba at war's end. The Congress was trying to make it clear that the Spanish-American War was not an "imperialist war," fought only to build America's empire.

Thus, with American help, Cuba won its struggle for independence from Spain, and soon became independent of the United States as well. The newly independent Republic of Cuba elected its first president and legislature in 1902.

FASCINATING FACTS: The Platt Amendment and Guantanamo Bay

Even after Cuba became independent in 1902, the United States did not relinquish all of its rights there. Congress's 1898 Teller Amendment, written before the Spanish-American War, had amended the U.S. declaration of war on Spain by insisting that the U.S. must not use the war as an excuse to annex Cuba. However, in 1901, Congress approved a new amendment regarding Cuba: the **Platt Amendment,** which contained a list of restrictions on the newly "independent" Cuba's rights. Among these restrictions:

- The U.S. retained the right to manage Cuba's foreign affairs if it wanted to.
- Cuba could not enter treaties that made it dependent upon foreign powers.
- Cuba could not borrow money in any way that made it dependent upon foreign powers.
- Cuba could not surrender any of its territory to foreign powers.

The United States had just succeeded in ejecting Spain from Cuba, and wanted to make it clear that it would allow no other foreign power to control any part of Cuba.

The Platt Amendment also included one other important restriction on Cuba: The United States would continue to hold a section of Cuba known as Guantanamo Bay. Guantanamo Bay (see picture) is a natural harbor at the southeast end of Cuba. The U.S. Navy used this harbor during the Spanish-American War, and the U.S. military has held about 45 square miles of Cuban territory near the harbor ever since. In 1903, the new government of Cuba granted the United States a permanent lease on Guantanamo Bay; and ever since 1903, the U.S. has faithfully sent a check for its lease payment every year.

The communists who took over Cuba in 1959 wanted the U.S. to leave Guantanamo Bay and give it back to Cuba. They claimed that the old lease was illegal, and refused to cash the United States' yearly lease checks. The U.S. insisted that the lease was still valid, and sent the checks anyway. This went on for decades; and, as of 2010, it is going on still. Cuba's communist leader Fidel Castro (see below) once opened one of his desk drawers in front of a television news crew to display a stack of un-cashed U.S. government checks, all sent in payment for the lease on Guantanamo Bay.

Unstable, Again

The new Republic of Cuba lasted only until about 1928. In that year its fifth president, Gerardo Machado, outlawed his opponents' political parties so that he would be sure to win a second term in office. Machado began to rule Cuba like a dictator, and Cuba's government became as unstable as it had been under Spain before the Spanish-American War. In 1933, the Cuban military overthrew Machado, and Cuba entered a 25-year period of chaos under corrupt governments. The central figure in most of those governments was a U.S.-supported anti-communist named Fulgencio Batista.

INTERESTING INDIVIDUALS: Fulgencio Batista (1901 – 1973)

As Chief of Staff of the Cuban Army, Fulgencio Batista had a great deal of power and influence. In the 1933 "Revolt of the Sergeants," Batista's military overthrew Cuba's dictatorial president Machado and took over the government. From 1933 - 1940, most of Cuba's several presidents were puppets of Batista's military. Then in 1940, Batista himself won election as Cuba's president. Four years later, however, his reelection campaign failed, and he lost the presidency. He spent the next several years living in exile in Florida.

In 1952, Batista returned to Cuba to run for president yet again. When it became clear that he would lose the election, he decided to use military power to take what Cuba's voters refused to give him. Batista's successful *coup d'etat* allowed him to return to the presidency, essentially as Cuba's dictator, in 1952. From then on, Batista allowed only staged presidential elections in which his victory was guaranteed.

At first, the U.S. government approved of Batista for two reasons: (1) because he opposed communism, cutting Cuba's ties to the USSR; and (2) because he favored American businesses. Cuba's economy grew and flourished during the boom years of the 1950s, just as America's did. America helped Cuba to prosper by buying most of the sugar and other goods Cuba produced. U.S. businesses built and operated the refineries that Cuba needed to process its sugar.

Later, however, the U.S. began to see more of Batista's dark side. Batista's Cuba was a poor example of freedom and democracy; it was more like a police state. Batista tortured and killed Cuba's communists to defeat their attempts at rebellion, just as China's Chiang Kai-shek and South Korea's Syngman Rhee did. He also ran a corrupt government that benefited from prostitution, gambling and deals with organized crime. Under Batista in the 1950s, Cuba's capital city of Havana became a "sin city" that was even more notorious than Las Vegas, Nevada.

Cuba's wealthy citizens did well under Batista, but the poor continued to suffer as they always had. The continual suffering of the poor opened their minds to the teachings of communists like Fidel Castro.

DASTARDLY DICTATORS: Fidel Castro

Fidel Castro was a law student at the University of Havana when he joined Cuba's communist movement. As a good communist, Castro hated Batista for his corrupt dealings with American capitalists and for his brutal attacks on communists. Like Lenin in Russia and Mao in China, Castro wanted to lead a revolution that would build an ideal communist society in Cuba, one in which the poor would have an equal voice and an equal share of Cuba's wealth.

The Attack on Mancado Barracks

Castro's first attempt at an armed communist revolution in Cuba was a July 26th, 1953 attack on the Mancado Barracks, a Cuban army base near Santiago de Cuba (see picture). The attack failed, and most of Castro's 100+ ill-armed troops were either killed or captured. After the attack, Castro and several others escaped into hiding in the hills around Santiago de Cuba.

In his eagerness to crush Castro's rebellion, Batista hunted down Castro and the other escaped revolutionaries with more than his usual brutality. In the week that followed the July 26th attack, Batista's troops accused anyone and everyone they found in the Santiago de Cuba area of being involved in the attack. They imprisoned anyone who bore a small bandage or a slight limp, torturing each victim for information about Castro and the other attackers. The people of Cuba began to take notice of Batista's excessive violence against innocent Cubans.

"History Will Absolve Me"

A week after the Mancado Barracks attack, Batista's men captured Castro. In October 1953, Batista's government tried Castro and sentenced him to 15 years in prison. But before he went to prison, Castro delivered a rousing four-hour speech entitled "History Will Absolve Me," in which he detailed everything that was wrong with Batista's Cuba and how he would like to set things right. As more and more Cubans learned the details of the "History Will Absolve Me" speech, Castro became more and more popular among poor Cubans.

Castro's growing popularity led to calls for his release. In 1955, Batista granted Castro and the rest of the July 26th attackers "amnesty," or official pardons for their crimes, and released them after less than 2 years in prison.

The Communist Revolution

Castro went from prison into exile in Mexico, where he planned his next attack on Batista. In December 1956, Castro boarded a yacht in Mexico on his way to reinvade Cuba. He named his new revolutionary campaign the "26th of July Movement" after his earlier attack on Mancado Barracks.

At its beginning, Castro's 26th of July Movement was no more successful than the attack on Mancado Barracks had been. Within a few days of his arrival in Cuba, about three fourths of his small band of troops were either dead or in prison. Once again, Castro was forced to retreat into the mountains of Cuba.

This time, however, was different: the people of Cuba remembered the **"History Will Absolve Me"** speech, and some of them viewed Castro with admiration. The Cuban public turned against Batista. More fighters joined Castro's cause, and he began to win battles against Batista's troops.

When the public turned against Batista, Batista turned against the public by torturing and killing more people. He attacked both the guilty and the innocent, trying to root out the ones who supported Castro's revolution. Batista's brutality in the fight against Castro only made him more unpopular.

By late 1958, Batista had lost the support of both the Cubans and the Americans. It was then that Batista realized that he was an extremely wealthy man who did not need all of this trouble just weeks before his 58th birthday. Batista cleared out of Cuba on January 1, 1959, and spent the rest of his life in exile. Castro took over as commander-in-chief of Cuba's military one week later, on January 8, 1959.

Enter the USSR

At first, Castro insisted to the United States that his new government was not a communist one, and that his revolution's only goal had been to eliminate the oppressive dictator Batista. Soon, however, he began to do the things that all communists did:

1. He broke up large farms and turned them into collective farms like the ones in the USSR and China;
2. He confiscated huge sugar farms that had belonged to U.S. companies, giving the companies little or nothing in return;
3. He took over control of Cuba's sugar refineries and other industries, many of which had been owned by U.S. companies; and

4. He nationalized (brought under government control) all Catholic schools, expelled more than 100 Catholic priests and began discriminating against Catholics.

Castro also grew friendly with the U.S.' Cold War opponent, the USSR. In 1960, Cuba began to receive arms, military advisers and large loans from the USSR. <u>Castro's friendship with the USSR placed Cuba on the center stage of the Cold War during the early 1960s.</u>

Cuban Exiles and the Bay of Pigs Invasion

Not everyone in Cuba was happy about the success of Castro's communist revolution. Over the months that followed Castro's takeover, Florida and other places became home to thousands of Cuban exiles who had fled Cuba to escape communism. Many of them were wealthy or middle class Cubans who had lost a great deal of valuable property when Castro confiscated their businesses, homes and farms.

In 1961, the U.S. Central Intelligence Agency (CIA) helped a group of these Cuban exiles organize an attempt to overthrow Castro and eliminate Cuba's communist government. The CIA's plan was to send this small army of exiles to invade Cuba at the Bay of Pigs, an inlet on the south side of the island. CIA planners believed that if their exile army could land secretly and capture a small part of Cuba near the Bay of Pigs, then Castro's enemies nearby would join them and help them overthrow Castro. They also believed that once their little army was on the ground in Cuba, President John Kennedy would feel obligated to send the U.S. military to help them complete their mission if necessary.

FASCINATING FACTS: The Bay of Pigs Invasion

On April 17, 1961, a small army of about 1,400 CIA-trained Cuban exiles attempted to invade Cuba at the Bay of Pigs. Their half-hearted, poorly-led invasion attempt was over almost before it began. The entire project quickly developed into a miserable fiasco, for two reasons:

- Sometime during the process of recruiting and training 1,400 Cuban exile soldiers in and around Miami, Florida, the secret of the planned invasion slipped out. The cat was out of the bag: Castro knew when and where the invasion would come, and he was ready for it.
- The small, poorly-trained army of Cuban exiles was unprepared for the opposition it met, so it was unable to capture and hold the beachhead at the Bay of Pigs as planned.

When the invasion began to fail, the CIA expected President Kennedy to send the warplanes of the U.S. Air Force to support them. Those warplanes could have driven off Castro's defenders and allowed the Cuban exiles to secure their tenuous hold on the Bay of Pigs beachhead. <u>However, when the moment of decision was upon him, President Kennedy surprised the CIA by backing down. He abandoned the Cuban exiles to their fate, and refused to send any air support.</u>

As a result, Castro's army quickly defeated the invasion force and captured nearly all of the Cuban exiles. The Bay of Pigs invasion was finished, and Castro had won. The whole affair was over less than 3 days after it began.

The failure of the Bay of Pigs invasion was terribly embarrassing for the United States and for President Kennedy. At the time of the invasion, President Kennedy had been in office for only about three months. Kennedy's critics blamed the fiasco of the invasion on the young President's inexperience, but for two different reasons:

1. Some felt that he should have stood up to the CIA and called off the invasion before it ever began.
2. Others felt that once he had decided to authorize the invasion, he should have stood behind his decision and backed up the Cuban exiles with the full force of the American military.

By choosing the middle road— by allowing the Cuban exiles to invade, but then not supporting them when they got into trouble— Kennedy reneged on promises the CIA had made to the Cuban exiles. He also allowed a gloating Fidel Castro to score a major victory.

As for Castro, he gleefully noted that more than half of the Cuban exiles he captured near the Bay of Pigs were "wealthy" property owners who were hoping to take back their property from the Cuban government. These were exactly the sort of people whom one would expect to attack a successful communist revolution-- a revolution which, Castro claimed, had taken property from the wealthy in order to give it to the poor people whom the wealthy had oppressed for so long.

THE NUCLEAR ARMS RACE

Scientists from the United States, Britain and Canada collaborated on the Manhattan Project (see Chapter 26) to develop the world's first atomic bombs. They conducted their first atomic bomb test, the "Trinity Test," on the desert sands of New Mexico on July 16, 1945. When the United States dropped its atomic bombs on Hiroshima (August 6, 1945) and Nagasaki (August 9, 1945), it was the only nation in the world that had the technology to build such terrible weapons. The U.S. naturally hoped to keep that technology secret for as long as possible.

Therefore the United States received a nasty surprise on August 29, 1949, when the USSR test-exploded its own first nuclear bomb, "Joe-1," nicknamed after USSR General Secretary Josef Stalin. This successful test came years before the United States expected it. Espionage (spying) had something to do with the USSR's early success: the USSR's spies had managed to get inside the supposedly secret Manhattan Project, and to bring their nation valuable information about U.S.-developed bomb technology. Thanks to espionage, "Joe-1" was almost identical to "Fat Man," the high-technology implosion bomb the U.S. dropped on Nagasaki.

When the USSR joined the "nuclear club" of nations, the Cold War race was on to see two things:

1. Which nation could build the most nuclear bombs, and
2. Which nation could develop the best airplanes and missiles to deliver those bombs farther and more accurately.

FASCINATING FACTS: Atomic Weapons Advancements

This is a very brief list of the United States' atomic weapons advancements during the Cold War nuclear arms race. The USSR had similar weapons in every category.

Fission bomb:

The Manhattan Project tested its first fission bomb at the Alamogordo Bombing and Gunnery Range, New Mexico, USA, on July 16, 1945. The fission bomb worked by compressing plutonium into a "critical mass," setting off a chain reaction that produced an explosive force equal to that of about 20,000 tons of TNT.

Fusion bomb:

The U.S. tested its first fusion bomb at Elugelab Island, one of the Marshall Islands of southeast Asia, on November 1, 1952. The fusion bomb used a fission bomb to trigger a nuclear fusion reaction in deuterium, an isotope of hydrogen. Fusion bombs were far more powerful than the earlier fission bombs: This first "hydrogen bomb" was about 450 times as powerful as the fission bomb used at Nagasaki. The bomb test completely obliterated tiny Elugelab Island; only a crater in the ocean floor remained where the island had once stood.

Long-range bomber:

The U.S. flew its first heavy-payload, long-range B-52 Stratofortress bomber in 1952. The huge B-52 was designed to drop heavy nuclear bombs on faraway targets like Moscow, the capital of the USSR, if the U.S. ever needed to do so. The threat of such unthinkable bombings was intended to "deter" a nuclear attack-- that is, to make the USSR think twice before attacking the U.S. or its European allies. During the height of the Cold War, the U.S. Air Force kept nuclear bomb-equipped B-52s in the air around the clock (24/7, 365) so that they could strike back at the USSR in case the USSR ever struck the U.S. first.

Nuclear missile:

The U.S. built its first nuclear-tipped missiles in 1953. For the first time, the U.S. could deliver nuclear bombs without dropping them from an airplane. Because nuclear missiles were faster than airplanes, they were harder for the enemy to find and shoot down.

Intercontinental Ballistic Missile (ICBM):

The U.S. built its first ICBM in 1959. Such missiles could deliver nuclear warheads between continents, against targets thousands of miles away, without endangering any pilots or airplanes.

Submarine-launched nuclear missile:

<u>The U.S. built its first Polaris submarine-launched nuclear missiles in 1960</u>. These long-range, highly accurate missiles could be hidden aboard submarines anywhere in the world's oceans. Such nuclear-armed submarines could launch their missiles at any target within range, then slip away undetected.

<u>M</u>ultiple <u>I</u>ndependently-Targeted <u>R</u>e-entry <u>V</u>ehicle (MIRV):

<u>The U.S. built its first MIRV in 1970</u>. MIRVs multiplied the threat of ICBMs by allowing them to carry multiple nuclear warheads, all of which could be programmed to strike separate targets. MIRV-equipped ICBMs flew high above the atmosphere and released their warheads; then each warhead re-entered the atmosphere to strike its selected target.

Mutually Assured Destruction

By the late 1950s, both the U.S. and the USSR had enough nuclear weapons to utterly destroy one another (and probably the rest of the world along with them). Both of the primary Cold War opponents understood that it would be pointless for one of them to attack the other-- because if either of them ever did, then the other would retaliate, and both would be destroyed. The assurance that both nations would be the losers in any nuclear war was called "Mutually Assured Destruction" (MAD), and it was a powerful reason for neither side to launch the "first strike" of a nuclear war.

Nevertheless, each side had to consider the possibility that the other side might gain some advantage that would save it from retaliation and destruction:

1. One nation might develop some new, superior nuclear missile technology that would outclass its opponent's technology, rendering the opponents' missiles obsolete.
2. Spies might sabotage one nation's missiles or reveal their locations to the enemy.

If an attacker could manage to destroy all of its opponent's missiles in a "first strike," then it might be possible for that attacker to destroy its opponent without being destroyed itself. Therefore, both sides hid their Intercontinental Ballistic Missiles (ICBMs) as carefully as possible: they built underground "missile silos" in far-flung regions, hoping to keep their locations secret; and they also moved their mobile missiles around constantly to avoid detection by spy planes and (later) spy satellites. Hiding ICBMs aboard submarines was also a good way to protect missiles against a first strike; however, each nation had to consider the possibility that the enemy might hunt down and destroy its submarines as well.

As both sides continued to build ever more nuclear missiles and warheads, it became clear that both had the capability to destroy the world many times over, leaving behind little but rubble where there had once been a great civilization.

British Prime Minister Winston Churchill summed up the situation with this quote:

"If you go on with this nuclear arms race, all you are going to do is make the rubble bounce."

FASCINATING FACTS: The Nuclear Club

As of 2010, these are the members of the "nuclear club" of nations and the years in which they first successfully tested nuclear weapons:

United States	1945	China	1964
USSR	1949	India	1974
Britain	1952	Pakistan	1998
France	1960	North Korea	2006

Israel may or may not have nuclear weapons; the Israelis refuse to say.

FASCINATING FACTS: The U-2 Crisis

Before the age of satellites, the U.S. relied on spy planes to discover the movements of the USSR's nuclear missiles and troops. The U-2 was a high-altitude airplane that the United States developed for spy missions during the Cold War. It was capable of flying at altitudes of up to 70,000 feet, heights which the military believed would render it difficult to detect and safe from the USSR's defenses. Unfortunately, the military was mistaken on both counts.

On May 1, 1960, a U.S. Central Intelligence Agency (CIA) U-2 flew over the USSR on a secret mission to learn more about the USSR's nuclear missiles. It was the second such mission within a number of weeks, and the Soviets were waiting for it. None of the USSR's fighter aircraft could reach the U-2's great altitude, but its anti-aircraft missiles could. A Soviet missile damaged the U-2, forcing its pilot, Gary Powers, to bail out and parachute to safety.

As a member of a spy organization (the CIA), Powers was trained to avoid capture at all costs, and to use a suicide capsule to kill himself if he couldn't escape. Powers didn't. The USSR captured Powers alive, but kept his capture a secret. USSR leader Nikita Khrushchev announced to the world that his air force had shot down a U.S. spy plane, but he neglected to mention that he had captured its pilot alive.

President Eisenhower and the CIA naturally assumed that Powers had either died in the U-2 crash or committed suicide as ordered; so, in an effort to keep the U-2's purpose secret, they tried to pretend that Powers' mission hadn't been a spy mission. They invented a cover story in which the U-2 was supposedly a weather research plane on a mission for NASA (America's space program). They even hastily painted another U-2 in NASA colors and rolled it out for a picture in order to back up their story.

A few days later, Khrushchev revealed three big secrets:

1. That he had captured Powers.
2. That he had recovered most of the crashed U-2.
3. That he had proof that the U-2 was a spy plane— in the form of a specially-designed high-altitude camera found only on spy planes. The USSR had even recovered the camera's film, which contained pictures of USSR missile sites.

President Eisenhower was caught in an embarrassing lie, and the purpose of the U-2 became obvious to everyone. As for Powers, he remained a prisoner until the USSR exchanged him for one of its own spies in 1962.

The Cuban Missile Crisis

The next Cold War crisis, the Cuban Missile Crisis, also involved U-2 spy planes.

After the U.S. developed its first medium-range nuclear missiles, it began setting up nuclear missile sites in Europe. The purposes of these sites were

1. To defend the U.S.' European allies, and
2. To make the USSR think twice before taking over West Berlin or any other western European territory.

Over the years from 1958 – 1961, the U.S. built nuclear missile sites in Britain, Turkey and Italy. These sites gave the U.S. the capability to attack targets and cities all over the western and central USSR, including the USSR's capital, Moscow.

Naturally, the USSR wanted to be able to target American cities as well; so it searched for a place to build sites from which its own missiles could attack the United States. It so happened that Fidel Castro had just completed his communist revolution in Cuba in early 1959, and was in the process of making an enemy of his powerful neighbor, the United States. Castro overcame the half-hearted Bay of Pigs invasion in April 1961; but after it was over, he suspected that the Americans might try to invade Cuba again. His response was to draw closer to his defender, the USSR. In mid-1962, the USSR made an agreement with Cuba's Fidel Castro and began building nuclear missile sites in Cuba.

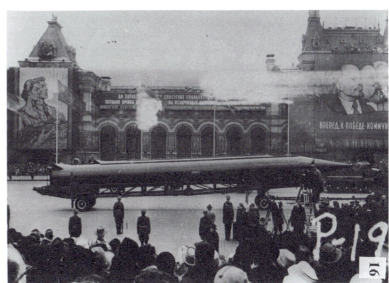

A Soviet-R-12-nuclear-ballistic missile

The U.S. didn't find out about these Cuban missile sites until October 14, 1962, when a U-2 spy plane first photographed them. The discovery stunned President Kennedy: suddenly, for the first time, the U.S. faced the threat of a nuclear attack on its home shores. Kennedy wanted those missiles out of Cuba and Castro gone, but he was wary of attacking Cuba because of the sequence of events that would probably follow:

1. The USSR would consider the U.S. attack on Cuba an act of war against the USSR, and might respond by attacking a city that it had wanted for a long time: West Berlin.
2. The U.S. would be forced to honor its commitment to defend Western Europe by trying to drive the USSR out of West Berlin.
3. China would view the war in Berlin as an attack on communism, and would enter the war on the side of the USSR and Cuba.
4. The whole world would be at war again, this time with globe-ravaging nuclear weapons in its arsenals.

To avoid this unfortunate sequence of events, Kennedy decided against invading Cuba. Instead, he decided to begin a "naval quarantine" of Cuba. On October 22, 1962, the U.S. Navy began boarding and inspecting all ships heading into Cuba, making sure that they carried no nuclear weapons. This partial blockade was as near as nations could come to war without actually declaring war. It also placed U.S. warships alarmingly close to Soviet warships, making a confrontation between the two navies far more likely. Any violent incident, accidental or otherwise, between the two navies could quickly have escalated into World War III. In all of the long years of the Cold War, the US and the USSR probably never came closer to nuclear war than during the thirteen days of the Cuban Missile Crisis.

Fortunately, both sides wanted to avoid nuclear war, and were willing to negotiate. On October 27, 1962, the two sides came to a compromise: the USSR agreed to remove its nuclear missiles from Cuba, and the U.S. agreed to remove its nuclear missiles from Turkey.

INTERESTING INDIVIDUALS: Che Guevara

Ernesto "Che" Guevara was an Argentinean doctor who believed that wealthy capitalist nations like the United States were at the heart of all of South and Central America's poverty problems. Guevara believed in communism with all of his heart, and his thinking helped shape Fidel Castro's.

Guevara met Castro in Mexico City in 1955, while Castro was training his band of revolutionaries for the invasion that started the Cuban Revolution. Guevara joined Castro's band as its combat medic, but he also received guerrilla warfare training along with the rest of Castro's group. During the revolution, he became a fearsome guerrilla warrior and Castro's most successful military commander. He also became well known for personally executing those whom he considered to be deserters or traitors.

Late in the Cuban Revolution, Guevara took charge of *La Cabana Fortress*, a military prison, and set about conducting the trials of defeated Batista supporters who had been accused of war crimes. Because Guevara considered it a crime not to support the communist revolution, these "trials" were often show trials that swiftly led to the executions of his anticommunist enemies. Cuba's Guevara was like Russia's Lenin and China's Mao: he wanted to set up an ideal communist society, and he was remarkably cold-blooded about killing anyone who stood in the way of that goal.

Guevara was more honest about his communist beliefs than Castro was. From the beginning of the Cuban Revolution, he freely admitted that he was a communist and that he hated the United States. He mocked President Kennedy for the failure of the Bay of Pigs invasion, and he dared the U.S. to attack Cuba during the Cuban Missile Crisis. He spent the rest of his life trying to promote communist revolutions in Africa and South America. In 1967, a Cuban exile who worked for the CIA executed Che Guevara for trying to start a communist revolution in Bolivia.

THE SPACE RACE

The Space Race was the race to become the most powerful nation in space as well as on earth. The Space Race ran side-by-side with the Nuclear Arms Race, for two reasons:

1. Because the US and the USSR wanted to use earth-orbiting satellites to spy on each other's nuclear weapons projects. Both realized that spy satellites could keep tabs on their enemies far better than spy planes could, and would be more difficult to destroy than spy planes.
2. Because the same technology that propelled nuclear missiles could also propel astronauts into space. Improvements in space technology would lead to improvements in guided missile technology, and better guided missile technology was key to winning the Nuclear Arms Race.

The USSR scored an early victory in the space race when it placed its first unmanned satellite, **Sputnik I**, into orbit around the earth on October 4, 1957. It scored a second victory on April 12, 1961, when it sent the first human being into space (cosmonaut Yuri Gagarin, aboard the *Vostok I*).

Clearly, the United States was falling behind in the Space Race.

To add insult to injury, USSR-supported Cuban communists overcame the U.S.-supported Bay of Pigs invasion within that same awful month of April 1961. These losses left President Kennedy defeated, embarrassed, and concerned that the U.S. was falling behind the USSR in both the Nuclear Arms Race and the Space Race. Kennedy knew that the U.S. would have to make some spectacular move if it was to get back on its feet and surpass the USSR.

The spectacular move Kennedy chose was to announce a new and inspiring goal: The United States, Kennedy said, must become the first nation to land a human being on the moon; and it must do so before the end of the 1960s. Kennedy announced this new goal in a speech before Congress on May 25, 1961, just weeks after Gagarin's successful space flight.

The U.S. achieved that goal, spectacularly, on July 20, 1969. On that day, astronaut Neil Armstrong became the first human being in history to set foot on earth's moon. As he stepped down onto the moon, Armstrong humbly announced that this was "One small step for (a) man, one giant leap for mankind." Sadly, President Kennedy did not survive to see his nation achieve the goal he had laid out for it in the Space Race: he was assassinated in Dallas, Texas on November 22, 1963 (see Chapter 32).

FASCINATING FACTS: Three American Space Projects

The space program that placed the first human being on the moon was divided into three major projects:

Project Mercury (1959 - 1963):
Mercury's goals were

1. To place an astronaut-manned space capsule into earth orbit, and
2. To recover both capsule and astronaut safely.

Project Mercury flew 20 unmanned missions (four of them with monkeys aboard) and 6 manned missions. The first two manned missions were "sub-orbital": they sent their astronauts into space, but not into earth orbit. The last four manned missions all carried astronauts into earth orbit.

The rockets that propelled the manned Mercury missions into space were the Redstone and the Atlas.

Project Gemini (1965 - 1966):
Project Gemini's goal was to prepare America's space program to land an astronaut on the moon. Trips to the moon would require complex maneuvers such as linking two spacecraft together in orbit. Engineers needed to perfect their equipment for such maneuvers, and astronauts needed to practice them in earth orbit. Project Gemini flew 2 unmanned missions and 10 manned missions.

The rocket that propelled the Gemini missions into space was the Titan II.

The Apollo Missions (1966 – 1972):
Apollo was the project that carried astronauts to the moon. Project Apollo flew 6 unmanned missions and 11 manned missions. Apollo 11, 12, 14, 15, 16 and 17, which flew from 1969 - 1972, all landed astronauts on the moon. Apollo 15 was the first to carry along the lunar rover, a four-wheeled, battery-powered "moon buggy" that allowed the astronauts to explore the surface of the moon up to 5 miles from their landing craft.

Apollo 13 was scheduled for a moon landing as well, but a serious equipment failure forced its astronauts to return to earth without completing their mission.

The rocket that propelled the Apollo missions into space was the Saturn.

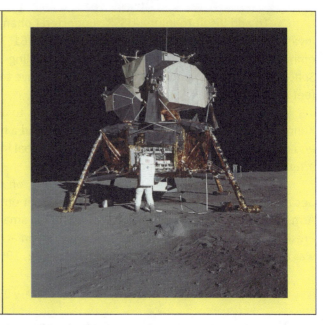

This is a short list of notable U.S. space flights during the Space Race:

Accomplishment	Command Astronaut	Mission	Launch Date
First American in space	Alan Shepard	Freedom Seven	May 5, 1961
First American in orbit	John Glenn	Friendship Seven	Feb. 20, 1962
First American to walk in space	Edward White	Gemini Four	June 3, 1965
First successful docking of two space vehicles	Neil Armstrong	Gemini Eight	March 16, 1966
First orbit around the moon	Frank Borman	Apollo Eight	Dec. 21, 1968
First moon landing	Neil Armstrong	Apollo Eleven	July 16, 1969
First use of the lunar rover	David Scott	Apollo Fifteen	July 26, 1971
Last moon landing	Eugene Cernan	Apollo Seventeen	Dec. 7, 1972

AMAZING AMERICANS

Alan Shepard (1923 – 1998), First American in Space:

Alan Shepard was a navy test pilot whom the National Aeronautics and Space Administration (NASA) chose as one of the "Mercury Seven," America's very first astronauts. Shepard became the first American in space when he flew the short, up-and-back Freedom 7 mission on May 5, 1961. Shepard's successful journey into space followed the Russian Yuri Gagarin's by less than one month. On his second spaceflight, Shepard commanded Apollo 14 and became the fifth man on the moon.

Shepard also became the unlikely holder of a world/moon record: the longest golf drive of all time. Shepard carried a golf club along on the Apollo 14 mission, and used it to drive two golf balls "miles and miles" in the moon's low gravity.

Neil Armstrong (1930 – 2012), First Man on the Moon:

Neil Armstrong was a U.S. Navy pilot who flew fighter planes during the Korean War. After the war, Armstrong returned home to study aeronautical engineering and became a test pilot. He was one of 16 lucky astronauts chosen for Project Gemini in 1962.

Armstrong's first space mission was Gemini 8, which launched on March 16, 1966. The flight began well, and Armstrong accomplished half of Gemini 8's mission when he successfully docked his spacecraft with a satellite. Then the mission turned into a near-disaster when one of Armstrong's thruster rockets malfunctioned, spinning the spacecraft out of control. Armstrong managed to regain control, but the incident cost him his chance to go outside the spacecraft on a planned spacewalk.

Armstrong made up for that lost chance when he commanded Apollo 11, the first mission that landed on the moon. NASA officials chose Armstrong to be the first man on the moon because of his skill and his humility. He slightly bungled his first words when he stepped down onto the moon: he meant to say "That's one small step for a man, one giant leap for mankind," but he accidentally dropped the word "a," leaving his meaning a bit unclear. Without the article "a" before the word "man," "man" and "mankind" mean the same thing.

After Apollo 11, Armstrong resigned from NASA and became a professor of engineering.

PRESIDENTIAL FOCUS

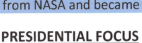

PRESIDENT #35: John F. Kennedy (1917 – 1963)	
In Office: January 20, 1961 – November 22, 1963	**Political Party:** Democratic
Birthplace: Massachusetts	**Nickname:** "JFK"

John Fitzgerald Kennedy was the son of an extremely wealthy Massachusetts businessman named Joe Kennedy. JFK served as a U.S. Navy PT boat commander during WWII, and won an award for his heroism in saving the lives of three crewmen after his vessel was sunk by a Japanese destroyer. His father's wealth helped JFK win election as a U.S. representative for Massachusetts, then as a Massachusetts senator. He defeated the outgoing President Eisenhower's vice president, Richard Nixon, in the Presidential election of 1960.

As Presidents go, JFK was young, attractive, and likable. He was wedded to the beautiful and glamorous Jacqueline Bouvier Kennedy, with whom he had two small children, Caroline and John Jr. The press adored the Kennedy family, and they swept into the White House in a scene reminiscent of King Arthur's legendary palace at Camelot. Their connections to the Hollywood movie industry only added to the romance of the Kennedy Presidency.

However, the harsh realities that Kennedy faced during his three years in office were anything but romantic. The Cold War crises began during his first months in office, and followed one after another:

1. The failed Cuban exiles' invasion of Cuba at the Bay of Pigs
2. The growing war in Vietnam
3. The USSR's early victories in the Space Race
4. The ongoing Nuclear Arms Race
5. The Cuban Missile Crisis

On November 22, 1963, the people of United States were shocked to learn that their young President had been shot to death in Dallas, Texas. The reasons for the JFK assassination were forever shrouded in mystery when his assassin, Lee Harvey Oswald, was himself murdered two days later (see Chapter 32). The 1964 Warren Commission concluded that Kennedy's assassin, Lee Harvey Oswald, had killed President Kennedy because of his hatred for American society, and that Oswald had done so without any outside help. Others concluded otherwise, believing that someone from Kennedy's long list of enemies must have helped Oswald plan and carry out the assassination. That list included (1) America's Cold War opponents, the USSR and Cuba; (2) large American businesses that resented Kennedy's interference in their affairs, and (3) organized crime.

Other interesting facts about John F. Kennedy:
- JFK won the Presidential election of 1960 at age 43. This made him the youngest President ever to win election, but not the youngest to serve in office. The youngest was Teddy Roosevelt, who took over the presidency after President McKinley's assassination in 1901.
- JFK was the first Roman Catholic President.
- JFK was responsible for creating the Peace Corps, a program in which educated young Americans volunteered to help poor people in struggling nations.

Notable quotes from John F. Kennedy:
- "The cost of freedom is always high, but Americans have always paid it. And one path we shall never choose, and that is the path of surrender, or submission."
- "My fellow Americans, ask not what your country can do for you, ask what you can do for your country."

PRESIDENT #36: Lyndon B. Johnson (1908 – 1973)	
In Office: November 22, 1963 – January 20, 1969	**Political Party:** Democratic
Birthplace: Texas	**Nickname:** "LBJ"

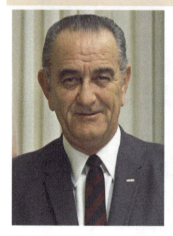

Lyndon Baines Johnson was a U.S. representative and a U.S. senator from Texas. During the Presidential election of 1960, Senator John F. Kennedy asked Senator Lyndon Johnson to be his vice presidential running mate. Johnson became Kennedy's vice president, then ascended to the Presidency after Kennedy's assassination. Johnson took the oath of office aboard the President's airplane, Air Force One, within hours of Kennedy's death. He won election in his own right about one year later, in 1964.

Johnson called his vision for America the "Great Society." The Great Society's social programs were part of Johnson's "war on poverty." These programs included (1) Medicare (government-funded health care for the elderly), (2) Medicaid (government-funded health care for the poor); and (3) federal funding for education. Johnson also signed the 1964 Civil Rights Act that outlawed racial discrimination (see Chapter 32).

Although the U.S. got involved in the Vietnam War under earlier Presidents (Eisenhower and Kennedy), Vietnam became President Johnson's war in 1965, when he sent a great number of American troops into South Vietnam to punish North Vietnam for the Gulf of Tonkin incident (see Chapter 32). Young Americans protested against the Vietnam War and against President Johnson constantly during the late 1960s. The President was hurt by their attitude, and felt that they were forgetting all of the good that he had done by standing up for the poor and for civil rights. When the time came to campaign for reelection in 1968, a discouraged President Johnson decided not to run, and retired from office.

Other interesting facts about Lyndon B. Johnson:
- Johnson owned a large ranch in Texas. He loved to drive around his ranch in a large Cadillac car at speeds of up to 90 miles per hour.
- During World War II, Johnson was one of several U.S. congressman who served in non-combat jobs in the military. Before one flight mission, Johnson left an aircraft named the *Wabash Cannonball* to relieve himself. When he returned, his seat was taken, so he rode in another aircraft. Later that day, the *Wabash Cannonball* was shot down, and everyone aboard was killed.

Notable quotes from Lyndon B. Johnson:
- "Until justice is blind to color, until education is unaware of race, until opportunity is unconcerned with the color of men's skins, emancipation will be a proclamation but not a fact."
- "Yesterday is not ours to recover, but tomorrow is ours to win or lose."

Chapter 32

Civil Rights Struggles in the United States, the Vietnam War

U.S. HISTORY FOCUS

CIVIL RIGHTS STRUGGLES IN THE UNITED STATES

The Reconstruction era began during the U.S. Civil War and ended with the election of President Rutherford Hayes in 1876. During that era, Radical Republicans in the U.S. Congress passed three "**Reconstruction amendments**" to the U.S. Constitution: the Thirteenth, Fourteenth and Fifteenth Amendments. All three amendments involved freeing black slaves and ensuring that blacks and whites had equal rights.

CRITICAL CONCEPTS: The Reconstruction Amendments

From the Thirteenth Amendment, adopted in 1865: "Neither slavery nor involuntary servitude, except as a punishment for crime whereof the party shall have been duly convicted, shall exist within the United States, or any place subject to their jurisdiction."

From the Fourteenth Amendment, adopted in 1868: "All persons born or naturalized in the United States, and subject to the jurisdiction thereof, are citizens of the United States and of the State wherein they reside. No State shall make or enforce any law which shall abridge the privileges or immunities of citizens of the United States; nor shall any State deprive any person of life, liberty, or property, without due process of law; nor deny to any person within its jurisdiction the equal protection of the laws."

From the Fifteenth Amendment, adopted in 1870: "The right of citizens of the United States to vote shall not be denied or abridged by the United States or by any State on account of race, color, or previous condition of servitude."

Despite the Reconstruction Amendments, the "Jim Crow" laws that made discrimination against blacks legal in the American South remained in effect from the Reconstruction era through the 1950s and beyond (see Chapter 11). Two well-known U.S. Supreme Court cases bracketed the era of federal-government-approved, legalized discrimination in the South. One marked the era's beginning, and the other marked the beginning of the era's end:

- ***Plessy v. Ferguson* (1896)**: Although the Fourteenth Amendment required "equal protection of the laws" for blacks and whites, the Supreme Court agreed with Southern lawyers that government services could be "separate, but equal." Under *Plessy v. Ferguson*, the Southern states could maintain separate (segregated) facilities for blacks and whites: separate schools, separate buses, separate drinking fountains and so on. The services Southern governments provided for blacks were indeed "separate," but they were rarely "equal": under Jim Crow laws, blacks nearly always had inferior schools, inferior treatment and inferior rights.

- ***Brown v. Board of Education of Topeka*** **(1954):** Lawyers for the NAACP (National Association for the Advancement of Colored People), the organization founded by W.E.B. DuBois and others to advance black rights, originally filed this lawsuit in Topeka, Kansas.

> FASCINATING FACTS: Brown v. Board of Education (1954)
>
> Oliver Brown was a black man whose young daughter, Linda Brown, had to travel far across town every day to attend elementary school because the school in her neighborhood was for whites only. The NAACP argued that this faraway "separate but equal" black school was really far inferior to the "whites only" school, and that Mr. Brown's daughter shouldn't have to travel across town every day to attend an inferior school when there was a better school just a few blocks from her home.
>
> The Supreme Court agreed. In 1954, the Supreme Court overturned its 58-year-old ruling in *Plessy v. Ferguson*. In *Brown v. Board of Education*, the Court ruled that segregation of public schools did, in fact, violate the Fourteenth Amendment by denying black students "equal protection of the laws." Under the new ruling, the Court required Topeka, Kansas to "desegregate" (or "integrate") its public schools and allow both black and white students to attend.

The new Court ruling meant that public schools all over the South would have to open their doors to black students as well as white ones. Not surprisingly, some Southerners still felt strongly about segregation (separation between the races), and many of them dug in their heels to resist the forced integration of their schools.

A Brief Timeline of the Black Civil Rights Movement, 1954 – 1968

1954, May 17: In ***Brown v. Board of Education***, the Supreme Court rules that it is illegal to segregate public schools.
1955, December 1: In Montgomery, Alabama, Rosa Parks refuses to give up her seat near the front of a city bus to a white rider. Rosa is arrested, and the Montgomery Bus Boycott begins.

> FASCINATING FACTS: Rosa Parks (1913 – 2005) and the Montgomery Bus Boycott
>
> Rosa Parks was a seamstress and a housekeeper from Montgomery, Alabama who also happened to be a volunteer secretary for the local chapter of the NAACP. On December 1, 1955, Rosa got into trouble with the law for refusing to surrender her seat on a Montgomery public bus to a white man.
>
> The public buses in Montgomery were divided into "white" and "colored" sections by a movable sign: whites sat in the front, near the white driver; while blacks sat in the back. Bus drivers could make the colored section larger or smaller whenever they chose, just by moving the sign. Blacks had to board the bus by the front door, pay their fare, then get off the bus and re-enter by the back door so that they wouldn't disturb any white riders sitting in the front. Blacks also could not sit across the aisle from whites. The system was designed to keep blacks and whites as separate as possible.
>
> Rosa Parks had long years of experience with the racism of white bus drivers in Montgomery. More than once, she had paid her

fare and got off the bus to re-enter through the back door, only to have the driver pull away before she could climb aboard. When this happened, she was forced to walk all the way home, a distance of five miles or more, sometimes in the rain. Once, after Rosa had paid her fare, she dropped her purse on her way out of the bus to board from the rear; so she sat down in the front seat (a "whites only" seat) to retrieve it. The driver got so angry with her for sitting in a seat reserved for whites that he forced her off of the bus and drove off-- leaving her to walk home yet again, even though she had paid her fare.

When Rosa boarded the bus on December 1, 1955, she recognized the same racist bus driver who had done such things to her many times. She boarded the bus as usual and sat in the first row of the "colored" section, right behind the sign. As the bus continued on its route, the "whites only" section filled up until some white men were left standing in the aisle. When the bus driver noticed this, he stopped the bus, got up and moved the "colored" sign back one row. Then he insisted that Rosa and three other blacks must give up their seats for the white men. The three other blacks did as the driver asked. Rosa, however, had reached her limit; so she refused. She continued to sit in her seat until the driver called the police onto the bus and had her arrested.

Rosa's trial came four days later. To protest this unfair treatment of Rosa, civil rights leaders in Montgomery asked all blacks in the city to stop riding the city's buses. For more than a year, Montgomery's blacks walked, carpooled or took black-owned taxis, but they did not ride city buses. Black taxi owners agreed to accept the bus system's 10-cent fare for the duration of the Montgomery Bus Boycott. The boycott wrecked the bus system's finances, because before the boycott, blacks had paid about three-fourths of its fares.

In the end, the city of Montgomery agreed to repeal its racist rules and integrate its buses.

The Montgomery Bus Boycott was special for two reasons:

1. Because it was the first of several successful efforts to integrate public buses.
2. Because it was the first successful non-violent protest organized, in part, by Dr. Martin Luther King.

1956, February 24: U.S. Senator Harry F. Byrd of Virginia responds to the Supreme Court's ruling in *Brown v. Board of Education* by announcing his policy of "Massive Resistance." Massive resistance is a set of laws and programs designed to prevent the federal government from forcing the public schools of Virginia and other states to integrate.

1956, December 26: The Montgomery Bus Boycott ends when a federal court rules that Montgomery's segregated bus laws are unconstitutional.

1957, January: Dr. Martin Luther King becomes the leader of the Southern Christian Leadership Conference (SCLC), an organization that will use the power of black churches to promote black civil rights through non-violent protests.

Soldiers escorting the nine Little Rock Students into Central High School

1957, September 4: The governor of Arkansas orders National Guard troops to prevent the integration of Alabama public schools by blocking the entry of Little Rock Central High School to black students.

1957, September: President Eisenhower "federalizes" the Arkansas National Guard, taking over control from the Arkansas governor. He then orders the U.S. Army to end public school segregation in Arkansas by escorting the "Little Rock Nine" inside Little Rock Central High School.

1957, September 27: President Eisenhower signs the **Civil Rights Act of 1957,** which is designed to grant more Southern blacks the right to vote. Senator Strom Thurmond of South Carolina tries to block this law's passage with a 24-hour "filibuster" (a long speech that delays debates and votes in the Senate).

1960, February 1: Lunch counter sit-ins begin in Greensboro, North Carolina.

FASCINATING FACTS: Sit-ins and other Non-violent Protests

Dr. King and other black civil rights leaders followed the example of India's Mohandas Gandhi (see Chapter 19): They believed that non-violent protests were the best way to draw attention to the righteousness of their cause. To protest unfair segregation laws, blacks simply pretended as if segregation didn't exist by sitting on "whites only" park benches or drinking from "whites only" water fountains. Then they allowed the authorities to embarrass themselves by enforcing harsh laws that were obviously unfair. Rosa Parks' refusal to leave her seat on a Montgomery city bus was a good example of a non-violent protest: when the Montgomery police arrested Rosa merely for continuing to sit in a seat that she had already paid for and occupied, they revealed the ugliness of their unfair prejudice.

Another popular type of protest was the lunch counter sit-in. Under segregation laws in some parts of the South, blacks weren't allowed to sit at the same lunch counters with whites. In protest of these unfair laws, some blacks simply sat at the counters anyway. Such sit-in protests forced businesses to make a choice:

1. They could call the police like Rosa's bus driver did, making an ugly scene and embarrassing themselves;
2. They could ignore the sit-in and serve their black customers, possibly angering white customers in the process; or
3. They could close their lunch counters altogether, hoping to re-open them later after the sit-in protesters went away.

When civil rights leaders organized lunch counter sit-ins throughout the early 1960s, businesses across the South tried all three of these choices.

1960, May 6: President Eisenhower signs the **Civil Rights Act of 1960,** another law designed to grant more Southern blacks the right to vote. A group of 18 Democratic U.S. senators from the South filibusters this law for more than four solid days before it finally passes.

1960, October 19: Dr. Martin Luther King is arrested at a sit-in (this is only one of many times Dr. King will be arrested).

1960, October 28: U.S. Attorney General Robert Kennedy (President Kennedy's brother) intervenes and wins Dr. King's release. Robert Kennedy will support black rights more than any other member of President Kennedy's administration.

1963, January 18: In his inaugural address, incoming Alabama governor George Wallace insists that his state will remain segregated: "…segregation now, segregation tomorrow, segregation forever!"

1963, April 12: Dr. King is arrested in Birmingham, Alabama for demonstrating against segregation without a permit.

1963, April 16: Dr. King writes his *Letter from Birmingham Jail*.

FASCINATING FACTS: Dr. King's *Letter from Birmingham Jail*

The *Letter from Birmingham Jail* was an open letter (a letter that anyone may read) addressed to a group of Birmingham, Alabama ministers who had criticized Dr. King for coming to Birmingham and disturbing the peace with his civil rights protests. Dr. King responded to these ministers by saying that "Injustice anywhere is a threat to justice everywhere." He also chastised them for being so upset by the protests, without being at all upset by the racism that caused the protests. Like his speeches "I've Been to the Mountaintop" and "I Have a Dream," the *Letter from Birmingham Jail* demonstrated Dr. King's skilled reasoning and eloquent rhetoric.

1963, June 11: Governor Wallace personally stands outside a door at the University of Alabama, trying to block integration of the school. When U.S. marshals approach, Wallace backs down and allows black students to pass.

1963, June 19: President Kennedy proposes a new Civil Rights Act to Congress.

1963, August 28: Several civil rights organizations sponsor the **Great March on Washington** in support of the new Civil Rights Act. At the Great March, Dr. King delivers his "I Have a Dream" speech, and declares his hope that the United States will one day become a nation in which his children will "not be judged by the color of their skin, but by the content of their character."

FASCINATING FACTS: The Great March on Washington

The Great March on Washington was a civil rights protest march that took place in the nation's capital on August 28, 1963, during the 100th anniversary year of President Abraham Lincoln's Emancipation Proclamation. Its purposes were:

- To promote President Kennedy's new Civil Rights Act, which had been proposed but had not yet become law; and
- To goad President Kennedy into doing still more for civil rights.

About a quarter of a million people flooded into Washington, D.C. for the march. The march began at the Washington Monument, then proceeded down Washington's Mall until it reached the Lincoln Memorial. President Washington represented a time of slavery in the United States, while President Lincoln represented the emancipation of the slaves. Thus the marchers were symbolically traveling out of bondage and into freedom.

When the marchers arrived at the Lincoln Memorial, they listened while a series of musicians, actors and speakers declared their support for black civil rights from atop the memorial's long stairs. The musicians included protest singers like Joan Baez, Bob Dylan and Peter, Paul and Mary; the actors included Sammy Davis Jr., Sydney Poitier, Charlton Heston and Marlon Brando; and the speakers included Dr. King, who delivered his famous "I Have a Dream" speech. The speech closed with a phrase from an old black spiritual song that described the joy King hoped to feel when segregation and racism finally came to an end: "Free at last! Free at last! Thank God Almighty, we're free at last!"

1963, November 22: President Kennedy is assassinated in Dallas, Texas.

1964, January 23: The **Twenty-Fourth Amendment** to the U.S. Constitution takes effect, outlawing the use of poll taxes to prevent citizens from voting in federal elections.

1964, July 2: President Johnson signs the **Civil Rights Act of 1964**.

> ### FASCINATING FACTS: The Civil Rights Act of 1964
>
> The Civil Rights Act of 1964 was the centerpiece and the highest achievement of the struggle for black civil rights during the 1960s. President Kennedy proposed the Civil Rights Act in a speech to the nation on June 11, 1963. It passed through the House of Representatives and the Senate only with great difficulty-- Southern Democratic senators fought the Act with a long filibuster, just as they had filibustered earlier civil rights laws in 1957 and 1960. President Johnson supported the Act's passage by saying that it would make a fitting memorial to the late President Kennedy, dead at the hands of an assassin. Johnson signed the Civil Rights Act into law on July 2, 1964.
>
> The Civil Rights Act banned racial and other kinds of discrimination in several areas:
>
> - It outlawed racial discrimination in voting laws.
> - It outlawed separate public facilities (schools, parks, drinking fountains etc.) for different races.
> - It outlawed racial discrimination by any restaurant, hotel, theater or other business engaged in "interstate commerce" (because under the Constitution, Congress has the power to regulate interstate commerce).
> - It outlawed racial discrimination by businesses hiring employees.
>
> The Civil Rights Act signaled the coming end of the Jim Crow laws that legalized discrimination against the blacks of the South. Unfortunately, that end didn't come immediately.

1964, December 10: Dr. King wins the Nobel Peace Prize.

1965, March 7: On "Bloody Sunday," police attack civil rights protesters who are marching from Selma, Alabama to Montgomery, Alabama.

> ### FASCINATING FACTS: The Marches from Selma and Bloody Sunday
>
> Selma, Alabama lies about 50 miles west of Alabama's capital, Montgomery. Selma is the county seat of Dallas County, a county that tried to hold on to its Jim Crow laws for as long as it could. Even after President Johnson signed the Civil Rights Act of 1964, Dallas County continued to prevent nearly all of its many black citizens from registering to vote.
>
> In early 1965, Dr. King and other civil rights leaders began to organize protests against the Jim Crow laws that were still in effect in Dallas County and other counties nearby. The local police wanted to put a stop to such protests for good, so they handled the protesters with far more than their usual brutality. Finally, the violence got out of hand: a white policeman shot a black protester, and the young man died a week later.
>
> The protesters could have met violence with violence, but they didn't. Instead, they organized yet another non-violent protest, a 51-mile march that would begin in Selma and end in Montgomery. When the marchers reached Montgomery, they planned to question Alabama Governor George Wallace about the young protester's death and ask him if he had ordered his police to be so brutal.
>
> Governor Wallace was ready for them. On March 7, 1965, as the marching protesters left Selma and crossed the Alabama River on the Edmund Pettus Bridge,

state police and their deputies were waiting to attack them with nightsticks and tear gas. Although the protesters had done nothing but march, the Alabama police beat them, kicked them and tear gassed them until they were forced to retreat back across the bridge. Television cameras recorded the police's brutality on "Bloody Sunday," and they showed the American people an extremely ugly image of Alabama's stand against black voting rights.

That image made Americans far more sympathetic to the protesters' cause. When Dr. King finally reached Montgomery on March 25th, he marched at the head of about 25,000 protesters from all over the United States and beyond. The marches from Selma to Montgomery encouraged the U.S. government to pass yet another civil rights bill: President Johnson signed a new Voting Rights Act into law just a few months later, on August 6, 1965.

1965, August 6: President Johnson signs the **Voting Rights Act** to enforce the Fifteenth Amendment and help more Southern blacks win the right to vote.
1968, April 4: Dr. King is assassinated in Memphis, Tennessee by James Earl Ray.
1968, June 6: Robert F. Kennedy is assassinated in Los Angeles, California by Sirhan Sirhan, a citizen of Jordan who is upset by Kennedy's support for Israel.
1972, May 15: Former Alabama governor George Wallace, a staunch opponent of integration, is shot five times by a mentally ill attacker who seems to be seeking attention. The attack leaves Wallace paralyzed from the waist down for the rest of his life.

AMAZING AMERICANS: Dr. Martin Luther King Jr. (1929 – 1968)

Martin Luther King Jr. was a Baptist minister from a family of Baptist ministers: both his father and his grandfather served as pastors of Ebenezer Baptist Church in Atlanta, Georgia. Martin's life lay slightly to the west, in Alabama: he met an Alabama girl named Coretta Scott and married her in 1953. In the following year, Martin took a job as pastor of Montgomery, Alabama's Dexter Avenue Baptist Church; and in 1955, he became "Dr. King" when he earned a doctorate in theology from Boston University.

Dr. King harnessed the power of churches like his to aid in the struggle for black civil rights. His Southern Christian Leadership Conference, founded in 1957, used church meetings to inspire and organize non-violent protests like lunch counter sit-ins, bus boycotts, voter registration drives and even the Great March on Washington. In 1959, he became even more convinced that non-violent protests suited his cause best when he traveled to India to learn more about Mohandas Gandhi. Dr. King organized and participated in non-violent protests in favor of black civil rights for 13 years, from 1955 - 1968. During those years, he was arrested nearly 20 times, and spent many days and nights in jail.

In late March 1968, Dr. King traveled to Memphis, Tennessee to support a protest for black workers' rights. On April 3, he delivered a speech in which he reminded his listeners of what happened to the great Hebrew prophet Moses in Deuteronomy 34: how God allowed Moses to see the Promised Land, but did not allow him to enter it. Dr. King's speech eerily predicted what was to come:

"...I've been to the mountaintop...Like anybody, I would like to live a long life. Longevity has its place. But I'm not concerned about that now. I just want to do God's will. And He's allowed me to go up to the mountain. And I've looked over. And I've seen the Promised Land. I may not get there with you. But I want you to know tonight, that we, as a people, will get to the Promised Land. And I'm happy, tonight. I'm not worried about anything. I'm not fearing any man. 'Mine eyes have seen the glory of the coming of the Lord.'"

On the next evening, April 4, 1968, a sniper named James Earl Ray shot and killed Dr. Martin Luther King as he stood on a second-floor balcony at Memphis's Lorraine Motel. Ray was a habitual criminal and an escaped convict; he was also a racist who supported Alabama governor George Wallace, Dr. King's opponent at Selma and other protests. Police captured Ray in London two months after the shooting. He pleaded guilty to the crime in order to avoid the death penalty; however, for the rest of his life, he denied that he had been the trigger man. Ray died in prison in 1998.

OTHER INTERESTING INDIVIDUALS FROM THE CIVIL RIGHTS STRUGGLE IN THE UNITED STATES

Ruby Bridges (1954 –)

Ruby Bridges was the first black child to attend a formerly all-white school in the South. When Ruby started first grade at William Frantz Elementary School in New Orleans, Louisiana on November 14, 1960, she was the only black child in her entire school.

At the time, some Southerners were still extremely unhappy about the Supreme Court's 1954 decision in the case of *Brown v. Board of Education*, which required the South to integrate (mix races at) its public schools. For Ruby's first several days, federal marshals escorted her to school amid loud protests and vicious threats from integration opponents. White parents all withdrew their children from Ruby's class; so the school hired a special teacher from Boston just for Ruby, and the two of them worked together in a classroom of their own throughout the entire school year. Ruby wasn't allowed to play with the white children at recess, so she and her teacher did jumping jacks while listening to music in their classroom. Ruby was so fond of her white teacher that she even picked up her Boston accent.

By the time the following school year began, more Southerners had accepted the idea of integration, and there were more black students at Ruby's school.

Bull Connor (1897 – 1973)

Bull Connor was the Commissioner of Public Safety (chief of police) for Birmingham, Alabama. He was also a member of the Alabama Ku Klux Klan, a revival of the original Ku Klux Klan founded during Reconstruction after the Civil War. Dr. Martin Luther King, Jr. described Bull Connor's Birmingham as "the most segregated city in America."

In 1963, Dr. King organized a large campaign of nonviolent protests against segregation in Birmingham. Bull Connor was determined to control these protests, and ordered the protesters to disperse. When the protesters refused, Bull Connor's police force attacked them with high-pressure fire hoses and police dogs. Connor's heavy-handed attacks against peaceful protesters appalled President Kennedy, and made him more determined to promote the Civil Rights Act.

A PRESIDENTIAL ASSASSINATION AND A PRESIDENTIAL SCANDAL

The Assassination of President Kennedy

On November 22, 1963, President John F. Kennedy traveled to Dallas on a political mission to soothe differences in the Texas Democratic Party. The plans for his trip included a Presidential motorcade, which would allow him to greet the people of Dallas. Newspapers published the route of his motorcade days in advance so that the people of Dallas could line up for a chance to see the popular President in person.

One of the people who studied the President's motorcade route was Lee Harvey Oswald, a communist sympathizer who was

angry about Kennedy's treatment of communist Cuba. Oswald noticed that the President's route passed through Dealey Plaza, which was directly in front of the Texas Schoolbook Depository building where he worked. On November 22, Oswald climbed to the sixth floor of that building and waited at a window for the President to pass beneath him. At 12:30 PM, Oswald used an Italian-made bolt-action rifle to shoot President Kennedy three times, striking him in the back, neck and head. Kennedy died before he reached the hospital.

GRIM FACTS about Lee Harvey Oswald (1939 – 1963)

- Oswald was interested in communism from an early age.
- At the age of 17, Oswald dropped out of high school to join the U.S. Marine Corps. He served in the Philippines and elsewhere from 1956 - 1959.
- Oswald moved to the USSR in 1959 because he believed that it was a communist utopia (ideal society). When the Soviets denied his application for citizenship at first, he tried to commit suicide.
- The USSR, which loved for people to "defect" from freedom to communism as long as they weren't spies, allowed Oswald to stay and assigned him a job as an assembler of radio and television parts.
- Oswald soon found that life in the USSR was drab, and that his communist utopia was not all that he had hoped it would be. With a new Russian wife and child at his side, he returned to the United States in 1962.
- Oswald continued to search for his communist utopia, and he hoped that Cuba would become that utopia. Months after the Cuban Missile Crisis, he opened a new Louisiana branch of an organization called the Fair Play for Cuba Committee (FPCC) and tried to recruit members. He considered moving to Cuba, where he hoped that the communism of Fidel Castro and Che Guevara would be more pure than that of the USSR.
- Oswald got a job at the Texas Schoolbook Depository in Dallas, Texas on October 16, 1963. The building was located on Dallas's Dealey Plaza, which would become part of President Kennedy's motorcade route on November 22.
- Oswald concealed his assassin's rifle by claiming that he was carrying a package of curtain rods.
- After he shot President Kennedy with the rifle at 12:30 PM on November 22, 1963, Oswald left the Depository on foot. At about 1:40 PM, a Dallas policeman stopped him about 3 miles from the Depository because he matched the description of the President's assassin. Oswald pulled out his second weapon, a revolver, and shot the policeman to death.
- Oswald then slipped into a darkened movie theater, hoping to hide there. Dallas police found him and arrested him. He repeatedly denied killing anyone, and complained of police brutality.
- Three days later, on November 25, police led Oswald out of the basement of their headquarters on his way to a cell in the county jail. Although he was surrounded by police and reporters, a Dallas nightclub owner named Jack Ruby rushed up to Oswald and shot him in the chest at point blank range. Ruby later said that he had killed Oswald for revenge and to spare the President's wife, whom he admired, the ordeal of testifying at Oswald's trial.
- Jack Ruby was arrested, convicted of murder and sentenced to death. He appealed his conviction, but died of cancer before his second trial could take place. Ruby claimed to know more about the Kennedy assassination than he had revealed; but if he did, he died without telling anyone.

President Nixon and the Watergate Scandal

Break-ins at the Watergate

The Watergate Complex is a set of five office, hotel and apartment buildings that lies on the northeast bank of the Potomac River in Washington, D.C. During the Presidential election of 1972, the Democratic National Committee (DNC) rented an office on the sixth floor of the Watergate Hotel and Office Building. In that election,

Democratic Party candidate George McGovern was making his bid to unseat Republican President Richard Nixon, who had been in office since his first inauguration in January 1969.

During the election campaign, certain shady members of President Nixon's reelection committee hatched an illegal scheme to gain an unfair advantage over McGovern: The President's men hired a team of five burglars to break into the Watergate and "wiretap" the DNC office by secretly attaching listening devices to their opponents' telephones. Such devices would allow the President's men to learn McGovern's election strategies well in advance, so that they could be prepared for whatever he might do.

The Watergate Complex

The burglars broke into the DNC office twice. The first break-in, on May 17, 1972, didn't bring the President's men as much information as they had hoped; so, one month later, they sent the burglars in again. This time, a security guard noticed the break-in and called the police, who arrested the five burglars in the early morning hours of June 17, 1972. At the time, the election was less than five months away.

Investigations, Firings and Resignations

The investigation into the crime took time. The newspapers published several facts about the burglaries before the election, but Nixon easily convinced the trusting public that he had had nothing to do with the burglaries. When Election Day arrived on November 7, Nixon defeated McGovern overwhelmingly; and Nixon was inaugurated for his second term as President on January 20, 1973.

Ten days later, a federal judge convicted all five burglars of attempted burglary and wiretapping. In the process of investigating the break-in, the police uncovered the fact that President Nixon's men had paid the burglars. This clearly meant that the burglars weren't the only ones who had broken the law. Several other men, including some of the President's closest advisers, were also involved in planning the break-ins and in trying to keep them secret ("cover them up"). In all, seven of President Nixon's close advisers, the "Watergate Seven," would eventually be accused of crimes in the Watergate scandal-- and so would President Nixon himself.

On April 30, 1973, Nixon made several bold moves in an effort to save his Presidency:

1. He fired his White House counsel, John Dean.
2. He asked for the resignations of his two favorite advisers, Bob Haldeman and John Erlichman.
3. He accepted the resignation of his attorney general, Richard Kleindienst.

Nixon hoped that the American people would blame these four, especially Dean, for all of the illegal things his campaign committee had done— letting their president off the hook.

Senate Hearings and Secret Recordings

By now, however, the angry public wasn't as easily appeased as it had been before the election. The next attorney general appointed a "special counsel," a prosecuting attorney whose only task was to investigate the Watergate scandal. Then the U.S. Senate launched its own investigation into the affair. The Senate's method of investigation was to hold hearings in which it publicly interrogated the President's advisers and everyone else who might have been involved in the scandal. These hearings appeared on live television from May 17 to August 7, 1973, and the things they revealed did a great deal of damage to President Nixon's already-tarnished image.

One of the things the Senate hearings revealed was that the President's offices were equipped with tape recorders, and that these recorders had automatically recorded every word of every meeting the President held throughout the Watergate scandal. When the special counsel found out about those recordings, he issued a subpoena (court order) demanding that the President turn them over to him.

President Nixon refused to release them. He claimed that the recordings contained classified information, and that their release would compromise national security. He also believed that they were private, and that he had a right to refuse the special prosecutor's subpoena. He ordered the special counsel to withdraw his subpoena, but the special counsel refused.

The Saturday Night Massacre

President Nixon responded to the special counsel's refusal with his boldest action yet, a stunning series of firings on October 20, 1973 called the "Saturday Night Massacre":

1. Nixon ordered his new attorney general to fire the special counsel. The attorney general refused, so Nixon fired him (or he resigned in protest, depending upon whose version of the story one believes).
2. Nixon ordered the attorney general's second-in-command, the deputy attorney general, to fire the special counsel. He also refused, so Nixon fired him as well.
3. Nixon ordered the next man in line, solicitor general Robert Bork, to fire the special counsel. It so happened that Bork agreed with Nixon, and believed that the President could legally (1) refuse to release the tapes and (2) fire the special prosecutor. Bork fired the special prosecutor as ordered, and the Saturday Night Massacre was over.

None of these bold moves would save Nixon. A new special prosecutor continued the investigation, and eventually the President agreed to release transcripts and edited portions of the recordings. With the release of those recordings, the American people saw a private image of President Nixon that completely contradicted the image he presented in public. In public, he was well-spoken, patriotic and inspiring; but in private, he was profane (foul-mouthed) and disrespectful. With the release of those tapes, Nixon began to lose what little loyal support he had left.

Near-Impeachment and Resignation

In late July 1974, the Judiciary Committee of the U.S. House of Representatives recommended "articles of impeachment" for three of Nixon's alleged wrongdoings in office:

1. Obstruction of justice.
2. Abuse of power.
3. Contempt of (lying to) Congress.

Convinced at last that the game was up, Nixon decided to resign. His resignation took effect on August 9, 1974, before the full House of Representatives could vote on the Judiciary Committee's articles of impeachment.

Nixon's successor, Vice President Gerald Ford, became the United States' next President on that same day. In order to spare the nation the embarrassment of trying and convicting one of its former Presidents, President Ford issued Nixon a formal pardon for any crimes he might have committed in the Watergate scandal.

Other interesting facts about the Watergate Scandal:

- <u>President Nixon resigned before the House could formally impeach him; so, technically, he was not impeached</u>. Nixon would have been only the second U.S. President to be impeached; the first was Andrew Johnson.

- Years after the Watergate scandal, Nixon's opponents took revenge on Robert Bork, the solicitor general who agreed to fire the Watergate scandal's first special counsel during the Saturday Night Massacre. When President Reagan nominated Bork to the U.S. Supreme Court in 1987, members of the U.S. Senate reminded the public of Bork's role in the Watergate scandal, and refused to allow him to become one of the nine justices on the Supreme Court.

WORLD HISTORY FOCUS

THE VIETNAM WAR

The nation of Vietnam occupies the eastern edge of the Indochina Peninsula, a large Asian peninsula that lies east of India and south of China (which is why it is called "Indo-China"). For 20 years, from 1955 - 1975, Vietnam was the battleground of a bloody Cold War conflict between the communists of North Vietnam (aided by communist China and the USSR) and the anti-communists of South Vietnam (aided by the United States and some of its allies).

French Indochina

France colonized most of the Indochinese Peninsula during the late 1800s. For decades, the French controlled Vietnam, Cambodia, and Laos from their capital city of Hanoi (in northern Vietnam). At the time, the Vietnamese people were far behind the Western world in technology and education, just as China and Japan had been before their confrontations with the West. During Vietnam's French colonial era, two Vietnamese leaders began to consider how they might expel the French colonial government and restore Vietnam's independence someday:

Phan Chu Trinh (1872 - 1926)	
	Sought a peaceful revolution against France. Phan Chu Trinh wanted to educate the backward Vietnamese people, then appeal to France to grant the Vietnamese the same rights that all French citizens possessed.
Phan Boi Chau (1867 - 1940)	
	Founder of the Vietnamese Reformation Society. Phan Boi Chau also wanted to educate the Vietnamese people, but in a different way: he wanted them to learn modern technology from the militant Japanese so that they could use force to drive the French out of Vietnam.

When Germany invaded France during World War II in 1940, imperial Japan also invaded French Indochina. Japan's invasion was part of the 1937 - 1945 Second Chinese-Japanese War, and was designed to prevent China from importing military supplies through Vietnam (see Chapter 26). Japan allowed German-collaborating Vichy France, the new government of occupied France, to control Vietnam during the war.

When the Allies defeated Japan at the end of WW II, the restored government of Free France tried to resume control of its former colony in Vietnam. The French colonial government wanted to rule Vietnam through the same "puppet emperor" it had used before the war, Vietnamese Emperor Bao Dai.

The North Vietnamese had other ideas.

In 1945, a Vietnamese communist who called himself *Ho Chi Minh* ("Bringer of Light") declared Vietnam's independence from the French colonial government and its puppet emperor.

Ho Chi Minh and his Vietnamese Independence League, the **Viet Minh**, fought for Vietnam's independence through the eight years of the First Indochina War (1946 - 1954).

The First Indochina War

The First Indochina War went poorly for the Viet Minh until 1949, when Mao Tse-tung and his Communist Party of China won the Chinese Civil War and took over China (see Chapter 29). With help from the Chinese communists, the Viet Minh began to win victories over the French colonial government. (Picture is of a French Legionnaire).

These Vietnamese victories made the First Indochina War increasingly unpopular in France. The age of European empires was ending, and the disillusioned, war-weary people of France no longer wanted to spend their soldiers' lives merely to preserve France's tenuous hold on the far-flung colonies of its declining empire. After eight years of war, France was ready to grant Vietnam an independent government.

The question remained, however: What sort of government? The Viet Minh wanted to build a communist government in the North Vietnamese capital of Hanoi; but there was also the anti-communist French colonial government in the South Vietnamese capital of Saigon. This anti-communist government had a Vietnamese emperor (the former puppet emperor Bao Dai) and a great deal of support all over Vietnam. The Cold War was in full swing, and South Korea had just managed to preserve itself from a communist takeover in the 1950 - 1953 Korean War. France and its allies, especially the United States, wanted to give Vietnam a chance to remain free of communism the way South Korea had.

The Geneva Conference Divides Vietnam

In 1954, the French colonial government and the Viet Minh negotiated a ceasefire at Geneva, Switzerland. The Geneva Conference presented a temporary compromise in which Vietnam would be divided, North from South, at the 17th Parallel north of the equator. North Vietnam would become the Democratic Republic of Vietnam under Ho Chi Minh; while South Vietnam would soon become the Republic of Vietnam under President Ngo Dinh Diem (Diem would quickly depose the self-absorbed Emperor Bao Dai).

From 1954 - 1956, Ho Chi Minh built his communist dictatorship in North Korea.

Nearly one million North Vietnamese tried to escape communism by migrating into South Vietnam, aided by the French colonial government and the United States in "Operation Passage to Freedom."

The Geneva Conference also proposed a plan to hold nationwide elections and reunite Vietnam's two halves in 1956. These planned elections would allow the people of Vietnam to choose for themselves which type of government they wanted. However, President Diem was certain that Ho Chi Minh would interfere with the voting in North Korea; so, when the time for the elections arrived in 1956, South Vietnam refused to participate.

Despite the aborted elections, Ho Chi Minh remained determined to reunite the two halves of Vietnam. To accomplish this, he developed a strategy to undermine and destroy South Vietnam's government by sending trained communist rebels into South Vietnam. Ho's communist rebels were the "Viet Cong"; their path into South Vietnam was the "Ho Chi Minh Trail"; and the war they fought against South Vietnam was the Second Indochina War, better known as the Vietnam War.

Operation Passage to Freedom

DEFINITIONS

Viet Minh: The League for the Independence of Vietnam, an organization of Vietnamese nationalists who accepted support from communist China and the USSR in their effort to cast the French colonial government out of Vietnam after World War II.
Tonkin: Vietnam's northern region; its primary city is Hanoi.
Annam: Vietnam's central region; its primary city is Hue.
Cochin China: Vietnam's southern region; its primary city is Saigon.
Viet Cong: Vietnamese communists, especially communists in South Vietnam who battled the South Vietnamese and the Americans. Some believe that the Viet Cong were mostly North Vietnamese soldiers trained by Ho Chi Minh and sent into South Vietnam over the Ho Chi Minh Trail. Others believe that the Viet Cong included a lot of South Vietnamese who rebelled against their government because they wanted to live under communism.
Ho Chi Minh Trail: A collection of transportation routes used by North Vietnam to move and supply communist rebels in South Vietnam. The trail passed through neighboring Cambodia and Laos, making it inevitable that war would come to those two nations as well as Vietnam.
ARVN: <u>A</u>rmy of the <u>R</u>epublic of <u>V</u>iet<u>n</u>am, the army of South Vietnam
NVA: <u>N</u>orth <u>V</u>ietnamese <u>A</u>rmy, the army of North Vietnam

FASCINATING FACTS: The Domino Theory

The Domino Theory was a Cold War political theory which said that if Vietnam fell under communism, then all of its neighbors-- Cambodia, Laos, Thailand, and perhaps others-- would fall under communism as well, one after another, like a line of dominos.

Presidents Eisenhower, Kennedy and Johnson were all convinced that the Domino Theory was correct. It was these Presidents' faith in the Domino Theory that brought the United States into the Vietnam War. The United States had fought to prevent the spread of communism into South Korea and West Germany, and it was ready to fight communism in South Vietnam as well. By saving the first "domino" in line, Vietnam, from being knocked down by the communists, the U.S. hoped to save all of the other "dominos" from being knocked down as well.

Stages of the Vietnam War

The U.S. got involved in the Vietnam War slowly, in stages. During the last four years of the First Indochina War, from 1950 - 1954, the U.S. provided money to help the French colonial government fight off the communist Viet Minh. After the French lost the First Indochina War and the Geneva Conference divided Vietnam, the U.S. began sending military "advisers" to train President Diem's South Vietnamese army. As long as the U.S. could call its troops "advisers," it could claim that they weren't truly fighting a war in Vietnam.

Over the years, the number of American military advisers in Vietnam grew steadily. President Eisenhower originally sent fewer than 1,000 military advisers to Vietnam. By 1963, President Kennedy had boosted that number to more than 15,000. Kennedy's advisers were stationed in Vietnam only to train the South Vietnamese army, which performed very poorly in battles against the North Vietnamese. All the same, the American presence in Vietnam was beginning to look like a small army.

In 1963, chaos erupted when members of the South Vietnamese army overthrew and assassinated President Diem. Over the months that followed this *coup d'etat*, the government of South Vietnam changed hands time and again. North Vietnam capitalized on this chaos by sending more Viet Cong rebels down the Ho Chi Minh trail and into South Vietnam, where they continued to stir up trouble for the South Vietnamese government and for the Americans who supported it.

The Gulf of Tonkin Incident

The Gulf of Tonkin lies off the coast of North Vietnam. On August 2, 1964, the U.S. Navy destroyer *Maddox* tangled with a trio of North Vietnamese torpedo boats in the Gulf of Tonkin. The *Maddox* suffered little damage in this short sea battle, but all three North Vietnamese torpedo boats suffered heavy damage. A second, similar tangle may or may not have come two days later. Each side disputed the other's story of the *Gulf of Tonkin Incident*, so very few of its details were certain.

U.S. Tanks in Vietnam

What was certain about the Gulf of Tonkin Incident was President Johnson's strong reaction to it: he considered it to be a deliberate and direct attack on the United States. Johnson responded to this attack by immediately launching the first aircraft carrier-based bombings of North Vietnam.

The U.S. Congress backed Johnson up by passing the Gulf of Tonkin Resolution. This Resolution granted the President the authority to use the full force of the American military in Vietnam, without a formal declaration of war from Congress. All of those American military "advisers" and "trainers" in South Vietnam were about to become real soldiers in an all-out war.

Napalm and Agent Orange

President Johnson used his new authority to launch a full-scale war against North Vietnam. He began with a long aerial bombing campaign called "Rolling Thunder," which was designed to destroy North Vietnam's ability to wage war. He also sent U.S. Marines and soldiers to battle the North Vietnamese on the ground. At the war's peak, there were more than 500,000 American troops in Vietnam.

But the Vietnam War wasn't like World War II, which the Americans won by winning major battles. The North Vietnamese were too clever to allow themselves to be drawn into large confrontations that the powerful American military would certainly win.

Instead, they took advantage of Vietnam's terrain. The dense jungles of Vietnam favored guerrilla-style warfare rather than large armies of tanks and infantry. The Viet Cong rebels launched vicious attacks by night, then slipped away into the Vietnamese jungle and went into hiding. Frustrated American patrols had great difficulty finding these well-hidden rebels. The Viet Cong struck from concealment again and again, waiting for the Americans to grow discouraged, give up and go home.

The U.S. military's answer to these tactics was to try to destroy the very jungle in which the Viet Cong hid. One of the Americans' weapons was napalm, a jellied gasoline that could burn away huge areas of the Vietnamese jungle and eliminate the Viet Cong's hiding places (see picture). Another was Agent Orange, a chemical "defoliant" that destroyed plant foliage (leaves) and laid great swaths of jungle bare.

With these new weapons and several victories under his belt, U.S. Army General Westmoreland predicted a U.S. and South Vietnamese victory by late 1967.

The Tet Offensive

Once again, the North Vietnamese had other ideas. Vietnam's celebration of the new year, known as *tet nguyen dan*, usually meant a temporary cease-fire of at least two days. For this reason, General Westmoreland was caught by surprise when his enemies chose the day of the *tet* to launch a major new assault on South Vietnam. On January 31, 1968, the North Vietnamese and the Viet Cong launched surprise attacks on five major South Vietnamese cities and about 100 smaller cities and villages, all at the same time.

The Tet Offensive was not a major military victory for North Vietnam: within only a few weeks, Westmoreland and his troops managed to recover all of the ground they had lost. <u>Nevertheless, the Tet Offensive was a major propaganda victory for North Vietnam</u>. The American people had been promised victory, followed by a swift homecoming of American troops. Instead, they had received an ongoing war with no end in sight against an enemy that had proved its determination. To many Americans, the Vietnam War began to seem as if it might never end; and some believed that President Johnson and General Westmoreland had deliberately lied to them throughout the war.

The "Vietnamization" of the War

The Tet Offensive destroyed President Johnson's chances of remaining in office. He decided not to run for reelection in 1968, and President Nixon replaced him in 1969.

Nixon's tactics were different than Johnson's. Nixon wanted to begin the "Vietnamization" of the war:

1. He wanted the South Vietnamese to fight their own war, with far less help from the American military; and
2. He wanted to spend far less U.S. money to aid the South Vietnamese in their fight.

Slowly, Nixon began to reduce the number of American troops fighting in Vietnam. The war continued to drag on throughout Nixon's nearly 6 years in office. However, with the U.S. steadily reducing its troops and its war budget, the North Vietnamese knew that it was only a matter of time before the U.S. withdrew from Vietnam altogether.

The Fall of Saigon

President Nixon resigned his office on August 9, 1974 because of the Watergate scandal. His successor, President Ford, made the final decision to give up the fight, abandon South Vietnam and withdraw all U.S. forces and aid. On April 30, 1975, the last U.S. forces departed Saigon by helicopter.

<u>Thus the Vietnam War ended in a loss for the United States and a victory for communism. South Vietnam fell to the communists, and North and South reunited to form one Socialist Republic of Vietnam.</u>

INTERESTING INDIVIDUALS: Ho Chi Minh (1890 – 1969)

Ho Chi Minh was a Vietnamese communist who founded the Viet Minh (the League for the Independence of Vietnam) in order to drive the French colonial government out of Vietnam and establish a new communist government there. Ho was born in French colonial Vietnam under the name Nguyen Sinh Cung. When Nguyen joined the French communist party in Paris, he became known as Nguyen Ai Quoc, "Nguyen the Patriot." While he was in his 30s, Nguyen studied communism in the USSR and became a member of the Comintern (Communist International), an organization that sought to spark communist revolutions against every capitalist government around the world. When Nguyen started Vietnam's communist revolution and founded the Viet Minh in 1941, he finally adopted the spectacular, messianic name *Ho Chi Minh*, "Bringer of Light."

Ho and the Viet Minh battled both of Vietnam's occupiers, Japan and Vichy France, throughout World War II. When that war ended, Ho declared Vietnam's independence and founded the Democratic Republic of Vietnam. With help from communist China and the USSR, Ho's Viet Minh defeated the French colonial government in the First Indochina War.

The 1954 Geneva Conference that ended the First Indochina War left Vietnam divided: Ho's communist Democratic Republic of Vietnam ruled North Vietnam; while the old French colonial government, led by Vietnamese puppet emperor Bao Dai, governed South Vietnam. Like every other communist dictator, Ho began his reign with "land reforms" in which he confiscated land from wealthy farmers and "redistributed" it to the poor. He also confiscated the property of North Vietnam's Catholic churches. A great number of North Vietnamese migrated south to escape Ho's communist dictatorship, aided by the French and American navies in a mission called "Operation Passage to Freedom." A much smaller number moved north, convinced by Ho's propaganda that he would create a communist utopia there.

The Geneva Conference scheduled a nationwide election for 1956 that was supposed to reunite Vietnam under one government. However, the government of South Vietnam was certain that Ho would interfere with the voting results in North Vietnam; so it cancelled the election. The border was sealed, and the migrations of the Vietnamese people ceased.

Nevertheless, Ho remained determined to destroy the government of South Vietnam, which was backed by Americans whom Ho called "imperialists" and "capitalists." Ho realized that he could never defeat the U.S. military in direct battle, so he decided on a different tactic: he sent rebels and weapons into South Vietnam over the "Ho Chi Minh Trail," a collection of routes that wandered through neighboring Laos and Cambodia. These "Viet Cong" rebels blended in with the people of South Vietnam, making it difficult for the U.S. military to know which villages were on which side. When the U.S. military tried to destroy the Ho Chi Minh Trail, it brought Cambodia and Laos into the war as well.

Ho's most brilliant success came in the Tet Offensive, which he launched during the Vietnamese New Year celebration in January 1969. Ho's health was failing, and the Tet Offensive was a desperate effort to win some sort of victory before he died. Militarily, the Tet Offensive was a disaster: it cost North Vietnam tens of thousands of soldiers it could not afford to lose; and in the end, it captured no territory. Politically, however, the Tet Offensive was a tremendous victory: when the war didn't go as President Johnson and General Westmoreland had promised, the American people turned against the war, and howled in protest until the U.S. government was forced to withdraw from Vietnam. Ho and the North Vietnamese realized that if they only waited long enough, the Americans would abandon South Vietnam to communism.

Ho Chi Minh died on September 2, 1969, long before the Vietnam War ended. In 1975, when the North Vietnamese finally overran South Vietnam, they renamed Saigon "Ho Chi Minh City" in Ho's honor.

FASCINATING FACTS: Protesting the Vietnam War

From 1964 until 1969 and beyond, America's young people protested the Vietnam War as they had never protested any war before. They protested for several reasons:

1. Because they believed that the U.S. government had lied to them about the war;
2. Because they believed that U.S. soldiers were murdering far too many innocent civilians;
3. Because the U.S. military was using cruel chemicals like napalm and Agent Orange in Vietnam; and
4. Because the U.S. was spending a great deal of money on the war that might have been spent for peaceful purposes.

Some Americans even protested because they supported the communism of Ho Chi Minh and Mao Tse-tung. Protesters made themselves heard in several ways:

1. Through marches and street demonstrations;
2. By burning their draft cards; and
3. By holding mock trials in which they convicted President Johnson of war crimes.

Three pacifists even burned themselves to death in protest of the Vietnam War.

These protests had their effect: after the Tet Offensive, public opinion turned against the Vietnam War so strongly that President Johnson lost his Presidency.

FASCINATING FACTS: Coolie Hats

A "coolie" is a laborer, especially an East Asian laborer. In order to protect their heads from sun and rain while they work outside, Vietnamese and other East Asians wear cone-shaped hats known as "coolie hats." Some people object to the word "coolie" because it can be taken to mean "slave"; so coolie hats are also known as "paddy hats," "rice hats" or "conical hats." The first conical hats appeared around the 1200s.

Conical hat making is an important craft in Vietnam. Hatmakers weave the hats from young forest leaves and a special kind of bamboo. Then they stitch them together with a thread called "doac," which is made from the leaves of a certain reed. Finally, they coat the hats with rose oil to keep them clean and smooth.

> A Vietnamese legend accompanies the coolie hat:
>
> In the time before humans had learned to clothe themselves, a giant goddess descended from heaven to protect them from the rain. On her head was a vast hat of giant leaves stitched over a conical bamboo frame. The goddess twirled her hat to send away the clouds and rain, then taught her people how to grow crops to feed themselves. One day they fell asleep listening to her stories; and when they awoke, she was gone. The Vietnamese built a temple in her memory, and honored her as the Rain-shielding Goddess. Following her lead, they made hats like hers by stitching forest leaves over a bamboo frame.

MISSIONARY FOCUS

GIANTS OF THE FAITH: Billy Graham (1918 –)

Billy Graham was born on a dairy farm in North Carolina. Billy gave his life to Jesus Christ at a revival meeting in 1934, when he was 16 years old. He studied the Bible at Bob Jones College in Tennessee and at Florida Bible College before graduating from Wheaton College in 1943. He married Ruth Bell in that same year, and the couple went on to have five children together. After college, Billy became a Southern Baptist minister, then began a career that would make him the most successful Christian evangelist of all time.

In 1944, Pastor Graham took over a failing Christian radio program and recruited a successful musician named George Beverly Shea as his music director. Shea's popularity helped the show, "Songs in the Night," take off; and radio listeners began to respond to Billy Graham's strong voice and eloquent preaching of the Gospel of Jesus Christ. George Beverly Shea stayed with Billy Graham's ministry from that time on, and his baritone vocal solos introduced Graham's messages countless times.

In 1949, Billy Graham held a major tent revival in Los Angeles. He had planned to hold meetings for three weeks, but instead the revival went on for eight weeks and drew about 350,000 listeners. The Los Angeles revival made Billy Graham a nationally-known evangelist. He began to hold revivals in locations around the world, even in places that were off-limits to most Christians, such as China and the USSR. Through these "Billy Graham Crusades," Billy spoke to a larger audience than any other Christian evangelist in history. Always his message was the same: that Jesus Christ, the Son of God, sacrificed his life to pay for the sins of God's beloved children; and that anyone who believes in Christ's sacrifice and gives his life to Christ will be saved from sin and will receive eternal life in heaven.

Among Billy Graham's other accomplishments:
- Billy Graham was a personal friend of Dr. Martin Luther King's. In 1952, Graham decided that he would no longer speak to audiences that insisted on segregating blacks from whites.
- He helped found Youth for Christ, a well-known youth evangelization society with branches on campuses all over the world.
- He helped establish *Christianity Today* magazine, a monthly magazine for evangelical pastors and other Christians.
- For over 50 years, he appeared on a weekly evangelical radio show called "Hour of Decision."
- He met and counseled every U.S. President from Eisenhower on.
- He spoke before a live audience of about one million listeners in Seoul, Korea.

A quote from Billy Graham:
- "Being a Christian is more than just an instantaneous conversion— it is a daily process whereby you grow to be more and more like Christ."

U.S. GEOGRAPHY FOCUS

FASCINATING FACTS about ALASKA:

- <u>Statehood</u>: Alaska became the 49th US state on January 3, 1959.
- <u>Bordering states and bodies of water</u>: Canada, Arctic Ocean, Pacific Ocean, Beaufort Sea, Bering Sea, Gulf of Alaska
- <u>State capital</u>: Juneau
- <u>Area</u>: 663,268 sq. mi (Ranks 1st in size)
- <u>Abbreviation</u>: AK
- <u>State nickname</u>: "The Last Frontier"
- <u>State bird</u>: Willow Ptarmigan
- <u>State tree</u>: Sitka Spruce
- <u>State flower</u>: Forget-me-not
- <u>State song</u>: *Alaska's Flag*
- <u>State Motto</u>: "North To The Future"
- <u>Meaning of name</u>: comes from an Indian word meaning "the mainland" or "shore"
- <u>Historic places to visit in Alaska</u>: Mount McKinley, Ketchikan, Tongass National Forest, Big Game Alaska Wildlife Park, Alaska Native Heritage Center, Alutiiq Museum, Bering Land Bridge, Halibut Cove, Kanuti National Wildlife Refuge, Godwin Glacier Dog Sled Tours
- <u>Resources and Industries</u>: farming (vegetables, livestock, dairy, plant nursery), fishing (salmon, crab, halibut, herring), mining (oil, coal, natural gas, uranium, platinum, gold), forestry and wood products, tourism

Mt. McKinley – North America's Highest Point

Flag of Alaska

- Alaska adopted this flag on July 9, 1927.
- The flag has a dark blue field with eight gold stars. Seven of the stars form the Big Dipper constellation, and the last two of these seven point to an eighth, larger star, the North Star. The North Star represents Alaska, the northernmost of the 50 states.

PRESIDENTIAL FOCUS

PRESIDENT #37: Richard Nixon (1913 – 1994)	
In Office: January 20, 1969 – August 9, 1974	**Political Party:** Republican
Birthplace: California	**Nickname:** "Tricky Dick"

Richard Nixon represented California in both the U.S. House of Representatives and the U.S. Senate before he became Dwight Eisenhower's running mate in the Presidential election of 1952. He served as Eisenhower's vice president for eight years, but then lost the Presidency to John Kennedy in the election of 1960. He also lost the race for the California governorship in 1962, and his political career appeared to be over.

Then came the Vietnam War, which made President Johnson so unpopular that he decided not to run for reelection in 1968. Johnson's vice president, Hubert Humphrey, who ran in Johnson's place, proved to be equally unpopular. Nixon defeated Humphrey to become America's 37th President in 1969.

Nixon's Presidency is best remembered for the Watergate scandal (see above). This election cheating scandal was particularly ironic because Nixon didn't need to cheat: he won reelection in 1972 by an enormous margin, and almost certainly would have done so even if he hadn't cheated. After the election, however, the Watergate tapes revealed Nixon as a profane, devious politician, and destroyed his popularity. He resigned from office on August 9, 1974.

Other interesting facts about Richard Nixon:
- Nixon suffered from both hay fever and motion sickness.
- Nixon won many admirers during the election of 1952, when he ran for election as Eisenhower's vice president. When his opponents accused him of accepting inappropriate gifts in return for political favors, Nixon replied that he had granted no political favors, and that one of those supposedly inappropriate gifts was nothing more than a cocker spaniel his small children had named "Checkers." The "Checkers Speech" saved Nixon's candidacy and probably his political career.
- Nixon blamed the press when he lost the 1962 race to become California's governor. After the loss, he told press reporters that they wouldn't "have Nixon to kick around anymore, because, gentlemen, this is my last press conference." Later, of course, he gave many press conferences as President of the United States.

Notable quotes from Richard Nixon:
- "Never let your head hang down. Never give up and sit down and grieve. Find another way. And don't pray when it rains if you don't pray when the sun shines."
- "Only if you have been in the deepest valley, can you ever know how magnificent it is to be on the highest mountain."
- "If you want to make beautiful music, you must play the black and the white notes together."

PRESIDENT #38: Gerald Ford (1913 – 2006)	
In Office: August 9, 1974 – January 20, 1977	**Political Party:** Republican
Birthplace: Nebraska	**Nickname:** "Jerry"

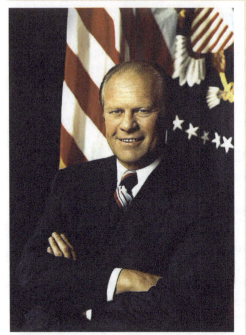

Gerald Ford was a lawyer who abandoned his law practice after the Japanese attack on Pearl Harbor to become a World War II naval officer. Ford won election to the U.S. House of Representatives in 1948, representing his home state of Michigan. He went on to serve in the House for 25 years, completing almost thirteen 2-year terms. From 1965 - 1973, he served as House Minority Leader, the highest-ranking Republican in the House of Representatives.

President Nixon's vice president, Spiro Agnew, got into legal trouble in 1973 because he had accepted bribes several years earlier, when he was the governor of Maryland. Agnew was forced to resign, so Nixon needed a new vice president. The 25th Amendment to the U.S. Constitution allowed Nixon to appoint a new vice president, subject to the approval of the U.S. Congress. President Nixon chose Gerald Ford because his 25 years of service in Congress had made him well-known and popular there. Congress easily confirmed Ford as the next vice president of the United States, and he took office on December 6, 1973.

When Ford took office as vice president, President Nixon was already involved in a scandal far worse than the one that had dragged Vice President Agnew down: the Watergate scandal (see above). Nixon submitted his resignation on the evening of August 8, 1974, and left office at noon on the next day. Vice President Ford took the oath of office and ascended to the Presidency on that same day, August 9, 1974. The Vietnam War, which had been winding down since the end of the Johnson Presidency in 1969, came to its final end under President Ford: on April 30, 1975, the last American troops left Saigon by helicopter, and South Vietnam fell to communism.

President Ford is best remembered for ending the misery of the Watergate scandal by granting Nixon a Presidential pardon for his crimes. Ford's supporters said that he pardoned Nixon to spare the United States the pain of putting a former President on trial; but his enemies said that he did it to save the Republican Party from further embarrassment. When the Presidential election of 1976 arrived, Ford's Republican Party was still trying to erase the stains of Watergate. Democratic Party candidate Jimmy Carter defeated President Ford, and Ford left office as the only person who ever served as President of the United States without having won any national election.

Other interesting facts about Gerald Ford:
- As a young man, Ford became an Eagle Scout and went on to play college football. He turned down offers to play professional football for both the Green Bay Packers and the Detroit Lions.
- Ford suffered from a rare medical condition that caused him to be left-handed while seated and right-handed while standing.
- Ford survived two botched assassination attempts, both of them by women.

Notable quotes from Gerald Ford:
- "There are no adequate substitutes for father, mother, and children bound together in a loving commitment to nurture and protect. No government, no matter how well-intentioned, can take the place of the family in the scheme of things."
- "I am acutely aware that you have not elected me as your President by your ballots, so I ask you to confirm me with your prayers."

Chapter 33

The USSR

WORLD HISTORY FOCUS

THE USSR AFTER STALIN
(See Chapter 20 for the USSR under Stalin)

The Death of Stalin

During the final months of World War II, the crafty USSR dictator Josef Stalin outmaneuvered his western Allies in their conferences at Tehran, Yalta and Potsdam (see Chapter 27). The West looked on helplessly as Stalin absorbed freedom-loving Eastern European nations like Poland and Czechoslovakia into his communist empire. The Western Betrayals of Eastern Europe, which had begun with British Prime Minister Neville Chamberlain's appeasement of Adolf Hitler before WW II (see Chapter 25), continued until all of Eastern Europe fell behind Stalin's "Iron Curtain" of strict, dictatorial communism.

Stalin and Mao Tse-tung together at Stalin's 70th birthday celebration

Stalin also promoted communism around the world. His Comintern trained the communists who fought Mao Tse-tung's communist revolution in China (see Chapter 22), then aided China and the communists of North Korea in the Korean War (see Chapter 29). As the successor to Vladimir Lenin, the great leader of Russia's own communist revolution, Stalin was the world's authority on communism. Communists in the USSR and China sought Stalin's approval for their every move; and if Stalin happened to disapprove, then they lived in constant fear of being denounced as "enemies of the people." Those whom Stalin disapproved usually faced either execution or a long stay in the Gulag prison system (see Chapter 20).

Near the end of the Korean War, Stalin's health failed. He suffered a stroke on March 1, 1953, and died on March 5. His successor as leader of the USSR was a former metal worker named Nikita Khrushchev.

INTERESTING INDIVIDUALS: Nikita Khrushchev (1894 – 1971)

Nikita Khrushchev was born near the Russia-Ukraine border in 1894. As a skilled metal worker, Khrushchev was involved in some of the many labor strikes that marked the last years of Tsar Nicholas II's reign (see Chapter 18). Through these strikes, Khrushchev became interested in communism; and in 1918, after the Bolshevik Revolution, he joined Vladimir Lenin's Bolshevik Party. Young Khrushchev became one of the Bolshevik/Communist Party's many "commissars," patriotic political operatives whose mission was to train the Russian people to think like good communists. In frequent political meetings all over the USSR, commissars like Khrushchev encouraged the Russian people to give up their possessions, join collective farms and sacrifice their own selfish desires for the good of the selfless, ideal communist society they would build in the USSR.

During the Stalin years (1924 - 1953), Khrushchev rose through the ranks of the Communist Party. He helped Stalin conduct his murderous Great Purge, which cleansed the Party of anyone whom Stalin denounced as an anti-communist "enemy of the people" (see Chapter 20). Like most communists, Khrushchev suffered little remorse over the executions of anti-communists at first, because he believed that those executions were necessary in order to scrub the USSR clean of the enemies of communism.

Later, however, Khrushchev began to believe that Stalin had gone too far. Khrushchev realized that Stalin had used the communist revolution as an excuse to murder his rivals for power and his personal enemies. He began to understand that Stalin's constant, arbitrary executions had made the USSR into a miserable place where everyone lived in constant fear, both of Stalin's secret police and of one's own neighbors. Whether one was a Communist Party official or an average citizen, life in the USSR was nearly unbearable under Stalin.

When Stalin died in 1953, Khrushchev was only one of several high officials in the Communist Party. Three years later, in early 1956, Khrushchev delivered a four-hour "Secret Speech" before the Party in which he revealed some of Stalin's many crimes. <u>He shocked the Communist Party by denouncing Stalin: he said that Stalin's reputation as a great communist leader had been a falsehood, and that what Stalin had truly been was a petulant and arbitrary dictator</u>. Khrushchev announced that he intended to "de-Stalinize" the USSR and lead his nation in a new direction. Khrushchev became the USSR's Premier, or highest official, two years later in 1958.

"De-Stalinization" meant fewer executions, fewer imprisonments and less torture for those who were denounced as "enemies of the people." It also meant a new emphasis on quality of life. Stalin had insisted that the modern conveniences of the West-- refrigerators, washing machines and so on-- were mere creature comforts for the weak, and that good communists didn't need such things. Khrushchev thought differently. He built pre-fabricated concrete apartment buildings called *khrushchyovkas* all over the USSR to house his people (see pictures). He tried to provide them with the things the people of the West had and elevate them out of their poverty. He allowed more of his people to visit nations outside the Iron Curtain, and he also allowed more outsiders to visit the USSR.

<u>Even though Khrushchev had denounced Stalin, he still believed in communism and hated capitalism</u>. To Khrushchev, the capitalists of the West were greedy people who cheated and mistreated poor laborers in order to make themselves rich. He never forgot his origins as a metal worker participating in labor strikes against the

tsars. He firmly believed that communism, in which everyone shared everything equally, was the best way for laborers like himself to get their fair share of the fruits of their labor and avoid being cheated by the rich. He wanted to prove to the world that communism was better than capitalism at providing for the needs of the poor. In a speech in late 1956, Khrushchev warned the West that communism would "bury" capitalism by building a selfless communist society that was far superior to the West's selfish capitalist society.

Khrushchev was the United States' most bitter Cold War opponent. He tried to force the western Allies out of West

Berlin again and again; and when he failed, he built the Berlin Wall to prevent his best young minds from escaping communism (see Chapter 31). During the nuclear arms race, when the United States placed medium-range nuclear missiles in Europe, Khrushchev responded by placing missiles of his own in Cuba, touching off the Cuban Missile Crisis (see Chapter 31). But Khrushchev understood the folly of nuclear war, and helped end the Cuban Missile Crisis by agreeing to withdraw his missiles. The USA and the USSR probably never came closer to nuclear war than they did during the thirteen days of the Cuban Missile Crisis from October 14 - 27, 1962.

Not everyone in the Communist Party agreed with Khrushchev's new, slightly more lenient version of communism. There remained plenty of party members who liked Stalin's ideas better than Khrushchev's, and wanted to return to strict Stalinist communism, both at home and abroad. <u>These Stalinist "hardliners" still wanted to destroy capitalism, using nuclear weapons if necessary, and spread their communist revolution all over the world</u>. To the hardliners, Khrushchev's decision to remove the USSR's nuclear missiles from Cuba at the end of the Cuban Missile Crisis made him look weak.

In 1964, Stalinist hardliners in the Communist Party formed a plan to overthrow Khrushchev and return to Stalinism. Premier Khrushchev could have resisted their *coup d'etat*; but instead, he simply agreed to step down. However, he did remind his enemies that if they had planned such a *coup* under their hero Stalin, they would certainly have been executed. It was only because of their new freedoms under Khrushchev, he said, that his enemies were free to plot against him.

Khrushchev voluntarily stepped down from his position as premier on October 14, 1964. He lived on a pension for the rest of his life, and died of a heart attack on September 11, 1971.

The Hungarian Revolution

Hungary became part of the Communist Bloc soon after World War II; its western border formed part of the Iron Curtain that hung between the communist East and the free West. Soon after Premier Nikita Khrushchev denounced Stalin in 1956, Hungary denounced Stalin as well. On October 23, 1956, the people of Hungary began a Hungarian Revolution against their USSR-controlled government. They tore down a huge statue of Stalin in their capital, Budapest, and announced that they were forming a new government-- a government that would grant them the freedoms that Stalin had denied them (see picture).

The USSR decided that the Hungarians had gone too far. Khrushchev may have denounced Stalin, but he never denounced communism, or stopped believing that communism was the best way for the workers of the world to receive fair treatment. Furthermore, the USSR could not allow Hungary to become free: a free Hungary, sitting in the midst of the Communist Bloc, would have been like a far larger version of free West Berlin, sitting in the midst of communist East Germany-- another unwanted thorn in the paw of the Russian bear.

Khrushchev sent USSR troops into Hungary to defeat the rebellion, and the Hungarian Revolution was over by November 10, 1956. Hungary remained part of the Communist Bloc until the Revolutions of 1989 (see below).

FASCINATING FACTS: The Kitchen Debate

In 1959, the US and the USSR participated in an exchange program designed to promote understanding and good feelings between their two nations. As part of this exchange program, the USSR built an exhibit in a

New York City park to demonstrate life in the USSR, and the US built an exhibit in Moscow Park to demonstrate life in the US. With the Cold War in full swing, neither side could resist using its exhibit to try to prove that its way of life was better than its enemy's.

Part of the American National Exhibition was a complete model home that was supposedly typical of the sort of home an American factory worker could afford to buy. This model home included a kitchen that was full of modern appliances, including an automatic dishwasher and an electric juice maker. On the night before the exhibit opened, Vice President Nixon and Premier Khrushchev took a tour of the model home. Nixon pointed out all of the kitchen's modern conveniences to Khrushchev and explained how they made life easier for American housewives.

Nixon's attitude offended Khrushchev. Khrushchev scoffed at the kitchen's unnecessary appliances, and asked sarcastically whether Americans also needed appliances to place food in their mouths and shove it down their throats for them. Khrushchev accused Nixon of trying to dazzle the people of the USSR with all of these modern conveniences, but insisted that they wouldn't be dazzled: the new *Khruschyovka* apartments the USSR was building, he said, were built to last longer than American homes, and were just as convenient.

These were the opening remarks of the Kitchen Debate, a testy argument between Nixon and Khrushchev on the merits of communism versus capitalism. Nixon replied to Khrushchev that he wasn't trying to "dazzle" anyone, but only to demonstrate that Americans had the freedom to choose what sort of home they wanted. Americans, Nixon said, weren't all required to live in identical apartments designed by a communist central committee. Khrushchev fired back that at least in the USSR every citizen had a home-- while in America, the homeless poor slept in the streets. Khrushchev criticized the American exhibit for being shoddy and incomplete, and said that the USSR would catch up to the US and surpass it within a few years. Nixon responded that Khrushchev shouldn't be so afraid of allowing his people to see new ideas. The two were still bickering as they left the kitchen.

The Chinese-Soviet Split

China's Premier, Mao Tse-tung, was no fan of Khrushchev. When Khrushchev denounced Stalin, Mao believed that he was denouncing strict communism as well.

Khrushchev angered Mao further when he backed down at the end of the Cuban Missile Crisis. Mao was not satisfied merely to see communism take over Asia-- he wanted to see communist revolutions all over the world. He wanted to attack capitalists everywhere; and he was sufficiently insane that he did not fear even a nuclear war. When Khrushchev settled for peaceful co-existence with the West instead of war with the West, Mao turned against him.

From the beginning of Khrushchev's Premiership in 1958 through the breakup of the USSR in 1991, China and the USSR were no longer allies. During the late 1960s, the USSR built and maintained a huge army on its border with China. The two nations nearly went to war in 1969, but both backed down before that could happen. China continued to resist the USSR's inferior brand of communism even after Khrushchev's forced retirement, in places like Cambodia (1979 - 1991) and Afghanistan (1979 - 1989).

The Prague Spring and the USSR's Invasion of Czechoslovakia

Like Hungary, Czechoslovakia formed part of the Iron Curtain border between the free West and the communist East. In early 1968, a Czechoslovakian leader named Alexander Dubcek tried to reform USSR-controlled Czechoslovakia in some of the same ways in which Khrushchev had tried to reform the USSR. Dubcek wanted to allow his people Western-style freedoms like freedom of speech, freedom of the press and the freedom to travel beyond the Iron Curtain. Dubcek named his reform program the "Prague Spring" after Czechoslovakia's capital city, Prague.

Khrushchev's successor, Leonid Brezhnev, would have none of it. On August 21, 1968, the USSR and several of its communist bloc allies invaded Czechoslovakia and took over its government.

Czechoslovakia offered little resistance to Brezhnev's 200,000-strong invasion force. Brezhnev repealed Dubcek's reforms, restored strict Stalinist communism and put an end to the Prague Spring.

Officers of the Polish army tank regiment – Prague Spring 1968

INTERESTING INDIVIDUALS: Leonid Brezhnev (1906-1982)

Khrushchev's successor, Leonid Brezhnev, believed that Khrushchev's anti-Stalinist reforms went too far and allowed too many freedoms. Brezhnev would lead the USSR in the opposite direction, back toward the harsh, strict communism of Stalin.

At the end of World War II, Leonid Brezhnev was a major general in the USSR's Red Army. Brezhnev won a place on the Communist Party's Central Committee in 1952 with help from Khrushchev, and began his career in politics as one of Khrushchev's biggest supporters. Later, however, Brezhnev began to agree with those who said that Khrushchev's brand of communism was too soft. He wanted to get the communist revolution back on track by returning to the strict rules of the Stalin years. Brezhnev helped organize the *coup d'etat* that deposed Khrushchev in 1964, and became General Secretary of the USSR's Communist Party in that same year.

Brezhnev insisted on strict, Stalin-style communism; he allowed neither freedom of speech nor any other Western-style freedoms. When Czechoslovakia tried to allow Western-style freedoms in its Prague Spring, Brezhnev invaded Czechoslovakia and restored a strict communist government there. He justified this invasion with the "Brezhnev Doctrine," a policy which said that the USSR had a right to intervene whenever outsiders tried to interfere inside communist nations. Brezhnev also used the Brezhnev Doctrine to justify the 1979 - 1989 Soviet War in Afghanistan (see below), claiming that outsiders were trying to interfere with Afghanistan's communist revolution.

Brezhnev was part of a group of aging communist leaders who desperately wanted to see communism defeat capitalism within their lifetimes. Brezhnev and his allies didn't want to co-exist with the capitalist West, as Khrushchev seemed willing to do; instead, they wanted to overwhelm and defeat the West. Throughout Brezhnev's time in office, he continued to provide weapons and support for communist revolutions like the ones in Vietnam and Afghanistan. He also prepared the USSR for war against the West by building nuclear missiles, weapons and armies until his military was the most fearsome on earth.

In the process of building his military, however, Brezhnev neglected the rest of his economy. During the Brezhnev years, the USSR fell behind the West in nearly every area except nuclear missiles and other weapons. The USSR could build the world's most advanced tanks, warplanes and nuclear missiles, but it still couldn't raise enough food to feed all of its people. Brezhnev sacrificed the needs of his people for the needs of his military-- he built too many guns, and made not enough butter. Despite all of Brezhnev's successes in the space race and the nuclear arms race, he left his people as poor as ever. His time in office became known as the "**Era of Stagnation**."

During the 1970s, Brezhnev damaged his health by developing addictions to sleeping pills, alcohol and cigarettes. When he died of a heart attack on November 10, 1982, the USSR honored its long-time leader with one of the largest funerals in world history.

The Soviet War in Afghanistan

In 1978, the communist party of Afghanistan led a revolution against Afghanistan's republican government. That government had been founded in 1973, when Afghanistan's prime minister overthrew the last

Barakzai Dynasty shah (see Chapter 3). The communists overthrew the republican government and formed the new Democratic Republic of Afghanistan as a communist state.

As soon as the communists took control of Afghanistan's government, they began to do what communists always did:

They began a program of "land reforms" in which they confiscated land from the wealthy and "redistributed" it to the poor; and they began teaching atheistic communism in the place of religion.

Their goal, as always, was to eliminate Afghanistan's old, backward traditions and replace them with the new traditions of socialism and communism. Community property, government ownership of businesses and atheism were the new rules in Afghanistan.

However, Afghanistan was different from other nations where communism had taken root in one important way: Afghanistan was a nation of Muslims.

Afghanistan's Muslims believed in Islam with all of their hearts, and they didn't appreciate the communist party's attempts to replace their religious faith with faith in communism. When the Afghanis began to protest against their new communist government, the communists responded to their protests as communists always did: by arresting, torturing and executing anti-communist rebels by the thousands and even tens of thousands.

In 1979, the USSR began sending weapons and troops into Afghanistan to support the communist government against the anti-communist rebels.

Afghanistan's anti-communist rebels became known as *mujahideen*, which means "warriors of the *jihad* (holy struggle)." Their rebellion against communism was the beginning of the Soviet War in Afghanistan.

The anti-communist United States began sending weapons and supplies to support the *mujahideen* in their struggle against communism.

An Afghan holding a Soviet-built surface to air missile

Surprisingly, the expensive and highly trained armies of the USSR had a great deal of trouble with the under-funded and untrained *mujahideen*. The caves and mountains of Afghanistan gave the *mujahideen* plenty of places to hide; while the U.S. and other nations supplied the *mujahideen* with weapons and kept them from starving. Even when the USSR sent more than 100,000 troops to Afghanistan in the mid-1980s, they simply could not put a stop to the rebellion of the *mujahideen*.

During the late 1980s, the USSR began to have problems that were far more important than a failing communist revolution in Afghanistan. When the Revolutions of 1989 threatened to dissolve the entire Communist Bloc (see below), the USSR began withdrawing its troops from Afghanistan and bringing them home. The last USSR troops left Afghanistan in 1989, shortly before East Germany tore down the Berlin Wall. The *mujahideen* had won, and Afghanistan was free to rebuild its Islamic government.

FASCINATING FACTS: The Boycott of the 1980 Moscow Summer Olympics

The United States and about 60 other nations protested the USSR's invasion of Afghanistan by refusing to participate in the 1980 Summer Olympics, which were to be held in the USSR's capital city of Moscow. The boycott was hard on these nations' athletes, who had trained for the Olympic Games for at least four years and might never have another chance to win an Olympic medal. Despite the boycott, the Olympic Games in Moscow went on; about 80 nations participated (the usual number of participating nations at the time was around 120).

Each boycotting nation had to decide how far to carry its protest:

1. Some nations refused to allow their athletes to participate at all. 29 of these nations participated in a special Olympic Boycott Games in Philadelphia instead.
2. Some nations supported the boycott, but allowed their athletes to compete if they chose to.
3. Other nations allowed their athletes to compete, but did not allow them to use their national flags. Most of these athletes appeared under the five-ringed Olympic flag instead of their national flags.

Andropov and Chernenko

Two more Stalinist general secretaries followed Brezhnev: Yuri Andropov and Konstantin Chernenko. Andropov died after only fifteen months in office, and Chernenko died after only thirteen months in office.

In 1983, while Andropov was general secretary, the U.S. and the USSR came close to war yet again. The threat of war came because of a realistic military training exercise that the U.S. and its allies conducted all over Western Europe. The exercise was codenamed "Able Archer," and it was designed to simulate all of the movements and steps the West would take if it ever went to war with the USSR. Such training was not unusual; peacetime armies spend much of their time conducting training exercises that mimic real wars. However, Able Archer was so large and realistic that the USSR wondered if this supposed "exercise" might really be a ruse (trick) to conceal troop movements leading up to a real invasion. The threat of war ended when the Able Archer exercise ended in late 1983.

Andropov's time as general secretary is also remembered for the letters he exchanged with a young American girl named Samantha Smith.

AMAZING AMERICANS: Samantha Smith (1972 – 1985)

Americans were concerned when the USSR chose Yuri Andropov to succeed Leonid Brezhnev. Andropov was Stalinist and a former member of the KGB, the USSR's infamous security and secret police organization. Americans expected Andropov to be a hardnosed, America-hating warmonger. Few suspected that the new general secretary's battle-hardened heart might be softened by a letter from a ten-year-old girl.

Samantha Smith of Maine was ten years old in 1982, when she wrote General Secretary Andropov a short letter asking him what he would do to avoid a nuclear war. Samantha asked Andropov why he wanted to conquer the world, and told him that "God made the world for us to live together in peace and not to fight."

Almost six months later, Samantha finally received Andropov's response. The General Secretary explained to her that the USSR had suffered terribly in the last Great War, World War II; and he reminded her that her country and the USSR had been allies in that war against Germany, a nation that had truly sought to conquer the world. Andropov told Samantha that, unlike Hitler's Germany, the USSR wanted "peace for ourselves and for all peoples of the planet. For our children and for you, Samantha." Then he invited her to visit him in the USSR that summer.

She did. In the summer of 1983, Samantha and her parents flew to the USSR, where they saw the best of everything the struggling nation had to offer. They attended a well-funded youth camp on the Crimean Peninsula and met several well-known Soviets. Samantha had a great time at the camp, and remarked that the

Soviets were "just like us." One Soviet whom Samantha did not meet was Yuri Andropov: his health was already failing, and he would die during the following winter.

Tragically, Samantha's own death followed Andropov's by only about a year and a half. Samantha was flying to her home in Maine on August 25, 1985 when the small passenger plane in which she was riding crashed short of its runway, killing Samantha, her father and six others on board. Samantha was 13.

Some Americans believed that Andropov's kindness to Samantha Smith was only more communist propaganda, designed to trick Americans into believing that it was America's leaders, not the USSR's, who wanted war. They reminded Americans of the terrible things Andropov and men like him had done-- how he had spied on his own people, how he had tortured and executed Stalin's political enemies, and how he continued to deny his own people basic human rights like freedom of speech and freedom of religion. Even so, the Samantha Smith episode was at least a small sign that the USSR was interested in peace.

Further signs of peace came with the arrival of the USSR's next general secretary, Mikhail Gorbachev.

INTERESTING INDIVIDUALS: Mikhail Gorbachev (1931 –)

When Stalinist hardliners like Andropov and Chernenko kept dying, the USSR's Communist Party decided to promote a much younger man. Mikhail Gorbachev was only 54 years old when the Communist Party elected him General Secretary in 1985, and he was the first General Secretary who had been born after the Bolsheviks' October Revolution in 1917.

Gorbachev's communism was less strict than that of Brezhnev, Andropov and Chernenko. He believed in communism, but he was more aware of his nation's shortcomings than his predecessors had been. Gorbachev wanted to reverse the hard times of the Brezhnev "Era of Stagnation": He wanted to reduce military spending, and instead concentrate on building a better government and better lives for his people. Gorbachev explained his reforms with two Russian words:

1. *Perestroika* ("restructuring"): Under *perestroika*, Gorbachev relaxed some of the USSR's strict rules about government ownership of businesses. He allowed private businessmen to own certain types of businesses, and to keep more of the money they earned when their businesses did well.
2. *Glasnost* ("openness"): Under *glasnost*, Gorbachev allowed the people of the USSR to speak more freely about their history and their government, without fear of ending up in the Gulag prison system.

Gorbachev didn't know what sort of monster he had let off the chain when he began to promote freedom of speech. Under Gorbachev and *glasnost*, the empire that had taken the USSR decades to build began to fall apart, piece by piece, within a few short months in 1989:

- **Poland, Hungary, Czechoslovakia** and other Communist Bloc nations declared their independence and opened the borders that had formed the Iron Curtain between the free West and the communist East.
- **East Germany** opened the gates of the Berlin Wall, and soon tore down the wall itself. **East Germany and West Germany reunited**.
- The Soviet Socialist Republics (SSRs) that made up the USSR began to declare independence.

Gorbachev found himself presiding over the demise of the Soviet Empire. When the USSR's largest SSR, Russia, began ignoring Gorbachev's commands, the USSR became irrelevant. Gorbachev resigned his office and dissolved the USSR in December 1991 (see below).

FASCINATING FACTS: Glasnost

The First Amendment to the U.S. Constitution guarantees U.S. citizens freedom of religion, freedom of speech and freedom of the press, as well as certain rights:

"Congress shall make no law respecting an establishment of religion, or prohibiting the free exercise thereof; or abridging the freedom of speech, or of the press; or the right of the people peaceably to assemble, and to petition the Government for a redress of grievances."

Under communism, citizens of the USSR possessed none of these freedoms or rights-- that is, until General Secretary Gorbachev began his policy of *glasnost*, "openness." *Glasnost* had an enormous effect on life in the USSR: Suddenly, the Soviets were more free to speak their minds than they had been since Tsar Ivan the Terrible launched Russia's first secret police force, the *oprichniki*, over 400 years before. Under glasnost, Gorbachev

1. Released political prisoners;
2. Allowed the people of the USSR more contact with the outside world through newspapers, radio broadcasts and visitors; and
3. Allowed honest discussion of the miseries of life under Stalin.

For decades, hard-line Stalinist leaders had relied on falsehoods to keep their people safely in the fold of communism. As soon as the Soviet people were free to tell the truth to one another, those falsehoods began to collapse. When the truth about communism was revealed, two things quickly became clear:

1. That socialism/communism was not the perfect system of government that the Stalinists had always claimed it was; and
2. That the leaders of the Communist Party had never been the selfless servants of the people that they claimed to be.

Glasnost was one of several things that helped unravel the Communist Bloc and the USSR in the late 1980s. That unraveling happened in just the way the secretive Stalinists had feared: Freedom of speech started a small tear in the fabric of the Iron Curtain; and before they could stitch the tear up, freedom of speech rent the entire Iron Curtain asunder.

FASCINATING FACTS: President Reagan at the Berlin Wall's Brandenburg Gate

A Prussian king built the grand Brandenburg Gate in the 1780s to mark one of the main entrances to the old city of Berlin. When Premier Nikita Khrushchev began building the Berlin Wall in 1961, he closed the Brandenburg Gate and made it part of the Berlin Wall. Both Gate and Wall would remain closed for 28 years. As the most recognizable part of the Berlin Wall, the Brandenburg Gate became an important symbol of the Cold War.

U.S. President Ronald Reagan took advantage of that symbolism on June 12, 1987, when he traveled to West Berlin to deliver a speech in front of the Brandenburg Gate. In his speech, Reagan used the contrast between prosperous West Berlin and floundering East Berlin to make a point: that freedom led to prosperity, while communism led to poverty. He pointed out that despite its advanced nuclear weapons arsenal, the USSR was still unable to produce enough food to feed all of its people. He acknowledged the USSR's new "openness" under General Secretary Gorbachev, but insisted that it didn't go far enough:

"We welcome change and openness, for we believe that freedom and security go together, that the advance of human liberty can only strengthen the cause of world peace. There is one sign the Soviets can make that would be unmistakable, that would advance dramatically the cause of freedom and peace. General Secretary Gorbachev, if you seek peace, if you seek prosperity for the Soviet Union and Eastern Europe, and if you seek liberalization, come here to this gate. Mr. Gorbachev, open this gate. Mr. Gorbachev, tear down this wall!"

The Revolutions of 1989

Although *perestroika* and *glasnost* were big changes for the USSR, they did little to change the fact that the economy Brezhnev had built was a wreck. The costs of maintaining Brezhnev's large military were simply too high for Gorbachev's struggling economy.

In 1988, General Secretary Gorbachev tried to reduce those military costs by withdrawing the USSR's troops from its "satellite" nations in the Communist Bloc of nations.

FASCINATING FACTS: The Sinatra Doctrine

By withdrawing his troops from the Communist Bloc, Gorbachev was repealing the Brezhnev Doctrine, which the USSR had used since 1968 to justify its strict control of the Communist Bloc. In the Brezhnev Doctrine's place, Gorbachev set up the "Sinatra Doctrine," which was jokingly named for the Frank Sinatra song "My Way": under the Sinatra Doctrine, the USSR would allow its former satellites to have their own way and make their own decisions about what type of government they should have.

Gorbachev's troop withdrawals and the so-called "Sinatra Doctrine" were the beginning of the end for the Communist Bloc. As soon as those satellite nations got the chance, they stopped obeying the USSR's strict communist rules. Nations like Hungary and Czechoslovakia, which had proven their readiness to rebel against the USSR in the past, began opening their Iron Curtain borders in 1989. People began to travel more freely between the West and the East, and the USSR did little to stop them.

One by one, **all seven of the former Communist Bloc nations** replaced their communist governments with freely elected ones. All of the Revolutions of 1989 except Romania's were peaceful, involving nothing more violent than street protests against communist governments that were no longer welcome. In all of these nations, elections replaced communist governments with freely elected governments in 1989 - 1990.

The Fall of the Berlin Wall

When the Iron Curtain began to come down in other parts of Eastern Europe, the Berlin Wall that isolated West Berlin from East Berlin and East Germany no longer made sense. As East Germany's neighbors began to open their borders, East Germany finally opened its border as well:

1. *Hungary*: First, Hungary opened its border with free Austria. With Hungary's border open, East Germans could escape to the West by traveling through Czechoslovakia and Hungary. East Germany responded by forbidding its citizens to travel to its former communist ally Hungary.

2. *Czechoslovakia*: Next, Czechoslovakia opened its border with free Austria. With Czechoslovakia's border open, East Germans could again escape to the West by traveling through Czechoslovakia. East Germany was forced to close its border with Czechoslovakia.

3. *East Germany*: East Germans began the "Monday Demonstrations," a series of street protests against the unfair laws that took away their freedom to travel. These demonstrations happened every Monday for ten weeks. Finally, on Thursday November 9, 1989, East Germany's communist government gave in to the protesters and announced its decision to open the gates of the Berlin Wall-- without telling its gate guards in advance, and without making any plans for what might happen next.

On November 9, 1989, East Germans listening to their radios and televisions heard their government announce that it would open the Berlin Wall's gates. Thousands of East Germans gathered at the Berlin Wall and demanded to be allowed to pass through its gates, just as other Eastern Europeans were being allowed to pass borders all along the rest of the wavering Iron Curtain. The overwhelmed guards had no orders to open the gates, and no way to refuse so many people at once; so they called their superior officers and waited nervously on telephones while the crowds at the gates continued to grow larger. Finally, at around 10:45 that evening, they opened the gates.

The guards' change in attitude was remarkable: A few hours before, merely to stand inside the lifeless, sandy "no man's land" on the East German side of the wall had meant certain death. Now, suddenly, East Germans were standing on top of the wall and even climbing down on the West German side. The stern rules that had been imposed by the USSR no longer applied, and the people of East Germany began to make their own rules. The Sinatra Doctrine was in full effect: East Germans began doing things "My Way" for the first time since the end of World War II in 1945.

Over the weeks and months that followed, the city of Berlin tore down and destroyed the wall that had sundered its two halves for 38 years. Only a few sections of the old wall remained as reminders of the city's dark past. East Germany and West Germany formally reunited in 1991.

The Romanian Revolution of 1989

Only the most rigidly communist state in the Communist Bloc, Romania, needed a violent revolution in order to overthrow its communist government. In November 1989, Romania's communist dictator, Nikolai Ceausescu (see picture), won reelection for another five years and announced that he intended to ignore the revolutions that were going on in the other Communist Bloc nations. Romanians protested against Ceausescu with loud street demonstrations in Bucharest, Romania's capital that began on December 16, 1989.

At first, Romania's military supported Ceausescu by firing into the crowds of people protesting in the streets. At least several hundred Romanians died, and many more were injured. However, on December 22, 1989, the military turned against Ceausescu, and he barely managed to escape by fleeing Bucharest in a helicopter. The military caught up with Ceausescu by grounding all flights in Romanian airspace. Romania executed its former dictator on Christmas Day, December 25, 1989.

These are the former USSR satellite states that became Independent after the Revolutions of 1989:

Albania	Hungary	Bulgaria	Poland
Czechoslovakia	Romania	East Germany	

Russia Declares Independence from the USSR

The USSR's economic problems did not end with the deaths of hard-line communists Brezhnev, Andropov and Chernenko, nor did they end when Gorbachev introduced *perestroika* and *glasnost*. Even under the more lenient Gorbachev, the USSR still had real trouble producing and distributing enough food to feed its people. USSR citizens grew used to waiting in long lines for chances to buy bread and other staple foods.

By 1990, the people of Russia had grown tired of communism's inability to supply even their most basic needs.

On June 12, 1990, Russia declared its independence from the USSR.

Russia's new president, Boris Yeltsin, resigned from the USSR's Communist Party on that same day-- Yeltsin had given up on communism. After 73 years under communism, Yeltsin planned to restore Russia's prosperity by returning Russia to communism's hated rival: capitalism. Almost immediately, Yeltsin and Russia began ignoring the USSR's strict rules against private ownership of businesses. Yeltsin would allow private businessmen to work for themselves. He believed that when private businesses were allowed to keep more of what they earned, they would work harder to refill the shelves of Russia's grocery stores.

Yeltsin's moves shocked the Communist Party of the USSR, because to lose control of Russia was to lose control of the USSR itself. In 1991, a group of hard-line communists who still believed in Stalinism made one last attempt to bind the disintegrating USSR back together.

FASCINATING FACTS: The August Coup Attempt of 1991

The Communist Party's few remaining hard-line Stalinists refused to let the USSR go without a fight. In August 1991, eight high Communist Party officials-- later known as the "Gang of Eight"-- formed a plan to convince Gorbachev to declare a state of emergency and reunite the USSR. Their plan became more urgent when their secret police overheard a conversation in which Gorbachev discussed removing the Gang of Eight from their high positions in the Communist Party.

Instead of waiting for Gorbachev to remove them, the Gang of Eight decided to act. In August 1991, when Gorbachev traveled to the Crimean Peninsula for a two-week vacation, the Gang of Eight confronted him and demanded that he declare a state of emergency and "restore order" to the USSR, reuniting it by force if necessary. When Gorbachev refused, they placed him under house arrest inside his own *dacha*, or vacation home. They also cut his telephone lines so that he couldn't communicate with his government.

With the unwilling Gorbachev out of the way, the Gang of Eight traveled to Moscow and declared a state of emergency themselves. Claiming that Gorbachev was ill, they took control of his government and closed down Russia's new free press. USSR tanks and troops rolled into Moscow and surrounded the White House, the seat of Russia's parliament and the symbol of Russia's independence from the USSR. As soon as the Gang of Eight gave the order, the military was prepared to attack the White House and anyone else who resisted the Gang of Eight's August Coup Attempt against Gorbachev.

But the Gang of Eight didn't account for Russia's new president, Boris Yeltsin. When Yeltsin arrived in Moscow on August 19, he announced to the public that the Gang of Eight's takeover was an illegal attempt to overthrow General Secretary Gorbachev. He begged the military not to support the Gang of Eight. Then he dared the military to attack him by climbing onto one of the tanks surrounding the White House and demanding to hear from Gorbachev himself. Gorbachev, of course, couldn't speak for himself because the Gang of Eight had imprisoned him in the Crimea.

When Yeltsin made his demands, the Russian military couldn't decide what it should do: some of its officers supported the Gang of Eight, and some supported Yeltsin. The Gang of Eight wanted to attack the White House anyway; but the few military officers who still supported them refused to try. When Gorbachev's communications were restored, he arrested the Gang of Eight and removed them from office.

The August Coup Attempt ended on August 22, 1991 with the arrests of the Gang of Eight. The entire

Boris Yeltsin on top of a military tank

episode was extremely embarrassing for Gorbachev, for two reasons: (1) because the Gang of Eight had succeeded in imprisoning him, rendering him powerless compared to Yeltsin; and (2) because the members of the Gang of Eight all worked for Gorbachev. Two days after the end of the August Coup Attempt, Gorbachev resigned his post as General Secretary of the Communist Party.

The Belavezha Accords and the Commonwealth of Independent States

The August Coup Attempt reminded every USSR citizen of the worst parts of life under Stalinist communism: the secret police who watched their every move, the lies that their government officials constantly told them, and the violence their government used to enforce its will. Few wanted to return to that.

In late 1991, leaders from three former SSRs met at a *dacha* (resort) in Belavezha Forest to discuss the end of the USSR. In the **Belavezha Accords**, signed on December 8, 1991, Russia, Belarus and Ukraine agreed to dissolve the USSR and form a new international organization known as the Commonwealth of Independent States (CIS). The CIS was not a central government like the USSR; instead, it was more like the Commonwealth of Nations, the loose association formed by Britain's former colonies. The members of the CIS agreed to work together, but remained fully independent.

At first, former General Secretary Gorbachev challenged the three former SSRs' legal right to dissolve the USSR. Then on December 21, eight more SSRs joined the CIS by signing a new agreement known as the Alma-Ata Protocol. Finally, Gorbachev accepted the SSRs' decision and resigned his office, formally dissolving the USSR on December 26, 1991.

The former USSR's largest SSR, Russia, took over most of the former USSR's responsibilities: its important position in the United Nations (including its veto power on the UN Security Council), its nuclear weapons and its international debts. Belarus, Ukraine and Kazakhstan transferred all of their nuclear weapons to Russia by 1995, becoming non-nuclear weapons states. As of 2010, Russia controls all of the former USSR's nuclear weapons.

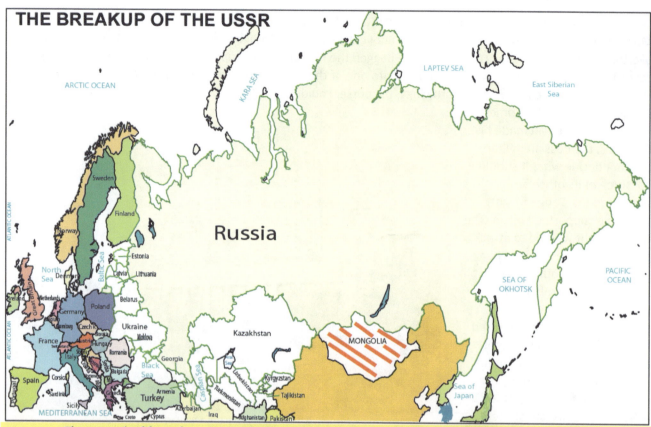

These are the fifteen former SSRs that became independent when the USSR dissolved in late 1991:

Russia	Ukraine	Lithuania	Belarus
Latvia	Kazakhstan	Estonia	Azerbaijan
Georgia	Tajikistan	Moldova	Kyrgyzstan
Armenia	Turkmenistan	Uzbekistan	

FASCINATING FACTS: Nuclear Arms Reduction Treaties

Over the decades, the members of the "nuclear club" of nuclear-weapons-armed nations have negotiated more than a dozen treaties designed to limit the number of nuclear weapons in the world. Nuclear arms reduction treaties can have several benefits:

- They can save nations the money that they would otherwise have spent developing and building new nuclear weapons, trying to keep up with their enemies;
- They can limit the amount of death and destruction that would happen if a nuclear war ever broke out;
- They can protect the earth's environment from the permanent damage a nuclear war might cause; and
- They can help enemies avoid war and learn to trust one another.

Unfortunately, nuclear arms reduction treaties also have their drawbacks:

- Nations that sign such treaties must constantly watch to be sure that their enemies aren't deceiving them by only pretending to honor the promises that they have made in the treaties; and
- They can actually make nuclear war more likely, not less likely: If an aggressive nation believes that a treaty has made its enemy weaker, it might try to take advantage of that weakness by attacking.

Here are several important nuclear arms reduction treaties from the Cold War years and beyond:

1. **Antarctic Treaty (1959):** Among other things, the Antarctic Treaty banned stationing or testing any nuclear weapons on the continent of Antarctica. It also banned using Antarctica as a place to dispose of nuclear waste.
2. **Direct Communications Agreement, aka the "Hotline" Agreement (1963):** In the "Hotline" Agreement, the US and the USSR agreed to maintain direct lines of communication between the White House and the Kremlin. With the hotline in place, the President of the United States and the General Secretary of the USSR were never more than a phone call away from each other. The two heads of state could use their hotline to avoid misunderstandings that might lead to a nuclear war.
3. **Limited Test Ban Treaty (1963):** The Limited Test Ban Treaty banned test explosions of nuclear weapons everywhere except underground. The treaty's purpose was to keep frequent nuclear explosions from damaging the environment and overloading the earth's atmosphere with radioactive carbon-14.
4. **Outer Space Treaty (1967):** The Outer Space Treaty banned stationing nuclear weapons in earth orbit, on the moon or anywhere else in space.
5. **Latin America Nuclear Free Zone Treaty (1968):** This treaty banned building, testing or stationing nuclear weapons anywhere in Latin America (Neither Argentina nor Cuba agreed to this treaty).
6. **Nuclear Non-Proliferation Treaty (1970):** In this treaty, nuclear-armed nations agreed not to make the threat of nuclear war worse by sharing nuclear weapons technology with other nations that didn't already have it. These nations also agreed to work toward the goal of reducing the number of nuclear weapons in the world, but the treaty didn't set any specific goals for nuclear arms reductions.

President Kennedy signing the Limited Test Ban Treaty

7. **The Seabed Arms Control Treaty (1972):** The Seabed Arms Control Treaty banned stationing nuclear weapons on the ocean floor anywhere outside a nation's 12-mile coastal border zone.
8. **The Strategic Arms Limitation Treaty, aka SALT 1 (1972):** For five years, from 1972 - 1977, the US and the USSR agreed not to add any more strategic (long-range) nuclear missiles to their already enormous arsenals. Under SALT 1, neither nation was allowed to build any new ground-based long-range nuclear missile silos to its arsenal; and if either nation wanted to add a submarine-launched long-range missile to its arsenal, it had to eliminate a ground-based missile first. The US and the USSR also negotiated a second SALT treaty, SALT 2, in 1979. However, SALT 2 never went into effect because after the USSR invaded Afghanistan in 1979, the US refused to ratify SALT 2.
9. **The Anti-Ballistic Missile Treaty, aka ABM Treaty (1972):** This treaty banned the creation of ground-based missile defense systems that could shoot an attacker's nuclear missiles out of the sky. It was designed to prevent one nation from gaining an advantage over the other in the nuclear arms race. The ABM Treaty preserved the deterrent of Mutually Assured Destruction (MAD; a "deterrent" is a reason not to do something). <u>As long as neither side could defend itself from its enemy's missiles, then neither could launch a nuclear first strike, because if either one did, then the other would retaliate and both would be destroyed</u>. However, if missile defense systems worked, they would take away the deterrent of MAD: if one side could protect itself from its enemy's missiles, then it might feel safe enough to launch a nuclear first strike without fear of retaliation. Therefore, by the twisted logic of MAD, it was better for neither side to have missile defense systems so that neither would feel safe from attack. Under the ABM Treaty, each nation was allowed just two ground-based missile defense systems: one to protect its capital, and another to protect some of its own nuclear missiles from a first strike.

10. **Intermediate-Range Nuclear Forces Treaty, aka INF Treaty (1988):** The INF Treaty eliminated nuclear missiles with ranges between 500 and 3,500 miles. <u>This treaty was particularly important because it was the first treaty in which both sides agreed to destroy existing nuclear weapons, not just to place limits on the creation of new ones.</u> As President Ronald Reagan signed the INF treaty for the US, he said that the US would "trust, but verify"-- by which he meant that the US would insist on inspecting every USSR missile as it was destroyed to be sure the USSR was really destroying nuclear missiles, not just pretending to do so. By 1991, the US and the USSR had destroyed a total of more than 2,600 tactical (intermediate range) nuclear missiles under the terms of the INF Treaty.

Reagan and Gorbachev signing the INF Treaty

11. **Strategic Arms Reduction Treaty, aka START (1994):** The START treaty placed limits on the number of strategic (long-range) nuclear missiles and bombers each nation could have. The US and the USSR signed the first START treaty in 1991; but by the time it was ratified in 1994, the USSR had dissolved, so Russia took the USSR's place in the treaty. <u>Like the INF Treaty, the START treaty actually eliminated existing nuclear weapons, instead of just limiting the creation of new ones.</u>

Communist Flags

The USSR was the home of the world's first successful communist revolution. Lenin and Stalin inspired and sponsored communist revolutions in several other nations, including China, North Korea, Vietnam and Angola (Africa). Those nations honored their communist connections by creating flags similar to the USSR's.

This was the USSR's flag from 1923 - 1991. The red field symbolized the blood of the revolutionaries who gave their lives for the communist revolution. The hammer symbolized the industrial workers, and sickle symbolized the farmers. The star at the top symbolized the Communist Party, which was supposed to be a union of those workers and farmers.	
This is the flag of the People's Republic of China, which first flew in Beijing's Tiananmen Square on October 1, 1949. The red field symbolizes the communist revolution. The large star represents the Communist Party of China, and the smaller stars represent the Chinese people.	
This is the flag of Russia, which took over most of the responsibilities of the former USSR. This flag is over 300 years old, and was first used by Tsar Peter the Great. It remained Russia's official flag until 1917, when the Bolsheviks deposed the Kerensky government (which had already deposed the tsars). When the USSR dissolved in 1991, Russia took back its old tri-color flag.	

U.S. HISTORY FOCUS

Three Disasters for the U.S. Space Program

The exploration of space is dangerous work in a hostile environment. The United States' many successes in space did not come without tragedy and sacrifice.

Apollo I Disaster (Jan. 27, 1967): The first of the manned, moon-seeking Apollo missions never got off the ground. During an important pre-launch test of the astronauts' space capsule, a fire broke out inside the capsule. The fire spread rapidly because the atmosphere inside the capsule was nearly pure oxygen. The three astronauts aboard-- Virgil Grissom, Edward White and Roger Chaffee-- all died in the fire.

Space Shuttle *Challenger* Disaster (Jan. 28, 1986): After the Apollo missions, NASA built a small fleet of five "space shuttles" to ferry satellites into earth orbit. The space shuttle blasted off into orbit like a rocket, then re-entered the earth's atmosphere and taxied to a landing like an airplane. The shuttle fleet had 24 successful missions before the *Challenger* disaster.

The space shuttle used two disposable solid-fuel rockets to boost it into orbit. The weather was cold on *Challenger*'s launch day, and one of the solid rockets' O-ring seals became brittle in the cold. Hot combustion gases leaked past the brittle seal and ignited the fuel in *Challenger*'s main tank, causing the entire spacecraft to explode 73 seconds after liftoff. All seven astronauts aboard died, including a civilian schoolteacher named Christa McAuliffe. NASA grounded its entire shuttle fleet for almost three years while it investigated the accident and looked for ways to make sure that such a thing could never happen again.

Space Shuttle *Columbia* (Feb. 1, 2003): The *Columbia* disaster came near the end of what would have been the 112th successful Shuttle mission. During takeoff on January 16, debris damaged the *Columbia*'s re-entry heat shield. No one noticed the damage to *Columbia*. At the end of its mission, as *Columbia* re-entered earth's atmosphere, the heat of re-entry caused a fire that burned through the damaged heat shield. The fire destroyed *Columbia* before it could land, killing all 7 astronauts aboard.

MISSIONARY FOCUS

GIANTS OF THE FAITH: Brother Andrew (1928 –), founder of Open Doors

Andrew van der Bijl was a Dutchman who volunteered for military service in the Dutch East Indies after World War II. A bullet wound shattered Andrew's ankle and landed him in the hospital, where he came under the care of Franciscan nuns. Those nuns encouraged him to read his Bible. The Word of God spoke to Andrew's heart, and he gave his life to Christ. Later, he attended a Bible college and devoted his life to mission work.

Andrew's mission was to carry Bibles into forbidden places so that God's Word could speak to the hearts of others as it had spoken to his. Around 1957, he began smuggling Bibles behind the Iron Curtain in a little Volkswagen Beetle. He called himself "Brother Andrew" to conceal his identity.

Brother Andrew's Bible smuggling was extremely perilous, because Iron Curtain border guards often tore cars apart looking for illegal items. The guards searched travelers' engine compartments and even removed car seats in their search for hidden contraband. Brother Andrew could easily have been arrested for trying to conceal forbidden Bibles; so, instead of concealing them, he often carried them in plain sight. He openly placed Bibles on the front seat of his car, where the guards could easily see them, and prayed for God's protection while they searched his car. Instead of arresting him, they simply waved him through. In this way, Brother Andrew smuggled Bibles into Poland, Czechoslovakia, Romania, the USSR and other Communist Bloc nations.

Brother Andrew also carried Bibles into other communist nations around the world. He carried Bibles into China during Mao Tse-tung's Cultural Revolution, and he carried Bibles into Cuba after Fidel Castro's communist revolution. Later, he published an autobiography called *God's Smuggler*. The book revealed his smuggling secrets and put an end to his own personal smuggling; but by then, he had founded a missionary organization called Open Doors to carry on his work. In a 1981 operation called "Project Pearl," Open Doors smuggled one million Bibles into communist China within a single night.

GIANTS OF THE FAITH: Richard Wurmbrand (1909 – 2001), founder of Voice of the Martyrs

Richard Wurmbrand was a Jewish-born Romanian who converted to Christianity and became an ordained Christian minister. In 1944, near the end of WW II, the USSR occupied Romania and began taking over churches like Richard's, trying to wipe out the Christian faith. Romania was already gaining a reputation as the most strictly communist of all of the Communist Bloc nations. Richard stood up to Romania's communists and continued holding church services anyway.

In 1948, the communists arrested Richard and made him pay for his defiance. He spent more than 8 years in prison, three of them in solitary confinement. While Richard was in solitary, he preserved his sanity by composing and delivering sermons to himself. As soon as he was released in 1956, he went right back to preaching.

In 1959, the communists arrested him and sent him to prison yet again. This time, they subjected him to regular, severe beatings. He spent another five years in prison, suffering unspeakable torture, before the communists finally released him again in 1964.

After this second release, a group of Richard's friends convinced him that he shouldn't return to preaching this time. Instead, they said, he should save himself, leave Eastern Europe behind and tell the free world how Christians behind the Iron Curtain were suffering for their faith. They managed to get Richard out of Eastern Europe by paying the communists a large bribe.

Richard moved to the United States, where he became a bold and extremely believable witness to the wrongs Christians were suffering under communism. He wrote a book called *Tortured for Christ* in which he detailed all of the tortures he had suffered at the hands of the communists. He testified before the U.S. Congress about the shameful way the communists had treated him, and showed the congressmen his torture wounds. He also founded a new ministry, Voice of the Martyrs, to tell the stories of Christians who were suffering at the hands of communist and Islamic governments around the world.

U.S. GEOGRAPHY FOCUS

FASCINATING FACTS about HAWAII:

- Statehood: Hawaii became the 50th US state on August 21, 1959.
- Bordering bodies of water: Pacific Ocean
- Main islands (eight): Niihau, Kauai, Oahu, Maui, Molokai, Lanai, Kahoolawe and the "Big Island" of Hawaii
- State capital: Honolulu
- Area: 10,931 sq. mi (Ranks 43rd in size)
- Abbreviation: HI
- State nickname: "Aloha State"
- State bird: Hawaiian Goose
- State tree: Kukui (Candlenut Tree)
- State flower: Red Hibiscus
- State song: *Hawaii Ponoi*
- State Motto: "The life of the land is perpetuated in righteousness"
- Meaning of name: means "homeland" in native Hawaiian.
- Historic places to visit in Hawaii: Kilauea Volcano, Haleakala Crater, the old whaling town of Lahaina, the road to Hana, Kaanapali Beach, Molokai Ranch Wildlife Park, Hulope Bay, Island of Lanai (world's highest sea cliffs, Hawaii's longest waterfall, largest white sand beach), USS Arizona memorial site at Pearl Harbor, Sprouting Horn
- Resources and Industries: farming (coffee, pineapples, livestock, sugarcane, flowers, bananas, macadamia nuts, taro), food processing, metal products and tourism

U.S.S. Arizona Memorial at Pearl Harbor, Hawaii

Flag of Hawaii
- Hawaii adopted this flag in 1816, long before Hawaii became a U.S. state.
- The eight red, white and blue stripes on the flag represent Hawaii's eight main islands.
- The "Union Jack" of Great Britain appears on the upper left corner of the flag, a reminder that Hawaii was a British protectorate until 1843.

PRESIDENTIAL FOCUS

PRESIDENT #39: Jimmy Carter (1924 –)	
In Office: January 20, 1977 – January 20, 1981	**Political Party:** Democratic
Birthplace: Georgia	**Nickname:** "Jimmy" and "Peanut Farmer"

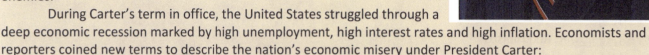

James Earl Carter served in the U.S. Navy as a nuclear engineer during the early years of the Navy's nuclear submarine program. When his father died in 1953, Carter resigned his Navy commission and returned home to operate the family peanut farm. His success at farming earned him the wealth he needed to enter politics. He served one term as Governor of Georgia before he won the Presidential election of 1976.

President Carter was a peace-loving man who sought to solve problems through negotiation, not through fighting. His greatest accomplishment as President came in 1978, when old enemies Egypt and Israel met at Carter's Camp David Presidential retreat to negotiate the Camp David Accords. This agreement led to the 1979 Egypt-Israel Peace Treaty, the first peace treaty in history between Israel and one of its former Arab enemies.

During Carter's term in office, the United States struggled through a deep economic recession marked by high unemployment, high interest rates and high inflation. Economists and reporters coined new terms to describe the nation's economic misery under President Carter:

1. *Stagflation*: a blend of "stagnation" (near-zero business growth) and "inflation" (rising prices). Before the Carter years, these two things had never happened at the same time. A certain amount of inflation is normal when businesses are growing and prospering, but prices usually remain steady or fall when businesses are suffering, as they were during the Carter years.
2. *Misery index*: A new economic measure that combined the high unemployment measure with the high inflation measure to show how bad the economic times were.

Carter was also beset by the Iran Hostage Crisis (see Chapter 34). In 1978, the angry Islamic cleric Ayatollah Khomeini took a group of 66 American diplomats stationed in Iran hostage, defying the United States to attack him. Foreign diplomats are protected by strict international laws; ordinarily, to attack a nation's diplomats is to declare war on that nation. However, Carter was reluctant to go to war over the hostage crisis; so he tried to resolve the crisis by negotiation instead. His negotiations failed. As the crisis wore on, news reporters embarrassed Carter every day by announcing the number of days the American hostages had been in captivity.

The combination of the poor economy and the hostage crisis damaged Carter's reputation. His opponent in the Presidential election of 1980, Ronald Reagan, suggested that Carter's reluctance to fight had made America look weak to its enemies. A majority of voters agreed: Reagan defeated Carter easily, and took his place as President in early 1981. Iran released its hostages minutes after Reagan took office.

Other interesting facts about Jimmy Carter:
- Carter signed the Panama Canal Treaty, in which the U.S. agreed to return the Panama Canal Zone to Panamanian control before the turn of the millennium.
- He issued a Presidential pardon for American "draft dodgers" who had avoided military service during the Vietnam War. Many draft dodgers had burned their draft cards and fled to Canada to escape the draft, but were able to return to the U.S. after Carter issued their pardon.
- He was a Sunday school teacher, and his favorite hymn was "Amazing Grace."
- He could read/scan 2,000 words per minute.

Notable quotes from Jimmy Carter:
- "We become not a melting pot but a beautiful mosaic. Different people, different beliefs, different yearnings, different hopes, different dreams."

PRESIDENT #40: Ronald Reagan (1911 – 2004)	
In Office: January 20, 1981 – January 20, 1989	**Political Party:** Republican
Birthplace: Illinois	**Nickname:** "The Gipper"

Ronald Reagan was a California actor before he began his political career. In the 1940 film "Knute Rockne, All American," Reagan played the role of George Gipp, a real University of Notre Dame football star who died in 1920 while he was still at college. Reagan's friends called him by Gipp's nickname, "The Gipper," for the rest of his life. Some of Reagan's films were considered "B movies," which meant that they were not the finest Hollywood had to offer. One of his worst was "Bedtime for Bonzo," a rather ridiculous film in which he co-starred with a monkey.

Reagan served two terms as Governor of California before he became President. He sought the Republican Party's Presidential nomination three times: once against Richard Nixon in 1968; a second time against sitting Republican President Gerald Ford in 1976; and a third time in 1980, when he finally won the nomination and the Presidency.

Reagan's first task in office was to reverse the miserable economy of the Carter years. Reagan proposed to apply the "trickle-down" economic theory, which said that if wealthy business owners prospered, then the benefits of their prosperity would "trickle down" to the rest of the nation in the form of jobs and opportunities. In order to help those business owners prosper, Reagan lowered the nation's tax rates dramatically.

Reagan's enemies called his theories "Reaganomics" or "voodoo economics" because they believed that his large tax cuts would mean less money for the government. Instead, U.S. businesses began to thrive under Reagan, and the government received more tax money than ever before because the American people earned more taxable income. Reagan's critics denied that his low tax rates were responsible for America's restored prosperity, and believed that he should have kept tax rates high so that he could spend more government money helping America's poor.

During his eight years in office, President Reagan was a tough Cold War opponent for four USSR general secretaries: Brezhnev, Andropov, Chernenko and Gorbachev. Through the Reagan Doctrine, Reagan refused to allow USSR-backed communists to gain a foothold in Central America as they had in Cuba (see Chapter 30). Reagan believed in "peace through strength": he sought to make the U.S. military an invincible fighting force so that the USSR would not dare attack America or its allies. The USSR struggled to keep up with Reagan's enormous military buildup. The strain proved too great for the USSR: Less than one year after Reagan left office, the Cold War ended with the unraveling of the USSR's empire.

Other interesting facts about Ronald Reagan:
- Whenever Reagan was on vacation, reporters photographed him splitting firewood with an ax.
- His Secret Service code name was Rawhide.
- Inaugurated within weeks of his 70th birthday, Reagan was the oldest person ever inaugurated as President. When he died in 2004, he had also lived longer than any other President.
- A mad gunman named John Hinckley tried to assassinate Reagan in 1981, but Reagan recovered from his bullet wound very well despite his advanced age.

Notable quotes from Ronald Reagan:
- "If we ever forget that we are One Nation under God, then we will be a nation gone under."
- "We must reject the idea that every time a law's broken, society is guilty rather than the lawbreaker. It is time to restore the American precept that each individual is accountable for his actions."
- "The problem is not that people are taxed too little, the problem is that government spends too much."

Chapter 34

Wars in the Middle East

WORLD HISTORY FOCUS

MODERN IRAN (PERSIA)
(see Chapter 16 for a discussion of Persia)

The Islamic religion began in 622 AD with the **Hegira**, the Prophet Muhammad's pilgrimage from Mecca to Medina (in Saudi Arabia). Over the ten years that followed, Muhammad united the Arab people and spread his new faith all over the Arabian Peninsula. But when Muhammad died in 632, his Muslim followers disagreed about how to choose the best person to succeed him as Islam's leader:

1. **SUNNI**: Some Muslims wanted to hold popular elections to choose Muhammad's successor. This branch of Islam elected *caliphs* as its leaders, and became known as **Sunni** Islam because its people followed Muhammad's *Sunnah*, or religious practices.
2. **SHIA**: Other Muslims believed that only God could choose the proper leader for Islam. These Muslims followed *Imams*, perfect, sinless leaders whom they believed were chosen for them by God. They named themselves **Shia**, "followers of Ali," after their first Imam, Ali ibn Abi Talib.

FASCINATING FACTS: Twelvers

The largest group of Shia Muslims is known (to outsiders) as the "Twelvers." The Twelvers believe that there have been exactly twelve perfect, sinless Imams since the death of Muhammad. The first was Ali, Muhammad's son-in-law and the husband of Fatima, Muhammad's favorite daughter. All of the next ten imams were murdered, nine of them reportedly by poisoning at the hands of Sunni caliphs. The eleventh imam, Hassan al-Askari, died in 874.

Most Iranians are Shia Muslims, and the majority of them are Twelvers.

FASCINATING FACTS: The Twelfth Imam

Most Twelvers believe that the twelfth imam is Muhammad al-Mahdi. Al-Mahdi was born in the year 869 to the eleventh imam, Hassan al-Askari. He was only a small child in 874, when his father died. According to Shia legend, upon his father's death, the five-year-old al-Mahdi showed wisdom far beyond his years. He claimed his place as the Twelfth Imam, conducted his father's funeral at the Jamkaran Mosque shown in the picture, and then promptly disappeared. No one has seen the Twelfth Imam since the Eleventh Imam's funeral.

Twelvers believe that Muhammad al-Mahdi still walks the earth, but that Allah has hidden (occulted) him until the End Times. The date of his coming reappearance is known only to Allah. When al-Mahdi reappears, they believe, he will bring order from chaos and create perfect justice on earth.

The absence of an authoritative Imam sometimes makes Iran difficult to govern. Modern Iran has two governments: an elected government and an Islamic government. When the two governments disagree, there can be chaos. Some Twelvers believe that if they create more chaos on earth, they can hasten the Twelfth Imam's reappearance (and the End Times as well).

Reza Shah Pahlavi

In 1921, Reza Khan captured Persia's capital city, Tehran, and ejected Ahmad Shah Qajar (see Chapter 16). By 1925, Reza Khan had overthrown Persia's old Qajar Dynasty to create a new dynasty of his own, the Pahlavi Dynasty. The new Shah of Persia took the name Reza Shah Pahlavi.

When Reza Shah took control of Persia, foreign powers dominated his nation. The 1907 Anglo-Russian Convention had brought an end to the "Great Game" between Russia and Britain by dividing Persia into a northern "sphere of influence" for Russia and a southern "sphere of influence" for Britain. Reza Shah had reason to resent both of these great powers:

1. Persia had fought several losing wars against Russia; and
2. Britain had purchased Persia's oil mining rights for a tiny fraction of what they were worth (in the D'Arcy Oil Concession, see Chapter 16).

Reza Shah wanted to modernize Persia so that it could become more independent of Britain and Russia. For help with his modernization projects, Reza Shah looked to another great European power: Germany.

INTERESTING INQUIRY: How did the outside world come to know Persia as "Iran"?

In 1935, Reza Shah Pahlavi sent a letter to the League of Nations with an unusual request: He wanted the rest of the world to begin referring to his nation as "Iran" instead of "Persia." Reza Shah might have had an innocent reason for his request: "Iran" was much closer to the word Persians used to refer to their own country in their own language.

However, there was also a less innocent reason for the Shah's request: the new name brought Iran closer to Adolf Hitler's Germany. Both Germans and Persians claimed to be descended from the elite ancient race known as the Aryans; and "Iran" means "land of the Aryans." By asking that outsiders call his nation "Iran," Reza Shah was declaring his Aryan pride and showing his support for Hitler's Germany.

Muhammad Reza Shah Pahlavi

After World War II began and the Allies declared war on Germany, Britain and Russia occupied Iran to prevent the oil-rich nation from falling to Germany. With the Allies in control of his nation, Reza Shah Pahlavi's friendship with Germany became a liability, not an asset. **In 1941, Britain forced the Hitler-friendly Reza Shah to give up his throne and replaced him with his 21-year-old son, who became Iran's new shah, Muhammad Reza Shah Pahlavi (see picture).** Throughout the rest of the war, the western Allies carried supplies into Russia through the "Persia Corridor" in occupied Persia.

Iran Nationalizes the APOC (The Abadan Crisis)

Throughout World War I, the interbellum (the period between the wars) and World War II, the British-owned Anglo-Persian Oil Company (APOC) grew extremely wealthy operating Iran's rich oil business. Iran was never satisfied with its share of the APOC's earnings, which was still the same share the old Qajar Dynasty shah had received in the 1901 D'Arcy Oil Concession: 16%, or about one sixth, of the APOC's net profits. Britain believed that 16% was fair because:

1. Iran had agreed to that amount in 1901;
2. Iran might never have discovered its oil without British engineers and businessmen; and
3. British companies owned and operated all of the equipment that produced and transported the oil.

Iran, on the other hand, believed that it deserved more than 16% because the oil came from Iranian lands. Iran was still a backward, impoverished nation, and it needed money to help solve its poverty problems. Iran's powerful Prime Minister, Muhammad Mosaddeq, believed that taking over Iran's oil business from the British was the best way to get that money.

In 1951, Iran's parliament solved the 16% problem by "nationalizing" the oil business. Iran's government simply took over the operation of every oil field and refinery in Iran, despite the fact that all of the oil-producing equipment in Iran was British-owned. Suddenly, Britain was out of the oil business in Iran and out a great deal of money and equipment.

Iran's Abadan Oil Company

Britain Boycotts Iranian Oil

The British considered Iran's nationalization of their oil business to be little more than theft of all of their expensive equipment and investments. Prime Minister Clement Attlee considered invading Iran to take back the oil business; but instead, he settled on the less violent tactic of a British boycott against Iranian oil.

Britain's boycott wrecked Iran's oil business. Britain refused to buy any Iranian oil, and it also refused to allow its engineers to work for the new Iranian national oil company. Mining and refining oil is a complex business, and Iran didn't have enough qualified engineers to keep its oil business working. As a result, Iranian oil production in 1952 was a tiny fraction of what it had been in 1951. Instead of making more money from its oil, as Prime Minister Mosaddeq had hoped, Iran was making far less.

Britain also began to confiscate every oil tanker that left Iranian waters, claiming that any oil aboard was stolen property. By eliminating Iran's best means of earning money, Britain's oil boycott slowly drove Iran into bankruptcy.

The Coup of 1953

In 1953, Britain asked the United States to help it solve its Iran problem. President Dwight Eisenhower, who took office in early 1953, was a Cold War warrior who thoroughly distrusted communists. Britain's new Prime Minister, the returning Winston Churchill, got the U.S. on Britain's side by warning Eisenhower that Iran might be falling to communism and growing closer to the USSR.

Some of Mosaddeq's actions as prime minister made it easy for Eisenhower to believe that Mosaddeq was a communist:

- Mosaddeq's 1951 government takeover of Iran's oil business was similar to what Fidel Castro would do to Cuba's sugar business in 1959 (see Chapter 31). It was a typical move a socialist/communist might make.
- Mosaddeq demanded and received from the shah full control of Iran's military.
- Mosaddeq demanded and received "emergency powers" to help Iran weather the crisis caused by Britain's oil boycott. These powers enabled him to pass laws without the approval of the Majles, Iran's parliament. This move was similar to the move Adolf Hitler made after the Reichstag Fire (see Chapter 24).
- With his emergency powers, Mosaddeq began a series of "land reforms" that took land from the wealthy and redistributed it to the poor.

Mosaddeq

With every step he took, Mosaddeq looked more and more like a communist dictator. When President Eisenhower became convinced that Iran might fall to communism, he ordered his Central Intelligence Agency (CIA) to form a plan to remove Mosaddeq from power. The plan the CIA chose became known as the **Coup of 1953**.

In the Coup of 1953, the CIA used the power of the Shah to topple Mosaddeq. CIA agents convinced Muhammad Reza Shah to remove Mosaddeq as prime minister and install a new, more freedom-friendly prime minister. They also hired mercenaries to handle the riots that they knew would come when the Shah made his move. The Shah was afraid to take such a bold step against the popular and powerful Mosaddeq, so he issued his removal order from the safety of Rome, Italy. The CIA hired revolutionaries to arrest and imprison Mosaddeq; he would spend the rest of his life under house arrest.

When Muhammad Reza Shah returned, he became the true power in Iran. He would remain so for the next 26 years, until the Islamic Revolution of 1979.

> The Coup of 1953 remains a sore spot on the troubled relationship between Iran and the United States. Prime Minister Mosaddeq was extremely popular with Iran's voters; they voted overwhelmingly to grant him his emergency powers. Because the freedom-loving United States claimed to support free elections for all nations, one might have expected the U.S. to support the freely-elected Mosaddeq. Instead, when Mosaddeq's communist leanings offended strong anti-communists like President Eisenhower, the CIA hatched a plot to overthrow Mosaddeq.

The White Revolution

The Shah was a "secular Muslim" who believed that the old traditions of Islam were holding his nation back. Like his father before him, Muhammad Reza Shah wanted to modernize his nation and make it more like the advanced nations of the West. To accomplish this, the Shah made several major changes in 1963:

- He gave women the right to vote and to hold office, even as judges over men, in his government.
- He gave non-Muslims to right to vote and to hold office.
- He built new schools modeled after those of the West.
- He made several other changes designed to elevate the poor out of their poverty.

The Shah called his reform program the "White Revolution" because he wanted to carry it out without any violence, which would have stained it blood-red instead of white.

The Islamic Revolution of 1979

Iran's religious Muslims hated the Shah's White Revolution. They had no interest in imitating the West, which they saw as an immoral enemy of Islam. They could not stand to see their children corrupted by the Shah's Western movies, Western clothing and loose Western morals. Religious Muslims learned to see the Shah as no more than a puppet of the dishonest, immoral Americans who had overthrown their elected government and placed their traitorous Shah in power as a near-dictator in 1953.

The greatest opponent of the Shah's White Revolution was an Islamic cleric named Ruhollah Khomeini.

INTERESTING INDIVIDUALS: Ayatollah Ruhollah Khomeini (1900 – 1989) and the Islamic Revolution

Ruhollah Khomeini was an Islamic cleric who was descended from the seventh of Shia Islam's Twelve Imams. Khomeini earned his title, "Ayatollah," when he became a high-ranking teacher of Shia Islam (an *ayatollah* is a highly educated religious leader of Shia Islam; his position is something like that of a Roman Catholic cardinal or a Jewish chief rabbi).

Khomeini was 62 years old when the Shah announced the White Revolution. Khomeini saw the Shah's White Revolution "reforms" as attacks on traditional Shia Islam. When he began to speak out against the White Revolution, the Shah's government arrested him and banished him from Iran. Khomeini's exile began in 1964, and would last for more than fourteen years.

During his time in exile, Khomeini continued to denounce the Shah and his government. Khomeini believed that Iran should follow only the laws of God, **Shariah** Law. He also insisted that only a leader well-trained in *Shariah* Law could hope to lead Iran in God's way. That leader, Khomeini said, was not the Shah. During the years of his exile, Khomeini became a national hero as he continued to call Iran's Muslims to a greater faith.

In 1977, Iranians began to show their unhappiness with the Shah's reign through public demonstrations and labor strikes. Khomeini organized some of these strikes from Iraq and from Paris, France, his last home in exile. The number of Iranians publicly protesting against the Shah climbed into the millions, then into the tens of millions.

When the chaos got out of hand, the ill and aging Shah did to himself what he had forced Khomeini to do: he left Iran and went into exile on January 16, 1979.

Khomeini returned to Iran in triumph on February 1, 1979. In late 1979, he won election as Iran's Supreme Leader and recreated Iran as an Islamic Republic. He declared that to disobey his new government was to disobey God Himself. Even so, it took Khomeini until 1982 to quiet the unrest that his revolution had unleashed in Iran.

Khomeini's successful Islamic Revolution meant a swift return to strict, conservative Shariah Law. Suddenly, women were required to cover their heads in public again and were no longer allowed to serve as judges over men. Men were forbidden to wear shorts and other sorts of Western-style clothing. The Ayatollah banned Western movies, alcohol, sunbathing, co-ed swimming and all non-Islamic music. Shariah Law punished immoral behavior with exile or even death.

Ayatollah Khomeini remained in power as Iran's Supreme Leader until his death in 1989.

The Iran Hostage Crisis

Shortly after the Shah fled into exile, his ill health caught up with him, and he needed expert medical attention. U.S. President Jimmy Carter reluctantly allowed him to enter the United States for a short time so that he could have surgery. The U.S. tried to keep the Shah's whereabouts secret, but Khomeini's new government soon discovered that the Americans were helping their hated Shah yet again. Khomeini and his followers felt that the United States should return the Shah to Iran for trial, not coddle him with expensive medical treatments. The help the Americans offered the Shah reminded the Iranians of the Coup of 1953, when the Americans had helped the Shah depose Iran's elected prime minister.

On November 4, 1979, a group of about 500 angry Iranians displayed their hatred for America by storming the United States embassy in Iran and taking 52 American embassy staffers hostage. Such an attack should have been unthinkable, because foreign embassies are usually considered untouchable. Under international law, the property of any foreign nation's embassy is considered to be just like a small piece of that nation's sovereign territory. An attack on any embassy is considered to be just like an attack on the nation it represents. Iran should have been terrified to attack its U.S. embassy, because doing so should have been just like declaring war on the mighty United States. Instead, Khomeini supported the renegade hostage takers and defied the U.S. to retaliate.

President Carter believed in peace, not war. Having just negotiated peace between Egypt and Israel in the 1978 Camp David Accords (see Chapter 28), Carter was extremely reluctant to add to the troubles in the Middle East by declaring war on Iran. Instead, he tried to win the hostages' release through negotiations and economic sanctions (punishments). He froze Iran's American bank accounts, blocking Iran's access to its money, while he sent negotiators to listen to Iran's demands. Often Carter's negotiators would agree to these demands, only to watch the Ayatollah change his mind and issue new demands. As the hostage crisis wore on, news reporters embarrassed President Carter daily by keeping a running tally of the American hostages' days in captivity.

Finally, Carter decided to act more forcefully, and ordered the U.S. military to rescue the hostages from the Iranian embassy. The rescue attempt, codenamed Operation Eagle Claw, went into action on April 24, 1980. Unfortunately, the military had trouble with its helicopters. Before the rescuers got anywhere near the hostages, one of their helicopters crashed into a transport plane, destroying both aircraft and killing eight servicemen. Khomeini declared that the failed rescue attempt proved that God was on his side. After Operation Eagle Claw, the Iranians held their hostages at separate locations to make any future rescue attempts even more difficult.

Partly because of his failures in handling the Iranian hostage crisis, Carter lost his bid for a second term as president. Ronald Reagan won election to the presidency in November, 1980. When the Iranians learned that a more militant president was coming into office, they were far less eager to defy the Americans. The hostage-release negotiations that had failed for so long finally succeeded; and Iran released its hostages just minutes after Reagan was inaugurated as president on January 20, 1981.

Wreckage from the crash during Operation Eagle Claw

MAGNIFICENT MONUMENTS: The Azadi Tower

The Shah of Iran dedicated Tehran's new *Shahyad* Tower in 1971. The dedication was part of an enormous celebration in honor of the 2,500th anniversary of the Persian Empire (which was founded by Cyrus the Great around 550 BC). Built from carven blocks of white marble, the tower stands about 150 feet tall. Beneath it lies a museum that houses some of Iran's finest ancient treasures. The tower stands at the center of a large public square that marks Tehran's western entrance.

After the Islamic Revolution of 1979, the people of Iran decided that the Shahyad Tower needed a new name. *Shahyad* is Persian for "memorial to the shahs"; but after their successful revolution against the foreign-influenced shahs, the people of Iran no longer wanted to honor the shahs. Instead, they chose to rename the tower and the square in which it stands *Azadi*, Persian for "freedom."

OTHER NATIONS OF THE MIDDLE EAST

During World War I, Britain and France convinced the Arabs of the Middle East to rebel against the Ottoman Empire. The Arabs' successful rebellion, known as the Arab Revolt, helped the Allies defeat one of their Axis Power enemies and finish off the tottering Ottoman Empire. One of the British army officers who helped encourage the Arab Revolt was T.E. Lawrence, now better known as "Lawrence of Arabia."

When WWI was over, the Arabs expected to create new governments of their own in Lebanon, Syria, Jordan, Palestine, Iraq and elsewhere. However, France and Britain had other plans. Instead of creating independent Arab governments, the new League of Nations partitioned much of the Middle East into three separate "mandates": The French Mandate for Syria and Lebanon, the British Mandate for Palestine, and the British Mandate for Mesopotamia. The new nation of Israel was formed from part of the British Mandate for Palestine in 1948 (see Chapter 28). Like Israel, several other nations of the Middle East would have to wait for their independence until after the end of World War II.

Oil Wealth: After Persia became a major oil producer in the early 1900s, explorers searched for oil in the other nations of the Middle East. Several of these nations turned out to have enormous oil reserves. The world's need for oil brought great wealth to several Middle Eastern nations, but not to all of them.

Lebanon	Capital: Beirut
Syria	Capital: Damascus

Oil Wealth: Lebanon is oil-dry. Syria has minimal oil wealth, about 2 billion barrels of proven reserves.

Both Lebanon and Syria were part of the Ottoman Empire until the end of World War I. After that war, France governed both nations as the French Mandate for Syria and Lebanon. They gained their independence from Free France during WWII, but remained under French control until 1946.

Jordan	Capital: Amman

Oil Wealth: Jordan is oil-dry.

After WWI, Transjordan (the area east of the Jordan River) became part of the British Mandate for Palestine. The Kingdom of Jordan became independent of Britain in 1946.

Saudi Arabia	Capital: Riyadh

Oil Wealth: Saudi Arabia has proven oil reserves of over 250 billion barrels, more than any other nation on earth.

The Arabian Peninsula was also part of the Ottoman Empire until the end of World War I. The king of the peninsula's Arabs, Abdul-Aziz of the royal Saud family, stayed out of the Arab Revolt against the Ottoman Turks in the north. Most of the Arabian Peninsula wasn't included in the British and French mandates established after World War I, so Abdul-Aziz managed to keep Arabia independent of the European powers. Abdul-Aziz united two smaller Arab kingdoms to form the independent Kingdom of Saudi Arabia in 1932.

Iran	Capital: Tehran

Oil Wealth: Iran has proven oil reserves of over 130 billion barrels.

Iraq	Capital: Baghdad

Oil Wealth: Iraq has proven oil reserves of over 110 billion barrels.

Iraq, too, was part of the Ottoman Empire until the end of WWI. After that war, Britain governed Iraq as the British Mandate for Mesopotamia. The Kingdom of Iraq gained independence from Britain in 1932.

King Faisal I and the Kingdom of Iraq had a major grievance against Britain: Kuwait. Iraq considered Kuwait to be a part of its territory, and that territory was home to all of Iraq's best coastline on the Persian Gulf. Iraq lost its best port city and a great deal of oil wealth when Britain made Kuwait a British protectorate.

| Kuwait | Capital: Kuwait City |

Oil Wealth: Kuwait has proven oil reserves of over 100 billion barrels.

Kuwait was a city-state on the Persian Gulf that was also part of the Ottoman Empire. Kuwait came under British protection in 1899 because Britain wanted to keep Kuwait's important Persian Gulf coastline out of German hands. It remained under British protection until 1961, when it finally became independent.

| Bahrain | Capital: Manama |

Oil Wealth: Bahrain is oil-dry.

Bahrain is a collection of 33 islands that lie near the western edge of the Persian Gulf. It is ruled by an Islamic dynasty.

| Oman | Capital: Muscat |

Oil Wealth: Oman has proven oil reserves of only about 5 billion barrels.

Oman is an independent nation ruled by an Islamic dynasty.

| Qatar | Capital: Doha |

Oil Wealth: Qatar has proven oil reserves of over 15 billion barrels.

Qatar is another independent nation ruled by an Islamic dynasty. It was a British protectorate until 1971.

| Yemen | Capital: Sana'a |

Oil Wealth: Yemen has proven oil reserves of only about 3 billion barrels.

Yemen's coast lies on the Gulf of Aden, which forms the southern outlet of the Suez Canal and the Red Sea. For decades, Britain maintained a colony at the port city of Aden, Yemen so that it could control the outlet of the all-important Suez Canal. Rebellions in Yemen finally forced the British to leave Aden in the late 1960s. Yemen was divided, north from south, until its two halves reunited as the Republic of Yemen in 1990.

| United Arab Emirates | Capital: Abu Dhabi |

Oil Wealth: United Arab Emirates has proven oil reserves of almost 100 billion barrels.

The United Arab Emirates is a confederation of seven small Islamic city-states ruled by Arab *emirs*, or princes. The Emir of Abu Dhabi is the UAE's official head of state. The seven "emirates" are Abu Dhabi, Ajman, Dubai, Fujairah, Ras al-Khaimah, Sharjah and Umm al-Quwain.

FASCINATING FACTS: Dubai's Khalifa Tower

As of 2010, Dubai is home to the tallest building in the world. The Khalifa Tower— aka the Burj, Arabic for "tower"— stands over 2,700 feet tall, contains more than 3 million square feet of floor space, and cost about $1.5 billion. It has 163 floors above ground, and a mosque on its 158th floor. Some of its elevators reach speeds of up to 40 miles per hour.

IRAQ

In 1958, Iraqi Arabs who were inspired by the success of Egypt's Abdel Nasser (see Chapter 28) overthrew King Faisal II and founded the new Republic of Iraq. Like Nasser, Iraq's new leaders were Arab nationalists who hoped to reunite all Arab nations under one government someday. The Ba'ath Party, an Arab nationalist party, took over the government of the Republic of Iraq in 1968. One of the Ba'ath Party's leaders was an Iraqi general named Saddam Hussein.

DASTARDLY DICTATORS: Saddam Hussein (1937 – 2006)

Saddam Hussein was born into a family of Iraqi shepherds. Saddam never knew his father, and spent most of his childhood living with an uncle in Baghdad. This uncle was a Sunni Muslim with a deep hatred for Iranians, Shia Muslims and Jews. Saddam inherited all of those hatreds from his uncle, along with a few more.

The success of Egypt's President Nasser during the 1956 Suez Crisis inspired Arabs all over the Middle East. Other Arab nationalists wanted to restore Arab pride and humiliate the Europeans as Nasser had done. Nasser and his followers were "pan-Arabists" who hoped to create a single Arab nation under one mighty ruler. Saddam Hussein nursed an ambition to become that mighty ruler.

Saddam joined the Arab nationalist Ba'ath Party in 1957. In 1968, when the Ba'ath Party took over the government of Iraq (in a "bloodless coup"), Saddam became the new president's deputy. Then in July 1979, he forced the ailing president to resign and became the new President of Iraq.

Under Saddam's presidency, the Republic of Iraq immediately transformed into a dictatorship. As soon as he took office, the ambitious Saddam did precisely what dictators Hitler and Stalin had done before him: he ordered a murderous purge of his political enemies. Within a few days, he had murdered several hundred high-ranking members of the Ba'ath Party, the very party that helped him rise to power. He removed every potential rival he could find. Also like Hitler and Stalin, Saddam used secret police to spy out any potential enemies. These spies turned neighbor against neighbor, friend against friend until no Iraqi could speak his mind without fear of arrest, torture and execution.

With Iraq firmly in his grasp, Saddam set about his ambitious campaign to become the leader of the Arab world.

The Iran-Iraq War (1980 – 1988)

Saddam Hussein's Iraq attacked Iran in 1980, while Iran was still in the midst of Ayatollah Khomeini's Islamic Revolution. As an excuse for his attack, Saddam used an old border dispute over the Shatt al-Arab River, the river that provided Iraq's only shipping access to the Persian Gulf. The Shatt al-Arab formed part of the border between Iraq and Iran, and both nations used it for shipping. However, Saddam claimed that the entire river had always belonged to Iraq. He wanted to be able to charge Iran fees for the use of his river; and when Iran refused to pay, he decided to attack Iran. Saddam also gave other reasons for his attack:

1. He wanted to stop Iran's Islamic Revolution from spreading into Iraq. Saddam was a Sunni Muslim who hated Iran's Shia Muslims, and he feared what might happen if the Shia revolution in Iran spread to Iraq.
2. He blamed Iran for an assassination attempt on his foreign minister, Tariq Aziz.

Iraq's attack led to the bloody, eight-year-long Iran-Iraq War. In that miserable, expensive war, neither side gained any territory, but both sides lost hundreds of thousands of citizens and soldiers.

FASCINATING FACTS: Operation Anfal and the Iraqi Kurds

It was near the end of the Iran-Iraq War that Saddam Hussein committed his very worst crimes: a series of genocidal (race-killing) attacks against the Kurdish people of northern Iraq.

The Kurds are the people of Kurdistan, an ancient land that lay in parts of modern-day Iran, Iraq, Syria and Turkey. When the Ottoman Empire broke up after WWI, some Kurds demanded an independent homeland; but the world ignored their demand. Throughout the rest of the 20th Century, the Kurds often rebelled against Iraqi rule.

During the Iran-Iraq War, Saddam Hussein decided that the Kurds' usual acts of rebellion were really acts of treason against his war effort. In order to punish the Kurds' treason, Saddam decided to solve his Kurdish problem once and for all by eliminating every Iraqi Kurd.

Kurdish Calvary

Saddam codenamed his attacks on the Kurds **Operation Anfal**. Operation Anfal included bombings of Kurdish villages, concentration camps for Kurdish prisoners of war and mass executions of Kurds. The operation destroyed about 4,000 Kurdish villages, and killed tens of thousands of Kurds.

Iraq's Operation Anfal is most notorious for its use of chemical weapons against the Kurds. Poison gas attacks had become extremely rare after World War I, but Saddam Hussein was bold enough to use a deadly nerve gas called Sarin against the Kurds. Sarin kills its victims horribly by causing them to lose control of their muscles, including the muscles that help them breathe. Sarin victims suffocate to death in a painful fit of convulsions. Sarin is an extremely inhumane weapon, and its use is a war crime of the worst order.

Saddam's attacks on the Kurds are considered acts of "genocide," attempts to wipe out an entire race of human beings.

Kuwait
(The green area on map is Kuwait. Kuwait is bordered by Saudi Arabia to the south, Iraq to the west and north and Iran to the northeast.)

When Saddam Hussein failed to defeat his large eastern enemy, Iran, he turned his attention to a much smaller prey: Kuwait. After the Iran-Iraq War, Iraq owed Kuwait and Saudi Arabia a great deal of money, and both nations refused to cancel Iraq's debts. Saddam accused Kuwait of making Iraq's difficulties worse by:

1. Overproducing oil, driving oil prices down and making it more difficult for Iraq to earn money by selling oil; and
2. "Slant-drilling," angling Kuwaiti oil drills into Iraqi territory so that they could steal oil that rightly belonged to Iraq.

More important to Saddam was the argument that Kuwait traditionally had belonged to Iraq, and that Kuwait only separated from Iraq because of British interference in 1899. The loss of Kuwait had cost Iraq a staggering amount of oil reserves, as well as all of its best shoreline on the Persian Gulf. Saddam wanted Kuwait back.

FASCINATING FACTS: The Persian Gulf War

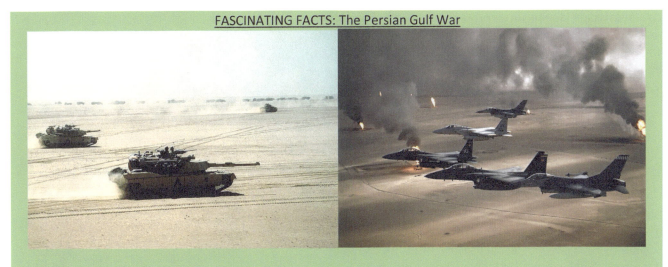

The Persian Gulf War began when Iraq invaded Kuwait on August 2, 1990. The conquest of tiny Kuwait required only about two days; and after 6 days, Saddam installed one of his cousins as the new governor of Iraq. In Saddam's eyes, the Persian Gulf War was over on August 8, and Kuwait had become a permanent province of Iraq.

The rest of the world saw the matter differently. Ever since World War II, the United Nations had frowned upon rogue nations that tried to take over other nations. In response to Iraq's attack on Kuwait, U.S. President George H. W. Bush assembled a coalition of 28 nations, including several Arab nations, to drive Iraq back out of Kuwait. Among the coalition nations were the United States, Britain, Canada, Australia, France, Saudi Arabia and Egypt. The American-led coalition drove the last Iraqi military units out of Kuwait on February 28, 1991.

As the Iraqis departed, they created a severe distraction for the victorious UN coalition army by setting several hundred Kuwaiti oil wells aflame. They also laid explosive mines around the burning oil wells so that the fires would be more difficult to extinguish. Kuwait worked for nearly a year and spent more than $1 billion to extinguish all of its oil well fires.

Economic Sanctions

Near the end of the Persian Gulf War, some members of the coalition that removed Iraqi forces from Kuwait felt that the Gulf War would fail in its purpose if it did not punish Iraq by removing Saddam Hussein from power. However, President Bush feared that the coalition's Arab nations would be offended at the idea of Western forces invading a Muslim country.

Instead, the coalition decided to punish Iraq with "economic sanctions": the world tried to force Saddam Hussein to step down as Iraq's dictator by refusing to trade with Iraq. These economic sanctions punished the Iraqi people far more than they punished Saddam. The sanctions made food and other necessities scarce in Iraq; but it was the poor who went without food, not Saddam and his cadre. While the sanctions remained in effect from 1990 - 2003, hundreds of thousands of Iraqis starved to death.

The Iraq War and the Demise of Saddam Hussein

Saddam Hussein, however, remained safely in power until 2003. In that year, the United States attacked Iraq again, for two reasons:

1. Because Iraq supported terrorist groups and allowed terrorists to operate training camps within its borders, and
2. Because the United States suspected that Iraq was trying to build nuclear weapons, and also suspected that Iraq was manufacturing more weapons of mass destruction like the Sarin gas it had used against the Kurds.

The U.S. attack overwhelmed and defeated the Iraqi army within about two weeks. Saddam escaped into hiding while a U.S. armored towing vehicle pulled down his statue in Baghdad, symbolizing the end of his tyrannical reign (see picture). After a long search, U.S. forces finally discovered Saddam's hiding place— a well-concealed, well-equipped hole in the ground near his home city of Tikrit, Iraq— in late 2003. In 2006, Iraq's new government executed Saddam Hussein for his genocidal attacks against the Kurds.

AFGHANISTAN

FASCINATING FACTS: The Taliban

Taliban is Arabic for "religious students." Afghanistan's Taliban was one of the *mujahideen* ("warriors of the holy struggle") groups that formed to fight off the USSR's invasion of Afghanistan in 1979. After the USSR departed Afghanistan in 1989, the Taliban emerged from the post-war chaos to take control of Afghanistan in 1996.

The members of the Taliban were a bit like Iran's Ayatollah Khomeini: they believed in strict attention to Islamic *Shariah* law. They forbade the education of women, and did not allow women to leave their homes unless male relatives accompanied them. They required all men to wear beards, and punished any man who appeared in the streets without one. They banned television, non-Islamic music, the internet and most other non-religious activities.

They were also like Khomeini in another way: they hated the West, and the United States in particular. Members of the Taliban believed that the West was immoral, and that it had committed terrible crimes against holy Islamic nations. The terrorists who attacked New York City's World Trade Center and Arlington, Virginia's Pentagon on September 11, 2001 trained in Taliban-controlled Afghanistan.

FASCINATING FACTS: Kite Battles and Kite Running

Kite battles are fun, sometimes dangerous games that are popular in several Asian nations, including India, Pakistan, Afghanistan, Iran, Iraq and China. The object of a kite battle is to use one's kite to knock opponents' kites out of the sky by cutting their kite strings. Before a kite battle, each kite flyer soaks part of his kite string in a mixture of glue and crushed glass. The glass makes the string sharp enough to cut. During a battle, the attacker maneuvers his kite into position near his opponent's kite, then uses his sharp string to try to saw through his opponents' string. Most fighter kites are made of paper fastened to bamboo frames. They are usually diamond-shaped, and they are made without tails so that they can be more agile in the air.

Boys who are too poor to buy or build a kite can hope to win a kite through "kite running." According to the rules of kite battles, after a kite's string has been cut, it belongs to the next person to find it, wherever it falls. Kite runners race through the streets where kite battles are fought, trying to be the first to find fallen kites.

When the Taliban came to power in Afghanistan, it banned kite flying and kite battles. After the United States deposed the Taliban in 2001, kites made a comeback. Friday is kite battle day: on Fridays in Afghani cities like Kabul and Kandahar, kite lovers pour out onto streets and rooftops and begin their kite wars.

PRESIDENTIAL FOCUS

PRESIDENT #41: George Herbert Walker Bush (1924 –)	
In Office: January 20, 1989 – January 20, 1993	**Political Party:** Republican
Birthplace: Massachusetts	**Nickname:** "Poppy," "Bush 41"

George H. W. Bush was the son of Prescott Bush, a wealthy U.S. senator from Connecticut. Bush was still in high school when the Japanese attacked Pearl Harbor in late 1941. He graduated from high school on his eighteenth birthday in 1942, then enlisted in the U.S. Navy on that same day. Less than one year later, while he was still 18, George Bush became the Navy's youngest pilot. Bush flew 58 World War II combat missions. During one of those missions, antiaircraft fire damaged the bomber he was piloting, setting one of its engines afire. With his engine still burning, Bush completed his mission, then bailed out over the Pacific Ocean and waited in an inflatable raft until a submarine rescued him. That mission won him the Distinguished Flying Cross, a medal awarded to heroic military pilots.

After the war, Bush earned millions of dollars in the Texas oil business. He entered politics as a member of the U.S. House of Representatives in 1966. He also served the federal government as U.S. ambassador to the UN, as U.S. ambassador to China and as director of the CIA. Republican presidential candidate Ronald Reagan chose George Bush as his vice presidential running mate in 1980. Bush served as vice president under Reagan for 8 years, then won election as President in his own right in 1988.

The four years of Bush's Presidency were eventful ones. In 1989, the Iron Curtain unraveled and East Germany tore down the Berlin Wall. In 1990, Russia declared its independence from the USSR. In 1991, the USSR dissolved, and the Cold War that had begun at the close of World War II in 1945 finally ended in victory for the West. Also in 1991, Bush led a coalition of nations to drive Iraq out of Kuwait in the Persian Gulf War. The United States won victory after victory overseas while Bush was in office.

Back home, however, Bush was less successful. He had won election in 1988 by promising that he would not raise taxes under any circumstances: when the Congress asked him to raise taxes, he insisted, he would tell lawmakers to "Read my lips: No new taxes!" Unfortunately, he also wanted to reduce America's budget deficit, the amount of money the nation was forced to borrow each year. Bush needed more tax money to balance the budget; so he agreed to compromise with Congress, break his promise and sign a tax increase into law.

That broken promise haunted Bush during the Presidential election of 1992. The Republican Party voters who had supported President Reagan so faithfully turned against Bush when he raised taxes. They gave all of the credit for America's Cold War victories to Reagan, and none of it to Bush. As a result, they didn't turn out to vote for Bush, and he narrowly lost the election to Arkansas governor Bill Clinton.

Other interesting facts about George H.W. Bush:
- In 1985, when President Reagan underwent a scheduled three-hour surgery, Bush became the first vice president to serve as acting President under the rules set out in the 25th Amendment.
- Bush's Secret Service code name was "Timberwolf."
- After he left office, Bush celebrated his 75th, 80th and 85th birthdays by going skydiving.

Notable quotes from George H.W. Bush:
- "America is never wholly herself unless she is engaged in high moral principle. We as a people have such a purpose today. It is to make kinder the face of the nation and gentler the face of the world."
- "I do not like broccoli. And I haven't liked it since I was a little kid and my mother made me eat it. And I'm President of the United States and I'm not going to eat any more broccoli."
- "We are a nation of communities... a brilliant diversity spread like stars, like a thousand points of light in a broad and peaceful sky."

PRESIDENT #42: William Jefferson Clinton (1946 –)	
In Office: January 20, 1993 – January 20, 2001	**Political Party:** Democrat
Birthplace: Arkansas	**Nickname:** "Bill," "Bubba"

Bill Clinton served five terms as Governor of Arkansas before he defeated President George Bush to become President in 1992.

President Clinton wanted to reverse the course America had taken during the Reagan and Bush years. With the Cold War over, Clinton wanted to stop spending so much money on weapons and start spending money on government programs designed to elevate America's poor out of their poverty. Early in his Presidency, Clinton pursued this goal by trying to "nationalize" health care in the United States. Had Clinton succeeded, his nationalized health care program would have brought every doctor, hospital and medical insurance company in the United States under government control. Instead, the overly ambitious effort backfired on Clinton: Congress rejected nationalized health care; and in the congressional election of 1994, the voters punished Clinton's overreaching by electing Republican majorities in both houses of Congress for the first time since 1955.

Despite these and other setbacks, Clinton remained a skilled politician. He compromised with the newly Republican congress by reforming America's welfare program. America's economy prospered, and he narrowly won reelection in the Presidential election of 1996.

Investigations and accusations of criminal wrongdoing marred much of President Clinton's second term in office. Both Clinton and his wife were accused of filling their bank accounts with money made through illegal investments in real estate (the "Whitewater Scandal"). Investigators never proved that the Clintons had made any illegal investments; however, during the investigations, several witnesses accused Clinton of immoral behavior with women. Clinton lied to cover up that immoral behavior more than once. When Clinton's lies were revealed, the U.S. House of Representatives voted to impeach him. The U.S. Senate acquitted Clinton at his impeachment trial, and he remained in office until the end of his two terms. Clinton was only the second U.S. President to be impeached by Congress (the first was Andrew Johnson).

Other interesting facts about Bill Clinton:
- Bill Clinton was only 32 years old when he won election as governor of Arkansas. He was the youngest Arkansas governor ever, and the youngest governor in America at the time.
- He was the first President who had studied at England's Oxford University under a Rhodes Scholarship.
- He played the saxophone.
- His family cat was named "Socks" because it had white feet on an otherwise all-black body.

Notable quotes from Bill Clinton:
- "If you live long enough, you'll make mistakes. But if you learn from them, you'll be a better person. It's how you handle adversity, not how it affects you. The main thing is never quit, never quit, never quit."
- "Work is about more than making a living, as vital as that is. It's fundamental to human dignity, to our sense of self-worth as useful, independent, free people."

APPENDIX: Presidents # 43 and 44

PRESIDENT #43: George Walker Bush (1946 –)	
In Office: January 20, 2001 – January 20, 2009	**Political Party:** Republican
Birthplace: Connecticut	**Nickname:** "Dubya" or "W"

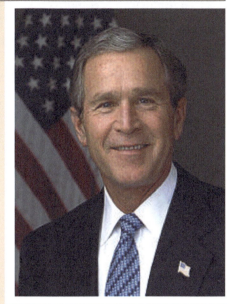

George Bush came from a family of politicians: his father was the 41st President, his brother was the Governor of Florida, and he himself was the Governor of Texas before he became President. Before he was a governor, he was a co-owner of the Texas Rangers baseball team.

Eight months after George Bush became President, terrorists attacked the United States at New York's World Trade Center and at the Pentagon on September 11, 2001. It fell to Bush to lead America's response to the 9/11 attacks, the worst attacks on American soil since Pearl Harbor in 1941. The investigation of the attacks led two places: (1) to a Middle Eastern terrorist group called Al Qaeda, and (2) to an Afghani political party called the Taliban. In response, Bush declared a new "war on terrorism," especially on Al Qaeda, and he ordered an invasion of Afghanistan. He also:

1. Established a new Department of Homeland Security to bring together information from all of the government's law enforcement departments in one place; and
2. Signed the "Patriot Act" into law, legalizing certain kinds of wiretapping and surveillance so that law enforcement officers could monitor suspected terrorists more easily. Some saw the Patriot Act as a violation of American citizens' Constitutional rights.

Bush's most controversial response to the 9/11 attacks was his invasion of Iraq, which began in March 2003. No evidence linked Iraq directly to the 9/11 terrorists. However, when Bush declared war on terrorism in 2001, he had vowed to punish any nation that gave aid to terrorists. Iraq (1) was home to suspected terrorist training camps; (2) had used chemical weapons against the Kurds in 1988; and (3) was trying to build nuclear weapons. Bush was unwilling to leave possible weapons of mass destruction in the hands of a rogue dictator like Saddam Hussein; so he led a pre-emptive strike against Iraq that toppled Iraq's government.

With American help, the Iraqis established a new republican government for Iraq. Unfortunately, terrorism and suicide bombings continued to plague the country and the U.S. troops stationed there for years after the invasion. America never discovered Iraq's feared weapons of mass destruction, although it did find hints of them, and Iraq certainly had them at one time. Bush suffered heavy criticism for his "pre-emptive war" for the remainder of his time in office.

Other interesting facts about George W. Bush:
- George experienced tragedy at a young age: when his sister Robin was three, she died of leukemia.
- George and his wife Laura had twin daughters who were teenagers when he began his first term. One of their daughters was married while Bush was still President, but the ceremony was held in Texas, not at the White House.

Notable quotes from George W. Bush:
- "Some folks look at me and see a certain swagger, which in Texas is called 'walking.'"
- "Terrorist attacks can shake the foundations of our biggest buildings, but they cannot touch the foundation of America. These acts shatter steel, but they cannot dent the steel of American resolve."
- "We will not waver; we will not tire; we will not falter, and we will not fail. Peace and Freedom will prevail."

PRESIDENT #44: Barack H. Obama (1961 –)	
In Office: January 20, 2009 –	**Political Party:** Democrat
Birthplace: Hawaii	**Nickname:** "Barry"

Barack Obama worked as a community organizer in Chicago, Illinois before studying at Harvard Law School to become an attorney. He won election to the Illinois state senate in 1996, and remained in that office until he won election as a U.S. Senator from Illinois in 2004. Obama's well-received keynote speech at the 2004 Democratic National Convention made him the Democratic Party's rising star. In 2008, he defeated Arizona Senator John McCain to become the first black President of the United States.

As President, Obama succeeded where the last Democratic Party president, Bill Clinton, had failed: He managed to pass the Patient Protection and Affordable Care Act of 2010, a law that requires universal health care for every citizen of the United States. He withdrew most American troops from Iraq, but he sent more American troops to Afghanistan in an effort to defeat the Taliban there. He also signed the American Recovery and Reinvestment Act of 2009, an act that spent nearly $800 billion in an attempt to elevate America out of an economic recession.

Other interesting facts about Barack Obama:
- Obama's father was from Kenya, and his mother was from Kansas. He was born in Hawaii and raised in both Indonesia and Hawaii.

Notable quotes from Barack Obama:
- "If you're walking down the right path and you're willing to keep walking, eventually you'll make progress."
- "If the people cannot trust their government to do the job for which it exists - to protect them and to promote their common welfare - all else is lost."

YEAR 4 OVERVIEW

Chapter	Missionaries	Heroes and Villains of History	Presidents	U.S. Geography	World Geography
1	George Mueller	Queen Victoria Harriet Tubman Frederick Douglass	Zachary Taylor		Continents Oceans
2		Florence Nightingale Clara Barton Muhammad Ali Pasha	Millard Fillmore Franklin Pierce	United States	Sevastopol Suez Canal
3	Mary Slessor David Livingstone	Ahmad Shah Durrani Dost Muhammad Khan Jefferson Davis	James Buchanan	Alabama	Afghanistan Khyber Pass Victoria Falls Devil's Pool
4		John Brown Robert E. Lee Thomas Jonathan "Stonewall" Jackson	Abraham Lincoln	West Virginia	Geography of the Civil War
5		Elizabeth Blackwell Joshua Chamberlain J.E.B. Stuart William Sherman John Wilkes Booth			Geography of the Civil War
6	Charles Spurgeon	De Francia Pedro II of Brazil	Andrew Johnson	Maine Alaska Purchase	Geography of South America
7	Abraham Kuyper	Louis-Napoleon Bonaparte Otto von Bismarck	Ulysses S. Grant Rutherford Hayes	Iowa	France Germany
8		Thomas Alva Edison Cyrus McCormick Jerome Case	James Garfield Chester Arthur	Arkansas Transcontinental Railroad Moving Out West	
9	Japanese Christians	Jane Addams Com. Matthew Perry	Grover Cleveland Benjamin Harrison	Michigan Ellis Island	Japan
10	Armenian Christians	Helen Keller Sultan Abdulhamid II		Wisconsin	Indonesian Islands Island of Sumatra
11		Booker T Washington W.E.B. Du Bois George W. Carver Ned Kelly Leopold II of Belgium Cecil Rhodes			Australia Dividing Africa Liberia Ethiopia South Africa
12		Tsar Alexander II Tsar Alexander III Nellie Bly	William McKinley Teddy Roosevelt	Panama Canal Territories/Possessions of the United States Philippine Islands	
13	Hudson Taylor Lottie Moon	Hong Xiuquan Empress Dowager Cixi		Minnesota	China Trans Siberian Railway Korea Port Arthur

14	Jonathan Goforth	Geronimo Chief Joseph Crazy Horse Buffalo Bill Cody		Overview of States Pioneer Trails Oregon	
15	Billy Sunday	John D. Rockefeller J.P. Morgan Andrew Carnegie Montgomery Ward John Deere		Kansas	
16		Henry Ford The Wright Brothers Naser al-Din Shah Qajar William D'Arcy Winston Churchill	William Taft	Nevada	Persia The Balkans
17		Maximilian I of Mexico Benito Juarez Porfirio Diaz Mori Pancho Villa Emiliano Zapata Kaiser Wilhelm Gavrilo Princip		New Mexico	Mexico Geography of World War I
18		Tsar Nicholas II Rasputin Vladimir Ilyich Lenin Sergeant York	Woodrow Wilson	Nebraska	Russia Geography of World War I
19	Sundar Singh Amy Carmichael	Babe Ruth William Gladstone Michael Collins Mohandas Gandhi	Warren G. Harding	Colorado	Ireland
20		Amelia Earhart Joseph Stalin		Washington	Dividing Europe after WWI The Alsace-Lorraine Yugoslavia USSR
21	Lillian Trasher	Guiseppe Garibaldi Benito Mussolini		Montana	Italy Vatican City Egypt
22	Eric Liddell Gladys Aylward	Sun Yat-sen Chiang Kai-shek Emperor Puyi Eleanor Roosevelt	Calvin Coolidge	North Dakota South Dakota Mount Rushmore	Manchuria
23		Charles Lindbergh	Herbert Hoover	Dust Bowl Route 66	
24	C.S. Lewis	Miguel Primo de Rivera Gen. Francisco Franco Adolf Hitler	Franklin Roosevelt	Oklahoma	Spain Spanish Morocco Germany
25	Corrie Ten Boom	Neville Chamberlain Ellen Nielsen Anne Frank			Geography of European Theater
26	Jacob Deshazer	Hirohito Tojo Yamamoto Erwin Rommel George S. Patton, Jr.			Geography of Pacific War and European Theater continued

27	Ida Scudder Mother Teresa	Ernie Pyle Indira Gandhi	Harry S. Truman	Idaho	Germany Divided India Pakistan Bangladesh Kashmir
28	C. T. Studd	Gamel Nasser Anwar Sadat	Dwight Eisenhower	Wyoming	Israel Palestine Aswan Dam
29	Robert J. Thomas Isobel Miller Kuhn	Mao Tse-tung Deng Xiaoping Douglas MacArthur		Utah	China, Hong Kong Macau Taiwan Korea
30	The Auca Missionaries	Juan and Eva Peron William Walker Patrice Lumumba Joseph Mobutu Nelson Mandela		Arizona	Geography of South America and Africa
31		Fulgencio Batista Fidel Castro Che Guevara Neil Armstrong Alan Shepherd	John F. Kennedy Lyndon B. Johnson	Guantanamo Bay	Iron Curtain countries Berlin Cuba
32	Billy Graham	Rosa Parks Martin Luther King Jr. Lee Harvey Oswald Ho Chi Minh	Richard Nixon Gerald Ford	Alaska	Vietnam
33	Brother Andrew Richard Wurmbrand	Nikita Khrushchev Leonid Brezhnev Samantha Smith Mikhail Gorbachev	Jimmy Carter Ronald Reagan	Hawaii	USSR to Russia
34		Ayatollah Khomeini Saddam Hussein	George H W Bush William J Clinton		Iran and Iraq

Bibliography

The 488th Port Battalion APO 6, 5th US Army. 5 August 2011 <http://www.488 thportbattalion.org/index.html>.

"Adolf Hitler." *Emerson Kent.* 10 May 2011 <http://www.emersonkent.com/history_notes/adolf_ hitler.htm >.

Ambrose, Stephen E. *Band of Brothers: E Company, 506th Regiment, 101st Airborne from Normandy to Hitler's Eagle's Nest.* New York: Simon & Schuster, 2001.

---. *Citizen Soldiers: The U. S. Army from the Normandy Beaches to the Bulge to the Surrender of Germany.* New York: Simon & Schuster, 24September 1998.

---. *Crazy Horse and Custer: The Parallel Lives of Two American Warriors.* New York: Simon & Schuster,1995.

---. *Nothing Like It In the World: The Men Who Built the Transcontinental Railroad 1863-1869.* New York: Simon & Schuster, 2001.

"American Civil War 1861-1865." *Emerson Kent.* 4 July 2011<http://www.emersonkent. comwars_and_battles_in_history/american _civil_war.htm>.

"American President: An Online Reference Resource." *Miller Center.* Rector and Visitors of the University of Virginia. 2011. 20 June 2011 <http://millercenter.org/president>.

"Ancient History." *BBC History.* 20 April 2010 < http://www.bbc.co.uk/history/ancient/>.

Arnold, James, and Robert Wiener, Ed. *The Timechart History of the Civil War (Time Charts).* Ann Arbor, Michigan: Lowe and B Hould Publishers, 2001.

Barbree, Jay, Alan Shepard, and Deke Slayton. *Moon Shot: The Inside Story of America's Race to the Moon.* Atlanta GA:Turner Publishing, 1994.

Bauer, Susan Wise. *The History of the Ancient World: From the Earliest Accounts to the Fall of Rome (1st Ed.).* New York: W.W. Norton & Co., Mar. 2007.

---. *The History of the Medieval World: From the Conversion of Constantine to the First Crusade(1st Ed.).* New York: W.W. Norton & Co., 22 Feb. 2010.

Blumberg, Rhoda. *Full Steam Ahead: The Race to Build a Transcontinental Railroad.* New York: Scholastic Inc., 1996.

"The Boer War." *Emerson Kent.* 7 May 2011 <http://www.emersonkent.com/wars_and_battles _in_history/boer_war.htm >.

British Battles. 25 July 2011 < http://www.britishbattles.com>."British History." *BBC History.* 6 Jan. 2011 <http://www.bbc.co.uk/history/british/ >.

Bristley, Eric, and Garry J. Moes. *Streams of Civilization Vol. 2: Cultures in Conflict Since the Reformation* 2nd edition. United States: Christian Liberty Press, 1995.

Brownstone, David M., Douglass Brownstone and Irene M Franck. *Island of Hope, Island of Tears.*New York: Barnes and Noble, 1979.

Bulliet, Richard, et al. *Volume II: Since 1500; The Earth and Its Peoples: A Global History.* Boston: Wadsworth Publishing, October 2006.

Burlingame, Michael. "Forward." *Abraham Lincoln: A Biography* by Thomas, Benjamin P. New York: Southern Illinois University Press, 26 September 2008.

Caney, Steven. Kids America. New York: Workman Publishing, 1978.

Chaikin, Miriam. *A Nightmare in History: The Holocaust 1933-194.* New York: Clarion Books, 1987.

"Chief Joseph." *Emerson Kent.* 2 Mar. 2010 <http://www.emersonkent.com/history_notes/chief_ joseph.htm >.

Coffey, Walter. "The U.S. Civil War in 1864." *American History Suite 101.*20 April 2011 <http://www.suite101.com/content/the-us-civil-war-in-may-1864-a364740>.

"The Cold War 1945-1991." *Emerson Kent.* 30 March 2011 <http://www.emersonkent. com/wars_and_battle_in_history/cold_war.htm>.

Cook, Jean, Ann Kramer, Theodore Rowland-Entwistle, and Fay Franklin, Ed. *History's Timeline Revised and Updated: a 40,000 Year Chronicle of Civilization.* New York: Barnes and Nobles Books, 1981.

"Crazy Horse." *Emerson Kent.* 2 Mar. 2010 < http://www.emersonkent.com/history_notes/crazy_ horse_Ta-sunko-witko.htm>.

"Crimean War 1853-1856." *Emerson Kent.* 30 March 2011<http://www.emersonkent.com/wars_ and_battles_in_history/crimean_war.htm>.

Davis, Burke.

They Called Him Stonewall. New York: Wings Book, 2006.Dolot. Miron. *Execution by Hunger: The Hidden Holocaust.* New York: W. W. Norton and Co. 1987.

Dolot. Miron. *Execution by Hunger: The Hidden Holocaust.* New York: W. W. Norton and Co. 1987.

Douglass, Frederick, and David Blight, Ed. *Narrative of the Life of Frederick Douglass: An American Slave, Written by Himself* (Bedford Series in

History & Culture). Boston: Bedford/St. 25 December 2002.

Dunnigan, James F. *Victory at Sea: World War II in the Pacific.* New York: Albert A Nofi William Morrow and Co., 12 Nov. 1995.

Egan, Timothy. *The Worst Hard Time: The Untold Story of Those Who Survived the Great American Dust Bowl.* Boston: Mariner Books, 1 September 2006.

Eidenmuller, Michael E. *American Rhetoric.* 5 August 2011 <http://www.americanrhetoric. com/>.

"Egypt: A Brief History." *MidEast Web.* 2 Dec. 2010 http://www.mideastweb.org/ egypthistory.htm >.

Elson, Robert, and Time-Life Books, Ed. *Prelude to War.* Alexandria, VA: Time Life Books, 1977.

Emerson Kent: World History for the Relaxed Historian. 25 July 2011< http://www.emersonkent. com>.

"Encyclopedia Virginia: Battle of Manassas or Bull Run." *Edsitement.* 10 April 2011 < http://edsitement.neh.gov/>.

Engels, Friedrich. *The Condition of the Working Class in England (Oxford World's Classics).* Chicago IL: Academy Chicago Publishers, 1994.

English, June, and Thomas Jones. *Encyclopedia of the United States at War.* New York: Scholastic Inc., 1998.

English Monarchs. 5 August 2011 < http://www.englishmonarchs.co.uk/>.

Fergurson, Ernest B. *Chancellorsville 1863: The Souls of the Brave.* New York: Alfred A Knopf Publisher, 1992.

"Fifth Arab-Israeli Wars 1982 ." *Emerson Kent.* 7 May 2011<http://www.emersonkent.com/war_and_battles_in_history/arab_israeli_wars. htm#Fifth_Arab-Israeli_War>.

"First Arab-Israeli War 1948-1949." *Emerson Kent.* 7 May 2011<http://www.emersonkent. com/wars _and_battles_in_history/arab_israeli_wars .htm#First_Arab-Israeli_War>.

Fox, Edward Whiting, Ed. *Atlas of European History.* New York: Oxford University Press, 1957.

"Fourth Arab-Israeli Wars (October War, Ramadan War), October 1973." *Emerson Kent.* 7 May 2011<http://www.emersonkent. com/wars _and_battles_in_history/arab_israeli_ wars.htm#Fourth_Arab-Israeli_War>.

Frank, Anne. *Anne Frank: The Diary of a Young Girl. New York: Pocket Books, 1953.*

Furgurson, Ernest B. *Chancellorsville 1863: The Souls of the Brave.* New York: Alfred A Knopf Publisher, 1992.

Gallagher, Gary W., Ed. *The Wilderness Campaign: Military Campaigns of the Civil War.* Chapel Hill, NC: The University of North Carolina Press, 5 July 2006.

"Georgia's Blue and Gray Trail Presents the Civil War." *Blue and Gray Trail.* 16 Oct. 2007. 25 July 2011 < http://blueandgraytrail.com/event /The_Civil_War>.

"Geronimo." *Emerson Kent.* 2 Mar. 2010 <http://www.emersonkent.com/history_notes/geronimo _goyathlay.htm>.

Gonzalez, Justo L. *The Story of Christianity: Volume 2: The Reformation to the Present Day.* New York: HarperOne, Dec. 2010.

Greek Gods Info: Gods and Goddesses of Ancient Greece. 2011<http://www.greek-gods.info/>.

Harries, Maggie. "Gerald Ford, Deserted by His Birth Father." *American History Suite 101.* 19 April 2011. 2 May 2011<http://www.suite101.com/ content/gerald-ford-deserted-by-his-birth-father-adopted-by-another-a364408 >.

Hakim, Joy. *Age of Extremes.* A History of US Book 8. New York: Oxford University Press, 2003.

---. *All the People.* A History of US Book 10. New York: Oxford University Press, 2003.

---. *The First Americans.* A History of US Book 1. New York: Oxford University Press, 2005.

---. *From Colonies to Country.* A History of US Book 3. New York: Oxford University Press, 2005.

---. *Liberty for All?* A History of US Book 5. New York: Oxford University Press, 2003.

---. *The New Nation.* A History of US Book 4. New York: Oxford University Press, 2005.

---. *Reconstruction and Reform.* A History of US Book 7. New York: Oxford University Press, 1999.

---. *The Thirteen Colonies.* A History of US Book 2. New York: Oxford University Press, 2005.

---. *War, Peace, and All That Jazz.* A History of US Book 9. New York: Oxford University Press, 2003.

---. *War, Terrible War.* A History of US Book 6. New York: Oxford University Press, 2003.

Harries, Maggie. "Gerald Ford, Deserted by His Birth Father." *American History Suite 101.* 19 April 2011. 2 May 2011

<http://www.suite101.com/content/gerald-ford-deserted-by-his-birth-father-adopted-by-another-a364408 >.

Hartshorne, Thomas L., Mark T. Tebeau, and Robert A. Wheeler. *Social Fabric, The, Volume 2 11 edition.* Upper Saddle River, New Jersey: Prentice Hall, 24 August 2008.

Hecht, Richard D., and Ninian Smart, Ed. *Sacred Texts of the World: A Universal Anthology.* New York: The Crossroad Publishing Company, 2002 edition.

Hickman, Kennedy. "Civil War 150th: Armies Clash at Bull Run." *About.Com Military History.* 25 July 2011<http://militaryhistory.about.com/od/civilwarintheeast/p/first-battle-of-bull-run.htm>.

"Historic Figures." *BBC History.* 6 Jan. 2011 <http://www.bbc.co.uk/history/british/ >.

"History Map Archive." *Emerson Kent.* 2011 <http://www.emersonkent.com/maps.htm>.

"History of Ireland."*History World.* 31 May 2011 <http://www.historyworld.net/>.

The History Place. 29 April 2011 <http://www.historyplace.com/>.

History World. 2011 <http://www.historyworld.net/>.

Hogan, Maggie, and Cindy Wiggers. *Ultimate Geography And Timeline Guide.* New York: GeoCreations Ltd., July 2000.

Hyper History Online. 2011 <http://www.hyperhistory.com/online_n2/History_n2/a.html>.

Indianetzone: Largest Free Encyclopedia on India with Lakhs of Articles. 20 June 2011 < http://www.indianetzone.com/>.

King, David C. *Children's Encyclopedia of American History (Smithsonian Institution).* New York: Roundtable Press Book, 2003.

King, Martin Luther."Letter from Birmingham Jail." *The Martin Luther King Jr. Research and Education Institute.*16 April 1963. 5 August 2011 <http://mlk- kpp01.stanford.edu/index.php/resources/article/annotated_letter_from_birmingha>.

Knappert, Jan. *Kings, Gods and Spirits from African Mythology.* Peter Bedrick Books, New York: 1986.

Koppy, Lawrence. "President Eisenhower and France's War in Viet Nam. *Military History Suite 101.* 21 April 2011<http://www.suite101.com/content/president-eisenhower-and-frances-war-in-vietnam-a366894 >.

Krull, Kathleen. *Lives of the Musicians: Good Times, Bad Times and What the Neighbors Thought.*New York: Harcourt Brace and Co., 1993.

Kuiper, B. K. *The Church in History.* Grand Rapids, Michigan: Wm. B. Eerdmans Publishing Company, June 1988.

Legends of America. 13 May 2011 <http://www.legendsofamerica.com/>.

Lincoln, Abraham, and T. Harry Williams, Ed. *Selected Writings and Speeches of Abraham Lincoln.* USA: Hendricks House, June 1980.

Martin, Goldsmith. *Islam and Christian Witness.* Illinois: Intervarsity Press, 1982.

Mao Zedong Reference Archive. *"*Mao Zedong Proclamation of the Central People's Government of the People's Republic of China." *Collected Works of Mao Tse-tung (1917-1949), Volume 9.* 1949 Oct. 1. 5 August 2011 <http://www.marxists.org/ reference/archive/mao /works/1949/10/01.htm>.

McKinney, Kevin. *Everyday Geography of the World: A Concise Entertaining Review of Essential Information with over 80 Maps and Illustrations.* Garden City, NY: Doubleday Direct Inc., 1993.

Mead, Gary. *The Doughboys - America and the First World War.* New York: Overlook Press, 2000.

"The Mexican Revolution." *Emerson Kent.* 30 June 2011 <http://www.emersonkent.com/wars _and_battles_in_history/mexican_revolution.htm>.

Mintz, S. (2007). *Digital History.* 12 March 2011<http://www.digitalhistory.uh.edu>.

Myers, Kraig. "Before Custer's Last Stand, There Was Fetterman's." *American History Suite 101.*20 April 2011<http://www.suite101.com/content /before-custers-last-stand-there-was-fettermans-a367287 >.

National Aeronautics and Space Administration NASA History Office. "The Decision to Go to the Moon: President John F. Kennedy's May 25, 1961 Speech before a Joint Session of Congress." *NASA.* 28 Jan. 2010. 5 August 2011 < http://history.nasa.gov/moondec.html>.

"Navy and Marine Living History Groups." *The Navy and Marine Living History Association. 20 June 2011*< http://www.navyandmarine.org/Navy Units/ByTimePeriod.htm>.

Osborn, William M. *The Wild Frontier: Atrocities During the American-Indian War from Jamestown Colony to Wounded Knee*. New York: Random House, 9 January 2001.

Ridpath, John Clark. *1-490 Egypt Babylonia, Ancient World Greece Vol. I.* Cincinnati, OH: History of the World Ridpath Historical Society, 1941.

---. *490-970 Greece, Macedonia, Rome Vol. II.* Cincinnati, OH: History of the World Ridpath Historical Society, 1941.

---.*971-1440 The Barbarian and Mohammedan Ascendency, Charlemagne, Feudalism, Crusades*, Vol. III. Cincinnati, OH: History of the World Ridpath Historical Society, 1941.

---.*1441-1912 New World and Reformation, The English Revolution*, Vol. IV. Cincinnati, OH: History of the World Ridpath Historical Society, 1941.

---.*1913-2410 Frederick the Great, The Age of Revolution, United States*, Vol V. Cincinnati, OH: History of the World Ridpath Historical Society, 1941.

---.*2411-2902 Europe in the 19 Century*, Vol. VI. Cincinnati, OH: History of the World Ridpath Historical Society, 1941.

---. *2903-3380 Minor American States, Oriental Nations, The Twentieth Century*, Vol VII. Cincinnati, OH: History of the World Ridpath Historical Society, 1941.

---.3381-3908 *The World War*, Vol. VIII. Cincinnati, OH: History of the World Ridpath Historical Society, 1941.

---.3909-4548.*The Period of Reconstruction*, Vol IX. Cincinnati, OH: History of the World Ridpath Historical Society, 1941.

Robertson, James I., Jr. *Soldiers Blue and Gray (Studies in American Military History).* South Carolina: University of South Carolina Press, 1 September1998.

Rubin, Gretchen. *Forty Ways to Look at Winston Churchill: A Brief Account of a Long Life.* New York: Random House Trade Paperbacks, 11 May 2004.

"The Russian Revolution of 1917." *Emerson Kent.* 2 Mar. 2010 <http://www.emersonkent.com/ wars_and_battles_in_history/russian _revolution_of_1917.htm>.

Saint, Steve. *End of the Spear.* Carol Stream, Illinois: Tyndale House Publishers, 2005.

Sansone, Stephen C., and Ethel Wood. *American Government: A Complete Coursebook.* Wilmington, MA: Houghton Mifflin Co., 2000.

Schultz, George F. Adaptation By. "The Sandlewood Maiden."*Viet Spring.* 5 August 2011 < http://www.vietspring.org/legend/sandalwood.html>.

"Second Arab-Israeli War 1956." *Emerson Kent.* 7 May 2011<http://www.emersonkent. com/wars _and_battles_in_history/arab_israeli_ wars.htm#Second_Arab-Israeli_War>.

Shi, David E., and George Brown Tindall. *America: A Narrative History (Eighth Edition) (Vol. 2).* New York: W. W. Norton & Company, October 2009.

Shotgun's Home of the American Civil War. 2 Sept. 2008. 11 May 2011< http://www.civilwar home.com/>.

Spungin, Raymond. "America's Five Greatest Presidents." *American History Suite 101.* 20 April 2011. 3 June 2011 <http://www.suite101.com/ content/americas-five-greatest-presidents-a366958>.

Teaching the Middle East: A Resource for Educators. 20 May 2011 < http://teachmiddleeast.lib uchicago.edu/ind ex.html>.

"Third Arab-Israeli War (Six Day War, June War) June 1967." *Emerson Kent.* 7 May 2011<http://www.emersonkent. com/wars _and_battles_in_history/arab_israeli_ wars.htm#Third_Arab-Israeli_War>.

Tuchman, Barbara W. *The Proud Tower: A Portrait of the World Before the War, 1890-1914.* New York: Ballentine Books, 1996.

Tucker, Phillip Thomas. "Introduction." *Memoirs of the Rebellion on the* Border by Wiley Britton. Lincoln Nebraska: Bison Books University of Lincoln Press, 1August 1993.

"The Two Boer Wars." *Emerson Kent.* 7 May 2011 <http://www.emersonkent.com/wars_and _battles_in_history/boer_war.htm#The_Two Boer_Wars >.

Van Loon, Hendrik Willem. *The Story of Mankind.* USA: Liveright Publishing, 1951.

"Victorian Political History." *The Victorian Web.*10 Feb. 2011. 20 June 2011 <http://www.victorianweb.org/history/>.

Vietnam Culture. 2006. 5 August 2011 < http://www.vietnam-culture.com/>.

Walsh, George. *Whip the Rebellion: Ulysses S. Grant's Rise to Command.* New York: Forge Books, 7 February 2006.

Walton, Robert C. *Chronological and Background Charts of Church History* (Zondervan Charts). Grand Rapids, Michigan: Zondervan, 2005.

"Wars in History: B-E." *Emerson Kent.* 28 April 2011<http://www.emersonkent.com/wars_and _revolutions_from_b.htm >.

Whiting, Edward, Ed. *Atlas of European History.* New York: Oxford University Press, 1957.

Wikipedia. 2011 <http://en.wikipedia.org >.

Wikimedia Commons. 2011<http://commons.wikimedia.org/wiki/Main_Page>.

"World Wars." BBC History. 3 Dec. 2010 <http://www.bbc.co.uk/history/worldwars/>.

World History. 2009. 10 March 2011 <http://worldhistory.com/ >.

"World History." *InfoPlease.* 2011 <http://www.infoplease.com/ipa/A0001196.html>.

PHOTO AND ILLUSTRATION CREDITS:

Public Domain Creative Commons License:

Chapter 1: The Young Queen Victoria, Crystal Palace from the northeast from Dickinson's Comprehensive Pictures of the Great Exhibition of 1851, Crystal Palace, British East India Company Flag from Rees, Pattern 1853 Rifle, Clive, Awan Sepoy, Flag of England, Union flag 1606 (Kings Colors), Flag of the United Kingdom, George Muller, Orphan-Houses-Ashley-Down, Brooklyn Museum - A Ride for Liberty -- The Fugitive Slaves - Eastman Johnson, Harriet Tubman, c1885, Uncle Tom's Cabin: Legree, Frederick Douglass, Dred Scott, Continental models

Chapter 2: Russo-British skirmish during Crimean War, Vernet - Taking of the Malakoff, Caton Woodville Light Brigade, Minie Balls, Florence Nightingale, Modern Egypt, Muhammad Ali by Auguste Couder, Clara Barton, Flag of the United States, Millard Fillmore by George PA Healy, 1857, Franklin Pierce by GPA Healy, 1858

Chapter 3: Ahmad-Shah-Durani, Afghan royal soldiers of the Durrani Empire, Dost Mohammad Khan of Afghanistan with his son, Great Game cartoon from 1878, David Livingstone preaching from a wagon, Henry Morton Stanley : How I found Livingstone, Mary Slessor, Victoria Falls, Jefferson Davis, Jefferson Davis in Prison, Jb15, Alabama State Capital

Chapter 4: Cottonfield panorama, Slave Dance and Music, Abraham Lincoln, John Brown portrait, 1859, John brown interior engine house, Sumter, Confederate Army Photo, Robert Edward Lee, Ricketts Battery Painting, Stonewall Jackson, Battle of Fort Donelson, CSS Virginia 1862, USS Monitor at sea, Battle of Shiloh Thulstrup, Dunker Church Antietam 1862, Stephens-reading-proclamation-1863, Slave children, Flag of West Virginia, U.S. flag, CSA FLAG 9, CSA Flag11, Second national flag of the Confederate States of America, Abraham Lincoln Oil Painting 1869

Chapter 5: Elizabeth Blackwell, Battle of Chancellorsville, Battle of Gettysburg, by Currier and Ives, Jeb Stuart, Battle of Vicksburg, Kurz and Allison, The Peacemakers 1868, The "Dictator" siege mortar at Petersburg, Waud-Petersburg-Crater, Ruins of Richmond April 1865, William-Tecumseh-Sherman, Sherman Atlanta, The burning of Columbia, South Carolina, February 17, 1865, Sherman sea 1868, Virginia Capitol 1865

McLean House parlor, Appomattox Court House, Lee Surrenders to Grant at Appomattox, Virginia, John Wilkes Booth, Abraham Lincoln, The Assassination of President Lincoln - Currier and Ives, Deathbed of President Lincoln, Great Seal

Chapter 6: 15th Amendment, or the Darkey's millennium - 40 acres of land and a mule, from Robert N. Dennis collection of stereoscopic views Carpetbagger, Freedman bureau Harpers cartoon, Mississippi Ku Klux, Flag of Paraguay, José Gaspar Rodríguez de Francia, Brazilian Soldiers, Flag of Brazil, The Emperor's speech (Peter II of Brazil in the opening of the General Assembly), Battalion No. 3 of the Chilean Army, formed in columns in the *Plaza Colon*, Antofagasta, Bolivia, in 1879, Combate naval, Angamos 2, Rainstick, John George Lambton, 1st Earl of Durham by Thomas Phillips, Charles Haddon Spurgeon by Alexander Melville, Alaska Purchase, Andrew Johnson

Chapter 7: Flag of France. Alexandre Cabanel: Napoleon III, Otto von Bismarck-Schönhausen, Grimm's Kinder- und Hausmärchen, Abraham Kuyper, Poll Tax Receipt Jefferson 1917, Thomas Nast from Harpers Weekly, Thomas Nast self-portrait, Merry Old Santa, Statue of Liberty 7, Iowa Flag, Ulysses Grant 1870-1880, R Hayes, Cheese platter

Chapter 8: Pony Express'60 West bound 1860, Pony Express Map William Henry Jackson, Locomotive made by Richard Trevithick and Andrew Vivian (1801), Transcontinental RR 1944-3c, The Last Spike 1869, Kane Assiniboine hunting buffalo, Homesteader NE 1866, Oklahoma Land Rush, Grabill - The Cow Boy, Thomas Alva Edison photo, Flag of Arkansas, James Garfield portrait, Chester Allen portrait

Chapter 9: Statue of Liberty, New York, Armenian-Americans-Boston-1908, Chinese Gold Miners, Ellis Island in 1905, Jane Addams in a car, Taisho enthronement, Sakoku Junk, Commodore Matthew Calbraith Perry, A Japanese print showing three men, believed to be Commander Anan, age 54; Perry, age 49; and Captain Henry Adams, age 59, who opened up Japan to the west, Satsuma-samurai-during-Boshin-war-period, Saigo With Officers, Three pictures of the same noh 'hawk mask' showing how the expression changes with a tilting of the head, Celebrating A Christian Mass In Japan, Grover Cleveland, Benjamin Harrison by Eastman Johnson (1895), Michigan Flag

Chapter 10: Votes for Women Poster, Votes For Women, Official program Woman Suffrage, Handicapped! Women's suffrage poster, 1910s, Procession Washington D.C. March 3 1913, The Drunkards Progress, The Moonshine Man of Kentucky Harper's Weekly 1877, Helen Keller, VOC, The Ottoman Constitution, December 1895, Courtesy of the University of Texas Libraries, The University of Texas at Austin: Ahamid, Young Turks first congress, March Armenians, Khatchkar at Goshavank Monastery in Armenia, Jugha-khachkar, Flag of Wisconsin

Chapter 11: Jim Crow, Jim Crow Car 2, Booker T Washington, WEB DuBois 1918, George Washington Carver, Ned Kelly in 1880, Eureka stockade battle, Leopold ii garter knight, Menelik II, Afrikaner Commandos, Punch Rhodes Colossus, Cecil Rhodes, Robert Baden Powell, Fleur de lys

Chapter 12: Tsar Alexander II, Yuriev day, Shilder Alexander III, Hep-hep riots, Columbus Taking Possession, Battleship Maine, USS Maine, Journal 98, World 98, Nellie Bly, Fil-American War Feb 04,1899, Rough Riders, President William McKinley, President Theodore Roosevelt, 1904

Chapter 13: Destroying Chinese war junks, by E. Duncan (1843), Hong Xiuquan, Chinese officers tear down the British flag on the arrow, Second Opium War-Guangzhou, Boxers Drawing By Koekkoek 1900, Boxer Rebellion, Siege of Peking, Boxer Rebellion, Photograph of China's Empress Dowager, Bound Foot, Bound Foot 2, Chinese Shoe, Bound feet (X-ray), Fire of the Oil Depot Caused by Our Gunfire, Chopsticks, Battle of Port Arthur, Hudson Taylor, Lottie Moon, Flag of Minnesota

Chapter 14: Oregon Trail 1907, Conestoga wagon on Oregon Trail reenactment 1961, Buffalo Soldiers, Five-Civilized-Tribes-Portraits, Cavalry and Indians, Crazy Horse in 1877 shortly before his death. Authenticity of the photo is disputed, Crazy horse c1877, Geronimo (Goyaałé), Edward S. Curtis Geronimo Apache, a Chiricahua Apache; full-length, kneeling with rifle, 1887, Chief Joseph tinted lantern slide, Nez Perce warrior on horse, Ghost Dance at Pine Ridge, En-chief-Sitting-Bull, Hotchkiss gun Wounded Knee, Pueblo, Buffalo Bill Cody ca1875, Buffalo Bill Wild West Show c1899, The Horse in Motion, Jonathan Goforth, Flag of Oregon, Flag of Oregon (reverse)

Chapter 15: Billy Sunday 1921, Sunday Preaching, B&O RR common stock, Wall street 1867,Yuan Emperor Album Genghis Portrait, Flag of the British East India Company (1801), John D. Rockefeller 1885, Puck Cartoon-TeddyRoosevelt-05-23-1906, John Pierpont Morgan, Andrew Carnegie circa 1878 - Project Gutenberg, Roper steam velocipede 1868 The Standard Reference Work, Flag of Kansas

Chapter 16: Henry Ford and the Model T, Ford assembly line - 1913, Wilbur Wright, Orville Wright, First flight 2, 1904 Wright Flyer, Battle of Issus 333BC - Mosaic, Lansereships, Live bridge, Nasseraldin Shah at Talare Ayneh (Mirror Hall), Naser kiss queen, Golestan Palace, Muzaffer-Ed-Din, BP Motor Spirit, 1922, First Majlis MPs, Mohammad Ali Shah, Ahmad Shah Qajar, Churchill portrait, Bulgarians overrun the Turkish positions, S-b war panting by Antoni Piotrowski, Nieuport, Sopwith F-1 Camel USAF, Fokker EIII 210-16, Nieuport 11, Photograph of Manfred von Richthofen, the Red Baron, Flag of Nevada, Taft Official Portrait

Chapter 17: StaCeciliaAcatitlan, Battle of Churubusco, Emperor Maximilian of Mexico, The Last Moments of Maximilian, Sombrero, Francisco I Madero, V Huerta, Carranza Postcard, Plutarco Salute, Titanic, Titanic-lifeboat, Titanic-lifeboat, Stöwer Titanic, French bayonet charge, Wilhelm II.

1905, Vickers IWW, Western front 1914, Christmas Truce 1914, Royal Irish Rifles ration party Somme July 1916, Gassed, Panorama de Verdun, vue prise du Fort de la Chaume, 1917, British Mark V-star Tank, Uncle Sam Wants You, New Mexico's Flag

Chapter 18: Nicholas II with St Vladimir order, Bloody Sunday, St. Petersburg, Russian Troops, Russian Royal Family 1911, Alexis, Rasputin, Kustodiev The Bolshevik, Alexander Kerensky, Lenin, Tov Lenin Poster, Grand Duchess Anastasia Nikolaevna, Lenin, Stalin Portrait, Zimmermann Telegram, 14 Points, Sheet music cover - Here's My Boy, Harry Colebourne and Winnie, 1917 World War I Poster, Flag of Nebraska, Woodrow Wilson

Chapter 19: Jolson black, Louise Brooks, Ernest Hemingway, Babe Ruth, Flag of the United Kingdom, Phytophtora infestans-effects, Irish potato famine Bridget O'Donne, William Gladstone, Hogan's Flying Column,Portrait of Micheál Ó Coileáin, Trifolium repens Leaf April 2, 2010, A Benet-Mercier machine gun section of 2nd Rajput Light Infantry in action in Flanders, during the winter of 1914-15, Major-Dyer-1903, M K Gandhi, Kipling cropped, Sadhu Sundar Singh, Amy Carmichael, Flag of Colorado, Warren G. Harding

Chapter 20: Amelia Earhart, AE and Vega, Council of Four Versailles, Child affected by malnutrition, Children starving during Holodomor, Lenin-office-1918, 1921-1923 Famine in Soviet Russia, Belomorkanal, Peter the Great Egg, Gulag Prisoners, Flag of Washington

Chapter 21: Jitterbugging in Negro juke joint, Saturday evening, outside Clarksdale, Mississippi, Brood (sliced bread), Margaret Gorman, 1801 Antoine-Jean Gros - Bonaparte on the Bridge at Arcole, Lama, Domenico (1823-1890) - Giuseppe Mazzini, Banner of Giovine Italia, Painting of Battle at Soufflot barricades at Rue Soufflot Street on 24 June 1848, Vittorio Emanuele II ritratto, Risorgimento, Giuseppe Garibaldi, Battle of Milazzo, With Victor Emmanuel, Italian infantrymen in 1916, Umberto of Italy, National Fascist Party logo, Benito Mussolini and Fascist Blackshirts in 1920, Ismail Pacha, Mohamed Tewfik, Abbas Hilmi II, Nationalists demonstrating in Cairo, Lillian Trasher, Flag of Montana

Chapter 22: South Manchuria Railway, Sun Yatsen, ROC calendar, Yuan Shikai, Communist star, Chiang Kai-shek, Mao, Communist purge, Mukden 1931, Puyi-Manchukuo, Boulier, Eric Liddell, Gladys Aylward, Anna Eleanor Roosevelt, flag of North Dakota, flag of South Dakota

Chapter 23: Stocks 29, NY stock exchange traders floor, Nixon Ticker TapeParade NYC 1960, 1930, Crowd outside NYSE, Bank Run c1933, Volunteers of America Soup Kitchen WDC, Hooverville Government Archives, Evacuation sales National Archives, . William Gropper's "Construction of a Dam" (1939), FDR fireside chat, New Deal NRA, WPA poster 1935 USA, color photo, Supreme Court 1932, Dust-storm-Texas-1935, Farmer walking in dust storm Cimarron County Oklahoma, Marble toy 2009, Lindbergh St Louis, Lindbergh baby poster, Correa-Martians vs. Thunder Child, Herbert Hoover

Chapter 24: Isabella II, Amadeo king of Spain, Primo-de-Rivera, Francisco Franco, Spanish 11 interbrigada in the battle of Belchev, The hammock, Handmade clay hamsa on a wall, inscribed with the Hebrew word "Behatzlacha" - Success, Stab-in-the-back postcard, Inflation, Hitler 1928 crop, Mein Kampf dust jacket, Firemen work on the burning Reichstag, Hitler Youth, Nazi Swastika, Hindu Swastika, Flag of Oklahoma, Portrait of Franklin Roosevelt

Chapter 25: A German and a Soviet officer shaking hands at the end of the Invasion of Poland, The Royal Castle in Warsaw - burning 17.09.1939, British troops lifeboat dunkerque, Never was so much owed by so many to so few, Inspection at Dachau, Herschel Grynszpan just after his arrest on nov. 7 1938, St Louis Havana, The Wall of ghetto in Warsaw - Building on Nazi -German order August 1940, Female prisoners in Ravensbruck chalk marks show selection for transport, Stroop Report - Warsaw Ghetto Uprising, Ebensee concentration camp prisoners 1945

Chapter 26: President Franklin Roosevelt, Japanese troops entering Saigon, Attack on Pearl Harbor Japanese planes view, The forward magazines of the U.S. Navy battleship USS Arizona (BB-39) explode shortly after 08:00 hrs during the Japanese attack on Pearl Harbor, Hawaii (USA), 7 December 1941, The March of Death, Army B-25 (Doolittle Raid), Jimmy Doolittle, USS Enterprise (CV-6) in Puget Sound, September 1945, SBDs and Mikuma, Lt. Yoshinori Yamaguchi's Yokosuka D4Y3 (Type 33) "Judy" in a suicide dive against the USS Essex (CV-9), Nagasaki bomb, Atomic Effects-Hiroshima, Cranes made by Origami, Sadako Sasaki in Hiroshima, Hiroshima Prefecture, Emperor Showa, Hideki Tojo, Yamamoto-Isoruko, Japan., Japanese fire balloon moffet, Japanese American Internment - Members of the Mochida Family Awaiting Evacuation 1942, Eichmann, Adolf, Herman Goering, Rudolf Hoess, Joseph Mengele, HMS Hood March 17 1924, 1944 Normandy LST, Normandy Supply, military parachutes, US 101st Airborne Division patch, 11th Airborne Division.patch, Patton photo, Patton in Sicily, DeShazer

Chapter 27: Teheran conference-1943, Yalta Conference (Churchill, Roosevelt, Stalin), Potsdam conference 1945, Flag of the United Nations, General George C. Marshall, official military photo, 1946, Ernie Pyle, Old Sikh man carrying wife1947, Ida S. Scudder 1899, Harry S. Truman, Flag of Idaho

Chapter 28: Israel-flag,, Theodore Herzl, Ottoman surrender of Jerusalem restored, Haganah troops on parade, Exodus, Zionist mortar team outside Zafzaf in October 1948, Palestinian refugees, Begin, Carter and Sadat at Camp David 1978, The Beta Yisrael village of Balankab, Dreidel, King Farouk1948, Nasser, Cairo Fire 1952 Revoli Cinema, Aswan dam, Suez Canal in February 1934, Destroyed Egyptian tanks, Anwar Sadat, Naguib and Nasser, C T Studd, Flag of Wyoming, Fort Laramie, Dwight D. Eisenhower

Chapter 29: Republic of China flag, China - Mao, Mao sitting, Peoples Republic of China flag, Mao, Mao flag, A scan of the cover of 1972 English language edition of "Quotations from Chairman Mao Tse-tung", Backyard furnace, People's commune, Tree Sparrow, Red Guards, Deng Xiaoping, Ceremony inaugurating the government of the Republic of Korea, Battle of Inchon, MacArthur Manila, Danwon-Ssireum, Delicate Arch, Flag of Utah

Chapter 30: Evita y Perón, William Walker, Mobutu, Black Hawk Down Super 64 over Mogadishu coast, Apartheid, Apartheid Sign English Afrikaans, Flag of Arizona

Chapter 31: A McDonnell Douglas F-4B Phantom II aircraft (BuNo 150479) from fighter squadron VF-151 Vigilantes intercepts a Soviet Tu-95 Bear D aircraft in the early 1970s, Berliners watching a C-54 land at Berlin Tempelhof Airport, 1948, Gail-Halvorsen-wiggly-wings, Berlin Wall 1961-11-20, Gitmo Aerial, Batista, Fidel Castro, Moncada barracks, Photo courtesy of Luis Korda: Fidel Castro and Camilo Cienfuegos, Havana, January 8, 1959, Joe One, Fat man, Ivy Mike, YB-52 side view, MGR-1 Honest John rocket, Peacekeeper missile, Trident II missile image, W87 MIRV, Alan Shepard, Neil Armstrong, John F. Kennedy, White House color photo portrait, Portrait of President Lyndon B. Johnson

Chapter 32: Constitution Pg 1 of 4, Segregation 1938, Rosa Parks, 101st Airborne at Little Rock Central High, Rodney Powell Nashville sit-ins 1960, I have a dream, Martin Luther King - March on Washington, Bloody Sunday-officers await demonstrators, Martin Luther King Jr, JFK limousine, Oswald in Minsk, Watergate From Air, Nixon edited transcripts, Nixon-depart, Phan Chau Trinh, Phan Boi Chau, A French Foreign Legionnaire goes to war along the dry rib of a rice paddy, during a recent sweep through communist-held areas in the Red River Delta, between Haiphong and Hanoi, Vietnamese refugees board LST 516, U.S Tanks in Vietnam, A U.S. Air Force Boeing B-52D-60-BO Stratofortress (s/n 55-0100) dropping bombs over Vietnam, US riverboat using napalm in Vietnam, from Colonel Hoang Ngoc Lung' The General Offensives of 1968-69. Washington DC: U.S. Army Center of Military History, 1981, CH-53 landing at Defense Attaché Office compound, Operation Frequent Wind, Ho Chi Minh 1946, Vietnamdem, Billy Graham photo, April 11, 1966, Flag of Alaska, Richard Nixon, Gerald Ford

Chapter 33: Mao, Bulganin, Stalin, Ulbricht Tsedenbal, Panel Khrushchev house in Tomsk, Cheboksary-Residential area, Nixon and Khrushchev, Warsaw Pact artillery unit in Czechoslovakia, 1968, Mujahid-MANPAD, Olympic flag, USSR stamp S.Smith 1985, Mikhail Gorbachev 1987, Reagan Berlin Wall, Nicolae Ceausescu, President Kennedy signs Nuclear Test Ban Treaty, 07 October 1963, Reagan and Gorbachev signing, Apollo 1's Command Module, Challenger explosion, STS-107 launch, Photo courtesy of Author Jako Jellema: Anne van der Bijl, Flag of Hawaii, Jimmy Carter, Ronald Reagan

Chapter 34: Reza Shah Pahlavi, Shah of Iran, Anglo-Iranian Oil Company, Abadan, Iran, Prime Minister Mohammed Mossadegh of Iran, Portrait of Imam Khomeini, Eagle Claw wrecks at Desert One April 1980, Iraq, Saddam Hussein, Kurdish Cavalry, Abrams in formation, USAF F-16A F-15C F-15E

Desert Storm, Saddam Statue, George H. W. Bush, William Jefferson Clinton

Creative Commons Attribution-Share Alike 2.5 Generic/GNU Free Documentation License/Copyright Free Use:

Chapter 1: Zachary Taylor
Chapter 2: The Saladin Citadel of Cairo
Chapter 3: Photo by James Mollison: Khyber Pass Pakistan, African beads Ghana, Flag of Alabama
Chapter 4: Photo courtesy of MamaGeek: John Brown's Fort
Chapter 5: Gettysburg national cemetery
Chapter 7: Photo courtesy of Benh LIEU SONG: Eiffel Tower, Fenlon Elevator
Chapter 8: Edison bulb, Cyrus McCormick engraving, Cyrus McCormick's reaper, Jerome Increase Case, Batteuse 1881, James Garfield portrait, Chester Arthur, Grover Cleveland
Chapter 9: Photo courtesy of Chris 73: Jesus on cross to step on, The Mackinac Bridge
Chapter 10: Photo courtesy of Wendy Kaveney:"Votes for Women" pennant, General van Heutz and staff, Ottoman Flag, The Red Cross and the Red Crescent emblems at the museum in Geneva, State Capital in Wisconsin
Chapter 11: Photo courtesy of Diliff: Koala climbing tree, Photo courtesy of Chensiyuan: Ned Kelly armor library, Photo courtesy of Robbie Sproule: Peach Melba
Chapter 12: Periodic table monument
Chapter 13: Prokudin-Gorskii-25, Photo courtesy of Timothy MN: Laura Ingalls Wilder House
Chapter 14: Photo courtesy of Mike Tigas from Columbia, MO, United States: Chimney Rock NE, Photo courtesy of Karthikc123: Shoshone Falls
Chapter 15: NYC NYSE, Photo courtesy of Eva K.: Bull and bear in front of the Frankfurt Stock Exchange, Short (finance), Scottish Tartan, 1909 White Steam car, Photo courtesy of Richard Webb: Re-Tyred, Moxie logo, Logo-mw, A. M. Ward, Abandoned Montgomery Ward, Sears, John Deere portrait, John Deere Model B, Chicago-fire1
Chapter 16: Oil rig, Gavrilo Princip
Chapter 17: Battle of Puebla, Porfirio Diaz, Rebels fighting during the battle for Mexico City, Poinsettia, Papel picado, Black hand cockade, Gavrilo Princip, A British gas bomb, This is a photograph of a young German soldier engaged in the Battle of the Somme, 1916. He wears a helmet, so the photo is from late in 1916
Chapter 18: Saint Isaac's Cathedral, 1915 painting depicting the sinking of the Lusitania by the German U-boat U 20, Photo courtesy of Maya Wildevuur: Poppies in the Field, Doughnuts cz, Winnie the Pooh, York, Portrait of Hugh A. Ball during his enlistment in the US Army as a WWI soldier
Chapter 19: Radio: Kosmaj 49, :(Ireland) Dublin Castle Up Yard, Bodiam murder holes
Chapter 20: Ederle, Gertrud: Schwimmerin, USA, Versailles Palace, The semi-official emblem of the League of Nations, used from 1939 to 1941. Vectors by Mysid, based on FOTW. This low-resolution vector logo is used to illustrate the League of Nations, Stalin Portrait, Photos courtesy of Stan Shebs: Moscow Kremlin Egg and Madonna Lily Egg and Equestrian Egg, Governor Mansion in Washington State
Chapter 21: Painted walls in the burial chamber (Tutankhamen's tomb) Valley of the Kings, Egypt, Benito Mussolini, Photo courtesy of François Malan: Panorama of St Peter's Square in Vatican City, Fes
Chapter 22: The Long March, Photo courtesy of Dean Franklin: Mount Rushmore Monument
Chapter 24: Columnas Plus Ultra, Hamsa, Adolf Hitler-1933, Adolf Hitler (Porträts), Ernst Röhm, Adolf Hitler and Eva Braun with dogs (German_Shepherd_Dog "Blondi"?) at the Berghof, Narnian World
Chapter 25: The Anschluss, British Prime Minister Neville Chamberlain arrives at Munich for the Munich Conference, 29 September 1938, Infobox collage for WWII, Poland, column of motorized German troops, Parade of German troops in Paris. View of the troops with the Arc de Triomphe in the background, Three German Junkers Ju 87D dive bombers over Yugoslavia, in October 1943, German soldier in front the 1918 monument, German Heinkel He 111 bombers over the English Channel 1940, The aftermath of a bombing raid in Stalingrad, Infantry and a supporting StuG III assault gun advance towards the city center, Auschwitz concentration camp, arrival of Hungarian Jews, Photo courtesy of Michael Hanke: Zyklon B container, Summer 1944, Roll-call of prisoners 20 July 1938, Treblinka Concentration Camp sign by David Shankbone, Yellow badge Star of David called "Judenstern". Part of the exhibition in the Jewish Museum Westphalia, Dorsten, Germany. The wording is the German word for Jew (Jude), written in mock-Hebrew script, Ravensbruck concentration camp
Chapter 26: USMC War Memorial Sunset Parade 2008-07-08, Joseph Goebbels, Rudolf Heß, Reinhard Heydrich, Heinrich Himmler, Schlachtschiff Bismarck, The Wolfsschanz e after the bomb, Ardennenoffensive,Grenadiere in Luxemburg, Erwin Rommel
Chapter 27: The United Nations Building, Nanga parbat, Kashmir Pakistan by gul791, Sikh man at the Golden Temple, Indira Gandhi, Rangoli in India, Flower kolam made at an office in Chennai for the Keralan festival Onam, Game-asia-kabadi, Photo courtesy of Wikimedia-Commons User Túrelio, Creative Commons BY-SA 2.0-de
Chapter 28: 6 days war, Bridge Crossing, Panorama of Jerusalem from the Mount of Olives, Egyptian flag
Chapter 29: Chinese Yoyo, Anapji Pond-Gyeongju-Korea, Photo courtesy of Steve Evans: Lisu Woman
Chapter 30: Lake Titicaca on the Andes from Bolivia, Rio Corcovado Pain de Sucre, Cristo Redeemer, Photo courtesy of Andrew Bertram: Muisca raft Legend of El Dorado Offerings of gold link: http://en.wikipedia.org/wiki/File:Muisca_raft_Legend_of_El_Dorado_Offerings_of_gold.jpg, Devil's Island, Photo courtesy of the Jonestown report: Jonestown Houses, Machu Picchu, Peru, Angel Falls, Bananas, Patrice Lumumba, Photo Courtesy of John Martinez Pavliga: Baidoa 1992 Somalia, Nelson Mandela-2008, Kente Weaver, Ewe kente stripes, Ghana, Photo courtesy of Jeff Dean: Arizona State Capital
Chapter 31: Juggling on the Berlin Wall, US Air Force U-2, Soviet-R-12-nuclear-ballistic missile, Che High, Sputnik asm, Mercury-Redstone 4 Launch, Gemini 7 in orbit, 5927 NASA
Chapter 32: Rosa Parks Bus, Young Vietnamese girl in aodai dress and non la hat
Chapter 33: Nikita S. Chruchtschow, Brezhnev, East German border guards look through a hole in the Berlin Wall in 1990, Photo Courtesy of Sue Ream: Berlin Wall-Brandenburg Gate, Photo courtesy of Reiche, Hartmut: Berlin, Wall in Mauer am Reichstag, Photo credited: attribute www.kremlin.ru: Boris Yeltsin 19 August 1991, Photo credited: attribute www.kremlin.ru: Boris Yeltsin, Photo courtesy of Cristo Vlahos: U.S.S. Arizona Memorial at Pearl Harbor, Hawaii
Chapter 34: Photo courtesy of Fabienkhan: Jamkaran Mosque, Imam Khomeini in Mehrabad, Azadi Monument, Shahyad, photo courtesy of Tobias Jäger: Two light-wind-kites in the sky close together

Fair Use:

Chapter 15: Rich Uncle Pennybags: source: http://en.wikipedia.org/wiki/File:GEM_Monopoly_box.jpg: This image is covered by fair use for use in Rich Uncle Pennybags because: Parker Brothers (the copyright holder) have released no freely licensed images of the cover so it cannot be replaced by a free image, It is used only to illustrate the cover of the board game, It is of low resolution preventing commercial re-use of this image, This image does not reduce the profits made from the sale of this game, also the game is no longer for sale

Chapter 18: Rin Tin Tin: source: http://en.wikipedia.org/wiki/File:Rintintin.jpg: This image is covered by fair use because no freely licensed images of the image have been released so it cannot be replaced by a free image. It is only being use to illustrate how the dog was featured as a leading performer in a film. It is of low resolution and does not reduce the profits made from the movie that is no longer in publication.

Chapter 19: Steamboat-Willie: source: http://en.wikipedia.org/wiki/File:Steamboat-willie-title2.jpg: This image is covered by fair use because no freely licensed images of the image have been released so it cannot be replaced by a free image. It is only being used to identify the film Steamboat Wille. It is of low resolution and does not reduce the profits made from the movie.

Chapter 20: Molotov-Ribbentrop Pact: source: http://en.wikipedia.org/wiki/File:Davidlowrendezvous.png: Though this image is subject to copyright, its use is covered by the U.S. fair use laws because: It's a low resolution copy of a drawing. It doesn't limit the copyright owner's rights to sell the drawing in any way, in fact, it may encourage sales. Because of the low resolution, copies could not be used to make illegal prints/copies of the artwork/image. The image illustrates a subject of discussion in the article.

Chapter 25: Anne Frank http://en.wikipedia.org/wiki/File:Anne_Frank.jpg - Though this Though this image is subject to copyright, its use is covered by the U.S. fair use laws because there is no free equivalent picture that could be created to give the same information.

Chapter 30: http://en.wikipedia.org/wiki/File:Hector_pieterson.jpg: Antoinette Sithole and Mbuyisa Makhubo carrying and 12-year-old Hector Pieterson moments after he was shot by South African police during a peaceful student demonstration in Soweto, South Africa. Though this image is subject to copyright, its use is covered by the U.S. fair use laws because: It's a low resolution copy and It is being used as an Iconic image discussed in the article in terms of the impact it had on changing the attitude of the nation and the world to the problems of Apartheid in South Africa. http://en.wikipedia.org/wiki/File:Jim_Elliot.JPG Jim Elliot: No free or public domain images have been located for this subject. http://en.wikipedia.org/wiki/File:Nate_Saint.JPG Nate Saint: No free or public domain images have been located for this subject. http://en.wikipedia.org/wiki/File:Ed_McCully.JPG Ed McCully: No free or public domain images have been located for this subject. http://en.wikipedia.org/wiki/File:The_Flemings.JPG Peter Fleming: No free or public domain images have been located for this subject. http://en.wikipedia.org/wiki/File:Youderian_Family.JPG Roger Youderian: No free or public domain images have been located for this subject.

Chapter 33: http://en.wikipedia.org/wiki/File:1956_hungarians_stalin_head.jpg: A photo of Hungarians crowded around the head of the 25-meter tall destroyed Stalin Monument in Budapest wrecked as part of the sixteen Demands of Hungarian Revolutionaries of 1956 during the 1956 Hungarian Revolution .No free or public domain images have been located for this subject. This is a historically significant photo - it is low quality and is being used to illustrate the destruction of the Stalin Monument in Budapest as part of the Demands of Hungarian Revolution.

Chapter 34: Burj Khalifa building - Though this image is subject to copyright, its use is covered by the U.S. fair use laws because: It is a historically significant photo of a famous building. The photo is only being used for informational purposes. Its inclusion in the article adds significantly to the article because the photo and its historical significance are the object of discussion in the article. Also this image can be copied in the United States under Freedom of panorama

MAP CREDITS:

Public Domain Creative Commons License:

Chapter 1: Imperial Federation, Map of the World Showing the Extent of the British Empire in 1886, India (orthographic projection)
Chapter 2: Sevastopol, Ukraine, Suez Canal, USA topographical
Chapter 3: Afghanistan (orthographic projection)
Chapter 4: Reynolds's Political Map of the United States 1856, USA Map 1864 including Civil War Divisions
Chapter 5: American Civil War Battles by Theater, Year
Chapter 6: Map of the War of the Pacific, Province of Quebec 1774, Canada (orthographic projection)
Chapter 7: EU-France, EU-Germany
Chapter 8: Transcontinental railroad route, Standard time zones of the world
Chapter 9: Japan-location-cia
Chapter 10: Sumatra Location, Territorial changes of the Ottoman Empire 1862, Switzerland
Chapter 11: Australia (orthographic projection), Australia, Scramble for Africa
Chapter 12: Russian Federation (orthographic projection), Location Cuba, The Philippines and ASEAN (orthographic projection), Pm-map, Kroonland in Panama Canal, 1915, US insular areas
Chapter 13: Korea, Port Arthur
Chapter 16: Balkan peninsula
Chapter 17: Viceroyalty of New Spain Location 1819, Division Politica Mexico
Chapter 18: Russian Federation (orthographic projection)
Chapter 19: Ireland 1450,India (orthographic projection)
Chapter 20: Alsace-Lorraine, Map courtesy of Hoshie: Location Yugoslavia, USSR (orthographic projection), Russia (orthographic projection)
Chapter 21: EU-Italy, Italy unification 1815 -1870, Triple Alliance
Chapter 22: China Shanxi Yuncheng
Chapter 23: Map of US 66
Chapter 24: Morocco-spanish-protectorate-1955, Map of the German Reich, (Republic of Weimar/Third Reich) 1919–1937
Chapter 25: second World War Europe 1941-1942 map
Chapter 27: Map-Germany-1945, Occupied Berlin, British Indian Empire 1909 Imperial Gazetteer of India, Partition of India, Kashmir map, Pakistan before the Bangladesh War in 1971
Chapter 28: Location Israel, UN Partition Plan Palestine, Cia-Israel-map, Ethiopia, Egypt (orthographic projection)
Chapter 29: Hong Kong, Taiwan, Korea, Korean dmz map
Chapter 30: Somalia, South African home lands map
Chapter 31: Map-Germany-1945, Occupied Berlin, Cuba, Bay of Pigs
Chapter 34: Kuwait

Julia Nalle:

Chapter 3: Travels of David Livingstone, Alabama
Chapter 2: Crimean War, Suez Canal
Chapter 4: West Virginia
Chapter 6: South America, Canada, Maine

Chapter 7: France, Iowa
Chapter 8: Arkansas
Chapter 9: Michigan
Chapter 10: Wisconsin
Chapter 13: Asia, Minnesota
Chapter 14: Oregon
Chapter 15: Kansas
Chapter 16: Persia, Nevada
Chapter 17: New Mexico
Chapter 18: Nebraska
Chapter 19: Ireland, Colorado
Chapter 20: Peace of Versailles, Washington
Chapter 21: Africa, Montana
Chapter 22: China, North Dakota, South Dakota
Chapter 24: Oklahoma
Chapter 27: Idaho
Chapter 28: Wyoming
Chapter 29: Asia, Utah
Chapter 30: South America, Central America, Africa, Arizona
Chapter 31: USSR
Chapter 32: Alaska
Chapter 33: RUSSIA, Hawaii
Chapter 34: Iran and Iraq

Cover and Logo Design by Poppies Blooming, London, England
www.poppiesblooming.co.uk

Index

Symbols

"separate but equal", *107, 153, 498*
11th airborne division, *405*
17th parallel, *509*
18th amendment, *139-141*
19th amendment, *138, 277*
101st airborne division, *404*
1906 san francisco earthquake, *223*
1980 summer olympics, *525*
21st amendment, *141*
22nd amendment, *366*
24th amendment, *107*
26th of july movement, *485*
38th parallel, *450-454*
40 acres and a mule, *76, 82, 84*

A

a.a. milne, *272*
abacus, *330*
abbas i, *32*
abbasid caliphate, *228*
abdul-aziz, *547*
abdulhamid ii, *143, 145-149, 235, 318*
abdulmecid i, *144*
able archer, *525*
abolition, *63, 137*
abolitionist, *20-22, 36, 52-53, 62, 111, 123, 137, 162, 208*
abolitionists, *19, 21-22, 35-36, 44, 51-53, 63, 66, 82, 122, 137, 162, 172, 465*
aborigines, *156*
abraham kuyper, *106*
abraham lincoln, *20-21, 23, 49, 51, 54, 62, 66-67, 77, 169, 334, 501*
aceh war, *142*
acerbo law, *315*
act of union, *92, 280, 284*
adana massacre, *149*
adlai stevenson, *440*
admiral chester nimitz, *388, 392*
adolf eichmann, *361, 398*
afghanistan, *37-42, 227, 229-230, 232, 250, 291, 437, 477, 522-524, 533,* 552, 555-556
afghans, *37*
africa, *11-13, 22, 24, 31-33, 37, 43-46, 82, 92, 124, 141, 153, 155, 159-167, 172, 193, 233-234, 253, 257, 269, 288, 294, 297, 312, 316, 319, 352, 372, 375, 377, 386, 400-403, 405, 414, 436-437, 439-440, 458, 461, 466-468, 470-474, 492, 534*
african national congress, *470-471, 473*
african trade beads, *46*
afrikaans, *164, 470, 472*
afrikaner national party, *470*
afrikaners, *164, 166, 470-473*
age of counter reform, *169*
agent orange, *511-512, 514*
agha muhammed khan, *229*
agustin de iturbide, *242*
ahmad shah, *37-38, 42, 233, 541*
ahmad shah durrani, *37-38, 42*
air force one, *496*
aircraft, *224, 226-227, 237-238, 296, 387, 390-393, 396, 401, 404, 408, 430, 477, 490, 496, 511, 545*
aircraft carriers, *387, 390-392, 396*
akbar, *14, 39-41*
akbar khan, *39-41*
al capone, *140, 340*
al jolson, *277*
alabama, *48, 54, 71, 139, 154, 201, 498-504*
alan shepard, *494*
alaska, *34, 95, 202, 259, 516*
albania, *31, 234, 236-237, 304, 411, 478, 530*
albert sydney johnston, *61*
alexander dubcek, *522*
alexander graham bell, *122*
alexander hamilton, *50*
alexander ii, *168-170, 180, 259-260, 263*
alexander iii, *169-170, 194, 259, 263, 266, 305*
alexander kerensky, *261, 263-264*
alexander solzhenitsyn, *305*
alexandria, *31, 402*
alfonso xii, *352*
alfonso xiii, *352-354*
alfred t. mahan, *173*
alfred, lord tennyson, *28-29*
aliyah bet ships, *427-428*
all-india muslim league, *415-416*
allied powers, *253, 269, 295*
allies, *26-27, 39, 103, 137, 146-147, 177, 192, 234, 236, 244, 250, 252-253, 268, 270, 275, 278, 284, 304, 313-314, 316, 318-319, 326, 357, 366-373, 375-377, 383, 385, 387, 392-395, 397-399, 401-406, 409-413, 424, 435, 440-441, 449-450, 477-482, 488, 491, 508-509, 519-520, 522-523, 525, 539, 542, 546*
alma-ata protocol, *531*
alsace-lorraine, *104, 250, 295-298, 357, 368*
alvaro obregon, *247*
alvin york, *273*
amadeo i, *351*
amelia earhart, *224, 294-295, 337*
american mutual defense treaty, *448-449*
american revolution, *50-51, 91-92, 98, 107, 109, 154, 156, 257, 263*
american samoa, *34, 179*
americas, *11, 178, 248*
amoy, *183*
amritsar massacre, *287*
amy carmichael, *291*
anarchist, *180*
anastasia romanova, *265*
anatolia, *31*
ancient regime, *97-98*
andersonville, *78-79*
andrew carnegie, *216, 218-219, 224*
andrew jackson, *202*
andrew johnson, *60, 76, 80, 82, 96, 110, 508, 554*
angel falls, *463*
anglicans, *280*
anglo-afghan war, *39-40, 42*
anglo-dutch treaty, *142*
anglo-german agreement, *370*
anglo-irish treaty, *283-285*
anglo-persian oil company, *231, 234, 542*
anglo-russian convention, *232, 250, 541*
anglo-zulu war, *163*
annam, *510*
anne frank, *382-383*
anne sullivan, *139*
annie oakley, *209*
anschluss, *368-369, 404*
antarctic treaty, *533*
anthony eden, *437*
anti-ballistic missile treaty, *533*
anti-saloon league, *139-140*
antirevolutionary party, *106*
antonio lopez de santa anna, *242*
anwar sadat, *431, 438*
apache, *199, 203, 205*
apartheid, *470-474*
apollo 11, *494-495*
apollo i disaster, *535*
apollo missions, *494, 535*
appeasement, *369, 453, 519*
appomattox, *47, 57, 66, 71, 77-79, 204*
april uprising, *144*
arab revolt, *427, 546-547*
arab-israeli war of 1948, *429-430, 432, 434*
arabia, *31, 426, 540, 546-547, 550-551*
arabian sea, *32*
arapaho, *115, 203*
archduke franz ferdinand, *250-251*
argentina, *85-87, 398, 458-459, 463, 533*
argentine revolution, *458*
arizona, *202-203, 205, 238, 258, 292, 348, 387, 456, 537, 556*
arkansas, *56, 72-73, 121-122, 199, 201, 365, 499-500, 553-554*
armenia, *143, 147, 149-150, 229, 478, 532*
armenian genocide, *148-149*
armistice day, *270*
army of retribution, *40*
arrow incident, *185*
art, *100, 110, 150, 182, 248, 305, 333, 400, 421, 446*
arthur macarthur, *176-177, 452*

arvn, *510*
asia minor, *11, 24, 31, 228*
assassinated, *37, 40, 66, 169, 180, 230, 247, 263, 289, 309, 312, 328, 353, 368, 399, 493, 501, 503, 511*
assassination, *66, 80-83, 96, 113, 123, 147, 169-170, 180-181, 230, 237, 250-252, 266, 288, 296, 300, 318, 325, 332, 405, 420, 495-496, 504-505, 518, 549*
assassination of president lincoln, *80, 82-83*
assembly line, *225-226*
aswan dam, *435-436*
atacama desert, *88-90, 459-460*
atlanta, *73, 75-77, 96, 503*
attorney general, *500, 506-507*
auca indians, *475*
august chapdelaine, *185*
august coup attempt, *530-531*
aurangzeb, *14*
auschwitz, *380-383, 399*
auspicious incident of 1826, *143*
australia, *13, 22, 92, 153, 156-159, 253-254, 269, 284, 286, 371, 377, 389, 401, 451, 461, 470, 551*
austria, *25, 99, 101-102, 104, 143, 146, 148, 150, 183, 187, 232, 235-237, 250-253, 257, 269-270, 295-296, 298, 308-310, 312-313, 350, 358, 368-369, 371, 404, 411, 426, 529*
austria-hungary, *146, 148, 232, 235-237, 250-253, 257, 269-270, 295-296, 298, 312-313, 368, 426*
austro-prussian war, *102, 104*
axis powers, *370, 375, 377, 386, 401, 403*
ayatollah khomeini, *538, 545, 549, 552*
azadi tower, *546*
azerbaijan, *229, 376, 478, 532*
aztec empire, *241*

B

b-25 bomber, *390, 408*
b-29 bomber, *393-394*
b-52, *488*
b.f. goodrich, *220*
ba'ath party, *549*
babe ruth, *278*
bahadur shah zafar, *17*
bahrain, *548*
baker island, *34*
bakufu, *129*
balfour declaration, *269, 427*
balkan league, *235-236, 251*
balkan peninsula, *105, 143, 145, 147-148, 234-237, 251, 259, 270, 312-313*
balkan wars, *148, 225, 234-235*
balkans, *11, 143-146, 234-235, 250, 259, 316*
baltimore, *72, 79, 113, 278*
banana republics, *464*
bangladesh, *418-419*
bangladesh liberation war, *418-419*
bank runs, *339-340, 343-344*
banks, *151, 157, 213, 218, 230, 264, 300, 336-337, 339-344, 358, 387, 401, 436*
bantu authorities act, *471*
bantustans, *472*
bao dai, *509, 513*
barakzai dynasty, *38-40, 524*
bastille, *98*
bataan death march, *389, 397*
bataan peninsula, *389*
batak massacre, *144*
batavian republic, *141*
battle of adwa, *163*
battle of antietam, *62-63*
battle of argonne forest, *273*
battle of balaclava, *26-28*
battle of bloody ridge, *454*
battle of britain, *234, 371, 374-375*
battle of bull run/manassas, *57*
battle of buxar, *15*
battle of chancellorsville, *58, 69, 71, 207*
battle of chickamauga, *73*
battle of cold harbor, *74*
battle of fort stedman, *74*
battle of france, *372-374*
battle of fredericksburg, *68-69, 71*
battle of gallipoli, *234*
battle of gettysburg, *70-72, 204*
battle of heartbreak ridge, *454*
battle of iwo jima, *393*
battle of leipzig, *308*
battle of leyte gulf, *392-393*
battle of little bighorn, *203-204*
battle of manila bay, *175, 178*
battle of moscow, *401*
battle of okinawa, *393-394, 414*
battle of old baldy, *454*
battle of plassey, *15*
battle of pork chop hill, *454*
battle of puebla, *243-245*
battle of rosebud creek, *204*
battle of santiago de cuba, *177*
battle of sedan, *99, 103-104*
battle of shiloh, *61-62*
battle of shiroyama, *132*
battle of sinop, *25*
battle of somme, *256*
battle of spotsylvania, *74*
battle of stalingrad, *376, 401, 409, 480*
battle of tennenberg, *253*
battle of the ardennes forest, *253*
battle of the bulge, *406-407*
battle of the crater, *74*
battle of the frontiers, *253*
battle of the marne, *253*
battle of the masurian lakes, *253*
battle of the philippine sea, *392*
battle of the wilderness, *73-74*
battle of tsushima, *193*
battle of verdun, *255-256*
battle of waterloo, *98-99*
battle of wounded knee, *203, 208*
bay of bengal, *14*
bay of pigs, *486-487, 491-493, 495*
beauregard, *58, 61*
beer hall putsch, *360-361, 399*
beijing, *100, 182, 186-188, 327-328, 442-443, 448, 534*
beiyang army, *324*
belarus, *265, 270, 478, 531-532*
belavezha accords, *531*
belgian congo, *160, 467*
belgium, *159-161, 166, 183, 252-253, 269-271, 297, 372-373, 376-377, 379-380, 401, 403, 406, 413, 466-468*
belize, *463-464*
belzec, *380*
bengal, *14-15, 287, 416, 418, 422*
bengali, *418*
benito juarez, *99, 243-244, 315*
benjamin harrison, *135-136*
bergen-belsen, *383*
berlin, *146, 161-162, 235, 239, 304, 361-362, 364, 370, 374, 378, 382, 400, 405-406, 411-412, 477-482, 491, 521, 524, 526-529, 553*
berlin airlift, *477, 480-481*
berlin blockade, *412, 479-481*
berlin conference, *161-162*
berlin wall, *412, 481-482, 521, 524, 526-529, 553*
beta israel, *432-433*
bey, *30*
bhopal, *421*
big foot, *207*
big three, *296, 409-411, 424, 479*
bill clinton, *553-554, 556*
billy graham, *515*
billy sunday, *212*
bismarck, *102-105, 132, 161, 173, 235, 297, 333, 400-401*
black hand, *237, 251-252*
black hawk down, *469*
black homelands act, *472*
black monday, *339, 344-345*
black sea, *17, 25-27, 143, 228, 236, 259, 303, 381, 409*
black thursday, *339*
black tuesday, *339*
blackface, *153, 277*
blacks, *21, 83-84, 107, 111, 124, 153-155, 162, 277, 288, 470-473, 497-500, 502-503, 515*
blackshirts, *314-315*
blitzkrieg, *372, 376*
blood libel, *377*
bloody kansas, *19, 36, 49, 52-53, 208*
bloody lane, *62*
bloody sunday, *260-261, 502-503*
bob haldeman, *506*
boer, *13, 163-167, 233, 470*
bolivia, *85, 88-90, 458-460, 462-463, 492*
bolsheviks, *261, 264-267, 269-270, 299-300, 303, 305, 357, 378, 410, 526, 534*
bombay, *15, 290*
booker t. washington, *154-155*
boomers, *118*
boris yeltsin, *530-531*
boshin war, *131*
bosnia, *144, 146, 234-237, 251-252, 270, 298*
bosnia and herzegovina, *144, 146*
boundary treaty of 1866, *89*
boxer rebellion, *100, 180, 186-190, 194-195, 210, 322, 330*
boy scouts, *167*
boycott, *378, 473, 498-499, 524-525, 543*
bozeman trail, *199*
brain trust, *343, 345*
brandenburg gate, *482, 527-528*
brazil, *85-88, 130, 311, 460, 463*
brazzaville, *468*
brezhnev doctrine, *523, 528*
brigham young, *199, 457*
britain, *12-15, 17, 24-26, 30-31, 33, 38-40, 42-47, 49, 62-63, 91-93, 98-100, 102, 113, 119, 142-144, 146-147, 156, 158, 160-161, 163-166, 182-184, 186-187, 193-194, 197, 200,*

229-234, 237, 243, 250, 252-257, 262, 268-269, 277-278, 280-285, 287-289, 296, 308-309, 313, 318-319, 330-331, 351, 364, 369-375, 377, 379, 381, 385-387, 399-401, 403, 407, 409, 411-417, 425-428, 434-437, 448-449, 451, 461, 463, 466, 468, 470-471, 479, 487, 490-491, 531, 537, 541-543, 546-548, 551
british, 11-17, 26-28, 30-31, 33, 35, 38-42, 44, 47, 50, 63, 80, 91-93, 105, 119, 141-142, 146-147, 154, 156-158, 163-167, 172, 182-188, 194, 197-198, 201, 216, 230-234, 238, 248, 250, 253-256, 268-269, 271, 273, 281-290, 307-308, 313, 317-319, 345-346, 364, 369, 371-375, 377, 381, 386, 399-401, 403, 405, 415-417, 420, 422, 425-428, 434-438, 441, 448, 453, 461, 463, 465, 468, 470-471, 490, 519, 537, 542-543, 546-548, 550
british columbia, 92-93
british empire, 11-15, 44, 92, 146, 158, 164-165, 233-234, 254, 271, 288, 290, 308, 317, 438, 470
british mandate for palestine, 426-428, 547
british petroleum, 231
british raj, 16-17, 286-287
british south africa company, 163, 166
brother andrew, 536
brown bess, 42
brown v. board of education, 498-499, 504
brownshirts, 315, 359-360, 362-363, 399
bucharest, 236, 529
budapest, 521
buddhism, 14, 183, 363, 454
buell, 61
buenos aires, 458-459
buffalo, 113, 115-116, 118, 180, 199, 202-204, 208-209, 292, 347
buffalo bill, 113, 116, 208-209, 292
buffalo soldiers, 199, 203
buford, 70
bugs moran, 140
bugsy siegel, 140
bulgaria, 143-148, 234-237, 251, 253, 269, 295, 304, 377, 401, 411, 426, 478, 530
bull connor, 504
bull market, 214, 336
bull moose progressives, 181, 240
bull run, 57-59, 62, 65, 75, 78
burma, 15, 17, 441
burnside, 59, 68, 110
bushido, 132
bushrangers, 157

C

c.s. lewis, 364-365
c.t. studd, 438-439
cairo, 31-32, 166, 320, 431, 434-435
cairo fire, 434-435
calabar river, 45
calcutta, 14-15, 416, 422-423
california, 19, 23, 34-35, 56, 112-115, 118-119, 125, 130, 199, 201, 209-210, 223, 238, 269, 273, 348, 387, 453, 461-462, 503, 517, 539
california gold rush, 113, 118, 125
california trail, 199
caliphs, 540-541
calvin coolidge, 334-336
cambodia, 100, 386, 508, 510, 513, 522
camp david peace accords, 431, 438
campaign to suppress counter-revolutionaries, 444
canada, 13, 19-20, 34, 79, 90-94, 123, 134, 140, 158, 196, 206, 253-254, 269, 272, 284, 286-287, 306, 321, 331, 333, 377, 379, 396, 401, 423, 451, 461, 470, 487, 516, 538, 551
canton, 182-183, 185, 324
cape colony, 43, 163-166, 470
cape of good hope, 43, 163
cape town, 163, 166
capitol, 34, 110, 214
carbonari, 309-312
carlos antonia lopez, 86
carpetbaggers, 83
carrie nation, 141
catherine the great, 24, 168, 170, 229, 455
catholic church, 11, 101, 242, 244, 247, 279, 308, 316-317, 351, 353-355, 378, 423, 459
catholics, 101, 133, 247, 279-280, 282, 285, 316-317, 351, 354, 357, 378, 455, 486
cattle, 16, 109, 116, 118-119, 121, 199, 208, 210, 224, 239, 258, 274, 292, 306, 321, 333, 347, 365, 423, 439, 457
causeway heights, 27-28
cawnpore, 17
cecil rhodes, 161, 163-167
cemetery ridge, 70
central america, 82, 112, 130, 178, 458, 463-465, 492, 539
central committee, 267, 300, 303, 522-523
central intelligence agency, 467, 486, 490, 543
central pacific railroad, 114-115, 125
central powers, 148, 253-254, 269, 296, 298, 318, 426
challenger disaster, 535
chancellor, 103-105, 173, 233, 235, 297, 315, 358-359, 361-362, 368, 378, 398, 406
charge of the light brigade, 26-27, 29
charlemagne, 101
charles albert, 310-311
charles de gaulle, 372
charles guiteau, 122-123
charles lindbergh, 294, 307, 337, 346, 363
charles spurgeon, 93-94, 106
charles x, 97-98
chattanooga, 73
che guevara, 492, 505
cheka, 264, 266
chelmno, 381
cherokee, 117, 202
chester arthur, 123
cheyenne, 115, 199, 203-204, 439
chiang kai-shek, 324-327, 441-443, 448, 477, 484
chicago, 52, 128, 140, 212, 221-223, 278, 340, 348, 424, 456, 556
chickasaw, 202, 365
chief joseph, 205-206
chile, 88-90, 460, 462
china, 11-13, 43, 100, 114, 125-127, 131, 141, 180, 182-195, 208, 210, 253, 269, 291, 293, 299, 322-331, 367, 385-387, 389-390, 401, 408, 413, 417-418, 420, 424, 435, 438-450, 452-453, 455-456, 477, 484-485, 490-492, 508-510, 513, 515, 519, 522, 534, 536, 552-553
china inland mission, 187, 194-195, 210, 291, 331, 438-439, 456
chinese, 116, 125-127, 130, 182-192, 194-195, 210, 248, 322-331, 386, 390, 394, 410, 435, 441-450, 452, 455-456, 509, 522, 534
chinese civil war, 326, 442, 509
chinese exclusion act, 125-127
chinese exclusion repeal act, 126
chinese revolution, 322-323, 325, 327-328, 448
chinese soviet republic, 326
chinese warlord era, 324, 328
chinook, 205
chisholm trail, 118
chlorine gas, 255
choctaw, 202
chopsticks, 190
christ the redeemer, 460
christmas truce, 254
chrysler building, 342
church of the holy sepulcher, 25
church of the nativity, 25
cia, 467, 486-487, 490, 492, 543-544, 553
cinco de mayo, 243-244
citadel of cairo, 31-32
citizenship, 124, 126, 315, 335, 378, 432, 472, 505
civil rights act of 1957, 500
civil rights act of 1960, 500
civil rights act of 1964, 83, 502
civil war, 18-24, 33-35, 38, 47, 49-60, 62-63, 66-68, 70-73, 76, 78-79, 82-84, 96, 99, 109-111, 113-114, 116, 118, 122-123, 135, 137, 154, 180, 199, 204, 207, 212, 217, 239, 242-244, 259, 264, 266-267, 269, 279, 284-285, 299-301, 303, 314, 326, 334, 350-351, 354-356, 428-429, 442, 459, 464-465, 467, 469-470, 497, 504, 509
civilian conservation corps, 344
clara barton, 33
claus von stauffenberg, 405
clement attlee, 411, 479, 543
cochin china, 510
cold war, 414, 440, 448, 459, 464, 477-479, 486-492, 495-496, 508-510, 520, 522, 528, 532, 539, 543, 553-554
collectivization, 301, 445
colombia, 178, 460-461, 463, 466
colorado, 138, 201, 224, 258, 274, 292, 347, 365, 439, 456
columbia disaster, 535
comanche, 199, 203
comintern, 325, 353, 367, 443, 513, 519
committee of union and progress, 148, 235
commodore matthew perry, 35, 130

commonwealth of independent states, *531*
communism, *125, 155, 184-185, 234, 265-266, 298, 300-302, 304-305, 322, 324-327, 355, 367, 410-411, 413, 424, 440-445, 447-448, 450-453, 459, 464-465, 467-468, 477, 479-482, 484, 486, 491-492, 505, 509-510, 513-514, 518-524, 526-528, 530-531, 536, 543*
communist bloc, *411, 477, 521, 523-524, 526-529, 536*
communist party, *155, 185, 267, 300-303, 305, 325-327, 331, 441, 443-447, 449, 509, 513, 519-521, 523-524, 526-527, 530-531, 534*
compiegne forest, *372-374*
compromise of 1790, *18*
compromise of 1850, *19, 35, 113*
compromise of 1877, *111*
concentration camps, *165, 172-174, 367, 376, 378-379, 388, 550*
confederacy, *47, 55-56, 58-59, 61-63, 65, 70, 72-73, 76, 78-79*
confederate, *34, 36, 47-48, 51, 54-63, 65, 69-79, 81, 84, 110, 122, 207, 279, 334*
confederate flag, *65*
confederate states of america, *36, 47, 54, 65, 122*
confucianism, *183*
congo, *160, 467-468*
congo free state, *160, 467*
congress, *18, 20, 22, 25, 49-50, 52, 60, 63, 65, 81-82, 84, 89, 96, 107, 111, 116, 118, 125-126, 135, 137-138, 146, 148, 151, 155, 199-200, 202, 244, 257, 269-270, 275, 286-289, 293, 299, 308, 343, 345, 366, 385, 415-416, 453, 466, 470-471, 473, 482-483, 493, 497, 501-502, 507, 511, 518, 527, 537, 553-554*
congress of vienna, *25, 151, 308*
connecticut, *53, 200, 433, 553, 555*
constantinople, *11, 24-25, 27, 31, 143, 145-147, 149, 168, 234, 236, 318*
constitution, *18, 21, 49-50, 52, 54, 66, 81, 83-84, 98-99, 107, 124, 132, 137-141, 145, 147-148, 153, 162, 169, 200, 212, 232, 239, 242-243, 245, 247, 260-261, 270, 275, 282, 285, 310-311, 319, 334, 343-345, 350-351, 353, 357, 362, 366, 435, 450, 497, 501-502, 518, 527*
constitutional revolution of 1906, *232*
continents, *22, 159, 257, 311, 458, 474, 488*
contract labor law, *126*
contras, *465-466*
convention of kanagawa, *131*
convention of tientsin, *191*
coolie, *514-515*
coolies, *125*
cornelius vanderbilt, *216*
corregidor, *389-390*
corrie ten boom, *384*
corvee labor, *31, 33*
costa rica, *172, 464-465*
cotton, *14, 31, 43, 48, 50, 121, 155, 161, 218, 288, 365*
count benedetti, *102*
coup d'etat, *354, 360, 435, 458-459, 484, 511, 521, 523*
coup of 1953, *543-545*
crassus, *216*
crazy horse, *203-205, 333*
creek, *48, 53, 57, 62, 78, 157, 202, 204, 207, 333*
crimea, *17, 30, 531*
crimean war, *13, 24-27, 29-31, 99, 143-145, 147, 168, 259, 310*
cristero war, *247*
crusades, *25, 32, 150, 425, 515*
csa, *54*
cuba, *36, 51, 171-177, 179-180, 350, 379, 459, 465, 477, 482-486, 491-492, 495-496, 505, 521, 533, 536, 539, 543*
cuban missile crisis, *477, 491-492, 495, 505, 521-522*
cuban revolution, *492*
cuban war for independence, *172, 174-175, 180*
cultural revolution, *446-447, 536*
cyrus mccormick, *120*
czechoslovakia, *270, 295, 297, 304, 360, 369-371, 399, 411, 478, 519, 522-523, 526, 528-530, 536*

D

d-day, *403-404, 406-407, 409, 414, 440*
dachau, *378*
dag hammarskjöld, *468*
daimyos, *129, 131-132*
dalai lama, *420*
danish underground, *382*
danube river, *25, 146*
dark ages, *11*
david livingstone, *43, 45-46, 159-160*
david lloyd george, *256, 296*
david scott, *494*
daylight savings time, *275*
de-stalinization, *520*
death marches, *149, 383-384*
declaration of sentiments, *137*
decree on land, *264*
decree on peace, *264*
delaware, *56, 200, 433*
democrat, *36, 110, 181, 240, 397, 554, 556*
democratic national committee, *505*
democratic party, *36, 49, 109, 366, 424, 440, 504, 506, 518, 556*
democratic republic of the congo, *160, 467-468*
deng xiaoping, *446-449*
denmark, *104, 269, 297, 377, 382, 400-401, 403*
desert fox, *407*
devil's island, *461*
devil's pool, *46*
diamond mining, *121, 163, 166*
dictator, *85-86, 88, 177, 246, 268, 302, 314-316, 349, 353, 358, 361-362, 402, 406, 459, 462, 466, 468, 478, 483-485, 513, 519-520, 529, 543-544, 551, 555*
diet of the german confederation, *104*
direct communications agreement, *533*
divan, *30*
divine right, *97-98, 104*
dmitri mendeleev, *171*
dmz, *454-455*
doctrine of lapse, *16*
dominican republic, *171-172*
domino theory, *510*
don miguel hidalgo y costilla, *242*
donner party, *199*
doolittle raid, *390-391, 408*
dost muhammad, *39-42*
doughboy, *273*
doughface, *36, 49, 51*
doughnuts, *272*
dow jones industrial average, *215, 338-339, 342*
dowager cixi, *188-190, 322, 327*
draft, *70, 269, 351, 514, 538*
draft dodgers, *538*
dred scott, *21-22, 49*
dreidel, *433*
dual alliance, *250*
dubai, *548*
dublin, *279, 283-284*
duke of wellington, *98*
duma, *260-261*
dunkirk, *372-373*
durrani dynasty, *38-39*
dust bowl, *347*
dutch, *13, 43, 106, 124, 130, 141-142, 156, 163-164, 214, 238, 383-387, 389, 401, 405, 462, 470, 536*
dutch east india company, *141, 163*
dutch reformed church, *106*

E

early, *12, 14-15, 21, 24, 30, 38-39, 41, 45, 52, 56, 58-59, 64, 71, 74-77, 80, 82, 86, 88-89, 93-94, 96, 104-105, 113, 117-118, 120-121, 126-129, 133, 136, 139, 142-143, 155, 160, 162, 164, 168, 170-172, 180-181, 197-198, 202, 208-209, 216, 218-219, 222, 225-226, 234, 236-237, 243-246, 249, 253, 259-260, 263, 268, 276, 278, 280-282, 284-285, 297, 308-309, 313, 324, 329-330, 332, 338-342, 346, 350, 355, 360, 363, 373, 380-381, 385, 391-392, 399-400, 403-407, 413, 415, 424, 426, 433, 443, 451-452, 477, 486-487, 491-492, 495, 500, 502, 505-506, 520, 522, 538, 543, 547, 554*
early modern era, *14, 24, 129, 143, 168, 308*
east africa, *31, 33*
east germany, *478-482, 521, 524, 526, 528-530, 553*
east india company, *13-17, 38, 141, 163, 166, 216, 286, 417*
east pakistan, *416, 418-419*
easter rising, *283-284*
eastern front, *255, 260-261, 304, 375-376, 402, 405*
eastern orthodox church, *11*
eastern question, *24-25, 31, 143*
eastern rumelia, *146, 235*
eastern thrace, *146, 236*
economic, *50, 89, 116, 218, 298-301, 337, 340-342, 345, 347, 353, 366, 413, 448, 530, 538-539, 545, 551, 556*
economy, *50, 168, 171,*

218, 245, 264, 276, 293, 297, 299, 301, 315, 318, 335, 338, 342, 348-349, 353, 357, 361, 366, 385, 412, 414, 472, 484, 523, 528, 538-539, 554
ecuador, 460-461, 463, 466, 475
ed mccully, 475
edo, 129-131
edward white, 494, 535
egypt, 11, 13, 24, 31-33, 143-144, 166, 178, 228, 295, 307-308, 313, 317-320, 400, 425-427, 429-432, 434-438, 459, 538, 545, 549, 551
egypt-israel peace treaty, 431-432, 438, 538
egyptian, 31-33, 307, 317, 319, 402, 430, 434-438
egyptian revolution of 1952, 434-435, 438
eiffel tower, 100, 108
eisenhower, 348, 407, 440, 453-454, 490-491, 495-496, 500, 510-511, 515, 517, 543-544
eisenhower doctrine, 440
el dorado, 460
el salvador, 464
eleanor roosevelt, 294, 332
elections, 83, 92, 96, 107, 138, 164, 245, 286, 314, 353, 361, 410-411, 435, 440, 450, 466, 468, 474, 484, 501, 509-510, 528, 540, 544
electoral college, 83, 111
elijah lovejoy, 53
elijah mccoy, 221
eliot ness, 140
elizabeth blackwell, 68, 422
elizabeth cady stanton, 137
ellen nielsen, 382
ellis island, 108, 126-128
emancipation manifesto, 168
emancipation proclamation, 20, 62-63, 66, 76, 154, 501
emergency quota act of 1921, 127
emilio aguinaldo, 176-177
emilio zapata, 246
emir, 38-39, 41, 548
emperor hirohito, 329, 395, 397
emperor pedro i, 87-88
emperor pedro ii, 87
emperor puyi, 324, 327, 329, 386
empire state building, 342
enabling act, 361-362
enfield 1853 rifle-musket, 16-17, 42
england, 11-13, 17-18, 20-21, 25, 30, 49, 64, 68, 90-91, 94, 98, 100, 195, 219-220, 243, 249, 272, 279-280, 288, 295, 323, 331-332, 335, 350,

365, 370, 554
english, 11, 14, 18, 30, 68, 90-93, 128, 141, 162, 187, 219, 243, 248, 254, 260, 268, 272, 279-280, 282, 290, 295, 314, 330-331, 364, 371, 373-375, 403, 422, 438, 467, 472
english channel, 295, 373-375, 403
enola gay, 394
entente cordiale, 250
era of stagnation, 523, 526
eric liddell, 330-331
eritrea, 163
ernest hemingway, 277, 355
ernie pyle, 414
ernst rohm, 362
ernst vom rath, 379
espionage, 217, 275, 487
espionage and sedition acts, 275
estonia, 265, 270, 297, 304, 478, 532
ethiopia, 161-163, 312, 318, 432-433, 466
eugene cernan, 494
eureka diamond, 163-164
eureka rebellion, 156-157
europe, 11-12, 22, 24-25, 42, 44, 46, 50, 79, 87-88, 91, 98-102, 104, 124, 126-127, 129, 143, 146-147, 150, 161, 169, 171, 193, 209, 216, 227, 230, 235, 237, 242, 244, 250-251, 254, 257, 262, 272, 275-276, 297, 304, 308-310, 312, 319, 349-350, 366-370, 372, 374, 377-381, 385-386, 398, 400, 403, 406-411, 413-414, 426-428, 431, 448-449, 453, 466, 478, 482, 491, 519, 521, 525, 528, 536
eva braun, 363-364
eva duarte, 459
exodus 1947, 428
extermination camp, 380-383, 399

F

f. scott fitzgerald, 278
famine, 125, 281, 301-302, 432, 446, 448, 469
far east, 14-15, 32-33, 37, 99, 130, 193, 216, 253, 348, 453
farabundo mari national liberation front, 464
farmers, 31, 82, 129, 155, 158, 164, 202, 222, 264, 280-282, 301-302, 341-342, 346-348, 356, 436, 445-446, 513, 534
farms, 50, 165, 203, 266,

280, 300-302, 325, 341, 347-348, 401, 436, 442-445, 467, 480, 485-486, 519
fascism, 312, 314-316, 355, 367
fatwa, 438
february revolution, 260, 263-264, 268-269, 299
federal, 22, 47, 49-54, 64, 96, 107, 124, 126-127, 135, 138, 140, 181, 214, 218, 246, 275, 298, 343-344, 464-465, 479, 496-497, 499, 501, 504, 506, 553
federal deposit insurance corporation, 344
federal republic of central america, 464-465
federal reserve, 218, 275
federated states of micronesia, 179
fence cutting war, 118
ferdinand de lesseps, 33, 178
ferdinand vii, 171, 350-351
fetterman massacre, 203
feudal system, 129, 131, 168
fez, 319, 352
fidel castro, 459, 483-484, 487, 491-492, 505, 536, 543
fifteenth amendment, 137, 497, 503
fifth encirclement campaign, 326
filibuster, 465, 500, 502
film, 273, 276-277, 294, 331, 490, 539
final solution, 378, 380-381, 400, 426
fire balloons, 396
fireside chats, 343, 345, 366
first balkan war, 236, 251
first boer war, 163-165
first carlist war, 351
first chinese-japanese war, 190-191, 328
first fleet, 156
first french empire, 97-98
first french republic, 97-98
first indochina war, 100, 509-511, 513
first italian war of independence, 310
first kashmir war, 417
first opium war, 13, 43, 182-185, 448
first phase offensive, 452
first spanish republic, 351
fission bomb, 487-488
five civilized tribes, 202
five year plan, 301
flags, 65, 71, 143, 185, 274, 378, 525, 534
flappers, 277
florence nightingale, 30, 68
florida, 48, 54, 172, 176, 201, 205, 294, 343, 484,

486, 515, 555
foot binding, 189-190, 322
forbidden city, 186, 327-329, 442
force publique, 160, 467
foreclosure, 341-342
fort donelson, 59-60
fort henry, 59
fort sumter, 54-55, 57
four old things, 446
fourteen points speech, 269
fourteenth amendment, 107, 153, 497-498
france, 11, 13, 24-27, 31, 35, 88, 91, 94, 97-104, 107, 122, 141, 143-144, 147, 150, 160-161, 163, 168, 171, 183, 185, 187, 192, 227, 237, 242-246, 250, 252-254, 256-257, 269-270, 272, 277, 280, 294-298, 308-313, 316, 346, 350, 352, 354, 357, 368-369, 371-374, 376-377, 379-380, 385-386, 400-401, 403-409, 412-414, 426, 428, 435-437, 449, 451, 461, 466, 468, 490, 508-509, 513, 544, 546-547, 551
francisco madero, 245-247
francisco solano lopez, 86-87
franco-prussian war, 27, 99, 102-105, 250, 295, 297, 312
franco-russian alliance, 250
frank borman, 494
franklin pierce, 36, 47, 49, 52, 172, 174, 465
franklin roosevelt, 141, 343, 345, 349, 366, 385, 424
frederick douglass, 20-21, 34, 53, 66, 82, 137
free officers movement, 434-435, 438
freedmen's bureau, 83-84
french, 11, 25-27, 30, 33, 85, 87, 91-93, 97-105, 107-109, 124, 129, 147, 150, 158, 163, 178, 181, 185-186, 197, 205, 219, 238, 243-245, 250, 253-254, 256, 269, 272, 280, 297-298, 308-309, 311, 351, 372-374, 386-387, 404, 437, 461, 468, 508-511, 513, 547
french guiana, 461
french indochina, 386-387, 508-509
french revolution, 11, 97-98, 100, 309
friedrich nietzsche, 315
friedrich wilhelm iv, 104
fuchou, 183
fugitive slave act, 19-20, 35
fulgencio batista, 483-485, 492
fumie, 133
fusion bomb, 488

G

g.k. chesterton, *364*
gadsden purchase, *202, 242*
gail halvorsen, *481*
gamal nasser, *435, 437, 459*
gang of eight, *530-531*
ganghwa incident, *190*
gary powers, *490*
gasalee expedition, *187-188*
gavrilo princip, *237, 251-252*
gaza strip, *429-430, 432*
general crook, *204*
general erwin rommel, *407*
general franco, *315, 354-356*
general george marshall, *413, 440*
general george patton, *406-407, 411*
general macarthur, *389, 450-453*
general o.o. howard, *206*
general westmoreland, *512, 514*
geneva, *94, 150, 509, 511, 513*
geneva conference, *509, 511, 513*
genghis khan, *37, 182, 216, 229*
genocide, *148-149, 281, 550*
geography, *22, 32, 34, 42, 46, 48, 63, 94, 109, 121, 134, 151, 178, 194, 196, 210, 224, 238, 258, 267, 274, 292, 306, 316, 321, 333, 347, 365, 423, 439, 456, 481, 516, 537*
george custer, *204*
george dewey, *173, 175-176, 178*
george h.w. bush, *553*
george macdonald, *364*
george mcgovern, *506*
george mueller, *18, 438-439*
george orwell, *355*
george wallace, *500, 502-504*
george washington carver, *155-156*
georges clemenceau, *296*
georgia, *47-48, 54, 73, 75-76, 78, 82, 200-201, 229, 303, 320, 334, 478, 503, 532, 538*
gerald ford, *397, 507, 518, 539*
gerardo machado, *483*
german, *12, 98, 101-106, 113, 125, 132, 150, 173, 212, 235, 238, 250-256, 264, 268-270, 272-273, 283, 287, 295-298, 304, 312-313, 315-316, 354, 356-363, 367-376, 378-384, 395, 400-407, 409, 412, 414, 478-481, 509, 529, 548*
german confederation, *101-102, 104*
german empire, *103-104, 250-251, 270, 295, 297, 312, 368, 405*
german revolution, *270, 297, 356-357*
german revolution of 1918-1919, *270, 297, 356-357*
germanic, *100-101*
germany, *12, 30, 97, 100-101, 103-105, 108, 125, 132, 148, 150-151, 160-161, 183, 187, 192, 232-234, 237, 250-253, 255-257, 260, 265, 268-270, 275, 287, 295-299, 301, 304, 310, 313, 315-316, 346, 350, 353-354, 356-363, 367-386, 388, 394, 398-406, 408-412, 414, 426-428, 441, 449-450, 454, 466, 477-482, 509-510, 521, 524-526, 528-530, 541-542, 553*
geronimo, *205, 208*
gertrude ederle, *295*
gertrude stein, *277*
gestapo, *362, 367, 382-384, 399*
gettysburg, *57, 67, 70-72, 75, 204*
gettysburg address, *67*
ghana, *155, 474*
ghazni province, *39*
ghettos, *378, 380, 382, 399-400*
ghost dance, *207-208*
gilded age, *216-217*
giuseppe garibaldi, *311*
giuseppe mazzini, *309*
gladys aylward, *331*
glasnost, *526-528, 530*
gleiwitz incident, *371*
glorious revolution, *280, 351*
golden gate bridge, *342*
golden temple, *419-420*
gospel of wealth, *219*
government, *11-12, 15-17, 21-22, 25, 30-32, 36, 41, 44, 47, 49-51, 53-55, 57, 62, 64, 67, 79, 82-84, 86-88, 92, 96-97, 103-104, 106-108, 110-111, 114, 116, 123-124, 126, 129-133, 135-136, 139-141, 143-145, 148, 151, 153, 156-158, 161-162, 164, 166, 168-172, 175, 177-178, 181-183, 188, 190-191, 202-204, 206, 216, 218, 227, 231-235, 242-248, 257, 261-266, 268-270, 275, 279-281, 283-284, 286-289, 295, 298-302, 304-305, 308, 310, 312, 314-316, 318, 322-324, 328-329, 335, 342-345, 348, 350-351,* 353-354, 356-363, 366, 368-373, 379-380, 384-386, 388, 397, 402-403, 405-406, 408, 410-411, 413, 415-416, 418-420, 426, 429, 432, 434-435, 438, 440, 442, 446, 448-451, 455, 458-459, 461, 464-465, 468-474, 479, 483-487, 496-497, 499, 503, 508-511, 513-514, 518, 521, 523-524, 526-531, 534, 539, 541-545, 549, 552-556*
government of india act, *289*
grant, *50, 57, 59-61, 68, 72-78, 80, 83, 92, 96, 110, 137-138, 142, 147, 162, 204, 281, 344, 361, 396, 428, 432, 463, 472-473, 500, 508-509, 521, 544*
grattan massacre, *203*
great britain, *12-15, 17, 31, 44, 92, 165, 280, 284, 296, 318, 364, 537*
great chicago fire, *221-223*
great chinese famine, *446*
great depression, *223, 307, 320, 335-336, 338-342, 345, 348, 361, 366, 369, 452*
great exhibition, *13-14*
great game, *37-40, 42, 230, 232, 250, 437, 541*
great irish famine, *281*
great lakes, *91, 134*
great leap forward, *171, 443-446*
great march on washington, *501, 503*
great purge, *301, 303-304, 326, 376, 520*
great schism, *11*
great sparrow campaign, *446*
greece, *11, 31, 105, 143-144, 234-237, 251, 253, 269, 295, 377, 401, 414, 424*
grimm brothers, *106*
group areas act, *471*
grover cleveland, *108, 135-136, 174, 218*
guam, *34, 171, 176-177, 179*
guangdong province, *324*
guangxu emperor, *322, 327*
guantanamo bay, *175, 177, 179, 483*
guatemala, *463-464*
guernica, *356*
guerrilla, *41, 142, 165, 172, 177-178, 205, 208, 283-284, 326, 372, 402, 419-420, 464, 492, 512*
guglielmo marconi, *276*
gulag, *304-305, 519, 526*
gulf of aden, *32, 548*
gulf of mexico, *48, 112, 243*
gulf of suez, *32*
gulf of tonkin incident, *496, 511*
gunboat diplomacy, *131, 178, 181, 190, 466*
guru, *419*
guyana, *461*

H

habeas corpus, *66*
haganah, *427, 429*
hague convention, *255*
hamas, *432*
hamidian massacres, *146-147, 149*
hamidiye, *147, 149*
hampton institute, *154*
hampton roads, *57, 60-61*
han chinese, *182-184, 190, 195*
hanoi, *508-510*
harper's ferry, *20, 54, 57, 64*
harriet beecher stowe, *20-21, 53, 139, 162*
harriet tubman, *19-20, 53, 137*
harry f. byrd, *499*
harry truman, *406, 424*
havana, *172-174, 379, 484*
hawaii, *34-35, 130, 173, 177-180, 193, 202, 323, 330, 387, 391, 408, 537, 556*
heart of darkness, *160*
heinrich himmler, *361, 399*
helen keller, *139*
henry dunant, *150*
henry ford, *225-226*
henry stanley, *44*
herbert hoover, *337, 340, 342, 348-349*
herman goering, *399*
hernan cortes, *241*
herschel grynszpan, *379*
herzegovina uprising, *144*
hideki tojo, *397-398*
hindu, *16, 42, 287, 289, 291, 415-417, 423*
hindu-german conspiracy, *287*
hinduism, *14, 289, 363, 415*
hiroshima, *394, 396, 424, 487*
history will absolve me speech, *485*
hitler, *105, 234, 299, 304, 314-316, 350, 354-355, 357-364, 367-371, 373-378, 380, 398-403, 405-407, 409, 411, 426-427, 443, 453, 459, 519, 525, 542-543, 549*
hitler youth, *362-363*
ho chi minh, *509-511, 513-514*
ho chi minh trail, *510-511, 513*
holocaust, *149, 367, 372,*

377-378, 380, 383-384, 398-400, 426-429, 437
holodomor, 301-302
holy alliance, 309
holy roman empire, 101-102, 350
home rule bill, 282
homestead act, 116-117
honduras, 463-465
hong kong, 183, 448
hong xiuquan, 183-184, 194
hood, 77, 400-401
hooker, 59, 68-70, 110
hoovervilles, 340-341
horace greeley, 116
horn of africa, 468
house of commons, 233, 281-282
house of lords, 281-282
house of representatives, 35, 66, 122, 180, 502, 507, 517-518, 553-554
howland island, 34, 294
hudson taylor, 187, 194-195, 210, 291, 331, 438, 456
hull house, 128
hundred days, 98, 188, 270, 322, 343
hundred days offensive, 270
hundred days reform, 188
hundred flowers campaign, 444
hungarian revolution, 521
hungary, 24, 102, 146, 148, 232, 235-237, 250-253, 257, 269-270, 295-296, 298, 304, 312-313, 368, 370, 377, 401, 411, 426, 478, 521-522, 526, 528-530
hunger, 138, 260, 289, 301, 338, 340, 370, 384
hut tax, 166

I

i have a dream, 155, 501
ida scudder, 422
ida tarbell, 217
idaho, 198-199, 201, 203, 210, 238, 306, 321, 423-424, 439, 456
illinois, 21, 66, 109-110, 128, 151, 199, 201, 221, 223, 348, 539, 556
imam, 540-541
immigrants, 87, 108, 124-128, 156, 212, 427
immigration, 50, 108, 124-128, 335, 379, 426-428
immigration act of 1917, 125, 127
immigration act of 1924, 127, 335
immigration and nationality act of 1965, 127
impeachment, 82, 96, 507,
554
imperialism, 173, 312, 367, 414
imperialists, 16, 513
incheon, 451-452
india, 11-17, 33, 37-40, 42, 127, 141-142, 163, 166, 216, 228, 230, 233, 268-269, 276, 278, 286-291, 294, 319-320, 371, 377, 401, 409, 415-423, 441, 470, 490, 500, 503, 508, 552
indian appropriations act of 1851, 202
indian appropriations act of 1871, 202
indian citizenship act, 335
indian councils act of 1909, 286
indian independence act, 289, 416
indian national congress, 286-289, 415-416, 470
indian ocean, 23, 32, 230
indian removal act, 202
indian wars, 197, 199, 202-205, 207-209
indiana, 134, 200
indira gandhi, 420
indo-pakistani war of 1947, 417
indo-pakistani war of 1965, 418
indo-pakistani war of 1999, 418
indonesia, 127, 137, 141, 556
industrial revolution, 14, 113, 160, 216, 222
industrialize, 445
inflation, 111, 171, 297, 357, 538
institutional revolutionary party (pri), 247
integration, 21, 498-499, 501, 503-504
intellectualism, 291, 447
intercontinental ballistic missiles, 489
interest rates, 538
intermediate-range nuclear forces treaty, 534
international african association, 160
internment camps, 397
interstate highway system, 348, 440
invasion of normandy, 403-404, 407
inventions, 119-120, 219, 225
iowa, 109, 151, 155, 196, 198, 201, 208, 212, 274, 307, 333, 348
ira, 283-285
iran, 37, 227, 229, 233, 409, 426, 465-466, 538, 540-547, 549-550, 552
iran hostage crisis, 538, 545
iran-contra scandal, 465-466
iran-iraq war, 549-550
iranian, 542-543, 545-546
iraq, 295, 544, 546-547, 549-553, 555-556
ireland, 12-13, 17, 125, 268, 276, 278-286, 291, 364, 467
irgun, 427, 429
irish assembly, 283
irish church act, 282
irish declaration of independence, 283
irish free state, 284-285
irish home rule, 281-282
irish land acts, 282
irish potato blight, 125
irish republican army, 283
irish republican brotherhood, 282
irish volunteers, 282-284
iron curtain, 304, 410-411, 478, 482, 519-522, 526-529, 536, 553
ironclad oath, 83-84
irredenta, 313-315
isabella ii, 350-351
islam, 11, 37, 144, 228-230, 352, 524, 540, 544
islamabad, 418
islamic empire, 24, 37, 142, 144, 228-229
islamic revolution, 233, 543-546, 549
island hopping, 392
ismail pasha, 32-33, 317
isobel kuhn, 456
isoruko yamomoto, 398
israel, 171, 269, 377, 379, 381, 384, 398, 425-434, 437-438, 490, 503, 538, 545, 547
italian, 90, 99, 124-125, 127, 150, 162-163, 234, 280, 308, 310-316, 351, 400, 402, 406, 469, 505
italian campaign, 316, 402
italian social republic, 316, 402
italo-ethiopian war, 163
italy, 30, 46, 99-100, 125, 142-143, 150, 161-163, 183, 187, 232, 250-252, 269, 296, 307-316, 350-351, 353-354, 369-371, 373, 375, 377, 385, 388, 400-403, 406-409, 413-414, 435, 440-441, 459, 466, 469, 491, 543
ivan iv the terrible, 168

J

j.r.r. tolkein, 364
jack ruby, 505
jacob deshazer, 390, 408
jacques cartier, 91
jahangir, 14-15, 417
jainism, 14, 363
jamaica, 463
james buchanan, 36, 49
james connolly, 283
james cook, 156
james earl ray, 503-504
james garfield, 122-123
jameson raid, 164-166
jane addams, 128
janissary corps, 24, 143
japan, 35, 100, 124, 128-134, 141, 182-183, 186-187, 190-194, 251, 253, 259, 261, 269, 299, 322-323, 328-330, 375, 377, 385-398, 401, 408, 410-411, 424, 441, 448-450, 452-453, 455, 508-509, 513
japanese, 35, 125, 127-133, 190-194, 251, 259, 261, 325-326, 328-331, 386-398, 405, 408, 410-411, 414, 440-443, 450, 452, 495, 508-509, 518, 553
jarvis island, 34
jawaharlal nehru, 419-420
jay gould, 216
jeannie lawson, 331
jefferson davis, 36, 47, 54, 57
jerome case, 120-121
jerusalem, 25, 228, 269, 377, 425-426, 428-430
jesuits, 133-134
jesus, 11, 18, 25, 44, 94, 106, 184, 248, 267, 408, 425, 439, 460, 475, 515
jewish question, 378
jews, 18, 143-144, 148-149, 169-171, 228, 259, 263, 277, 281, 315, 352, 354, 357, 359-360, 363, 367, 372-373, 376-384, 398-400, 407, 425-430, 432-433, 435, 549
jezail, 42
jfk assassination, 495
jihad, 524
jim crow laws, 83, 107, 153-155, 498, 502
jim elliot, 475
jim jones, 461-462
jimmy carter, 431, 438, 449, 518, 538, 545
jimmy doolittle, 390
jintian uprising, 184
johannesburg, 471-472
john bell hood, 77
john brown, 20-22, 36, 53-54, 57, 64
john cabot, 90
john calvin, 94, 106, 335
john conroy, 13
john d. rockefeller, 216-218, 221
john dean, 506
john deere, 221, 347
john erlichman, 506
john f. kennedy, 482, 495-496, 504

john george lambton, *91*
john glenn, *494*
john hinckley, *539*
john jacob astor, *216*
john maynard keynes, *345*
john mccrae, *271*
john pierpont morgan, *218*
john steinbeck, *348*
john wilkes booth, *66, 79-80*
johnston atoll, *34*
jonathan goforth, *210*
jonestown, *461-462*
jordan, *428-430, 432, 503, 546-547*
jordan river, *428-429, 547*
jose gaspar rodriguez de francia, *85, 462*
jose rizal, *176*
joseph conrad, *160*
joseph e. johnston, *58, 72*
joseph goebbels, *361, 378, 398, 406*
joseph mengele, *361, 399*
joseph pulitzer, *174-175*
joshua chamberlain, *70-71, 78*
josiah tattnall, *186*
juan peron, *458-459*
judicial procedures reform bill of 1937, *345*
july monarchy, *97-98*

K

kabaddi, *421*
kabul, *39-42, 552*
kaiser friedrich iii, *105*
kaiser wilhelm ii, *12, 105, 237, 251, 260-261, 268, 270, 356*
kalahari desert, *44*
kamikaze attacks, *393-394*
kansas, *19, 36, 49, 51-53, 118, 198, 201-202, 208-209, 224, 274, 292, 347-348, 365, 453, 498, 556*
kansas-nebraska act, *19, 36, 52-53*
karachi, *418*
kargil war, *418*
karl marx, *264, 303, 315*
kashmir, *415, 417-418*
katipunan, *176*
kazakhstan, *478, 531-532*
kelly gang, *158*
kensington system, *13-14*
kente cloth, *474*
kentucky, *20, 47, 55-56, 59, 63, 65-66, 82, 200*
kgb, *525*
khachkars, *149-150*
khalifa tower, *548*
khamsa, *352*
khedive abbas ii, *318*
khedive ismail, *317-318*
khedive tewfik, *317-318*
khodynka tragedy, *259*
khrushchyovka, *520, 522*

khyber pass, *40-42*
kim, *38, 290, 451*
kim il-sung, *451*
king charles ii, *15, 280*
king farouk, *319, 434-435*
king fuad, *319, 434*
king george iii, *12, 280*
king william iv, *12-13*
kingman reef, *34*
kinshasa, *467-468*
kiowa, *115, 203*
kitchen debate, *521-522*
kite battles, *552*
kite running, *552*
kmt, *324-326, 441-444*
kojong, *191*
konstantin chernenko, *525*
korea, *99-100, 132, 182, 190-194, 210, 259, 328, 386, 424, 450-456, 477, 484, 490, 509-510, 515, 519, 534*
korea's demilitarized zone, *454*
korean, *130, 190-192, 328, 424, 440-441, 448-449, 451-455, 477, 495, 509, 519*
korean armistice agreement, *454*
korean war, *424, 440-441, 448-449, 451-454, 477, 495, 509, 519*
kristallnacht, *379, 398, 400*
ku klux klan, *84, 110, 154, 504*
kulaks, *301-302*
kung fu, *187*
kuomintang, *324-325, 441, 448*
kurds, *550-552, 555*
kurt schuschnigg, *368*
kuwait, *547-548, 550-551, 553*
kyrgystan, *478, 532*

L

lake titicaca, *459*
land run, *117-118*
laos, *386, 508, 510, 513*
lateran treaty, *316*
latin america nuclear free zone treaty, *533*
latvia, *265, 270, 297, 304, 478, 532*
law for the encouragement of marriage, *363*
law of unintended consequences, *446*
league of nations, *270, 275, 296-299, 329-330, 368, 410, 413, 426, 542, 547*
lebanon, *429, 546-547*
lee, *47, 54, 56-58, 62, 66, 69-74, 76-80, 110, 204, 224, 272, 495, 504-505*
lee harvey oswald, *495, 504-505*

leland stanford, *115, 209, 216*
lend-lease act, *385, 387*
leon cgolcosz, *180*
leonid brezhnev, *523, 525*
leopold ii, *159-160, 166, 467*
letter from birmingham jail, *500-501*
liberal party, *282*
liberia, *82, 161-162, 466*
lillian trasher, *320*
limited test ban treaty, *533*
lindbergh baby, *346*
line of contact, *479*
line of control, *418*
lisu people, *456*
lithuania, *265, 270, 297, 304, 478, 532*
little red book, *444*
little rock nine, *500*
lombards, *100*
lombardy, *308-311*
london blitz, *374*
london missionary society, *43*
london pact, *313-314*
long march, *326-327, 384, 443*
lookout air raid, *396*
lord melbourne, *12*
lord raglan, *27*
lost generation, *277-278, 447*
lottie moon, *195*
louis joseph papineau, *91*
louis xiv, *97, 103-104, 129, 295*
louis xv, *97*
louis xvi, *98, 309*
louis xviii, *97-99*
louis-napoleon, *97-99*
louis-philippe, *97-98*
louisiana, *18, 52, 54, 72-73, 109, 121, 171, 200-201, 334, 350, 504-505*
louisiana purchase, *18, 109, 200-201, 334*
lower canada, *91-92*
lucky luciano, *140*
luftwaffe, *367, 372-373, 375-376, 399-400, 402, 404, 480*
lusitania, *255, 268*
luxembourg, *372, 377, 401, 403, 406*
lyman beecher, *139*
lynching, *154*
lyndon b. johnson, *496*
lytton report, *329-330*

M

macau, *182, 448*
macedonia, *146, 234-236, 298, 422*
machu picchu, *462*
maginot line, *372*
mahmud ii, *143*
maine, *70-71, 94-95, 172-175, 180, 201, 525-526*
majles, *232-233, 543*
major anderson, *55-56*
major rathbone, *81*
malaria, *30, 45, 47, 178-179*
malaysian peninsula, *142*
malmedy massacre, *406*
mamluk, *31, 425*
manchu, *182, 184, 189, 322, 328*
manchukuo, *328-330, 386, 394*
manchuria, *182, 186, 189, 191-192, 194, 299, 322, 328-330, 386, 394, 410, 442*
manchurian incident, *329-330, 386, 394*
mandarin, *194, 455*
manhattan project, *394, 411, 487*
manifest destiny, *334, 465*
manila bay, *175-176, 178, 388-390*
manitoba, *92-93, 272*
manuel noriega, *466*
mao, *155, 185, 325-328, 441-448, 451-452, 477, 484, 492, 509, 514, 519, 522, 536*
maple leaf, *93*
marbles, *345-346*
march to the sea, *74-77, 288*
margin buying, *336-337*
marie antoinette, *98*
mark twain, *160, 177, 216*
marshal tito, *298, 478*
marshall plan, *413-414, 440*
martin luther king, *155, 499-500, 503-504, 515*
mary slessor, *45-46*
maryland, *19-21, 56, 62-63, 66, 69, 71, 79-80, 82, 200, 278, 431, 518*
mason dixon line, *19, 465*
massachusetts, *33-34, 139, 155, 200-201, 335, 495, 553*
massacre of elphinstone's army, *39-40*
massive resistance, *499*
maximilian i, *99, 244*
may laws, *170, 259*
mcclellan, *59, 62, 68, 110*
mcdowell, *57, 59*
mckinley tariff of 1890, *135*
meade, *70*
mediterranean sea, *11, 24-26, 32-33, 168, 319, 350, 403, 426*
meiji, *131-132, 134, 190, 397*
meiji restoration, *131-132, 134, 190, 397*
mein kampf, *105, 360, 399*
memphis, *61, 503-504*
menachem begin, *431, 438*
menelik ii, *162-163*
mensheviks, *266*

mercenary, *465*
merrimack, *60-61*
mexica indians, *241*
mexican cession, *201-202, 242, 269*
mexican civil war, *242-244*
mexican empire, *99, 242, 244, 464*
mexican hat dance, *248*
mexican revolution, *245-248*
mexican-american war, *23, 36, 57-58, 110, 113, 198, 242-243, 269, 273*
mexico, *23, 34, 48, 57, 73, 80, 99, 112, 197, 199, 201-203, 205, 241-248, 258, 269, 273, 283, 292, 348, 365, 456, 464-465, 485, 487, 492*
michael collins, *283-285*
michigan, *119, 134, 140, 151, 201, 223, 518*
mickey mouse, *277, 397*
middle ages, *11, 14, 31, 279*
middle east, *11, 24-25, 141, 228, 352, 426, 435, 437, 540, 545-547, 549*
midway island, *391*
midway islands, *34, 179*
miguel primo de rivera, *352-353*
mikhail gorbachev, *482, 526*
military demarcation line, *454*
millard fillmore, *35-36, 130*
millets, *143*
minie ball, *29*
minnesota, *109, 134, 151, 196, 201, 333*
mirza reza kermani, *230*
misery index, *538*
missiles, *391, 393, 487-492, 521, 523, 533-534*
mississippi, *20, 23, 47-48, 54, 61, 72, 121, 200-202*
mississippi river, *20, 72, 202*
missouri, *18-19, 22, 36, 52-53, 56, 65, 109, 112, 121, 155, 197-199, 201, 224, 274, 348, 365, 395, 424, 452*
missouri compromise, *18-19, 22, 36, 52*
missouri river, *198*
mobutu sese seko, *468*
model t, *225-226*
modern war, *29, 355*
modernize, *24, 31, 142-143, 148, 301, 318, 445, 541, 544*
mogadishu, *468-469*
moghul dynasty, *14, 17, 37, 417*
mohandas gandhi, *287-289, 415, 420, 470, 500, 503*
moldavia, *25-27*
moldova, *478, 532*
molotov-ribbentrop pact, *304, 370-371, 409*
mongol, *37, 42, 169, 182, 216, 229*

mongols, *37, 227, 229*
monitor, *60-61, 360-361, 555*
monopoly, *223*
monroe doctrine, *130, 244*
montana, *199, 201, 203-204, 293, 321, 333, 423, 439*
montenegro, *146, 234-235, 237, 252-253, 269, 298*
montezuma, *241*
montgomery bus boycott, *498-499*
montgomery ward, *221, 223*
montreal, *79, 91*
mormon trail, *199, 203*
moro guerrillas, *178*
morocco, *319, 352, 354*
moscow, *194, 259, 266-267, 303-305, 325, 376, 401, 488, 491, 522, 524-525, 530-531*
mother teresa, *422-423*
motorcycle, *220, 333*
mount rushmore, *333-335*
moxie cream soda, *220*
mozaffar ad-din shah, *230-232*
ms st. louis, *379*
muckraker, *217*
muhammad al-mahdi, *541*
muhammad ali jinnah, *415-416*
muhammad ali pasha, *31-32, 143-144, 317*
muhammad ali shah, *232-233*
muhammad farrah aidid, *469*
muhammad mosaddeq, *542*
muhammad reza shah pahlavi, *542*
mujahideen, *524, 552*
munich agreement, *369*
munich conference, *370*
murad iv, *24*
murad v, *144-145*
muslim, *11, 14, 25, 31, 38, 142, 149-150, 228-229, 235-236, 287, 289, 319, 384, 415-417, 422, 425, 438, 469, 540, 544, 549, 551*
mussolini, *314-316, 355, 367, 370, 402, 406, 459*
mustard gas, *255, 359*
mutsuhito, *131-132*
mutually assured destruction, *489, 533*

N

naacp, *155, 498*
nader shah, *37*
nagasaki, *133-134, 394-395, 424, 487-488*
nanking, *183-186*
napalm, *511-512, 514*
napoleon i, *242, 304, 308-309, 350*

napoleon iii, *25, 35, 97-100, 102-104*
napoleonic wars, *11, 25, 98-99, 151, 308*
nasa, *490, 494-495, 535*
naser al-din shah, *230*
natal, *163, 165, 470*
natalia republic, *163*
nate saint, *475*
nathaniel hawthorne, *36*
national association for the advancement of colored people, *155, 498*
national fascist party, *314-315*
national origins act of 1924, *128*
national origins formula, *127*
national recovery administration, *344-345*
national woman suffrage association, *138*
nationalist, *132, 308, 314, 318-319, 323, 325, 353-355, 358-359, 434, 441, 443, 448, 450-451, 549*
nationalist party, *353, 355, 441, 443, 549*
native american, *59, 202, 241*
native lands act, *470-471*
navajo, *203*
navassa island, *34*
nazi party, *151, 359, 361-362, 368-369, 378, 398-399, 454*
nazis, *359-361, 363, 367, 372, 375-376, 378-386, 398-401, 407, 410, 427, 459, 482*
nebraska, *19, 36, 52-53, 109, 114, 198-199, 201, 209, 224, 274, 292, 333, 439, 518*
ned kelly, *157-158*
neil armstrong, *493-495*
nellie bly, *175*
nellie melba, *158-159*
nelson mandela, *471, 473-474*
netherlands, *11, 106, 141-142, 160, 163, 270, 350, 356, 372, 377, 380, 383-384, 387, 401, 403, 462, 466*
nevada, *114, 199, 201, 207, 210, 223, 238-239, 423, 456, 484*
neville chamberlain, *234, 369, 453, 519*
new brunswick, *90, 92-93*
new deal, *342-345, 366*
new economic policy, *300-301*
new england, *20-21, 220, 335*
new hampshire, *36, 94, 200*
new jersey, *33, 119, 128, 135, 200, 274, 307, 343, 346*

new mexico, *23, 199, 202-203, 205, 258, 292, 348, 365, 456, 487*
new world, *11, 91, 124, 130, 171-172, 241, 350, 458*
new york, *21, 35, 44, 47, 53, 57-58, 91, 107, 109-110, 116, 119, 121, 123, 126-128, 135, 137, 153, 174-175, 179-180, 200, 213-214, 218-219, 249, 257, 277-278, 294-295, 332, 336-339, 342, 346, 348, 366, 413, 438, 440, 522, 552, 555*
new york city, *109-110, 213, 218-219, 249, 277, 294-295, 337, 342, 438, 440, 522, 552*
new york stock exchange, *213-214, 336-339*
new zealand, *13, 92, 156, 269, 371, 377, 401*
newfoundland, *90, 93*
ngo dinh diem, *509*
nicaragua, *36, 51, 112, 197, 464-465*
nicholas i, *24-25, 259*
nicholas ii, *170, 193, 255, 259-265, 268-269, 519*
nicolai yezhov, *304*
night of the long knives, *362, 399*
nikita khrushchev, *302, 481, 519-523, 527*
nikolai ceausescu, *529*
nile river, *32-33, 44, 159, 320, 436*
ningbo, *183*
nkpa, *451-453*
nobel peace prize, *128, 193, 275, 423, 502*
noh masks, *133*
non-aligned movement, *478*
north, *11, 18-19, 22, 24, 31, 33-38, 43, 47, 49-52, 55-58, 61-63, 66, 69-72, 74-75, 79, 82-83, 90-92, 95-96, 102, 104, 112, 114, 122, 124, 136, 140, 150-151, 156, 163, 166-167, 169, 171, 196-198, 200-201, 223, 226, 228-230, 234, 246, 253, 294, 297, 308-310, 313, 316, 319, 321, 324, 327, 333-334, 350, 352, 372, 375, 381, 389, 391, 396, 400, 402-403, 405, 407, 412, 414, 424, 433-434, 437, 440, 443, 450-455, 465, 490, 496, 500, 508-516, 519, 534, 547-548, 550*
north america, *11, 22, 34, 52, 90-92, 112, 122, 124, 156, 171, 294, 391, 396, 516*
north carolina, *56-57, 61, 96, 200, 226, 500, 515*

north dakota, *196, 201, 321, 333*
north german confederation, *102, 104*
north korea, *424, 451-455, 490, 509-510, 519, 534*
north korean, *451*
north korean people's army, *451*
north vietnam, *151, 496, 508-514*
northern, *14, 17, 19, 22, 25, 34, 36, 38, 48, 50-52, 56-58, 62-63, 69-70, 77, 79-80, 99-100, 102, 110, 113, 142, 162-163, 166-167, 179, 192, 228, 231-232, 236, 241-242, 256, 270, 279, 282, 284-285, 290-291, 304, 308, 310-311, 316, 324-325, 352, 358, 364, 372-373, 387, 402-403, 406, 417, 425, 432, 442-443, 450-451, 460, 469, 474, 508, 510, 541, 550*
northern expedition, *324-325, 442-443*
northern ireland, *17, 279, 282, 284-285, 291, 364*
northern mariana islands, *34, 179*
northwest ordinance, *200*
norway, *269, 371, 376-377, 401, 403*
nova scotia, *90, 92-93*
nuclear arms race, *477, 487, 490, 492-493, 495, 521, 523, 533*
nuclear arms reduction, *532*
nuclear non-proliferation treaty, *533*
nuremburg race laws, *378*
nuremburg trials, *398-399*
nva, *510*

O

obstruction of justice, *507*
oceans, *23, 115, 229, 270, 294, 296, 350, 489*
october revolution, *233, 261, 264-266, 299-300, 303, 526*
ohio, *61, 63, 75, 110-111, 113, 119, 122, 134-135, 180, 200, 217, 226, 239, 293*
okies, *348*
okinawa, *393-395, 414*
oklahoma, *117-118, 121, 199, 202, 205, 224, 258, 292, 347-348, 365, 387*
okubo toshimichi, *132*
olmecs, *241*
omaha beach, *403-404*
oman, *548*
omar abdel-rahman, *438*

one-child policy, *449*
opec, *431*
operation anfal, *550*
operation barbarossa, *375-376, 401*
operation blue star, *419-420*
operation dynamo, *373*
operation eagle claw, *545-546*
operation little vittles, *481*
operation musketeer, *437*
operation neptune, *403*
operation passage to freedom, *509-510, 513*
operation restore hope, *469*
operation unthinkable, *410-411, 479*
operation valkyrie, *405, 407*
orange free state, *163-166, 470*
orange river convention, *163*
ordinance of nullification, *50*
oregon, *114, 197-199, 201, 203, 205-206, 210-211, 223, 238, 306, 396, 423*
oregon trail, *114, 197-199, 205-206*
oregon treaty, *198*
origami, *396*
orville wright, *226*
otto von bismarck, *102-105, 132, 161, 173, 235*
ottoman capitulations, *25, 149*
ottoman empire, *24-27, 30-33, 38, 99, 137, 142-149, 229, 233-237, 251-254, 259, 269-270, 295, 312-313, 317-319, 422, 425-426, 546-548, 550*
ottomans, *25-27, 31, 143-149, 235, 237, 318, 425-426*
outback, *157, 159*
outer space treaty, *533*

P

pablo picasso, *356*
pacific ocean, *23, 89, 130, 173, 178, 192, 194, 210, 294, 306, 391, 396, 516, 537, 553*
pacific railway act, *114*
pacific theater of world war ii, *385*
pact of steel, *315, 370-371*
pahlavi dynasty, *233, 541*
paiute indians, *207*
pakistan, *40, 42, 289, 415-421, 490, 552*
pale of settlement, *170-171*
palestine, *25, 171, 269, 381, 425-429, 434-435, 546-547*
palmyra atoll, *34, 179*
panama canal, *178-179, 181, 390, 466, 538*

panama canal treaty, *538*
pancho villa, *246*
panic of 1893, *218*
panic selling, *338-339*
panzers, *367, 376*
papal states, *99, 308-309, 311-312, 316*
papel picado, *248*
parachutes, *404*
paraguay, *85-88, 130, 133, 458, 462-463*
paratroopers, *316, 402-405, 408*
parliament, *12, 15-16, 91-92, 104-106, 132, 145, 147-148, 158, 160, 233-234, 280-284, 286, 310-311, 315, 319, 357, 361-362, 372, 402, 416, 435, 438, 450, 467, 470-472, 530, 542-543*
pashtun, *41, 229, 418*
patrice lumumba, *467*
pax britannica, *25*
peace corps, *332, 496*
peace of prague, *102, 104*
pearl harbor, *193, 330, 387-391, 397-398, 408, 440-441, 452, 518, 537, 553, 555*
peking, *100, 187, 442-443*
penal laws, *279-280*
pendleton act, *123*
peninsula campaign, *26, 71*
pennsylvania, *19-20, 49, 63, 67, 69-70, 75, 200, 218, 223-224, 276*
penny auctions, *341-342*
people's liberation army, *442*
people's republic of china, *442-443, 448, 534*
perestroika, *526, 528, 530*
periodic table of the elements, *171*
persia, *11, 37-40, 142, 225, 227-233, 250, 426, 437, 540-542, 547*
persian, *16, 37, 39, 41, 227-234, 318, 425, 472, 542, 546-551, 553*
persian gulf, *229-230, 547-551, 553*
persian gulf war, *551, 553*
peru, *89-90, 460, 462*
peter faberge, *305*
peter fleming, *475*
peter the great, *24, 229, 267, 305, 534*
petersburg, *57, 73-77, 260, 267*
phan boi chau, *508*
phan chu trinh, *508*
philadelphia, *20, 212, 214, 525*
philippe petain, *372*
philippine islands, *179, 350, 388-390*
philippine revolution, *174-176*
philippine-american war, *175, 177-178, 180, 452*

philippines, *171, 173, 175-178, 180, 239, 388-390, 392, 405, 451-453, 505*
phosgene gas, *255*
pickett's charge, *70*
plantation, *23, 50, 56, 154, 195, 279-280, 282*
plantation system, *280, 282*
platt amendment, *177, 483*
plessy vs. ferguson, *107, 153*
plo, *432*
plutarco calles, *247*
pogroms, *125, 170, 263*
poison gas, *255, 296, 381, 550*
poland, *170, 255, 265, 270, 295, 297, 304, 360, 370-372, 375, 377, 379-383, 394, 399, 401-403, 405, 409-413, 427, 450, 478-479, 519, 526, 530, 536*
polish, *135, 180, 297, 371, 379-380, 413, 523*
poll tax, *107*
pontifical swiss guard, *317*
pony express, *112-114, 118, 208-209*
pope, *101, 110, 308, 311, 316-317, 351, 357, 459*
popular front, *353-356, 459*
popular sovereignty, *52, 66*
population registration act, *471*
porfiriato, *244-245*
porfirio diaz, *244-246*
port arthur, *192-194, 251, 259, 261, 328, 410*
portugal, *11, 87-88, 133, 161, 182-183, 269, 448, 460, 466*
portuguese, *46, 87, 130, 133, 163*
potato blight, *125, 281, 301*
potsdam conference, *411-412, 479*
potsdam declaration, *411*
pows, *389, 453*
prague spring, *522-523*
preservation of separate amenities act, *471*
president, *20, 23, 33-36, 47, 49, 52, 54-57, 59-64, 66-68, 70, 72-73, 75-77, 79-83, 96, 98-99, 107-108, 110-111, 113, 115, 122-123, 127, 130-131, 135-136, 138, 141, 154, 169, 172-174, 176, 178, 180-181, 193, 197, 202, 206, 214, 217-218, 226, 239-240, 242-247, 251, 256-257, 268-269, 274-275, 285, 288, 293, 295-296, 298-299, 306, 313-314, 323-324, 332, 334-337, 340, 342-343, 345, 348-349, 360-362, 366,*

385-390, 394-395, 397-398, 406, 409-411, 413-414, 423-424, 431, 435-436, 438, 440, 449-450, 452-454, 458-459, 464-467, 473-474, 482-484, 486, 490-493, 495-497, 500-515, 517-518, 522, 527-528, 530-531, 533-534, 538-539, 543-546, 549, 551, 553-556

president hindenburg, *360-362*
pri, *247*
prime minister, *12, 17, 91, 102-106, 164-166, 233-234, 256, 269, 281-282, 296, 310, 314-316, 324, 352-353, 369-370, 372, 375, 397-398, 402, 409-411, 419-420, 431, 437-438, 450, 453, 467, 471, 479, 490, 519, 523, 542-545*
prince albert, *12, 14*
prince edward, *12, 92-93*
prince edward island, *92-93*
prince leopold, *102*
progressive party, *181*
prohibition, *137, 139-141, 340*
project gemini, *493, 495*
project mercury, *493*
promontory summit, *115*
propaganda, *105, 302-304, 314, 326-327, 355, 360, 362-363, 367, 371, 378-379, 398, 442-443, 445, 512-513, 526*
propagandist, *302*
protestant reformation, *11*
protestants, *101, 279-280, 282*
prussia, *25, 27, 99, 101-105, 132, 235, 251, 253, 297, 308-309, 312*
public works administration, *343*
publicly traded companies, *213*
pueblos, *208*
puerto rico, *34, 171-172, 177, 179, 350*
pullman car, *113*
punjab, *38, 40, 287, 290, 415-417, 419-420*
pyongyang, *452*

Q

qajar dynasty, *229-230, 233, 541-542*
qatar, *548*
qing dynasty, *182-185, 188-191, 322-324, 327-329, 443*
quebec, *91-93, 124*

quebec act, *91*
queen maria christina, *352*
queen victoria, *12, 16-17, 44, 46, 49, 230, 262, 286*
quotas, *127, 160, 302, 444-446*

R

race to the sea, *253*
racial discrimination, *496, 502*
radio, *100, 218, 275-277, 294, 343, 347, 355, 366, 371-372, 385, 392, 395, 398, 438, 505, 515, 527*
railroads, *76, 88, 113, 115, 118-119, 166, 175, 189, 216, 304, 323, 328, 347, 386*
railway time, *119*
rainstick, *90*
rangoli, *421*
ranjit singh, *38, 40*
rappahannock river, *58, 69*
rasputin, *256, 261-263*
ravensbruck, *382, 384*
re-education, *444, 447*
reaganomics, *539*
realpolitik, *105*
reaper, *120*
rebel yell, *59*
recession, *345, 538, 556*
reconstruction, *66, 76, 82-84, 107, 109-111, 116, 122, 137, 153-154, 497, 504*
red army, *264, 266-267, 299, 354, 371, 401-402, 409, 523*
red baron, *238*
red crescent, *150*
red cross, *17, 33-34, 150, 272, 275, 382*
red guards, *446-447*
red kelly, *157*
red remembrance poppy, *271*
red sea, *32-33, 548*
red terror, *265-266, 354*
reginald dyer, *287*
reginald fessenden, *276*
reichstag fire decree, *360-361*
reichswehr, *362*
reign of terror, *98*
reinhard heydrich, *361, 399*
renaissance, *11, 97, 106*
repatriation, *162*
report on the affairs of british north america, *91-92*
republic of china, *190, 323-324, 331, 442-443, 448, 534*
republic of gran colombia, *460-461, 463, 466*
republic of palau, *179*
republic of rif, *352*

republic of the congo, *160, 467-468*
republic of the marshall islands, *179*
republican, *49, 66, 83-84, 96, 98, 109-111, 122-123, 135, 138, 180-181, 239-240, 242, 270, 274-275, 282-283, 293, 311, 323-324, 332, 335, 348, 356, 366, 424, 435, 440, 450, 506, 517-518, 523-524, 539, 553-555*
republican party, *49, 84, 109-110, 181, 240, 366, 518, 539, 553*
revenue act of 1936, *345*
revolutionary command council, *435*
reza shah pahlavi, *233, 541-542*
rhine river, *297, 368*
rhineland, *296, 368*
rhode island, *34, 200, 433*
rhodesia, *166-167*
richard kleindienst, *506*
richard nixon, *440, 495, 506, 517, 539*
richard wurmbrand, *536*
richmond, *47, 57, 69, 72-74, 77*
rif war, *352*
rin tin tin, *272-273*
rio de janeiro, *460*
rio grande river, *34*
roaring twenties, *276-278, 293, 307, 335-337*
robber barons, *212, 216-218, 224*
robert baden-powell, *167*
robert bork, *507-508*
robert clive, *15*
robert jermain thomas, *455*
robert kennedy, *500*
robert moffat, *43-44*
robespierre, *98*
rockefeller center, *342*
roger b. taney, *22*
roger youderian, *475*
rolling thunder, *511*
roman catholic church, *11, 101, 247, 279, 308, 317, 459*
roman empire, *11, 101-102, 308, 314, 350*
romania, *25, 146, 234, 236, 269, 304, 377, 381, 401, 411, 478, 528-530, 536*
romanov dynasty, *168, 259*
rome, *11, 99, 216, 230, 308-309, 311-312, 314-316, 351, 370, 402, 543*
ronald reagan, *423, 464-465, 482, 528, 534, 538-539, 546, 553*
rosa parks, *498, 500*
rough riders, *176, 180*
rousseau, *85, 97-98*
route 66, *348*

rowlatt act, *287*
royal air force, *373-374*
royal navy, *105, 249, 400-401*
royal proclamation of 1763, *91*
ruby bridges, *504*
rudolf hess, *360, 399*
rudolf hoess, *361, 399*
rudyard kipling, *38, 42, 290*
rudyard kipling, *38, 42, 290*
russia, *11, 13, 24-27, 37-40, 42, 49, 95, 98-99, 102, 104, 125, 143, 145-149, 151, 163, 168-170, 180, 183, 185-187, 189, 192-194, 197, 202, 229-233, 237, 250-255, 257, 259-270, 296-297, 299-301, 303-305, 308-309, 325, 328, 357, 360, 371, 376, 378, 410, 426, 443, 477-478, 484, 492, 519, 526-527, 530-532, 534, 541-542, 553*
russia's bloody sunday, *260-261*
russian, *24-29, 39, 125, 143, 146-147, 151, 168-171, 192-194, 229-230, 232-233, 250, 255-256, 259-261, 263-267, 269, 299-301, 303-305, 325-326, 328, 376, 401, 403, 406, 410, 435, 451, 455, 479, 494, 505, 519, 521, 526, 531, 541*
russian civil war, *264, 266-267, 269, 299-301, 303*
russian revolution, *193, 260-261*
russian-japanese war, *192-194, 328*
russo-persian wars, *229*
russo-turkish war, *145-148, 150, 229, 234-235, 259*
rutherford b. hayes, *82-83, 111*

S

saad zaghloul, *319*
saddam hussein, *549-552, 555*
safavid dynasty, *37, 229*
sahara desert, *43*
said pasha, *32-33*
saigo takamori, *132*
saigon, *386, 509-510, 513-514, 518*
sakoku, *35, 129-131, 133, 141*
saladin, *31-32*
salic law, *97*
sallie gardner, *209*
salt lake city, *114, 199, 456*

salvadoran civil war, 464
samantha smith, 525-526
samuel de champlain, 91
samurai, 129, 132, 393
san francisco, 179, 223, 294, 342, 450
san francisco peace treaty, 450
sanctions, 298-299, 413, 545, 551
sand river convention, 163
sandinista, 464-465
santa fe trail, 199
saratoga chips, 220
sarin, 550-551
sassanid empire, 228
sati, 16
satsuma rebellion, 132
saturday night massacre, 507-508
satyagraha, 288
saudi arabia, 540, 547, 550-551
savannah, 76
scalawags, 83
schlieffen plan, 250
sclc, 499
scorched earth policy, 165, 395
scotland, 17, 45, 218-219, 279, 281, 399
scottish, 27, 43, 45, 59, 219, 254, 282
scottish highland brigade, 27
scramble for africa, 153, 161-163, 166, 312, 352, 437, 466-468
screaming eagles, 404
seabed arms control treaty, 533
sears, roebuck and company, 221
secession, 47, 51, 54-56, 60, 64-65, 96, 110
secessionist, 79, 82, 96
second balkan war, 236, 251
second battle of bull run, 62
second battle of el alamein, 402
second boer war, 13, 165-167, 233
second chinese-japanese war, 330, 441, 443, 509
second french empire, 97-99, 243
second french republic, 97-98
second indochina war, 510
second kashmir war, 418
second opium war, 100, 185-189, 195
second phase offensive, 452
second spanish republic, 352-353
second war of italian independence, 310-311
second war of schleswig, 104
secret police, 147, 169, 263-264, 266, 303-305, 399, 520, 525, 527, 530-531, 549
secret speech, 520
segregation, 83, 154, 498, 500-501, 504
selective service act, 269
selma, 502-504
seminole, 202
senate, 36, 47, 66, 95-96, 500, 502, 506, 508, 517, 554, 556
senator, 36, 47, 49, 66, 96, 107, 293, 424, 495-496, 499-500, 553, 556
seneca falls, 137
seoul, 451-452, 515
sepoy rebellion, 13, 15-17, 39, 286
seppuku, 132, 393
serbia, 143-146, 234-237, 251-253, 269, 298
serbo-bulgarian war, 235
serfs, 168-169, 259, 263
sevastopol, 26-27
seven laws, 242
seward's foly, 95
seymour expedition, 187-188
shah ismail, 229
shah jahan, 14
shah shuja, 40
shahyad tower, 546
shaka, 163
shamrock, 286
shanghai, 183-184, 194, 324, 326
shariah law, 544-545, 552
sharpeville massacre, 471, 473
sharpsburg, 57, 62, 71
shenandoah valley, 58, 74, 77
sheridan, 72, 77, 116, 204
sherman, 61, 73-77, 79, 82, 84, 96, 135-136, 181
sherman antitrust act of 1890, 135, 181
shia, 229, 540-541, 544, 549
shinto, 129, 397
shoguns, 129-131, 133
short selling, 214-215
shoshone, 115, 198, 423
shtetls, 170
siberia, 169, 192-194, 301-305
sichuan province, 323
siege of leningrad, 401
siege of paris, 103-104
siege of petersburg, 73-77
siege of the international legations, 187
siesta, 356
sikhism, 14
sikhs, 38-40, 42, 417, 419-420
silents, 276-277
simon bolivar, 459
sinai peninsula, 430-432, 437-438
sinatra doctrine, 528-529
singapore, 142, 386
sinn fein, 282-283
sioux, 121, 203-205, 207-209
sioux wars, 203, 207-208
sirhan sirhan, 503
sistine chapel, 317
sit-ins, 500, 503
sitting bull, 204, 207, 209, 333
six-day war, 430, 432, 437-438
slave, 18-23, 35, 44, 50-53, 55, 63, 82-83, 88, 96, 154, 161, 172, 189, 208, 462, 465, 514
slavery, 11, 18-23, 35-36, 44, 47, 49, 51-54, 56, 63, 66, 81, 84, 88, 96, 113, 154-155, 208, 302, 461-462, 465, 471, 497, 501
slaves, 19-23, 31, 35, 44, 46, 50-51, 53, 62-63, 66, 76, 80, 82-84, 87-88, 96, 110, 116, 124, 137, 153-154, 162, 164, 169, 247, 461, 463, 497, 501
sliced bread, 307
sobibor, 382
social contract, 98
social gospel, 128, 139
social security administration, 344
socialism, 155, 265-266, 300-302, 323, 325, 359, 411, 448, 524, 527
society of united irishmen, 280
solicitor general, 507-508
somali civil war, 469-470
somalia, 468-470
sooners, 118
south, 11-14, 18-24, 33-38, 43-44, 47, 49-52, 54-59, 61-63, 65-66, 69-72, 74-77, 79-80, 82-90, 92, 96, 104, 107, 109-111, 113-114, 121-122, 130, 133, 136-137, 141-142, 150-151, 153-154, 156, 158-159, 161, 163-167, 171-172, 178, 192, 194-198, 200-201, 203, 207, 220, 223, 233, 241, 246, 253, 269, 274, 288, 291, 308, 311, 320-321, 323-324, 328-330, 333-334, 350, 372, 377, 386, 389, 393, 399, 401, 421, 424, 433, 439, 448, 450-455, 458-463, 467, 470-474, 477, 484, 486, 492, 496-498, 500, 502, 504, 508-514, 518, 548, 550
south africa, 12-13, 43-44, 92, 163-167, 172, 233, 253, 269, 288, 377, 401, 458, 470-474
south africa act, 470
south america, 22, 82, 85-86, 88, 90, 113-114, 130, 133, 178, 197, 241, 311, 399, 458-463, 492
south carolina, 20, 50-51, 54-55, 57, 76, 82, 200, 500
south china sea, 389, 448
south dakota, 109, 136, 196, 201, 203, 207, 274, 321, 333-334, 439
south korea, 424, 451-454, 477, 484, 509-510
south vietnam, 151, 496, 508-514, 518
southern, 17-23, 32, 37, 39, 42, 47, 49-52, 55-57, 65, 70, 72, 76, 80, 82-84, 90, 96, 107, 110-111, 125, 153-155, 159, 163, 166-167, 182, 184, 187, 195, 228-229, 232, 236, 258, 270, 291, 298, 301, 308, 316, 323-324, 394, 402-403, 406, 409, 425, 436-437, 442, 450, 469, 472, 474, 497-500, 502-503, 510, 515, 541, 548
southerner, 23, 49, 83, 96
soviet bloc, 411
soviet war in afghanistan, 523-524
soweto, 471-473
space race, 477, 492-495, 523
spain, 11, 86-87, 100, 102, 122, 133, 161, 171-177, 180, 201, 241-243, 258, 269, 308-309, 315, 350-356, 367, 458-466, 482-483
spanish empire, 171-172, 241, 350
spanish-american war, 171-180, 239, 334, 350, 352, 482-483
speakeasies, 140
spear of the nation, 471, 473
special counsel, 506-508
spiro agnew, 518
spring offensive, 270
sputnik i, 492
square deal, 181
ss, 362-363, 367, 371-372, 381-383, 398-399, 406
ss struma, 381
ssireum, 455
st. louis, 52, 346, 379-380
st. patrick, 17, 282, 286
st. peter's basilica, 317
st. petersburg, 260, 267
st. valentine's day massacre, 140
stagflation, 538
stalin, 155, 267, 294, 300-305, 325, 355, 367, 370, 376, 402-403, 409-413, 443, 445, 450, 477-480, 487, 519-523, 526-527, 534, 549
stalingrad, 304, 376,

401-403, 409, 480
standard oil, 217
star of david badge, 384
states' rights, 49-51, 54
statue of liberty, 100, 107-108, 120, 127, 337
steal treaty, 206
steam locomotive, 113
steamboat willie, 277
steel, 64, 105, 108, 121, 216, 218-219, 222, 238, 240, 296, 301, 303, 315, 343-344, 347, 370-371, 444-446, 457, 555
steven douglas, 66
stock exchanges, 213
stock market crash of 1929, 335, 338, 340, 342
stonewall jackson, 54, 58-59, 69, 207
strait of gibraltar, 352
strategic arms limitation treaty, 533
strategic arms reduction treaty, 534
strom thurmond, 500
struggle sessions, 444, 447
stuart, 54, 71-72, 280
sublime porte, 30
subpoena, 507
sudan, 31-32, 162, 233, 295
sudetenland, 369-370
suez canal, 24, 32-33, 178, 193, 318-319, 431, 434-437, 548
suez canal company, 33, 318, 436
suez crisis, 319, 425, 434, 436-437, 477, 549
suffragists, 138-139
suleiman the magnificent, 24
sultan, 24, 31, 142-145, 147-149, 235, 318-319, 434
sultan kamel, 318
sumatra, 142
sumatra treaty, 142
sun yat-sen, 322-325
sundar singh, 290-291
sunni, 229, 540-541, 549
supreme court, 22, 49, 107, 153, 217, 240, 344-345, 366, 397, 497-499, 504, 508
suriname, 462
susan b. anthony, 20, 34, 137, 139
swaraj, 288
swastika, 363, 454
sweden, 269, 382
swiss, 150-151, 317
switzerland, 94, 98, 150-151, 269, 316-317, 509
sylvester roper, 220
syngman rhee, 450-451, 453, 477, 484
syria, 31, 295, 429-432, 437-438, 546-547, 550

T

t.e. lawrence, 546
t.s. eliot, 278
taiping rebellion, 125, 183-185, 194
taiwan, 323-324, 331, 442, 448-449
taj mahal, 14
tajikistan, 478, 532
taliban, 552, 555-556
talkies, 276-277
tanzimat, 143-145, 147-148
tariffs, 50, 180
tariq aziz, 549
tartan, 219
teapot dome scandal, 293
tear gas, 255, 503
tehran conference, 409
telegraph, 30, 113, 119, 158, 166, 175, 218, 276, 287
teller amendment, 482-483
temperance, 139, 141, 212
ten percent plan, 82
ten tragic days, 246
ten years war, 172
tennessee, 48, 56, 59-61, 73, 77, 82, 96, 121, 200, 273, 344, 503, 515
tennessee valley authority, 344
tennos, 128-129, 397
tet offensive, 512, 514
texas, 54, 56, 72-73, 118, 121, 176, 201-203, 205, 209, 242, 245, 258, 347-348, 365, 440, 465, 493, 495-496, 501, 504-505, 553, 555
texas cession, 242
texas war for independence, 242
thailand, 456, 510
the chronicles of narnia, 364
the diary of a young girl, 383
the grapes of wrath, 348
the gulag archipelago, 305
the influence of sea power upon history, 1660-1783, 173
the jazz singer, 277
the red badge of courage, 69
the sun also rises, 277
the untouchables, 140
theodore herzl, 426
theodore roosevelt, 154, 173, 176, 178, 180-181, 193, 217, 239, 332-334, 466
third battle of petersburg, 74, 77
third french republic, 97, 99, 104
third war of italian independence, 311-312
thirteen colonies, 11, 35, 91-92, 156, 200
thirteenth amendment, 81, 497
thomas edison, 119, 209
thomas jefferson, 50, 162, 172, 334-335
thomas nast, 108-109
three principles of the people, 323-324
three-fifths compromise, 18
threshing machine, 121
tiananmen square, 442-443, 448, 534
tibet, 291, 390, 420
time zones, 119
tires, 220
titanic, 248-250
tokugawa, 129-131, 133
tokyo, 129-131, 390, 393, 395
tonghak rebellion, 191
tongmenghui, 322-324
tonkin, 496, 510-511
trail of tears, 202
trans-siberian railway, 192-194, 328, 331
transcontinental railroad, 112-116, 125, 185, 197
transvaal republic, 163, 166
treaties of tianjin, 186
treaty, 13, 15, 17, 25, 27, 39-40, 89-91, 100, 102, 104-105, 126, 131, 142, 146, 151, 161-163, 165-166, 168, 177-178, 183-186, 191-194, 197-198, 203, 205-206, 232, 235-236, 255, 265, 270, 275, 283-285, 294-299, 313-314, 316, 319, 323-324, 326, 328-329, 350, 352, 357, 359, 367-370, 386, 431-432, 438, 448-450, 453-454, 463, 532-534, 538
treaty of addis ababa, 163
treaty of berlin, 146, 235
treaty of brest-litovsk, 265, 270, 297
treaty of ganghwa, 191
treaty of lausanne, 295
treaty of london, 236
treaty of nanking, 183, 185-186
treaty of paris, 27, 91, 168, 177
treaty of peace and amity, 131
treaty of peshawar, 39-40
treaty of portsmouth, 193-194
treaty of saint germain, 295
treaty of san stefano, 146
treaty of sevres, 295
treaty of shimonoseki, 191-192
treaty of trianon, 295
treaty of vereeniging, 165-166
treaty of versailles, 105, 270, 275, 294-299, 313-314, 319, 357, 359, 367-369
treaty of wuchale, 162-163
treaty ports, 13, 100, 183-185, 191-192, 323-324, 328, 386
treaty with the nez perce, 203
treblinka, 380-382
trenches, 176, 234, 253-254, 256, 271, 414, 481
trickle down, 539
tripartite pact, 375, 386, 388, 401
triple alliance, 86-88, 232, 250-252, 312-313, 371, 462
triple intervention, 192
truman doctrine, 413-414, 424
trust-busting, 217
tsar nicholas, 24-25, 170, 193, 255-256, 259-265, 268-269, 519
tsarevich alexis, 261-262
tsars, 151, 168-169, 194, 260, 263-264, 266, 268, 299, 302-305, 410, 477, 520, 534
tuberculosis, 88, 99, 252, 352
turkey, 30-31, 48, 127, 149, 295, 381, 414, 424, 426, 491-492, 550
turkish, 27, 143, 145-150, 229, 234-235, 259
turkmenistan, 478, 532
tuscany, 308-311
tuskegee airmen, 48, 332
tuskegee institute, 154-155
twelvers, 540-541
twenty-one demands, 328
twenty-six martyrs, 133
twin murder, 45

U

u-2, 490-491
u.s. army, 21, 36, 47, 54, 56-57, 80, 116-117, 176, 178, 199, 202-204, 206, 257, 332, 346, 394, 396, 404, 408, 413, 452, 500, 512
u.s. government, 11, 21, 53, 55, 57, 83-84, 116, 130, 178, 204, 206, 257, 275, 366, 483-484, 503, 514
u.s. income tax, 275
u.s. navy, 130, 173, 175, 177-178, 180, 387, 390-393, 441, 452, 483, 491, 495, 511, 538, 553
u.s. steel, 219, 240
u.s. virgin islands, 34, 179
ukraine, 265, 270, 301-302, 376, 401, 478, 519,

531-532
ulster, 279, 282, 284-285
umberto i, 312-313
un, 69, 127, 155, 413, 415, 417, 426, 428-429, 450-453, 467-470, 483, 531, 551, 553
un security council, 531
uncle sam, 109, 257
uncle tom's cabin, 20-21, 51, 53
underground railroad, 11, 19-20, 53
unemployment, 293, 340, 349, 538
union, 17, 19-20, 23, 34-36, 47, 49-52, 54-66, 69-84, 92, 95-96, 110, 112-116, 122-123, 135-136, 148, 165-166, 200-201, 204, 235, 265, 267, 274, 280, 284, 299, 333-334, 355, 368, 421, 437, 464, 470, 478, 528, 534, 537
union jack, 17, 280, 537
union of soviet socialist republics (ussr), 265, 299
union pacific railroad, 114, 274
united arab emirates, 548
united arab republic, 436-437
united fruit company, 464
united kingdom, 12-13, 17, 219, 280-281, 284-285, 369, 425
united nations, 332, 409-410, 413, 415, 425, 428, 432, 437, 449-451, 453, 467-469, 531, 551
united states, 11, 18, 20, 22-23, 34-36, 47, 50-51, 53-56, 63, 66, 68, 71, 81-82, 85, 91-92, 95-96, 99, 107-110, 113, 119, 122, 124-128, 130-131, 135, 137-142, 153-155, 162, 172-173, 175-180, 183, 185-186, 197, 200, 202-203, 211-212, 216-218, 223, 240, 242-244, 246, 248, 251, 253, 256-258, 268-269, 273, 275-276, 281, 287, 295-296, 299, 301, 306, 313, 330, 332, 334-336, 338, 340, 342, 366, 379, 385-388, 390, 395-398, 401, 404, 408-409, 413-414, 424, 431, 435, 437, 448-450, 452-453, 462, 465, 467-469, 477, 482-483, 485-487, 490-493, 495, 497, 501, 503-505, 507-510, 513, 517-518, 520-521, 524, 533, 535-536, 538, 543-545, 551-556
up from slavery, 154
upper canada, 91-92
urabi rebellion, 318

uruguay, 86, 311, 458, 463
uss maine, 172-174, 180
ussr, 149, 234, 265-267, 294, 298-305, 324-326, 328, 331, 353-354, 370-371, 375-377, 381, 383, 385, 390, 394, 401-405, 409-414, 431, 435-437, 440, 443-445, 449-451, 453, 459, 465, 467-468, 477-482, 484-493, 495-496, 505, 508, 510, 513, 515, 519-534, 536, 539, 543, 552-553
utah, 115, 199, 201, 238, 258, 292, 403-404, 423, 439, 456-457
uzbekistan, 478, 532

V

v-e day, 406, 411, 449
v-j day, 395, 449, 452
vatican city, 316-317
venezuela, 459-461, 463, 466
venice, 308-309, 312
venustiano carranza, 246-247
vermont, 123, 200, 221, 335
versailles, 97, 103-105, 129, 250, 270, 275, 294-299, 313-314, 319, 357, 359, 367-369
viceroy, 17, 31, 241, 286, 289, 308
vichy france, 372, 386, 509, 513
vicksburg, 72-73, 75
victor emanuel iii, 313-315
victor emmanuel ii, 310, 351
victoria, 12-14, 16-17, 44, 46, 49, 156, 159, 230, 262, 286
victoria falls, 44, 46
victorian, 12-15, 93, 156, 175, 233
victorian gold rush, 156
victoriano huerta, 246
viet cong, 510-513
viet minh, 509-511, 513
vietnam, 99-100, 151, 385-386, 440-441, 477, 495-497, 508-514, 517-518, 523, 534, 538
vietnam war, 477, 496-497, 508, 510-514, 517-518, 538
vietnamese, 508-515
vietnamese independence league, 509
vietnamese reformation society, 508
virginia, 21, 23, 47, 53-54, 56-58, 60-66, 68-70, 73-74, 77-78, 80-81, 96, 120, 124, 154, 195, 200-201, 239, 274, 387,

499, 552
visigoths, 100
vittorio orlando, 296, 314
vizier, 30, 143
vladimir lenin, 151, 261, 264, 266-267, 299, 303, 325, 443, 519
voc, 141-142
voice of the martyrs, 536-537
voltaire, 85, 97
voortrekkers, 163-164

W

w.e.b. du bois, 155
wafd party, 319
wagon box fight, 204
wagonways, 113
wake island, 34, 179
wales, 17, 93, 156, 158, 279, 281, 400
wali, 317
wall street, 213-215, 337
wallachia, 25-27
walt disney, 277
war, 12-13, 18-27, 29-31, 33-43, 47, 49-63, 66-79, 82-84, 86-89, 91, 96-97, 99-105, 109-111, 113-114, 116, 118, 120, 122-124, 126, 128, 131-132, 135, 137, 142-151, 154, 158, 161-168, 171-195, 198-199, 201, 203-205, 207, 212, 217, 229, 231-239, 241-244, 247, 250-257, 259-273, 275-285, 287, 289, 293, 295-301, 303-305, 308, 310-316, 318, 326, 328-332, 334, 338, 342, 347-359, 361, 363-364, 366-378, 380-395, 397-415, 417-420, 424-432, 434-435, 437-438, 440-443, 447-454, 459-460, 462, 464-465, 467, 469-470, 477-480, 482-483, 486-492, 495-497, 504, 508-514, 517-526, 528-529, 532-533, 536, 538-539, 542-543, 545-547, 549-555
war between the states, 50-51, 68
war of the pacific, 88-89, 459-460, 462
war of the triple alliance, 86-88, 462
war of the worlds, 347
warren g. harding, 293
warsaw ghetto, 380-381
washington d.c., 34, 307
watergate, 505-508, 513, 517-518
watergate seven, 506

weimar republic, 270, 297, 350, 356-358, 360-361
well of joseph, 32
west bank, 61, 297, 429-430, 432
west germany, 479-480, 482, 510, 526, 529
west pakistan, 416-419
west virginia, 53, 56, 58, 63-65, 154, 201, 387
western europe, 24-25, 143, 169, 372, 385, 403, 406-410, 413-414, 431, 466, 491, 525
western front, 253-254, 269-270, 313, 364, 405, 407-408
whig, 23, 35
white army, 264, 266-267, 299
white revolution, 544
whitewater scandal, 554
wilbur chapman, 212
wilbur wright, 226
wilhelm i, 102-105
willem janszoon, 156
william dampier, 156
william gladstone, 281-282
william howard taft, 239
william knox d'arcy, 231
william lloyd garrison, 20-21
william lyon mackenzie, 91
william mckinley, 172, 176, 180, 226, 239, 313
william randolph hearst, 174
william walker, 465
winfield scott, 36, 57
winnie-the-pooh, 272
winston churchill, 233-234, 370, 372, 375, 479, 490, 543
wisconsin, 21, 109, 134, 151-152, 196, 201
women's rights, 137, 139, 209, 332
women's suffrage, 137-138
woodrow wilson, 181, 240, 246-247, 251, 256-257, 268-270, 274-275, 296, 299, 313, 467
works progress administration, 343
world war i, 12, 105, 147-149, 151, 179, 231-234, 237-238, 241, 250-251, 253, 255-257, 259-265, 268-273, 275-278, 281-283, 287, 293, 295-297, 308, 313-315, 318, 329, 348, 352-354, 356-359, 364, 367-368, 372-374, 378, 381, 404, 410, 413, 425-427, 434, 467, 542, 546-547, 550
world war ii, 97, 105, 126, 132, 149, 151, 176-177, 234, 272, 289, 298-299, 304-305, 314-316, 326, 328, 330-332, 338, 342, 354-355, 361, 363-364,

366-369, 371, 375-378, 380, 382-387, 397-398, 400, 406, 409, 413-415, 427-428, 434-435, 440-441, 443, 449, 452, 467, 478, 496, 509-511, 513, 518-519, 521, 523, 525, 529, 536, 542, 547, 551, 553

world's fair, *14, 100, 108, 356*
wovoka, *207*
wright brothers, *226-227, 237, 254, 404*
wright flyer, *226-227*
wyatt earp, *116*
wyoming, *114, 198-199, 201, 203, 274, 292-293, 321, 333, 423, 439, 456*

Y

yalta, *304, 409-411, 450, 519*
yangtze river, *323*
yellow journalism, *174*
yemen, *548*
yom kippur war, *430-431, 438*
young italy, *309-312*
young turk revolution, *148-149, 235*
young turks, *146-149, 235, 309*
yuan shikai, *324, 327-328*
yugoslavia, *270, 295, 298, 377, 401, 478*
yukon gold rush, *95*
yunnan province, *456*
yuri andropov, *525-526*
yuri gagarin, *492, 494*

Z

zachary taylor, *23, 35, 47, 113*
zaire, *468*
zambezi river, *46*
zambia, *46, 167*
zand dynasty, *229*
zemstvo, *168-169*
zimbabwe, *46, 167*
zimmerman telegram, *256, 268-269, 283*
zionism, *426*
zionists, *426-428*
zoroastrian, *228*
zulu, *163*
zululand, *163*
zyklon-b, *381*